THE CAMBRIDGE HISTORY OF SOUTHEAST ASIA

VOLUME FOUR

From World War II to the present

THE CAMBRIDGE HISTORY OF SOUTHEAST ASIA

THE CAMBRIDGE HISTORY OF SOUTHEAST ASIA

VOLUME FOUR

From World War II to the present

edited by

NICHOLAS TARLING

CAMBRIDGE
UNIVERSITY PRESS

PUBLISHED BY THE PRESS SYNDICATE OF THE UNIVERSITY OF CAMBRIDGE
The Pitt Building, Trumpington Street, Cambridge, United Kingdom

CAMBRIDGE UNIVERSITY PRESS
The Edinburgh Building, Cambridge CB2 2RU, UK www.cup.cam.ac.uk
40 West 20th Street, New York, NY 10011–4211, USA www.cup.org
10 Stamford Road, Oakleigh, Melbourne 3166, Australia
Ruiz de Alarcón 13, 28014, Madrid, Spain

The Cambridge History of Southeast Asia was first published in hardback
in two volumes in 1992, reprinted 1994
Volume One ISBN 0 521 35505 2 (hardback)
Volume Two ISBN 0 521 35506 0 (hardback)

The Cambridge History of Southeast Asia is first published in paperback
in four volumes in 1999
Volume One Part One: From early times to c. 1500
ISBN 0 521 66369 5 (paperback)
Volume One Part Two: From c. 1500 to c. 1800
ISBN 0 521 66370 9 (paperback)
These two volumes contain the contents of 0 521 35505 2 (hardback),
with additional supplementary material
Volume Two Part One: From c. 1800 to the 1930s
ISBN 0 521 66371 7 (paperback)
Volume Two Part Two: From World War II to the present
ISBN 0 521 66372 5 (paperback)
These two volumes contain the contents of 0 521 35506 0 (hardback),
with additional supplementary material

The set of four paperbacks, containing the complete contents of *The Cambridge History
of Southeast Asia*, ISBN 0 521 77864 6 (paperback).

Printed in Singapore by Craft Print Pte Ltd

Typeface Palatino 10/11 pt. *System* Penta [MT]

A catalogue record for this book is available from the British Library

National Library of Australia Cataloguing in Publication data
The Cambridge history of Southeast Asia.
Bibliography.
Includes index.
ISBN 0 521 66369 5 (Volume One Part One).
ISBN 0 521 66370 9 (Volume One Part Two).
ISBN 0 521 66371 7 (Volume Two Part One).
ISBN 0 521 66372 5 (Volume Two Part Two).
ISBN 0 521 77864 6 (set).
1. Asia, Southeastern – History. I. Tarling, Nicholas.
959

ISBN 0 521 66372 5 paperback

CONTENTS

NOTE ON SPELLING

The spelling of proper names and terms has caused editor and contributors considerable problems. Even a certain arbitrariness may have not produced consistency across a range of contributions, and that arbitrariness contained its own inconsistencies. In general we have aimed to spell place-names and terms in the way currently most accepted in the country, society or literature concerned. We have not used diacritics for modern Southeast Asian languages, but have used them for Sanskrit and Ancient Javanese. We have used pinyin transliterations except for some names which are well known in English in the Wade–Giles transliteration.

ABBREVIATIONS

AFPFL   Anti-Fascist People's Freedom League, Burma.

ASEAN   Association of South-East Asian Nations.

BKI   *Bijdragen van het Koninklijk Instituut voor de Taal-, Land- en Volkenkunde*, 's-Gravenhage.

BSPP   Burma Socialist Programme Party.

BWS   Burmese Way to Socialism.

DAP   Democratic Action Party, Malaysia.

DRV   Democratic Republic of Vietnam.

GCBA   General Council of Burmese Associations.

ICP   Indochina Communist Party.

ISDV   Indische Sociaal-Demokratische Vereeniging (Indies Social-Democratic Association).

ISEAS   Institute of Southeast Asian Studies, Singapore.

JAS   *Journal of Asian Studies*, Ann Arbor.

JMBRAS   *Journal of the Malay/Malaysian Branch of the Royal Asiatic Society*, Kuala Lumpur.

JSEAH   *Journal of Southeast Asian History*, Singapore.

JSEAS   *Journal of Southeast Asian Studies*, Singapore.

JSS   *Journal of the Siam Society*, Bangkok.

MAS   *Modern Asian Studies*, Cambridge, UK.

MCP   Malayan Communist Party.

MNLF   Moro National Liberation Front.

MPAJA   Malayan People's Anti-Japanese Army.

NLF   National Liberation Front, Vietnam.

NPA   New People's Army, The Philippines.

PAP   People's Action Party, Singapore.

PAS   Partai Islam se Tanah Malaya (Pan-Malayan Islamic Party).

PKI   Partai Komunis Indonesia (Indonesian Communist Party).

PNI	Perserikatan Nasional Indonesia (Indonesian National Association).
RVN	Republic of Vietnam.
SEAC	South-East Asia Command.
SEATO	South-East Asia Treaty Organization.
SRV	Socialist Republic of Vietnam.
UMNO	United Malays National Organization.

PREFACE TO THE PAPERBACK EDITION

Two ideas came together in the project for a Cambridge History of Southeast Asia. One was the concept of the Cambridge Histories themselves. The other was the possibility of a new approach to the history of Southeast Asia.

In the English-speaking and English-reading world the Cambridge Histories have, since the beginning of the century, set high standards in collaborative scholarship and provided a model for multi-volume works of history. The original *Cambridge Modern History* appeared in sixteen volumes between 1902 and 1912, and was followed by the *Cambridge Ancient History*, the *Cambridge Medieval History*, the *Cambridge History of India* and others.

A new generation of projects continues and builds on this foundation. Recently completed are the Cambridge Histories of Africa, Latin America and the Pacific Islanders. Cambridge Histories of China and of Japan are in progress, as well as the New Cambridge History of India. Though the pattern and the size have varied, the essential feature, multi-authorship, has remained.

The initial focus was European, but albeit in an approach that initially savoured rather of the old Cambridge Tripos course 'The Expansion of Europe', it moved more out of the European sphere than the often brilliant one-author Oxford histories. But it left a gap which that course did not leave, the history of Southeast Asia.

Southeast Asia has long been seen as a whole, though other terms have been used for it. The title Southeast Asia, becoming current during World War II, has been accepted as recognizing the unity of the region, while not prejudging the nature of that unity. Yet scholarly research and writing have shown that it is no mere geographical expression.

There have indeed been several previous histories of Southeast Asia. Most of them have been the work of one author. The great work of the late D. G. E. Hall dates back to 1955, but it has gone through several editions since. Others include B. Harrison, *South-east Asia, A Short History*, London, 1954; Nicholas Tarling, *A Concise History of Southeast Asia*, 1966; and D. J. Steinberg, et al., *In Search of Southeast Asia*, 1971. The authors of these works faced difficult tasks, as a result of the linguistic diversity of the area; the extent of the secondary material; and the lacunae within it.

Given its diversity, Southeast Asia seemed to lend itself to the Cambridge approach. A magisterial single-volume history existed; others had also made the attempt. A single volume by several authors working together had also been successful. But a more substantial history by a larger number of authors had not been attempted.

The past generation has seen a great expansion of writing, but Southeast Asia's historiography is still immature in the sense that some aspects have been relatively well cultivated, and others not. The historical literature on the area has become more substantial and more sophisticated, but much of it deals with particular countries or cultures, and many gaps remain. A range of experts might help to bring it all together and thus both lay the foundation and point the way for further research effort.

The Cambridge approach offered a warning as well as an invitation. There were practical obstacles in the way of histories on the scale of the original European histories. They got out of hand or were never finished. A summation that was also to lead other scholars forward must be published within a reasonable time-span. It must not be too voluminous; it must not involve too many people.

Practical indications of this nature, however, coincided with historiographical considerations. There were some good histories of Southeast Asia; there were also some good histories of particular countries; but there was, perhaps, no history that set out from a regional basis and took a regional approach. This seemed worthwhile in itself, as well as establishing a coherence and a format for the volumes.

In almost every case—even when chapters are the work of more than one person—authors have been taken out of their particular area of expertise. They were ready to take risks, knowing that, whatever care they took, they might be faulted by experts, but recognizing the value all the same in attempting to give an overview. Generally contributors felt that the challenge of the regional approach was worth the hazardous departure from research moorings.

Authors invited to contribute recognized that they would often find themselves extended beyond the span of the published work which has made them well known. The new history did, however, give them a chance—perhaps already enjoyed in many cases in their teaching—to extend into other parts of the region and to adopt a comparative, regional approach. The publishers sought a history that stimulated rather than presented the last word. Authors were the more ready to rely where necessary on published or secondary works, and readers will not expect equally authoritative treatment of the whole area, even if the sources permitted it.

At the same time, the editor and the contributors have had, like any historians, to cope with problems of periodization. That is, of course, always contentious, but particularly so if it seems to result from or to point to a particular emphasis. In the case of Southeast Asia the most likely temptation is to adopt a chronology that overdoes the impact of outside forces, in particular the Europeans. The structure of this history is not free from that criticism, but the contributors have sought, where appropriate, to challenge rather than meekly to accept its implications.

A similar risk is attached to the division of the material into chapters. The scope of a work such as this makes that all the more difficult but all the more necessary. Sometimes the divisions appear to cut across what ought to be seen as a whole, and sometimes repetition may result. That has been allowed when it seemed necessary. But it may still be possible to pursue certain themes through the book and not to read it merely in chronological sequence. Within the four major chronological divisions, chapters are in general organized in a similar order. The work may thus in a sense be read laterally as well as horizontally.

Some topics, including treatment of the arts, literature and music, have been virtually excluded. The focus of the work is on economic, social, religious and political history. But it will still be difficult to pursue the history of a particular people or country. The work does not indeed promise to offer this; though it offers guidance to those who wish to do this in its apparatus, the footnotes and bibliographic essay to each chapter, the historiographical survey, the list of bibliographies, and the index.

* * *

The work was originally published in 1992 in two hardbound volumes. The paperback edition is a reprint in four volumes with minor revisions. While the work in its two-volume format has been quite widely welcomed, it is hoped that the new format will make it more accessible, and in particular bring it more readily within reach of those who teach and are taught about the region, as well as those who are simply curious about it. The four paperbacks may stand on their own, though it is also the case that the whole is greater than the sum of the parts.

The first volume contains an essay on the historiography of Southeast Asia and Part 1 of the original Volume 1, 'From Prehistory to c. 1500 CE'. The second volume contains Part 2 of the original Volume 1, covering the years c. 1500 to c. 1800, and the third volume covers the period from c. 1800 to the 1930s. The present volume deals with World War II and since, and also contains a bibliography of bibliographies on Southeast Asia.

Discussions about the work, both in the course of its preparation and since, have raised questions both about its regional approach and its periodization, questions that are indeed of enduring interest to historians and their readers, though not susceptible of enduring answers. The prefaces to the previous paperback volumes have again taken up those questions. They put forward the suggestion that 'Southeast Asia' is still a useful category, though we should always be on our guard lest we are tempted to over-emphasize either its cohesion or its diversity. They offer a similar defence of the periodization the work adopted, all the more necessary, perhaps, now that those periods may now divide one book from another rather than one part of a book. The defence comes as it were in the form of a health warning. The divisions cannot be hard and fast, implying, say, an over-emphasis on external factors rather than indigenous, or precluding a differential relationship among them in different parts of the region.

The debate on such matters is symptomatic of the historical approach. The advances the discipline has made depend partly on the application of its methods, designed as they are to maximize the objectivity with which the various materials at hand must be tackled, however elusive this objective may be. They also depend on the conditions under which an historian works and on the concerns of the society to which the historian belongs. 'Present-mindedness', though it has been responsible for major errors, has often brought with it a major access of new insight—bearing error and distortion not in arbitrary solitude but in a kind of fertile if illicit union with intellectual discovery' (R. Hofstadter, quoted in Peter Novick, *That Noble Dream: The 'Objectivity Question' and the American Historical Profession* Cambridge University Press, 1988, p. 407). The paradox is thus less complete than it seems. No view can be final, since we cannot know all the 'facts', and cannot be entirely objective in interpreting them. Successive revisions of the past are not therefore a reason for condemning the historical discipline: they are, as Barzun and Graff suggest, 'additive' (J. Barzun and Henry F. Graff, *The Modern Researcher* 4th edition, New York: Harcourt Brace, 1985, p. 191). They are, too, a sign of its vitality.

The nature of the debate about the present volume, like that about the earlier volumes, reflects these issues, but in a somewhat different way. It covers a relatively recent period, all of it within the adulthood of many living people, and some of it at least widely regarded as contemporary. To write its history may seem somewhat foolhardy. Not to do so, however, would be to fail to respond to a widespread curiosity about the recent as well as the distant past of the region, or to endeavour at least to keep the record straight at a time when the past, recent and distant, is often invoked, but almost as often misrepresented or even traduced. A great deal of material is available, it will be said, and its copiousness is indeed as daunting to the historian as its paucity in earlier periods. But much of what is available, particularly in respect of the last three decades, is only what can be found in the public domain, or has been dragged more or less reluctantly or partially into that domain. That is, however, not a reason to avoid the attempt. Later historians can put us right, and meanwhile survivors of the recent past may be prompted to comment, digging, with whatever degree of reliability, into the sands of memory.

The open-endedness of the venture presents, however, yet another difficulty. Without a longer-term perspective, we may be even less sure about the framework of our history. At the time this work was conceived, for example, the region was perceived in terms of economic growth, and some of its countries were, in actuality or potentially, among the 'tigers'. That affected the focus of historians. Were we right to choose a periodization that stressed the significance of the political changes brought about by the Pacific War? Now we may be asking ourselves whether or not the economic crisis that began in 1997 is marking off a new division in Southeast Asian history.

It may also lead us to question the regional concept. In this period it did indeed gain a new measure of acceptance. Initially that seemed rather to echo the political and military concerns that had popularized the concept of 'Southeast Asia' during World War II. Now it became a part of the world which was contested in the Cold War, the countries of which might fall like dominoes to the communists as they once had to the Japanese. Even before that war came to an end, however, the newly independent countries in the region had seen the possibility of an unprecedented degree of cooperation among themselves, partly in order to limit the penetration of outside powers, and partly to enhance the economic prospects of the region. Will that be sustained in the years of economic crisis? The answer may again shape the attitude of historians, among whom the regional concept has been both contested and stimulating.

The outbreak of the Pacific War, in which the resources of the region had a crucial role, has been the source of deep controversy and also of much historical argument. Among the most recent works is A. Best, *Britain, Japan and Pearl Harbor: Avoiding War in East Asia, 1936–41* (London and New York: Routledge, 1995). Two recent authors have focused on the place of Southeast Asia in the diplomacy of the period: Richard J. Aldrich, *The Key to the South* (Kuala Lumpur: Oxford University Press, 1993) and myself, *Britain, Southeast Asia and the Onset of the Pacific War* (Cambridge University Press, 1996).

The Japanese occupation has continued to attract attention, not only because of its intrinsic interest, but also because of its position in the long-term history of the relationships between Southeast Asia and Japan. Most of the recent work takes a country-by-country approach. That applies even to the collection edited by Grant Goodman, *Japanese Cultural Policies in Southeast Asia during World War 2* (Basingstoke: Macmillan, 1992). Among the contributors to that volume are Aiko Kurasawa, whose thesis on occupied Java dates from 1988, Kenichi Goto, and Yoji Akashi. Goto also contributes to a collection edited by Peter Post and Elly Touwen-Bouwsma, *Japan, Indonesia and the War: Myths and Realities* Leiden: KITLV Press, 1997), as does Sato Shigeru, author, too, of *War, Nationalism and Peasants: Java under the Japanese Occupation* (Sydney: Allen & Unwin, 1994). Another collection on the Japanese occupation appeared in *Journal of Southeast Asian Studies* March 1996, and its editor, Paul Kratoska, a contributor to Volume 3 of *The Cambridge History of Southeast Asia*, has published *The Japanese Occupation of Malaya 1941–1945* (Sydney: Allen & Unwin, 1998). E. Bruce Reynolds revised his thesis as *Thailand and Japan's Southern Advance* (New York: St Martin's Press, 1994), and the completion of David Marr's masterly trilogy on Vietnamese nationalism came with *Vietnam 1945* (Berkeley: University of California Press, 1995).

The historiography of decolonization in Southeast Asia has benefited both from the official publication of extracts from the records in the US, the UK, the Netherlands and Australia, and from monographs relating to particular countries. Among those are Albert Lau, *The Malayan Union Controversy* (Singapore: Oxford University Press, 1991), and Simon C. Smith, *British Relations with the Malay Rulers from Decentralization to Malayan Independence* (Kuala Lumpur: Oxford University Press, 1995). Those concerned with Indonesia may look at two ends of the spectrum of leadership with Robert Cribb's *Gangsters and Revolutionaries* (Sydney: Allen & Unwin, 1991) and Rudolf Mrazek's biography of Sjahrir (Ithaca: Cornell University Press, 1994). A useful collection, edited by Robert Holland, is *Emergencies and Disorder in the European Empires after 1945* (London: Cass, 1994). My *Britain, Southeast Asia and the Onset of the Cold War* (Cambridge University Press, 1998) attempts an overview. The role of the USA in this period has been well discussed in William J. Duiker, *US Containment policy and the Conflict in Indochina* (Stanford University Press, 1994) and Daniel Fineman, *A Special Relationship. The United States and Military Government in Thailand, 1947–1958* (Honolulu: University of Hawaii Press, 1997).

The nature of the régimes that consolidated themselves in the 1970s and 1980s is well analyzed in David Brown, *The State and Ethnic Politics in Southeast Asia* (London and New York: Routledge, 1994). William Case offers an interpretation of Malaysian politics in *Elites and Regimes in Malaysia: Revisiting a Consociational Democracy* (Melbourne: Monash Asia Institute, 1996), and a number of regional studies are among those that dealt with Suharto's Indonesia, such as Ichlasul Amal, *Regional and Central Government in Indonesian Politics: West Sumatra and South Sulawesi 1949–79* (Yogyakarta: Gadjah Mada University Press, 1992) and Tim Kell, *The Roots of Acehnese Rebellion, 1989–1992* (Cornell Southeast Asia Program, 1995). Separatism is the focus of Clive Christie's *A Modern History of Southeast Asia: Decolonization, Nationalism and Separatism* (London and New York: Tauris, 1996), and ethnicity the focus of Anthony Reid's new research project.

Recent books on the development of ASEAN include Sueo Sudo, *The Fukuda Doctrine and ASEAN* (Singapore: ISEAS, 1992), Leszek Buszynski, *Gorbachev and Southeast Asia* (London and New York: Routledge, 1992), and, particularly perceptive, Dewi Fortune Anwar, *Indonesia in ASEAN: Foreign Policy and Regionalism* (New York: St Martin's Press, and Singapore: ISEAS, 1994).

So brief a selection only suggests the quantity and quality of the work now being done on contemporary Southeast Asia. Like its longer-term history, it offers plenty of challenge to the student. Bringing the two together is the special task of the historian. The present volumes represent only one of the ways in which it may be done. The door is open both to new work and to new interpretation from within the region, from without, or from both.

Nicholas Tarling 1999

FROM WORLD WAR II
TO THE PRESENT

INTRODUCTION

Writing a history of Southeast Asia as a region presents many challenges: the diversity the region displays in so many fields of human endeavour makes its history exciting but intractable. But if this is true throughout, the period during and since World War II presents the historian with special problems. By contrast to much of the earlier history, the period is copiously covered in written and printed documents. But they tell only part of the story. The period is, too, relatively recent, so that, in assimilating and analyzing the material, it is hard to be sure that the right themes have been chosen. Even determining the date at which to stop is fraught with difficulty. The authors of this part have accepted that their approach must be tentative. At times they must content themselves more with narrative than interpretation.

The period indeed opens with an event the impact of which is still clearly being felt, the Japanese invasion and the collapse of the European empires. This is discussed in Chapter 1. Once more the fortunes of Southeast Asia were profoundly affected by forces outside the region. Once more its peoples reacted in a variety of ways. The colonial régimes were destroyed. In the Japanese phase new social and political opportunities were opened up for some, new constraints placed on others. The economy of the region, damaged in the Great Depression, was profoundly dislocated. Parts of it were fought over, parts not. The attempts of the colonial powers to return were again variously successful. Nationalist movements contended for power. They faced not only returning colonial rulers, but new local rivals. Their success was also partly dependent on the impact of changes outside the region, the decline of British and the rise of US power, the Cold War, the triumph of Chinese communism, the independence of India.

In general the nationalist élites inherited the colonial states. Their task was now to govern them. The political structures that they used are surveyed in Chapter 2. It argues that some structures were particularly shaped by war and revolution. Others were plural in nature, particularly those set up in the early years of independence. A third category the analysis discerns is maximum government. Its emergence may at least in part relate to the impact of and opportunities offered by the Asia-Pacific economic boom from the 1960s.

Chapter 3 discusses economic and social change in Southeast Asia. The leadership of the new states had to argue that independence would mean the end of poverty and developmental backwardness. Most sought growth, generally involving a good deal of direct government involvement in the economy. Different ideologies affected government policy. But so did the changing international environment, to which as ever Southeast Asia had to respond. That in turn was affected both by the economic policies of particular outside powers and by global economic trends. The search for growth met varying success, but urbanization and industrialization were often accompanied by degradation of the environment. Traditional hierarchy and community were challenged, sometimes enthusiastically, sometimes more doubtfully. Most Southeast Asians achieved some compromise between the old and the new. The other options were protest and, rarely successful now that the state was unprecedently strong, rebellion.

The region remains a site of encounter between divergent world-views, and its peoples experience a rich variety of religious experiences. Earlier transformations in Southeast Asian history had been attended by changes in religion, and, Chapter 4 suggests, pragmatic utilitarianism may be the most powerful missionary force in the Southeast Asia of the late twentieth century. But older patterns persist, particularly at the village level. They have also been taken up by the state, as governing élites seek to turn them to account, and in particular to integrate the states they have inherited. They continue, however, to have a vitality of their own. In effect, traditionalism, magic, millenarianism, mysticism, scripturalism and fundamentalism exist within all the world religions of the region. The experience of the spiritual among Southeast Asians remains intense, but increasingly they are likely to have faith in religion rather than accept it as an integral part of a whole system.

Throughout this work the authors have sought to adopt a regional approach to the history of Southeast Asia. The majority of them come from outside Southeast Asia, and it may be easier for those who live elsewhere to conceive of it as a region than for those who live in a Southeast Asian country. Chapter 5, which is the last chapter of the work as a whole, suggests that regionalism was slow to develop both because of the concern of the nationalist governments with consolidating the new states and because of the continued intervention of outside powers. But by the last decade of the century Southeast Asia had substantially determined the character of its nations and established a degree of regional cohesion. Though the region was as ever an object of interest to the great powers, its states had secured some control over their fate.

CHAPTER 1

SOUTHEAST ASIA IN WAR AND PEACE: THE END OF EUROPEAN COLONIAL EMPIRES

So marked is the diversity of Southeast Asia that even the recent history of each country, indeed of each community, possesses its own periodization and invites examination as a more or less autonomous entity. Nonetheless, the separate territories and societies do have sufficient shared experiences to allow a level of generalization for the area as a whole. The developments which provide a degree of regional coherence are not themselves, however, necessarily unique to the region. On the contrary, the outstanding landmarks in the closing chapter of Southeast Asia's colonial period are also features of the broader terrain of world history, notably the rise and fall of the Japanese empire, the postwar restoration of European colonialism and the achievement of national independence during the Cold War. Indeed, given that the focus of this chapter is upon the end of European empires in Southeast Asia, it is only to be expected that the momentous events and key decisions which are both the determinants and the symbols of its periodization are of major significance for, since they partly emanated from, the world beyond Southeast Asia.

WORLD WAR II AND JAPANESE OCCUPATION

World War in Southeast Asia, 1941–1945

Few historical events in the history of Southeast Asia appear so definitive as the Japanese invasion in December 1941.[1] By a stroke more compelling than the fall of Melaka to the Portuguese in 1511, the balance of power between Europe and Asia seemed to have been immediately and permanently transformed. The reasons for this invasion are to be found largely,

---

[1] A selection of titles on the outbreak of World War II in Asia and on other topics covered in this chapter is to be found in the bibliographical essay.

but not entirely, in events outside the region; in, for example, the growth of militarism in Japanese society during the 1930s, in the imperialist expansion of Japan and the course of the war in China, and in Japan's economic needs and the ideology of Co-prosperity. One must also take into account the weaknesses of European powers which, despite the apparent confidence and stability displayed by their governments in the colonies during the late 1930s, were at home distracted, and in the case of France and the Netherlands overwhelmed, by the war in the West. An additional dimension to any explanation of Japanese success and European failure in 1941–2 is that of the 'imperial periphery'. Amongst its more noteworthy features were, first, the raw materials which the region itself offered to the Japanese; second, the realities of the colonial position which, in contrast to appearances of virtual omnipotence, was marked in all instances by a fundamentally rickety network of collaborative ties with local peoples; and, third, the absence of any co-ordinated resistance to the Japanese advance.

In May–June 1940, when first the Netherlands and then France fell to Germany, Japan signed an agreement with Phibun Songkhram's government in Siam and also began to demand special privileges whereby it might land forces in French Indochina. In August the new régime of Vichy France permitted the Japanese the use of ports in Indochina and in September Japan joined the Axis in a ten-year tripartite pact, although this would not prevent it from upholding a neutrality agreement with Moscow (concluded in April 1941) when Hitler invaded the Soviet Union in June 1941. Early in 1941 Japan acted as 'mediator' between France and Siam in Indochina. One result of these negotiations was the convention in March whereby Siam regained territory on the west bank of the Mekong which it had lost to France in the Paknam incident of 1893. A second consequence was the further extension of Japan's territorial position in the region and the consolidation of its position for another leap forward, since it had succeeded in obtaining supplies of rice, rubber, coal and other minerals from Indochina, and also had won the formal confirmation of its military occupation of French territory. By the end of July Japan had effectively occupied Indochina, and the army and navy were preparing for operations in Southeast Asia and the Pacific. Japan nonetheless held back from military hostilities while at the same time Western powers, and especially the USA, attempted to block its advance with a combination of negotiations and embargoes.

The period of expansion through diplomatic means ended soon after mid-October when Prince Fumimaro Konoye was replaced as premier by General Hideki Tojo, the Minister of War, who had previously served as chief of staff with the occupation force in China. Feeling the pressure of the economic blockade, particularly as regards oil supplies, determined not to lose international status and mindful that the US would be likely to assist Britain and the Netherlands in the defence of their colonies, Tojo's government decided at the start of November on an early military strike. During the night of 7–8 December Pearl Harbor, Malaya, the Philippines and Hong Kong were attacked, and on 8–9 December the United States, Britain and the Netherlands declared war on Japan. But the US Pacific Fleet had been crippled in Pearl Harbor, half the American air force in the Far East was destroyed at Clark airfield, and British naval power in Asia was wiped out when HMS *Repulse* and HMS *Prince of Wales* were sunk off the coast of Pahang on 10 December. Japan had achieved supremacy in the air and at sea.

The military advance continued remorselessly and in several directions at the same time. On 2 January Japanese troops captured Manila and Cavite, though the island-fort of Corregidor at the entrance to Manila Bay held out some months longer. British and Commonwealth troops were unable to make an effective stand in the Malayan peninsula; Kuala Lumpur was captured by troops of General Yamashita's Twenty-fifth Army on 11 January, and 'fortress Singapore' came under siege on 31 January when the causeway between Johor Bahru and the island was blown up by departing Commonwealth forces. The Japanese had for a time hoped to occupy the Netherlands East Indies in the same manner that they had taken over French Indochina, that is without a military campaign which would waste Japanese resources and endanger the most valued of Indonesia's assets, namely the oil industry. Dutch stubbornness, however, forced Japan in January to launch a campaign for the occupation of the Netherlands East Indies. Towards the end of the same month a two-pronged invasion of Burma was mounted from Thailand which, having revised its relationship with Japan in the form of a ten-year alliance on 21 December, declared war on the Allies on 25 January.

The climax of the blitzkrieg came with the fall of Singapore on 15 February. Secure in the air, at sea and on land, controlling the major strategic point in the region, divested of effective enemies, Japan could now proceed to mop up residual colonial resistance. The battle of the Java Sea (27 February—1 March) opened up the Netherlands East Indies to the Japanese who, having captured Batavia on 6 March, virtually completed their occupation of Dutch possessions by early May. Meanwhile the British had evacuated Rangoon on 7 March, and the conquest of Burma culminated with the seizure of Mandalay on 2 May; the campaign in the Philippines ended with the fall of Corregidor on 6 May. This was the furthest extent of the Japanese conquests.

Surprise is said to have been a key reason for Japan's military successes. Tokyo recognized the need to avoid at all costs a war of attrition which would have allowed its enemies, and particularly the USA, a breathing space during which they could have blocked the Japanese advance upon the prime targets of Southeast Asian mineral supplies and the region's defensible strategic points. Second, though some of Japan's triumphs were close-run things—even the victory in Singapore was one of these—we must not underestimate what so many purblind decision-makers in Western governments did at the time, namely Japan's real strengths. During the months before armed conflict, Japanese diplomats displayed immense skill in obtaining Russian neutrality in the Far East, in exploiting American isolationism for as long as possible and in taking advantage of Thai territorial revanchism. Preparations for war were thorough, military morale was high, and the conduct of the campaigns themselves benefited from knowledge of local conditions. Conversely, and here is a third factor in Japan's success, Europeans were insufficiently mindful of the threat of war in the East and their response was further weakened by the lack of co-ordinated resistance on the part of colonial governments in Southeast Asia. More important still in determining the outcome of events in the East was the impact of the war in the West: the gathering storm in Europe from the late 1930s onwards distracted Europeans from forearming themselves in Southeast Asia, while Hitler's military success in 1940–1 prevented an adequate response to Japan from Britain, France and Holland. In the end, revelations of the fragility of the power and the superficiality of the support which Europeans enjoyed in Southeast Asia provoked an outcry at home. In addition to military scapegoats, 'effete' colonial rulers and 'treacherous' colonial subjects were blamed in turn, although in fact fifth-columnists made an insignificant contribution to the outcome of the campaigns of 1941–2.[2]

Almost as soon as it had reached its greatest extent, the Japanese empire was forced on to the defensive and soon afterwards into retreat. The day after the fall of Corregidor, Japan's advance was arrested at the Battle of the Coral Sea (7 May 1942). A month later came the turning-point of the Pacific War when, by their victory at Midway (4–7 June), the United States established ascendancy at sea and in the air. Cutting two swathes across the Pacific, the Americans launched the Allied counter-offensive. General MacArthur, at the head of the Southwest Pacific Command, advanced through the Solomon Islands (August–November 1942) and the eastern archipelago (1943–4) to land on Leyte in October 1944, while the Central Pacific Command under Admiral Nimitz pursued a similar 'island-hopping' course through the Marshall Islands, Guam and the Carolines. Both forces converged on Okinawa and the home islands in the spring of 1945.

On the Burma front the campaign was at first more sluggish. In the summer of 1942 General Wavell proposed Operation Anakin to retake Rangoon. This came to nothing. Although Orde Wingate's First Chindits demonstrated in early 1943 the possibility of survival behind Japanese lines, albeit at enormous human cost, the Allies were dogged by disease, low morale and poor liaison between the British, American and Chinese contingents. The appointment of Louis Mountbatten as Supreme Allied Commander Southeast Asia (SACSEA) in August 1943 breathed new life into this theatre. Although Plan Culverin for the reconquest of Sumatra in 1944 was not proceeded with owing to Anglo-American disagreements, General Slim's Fourteenth Army withstood Japanese offensives at Imphal

---

[2] Major Iwaichi Fujiwara was, for example, the leader of a special agency (the *F Kikan*) set up to recruit overseas Indians to the Japanese side, but its contribution to the 1941–2 campaign was negligible. As regards Malaya, an enquiry by the non-official Association of British Malaya concluded that there was little evidence of fifth-column activity: see Sir George Maxwell, ed., *The Civil Defence of Malaya*, London, 1944. It appears that the only significant outbreaks of local armed opposition to Europeans in Southeast Asia during the Japanese invasion were the activities of Aung San's Burma Independence Army and the Muslim rebellion in Aceh in Feb.–Mar. 1942: Jan Pluvier, *South-East Asia from Colonialism to Independence*, Kuala Lumpur, 1974, 195. See also Eric Robertson, *The Japanese File: Pre-war Japanese Penetration in Southeast Asia*, Hong Kong, 1979.

and Kohima in March–June 1944. Then, destroying the resistance of the Japanese Fifteenth, Twenty-eighth and Thirty-third Armies, and expecting support from Aung San's Anti-Fascist Organization, Allied troops swept south and entered Rangoon early in May 1945. Southeast Asia Command (SEAC), whose headquarters had moved from New Delhi to Kandy in April 1944, now set about preparing Operation Zipper, the seaborne invasion of Malaya which was to be assisted from within the peninsula by Force 136 in liaison with the Malayan People's Anti-Japanese Army (MPAJA).

The war came to an end, however, before Operation Zipper got under way. Air-raids upon Japan from November 1944 onwards reached a crescendo in the massive offensive on Tokyo and other cities in May–August 1945. On 6 August the first atomic bomb was dropped upon Hiroshima, and this was followed by the second on 9 August. On 8 August 1945, the USSR declared war on Japan and swept into Manchuria. On 10 August Kuniaki Koiso's government offered to surrender provided the emperor kept his throne. Four days later the Japanese accepted the Allied terms of capitulation and on 15 August the emperor announced his surrender. Territorial expansion had brought them military burdens without commensurate economic gains, and the Japanese were in the end worn down by the economic, military and technological power of the Allies, who turned their full might upon the Pacific theatre after victory in Europe.

The Japanese Occupation

A decade of expansion had resulted in the creation of the 'Greater East Asia Co-Prosperity Sphere' embracing Japan itself, Manchuria, Korea, and territories of China and Southeast Asia. 'Asia for the Asians' was the avowed objective of Japan's mission to eradicate Western influence over, and bring freedom and prosperity to, all races living in the Sphere, and many Southeast Asians at first hailed the Japanese as liberators. This ideology was intended both to inspire front-line troops and to win local support. In fact it meant the subjection of Southeast Asian communities to the Japanese way, including the veneration of the emperor, mass celebrations of anniversaries in the imperial calendar and compulsory language classes in *nippon-go*, as well as the subordination of their interests to Japanese military and material requirements.

Directing affairs on behalf of Emperor Hirohito, Premier Tojo was the architect of imperial policy until July 1944. Conquered territories in Southeast Asia immediately came under military control. The commander of the Southern Army, Field Marshal Terauchi, established his headquarters at Saigon. Java, Sumatra and Malaya were in the charge of the army (Sumatra and Malaya being united under the Twenty-fifth Army until 1943) while the rest of the Dutch East Indies was placed under the navy. Although it was their intention, and well within their capacity, to retain as a colony the strategically vital island of Singapore (renamed Syonan or Light of the South), the Japanese clearly lacked the manpower to rule all their dependencies directly. As regards Siam, attempts were made to subordinate the country's economy to Japanese needs—which were resented by the Thais—but the Japanese made no move to intervene in the internal government of the country. Elsewhere the pragmatic adaptation of the institutional structures and administrative methods of the previous colonial régimes was a feature of the new colonialism. In each state vacated by Europeans, the Japanese inherited and utilized institutions and instruments that came to hand, though their task was made difficult by wartime damage to administrative fabric and the lack of experienced personnel.

Former Dutch and British territories, where Europeans were interned, were bereft of senior administrators; but in Indochina the Japanese retained French officials until March 1945, Governor-General Decoux arguing that in this way France saved its colonies. In the Philippines, where Filipinos had managed affairs since the inauguration of the Commonwealth in 1935, the local élite continued in post, and in other parts of the region where Southeast Asians had occupied junior echelons of government, local officials were advanced to fill gaps at higher levels. So, too, were former critics of colonialism and nationalist politicians who previously had either been imprisoned by Europeans or fled from them. Sukarno and the Malay radical Ibrahim Yaacob, for example, were released from detention and each was active in the mobilization of grassroots support for the military objectives and economic policies of the Co-prosperity Sphere in Indonesia and Malaya respectively, while Aung San, having returned to Burma from exile as one of the Thirty Comrades, placed the Burma Independence Army at Japan's disposal. The younger generation was also groomed for public duties. In Malaya, for example, some of the more able young men were sent for training at the *Kunrensho* colleges at Melaka and Singapore, or participated in paramilitary organizations such as *Giyu Gun* and PETA (a Malay acronym for Defenders of the Fatherland), or were even sent for further education in Japan itself.[3]

In June 1943, as the Japanese took the strain of a war on several fronts and anticipated Allied counter-offensives, Tojo declared his intention to delegate civil administration. Consequently on 1 August Burma became 'independent' under Ba Maw as 'Adipadi' (or Fuehrer); in September the Central Advisory Council was set up in Java under Sukarno; a Malayan Consultative Council was established in Singapore; and on 15 October José P. Laurel became head of an 'independent' régime in the Philippines. At the same time Japan rewarded Siam with the restoration of land: in July 1943 the four northern Malay states (Perlis, Kedah, Kelantan and Terengganu) were added to the territory of two Shan states and parts of Cambodia and Laos which Siam had already regained thanks to Japan. In 1944 continuing military reverses led to further political changes: in July Tojo was replaced as prime minister by General Koiso and in the same month Phibun Songkhram was forced to resign as Thai premier; he was replaced by Khuang Aphaiwong who served until September 1945 more or less under the direction of Nai Pridi Phanomyong and the anti-Japanese and

---

[3] See Yoji Akashi, 'The Japanese Occupation of Malaya' in Alfred W. McCoy, ed., *Southeast Asia under Japanese Occupation: Transition and Transformation*, New Haven, 1980.

American-sponsored Free Thai. In September 1944 Koiso promised, though he was never to have the time to grant, independence for Indonesia. In the following March the administration of Indochina was removed from French hands, and a nominally independent government was set up in Vietnam under Emperor Bao Dai.

Although these changes reflected Japanese needs rather than any sympathy for the aspirations of nationalist movements or, indeed, any acknowledgement of the latter's strength, the Japanese accepted that they risked damaging their own position by the gratuitous alienation of communities upon whose co-operation day-to-day rule depended. After all, the imposition of Japanese culture and insistence on emperor-worship were affronts to local customs and beliefs, particularly of the Buddhist and Moslem communities. With respect to the latter, the Japanese, like the Dutch and British before them, took account of these feelings by institutionalizing consultative processes. Towards the end of 1943 they sponsored the formation in Java of the Majlis Sjuru Muslimin Indonesia or Masjumi (Consultative Council of Indonesian Muslims).[4] Similarly the régime expressed respect for Islam in Malaya: the sultanates were left intact and a convention of religious councils was held at Kuala Kangsar in December 1944. The religious movement in Malaya, however, was anodyne compared with that in Java, which, having been legitimized by the régime, came to compete for the soul of the Indonesian nation with *priyayi* administrators, politicians such as Sukarno and Hatta, and the militant youth of PETA.

The primary objective of the military occupation of Southeast Asia had been economic, but the systematic exploitation of the region's assets was baulked from the outset by the wartime disruption of communications and devastation of shipping. The invasion and, more particularly, the scorched-earth tactics of the retreating Allies had destroyed or badly damaged much of the infrastructure of colonial states and wrought considerable havoc in the estates and mines of the colonial economy. The basis of the former colonial economies of Southeast Asia was further undermined by the different demands which the new colonial power made of the region. According to Japan's Commodity Materialization Plan the value of Malaya, for example, lay in its coal and iron rather than its rubber and tin, while the intention was to extract oil, nickel and bauxite from Indonesia. The effectiveness of Japan's command economy, however, rested on command of the sea and air; yet this was shortlived, being rolled back day by day after the US victory at Midway in June 1942. The consequent collapse of trade in turn resulted, as far as Southeast Asian countries were concerned, in a surfeit of traditional exports and a dearth of vital imports. There were gluts of rice in Burma and Thailand but dire food shortages elsewhere, especially in those areas which had become dependent upon food imports during the prewar period. Insufficient goods led to rationing, hoarding, a rampant black market and galloping inflation. This economic upheaval meant that, except for the small minority who won contracts

---

[4] See H. J. Benda, *The Crescent and the Rising Sun: Indonesian Islam under the Japanese Occupation*, The Hague, 1953.

with the forces of occupation, Southeast Asians in general suffered unemployment, poverty and the loss of basic necessities. In desperation government dragooned people into agricultural schemes, while former plantations were given over to food programmes.

The social consequences of war and occupation cannot be quantified with any degree of accuracy, though the loss of life was on a scale unknown in the region since the beginning of modern government records, and the atrocities committed by occupying forces upon Southeast Asians verged on genocide in the case of Singapore's Chinese.[5] Subsequent food shortages reached starvation proportions in some areas and diseases (particularly malaria) were on an epidemic scale throughout the region by the time of the Allied reoccupation. In addition, communities were uprooted. Families fled the towns to escape direct contact with the régime and squatted on forest fringes to scrape together a livelihood from subsistence cultivation. Labour was forcibly recruited from, for example, the Burmese, the overseas Indian community and amongst Indonesians in order to build such projects as the Burma railway or military defences. In addition, men were conscripted for military or paramilitary service or for the Indian National Army.[6] Furthermore, the occupation aggravated the latent hostility between ethnic communities (between, for example, Malays and Chinese or Burmans and Karens) and also provoked struggles between competitors for power within individual communities. Communal conflict was less the result of deliberate policy or totalitarian manipulation on the part of the Japanese—on the contrary, the Japanese practice of divide-and-rule was grossly exaggerated by their enemies. Conflict was far more the outcome of economic hardships, changes in political patronage, the erosion of local government, and the sheer mutual mistrust of those unaccustomed to indigence. These were the conditions which would spawn violent conflict whenever Japanese rule was relaxed or after it had finally disintegrated.

Southeast Asian Nationalism, 1941–1945

Violence and oppression, the ideology of liberation and the taste of opportunity, the experience of arbitrary rule in some parts of the region and the collapse of government in others, all these features of 1941–5 sharpened political perceptions and stimulated nationalist activities in Southeast Asia.[7] War and the Japanese occupation, however, contributed as much to the dissipation of political energy as to its generation, and as

[5] See C. M. Turnbull, *A History of Singapore 1819–1975*, Singapore, 1985, 190–4, though see also Yoji Akashi, 'Japanese policy towards the Malayan Chinese 1941–1945', JSEAS, 1, 2 (1970).
[6] For an account of this army recruited from amongst the Indians of Southeast Asia see J. C. Lebra, *Japanese-trained Armies in Southeast Asia*, Hong Kong, 1977, and K. K. Ghosh, *The Indian National Army: Second Front of the Indian Independence Movement*, Meerut, 1969.
[7] The young Ahmad Boestamam in Malaya, for example, later recalled the exciting challenges of these years whereas the experience of 'Co-prosperity' taught the older U Nu in Burma to 'beware of Pied Pipers!'. See Ahmad Boestamam, trans. W. R. Roff, *Carving the Path to the Summit*, Athens, Ohio, 1979, and Thakin Nu, *Burma under the Japanese. Pictures and Portraits*, London, 1954.

much to the fragmentation of nationalist movements as to their consolidation. Rather than square up directly to alien control, the nationalists' priority was the cultivation of local support; this they often pursued in competition with each other. Since at this time none possessed the strength to achieve power unaided, most accepted the need to seek outside assistance; the result was that the calculations of nationalist leaders and their capacity to act largely hinged on the outcome of the war and the fates of their respective sponsors.

Although they may not have assessed their long-term interests and those of the communities they aspired to lead purely or even primarily in terms of the aims of the principal combatants in World War II, Southeast Asian political activists nonetheless faced up to the questions as to whether they stood to gain or lose by supporting the Axis or the Allies, and whether their fortunes would be further advanced through painstaking negotiation or armed struggle. Such issues caused debate, frequent divisions and long-lasting feuds within their ranks. In Indonesia Islamic élites and militant youths came to jostle for Japanese favours with nationalists of the prewar Indonesian National Association (PNI), whose leaders anyway hedged their bets on the outcome of the war: Sukarno openly co-operated with the Japanese, while Mohammed Hatta acted as intermediary with Sutan Sjharir's small underground organization. Asian communists were particularly taxed by the ideological and practical implications of collaboration and resistance, and split over the Comintern directive (issued after Hitler's invasion of Russia in June 1941) to ally with imperialism in opposition to fascism. Of Burma's Marxist Thakins, some, like Thein Pe Myint, were prepared to form an anti-fascist alliance with Britain whereas others, notably Aung San, argued that the interests of the Burmese pointed to joining with the enemies of Britain.[8] Meanwhile the perfidious secretary-general of the Malayan Communist Party (MCP), Lai Teck, kept his options open, following Moscow's line of 'united front' yet betraying his anti-Japanese comrades when it suited him.[9]

The choice between collaboration and resistance at any given time was determined by a mixture of considerations. Some were attracted by the prospect of rewards, seduced by the ideology of the Co-prosperity Sphere or bewildered by the apparent omnipotence of the Japanese empire. Selection of sides was also affected by ethnic allegiances, kinship ties and conflicts far more localized than the global struggles between fascism, communism and imperialism. Collaborators were not necessarily drawn from those who had previously opposed Western rule; as we have seen, Asian functionaries of European governments, who may be thought to have had vested interests in the old régime, generally submitted to employment under the new one. Moreover, the critics of colonialism who at first were eager to espouse the Japanese cause grew to doubt Japan's willingness and ability to transfer power to Southeast Asians.

[8] See Robert H. Taylor, *Marxism and Resistance in Burma 1942–1945. Thein Pe Myint's 'Wartime Traveler'*, Athens, Ohio, 1984.
[9] Cheah Boon Kheng, *Red Star over Malaya. Resistance and Social Conflict During and After the Japanese Occupation of Malaya, 1941–1946*, 2nd edn, Singapore, 1987, 56–100.

To be effective, a collaborative relationship must bring advantages to both parties involved. The Japanese used Southeast Asians to run routine administration and mobilize support for political demonstrations, public works and agricultural schemes. The extent to which Southeast Asians themselves derived political benefits from these activities is, on the other hand, difficult to measure. Co-operation with the régime did not in itself guarantee concessions from it. Aung San, for example, lost faith in Japanese promises so much so that in 1944 he formed the Anti-Fascist People's Freedom League (AFPFL) whose services he offered to Mountbatten in June 1945. Sukarno was abandoned by the Japanese before they were able to inaugurate Indonesia's independence, and it was the Pemuda (youth) who forced him to declare *merdeka* (independence) two days after the emperor's surrender. Moreover, Japanese patronage could not for long compensate adequately for lack of local support and credibility. Parties, like Masjumi in Indonesia, which represented significant constituencies were able to capitalize on the relationship, but shallow-rooted organizations failed to survive if the Japanese prop was removed. Whereas Sukarno's republican movement had the ballast to ride the storms of 1945, Ibrahim Yaacob's KRIS (Union of Peninsular Indonesians) was flat-bottomed and easily overwhelmed: Ibrahim, who tried to take over the helm in mid-August, was powerless to guide the Malayan vessel and soon abandoned ship for refuge in Jakarta. Similarly, when the Japanese replaced the French-manned administration of Vietnam with an 'independent' government in March 1945, it was not the incumbent Bao Dai but the revolutionary Ho Chi Minh who made the most of Japan's weakening grip upon Vietnam.

If collaborators were not synonymous with the opponents of European colonialism, then resisters were by no means its natural allies. The backbone of anti-Japanese resistance movements was, on the contrary, provided by historic enemies of Western imperialism, namely Kuomintang cells and especially Southeast Asia's communist parties, who shrewdly calculated on an eventual Allied victory, but also set their faces against the restoration of European rule.[10] Their first priority, however, was to muster lasting local support and they did this by harnessing rural unrest and concealing their communist creed within a nationalist front of more widespread appeal. Thus in Burma communists were active in the AFPFL until the Burma Communist Party was expelled from the League in 1946. In Malaya the Chinese-dominated MCP, influenced not least by ingrained Sino-Japanese enmity, followed the Comintern line, setting up the Malayan People's Anti-Japanese Army and making contact with Force 136 agents. In Vietnam between May and October 1941, Nguyen Ai Quoc (Ho Chi Minh) launched the Vietminh (League for Vietnam's Independence) as a broad-based resistance organization comprising all anti-Japanese nationalists. Although the Vietminh's programme was not communist (its goal

---

[10] For local resistance movements see Taylor, *Marxism and Resistance in Burma*; Cheah Boon Kheng, *Red Star over Malaya*; Benedict J. Kerkvliet, *The Huk Rebellion. A Study of Peasant Revolt in the Philippines*, Berkeley, 1977; and Greg Lockhart, *Nation in Arms: The Origins of the People's Army of Vietnam*, Sydney, 1989. Cf. Charles Cruickshank, *SOE in the Far East*, Oxford, 1983.

was a democratic republic of independent and united Vietnam) and although the Indochinese Communist Party was officially disbanded, communists like Ho Chi Minh and Vo Nguyen Giap were nonetheless its principal leaders. Seeing the danger of nurturing communists on their southern flank, Chiang Kai-shek's Kuomintang detained Ho between 1942 and 1944; the Vietminh trod a difficult path between allaying the suspicions of the Kuomintang and other non-communists and succumbing to neutralization. In the struggle for power in Tonkin, the Vietminh secured their position by developing the tactics of guerrilla warfare, appealing to the peasantry and cultivating US assistance. In the Philippines Luis Taruc led the Hukbalahap (or People's Anti-Japanese Army) which turned out to be the best-organized and most effective of the resistance forces in Southeast Asia. Furthermore, capitalizing on the polarization of Filipino society and particularly the peasant discontent of central Luzon, the Huk went much further than either the Vietminh or the MPAJA (the one being impeded by continuing French colonialism and the other by Sino-Malay communalism) in implementing a programme of social revolution aimed at breaking the economic power of great landlords. By the end of 1944 the Huk were in undisputed control of most of central Luzon. They undermined Japanese power elsewhere in the Philippines too, and greatly assisted the USA in its reconquest of the country. Finally we might mention 'non-occupied' Siam where the left wing, led by Nai Pridi, kept in touch with the Free Thai in exile and, after the enforced resignation of Phibun in July 1944, controlled the governments first of Khuang Aphaiwong and then of Seni Pramoj (the former leader of the Free Thai in the USA), who became prime minister in September 1945.

Although resistance armies received military supplies from the Allies and were able to establish control over certain rural areas, these country-based and largely communist-led organizations were something of an unknown quantity in the calculations of Americans, British and Chinese. We have noted Kuomintang mistrust of the Vietminh; the Allied commanders in the SEAC and Philippines theatres were similarly suspicious of the reliability and intentions of the AFPFL, MPAJA and the Hukbalahap. They were wary of making any great use of them, though in this respect Mountbatten was of necessity as well as temperamentally more inclined to be accommodating than was MacArthur. Whereas Aung San's offer of cooperation was accepted by Mountbatten whose officers also liaised with Chin Peng's MPAJA force, MacArthur rounded up the Huks despite the fact that they had mounted the most strenuous resistance to the Japanese. Like the Katipunan in 1898, the Hukbalahap was unable to thwart an American invasion. On his return, MacArthur immediately disbanded the Huk and imprisoned Luis Taruc. Although resistance armies seemed poised to seize power and were in actual control of some areas by August 1945, they were not in a position to prevent the reoccupation of the region by the Allies. Indeed, their leaders hoped to enhance their claims for a place in the postwar world by facilitating that reoccupation, and it is clear that their influence upon the course of the European return was more marked than had been the contribution of fifth columnists to the Japanese advance in 1941-2.

Neither collaboration nor resistance invariably brought their expected rewards. The fortunes of nationalists rested on the amount of assistance they received from outsiders and the extent of support they enjoyed locally; the absence or the removal of either factor could bring about their eclipse. Great Power patronage on its own was not enough to secure a party's success, although Great Power opposition could block its progress. Nationalist activity, on the other hand, did not determine the outcome of the campaigns of 1941–2 and 1944–5, although it did affect the manner of Japanese rule and Allied reconquests. Allegiances were volatile during World War II since nationalists were as anxious to distance themselves from their sponsors as the latter were inclined to ditch them.

While it is generally accepted that the Japanese invasion and occupation turned Southeast Asia upside down,[11] the nature, extent and permanence of the changes of these years have all been viewed from sharply differing angles. While many have judged it to have been the climacteric in the modern history of Southeast Asia, contrasting images jostle for attention. One is of a dark age of barbarism quenching the 'Roman' legacy of colonial government; another is of the dawn of a new age, heralding the triumph of national self-determination. On the other hand, those who are less inclined to be startled by big bangs and prefer an interpretation that places more emphasis on continuous development, if not a steady state, have kept in mind the deep-rooted patterns and particularities of the region's past when making their assessment of what was, after all, but a brief chapter in its history.

So far as the place of Europeans in Southeast Asia was concerned, the military disasters of 1941–2 were profoundly humiliating as well as materially damaging. Furthermore, the Japanese invasion, occupation and eventual defeat vitiated those conditions which had been fundamental to the viability of the old-style colonial régimes. The international isolation and economic equilibrium of the region disappeared; the fabric of government was eroded; and political relations became more intense. In short, the events of 1941–5 led to the destabilization of every country in the region: the circumstances of August 1945 were not propitious for the restoration of colonial systems. So intrusive and extensive was the disruption that the collaborative networks as well as the infrastructure of pre-colonial states were now in disarray. In addition, the demands of world war, and not just those of the Southeast Asian campaigns, dramatically affected the ability of Europeans to regain their colonial territories. It was clear that the restoration of colonial rule would be impossible without the deployment of men, materials and military power on a far larger scale than Europeans had ever found the need to wield before or were likely to be in a position readily to command in the straitened circumstances of the postwar world.

In considering the impact of war upon the colonial empires one should not focus on the Southeast Asian 'periphery' to the exclusion of the European metropole. Just as loss of colonies in Southeast Asia undermined

---

[11] cf. the near contemporary account by Chin Kee Onn, *Malaya Upside Down*, Singapore, 1946.

European pretensions to empire in other parts of the world, so the war in the West had a major impact upon the future of Europeans in the East. By weakening the economies of European states, it reduced their capacity to fulfil an imperial role. Paradoxically, it also increased their determination to resurrect their overseas empires in order to compensate for injuries inflicted upon the wealth and the prestige of the nation. Thus it was that the Japanese period did not put paid to colonial empires for ever, and that after 1945 there were vigorous and not completely unsuccessful attempts to reassert the European presence in the region.

The notion of a watershed in the imperial relationship, a turning-point in the relative positions of Europeans and Southeast Asians, is illustrated in those studies of nationalist movements which emphasize the changes that occurred in political ideology, leadership and organization during a period whose significance for the region was, it has been argued, out of all proportion to its length. Conversely, other writers have drawn attention to the large measure of continuity in indigenous political activity and state development, and have claimed that the Japanese made few initiatives and left little lasting impact in these areas.[12] In distinction from either of these interpretations—the one suggestive of a clean break, the other of linear progression—this discussion has stressed the veritable confusion that engulfed Southeast Asia in 1941–5. Up to a point, of course, the problems encountered by the returning Europeans invited nationalists to assert themselves more defiantly in the face of any attempt to restore colonialism. Indeed, all demonstrations of over-rule, it might be thought, could only have been counterproductive, encouraging amongst Southeast Asians the very resistance which they were intended to contain. But the havoc of war had added to the difficulties of nationalists too. It had shorn rungs from the ladder they hoped to climb and had damaged the citadel they aspired to take. Furthermore, since the upheaval had also multiplied the contestants for power, there was the prospect of the struggle for national independence dissipating itself in civil strife. The race was on, but in the stampede following the Japanese surrender few winners and losers were yet discernible.

COLONIAL RESTORATION AND STRUGGLES FOR INDEPENDENCE, 1945–1948

Colonial Planning for Postwar Southeast Asia, 1942–1945

Almost as soon as they had lost their empires, Europeans began to draw up plans for their recovery. They did so according to their respective assessments of their joint and individual interests, and in the light of their

---

[12] The emphasis laid by, for example, H. J. Benda on the significance of the Japanese period (e.g. *The Crescent and the Rising Sun* and 'The Japanese Interregnum in S.E. Asia' in Grant K. Goodman, comp., *Imperial Japan and Asia. A Reassessment*, New York: Occasional Papers of the East Asia Institute, Columbia University, 1967) has been reconsidered in Alfred W. McCoy, ed., *Asia under Japanese Occupation: Transition and Transformation*, New Haven, 1980.

perceptions of the region's future. Two factors in particular determined the planning for colonial restoration: the value of overseas possessions, and the capacity to tap their worth. Indochina and Indonesia had formed the core of the overseas empires of France and the Netherlands before the war, and their governments-in-exile had no doubts about their importance for national recovery. De Gaulle's colonial policy was geared to the re-establishment of French power in a postwar world, while the identity as well as the well-being of the now hapless Holland had been nurtured by three and a half centuries in the East Indies. Britain's possessions in Southeast Asia were, by contrast, on the fringe of an imperial system which centred upon India. Nevertheless, Churchill made no secret of his belief that the recovery of Singapore was 'the supreme British objective in the whole of the Indian and Far Eastern theatres . . . the only prize that will restore British prestige in this region'.[13]

If it was clear that Europeans had not yet lost the will to rule non-Europeans, in 1942 it was still uncertain how they would set about realizing their intentions, especially since to a greater or lesser extent the restoration of British, Dutch and French colonies in Southeast Asia hung on the might of the United States, whose president was convinced that the age of imperialism was dead. Running through the wartime Grand Alliance was a vein of mistrust born of the colonial issue. Americans were predisposed to regard European colonialism as a mark of decadent societies, as ideologically misguided because it stood in the way of national self-determination, and as an obstruction to the pursuit of the American way and especially American trade. Britain's 'imperial preference' had particularly galled Americans during the 1930s and US anti-imperialism came to focus upon the British imperial record, although the Dutch and the French were by no means immune. Europeans, for their part, dismissed their colonial critics as, at best, naive or, at worst, mischievous. Trans-Atlantic sententiousness and ready-made blueprints, it was held, failed to disguise American self-interest; nor did they make a constructive contribution to the solution of the more intractable colonial problems. As the British were keen to point out at the time, the Americans themselves had had colonial responsibilities in Southeast Asia and the Pacific which they had singularly failed to meet in 1941–2.

Differing approaches to the issue of European imperialism were apparent, for example, in divergent Anglo-American interpretations of the Atlantic Charter of August 1941, particularly of Article 3 which recognized 'the right of all peoples to choose the form of government under which they will live'. These differences affected the conduct of military operations. Because of his avowed commitment to the integrity of the British empire, Churchill was suspected by well-placed Americans of being less than whole-hearted in the pursuit of Allied war aims and was accused of delaying the second front in Europe until circumstances were suited to the preservation of the British empire. Likewise in the Southeast Asian theatre Mountbatten's American deputy, General Stilwell, was a bitter

---

[13] Quoted in John Darwin, *Britain and Decolonisation. The retreat from empire in the postwar world*, London, 1988, 42.

Anglophobe, and a number of operation plans (for example, Culverin in 1944) snagged on Anglo-American differences. In the closing stages of the war the US administration, preferring to treat the French as an associate rather than an allied power, placed all sorts of obstacles in the way of the participation of Free French units in the battle for Indochina. These misgivings infected joint planning for postwar Southeast Asia. In 1942–3 Roosevelt (echoing Woodrow Wilson in the closing stages of World War I) advocated some kind of international trusteeship council to administer former Southeast Asian colonies on behalf of subject peoples. The French and Dutch would have been powerless to resist had the White House pressed ahead with such a scheme while even Britain, it was feared in some quarters of Whitehall, might have been pushed to the point of sacrificing its colonial claims on the altar of the Anglo-American 'special relationship'.[14]

As it happened, American anti-imperialism moderated with the prospect of peace. Its fire faded with the death of Roosevelt in April 1945. Moreover, as their forces hopped across the Pacific in 1943–5 the United States swept up new islands (such as the Marianas and Marshalls) which they would be reluctant to relinquish. In addition, the demands of global policing and the residual American inclination to return to hemispherical isolation contributed to growing indifference in Washington to the recovery of 'colonial' Southeast Asia once the fighting stopped. We should not anticipate the sea-change in American attitudes to both European colonialism and regional security caused by the advent of Cold War in Asia several years later. Nevertheless, American military planners came to accept that the strategic interests of the USA would be better served in several turbulent regions of the world (Southeast Asia included) by the restitution of the apparently stable order of colonialism than by the institution of potentially fragile nation-states. One consideration in this respect was the opportunities which colonial governments, starved of funds from home and hungry for American investment in the postwar rehabilitation of devastated territories, might afford American business. Furthermore, the US administration recognized that in the end it could not afford to antagonize or, more seriously, to undermine those Allied leaders like De Gaulle and especially Churchill who were implacable imperialists. Finally, US antagonism to European empires diminished as Americans allowed themselves to be persuaded that Europeans were revising the ideology and reforming the structures of their empires.

For these reasons, although colonial régimes would be subject to unprecedented international scrutiny by the United Nations after the war (and increasingly so as more Afro-Asian countries became members of the organization) and although their survival in postwar Southeast Asia would hang in large measure upon the acquiescence (if not the active support) of the USA, the acid seeped out of Washington's strictures. Thus, while the

---

[14] For extensive examinations of Anglo-American differences over empire see Christopher Thorne, *Allies of a Kind: The United States, Britain and the War against Japan, 1941–1945*, London, 1978, and Wm Roger Louis, *Imperialism at Bay 1941–1945: the United States and the decolonization of the British Empire*, Oxford, 1977.

Yalta Conference in February 1945 set up new mechanisms of accountability to the United Nations with respect to the administration of certain trust territories in Africa and reaffirmed the principles of the Atlantic Charter, it abandoned the demand for the general internationalization of colonies.

So it was that during their three and half years of exile from Southeast Asia the Americans, British, Dutch and French considered their respective roles in the region in an atmosphere of interdependence yet mutual mistrust. All planning took place within military parameters in the first instance, but policy-makers looked beyond the requirements for successful invasion, reoccupation and military administration to the longer-term objectives of civilian rule.

Despite Britain's scuttle from Burma in 1942, plans for the restoration of colonial rule were drafted with confidence. Governor Reginald Dorman-Smith, supported by a staff of British officials who had evacuated the country as the Japanese had marched in, set up his court-in-exile at Simla, and it was here rather than in London that much of the preparation for reoccupation was laid. Separation from India and the inauguration of the ministerial system in 1937 had amounted to a radical departure in British policy for Burma: the priority of the wartime planners was Burma's economic rehabilitation, not its political advance. Consequently, the proposals which were published in May 1945—after the reoccupation of Burma and victory in Europe but when the war in Asia still seemed to have a year or two to run—merely held out the prospect of eventual dominion status for Burma (i.e. self-government within the British Commonwealth, which at this time was also the British intention for India). If anything, the white paper regressed beyond the *status quo ante bellum*, since it envisaged suspending the ministerial system of 1937–42, putting the country under the direct rule of British officials until December 1948, and allowing the Scheduled Areas of ethnic minorities to remain under British control until they themselves opted for amalgamation with 'Burma proper'. In short, wartime plans for Burma aimed at the restoration of British power and commercial interests, but were justified by reference to the well-being of Burma and the Burmese.

British preparations for postwar Burma and the Malayan region followed dissimilar courses. The circumstances in which policy was worked out for British Malaya and Borneo were very different, and the planning itself was far more radical than in the case of Burma. Fewer colonial officials had escaped Japanese detention in Malaya and Borneo, and the initiative was seized in London by the Colonial Office (and the Malayan and Borneo Planning Units). The result was a fresh departure designed to bring about the administrative consolidation of British territories, facilitate the economic development of the region and eventually lead to the creation of a self-governing nation (or nations) out of the plural societies of the 'Malaysian' region. The first steps down this road were taken during the war: in May 1944 the Cabinet approved proposals for, first, a Malayan Union of the peninsular Malay States and the former Straits Settlements of Penang and Melaka; second, for Crown Colony rule in Singapore, Sarawak and North Borneo; and third, for a governor-general supervising British colonial interests throughout the region. Although these proposals were drawn up in secret and were destined to arouse considerable local opposition, they were part of a radically different and avowedly more progressive approach by the British to colonial affairs.

In December 1942, when Britain was itself making great efforts to present the acceptable face of imperialism to the American government and people by publicizing the ideology of 'partnership', Queen Wilhelmina delivered a speech which promised the convention of a postwar conference for the reorganization of the Kingdom of the Netherlands into a Commonwealth. This was to consist of the Netherlands itself, the Netherlands East Indies, Surinam and Curaçao, and was based on the principles of 'complete partnership' and 'self-reliance' (or internal self-government). The East Indies were the centrepiece of Dutch overseas interests and the Dutch government-in-exile was determined to return there, even at the cost of giving hostages to fortune. The scheme had a considerable impact in the West and went a long way to counter US criticism of European overseas empires. Indeed, Americans held up the Dutch as exemplars to the British. In Indonesia, however, Queen Wilhelmina's speech went unnoticed at the time it was delivered. Moreover, it was overtaken by the events of the next three years and, although used by the Dutch as their point of departure in postwar negotiations with Indonesians, in the event it contributed little to the postwar restoration of Dutch colonialism in Southeast Asia. Thereafter, the Dutch government-in-exile—most prominently Dr H. J. van Mook who was Minister for Colonies and Lieutenant-Governor of the provisional government of the Netherlands East Indies—was hamstrung in its planning by its material weakness. When it became clear that the British and not the Americans would be responsible for the Allied reoccupation of the Netherlands East Indies, the Dutch were aggrieved that their interests were increasingly neglected.

The emergence of De Gaulle as undisputed leader of the Free French by mid-1943 confirmed Roosevelt in his opposition to entering into any commitment to restore Indochina to France in advance of the Japanese defeat. On this issue the French government-in-exile and the British government maintained a common front: it was, after all, as much in Britain's interests to build up a strong France, as well as a strong Holland, for the rehabilitation and security of Western Europe, as it was to safeguard the generality of European colonialism in postwar Asia. De Gaulle, however, did little to endear the French to progressives, let alone to critics of colonialism. The Brazzaville Declaration of January 1944 ruled out 'all idea of autonomy and all possibility of development outside the French Empire'.[15] The Japanese coup replacing residual French administration in Vietnam with the 'independent' régime of Emperor Bao Dai only stiffened French imperial resolve. On 24 March 1945 De Gaulle's government issued a statement spelling out a future in which an Indochinese Federation (of Tonkin, Cochinchina, Annam, Laos and Cambodia) would rest within a French Union concentrated upon and controlled from Paris.

---

[15] 'Brazzaville Declaration of 1944' quoted in Anthony Short, *The Origins of the Vietnam War*, London, 1989, 40, and J. D. Hargreaves, *Decolonization in Africa*, London, 1988, 64–6.

The statement of 24 March seemed to reinforce the antipathy of the Americans (whose Office of Strategic Services or OSS had recently discovered Ho Chi Minh) to French participation in the war against the Japanese. Nevertheless, in the longer perspective, the beginning of the end of American resistance to the restoration of French rule in Indochina can be dated from this point. De Gaulle was later persuaded by colonial reformers and American critics to moderate the strongly imperialist sentiment of the March statement and modify the structure of the Union Française in such a way that the status of a number of French colonies was altered to that of 'Associated States'. According to this formula the more 'advanced' dependencies outside tropical Africa, such as Morocco, Tunisia and Indochina, would be set on the road to internal autonomy within the French Union. 'Reculer pour mieux sauter': the French government believed that these concessions would do nothing to undermine the international standing of France, and anyway many French people, including senior army officers, did not foresee a genuine loosening of ties between Paris and the colonies. In order to work, however, these constitutional arrangements required a large degree of metropolitan control over local colonial affairs, and this the postwar Fourth Republic was not destined to enjoy.

The Western powers returned to Southeast Asia determined to impose a colonial system of some kind. For Burma the British prepared for an immediate period of direct rule, while they planned a similarly assertive role for themselves in Malaya and Borneo. Over-rule in both areas was intended to be preliminary to the construction of eventually self-governing members of the British Commonwealth. Building on Queen Wilhelmina's declaration of 1942, the Dutch also drew up a Commonwealth arrangement allowing for a degree of local autonomy within a Netherlands-centred imperial system. The French Union was, in theory, an even more coherent arrangement for the integration of an overseas empire. Of the colonial powers in Southeast Asia, only the USA expected to make an early transfer of power to its subject peoples once they had been liberated from the Japanese. The American commitment to grant independence to the Philippines on 4 July 1946, however, did not come about in response to developments since Pearl Harbor, nor did it amount to the surrender of imperial control. It was, in fact, a stipulation of the Tydings–McDuffie Act of 1934, which had established the Commonwealth of the Philippines, and was intended to secure American interests and continuing influence in the country beyond the date of formal independence.

Colonial Restoration and Nationalist Resistance: Confrontation and Negotiation, 1945–1948

The brevity of the colonial reoccupation and the speed with which the colonial empires were cleared out of Southeast Asia has tempted commentators on the immediate postwar years to present nationalists as the victors, colonialism as a lost cause, and Malaya as a temporary exception to the inevitable success of region-wide resistance to European rule. Such blunt conclusions, however, cannot be allowed to stand without important modifications. First of all, although it would be misleading to underrate the difficulties faced by Europeans bent on restoring their power in Southeast Asia in 1945–8, we should beware of anticipating the end of their empires. It is true that their homelands were bled white, their colonies were broken-backed and that reoccupation turned out to be neither smooth nor permanent. It must also have been the case that scarcely any Europeans in positions of authority could have expected to find their colonial inheritance unmarked by the tumult of war or imagined that they would reconstruct old forms of control. Indeed, the British took care to dress up their plans in progressive language, and the Dutch and French were persuaded to modify the methods and rhetoric of prewar colonialism. Nonetheless, European morale had recovered sufficiently since 1941–2 to foster a widely-held belief that the obstacles in the way of their return were surmountable and that the re-establishment of their régimes would be in the best interests of Southeast Asians as well as to their own advantage.

In arguing that there was something resembling a common colonial purpose in Southeast Asia, we should not forget the nuances, sometimes tensions, between European viewpoints. Not only did discussions between London, Paris and The Hague often lack unanimity, but the policies of each of these governments themselves frequently changed tack. Government policy, of course, is rarely doctrinally coherent, since the art of the possible necessitates compromise. Inconsistencies in the respective British, Dutch and French positions become more intelligible when reference is made to personality clashes and the complexities of decision-making. There was a variety of interested groups—including politicians and civil servants, military officers and businessmen, metropolitan authorities and those on the spot—and they adopted different approaches to the problems of reoccupation. For example, directors of rubber and tin companies requested more public expenditure than British Treasury officials could contemplate; Governor Gent was keenly disliked by 'old Malayan hands', and Governor Dorman-Smith in Burma was sacked by Attlee; van Mook in Jakarta occasionally tried to rush The Hague into decisions; and Léon Blum, the premier of France, juggling with a precarious coalition, found himself presented with a fait accompli in Indochina by Admiral d'Argenlieu in November 1946.

A factor that assisted the European return was the distraction of Great Power attention from Southeast Asia by problems in Europe, the Middle East and South Asia. Palestine and India were the major imperial issues where Britain risked (and, in the case of the former, actually suffered from) American criticism, while Greece and Iran levered apart the superpowers of the wartime Grand Alliance, thus paving the way for Cold War. If the USA took an interest in Southeast Asia in 1945–8, it was largely to give encouragement (but not, at this stage, material assistance) to Europeans, rather than lend support to their nationalist challengers.

In querying familiar assessments of colonial weakness we should likewise be careful not to exaggerate the strength of nationalist movements in the immediate postwar years. Nationalism did not carry all before it to complete the business which had been started, but left unfinished, in the upheaval of 1941–2. On the contrary, there is a strong case for arguing that Southeast Asia experienced a 'new imperialism' in the immediate postwar years and that colonialism was not the preserve of the mentally inert and those who had lost touch with the reality of world affairs. Neither in the Philippines, where independence was transferred with apparent grace, nor in Indonesia and Indochina where it was bitterly contested, did the Western presence show signs of abatement. Since nationalist movements were themselves fragmented, it would be as unwise to present them as unstoppable forces in Burma, Indonesia and Vietnam as it would be to assume the immovability of colonialism in Malaya. It was the best and the worst of times for all and everywhere.

Given the similar ends and shared problems of Europeans seeking to restore the fundamentals, if not the prewar forms, of colonial control in the unstable circumstances obtaining throughout the region, and bearing in mind the unprecedented efflorescence yet diffusion of nationalist move- ments in every territory, it is not surprising that Europeans and Asians explored ways of advancing their respective positions by striking bargains with each other. From September 1945 to early 1948, the British, Dutch and French were engaged in attempts to enlarge their political control, subdue rebellion and rehabilitate their dependencies. One of their tasks was to win the co-operation of nationalist leaders who, for their part, showed a similar willingness to collaborate in order to gain valuable European assistance in the competition with rivals, the consolidation of power and the quest for legitimacy. Indeed, if one is to identify a common theme in the confused politics of Southeast Asia during the aftermath of war, it is the pattern of alternate phases of confrontation and negotiation as Asians and Europeans sought a modus vivendi.

Malaya is sometimes cited as the exception to a trend best exemplified by Burma during the aftermath of war. In Malaya, it is said, colonialism was reinstated without apparent difficulty, while elsewhere nationalism forced it into retreat. Although we now know that the British position in Malaya was more secure than that of the Dutch or French in their territories, we should beware of drawing too stark a contrast between these colonial experiences by underplaying the difficulties of one in order to highlight those of others. Instead of the 'triumph of nationalism', 1945–8 wit- nessed—to borrow a phrase from the historiography of postwar Africa— 'the second colonial occupation' of Southeast Asia.[16] Since it was the case that, in spite of the constitutional changes that occurred in the Philippines after the war, Burma was the only territory from which Western imperial- ism had been eradicated by 1948, colonial Malaya rather than nationalist Burma might well be taken as the paradigm of the period.

It was decided at the Potsdam Conference in July 1945 to divide the responsibilities for the military administration of Japan's empire between American, British and Chinese commands. According to these arrange- ments the United States would repossess the Philippines, occupy Japan, liberate Korea and assist Chiang Kai-shek in China, while the British-led

---

[16] See, for example, D. A. Low and J. Lonsdale, 'Towards the New Order, 1945–1963' in D. A. Low and Alison Smith, eds, *History of East Africa*, III, Oxford, 1976, 12–16.

SEAC would assume charge of 'colonial' Southeast Asia (apart from North Vietnam which was to be occupied by Chinese troops as far south as the sixteenth parallel).

Independence in the Philippines

The Americans were confident that the Philippines would remain within their informal empire in the Pacific whatever constitutional concessions were made to Filipinos; they had set up the Commonwealth of the Philippines in 1935 with the promise that independence would follow after ten years. The Japanese Occupation did not deflect them from this strategy, principally because it scarcely altered the social basis and composition of the Filipino ruling class through which American influence had been exercised. On their return, the Americans ignored both the claims of guerrillas who had resisted the Japanese and the misdemeanours of élites who had assisted them. As we have seen, General MacArthur swept aside the pretensions of the Hukbalahap, relegating them to the status of rebels. Moreover, he did not pursue the punishment of enemy collaborators but went about restoring civil administration as early as February.

MacArthur at first worked through President Sergio Osmena who had been a leading member of the government-in-exile and represented the pro-American leadership that had dominated Filipino politics before 1942. Meanwhile, however, Manuel Roxas, a member of the land-owning oligarchy who had managed to serve the Japanese régime without breaking his links with the Americans, was officially cleared of the taint of treachery and encouraged to mount a challenge to the Osmena administration. Flush with funds, Roxas and his Liberal Party conducted a vigorous campaign against Osmena's Democratic Alliance which reluctantly fell back on left-wing, even Huk, support. In the April elections the Liberals won majorities in the House of Representative and Senate, and Roxas beat Osmena for the presidency. So far as the Americans were concerned, Roxas proved more compliant than Osmena might have been; he could be relied upon to secure the country against radical social change and to provide for American economic and strategic requirements. After the passage of the Bell Act, ensuring free trade between the two countries, and the Tydings Act, providing financial aid to the Philippines, the Philippines was proclaimed an independent republic on 4 July 1946. The strong links between Washington and Manila which survived both the Japanese Occupation and the achievement of independence suggest that, as Pluvier has commented, 'there was, in fact, hardly any fundamental difference between the policy of the United States in South-East Asia and that of the European colonial powers'.[17] The grant of formal independence to the Philippines, however, did signify a greater willingness on the part of Washington than of Paris, The Hague or even London at this time to experiment with informal methods of imperialism in postwar Southeast Asia.

Southeast Asia Command (SEAC), 1945–1946

As soon as Emperor Hirohito surrendered, SEAC's frontier was extended to embrace Thailand, southern Indochina and the greater part of Indonesia

[17] Pluvier, 386.

in addition to Burma, Malaya and Sumatra, and its headquarters were transferred from Kandy to Singapore. SEAC's task was to accept the Japanese surrender and repatriate Japanese personnel, to evacuate Allied prisoners of war and others in detention, to keep the peace and assist the restoration of colonial rule at least until the future status of liberated areas had been fully worked out. It appeared, therefore, that the extension of SEAC's authority guaranteed not only British interests in the region but those of the Dutch and the French as well. In fact, however, the assumption of sole responsibility for the reoccupation saddled Britain with heavy burdens and obligations, some of which it would be hard-pressed to fulfil.[18]

Though an enormous enterprise by any standard, SEAC's resources were inadequate to its tasks. The Americans were not willing to make substantial contributions to it and the British government found that its own resources were already overstretched by military commitments in Europe, the Middle East and South Asia. Loss of initiative in India meant that Britain could no longer freely deploy Indian troops in policing imperial territories elsewhere in the world, as it had done, for example, in the Middle East after World War I. Moreover, the need to place Britain's economy on a peacetime footing and the promises made to the electorate meant that the Labour government was under domestic pressure to demobilize Britain's conscript army as soon as possible.

Furthermore, despite the contemporary reports of joyous welcomes accorded to the returning Allies, their reoccupation of the region was something of a shabby scramble. From the outset SEAC was wrong-footed by the unexpected swiftness of the war's end. Its troops were deprived of the opportunity of redeeming their military reputation in the eyes of locals by force of arms; its administrators were called upon to set up military governments over the whole region immediately instead of step by step. An understandable lack of preparedness largely accounted for that anarchic hiatus between the Japanese surrender and the Allied 'liberation'. The landings on the coast of Malaya (Operation Zipper) could easily have turned into a military debacle had SEAC met with resistance, and when British troops eventually arrived in Java they encountered armed opposition and lawlessness on a large scale.

SEAC's position did not improve significantly after headquarters and a framework of military administration had been established in each territory. Throughout the region food shortages, worthless currency, political uncertainty and administrative collapse resulted in SEAC's having few footholds from which to assert itself over profiteering and banditry, vigilantes and kangaroo courts, communal conflict and competing bids for power of various nationalist groups. The army of occupation was unable, therefore, to confine itself to military administration *tout court*; it became increasingly involved in regional politics both at local and international levels. In September the British government, through Mountbatten, put heavy pressure on Thailand for the return of lands wrested from Burma

---

[18] See Peter Dennis, *Troubled days of peace. Mountbatten and South East Asia Command, 1945–46*, Manchester, 1987.

and Malaya, the full restitution of British property, trading privileges, free rice and the right to station troops indefinitely. These punitive 'Twenty-one Demands' struck Pridi, who had been leader of the wartime Free Thais and was now acting as regent, as a blatant attempt to reduce his country to colonial or neo-colonial status. The Americans who had other ideas about winning the co-operation of postwar Siam (as the country was again called in 1945–7), intervened to secure a substantial dilution of the terms of the Anglo-Thai treaty. The Anglo-Thai treaty, which was eventually signed in December 1945, was one aspect of SEAC's contentious political role in postwar Southeast Asia.[19] As regards 'colonial South-East Asia', Mountbatten appeared more liberal than he did to many Thais but his position was made the more onerous by diplomatic pressure from the governments of France and the Netherlands. They suspected that a British supremo who could bring himself to accept for an ally the 'war criminal' Aung San in Burma and to decorate the communist Chin Peng in Malaya was half-way to endorsing the claims of Sukarno and Ho Chi Minh as well.

Transfer of power or struggle for independence in Burma?
On 17 May 1945, a fortnight after Rangoon had fallen to Slim's Fourteenth Army, the British government published the White Paper announcing its postwar policy towards Burma. Full self-government within the British Commonwealth was accepted as Britain's long-term objective for Burma as it was for India, but no timetable for political advance was spelled out. Instead, as we have seen, it was proposed to return, for the interim at least, to the position established by the 1935 constitution except in one major respect: the ministerial system would be temporarily replaced by direct rule in order to facilitate the speediest economic reconstruction of the country. The British were, however, soon forced to abandon this measured approach. Mountbatten was particularly sensitive to the local appeal and nationalist demands of AFPFL, and recognized that it was imperative to reach an understanding with Aung San. Well aware that the White Paper for Burma was inappropriate to the circumstances which reoccupation revealed, he tried to push Dorman-Smith faster and further down the road to self-determination than the governor was inclined to go. In August 1946 Dorman-Smith, who had only antagonized Aung San, was replaced by Sir Hubert Rance.

The police strike in Rangoon soon after Rance's inauguration as governor revealed the poverty of British imperialism in no uncertain terms. Government was on the verge of breakdown and the political initiative fast slipping from Britain's grasp. Rance was convinced that he would have to bring Aung San into his Executive Council, and that the White Paper had to be scrapped. Thereafter British rule was rapidly wound up. An AFPFL delegation went to London in January 1947 and reached an agreement with Attlee's government on the election of a constituent assembly to draft the constitution for independent Burma. When AFPFL won a resounding victory in these elections in April, it seemed that the British had achieved a stay of execution: they had found a strong man with whom to do business

[19] See Judith A. Stowe, *Siam becomes Thailand. A Story of Intrigue*, London, 1991, 337–59.

and looked forward to a future of cordial relations with the new Burma.

Such hopes soon receded. The Aung San–Attlee agreement on independence triggered a struggle for the spoils between a myriad of Burmese groups, notably AFPFL itself, the Burma Army, the Burma Communist Party, the Karen National Union, and others besides. The assassination in July 1947 of Aung San and six Cabinet colleagues removed the one nationalist leader who might have had a chance of uniting Burma and maintaining close relations with Britain.[20] As it turned out, AFPFL remained in office and fashioned the constitution for independent Burma. However, its commitment to both republicanism and centralism ensured, in the one case, complete severance of Commonwealth membership and, in the other, the hostility of Burma's minorities. Moreover, Aung San's successor, U Nu, was unable to establish his authority effectively beyond Rangoon when civil war, not least communist insurrection and Karen secessionism, engulfed the Union of Burma following the achievement of independence on 4 January 1948.

Why had British interests and influence in Burma been overturned so precipitately? Part of the explanation, but not the whole of it, lies in the strength of the nationalist challenge. AFPFL's struggle for independence, it should be noted, succeeded because it conjoined with other major developments in and beyond Burma. First of all, Aung San's bid for power was launched at a time when conflict among the Burmese themselves placed overwhelming strains on Britain's ability (and ultimately its military capacity) to determine political advance. As Hugh Tinker has commented, 'Power was surrendered by the British to the Burmese long before the Union Jack was lowered on 4 January 1948.'[21] The British might well have coped with opposition had it come from a single source; what undermined the structure of the colonial state and British efforts to keep it in good repair was the extensiveness of the damage and rapidity of its deterioration. What weakened the landlord's determination to hang on to that which he felt was his entitlement was the apparently unanimous opposition of tenants who otherwise squabbled with each other to secure the whole property or squat in parts of it. This political confusion was to AFPFL's immediate advantage since, short of old-time collaborators, Britain realistically negotiated with the strongest of its opponents; the result was that, of the several competitors for the colonial inheritance, AFPFL manoeuvred itself into the best position to win possession of the tottering structure of British Burma. In the longer term, however, Burma's confusion was to AFPFL's disadvantage; the paint and plaster that had been slapped on to get a quick sale soon peeled away, and disagreement abounded amongst the new owners over the question of multiple occupancy.

---

[20] For fresh light on the assassination of Aung San see Louis Allen, 'The Escape of Captain Vivian. A Note on Burmese Independence', Journal of Imperial and Commonwealth History, 19, 2 (1991).

[21] Hugh Tinker, 'Burma: power transferred or exacted? Reflections on the constitutional process' in R. B. Smith and A. J. Stockwell, eds, British Policy and the Transfer of Power in Asia: Documentary Perspectives, London: School of Oriental and African Studies, 1988, 24; see also Tinker, 'The Contraction of Empire in Asia, 1945–48: The Military Dimension', Journal of Imperial and Commonwealth History, 16, 2 (1988).

A second factor to take into consideration is the British Labour government's reappraisal of the importance of Burma as an imperial asset. Although the reforms of 1935–7 had cut the constitutional ties between Burma and India, Burma still remained an appendage of the Indian Raj in the official mind, and British policy for Burma continued to shadow developments in South Asia. Having decided in the winter of 1946–7 upon an early withdrawal from India, Attlee's administration looked at Britain's other Asian dependencies in a new light. Whereas the strategic and economic value of Malaya had never stood higher, Burma, which had been acquired and maintained in the interests the Indian empire, now lost its imperial raison d'être.[22] The end of British rule in India was publicly announced on 24 February 1947, when the deadline was set for June 1948 (a date later brought forward to 14–15 August 1947), and coincided with the decision to seek escape from formal empire in Burma as well. That the escape route turned out to be an uncomfortable one is indicative not so much of the British reluctance to leave, as their inability to determine the manner of their going.

Although a certain amount of Anglo-Burmese goodwill was for a time retained, not least because the new leadership required outside assistance in coping with its internal problems, the British were soon citing the transfer of power to Burma as an object-lesson whose repetition in other territories was to be avoided at all costs. For Britain decolonization in Burma proved to be a failure on economic and strategic grounds: civil war, neutralism and isolationism threatened the rice trade and weakened Western defence in the gathering Cold War. An exception so far as British decolonization was concerned, British policy towards Burma did not altogether reflect the new colonialism which was a feature of the postwar settlement of Southeast Asia as a whole. Between September 1945 and early 1948, Burma was the only territory where the former colonial power failed to secure its position even in an informal capacity.

New imperialism in Malaya
Withdrawal from South Asia was matched by swings to the Middle and Far East in Britain's interests and influence. As regards their dependencies in Southeast Asia, the British returned with plans for direct rule and promises of self-government. In addition they assumed responsibility for supervising the restitution of colonialism in Indonesia and Indochina, and for co-ordinating the rehabilitation of the region as a whole.

The British Military Administration was established in Malaya in September and lasted until the inauguration of the Malayan Union under Governor Gent on 1 April 1946. Just as he was identified with liberal colonialism in Burma, so with regard to Malaya, Mountbatten was anxious that the British should command the moral high ground by giving full publicity to the progressive aspects of the Malayan Union scheme which appeared to meet the eight-point programme of the Malayan Communist Party on every count. Even so, however, the period of military occupation

---

[22] See R. B. Smith, 'Some contrasts between Burma and Malaya in British policy in South-East Asia, 1942–1946' in Smith and Stockwell, eds, *British Policy*, 30–76.

was costly in terms of local goodwill as well as in manpower and material resources. Like Burma, Malaya was plagued by lawlessness and ethnic conflict. Malaya differed from Burma, however, in three important respects which go a long way to explain the differing outcomes of colonial reoccupation in the two countries. First, Malaya acquired an enhanced value after 1945 and even more so after the demission of empire in India; Malayan rubber and tin were major commodities feeding British factories and, more importantly, earning dollars for the sterling area. Secondly, Malaya (together with Singapore) was the base of British power in a region of contiguous Great Power rivalries. Thirdly, the British were not under the same economic, political and military pressures in Malaya as they were in Burma: Malayan mines and plantations were swiftly rehabilitated; the unprecedented Malay opposition to the Malayan Union was readily appeased; Indonesian-inspired radicalism fizzled out; and the leadership of the MCP for the time being chose to pursue the 'united front' strategy of infiltration in preference to armed struggle.[23] While the self-determination of a Dominion of Southeast Asia, embracing the Malayan peninsula, Singapore and the Borneo territories, was Britain's ultimate objective, the time-scale of political advance was indistinct and nationalist forces were inchoate. In any case Britain was on its guard against making any move which might suggest repetition of the humiliating scuttle of 1941–2.

This is not to say that the wartime plans for a Malayan Union in the peninsula or for Crown Colony rule in Singapore, North Borneo and Sarawak were implemented without protest. The surrender of Sarawak by the Brookes to the Crown in 1946 provoked anti-cessionist protest, principally from Malays in the Kuching area. This opposition failed to deflect the British from their course of action, and died away when the assassination of Governor Stewart in 1949 induced Anthony Brooke to renounce all claims to his patrimony. More significant was the unprecedented Malay opposition aroused by the Malayan Union and especially the proposal to award citizenship to non-Malays. Frightened by the prospect of the loss of traditional Malay support on the one hand and the emergence of Indonesian-inspired or communist-led opposition on the other, the British decided to appease the Malay Rulers and Dato Onn bin Jaafar's newly formed United Malays National Organization (UMNO). In July 1946 constitutional negotiations got under way; insistent that a strong central government and some form of common citizenship should be retained, the British nonetheless accepted the Malay case as regards the Rulers' sovereignty and a more restrictive citizenship scheme. Although the British never lost sight of the multiracial principle underlying the Malayan Union, the Federation of Malaya, which was inaugurated on 1 February 1948, was essentially a reaffirmation of Anglo-Malay collaboration, ensuring British domination at the centre, securing Malay control over the separate states, and further alienating Malaya's Chinese community.

The island-colony of Singapore resumed its role as the headquarters of British military power in the region. It also became the centre for the diffusion

---

[23] See Cheah Boon Kheng, *The Masked Comrades: A Study of the Communist United Front in Malaya, 1945–1948*, Singapore, 1979.

of Britain's political, economic and cultural influence throughout postwar Southeast Asia. The systematic disposition of British interests and activities, which had been the priority of Duff Cooper's short-lived ministry in 1941–2, was the major recommendation of Mountbatten's political adviser, M. E. Dening. When SEAC was wound up, Lord Killearn was appointed as the Foreign Office's special representative having the prime task of restoring the region's rice trade, while Governor-General Malcolm MacDonald supervised the affairs of Britain's various colonial dependencies. Between them they sought to secure the postwar settlement of the region, bringing pressure to bear on colonial partners in some instances and wooing the leaders of emergent Asia in others. In 1948 Killearn left Southeast Asia and thereafter MacDonald, as Britain's Commissioner-General 1948–55, fulfilled the dual function of co-ordinating British colonial and foreign policies in addition to chairing the British Defence Co-ordinating Committee.[24] Since the USA was comparatively indifferent to the region's affairs at this time, 1945–8 amounted to Britain's moment in Southeast Asia.

Negotiation and war in Indonesia, 1945–1948
The reassertion of imperial power by the Dutch was made difficult—some would say impossible—by the changes which had occurred during their absence and Dutch inability to make adequate adjustments to them. First among these we must count the fragmentation of the colonial state under the looser control which the Japanese had exerted over the archipelago. Added to this was the emergence of correspondingly divisive nationalist forces and anarchic, albeit highly localized, groups such as those who toppled the sultanates in east Sumatra or plunged into civil war the Javanese town of Bandung.[25] Dutch problems were further compounded by the hiatus that was allowed to intervene between the Japanese surrender and the arrival of the SEAC reoccupation force. This was delayed by troop shortages, with the result that General Christison did not land in Java until late September 1945, some six weeks after Sukarno had proclaimed *merdeka*. In response to the nationalists' partial establishment of an independent republic of Indonesia, the furthest van Mook was prepared to go was to offer a variation on the theme of Queen Wilhelmina's 1942 speech, that is the creation of a Netherlands Commonwealth or imperial federation in which semi-autonomous colonial states would remain bound to Holland. The Dutch, for their part, have apportioned blame differently: Prime Minister Attlee, Supreme Allied Commander Mountbatten and General Christison between them failed to provide an adequate platform

---

[24] For aspects of Britain's postwar regional policy see N. Tarling, '"Some Rather Nebulous Capacity": Lord Killearn's Appointment in Southeast Asia', MAS, 20, 3 (1986), and Tilman Remme, 'Britain, the 1947 Asian Relations Conference, and regional co-operation in S.E. Asia', in A. Gorst, L. Johnman and W. S. Lucas, eds, *Postwar Britain, 1945–1964. Themes and Perspectives*, London, 1989.

[25] See Benedict R. O'G. Anderson, *Java in a Time of Revolution: Occupation and Resistance, 1944–1946*, Ithaca, 1972; John R. W. Smail, *Bandung in the Early Revolution 1945–6. A study in the social history of the Indonesian Revolution*, Ithaca, 1964; Anthony Reid, *The Blood of the People: Revolution and the End of Traditional Rule in Northern Sumatra*, Kuala Lumpur, 1979; and R. B. Cribb, 'Jakarta in the Indonesian Revolution 1945–1949', Ph.D. thesis, University of London, 1984.

from which Holland might mount its return to the Indies. In contrast to General Gracey's firm action allowing General Leclerc's early take-over in Vietnam, Christison appeared to sympathize with Indonesian nationalists, while shipping shortages and other problems so delayed the return of the Dutch in adequate numbers that some bitterly complained that the British deliberately conspired to prevent the restoration of the Dutch empire in Southeast Asia.

It is true that in 1945–6, as in 1815–16, the Dutch were dependent on the British for the restoration of their possessions in the East. The British, it should be noted, were as anxious to assist the Netherlands after the surrender of Emperor Hirohito as they had been after the defeat of Emperor Napoleon; on both occasions the British were largely motivated by the need to assist in the resurrection of the Netherlands in Europe. In 1945 Attlee's Labour government had no wish to be associated with any action which added to Holland's appalling plight of penury and near starvation. On the other hand, the British government was not keen to commit men and materials which they could ill afford to a prolonged and debilitating military operation and one which also threatened to damage Britain's international reputation. Moreover, since the theory and practice of Dutch colonialism did not altogether coincide with their own, they were embarrassed by, and increasingly resented involvement in, actions that pointed to the return of Indonesia to unreconstructed Dutch colonialism. Mountbatten and Christison, like their masters in London, were predisposed to seek the political co-operation of the nationalists rather than risk military confrontation with them; but Lieutenant Governor-General van Mook refused to countenance dealings with Sukarno, while Sjharir, who presented the Dutch with a slightly more acceptable face of nationalism, rejected outright the Dutch olive branch of 'partnership' within the Netherlands 'Commonwealth'. Bogged down in political stalemate and a maelstrom of disorder, Christison and his men were distracted from the task of evacuating internees and repatriating Japanese. They found themselves in some instances relying on Japanese to hold the line against lawlessness, while in others, they formed the target of nationalists' resistance, as in the bitter fighting over Surabaya where General Mallaby was murdered in October 1945. Indeed, the British looked forward to the end of this rather tawdry episode and, though they had had little influence on the way the Dutch approached the political problems, it was with relief that they transferred authority over the outer islands to the Dutch in July 1946 and completed the evacuation of Java and Sumatra by the end of November.

Like Europeans elsewhere in the region, until 1948 the Dutch significantly advanced their position in Indonesia. Being beneficiaries as well as victims of times that were out of joint, they were able to call upon the allegiance of the outer islands whose leaders were mistrustful of the Java-centred republic. Such indeed was their hold over the outer islands by mid-1946 that van Mook went ahead with the 'Commonwealth' scheme, and at the Malino conference with Indonesian leaders of the Dutch sector in July he set about organizing 'autonomous' states which would form components of a Netherlands Federation. Controlling the outer islands, the Dutch could bring economic pressure to bear on the Republican government (now based in Yogyakarta) since the latter were desperate for food imports and also lacked the necessary exports to generate foreign exchange. Parleying with rebels and traitors did not appear to come naturally to the Dutch, who resented yet succumbed to British pressure to negotiate with nationalists; but it was the relative strength of the Dutch rather than their weakness which induced republicans to come to the conference table at Hoge Veluwe in the Netherlands in April 1946 and at Linggajati near Cheribon (Cirebon) in November 1946. By the Linggajati agreement (provisionally signed on 15 November) the Dutch recognized the Republican government's writ in Sumatra and Java, and both sides agreed to co-operate in establishing a sovereign, democratic and federal 'United States of Indonesia'. Linggajati saw the Dutch relax their previous insistence upon the 'imperial' connection, and ensured that future debate would revolve round the distribution of power within the proposed federation. Nonetheless the Dutch emerged from the talks materially unscathed and in no mood to abandon their claims to the East Indies. Had they worked harder at cultivating nationalist leaders, it is conceivable that they might have won genuine collaborators in their commonwealth experiment. Instead, they preferred to play upon the divisions within the nationalist movement while preparing to do battle with it should the agreement come to naught.

The Dutch were assisted by the structural diversity of the nationalist movement and by feuds between Republican politicians. As in many another 'nationalist revolution', the ideology of struggle (*perjuangan*) against imperial rule was propagated in order to distract attention from simultaneous conflicts between Indonesians. From within the fledgling government Sukarno, Sjharir and Hatta respectively appealed to the populist, socialist and Islamic strands of Java-centred Indonesian nationalism. Even so, the tapestry which they wove, or rather their attempt at patchwork, did not entwine all colours of opinion without some violent clashes, nor did they succeed in stitching together such a variety of political textures without rents and tears here and there. The movement threatened to come apart at the seams, indeed, under the strain imposed on it by the *pemuda*, the Indonesian Communist Party (PKI) and Masjumi. Moreover, if the Dutch were initially dependent upon British troops, the Republican government had fewer resources at its command. Its legitimacy was in dispute, its military strength unreliable, its economic base was in shreds; it was forced to withdraw from Jakarta to Yogyakarta early in 1946.

The fissiparous tendencies within the nationalist movement were encouraged, and the Republic was further weakened, by a long-running disagreement between those who urged *diplomasi* or negotiation with the Dutch and the advocates of *konfrontasi* or armed confrontation. That Sjharir was willing to negotiate at all indicated in the first place his lack of confidence in the nationalists' ability to repulse the Dutch by military means; it also evinced his preparedness to co-operate in the creation of some kind of a federation and an appreciation of the value of Dutch assistance in the fashioning of a viable successor state. As it was, the Republicans' failure to extract Dutch recognition of their claims to independence and sovereignty fostered mutual mistrust, aggravated political feuds within the nationalist camp, and undermined Sjahrir's authority; the result was that he was forced out of office in June 1947 and the Linggajati agreement lapsed. The Dutch turned these divisions to their advantage and followed up the collapse of the agreement by deploying some 150,000 troops in the Police Action or First Military Action. Their forces made territorial inroads into the Republican heartland of Java, and the stranglehold they managed to impose upon Yogyakarta strengthened their hand at a further round of talks which got under way at the end of the year and culminated in the Renville agreement (January 1948). The Republic could do no other than accept the current lines of demarcation and the plan to set up a United States of Indonesia in advance of any Dutch commitment to withdraw militarily. Like the conference at Linggajati, that of Renville exacerbated fissures within the nationalist movement and forced the resignation of a major politician, this time the foreign minister Amir Sjarifuddin.

Another aspect of the survival of Dutch colonialism during this period was its resilience in the face of 'world opinion'. It is true that Britain was instrumental in persuading the Dutch to open negotiations towards the end of 1946; Lord Killearn played an important part in setting up the Linggajati conference. Similarly, it was criticism in the United Nations of the Police Action which persuaded the Dutch to mount the Renville talks. Nevertheless the Dutch made few significant concessions to their opponents at either encounter, and their ability to withstand international opprobrium at this time is in marked contrast to the constraints placed by the United States on their freedom of action after the abortive Madiun coup later in 1948.

Revolution and resistance in Vietnam

In Vietnam the respective positions of nationalists and imperialists were more rapidly staked out and more firmly entrenched than in Indonesia, with the result that war between them occurred sooner and became more prolonged. The Vietminh moved fast in order to anticipate colonial reoccupation and to confront the Chinese entering from the north and the French in the south with a fait accompli. The key moments in the August revolution were the election of Ho Chi Minh by the Vietminh Congress as chairman of the National Liberation Committee in Hanoi on 13 August; the enforced abdication of Emperor Bao Dai as head of state on 25 August; and the proclamation in Hanoi of the independent Democratic Republic of Vietnam (DRV) on 2 September. At the same time the Vietminh in Saigon established a Liberation Committee which sent representatives to meet General Gracey when he flew into Saigon on 13 September.

Gracey's objectives were to disarm the Japanese in SEAC's sector (that is south of the sixteenth parallel); to restore order in the Saigon area; and to assist in the restoration of French control. General Leclerc, who reached Saigon on 5 October, was looking forward to an early revival of the French colonial régime which was assumed to have been merely in abeyance since the Japanese coup of the previous March. This task was not complicated to the same extent as was Christison's in the Netherlands East Indies by the problems of finding, liberating and repatriating large numbers of European detainees. Still, Gracey was troubled by indiscipline amongst French troops who provoked a good deal of Vietnamese unrest, and by the activities of guerrillas who dominated the countryside in the south. British and French officers saw eye to eye in rejecting the claims of the Vietminh in Saigon, and, soon after his arrival, Gracey set about disarming them and re-establishing French control over Cochinchina. Firmly, though not undisputedly, based on the Cochinchina bridgehead, the French proceeded to reassert themselves in Cambodia, Laos, Annam and Tonkin. By the first week in March, Gracey was in a position to hand over the civil administration to Governor-General d'Argenlieu, and the military command to General Leclerc.

During the next nine months relations between the French and the Vietminh deteriorated from uneasy negotiations into outright war. At first Ho tacitly accepted the reimposition of French authority over Indochina, while the French did all they could to avoid military engagements with the Vietminh. Since Ho Chi Minh was consolidating his support, he also avoided armed confrontation and hoped to win advantages through diplomacy. Like the Dutch, the French tried to restore their power (though not the prewar colonial order) by building up a coalition of collaborators and hemming in their opponents. Within the projected Federation of Indochina (which itself would lie within the French Union) they envisaged direct control over the most economically valuable area of Cochinchina and effective, if less formal, control over the monarchies of Cambodia and Laos. This, they felt, would more than compensate for political concessions to the Vietminh in famine-stricken Tonkin. On 6 March Ho Chi Minh and Jean Sainteny concluded an agreement whereby the former accepted the deployment of French troops in Tonkin, while the latter recognized the DRV as a free and self-governing state, though with the proviso that it remained a part of the Indochinese Federation and the French Union. The French also promised to hold a referendum on the issue of the territorial unity of the three parts of Vietnam. France appeared magnanimous, but in reality it made more gains than did the Vietminh by this arrangement: in exchange for paper promises it had achieved a distinct military advantage in the north. Further conferences—at Dalat from 17 April to 11 May and at Fontainebleu from 6 July to 10 September—did not, however, break the stalemate over three vexed issues, namely: French insistence on the integrity of the Union, the Vietminh's demand for the reunification of Vietnam, and the place of Vietnam in the federation of Indochina.

This diplomatic phase ended dramatically when d'Argenlieu ordered the bombardment of Haiphong on 23 November 1946. The Vietminh retaliated by blowing up the power station in Hanoi on 19 December, and the next day Ho Chi Minh declared a 'war of nationwide resistance' against the French. So began the First Vietnam War.[26] Its opening offensive, known as the battle for Hanoi, lasted until mid-February 1947, when

---

[26] But R. B. Smith has written: 'One of the most remarkable features of the Vietnam War is that no one can say precisely when it began': *An International History of the Vietnam War*, I: *Revolution versus Containment, 1955–61*, London, 1983, 3ff.

Vietnamese resistance collapsed and the French completed their occupation of the city.

It is generally supposed that the French *coup de main* was intended to force Ho Chi Minh back to the conference table, not on to the battlefield. The bombardment, indeed, can be interpreted as the continuation of diplomacy by other means, rather than its abandonment. The French had witnessed both the steady reinforcement of Ho's position in the north (following his electoral victory, the inauguration of a new constitution and the appointment of a new cabinet earlier in November) and the growing disruptiveness of Vietminh units in the south. The longer he was allowed to consolidate his position, it was argued, the less amenable he would be politically and the more elusive he would become militarily. The resort to force was, however, a cardinal error. The short, sharp shock neither extracted political concessions from Ho Chi Minh, nor did it knock out his army. French troops may have succeeded in taking Hanoi and other towns, but in so doing they drove the Vietminh into the hills whence came their strength. That the French failed to foresee Ho Chi Minh's reactions— he was provoked into doing the very things which violence was intended to prevent—reveals a profound lack of understanding of both Vietminh strategy and the deep rural roots of their support, for, whereas the French cultivated anti-communist élites in the towns, the Vietminh fomented social revolution in the countryside.

French actions in Vietnam at the end of 1946, like their intervention ninety years earlier, are to be explained largely by reference to three factors: the fluidity of metropolitan politics, the impetuosity of the military on the imperial frontier, and the poor control exerted by Paris over the man on the spot. The socialist premier of France, Léon Blum, laid the blame on d'Argenlieu, but Blum's commitment to peaceful methods was also compromised by the imperialism of his coalition partners and even that of the generation of 'radicalized socialists' who had emerged in postwar France.[27] This war was no exception in arising from the miscalculations of decision-makers and their uncertain grip on events. The battle for Hanoi, once joined, committed France to a war which during the next seven and a half years would come to dominate its overseas policy, debilitate its postwar economic recovery, and jeopardize its position in the defence of Western Europe. On occasions it would determine the fates of governments and shake the very foundations of the republic.

All this was for the future, however, for 1945–8 witnessed the colonial reoccupation of Southeast Asia. In the aftermath of war the British, Dutch and French were determined to regain their assets and influence in the region, notwithstanding domestic problems and the progressive vapourings of some politicians. During these years the British may have relinquished Burma but they established direct rule over the 'Malaysian' territories; the French in Indochina, like the Dutch in Indonesia, managed to match local resistance, and refused to let expressions of international disapproval deflect them from their chosen course.

---

[27] See Miles Kahler, *Decolonization in Britain and France. The Domestic Consequences of International Relations*, Princeton, 1984, 165ff., 171–6.

REVOLUTION AND DECOLONIZATION IN THE COLD WAR, 1948–1957

The Cold War did not break upon the world like a clap of thunder but rather, it came like rolling fog. It gradually enveloped first Europe and then Asia from the time when the Big Three partitioned the world between them at Yalta (February 1945) and Potsdam (July 1945) to the invasion of South Korea by the North in late June 1950.[28] During these five years the wartime Grand Alliance was replaced by two hostile blocs. In 1947 the Truman Doctrine (March) committed the United States to the defence of Greece, and Zhdanov's 'two-camp' doctrine (September) replaced the communist strategy of 'united front' with a call to world revolution. A communist coup in Czechoslavakia, the Brussels Treaty and the Berlin airlift during 1948 marked a hardening of lines in the West, while communists in Burma, China, Indonesia, Malaya, the Philippines and Vietnam sought power through the barrel of the gun. In 1949 the establishment of the North Atlantic Treaty Organization (NATO) represented a triumph for regional containment, but the defeats and retreat of Chiang Kai-shek in China convinced the US Secretary of State, Dean Acheson, of the need to prevent 'further communist domination on the continent of Asia or in South-east Asia'.[29] At first it seemed that the strategy of containment gave the European colonial empires a reprieve; if so, it was to be brief, for the last scenes in the drama of decolonization in Indonesia, Vietnam and Malaya were played out against the backdrop of Cold War.

The Achievement of Indonesian Independence, 1948–1949

At the Renville conference (named after the warship on which it took place in January 1948) it was agreed to set up the United States of Indonesia *before* the Dutch withdrew their forces from the country and to accept for the time being the current lines of demarcation between Dutch (or Malino) territory and that held by the republic. The Dutch had, therefore, established a strong position and they pressed home their advantage in August during talks in The Hague, where they worked out details of the USI with the BFO (the Federal Consultative Council of representatives from Malino territories). Their hand was reinforced, in the short term at least, by dissension in Republican ranks which came to a head the following month in the attempt by the PKI to hijack the nationalist movement. The Madiun coup of September, led by Musso who had recently returned from the Soviet Union, proved unsuccessful and, as we shall see, enhanced the non-communist credentials of Sukarno and Hatta in the eyes of the Americans. The immediate effect of this conflict between Republicans,

---

[28] See, for example, Robert L. Messer, *The End of an Alliance. James F. Byrnes, Roosevelt, Truman, and the Origins of the Cold War*, Chapel Hill, 1982; Richard M. Freeland, *The Truman Doctrine and the Origins of McCarthyism. Foreign Policy, Domestic Politics, and Internal Security 1946–48*, New York, 1985; and Marc S. Gallicchio, *The Cold War Begins in Asia: American East Asian Policy and the Fall of the Japanese Empire*, New York, 1988.

[29] Memorandum by Dean Acheson, 18 July 1949, cited in Short, *Origins*, 73.

however, was to weaken their resistance to the Dutch. It correspondingly encouraged the Dutch to take an even tougher line against the Yogyakarta government. Further negotiations in The Hague in October between the Dutch and the BFO revealed the determination of the Netherlands to employ counter-revolutionary nationalists in the imposition of a settlement upon Indonesia.

The initiative in Dutch policymaking had by now shifted from Batavia to The Hague. Lt Governor-General Van Mook was forced to resign and was replaced by Louis Beel, High Representative of the Crown. In November Hatta could do little other than agree to place the Republican army under the control of the federal authorities until the USI was formally inaugurated. The Dutch were nonetheless uneasy about Republican participation in the interim government; as a result, not content with the sizeable political gains they had won since the beginning of the year, they determined on a course of action which would crush the republic once and for all. On 18 December the Dutch government revoked the Renville agreement and the next day launched the Second Police Action (or Second Military Action). It was startlingly successful in military terms: Yogyakarta was occupied and key Republican leaders, including Sukarno and Hatta, were detained.

The year 1948 appeared to have been a good one for the Dutch offensive against the Republic of Indonesia. The Second Police Action, however, revealed the inadequacy of military imperialism—whatever the military superiority the Dutch enjoyed over the republicans—for securing their political objectives. Immediately after they launched their offensive, the Dutch were subjected to international criticism which reached such a pitch as to have a decisive effect on the decolonization of Indonesia. On Christmas Eve the United Nations passed a resolution calling for a cease-fire in Indonesia, and at the end of January the Security Council decided to set up the UN Commission for Indonesia to supervise the provision of an interim federal government. The Dutch bowed to this pressure to the extent of officially calling off their military action. Although operations continued against Republican forces, nationalist guerrillas succeeded in making inroads into Dutch-controlled territory, upsetting Dutch communications and tying down their 140,000-strong army, with the result that by August the Dutch accepted the impossibility of bringing off a conclusive military victory. They now took the diplomatic path, and in mid-April informal negotiations got under way with republican leaders.

The Second Police Action, however, had scarcely improved Holland's political position. In their dealings with Indonesians the Dutch had become over-dependent upon the support of the 'Malino group' (as represented in the BFO), whose influence, hitherto confined to the outer islands, was increasingly challenged even there by growing support for the republic. Nor did the Dutch fully extract the potential of an alliance with an alternative, albeit counter-revolutionary, coalition of nationalist interests. On the contrary, Holland's resort to armed aggression tarnished any legitimacy the Malino group may have enjoyed in Indonesia and also alienated its leaders. Suspicion of Dutch federalism was aroused, and this in turn cut the chances of Holland achieving its objectives at the negotiating table.

Republican leaders, by contrast and despite the setbacks of the Second Police Action, entered the talks politically more buoyant than they had been in the conferences that had produced the short-lived Linggajati and Renville agreements. In 1947–8, as we have seen, unity in the cause of home rule had been offset by disunity over the question of who should rule at home with the result that Indonesian divisions had assisted the restoration of Dutch colonialism. As 1949 unfolded, however, the Republican movement suffered less fragmentation and its leaders asserted themselves more confidently over rebels and revolutionaries. After the PKI's abortive coup at Madiun and the suppression of the attempt by Darul Islam (launched at the time of the Second Police Action) to pursue its goal of the Islamic state, Indonesian opposition to the Dutch became firmly non-communist and secular. The Republican leaders did not shrink from employing harsh methods in rooting out opposition to their authority and, in the twin struggles against Dutch colonialism and challenges from within, the army established itself as guardian of the state.

The publication of the Roem–Van Royen statement on 7 May 1949 marked a significant shift in the relative positions of Holland and the republic and a milestone in the decolonization of Indonesia. In being a party to it the Dutch accepted the need to seek a political settlement. Moreover, in contrast to the Renville agreement, they were now prepared to adopt the nationalist line that transfer of power should take place in advance of the integration of the republic into a federation. The political impact of this was momentous: the hardliner, Beel, resigned as governor-general and the BFO of Malino leaders now shifted from supporting the Dutch to cultivating the Republicans.

Thereafter the Dutch retreat was inexorable. An agreement on military withdrawal was reached on 22 June 1949 and Dutch troops pulled out of Yogyakarta a week later (30 June). The armistice was signed on 1 August and the peace conference opened in The Hague on 23 August. The major issues here concerned the extent of the financial obligations with which the successor state should be saddled, and the position of West New Guinea (West Irian). At the same time as the Dutch–Indonesian negotiations were going on, talks were taking place between Republican and BFO delegations; there was an inter-Indonesian conference between 20 July and 2 August, and by the end of October the two sides had reached agreement on the federal structure of the USI. On 2 November agreements on the transfer of sovereignty were signed by Dutch and Indonesian leaders. They provided, first, for the federation of a Republican unit (embracing Java and Sumatra) with the fifteen outer islands which the Dutch had sponsored; second, a prospective Netherlands-Indonesian Union; third, guarantees for Dutch property and personnel; and, fourth, the assumption by the new Indonesian régime of some four million guilders of debt. On 28 December 1949, the day after the instruments of transfer had been signed, Sukarno entered Jakarta as president of the United States of Indonesia.

The way in which power had been transferred provoked much nationalist criticism; the economic arrangements and the project for a loose union with the Netherlands were attacked as forms of neo-colonialism. In fact, the constitutional arrangements were soon superseded; in August 1950 the federal scheme came to an end and, except for continuing Dutch claims over West Irian, Indonesia emerged free of alien control. Even so, the extent to which the country was set on a new course by these events became the subject of much scholarly debate, as well as remaining the stuff of polemic.[30]

The Indonesian revolution meant the overthrow of Dutch rule. Coming on top of the Japanese Occupation, the upheavals of 1945–9 left indelible marks on the political consciousness of Indonesians, the social relations between them, and the policies of their leaders. The ideology of the struggle (*perjuangan*) was, because of its real potency, more than a useful political myth: it has fashioned the shape of the modern history of Indonesia. On the other hand, with the removal of the Dutch, nationalists were robbed of a common enemy, and what had been a temporarily unifying factor: in adopting the motto 'Unity in Diversity' the new régime was in large measure whistling in the dark. Moreover, the structural weaknesses of the state were by no means removed on the achievement of independence; nor did the post-colonial government launch a transformation of government or society. Firmly ensconced in Jakarta and heir to colonial institutions, it faced in the rest of the archipelago the perennial problems encountered by the Dutch and resorted to the techniques of its predecessors in order to suppress opponents and safeguard the régime against political, regional and religious dissent. In short, pre-colonial patterns, the Dutch legacy and the experience of the struggle for independence combined to determine the political history of Indonesia in the first decade of independence.

Another point of contention is more central to the subject of this chapter than is the nature of the post-colonial Indonesian state: it concerns the relative significance of nationalist and international pressure in forcing the pace of Dutch decolonization in 1949. Those who adopt the perspective of an area-study are inclined to stress the importance of 'developments in Indonesia itself' rather than 'the actions of the Security Council' in New York.[31] Nonetheless, it should be noted that in 1949 the Dutch were better placed in Indonesia both militarily and possibly politically than were the French in Indochina, yet a colonial war was to be prosecuted in Vietnam for four and a half years after the departure of the Netherlands from Indonesia. More significant than UN actions in themselves, however, was the US line on Indonesia; this partly guided, and was partly reflected in, the UN resolutions. That Holland's colonial régime collapsed earlier than that of French Indochina cannot be explained without reference to the international politics of 1948–50.

In 1949 neither France nor Holland was able to continue its colonial campaign without at least the approval and preferably the tangible support of the United States. Each, however, carried different weight in world affairs: French influence was reduced at this time by the instability of the Fourth Republic, but Holland was much weaker still, displaying to a

---

[30] For introductions to this debate see M. C. Ricklefs, *A History of Modern Indonesia*, London, 1981, 200–21, and Anthony Reid, 'Indonesia: revolution without socialism' in R. Jeffrey, ed., *Asia, The Winning of Independence*, London, 1981, 113–62.

[31] Pluvier, 487.

greater degree than at any time in the past two centuries the characteristics of 'a colonial giant but a political dwarf'.[32] Moreover, in the foreign policy calculations of the US administration for the conduct of the Cold War and the containment of communism, France and Holland were assigned dissimilar roles. While Washington argued that a French victory in Indochina would allow France to play a fuller part in the defence of Western Europe and was, therefore, prepared to allocate Marshall Aid to the war in Indochina, the same concern for European security led the Truman administration to a very different line on the resolution of the Indonesian conflict. Convinced that the overseas venture was draining Holland's lifeblood and impairing its domestic recovery as well as its contribution to the stability of Europe, the United States not only refused to assist the Dutch in Southeast Asia but went so far as to threaten to withhold Marshall Aid from programmes for the rehabilitation of the Netherlands.

Thus European affairs went a long way in determining US policies to (and, hence, the fates of) Dutch and French colonialism in Southeast Asia; American attitudes were reinforced when Asian circumstances were taken into account. In 1948–50 European colonialism continued to jostle with Asian nationalism in the competition for American approval, and, as in the earlier 1940s, the US administration was still more inclined to frown on the one and smile on the other. In the late 1940s, however, neither ideology commanded as much American attention as did communism, the existence or threat of which came to determine the disposal of American favours in the world and in Southeast Asia in particular. It became an axiom of US foreign policy that American interests in Asia rested on the survival of non-communist régimes, and, whereas the momentum of the CCP advance in China persuaded the US administration to regard French Indochina as the front line of the free world, Sukarno's stand against Indonesian communists at Madiun won for the republic the seal of American approval. From the middle of 1949, US policy shifted from non-intervention to intervention in Southeast Asia; in early 1950, with Mao Zedong (Mao Tse-tung) established in Beijing (Peking), Washington was persuaded that 'Southeast Asia was the fulcrum on which the recovery of the developed nations rested'.[33] This meant offering assistance to the non-communist Republic of Indonesia as well as to the French in their war against the Vietminh.

The End of the French Empire in Indochina, 1948–1954

Neither the French nor the Vietminh attracted significant outside assistance during the first two years of the Vietnam War. Far from the battle for

[32] Because of this unique position amongst European imperial powers, the makers of Dutch foreign policy during the twentieth century 'knew all too well that in a world full of dangers a small nation can only walk on tiptoe'. H. L. Wesseling, 'The Giant that was a Dwarf, or the Strange History of Dutch Imperialism', *Journal of Imperial and Commonwealth History*, 16, 3 (1988) 69.
[33] Andrew J. Rotter, *The Path to Vietnam. Origins of the American Commitment to Southeast Asia*, Ithaca and London, 1987, 2.

Hanoi (1946–7) being provoked by a conspiracy of international communism, the Vietminh found themselves neglected by the Soviet Union, the Chinese Communist Party and the Communist Party of France, while the French were too obviously pursuing colonial goals for the comfort of the United States. The aims of the Vietminh were to force the French out of Indochina as a whole (hence their support for Son Ngoc Thanh in Cambodia and Prince Souphanouvong's Pathet Lao insurgents in Laos) and to unify Vietnam as an independent sovereign state. Neither their programme nor their support was starkly clear-cut, however. There were disputes amongst Vietnamese communists over tactics, differences being particularly in evidence as regards operations in the north and the south, whereas their nationalist goals attracted Vietnamese of all persuasions and backgrounds except French-trained army officers, some Catholics, and those with personal stakes in a continued French presence. French objectives were, by contrast, to construct an Indochinese federation within the French Union and maintain the regional distinctiveness of the territorial components of Vietnam. Victory against the Vietminh was regarded as essential for the survival of their wider empire and for the revival of French influence in Europe.

In September Bollaert, who had replaced d'Argenlieu as French High Commissioner soon after the battle for Hanoi, attempted a political initiative with his 'final offer' of 'freedom and autonomy within the French Union'. This was rejected by the Vietminh with the result that Bollaert began to cultivate the 'Bao Dai solution'. On 7 December 1947 he concluded the so-called Along Bay accord whereby Vietnam would become 'independent' as an 'associated state within the French Union', and Cochinchina would be reincorporated within the other two parts of Vietnam preparatory to the return of Emperor Bao Dai from self-imposed exile in France. The Along Bay accord signified a concession on the part of Bollaert who referred to Vietnam's right to independence and territorial unity—objectives shared by Vietminh and anti-Vietminh nationalists alike. It failed, however, to outflank the Vietminh or to bridge the gap between them and Vietnamese non-communists, or even to provide the foundations for the construction of a solid alternative to the DRV. It led, instead, to the formation of General Xuan's provisional government which proved to be ineffective. Its 'independence' was compromised from the outset by the obligation to co-operate with the French in restoring peace to Vietnam, its authority was disputed by Bao Dai's adherents, and its very existence finally put paid to the possibility of co-operation with Ho Chi Minh. No nearer to breaking the deadlock, Bollaert resigned in September.

The war continued. By the end of the year the French were not only bogged down in Tonkin but fearful that the Chinese might intervene to tip the military balance in favour of the Vietminh who, for their part, were no nearer to attaining their objectives. They felt that their cause was neglected by nationalist sympathizers in the United Nations, while the mounting successes of Mao Zedong had not led to substantial military aid flooding south across China's border with North Vietnam. In any case, they were wary that indebtedness to the Chinese communists might result in the CCP taking over the direction of the Vietnamese liberation struggle or provoke American intervention on behalf of the French.

Throughout 1949 the French government worked at the Bao Dai formula. In March President Auriol and Emperor Bao Dai concluded the Elysée agreement whereby France formally acceded to the Vietnamese goals of national unity and national independence. On Bastille Day, Bao Dai returned to Vietnam as 'head of state'; on 30 December talks, which had been going on in Paris since 1 September, resulted in the Convention of Saigon (ratified by the French Assembly on 2 February 1950) providing for the transfer of sovereignty to the 'State of Vietnam'. The extent of the independence now granted to Bao Dai, however, was as limited as the support he enjoyed in Vietnam. Whatever traditional allure the emperor may have exuded, he lacked a base in popular politics and was in any case too tainted by a long record of equivocation to command the respect of either Vietnamese nationalists or French imperialists. The latter were half-hearted in support of him, suspecting that he might attempt a deal with the Vietminh or, alternatively, claim more concessions from the French than were compatible with the lingering dream of French Union. Real power, therefore, remained with the French who continued to shoulder the burden of the war.

At the same time, however, the dimensions of the war were expanding. Between the spring of 1949 and the end of 1950 international polarization was distinctly etched by various events: the formation of NATO (April 1949), knowledge of Russia's possession of the hydrogen bomb (30 September 1949), the inauguration of the People's Republic of China (1 October 1949), the Sino-Soviet Treaty (14 February 1950), the Schuman Plan (8 May 1950), the outbreak of the Korean War (25 June 1950) and the entry of China into the Korean War (November 1950). Against this background, the USA and China committed themselves to help Bao Dai and Ho Chi Minh respectively. The lines of Cold War, of Great Power confrontation and containment, now underscored the demarcation between the forces of colonialism and the 'liberation struggle' in Vietnam. The USA recognized Bao Dai's Vietnam as an 'independent state within the French Union' on 7 February 1950, and on 8 May Dean Acheson announced Truman's programmes of $13 million of military assistance to Southeast Asia, $10 million of which were being allocated to the French.[34] China had recognized the DRV on 18 January 1950 (being followed by the USSR twelve days later) and by the middle of the year had drawn up an aid programme involving the supply of arms and military training. China contributed to the preparations for the Vietminh's Le Hong Phong II offensive in northern Tonkin in the autumn of 1950 which resulted in defeats for the French (notably at Cao Bang) and left the People's Army of Vietnam in control of the border area of central Tonkin.[35]

Although established in Hanoi and the Red River delta, the French had failed to dominate the countryside of Tonkin where Giap pursued guerrilla

[34] This was the beginning of a commitment which would rapidly expand; by 1952 the US was funding 40 per cent of the French war effort; two years later its share had risen to 70 per cent.

[35] Laura Calkins, 'Sino-Viet Minh Relations, 1948–52', Ph.D. thesis, University of London, 1990, 120ff.

tactics effectively and prolonged the war to France's ultimate disadvantage, for time was not on the side of the French. Yet, while the military debacle of the autumn of 1950 revealed real weaknesses, the French presence was now sustained by America. Once they learned to present themselves as the defenders of a legitimate Vietnamese régime in its struggle against world communism, the French were able to exploit the geopolitics peculiar to Indochina and, somewhat fortuitously, to identify their cause with that of the 'free world'. At the end of 1950 the French military position was desperate; had they not won US assistance (taking the form of an extension of the Marshall Plan to Indochina) and had the Vietminh not called off their general offensive (in deference to China's anxiety over border security), their chances of survival would have been slim.

Of the three options in Indochina—colonialism, communism or monarchy—the Americans relished none, though they were persuaded to stomach the last when it was garnished with the rhetoric of self-determination. That the US administration shifted its position from opposing French colonialism to supporting the puppet of French colonialism is not to be explained totally or even primarily by reference to French machinations or to French needs. Of central importance in US calculations was their diagnosis of what the administration, Congress and American public all took to be an underlying global conflict between communism and the 'free world'. In 1949–50 Americans felt threatened by the Sino-Soviet bloc in Asia as well as in Europe, and the survival of France appeared crucial to US interests in, indeed to the very security of, both continents. Assistance to France in Indochina would not only block the advance of Chinese communism, it was argued, but would also release French troops for the containment of Soviet expansion in the West. The American strategy of containment in Southeast Asia, therefore, arose both from the seeds of West European union and from 'the ashes' of its policy in China.[36]

Although American military involvement in Vietnam would not become irrevocable for several years to come, in May 1950 the US entered into a momentous commitment to grant military assistance to the French. Whether the turning-point in US policy towards Vietnam is to be identified with the May decision itself or whether the switch occurred a year earlier with the collapse of Chiang Kai-shek in China and the unfolding of NATO in Europe, it is clear that by May 1950 US support for the French was out in the open and that the connections between Western defence and the stability of Southeast Asia were as firmly established in the official mind of Washington as in the political consciousness of the American public. The conjuncture rather than coincidence of developments in the West and East, so far as US policymaking went, is illustrated by the fact that, in order to win Congress support for NATO, the administration was prepared to accede to the request of Congress for a military budget covering the 'general area of China'. Again, it is noteworthy that Acheson announced the grant of American aid to Indochina on the same day that Schuman published his plan for Franco-German reconciliation.

---

[36] Robert Blum has argued that 'the American containment policy in South-East Asia arose from the ashes of its failed policy in China': cited in Short, *Origins*, 74.

The emergence of American anti-communism in 1949–50 had, therefore, decisive and contrasting effects on the colonial fortunes of the Dutch and the French. US pressure upon the Dutch from late 1948 hastened the arrival of Indonesian independence, while US support for the French gave a lease of life to the colonial régime. Whereas Madiun established a congruity between the anti-colonialism and anti-communism of the Indonesian Republic, with regard to Indochina the US had for some years oscillated between sympathy for the Vietminh's anti-colonialism and hostility to their communism. There are, indeed, grounds for arguing that until the middle of 1949 American policy towards Indochina suffered more tensions and contradictions than did their Indonesian policy. For example, although an American commitment to intervention in Indochina was shaping up as early as 1947, there was to begin with something of an even-handedness in American approaches to the French and Vietminh and a residual mistrust of French colonialism. Bit by bit, however, the US managed to reconcile its hope for a 'democratic' Vietnam with support for the new-style colonialism professed by the French, and was persuaded that the French Union would shore up the French position in Europe's defence and stand as a bastion against communism in Asia. After May 1950 France relied upon the Americans for the tools, while the US expected it to finish the job. It was an awkward division of labour and, as the prospects of French victory faded following the false dawn associated with de Lattre de Tassigny, Franco-American co-operation was dogged by mutual recrimination.

The US administration decided to support the French position in Vietnam against a probable Vietminh offensive launched with the full-blooded backing of the Chinese Communist Party and People's Liberation Army. As is now well known, at the time their judgment rested on an incorrect assessment of the homogeneity of the communist world and a misreading of the likely effects of Mao's victories upon the fighting capacity of the Vietminh. Despite the Sino-Soviet treaty and expressions of solidarity between Asian communists, each party had its individual needs and interests, and there were wide variations between communist organizations in the tactics and even the strategies which they adopted in the liberation struggle. Contrary to the expectations of Western powers, and it should be added those of the Vietminh too, the Chinese undertook no major assistance to the Vietnamese between mid-1948 and early 1950, while the extent of support afforded by the USSR at the same time was insubstantial. It was only after the outbreak of the Korean War that Chinese military aid to the Vietnamese was expanded. When this occurred, it became clear that Chinese and Vietnamese communists had different views on its deployment, stemming from their separate strategic perspectives on the Far East and Southeast Asia.

The road to Geneva
Following China's entry into the Korean War (November 1950) the Vietnam conflict entered a new phase. Fear of Chinese intervention stiffened the US commitment which in turn led to the transformation of General Giap's army and his greater dependence upon outside assistance. The arrival of de Lattre de Tassigny as civil and military supremo in December

had an inspirational effect upon the French war effort. By June 1951 he had halted the Vietminh offensive in Tonkin, thereby encouraging the French to demand further assistance from the Americans and to resist political concessions to the Vietnamese. By the end of the year, however, de Lattre was dead. In February 1952 the Vietminh, benefiting from military aid which now reached them on an unprecedented scale from China, forced French forces to withdraw from Hoa Binh. The build-up of communist military strength now made victory in Tonkin a distinct possibility.[37]

The French were trapped in a dilemma. Upon the outcome of the war appeared to hinge the future of the French Union and the fate of the Fourth Republic, yet war-weariness progressively enveloped the nation and its leaders. The loss of life and economic strain were taking their toll. The public, disillusioned by what they increasingly took to be sacrifices for an American cause, opposed suggestions of conscription for Indochina, while successive governments were only too aware that Vietnam was aggravating political instability at home and weakening them in relation to a reviving and rearming West Germany. As their inability to continue the fighting on their own was revealed day by day, the French played upon the convergence of the Vietnam War and European defence to extract further assistance from the USA. In exchange for their participation in the European Defence Community (which was agreed in May 1952 but never ratified by the French Assembly) they demanded such aid in Indochina as would enable them to win the war or at least to release sufficient troops to ensure French military equality with West Germany. Nonetheless, doubts grew as to the reliability of American support, for not only did the US administration make aid conditional upon French participation in the EDC but in Southeast Asia it was becoming ever more fixated by communist China. Moreover, it seemed to many French people that the ironic logic of military victory meant political defeat, since the confirmation of the independent state of Vietnam would spell the end of the French empire.

At the end of Truman's term as president the United States' involvement in Vietnam was not yet direct, inevitable or irrevocable and, like the French, it was uncertain in its approach to the war. Before it could decide whether to respond to the communist threat directly or through surrogates, it had to identify the enemy and choose between the Vietminh and the Chinese as the target. In theory, four courses were open to the US government: it could ungrudgingly assist the French effort; it could shift its support to Bao Dai and focus on the Vietnamization of the war; it could intervene directly and unilaterally; or, fourth, it could work for an international solution either militarily or at a peace conference. Each option had its drawbacks. In identifying with a French war, for example, the US risked losing the war itself or alienating Asians who would be essential to a permanent political settlement. Yet the second course was no less hazardous, since the Vietnamese preferred 'to sit on the fence' rather than support Bao Dai. The third and fourth options were not seriously contemplated by Truman's administration, but they received considerable attention from his successor.

[37] Calkins, 'Sino-Viet Minh Relations', 211–37.

In January 1953 Eisenhower was inaugurated President of the United States. The Republican administration and especially the secretary of state, John Foster Dulles, seeing the French flagging and the Vietminh expanding into Laos, determined to take over the direction of the war. They became irrevocably committed to victory in August–September 1953; when the Navarre plan of the summer of 1953 to throw more French troops into the campaign fizzled out, they began to contemplate the possibility of direct military involvement. Throughout the period from the start of the battle of Dien Bien Phu to the conclusion of the Geneva Conference (March–July 1954) the Eisenhower government discussed the feasibility and, in particular, the objectives, preconditions and extent of US armed intervention. Each of these issues raised a host of questions. Should American aims be to keep France in the war, or support 'independent' Vietnam, or again to take over completely from the French? Should intervention depend upon the prior grant by the French of independence to the Associated States or on 'united [i.e. international] action'? As regards the preferred or permissible level of military activity, the spectrum ranged from the existing programme of providing weapons and advisers to the despatch of land, sea and air forces through to bombing operations, the actual engagement of ground troops and the use of nuclear weapons. Vice-Admiral Davis summed up their problem: 'One cannot go over Niagara Falls in a barrel only slightly.'[38]

As the French reeled under the Vietminh onslaught at Dien Bien Phu, the US attempted to draw others, especially the British, into a joint military operation. Internationalizing the war by involving other Southeast Asian states and members of the British Commonwealth became the prerequisite of US entry as Dulles announced in his 'united action' speech on 29 March 1954. However, America's allies had different approaches to the problem. The UK in particular resisted the internationalization of the war; it refused to participate in Dulles' proposal for a joint air-strike on the grounds that this would alienate Asian nations, provoke China, activate the Sino-Soviet pact and risk a third world war. Whereas Britain suggested an international conference on the Indochina question, Dulles argued that only 'united action' in advance of talks would ensure an acceptable political settlement. In January 1954 at the Berlin Conference of foreign ministers, Anthony Eden, in the face of US resistance, managed to include Indochina on the agenda for the conference on Korea scheduled to take place a few months later at Geneva. When it became clear at the end of April (on the eve of the Geneva talks) that the British government would not participate in joint military action over Indochina, Eisenhower acted decisively to prevent the US administration sliding into unilateral intervention.[39]

The Geneva settlement, 1954

In the 1950s Southeast Asia was a less important region in British global strategy than, say, the Middle East; until the spring of 1954 Britain had shown comparatively little interest in the Vietnam War, nor had it prepared a coherent policy with regard to Indochina. Britain was, however,

[38] Cited in Short, *Origins*, 126.
[39] ibid., 146–7.

eager for a settlement one way or another in order to safeguard its own interests in Southeast Asia (notably Malaya which appeared threatened by the escalating conflict) and strengthen the position of France in the arrangements for European defence. When the reports from Dien Bien Phu ruled out the possibility of a French victory, the British government pushed for a negotiated settlement rather than risk Great Power conflict over the issue. Britain's role at Geneva was not, therefore, the outcome of a long-considered strategy for Indochina, nor did it reflect its power to influence events in the region. That the conference took place and managed to produce any agreement at all was due as much to the compliance of France, the USSR and China. It was these four powers, not the Americans nor the Vietnamese, who were the principal participants in the talks and the architects of the Geneva settlement.[40]

Pierre Mendès France, who became French prime minister in June, declared his aim to achieve peace within a month. He instilled decisiveness and direction into the French quest for an escape route from Indochina by which it would yet retain access to influence and interests. In the somewhat more relaxed international atmosphere following the death of Stalin (March 1953), Molotov and Zhou Enlai were anxious to find a peace formula; each needed to avoid antagonizing the other in Southeast Asia and both wished to contain American expansionism. It has been suggested that Russia was induced to go along with the Geneva settlement by a French promise to sabotage the European Defence Community (EDC), though there is little, if any, evidence of such a conspiracy.[41] The DRV later claimed (in 1979) to have been betrayed by China at Geneva, arguing that Zhou Enlai had been primarily concerned with the security of China's southern perimeter and, as a consequence, had been agreeable to the more or less indefinite partition of Vietnam so long as the Geneva settlement was guaranteed by the United States. If this was China's objective, then the outcome of Geneva must have been a disappointment to it, for Dulles, thoroughly frustrated by the proceedings, chose to have nothing to do with the conference agreements. In the early summer of 1954 Dulles was resisting a negotiated settlement in Vietnam and urging the launch of the European Defence Community with equal passion, and he acquiesced in the conference as the price for the prospect of French ratification of the EDC treaty. In the event he was disappointed on both fronts: unable to call the shots at Geneva, the US dissociated itself from the final declaration, while the following month the French Assembly threw out the EDC.

Although its proceedings were irritable and hesitant, the conference did in the end produce a ceasefire agreement between France and the DRV; it established an International Supervisory Commission (to implement the cessation of hostilities); and it issued a final declaration on behalf of all delegations excluding the United States. As a result, a provisional military demarcation line was drawn across the country at the seventeenth parallel and French military withdrawal was put in train. At the same time the independence, integrity and security of Cambodia and Laos were

[40] See James Cable, *The Geneva Conference of 1954 on Indochina*, London, 1986.
[41] ibid., 129ff.

underwritten, while the prospect of the political settlement and reunification of Vietnam was held out, once elections (proposed for July 1956) had been held. Beyond this the conference is said to have prevented the internationalization of the war, brought to an end the French colonial empire in Southeast Asia, and contributed to the long march of the peoples of Indochina towards self-determination.

The Geneva settlement marked a pause in the conflict, however, not an end to it. In international relations it represented the pursuit of war by other means. Predicated upon a Manichean division of the world into two hostile blocs, it reinforced belief in the existence of Western and communist monoliths. Instead of providing for the agreement of the Great Powers, it set the scene for another phase in their future confrontation. None of the participants (including the co-chairmen, Britain and the USSR) had either the will or the means to stand firm on the implementation of the Geneva settlement and to convert the ceasefire into a political agreement. The United States came to hate everything Geneva stood for; China soon claimed it had been duped as regards the position of Cambodia and Laos; and the opposing Vietnamese felt betrayed by their respective sponsors. Some weeks later the creation of the Southeast Asia Treaty Organization (SEATO) at the Manila Conference (September 1954) introduced a new phase in the conduct of containment in the region by replacing the outworn structures of French colonialism and military imperialism with a system of 'collective security'. Geneva may have prevented the internationalization of the Vietnam War in the summer of 1954, but it provided for the formal entanglement of Indochina in the international relations of Cold War.

A second consequence of the Geneva Conference was the end of the French colonial empire in Southeast Asia. Usually portrayed as truculent imperialists, atavistically seeking to revive a glorious past and oblivious to postwar realities, the French failed to construct a viable alternative to the DRV. The Vietminh were militarily vigorous—winning battles in Tonkin, conducting guerrilla operations in the south and extending their campaign elsewhere in Indochina—and Ho Chi Minh established an alternative administration not only in the territory directly under his control but also clandestinely in the south; in contrast, the claims of the Bao Dai régime to be nationally representative rang hollow. It is true that there was considerable tension within the Vietminh over optimum military strategies for Tonkin and Nambo (Cochinchina) and that they needed external military assistance if they were to win decisively; but the internecine feuding on Bao Dai's side was indicative of its divorce from popular forces, while his very survival (let alone any military success) depended upon French troops and American money. As regards Indochina as a whole, the French attempt to build up a bloc of Associated States was half-hearted and came too late to have a material effect upon the war in Vietnam. Here, although they managed to cling to the towns and the Red River delta, the French had surrendered the northwest of Tonkin by the middle of 1952, and the costly sacrifices incurred in holding their position thereafter destroyed the commitment back home to continue the fighting. All that said, however, the French did manage to curb the Vietminh advance and, when they departed, they in effect transferred to the United States the responsibility of sustaining the non-communist State of Vietnam.

While the Geneva settlement may have given respite to the peoples of Indochina, it did not provide a lasting peace; nor did it achieve the goals of national self-determination in Vietnam. The questions of the independence and sovereignty, the unity and integrity of the country remained the unfinished business of the conference. To the Vietnamese contestants Geneva was a postponement, not the fulfilment, of their respective programmes for the achievement of national liberation. Ngo Dinh Diem, who became prime minister in South Vietnam in June 1954 and would remain leader until his assassination in 1963, was as bitterly anti-French as he was anti-communist. He resented the fact that his government was not a party to the Geneva arrangements. The ambiguity of his consequent position— was it the government of the state of Vietnam or its temporary administration which he led?—riled him, and he protested against the partition of his country. The DRV were similarly dissatisfied; the Vietminh had made huge sacrifices to win resounding victories, yet the liberation of a united Vietnam had eluded them. Giap's military campaigns had been greatly assisted by supplies from China in particular; now at the peace talks the DRV felt diplomatically repressed by China and the USSR, which insisted on the subordination of the national liberation struggle to the wider interests of the communist world. The Vietminh struggle had only half succeeded. The fact that the independence and unity of Vietnam remained unresolved meant that the programme for social revolution would continue to be subordinated to military objectives. Yet their military position was not promising, since they were now directly confronted by the United States.

A comparison with the Indonesian struggle may be instructive here; while Ho and Giap were more successful militarily than Sukarno and Hatta, yet the Dutch were hustled out of Indonesia and the Vietminh were thwarted in victory. In both instances, however, it was wider international issues that determined the way colonial empires ended. In the case of Indonesia, Great Power involvement was one-sided: concerned for the defence of Western Europe and convinced by the anti-communist credentials of the republic, the United States took it upon itself to force the pace of decolonization. In Indochina, by contrast, the Great Powers were in competition with each other: in blocking the moves of their rivals' satellites they also blunted the aspirations of their own clients without assuming responsibility for the implementation of the arrangements which were cobbled together at Geneva in the summer of 1954.

Malaya: Decolonization and Counter-insurgency, 1948–1957

By the time the Geneva Conference had ended, the Malayan communists were a spent force militarily and Malaya was well on course for independence within the British Commonwealth. At the end of May 1954, Sir Gerald Templer, who had broken the Malayan Races Liberation Army, was succeeded as High Commissioner by Sir Donald MacGillivray, who swiftly met the constitutional demands of the non-communist Malayan Alliance. A year later the Alliance won a landslide victory in the federal elections, formed a government under Tunku Abdul Rahman, and, having refused to make political concessions to the Malayan communists in talks held at the end of 1955, conferred with the British on the early conversion of internal self-government into complete independence. The extent to which there are discernible connections between insurgency and decoloni-zation on the one hand, and between local and international developments in Southeast Asia on the other, are themes central to a discussion of the Malayan Emergency.

Enquiry into the outbreak of the communist uprising in Malaya has been dominated by two debates. One has been over the relative significance of local and international factors in determining the course of events; the other concerns the extent to which either the Malayan communists or the British authorities were prepared for the outcome.[42] Following hard on the heels of the Calcutta Youth Conference (February 1948), which issued the call for 'armed struggle' in Asia, and more or less coinciding with the uprisings of the Burma Communist Party, Hukbalahap and PKI, the decision of the MCP to take to the jungle and resort to armed violence was interpreted from the outset as part of the Cominform's pursuit of world revolution. The causal links between deliberations in Calcutta and decision-making within the MCP have, however, been largely discounted by some historians. Focusing upon Malayan circumstances, they have emphasized the importance of the economic hardships and political mar-ginalization of Malaya's Chinese; of changes in party leadership with the flight of the 'moderate' Lai Teck and the emergence of Chin Peng as general secretary; and of MCP frustration with the 'united front' strategy in the face of counter-revolutionary activity by the police and the reformed trade union movement. They have also drawn attention to the almost accidental manner in which the Sungei Siput murders committed the MCP to 'armed struggle', tipped the scales against British toleration of the party, and triggered a twelve-year Emergency. Accurate intelligence was to be vital to the eventual success of counter-insurgency, but it is doubtful whether in 1948 the authorities were provided with sufficiently precise warnings as to MCP intentions or information which could be relied upon as the basis for appropriate action. The High Commissioner, Gent, whose reputation had suffered from the Malayan Union debacle, was blamed for failing first to anticipate and then to counter MCP violence. At the end of June he was recalled for 'consultations', but he died in an air accident as his plane approached London.

During the next three and a half years the British mood swung between hope and despair as a force of some 4000 guerrillas tied down increasing numbers of police and troops. Malaya's strategic position and its economic

[42] See A. Short, *The Communist Insurrection in Malaya, 1948–1960*, London, 1975. For a recent review of the outbreak of the Emergency from the perspective of Malaya see Richard Stubbs, *Hearts and Minds in Guerrilla Warfare: The Malayan Emergency 1948–1960*, Singapore, 1989, 42–65, and for a discussion of China's involvement in communist-led uprisings in Southeast Asia see R. B. Smith, 'China and Southeast Asia: The Revolutionary Perspective, 1951', JSEAS, 19, 1 (Mar. 1988).

importance—it was the sterling area's largest dollar-earner—meant that its surrender was unthinkable to the British government. Periodically parliament was reassured that there would be no repetition of 1941–2, that the strike-rate against insurgents was improving, that plans for the long-term development of the territory were in hand, and that Britain would not withdraw until conditions were ripe for Malayan self-government within the Commonwealth. At the same time, however, the Cabinet worried about the increasing costs of the Emergency when Britain was hard-pressed to repay loans, rehabilitate the domestic economy, create a welfare state at home, and meet its commitments to global security. The Korean War aggravated their problems: by January 1951 defence estimates for 1951–4 stood at approximately double the level envisaged before the outbreak of the conflict, yet, given the fear of tumbling Southeast Asian dominoes, Malaya offered no prospect of retrenchment. The new High Commissioner, Henry Gurney, appeared to fare little better than Gent in the suppression of insurrection; the military, police and administration, and liaison between them, were all subjects of grave concern, while the authorities made little progress in winning the active co-operation of the Chinese community. British morale reached its nadir with the assassination of Gurney in October 1951.

The apparent drift in Malaya, which some attributed to the lack of direction provided by Britain's Labour government, seemed to end when the Conservatives under Churchill returned to office and General Templer was appointed High Commissioner and Director of Operations early in 1952. Like General de Lattre de Tassigny in Indochina, Templer was put in charge of both military matters and civil administration, and he had an immediately electrifying impact upon the war. In contrast to the French experience, however, the arrival of the new supremo coincided with a lasting improvement in British fortunes.

Clearly personalities and their policies had a role to play in the ebb and flow of the Malayan Emergency and the eventual defeat of the communist insurgents. Nevertheless, it should be noted that the Conservatives continued the policies of their Labour predecessors in all essentials: both parties emphasized the need for political development and nation-building, and both set great store on the Malayan Union principles of the consolidation of the discrete territories of the region (particularly the closer association of Malaya and Singapore) and the growth of multiracialism as opposed to communal politics.[43] Moreover, Templer himself brought to fruition plans whose seeds had been sown during Gurney's time, notably Briggs's scheme to resettle in New Villages half a million Chinese squatters upon whom the communists relied for supplies and information. Indeed, Templer's 'hearts and minds' strategy, with its accent upon the political and social advance of the Malayan people, had been foreshadowed by various moves made under Gurney: they included the quasi-ministerial Member system (April 1951); the bill to increase the number of non-Malays eligible for federal citizenship (which came into effect in September 1952,

[43] A. J. Stockwell, 'British imperial policy and decolonization in Malaya, 1942–52', *Journal of Imperial and Commonwealth History*, 13, 1 (1984).

seven months after Templer arrived); and attempts to improve the economic lot of the Malays (for example through the Rural and Industrial Development Authority set up in 1950).

The British never lost sight of the fact that, as Eden put it, 'Communism in Asia cannot be checked by military means alone.'[44] The press statement made by Colonial Secretary Oliver Lyttelton during his visit to Malaya in December 1951 stressed the prime need to restore law and order and was welcomed by some as a commitment to reassert British authority, but in fact it did not breach the bipartisan pledge 'to guide Colonial people along the road to self-government within the framework of the British Empire'. The directive issued to Templer a few weeks later started with the declaration that '[t]he policy of His Majesty's Government in the United Kingdom is that Malaya should in due course become a fully self-governing nation'; it expressed the hope that 'that nation will be within the British Commonwealth'; it pointed to the need to 'achieve a united Malayan nation ... [through] a common form of citizenship for all who regard the Federation or any part of it as their real home and the object of their loyalty'; and it instructed the High Commissioner 'to guide the peoples of Malaya towards the attainment of these objectives and to promote such political progress of the country as will, without prejudicing the campaign against the terrorists, further our democratic aims in Malaya'.[45]

If the aims of British policy were not in doubt, the timing, manner and very chances of their realization were by no means certain. 'Nation-building' involved the cultivation of multiracial as well as popular politics, and a British precondition for the transfer of power was the emergence of a responsibly-led, democratically-endorsed and multiracial party of government. Alarmed at the politicization of communal antagonisms resulting from the successive crises of the 1945 interregnum, Malayan Union and the Emergency, Commissioner-General MacDonald sponsored the Communities Liaison Committee and approved of Dato Onn's attempts to broaden the appeal of the communally exclusive United Malays National Organization (UMNO). But neither of these initiatives put down firm roots in the political subsoil, while Onn's avowedly non-communal Independence of Malaya Party flopped within a year of its inauguration in the second half of 1951. Like the Americans in their attitude to the Vietnamese, the British were dismayed by the propensity of Malaya's Chinese community to 'sit on the fence'. To win their allegiance, Gurney had encouraged the launch of the Malayan Chinese Association (MCA) in 1949, although until his death he remained unconvinced that its leaders possessed sufficient determination effectively to counter the MCP appeal to the poor and disenfranchised majority of Malaya's Chinese. In short, from its start in June 1948 to the end of 1951 the Emergency appeared to retard the prospects of British withdrawal and to constrain the development of Malayan politics.

From 1952, the essential ingredients of counter-insurgency operations— intelligence, policing and civil-military co-ordination—all improved and,

---

[44] Sir Anthony Eden, *Memoirs: Full Circle*, London, 1960, 109.
[45] Public Record Office, PREM 11/639, 1 Feb. 1952. See also John Cloake, *Templer. Tiger of Malaya. The life of Field Marshal Sir Gerald Templer*, London, 1985, 457–8.

with the achievement of more tangible successes against the guerrillas, the pace of political advance resumed. In order to prevent victory by the Independence of Malaya Party in the Kuala Lumpur municipal elections of February 1952, the local branch organizations of UMNO and MCA struck an ad hoc alliance. In March 1953 this arrangement was formalized by the central leadership of both parties, and the Alliance was augmented by the accession of the Malayan Indian Congress in 1954. As Templer rolled back the insurrection, declaring the first 'white area' (where Emergency regulations were relaxed) in Melaka in September 1953, so the Alliance pressed for the early grant of independence. The British were mistrustful of a political coalition, which if it survived at all threatened to institutionalize communalism, and dubious of the ability of UMNO and MCA leaders to discipline their respective supporters; for these reasons the British at first cold-shouldered Alliance exuberance. Though not severely shaken by the non-cooperation campaign which the Alliance mounted in May–June 1954 in order to hammer home their demand for an elected majority on the Federal Legislative Council, the British were nonetheless conscious of the absence of any popular alternative. The upshot was that High Commissioner Donald MacGillivray (1954–7) reached a compromise with the Alliance on the composition of the new Federal Council in July 1954.

The pace of decolonization hereafter gathered such momentum as to leave officials breathless. By the end of 1955 the Alliance appeared to have met British requirements in bridging racial divides, commanding electoral support in the federal elections of July 1955, and standing firm against communism at the Baling talks with Chin Peng in December. When British and Malayan delegations conferred in London in January–February 1956, the former conceded the Alliance timetable for independence by the end of August 1957, while the latter accepted the need for a continuing British presence in post-independent Malaya for the defence and economic well-being of the country. The next eighteen months saw a hectic round of negotiations with respect to the financial aspects of independence, the Anglo-Malayan Defence Arrangement, and the balances to be struck between Malay privileges and non-Malay rights and between state autonomy and central powers in the constitution of the new state. All these issues provoked disagreements and there was some hard bargaining over the defence treaty, but on the fundamentals of security and subversion both sides thought alike.

If the communist insurrection had forced the pace of political change in Malaya, it had fortuitously played into British hands by throwing up a staunchly anti-communist leadership which not only valued continuing close relations with Britain but also enjoyed overwhelming popular support. This had not occurred in either Indonesia or Vietnam, where the Dutch and French had failed to find secure footholds in the shifting sands of local politics. The contrast in the respective fortunes of European colonial régimes, however, is not to be attributed solely or even mainly to British skill in manipulating nationalist politicians. After all, the Alliance was not a colonial stooge but a product of ingrained communalism, for which the activities of British colonialists in the past may have been partly responsible, but to which British decolonizers were now forced to reconcile themselves. The structure of Malaya's plural society, indeed, virtually predetermined the failure of the Chinese-dominated MCP to rouse anything more than token Malay support; this in turn explained their inability to sustain a rural revolution or to present a convincingly nationalist programme. In addition, and in contrast with the Vietminh, the Malayan communists did not receive significant help from outside the country; they waged the 'armed struggle' more or less in isolation. In view of its meagre triumphs and the slow progress towards victory, the MCP leadership decided in October 1951 to end indiscriminate violence (but not to abandon the military campaign) and to focus on the political organization of the masses. In this area, too, it could not compete with the Anglo-Malayan authorities at federal, state and district levels. What support the MCP had once mustered slipped away, and Chin Peng had no trump cards to play when he parleyed with Tunku Abdul Rahman, chief minister of the elected Malayan government.

Just as the MCP waged the liberation struggle without significant aid from China or the USSR, so Britain was left more or less to its own devices in this theatre of the Cold War. Although Malaya was central to British influence in the region, it was peripheral to the interests of other Great Powers. The Malayan Emergency did not attract international attention to nearly the same degree as did Indonesia in 1948–9 and Indochina in 1950–4. The British were not eased out of their colony by American political pressure, as the Dutch were; nor, like the French, were they propped up by US military assistance. Of course, the British government was gratified by Washington's approval of its efforts and more material expressions of support in the form of non-military supplies. The costly Malayan operation also carried some advantages for British diplomats treading the tightrope of the special relationship; on the one hand, it demonstrated British anti-communist bona fides while, on the other, it provided an excuse for not joining the US in a strike on Indochina. As time went on, indeed, the British became increasingly worried by American militarism which, as the events surrounding the Geneva conference revealed, jeopardized good relations with the independent and emergent states of Asia.

The closeness of Anglo-Malayan relations in the aftermath of the transfer of power raised all sorts of questions as regards the degree of independence which was actually achieved by the successor state. Although Malaya refused to join SEATO, it remained central to British interests in Southeast Asia for at least another decade. It participated in the internal security of colonial Singapore, and then provided the stem of Malaysia on to which the remaining colonies of Singapore, Sabah and Sarawak were grafted as Britain relinquished responsibility for them in 1963. Britain, for its part, directly assisted Malaya in Emergency operations until they officially ended in 1960; it rushed to the defence of Malaysia in its Confrontation with Indonesia in 1963–6; it was the dominant partner in the Anglo-Malayan Defence Arrangement[46] (to which Australia, New

---

[46] See Chin Kee Wah, *The defence of Malaysia and Singapore. The transformation of a security system 1957–1971*, Cambridge, 1983.

Zealand and Singapore also adhered); and it took charge of the defence of Western interests in maritime Southeast Asia. In the 1960s, however, the Wilson government decided on economic grounds to run down its military commitment east of Suez and to embark upon a phased withdrawal from the Singapore naval base. Domestic realities forced post-imperial Britain to come to terms with the regional realities of post-colonial Southeast Asia, whose international affairs were by now dominated by the US presence.

CONCLUSION

Since the main theme of this chapter has been the ending of European empires in Southeast Asia, it is appropriate to conclude with some general reflections on their decline and fall. Libertarians through the ages have detected philosophical lessons in the hubris and subsequent nemesis of successors to Ozymandias King of Kings, the glory and grandeur of their rise being followed by the folly and degeneracy of their fall. In unravelling the tangled skein of imperial fortunes over centuries, determinists have, in contrast, constructed cyclical historical models; others, seeing neither rhyme nor reason in these ephemeral phenomena, have concluded that if, like Topsy, empires 'just growed' or were acquired 'in a fit of absence of mind', then it might follow that they waned as they had waxed, it being neither a morally justifiable nor a rationally predictable process.

Perhaps the key to an understanding of the decline and fall of empires lies in the essential nature of empire itself, the suggestion here being that such gangling growths somehow carry within them the seeds of their own destruction. Or perhaps it is rather to be discovered in the systematic analysis of individual cases: some empires being things of shreds and patches swiftly succumbed to adversity, whereas more elaborate structures collapsed under their own weight as territorial responsibilities increased beyond the metropolitan capacity to sustain them. A different explanation would connect the strength of a state's commitment to the expansion and retention of its overseas empire with troubles and weaknesses on the home front. In some instances domestic policies eroded the imperial bond; in others they served to strengthen it. As we have seen, metropolitan difficulties after 1945 did have the effect of enhancing the value of overseas possessions and of stiffening British, Dutch and French determination to hold on to them. In times of national crisis, imperialists perceived a route to salvation through the development of the deceptively prodigious potential of colonies; reactionaries opposed any concessions which suggested lack of imperial spunk; progressives and pragmatists advocated tactical retreat as the best means of saving trade, investments, the goodwill of emergent nations and prestige in the international community. Indeed, there is a case for arguing that empires never ended but merely changed their form as colonialism was succeeded by neo-colonialism, as formal imperialism gave way to informal imperialism, and as the baton of Western dominance passed from Europe to the USA and USSR.

If the reasons for the ebb and flow of Europe's influence overseas are located by some in the metropole, others focus on developments on the periphery and challenges from outside.[47] Thus, as war and peace swept across Southeast Asia in the 1940s and 1950s, so there were dramatic twists in the fortunes of alien régimes and nationalist movements, and major adjustments in the 'collaborative relationship' between local élites and foreign forces. Indeed, a more obvious explanation for the fall of empires would appear to lie in the force of local and nationalist movements provoked by prewar colonial rule and unleashed in the disturbed conditions of world war and its aftermath.

Imperial weakness is sometimes regarded as a cause, and sometimes as an effect, of nationalist strength. Colonialism and nationalism often appear in the mind's eye to be positive and negative images of a single phenomenon, repellent poles, opposite ends of a spectrum, extremities of the arc described by a pendulum. The juxtaposition of colonialism and nationalism through scientific metaphor is, however, too mechanistic to bear an exact resemblance to the historical experience. Those who highlight the force of nationalism in the deposition of colonial empires have an obligation to peer into the penumbra of such presumptions in order more precisely to identify its nature and assess its power.

Nationalism, like class, is a boundary phenomenon, a social category easy to recognize yet difficult to define.[48] Its characteristics are imprecise and subjective, varying over time and from place to place. Ethnicity and race, religion and language, geography and the concept of 'homeland', history and an awareness of shared traditions, all these are among the main features of nationalism, though their mix and relative significance vary from case to case. It is generally accepted that nationalism is expressed through political organization and that nations aspire to, or actually enjoy, separate statehood. In some cases the nation-state might include several ethnic and linguistic groups, as in Switzerland or Indonesia; in others the political movement may be the creature of just one such group, as in Zionism or Malay nationalism. Again, it is usual for the nation to occupy a distinct territory, for example in Ireland or Thailand, although some movements embrace a number of states and gather a momentum from the very absence of any clear territorial frontiers as in the case of pan-German or pan-Malay nationalism. Conversely, groups which some identify as 'minorities', 'clans', 'tribes' or 'districts' might, like the Karens of Burma or the Ambonese of Indonesia, claim separate nationhood and strive to secede from a larger so-called 'national' entity. The nationalist has, indeed, a dual concern to safeguard the nation from the fissiparous tendencies of its parts and from external threats to its autonomy.

Nationalism is associated with the struggle for independence, the concept originating in Europe's political ferment of the 1840s. We will

---

[47] Recent literature on European decolonization includes: R. F. Holland, *European Decolonization 1918–1981: an introductory survey*, London, 1985; Darwin, *Britain and Decolonisation*; A. N. Porter and A. J. Stockwell, *British Imperial Policy and Decolonization*, I: *1938–51*, II: *1951–64*, London, 1987 and 1989, and Franz Ansprenger, *The Dissolution of the Colonial Empires*, London, 1989.

[48] For a recent essay on this much discussed subject see E. J. Hobsbawm, *Nations and Nationalism since 1780. Programme, myth, reality*, Cambridge, UK, 1990.

leave aside the question of the applicability of European terminology and political categories to non-European circumstances; there are to hand, anyway, a number of models of national identity specifically derived from Afro-Asian case-studies, ranging from the 'primordial' to the 'functional-ist', from 'resistance' to 'collaboration', from 'traditional' to 'modern' and from 'élitist' to 'mass'. The mobilization of peoples as nations owes much to their sense of alienation, that is their experience of political, economic and cultural subjugation.

Before World War II colonialism, in its political and economic forms of power and ownership, had already become the target of protest in South-east Asia. Wars in Java and Aceh, risings in Perak and Pahang, the disaffection of Vietnamese scholar-gentry and Saya San's millenarianism in the Irrawaddy delta are a few examples of traditionalist resistance. With the extension of Western influence, however, forms of nationalism devel-oped not so much in opposition to the colonial state but in many ways as a function of it. Here, Western-educated élites, having espoused European values and being eager to manage their own affairs, were essentially 'collaborators'. They wrestled with their colonial masters in the hope, not of destroying, but rather of wrenching from them the panoply of state power. Both manifestations of nationalism resembled each other in being reactions to imperial authority. The nationalist activity of 1941–57 still bore the hallmarks of 'collaboration' and 'resistance', yet was clearly distin-guishable from the prewar responses to colonial rule by the administrative disintegration, economic dislocation and social maladjustment that scarred the later period. Conditions which oscillated between arbitrary rule and anarchy, such as obtained throughout Southeast Asia between 1942 and 1946, and in many parts of the region in the decade that followed, spawned a host of nationalisms as communities struggled to survive through the articulation of identity and common cause. The disturbed conditions which impeded the restoration of colonial rule also, therefore, added to the problems of those wider nationalist movements that aspired to inherit the colonial state in its entirety and envelop it in the mantle of the nation-state.

Related to the termination of colonial empires in Southeast Asia and the achievement of national independence was the transformation of the region's position in international affairs. On the eve of our period South-east Asia had been isolated from the major trouble-spots of the world and, if anything, had stood as a buffer between the spheres of interest of the Great Powers. In international affairs Southeast Asia was then little more than a geographical expression; its separate countries had been closely linked to their various colonial masters but scarcely at all with each other.

War and its aftermath resulted in attempts to create a regional order in Southeast Asia first by the Japanese, then by the Allies and subsequently by opposing Cold Warriors. In the 1940s, for the first time in modern history, the area acquired an international identity. The Allies matched the ideology and organization of the Co-prosperity Sphere with the principles of the United Nations and the machinery of Southeast Asia Command. After the defeat of Japan it was clear that world war had brought about major changes in the relative influence which individual Western powers were able to assert, and in the relations that subsisted between them, in Southeast Asia. Although the Japanese occupation did not prevent the restoration of former colonial régimes, following the 1941–2 debacle the European presence hinged on US military and economic power and on decisions taken in Washington. After 1945 West Europeans to a greater or lesser degree became clients of the USA through the Marshall Plan, within NATO and, by extension, in Southeast Asia as well. Conversely, the emergence of nation-states in the 1950s was moulded by the political, economic and military assistance received from America or China or Russia. While it is true that, even after the demise of formal colonialism, Britain in particular was able to exert considerable influence over its former dependencies and the region beyond, the international relations of Southeast Asian countries now revolved round Cold War rather than neo-colonial considerations. By the time of the Geneva Conference, Southeast Asia had emerged as one of the world's major trouble-spots largely because Great Power rivalries abutted there.

BIBLIOGRAPHIC ESSAY

A general survey is contained in Milton Osborne, *Southeast Asia. An Illustrated Introductory History*, Sydney, 1988. John F. Cady, *The History of Post-war Southeast Asia*, Athens, Ohio, 1974, is fuller on the period after 1957, but more detailed coverage is provided by Jan Pluvier, *South-East Asia from Colonialism to Independence*, Kuala Lumpur, 1974. Developments in specific countries are introduced by Alfred W. McCoy, 'The Philippines: independence without decolonisation', Anthony Reid, 'Indonesia: revolution without socialism', David Marr, 'Vietnam: harnessing the whirlwind' and Lee Kam Hing, 'Malaya: new state and old elites' in Robin Jeffrey, ed., *Asia. The Winning of Independence*, London, 1981. European decolonization is introduced by R. F. Holland, *European Decolonization 1918–1981: an introductory survey*, London, 1985, and Franz Ansprenger, *The Dissolution of the Colonial Empires*, London, 1989.

For World War II see Akira Iriye, *The origins of the Second World War in Asia and the Pacific*, London, 1987; S. Woodburn Kirby et al., *The War against Japan*, 5 vols, London, 1957–69; Christopher Thorne, *Allies of a Kind: The United States, Britain and the War against Japan, 1941–1945*, London, 1978; Wm Roger Louis, *Imperialism at Bay 1941–1945: the United States and the decolonization of the British Empire*, Oxford, 1977. There is a mass of published material on the failure of British naval strategy and the fall of Singapore 1942, for example: W. David McIntyre, *The Rise and Fall of the Singapore Naval Base, 1919–1942*, London, 1979; James Neidpath, *The Singapore Naval Base and the Defence of Britain's Eastern Empire, 1919–1941*, Oxford, 1981; Malcolm Murfett, *Fool-proof relations: the search for Anglo-American naval co-operation during the Chamberlain years, 1937–40*, Singapore, 1984; Arthur J. Marder, *Old Friends, New Enemies: The Royal Navy and the Imperial Japanese Navy, Strategic Illusions, 1936–41*, Oxford, 1981; Louis Allen, *Singapore 1941–1942*, London, 1977. For the Burma campaign see R. Callahan, *Burma 1942–1945: the policies and strategy of the Second World*

War, London, 1978; Louis Allen, *Burma: The Longest War 1941–45*, London, 1985, and *The End of the War in Asia*, London, 1976. See also Charles Cruickshank, *SOE in the Far East*, Oxford, 1983.

The Japanese occupation and its impact on Southeast Asia are discussed in the following: F. C. Jones, *Japan's New Order in East Asia, 1937–1945*, London, 1974; W. H. Elsbree, *Japan's role in Southeast Asian Nationalist Movements*, Cambridge, Mass., 1953; Josef Silverstein, ed., *Southeast Asia in World War II*, New Haven, 1966; H. J. Benda, *The Crescent and the Rising Sun: Indonesian Islam under the Japanese Occupation*, The Hague, 1953; Alfred W. McCoy, ed., *Southeast Asia under Japanese Occupation: Transition and Transformation*, New Haven, 1980; Robert H. Taylor, *Marxism and Resistance in Burma 1942–1945. Thien Pe Myint's 'Wartime Traveler'*, Athens, Ohio, 1984; J. C. Lebra, *Japanese-trained Armies in Southeast Asia*, Hong Kong, 1977; Benedict R. O'G. Anderson, *Java in a Time of Revolution: Occupation and Resistance, 1944–1946*, Ithaca, 1972; John R. W. Smail, *Bandung in the Early Revolution 1945–6. A study in the social history of the Indonesian Revolution*, Ithaca, 1964; Cheah Boon Kheng, *Red Star over Malaya. Resistance and social conflict during and after the Japanese occupation, 1941–1946*, Singapore, 1983; Benedict J. Kerkvliet, *The Huk Rebellion. A Study of Peasant Revolt in the Philippines*, Berkeley, 1977; Judith A. Stowe, *Siam becomes Thailand. A Story of Intrigue*, London, 1991.

Aspects of Allied wartime planning for postwar Southeast Asia and reoccupation of the region are covered in the following works: Hugh Tinker, ed., *Burma: The Struggle for Independence, 1944–48*, I, London, 1983; Nicholas Tarling, ' "A New and a Better Cunning": British Wartime Planning for Post-War Burma', JSEAS, 13, 1 (1982), ' "An Empire Gem": British Wartime Planning for Post-War Burma', ibid. 13, 2 (1982), and 'Lord Mountbatten and the Return of Civil Government to Burma', *Journal of Imperial and Commonwealth History*, 11, 2 (1983); C. Mary Turnbull, 'British Planning for Post-war Malaya', JSEAS 5, 2 (1974); A. J. Stockwell, *British policy and Malay politics during the Malayan Union experiment, 1942–1948*, Kuala Lumpur, 1979; R. B. Smith, 'Some contrasts between Burma and Malaya in British policy in South-East Asia, 1942–46', in R. B. Smith and A. J. Stockwell, eds, *British Policy and the Transfer of Power in Asia: Documentary Perspectives*, London, 1988; F. S. V. Donnison, *British Military Administration in the Far East, 1943–45*, London, 1956; Peter Dennis, *Troubled days of peace. Mountbatten and South East Asia Command, 1945–46*, Manchester, 1987.

For postwar developments culminating in the independence of Burma see Hugh Tinker, ed., *Burma: The Struggle for Independence, 1944–1948*, 2 vols, London, 1983–4, and 'The Contraction of Empire in Asia, 1945–48: The Military Dimension', *Journal of Imperial and Commonwealth History*, 16, 2 (1988); Robert H. Taylor, *The State in Burma*, London, 1987; Louis Allen, ' "Leaving the Sinking Ship". A Comment on Burma and the End of Empire' in D. K. Bassett and V. T. King, eds, *Britain and South-East Asia*, Hull: Centre for SE Asian Studies, 1986; and Smith, 'Some contrasts between Burma and Malaya' in Smith and Stockwell, eds, *British Policy*.

Of the wealth of literature on the tumultuous aftermath of war in Indonesia and the Indonesian revolution, the following are particularly important: Anderson, *Java in a Time of Revolution*; Smail, *Bandung in the*

Early Revolution; George McT. Kahin, *Nationalism and Revolution in Indo-nesia*, Ithaca, 1952; and Anthony Reid, *The Blood of the People: Revolution and the End of Traditional Rule in Northern Sumatra*, Kuala Lumpur, 1979. See also Reid, 'Indonesia: revolution without socialism' in R. Jeffrey, ed., *Asia*.

Indochina has been examined from a number of angles although the focus has been the First Vietnam War, viz: French decolonization, the origins of American involvement, the Vietminh struggle for liberation, and the international settlement of 1954. These different perspectives are reflected in the following selection of titles: Marr, 'Vietnam' in R. Jeffrey ed., *Asia*; Bernard B. Fall, *Street without Joy*, Harrisburg, 1961; R. E. M. Irving, *The First Indochina War*, London, 1975; R. B. Smith, *An International History of the Vietnam War*, I: *Revolution versus Containment, 1955–61*, London, 1983; Peter M. Dunn, *The First Vietnam War*, London, 1985; James Cable, *The Geneva Conference of 1954 on Indochina*, London, 1986; Andrew J. Rotter, *The Path to Vietnam. Orgins of the American Commitment to Southeast Asia*, Ithaca and London, 1987; Anthony Short, *The Origins of the Vietnam War*, London, 1989; Greg Lockhart, *Nation in Arms: The Origins of the People's Army of Vietnam*, Sydney, 1989; Laura Marie Calkins, 'Sino-Viet Minh Relations, 1948–1952', Ph.D. thesis, University of London, 1990.

Imperial policy and Malayan politics from the inauguration of the Malayan Union to the achievement of independence are discussed in the following: Mohd. Noordin Sopiee, *From Malayan Union to Singapore Separa-tion*, Kuala Lumpur, 1974; J. de V. Allen, *The Malayan Union*, New Haven, 1967; Stockwell, *British Policy and Malay Politics*, and 'British Imperial Policy and Decolonization in Malaya, 1942–52', *Journal of Imperial and Common-wealth History*, 13, 1 (1984); Anthony Short, *The Communist Insurrection in Malaya, 1948–1960*, London, 1975; R. Stubbs, *Hearts and Minds in Guerrilla Warfare. The Malayan Emergency 1948–1960*, Singapore, 1989; Heng Pek Koon, *Chinese Politics in Malaysia: A History of the Malaysian Chinese Associa-tion*, Singapore, 1988. For the cession of Sarawak to the Crown in 1946 see R. H. W. Reece, *The Name of Brooke: The end of White Rajah Rule in Sarawak*, Kuala Lumpur, 1982.

CHAPTER

2

THE POLITICAL STRUCTURES OF THE INDEPENDENT STATES

Writing about recent history can be an incautious exercise. The closer the past gets to the present, the more insecure it is for the historian. The natural instinct is to withdraw from the present, which is precariously perched on the edge leading to the future, and find that comfortable distance between the writer and the brink. The aim is to gain the security that is often professionally called 'perspective'. From the historian's point of view, the trouble with the contemporary past is that it is still happening and there are no reliable records ('primary sources') to cite. Equally problematic is the possibility that the people described in the narrative may still be alive, and writing about living personalities can be notoriously insecure for the historian. Another dilemma is the fact that readers— fellow historians and others—bring to bear on that same narrative their own experiences and interpretations.

Couple these built-in disabilities in writing contemporary history to a description of the political structure of the independent states of Southeast Asia and there will emerge a veritable nightmare. So much needs to be discussed. So many themes can be presented. It is like a Balinese painter at work. He tries to depict as much as possible so that the canvas is completely covered, including the corners. The viewer then faces the task of relating the numerous features to each other. Very often, especially to the uninitiated, the end product merely registers as a patchwork of colours and shapes with no discernible message.

Within each state of Southeast Asia are legislative and executive institutions: the military, the bureaucracy, religious hierarchies, interest groups and others. All these constitute 'political structures'. However, they often bear little relationship to one another, much like the variety in a Balinese painting. The Balinese style is therefore not the preferred mode of expression. Rather, like Chinese calligraphy, a few strokes here and there on a broad canvas will be applied in order to suggest to the reader what can be perceived.

How should political structures in Southeast Asia be studied? Should they be simply described? But if that alone is attempted, the links connecting those structures would be lacking, and those interlinkages are themselves a matter of historical truth. The structures cannot be viewed simply

The author is grateful to those who evaluated the draft of this chapter and made comments for improvement. In particular, the following were especially helpful: Associate Professor Cheah Boon Kheng and Dr Abu Talib Ahmad, both of Universiti Sains Malaysia, and Professor Sombat Chantornvong of Thammasat University.

as external expressions of human behaviour: the milieu in which they function must also be studied.

For analytical purposes, it is convenient to identify three categories of political structures: those affected by revolution and war; the 'plural' ones; and 'maximum' government. Structures affected by revolution and war are relatively unfamiliar because they have been obscured by the more recognizable, distinctive and newsworthy 'events' of violence characterizing those phases of history. In Southeast Asia, those structures were largely found in the Indochina states and Indonesia during the early postwar years. To a large extent, they were fashioned by the milieu of war and violence that imposed constraints and demanded makeshift arrangements. Plural political structures were initially predominant in the first flush of independence. They catered for various elements of stresses and strains in society, allowing for dominant and subordinate structures not necessarily sharing common value systems to exist side by side in a plurality. In such political structures, attempts were made to accommodate counter-structures or counterpoints.[1] With the passage of time, however, conditions emerged which rendered these plural structures less than efficient. Apart from the Indochinese states, most of the other societies experienced a period of history during the years of independence that coincided with the great Asia-Pacific economic boom. Further research on its impact on political structures is required. However, for present purposes, it can be argued that political structures had to change in scale to adjust to the demands of the new economic conditions. Plural structures with their niches for local interest groups began to make way for maximum governments—pervasive, omniscient, all-powerful, often the fount of authority.

REVOLUTION AND POLITICAL STRUCTURES

Revolution impacted on the political structures by providing the consensus that transformed society from disparate and separate units into a united whole. It was possible to achieve consensus through revolution because, in the main, Southeast Asian leaders exploited nationalism and focused attention on eliminating a common enemy—usually the colonial power. This nationalism was still very much an extended version of the old anti-colonialism that was prevalent before the states of Southeast Asia became independent. It was especially widespread in Vietnam where the contest against the French and the United States was carried out in a continuous struggle, and it is to Vietnam that attention should first be given.

Northern Vietnam

Vietnam is not an easy country to understand. Much of what transpired in the society was so enveloped in mystery and secrecy that one could be forgiven for failing to delineate the specific segments of the political structure and give each part its due importance. For a great part of its

---

[1] The term was used in W. F. Wertheim, *East-West Parallels: Sociological Approaches to Modern Asia*, The Hague, 1964, 26, 34.

history as an independent state, from 1945 till well into the 1980s, Vietnam was, moreover, at war. The military enemies included France, the United States, China, and then the Cambodian guerrillas. How the constant warfare shaped the political structures is particularly difficult to ascertain: given the nature of war, it is difficult to collect data about most issues. Moreover, Vietnam experienced war for such a long period that analytical approaches applicable to other states at peace cannot be simply grafted on to the Vietnamese case.

In other Southeast Asian states, leaders played significant roles in moulding political structures. In Vietnam, during the formative years from 1945 to 1960, this does not seem to have been the case. Although Ho Chi Minh remained the towering nationalist leader, there appeared to be no personality cult and no attempt by him to adopt a high profile. Similarly, the communist party kept in the background. The reasons for this state of affairs are not difficult to fathom. The need to reconcile differences among the splintered Vietnamese élite meant that Ho had to work behind the scenes until the situation was sorted out. Also, in the years from 1945 to 1960, the leader of Vietnamese communism—Ho himself—was not firmly established and he had to depend on the support of the non-communists. Much of the work of government was therefore carried out by committees which formed the main segments of the political structure.

As long as matters did not get out of hand, Ho took a back seat. Before 1960, he emerged only twice to decide on matters of national importance. The first was the partition of Vietnam into north and south along the seventeenth parallel in 1954. It is still not clear why Ho settled on this concession to the French, especially when the military victory of Dien Bien Phu (1954) clearly promoted the Vietnamese cause at the negotiating table. Most likely, he was under pressure from the Soviet Union to make concessions to the French in order to induce Paris to oppose the creation of a European defence community. Equally probable was a pragmatic decision taken by Ho to settle for the northern half of Vietnam in order to win some years of peace for reconstruction after a long period of war and destruction.

The second occasion when Ho showed his hand was his intervention during the November 1956 Nghe An peasant rebellion which arose principally over discontent with land reform. Issues like land reform reveal more about political structures than a plain description. From the earliest days of its inception, the party had concerned itself with the issue of land and the related problems of indebtedness, fragmentation of plots, rents and loans. In 1955, a major attempt at land reform was launched. In accordance with its goals, some cadres were specially designated to expropriate land without compensation, to redistribute the lands of the Catholic Church, and to confiscate communal lands which village elders could assign, thus boosting their prestige and power. Poor peasants were invited to classify their neighbours, denounce them and then move to have their lands confiscated. In the confusion, many people—including party members, government officials and supporters of the revolution—were branded as landlords and thus lost their properties, positions and sometimes their lives. The Nghe An rebellion was the result.

The opposition that was aroused led Ho to discontinue the forced collectivization of peasant land. Again, it was a crucial situation that he felt required his intervention. But Ho intervened without at the same time alienating the hardliners in the party: they were soon rehabilitated. Ho's role in the political structure before 1960 was not therefore a pervading presence. In fact, interestingly enough, the task of explaining the errors of the land reform programme was given to General Giap, the defence minister.

The low profile Ho assumed could be traced to the historical development of the Vietnamese revolution. Ho's quick action to correct the mistakes of the collectivization programme was an honest admission of the fact that the enemies of the revolution were not a feudal society and a feudal tradition. The French had already destroyed elements of the old feudal régime by reducing the royal court to insignificance and by commercializing agriculture. At the same time, the French did not contribute to the formation of a capitalist régime. In this environment, Ho could afford to de-emphasize class conflict and class struggle. His aim, before and after 1945, was to emphasize continuity with peasant opposition to foreign rule led by the gentry. What was important was the formation of an anti-foreign united front in the interim. Given these basic premises, most political structures remained essentially makeshift wartime innovations.

The Vietminh, a united front with the non-communists, was one example. The exigencies of war meant that party and state apparatus had to be decentralized, and this gave the middle and lower level cadres some impression of broad-based participation. This coincided with the traditional political structure which was decentralized with the village as the basic unit. The village was therefore the real political structure, and in 1945 the Vietminh made the wise decision to consolidate its control of the country by exploiting this traditional institution. As each village fell under Vietminh control, a committee of liberation was set up there. Following this decentralized approach, similar committees were established for 'liberated' factories, mines, barracks, towns, districts or provinces. As expected, the duties of the committees concentrated on gathering support for the national liberation movement. By ensuring that each local committee had its share of Vietminh cadres, the entire system guaranteed that a political infrastructure was developed by the Vietminh that could constitute the basis of a nascent authority.

However, as peace returned to the countryside after the Nghe An rebellion and after a spate of good harvests in 1958 and 1959 (always an important factor in the food-deficient north cut off from the rice granaries of the south), the stage was set for changes to make the political structure more permanent. But, even when communism was stressed, provocative issues like class conflict were not emphasized.

At the level of the central government in Hanoi, Ho commissioned and, in fact, played a personal role in the framing of a new constitution which was finally adopted on 1 January 1960. The new constitution was noted for the prominence it gave to commmunism. No longer was the facade of a broad national front with the non-communists deemed necessary. However, there was also no evidence that the constitution established a fanatical, class-conscious political system. The other distinguishing feature was the recognition it gave to the contribution of Ho to the Vietnamese nation. As president, Ho was invested with absolute powers. However, he practised collective leadership. The principal party leaders were given charge over major power bases. Pham Van Dong was given control over the government machinery; Vo Nguyen Giap control over the defence forces; and Truong Chinh control over the National Assembly. Elections for the Assembly were held after the promulgation of the new constitution. The powers given to this body did not suggest, however, that it would wield much influence.

It must be noted that the history of national assemblies as a political structure in north, as well as south Vietnam, was chequered. The first colonial council had been formed in the 1880s in Tonkin. When independence was declared in 1945, one of the earliest actions taken was the formation of a National Assembly to provide an institution in which all political groups could be represented. With the partition in 1954, the north elected a new assembly, the south following in 1956. However, whether north or south, national assemblies were co-optative bodies appended to an élite or party decision-making process, not totally unlike the bodies set up by the French colonial authorities. Thus Vietnam in 1960 emerged as a totalitarian political structure with a dominant president, a disciplined party and the largest army in Southeast Asia to boot.[2] The system remained essentially unchanged through the 1960s and as the war intensified; further administrative changes were placed on the back burner until after the reunification of the north and the south in 1975.

The significance of the National Assembly as a component of the political structure, however, should not be dismissed just because the institution appeared powerless. Since the election of the first National Assembly in January 1946 and through the subsequent elections of 1960 and 1964, there were always southern deputies who supposedly represented constituencies in the south. The National Assembly therefore presented a powerful symbol of Vietnamese political unity. However, in 1971, for the fourth National Assembly, these deputies were not re-elected and the National Assembly became a strictly northern body. This was probably a consequence of the formation in 1969 of the Provisional Revolutionary Government (PRG) by the Vietcong in the south. The re-election of the southern deputies was therefore rendered irrelevant. This move was also designed to give credibility to the PRG as a political structure independent of Hanoi.[3]

The party and the army were also important segments of the political structure. The Vietnam Dang Lao Dong (Workers' Party) had always claimed to be the sole legitimate leader of the proletariat and the instrument of the will of that class. All other interests must be subordinated to the party and even professional military interests and attitudes had to conform to the party ideology. The party grew in strength from 1946 to

[2] Bernard B. Fall, 'North Vietnam: a Profile' in Robert O. Tilman, ed., *Man, State, and Society in Contemporary Southeast Asia*, New York, 1969, 382–92.

[3] Tai Sung An, 'The Fourth National Assembly of North Vietnam: Significant Developments', *Asian Survey*, XII, 4 (1972).

1960. Numbers and ubiquity alone, though, are insufficient criteria for an appreciation of the important role of the party in the political structure. Several key members of the Lao Dong's central committee also doubled as important leaders of the north Vietnamese government. Thus party beliefs could easily be translated into national policies. The party itself was not a homogeneous monolith: internal differences related to the Sino-Soviet conflict. In 1956, when Ho replaced Truong Chinh as Secretary-General of the Lao Dong, this was interpreted as a setback for the pro-Chinese wing. In September 1961, when Ho relinquished this top political post in favour of Le Duan (who was not considered objectionable by the pro-Chinese wing), this was viewed as a renewed sign of weakness of the pro-Moscow wing. There were also generational differences. Ho and Ton Duc Thanh belonged to the 'old Bolsheviks' who had fought the French. Le Duan belonged to the group of party bureaucrats who were not combatants in the revolution.

According to Marxist theory, the army was the handmaid of the party in the political structure. Control over the army by the Lao Dong was exercised by recruiting the commanders as party members. In fact, promotions in the military had to be approved by the party. Also, party cells were organized within the military for surveillance. Notwithstanding the theory, it would be difficult to understand how the Lao Dong could exercise authority over the army. After all, the army's magnificent victory at Dien Bien Phu against the French in 1954 gave it a high status. It was also more representative of the population than the Lao Dong because its soldiers were mainly peasants, and its officer corps consisted of a sprinkling of intellectuals (General Vo Nguyen Giap) and minorities (e.g. Major General Chu Van Tan from the Tho tribe). However, the fact that it agreed to the division of Vietnam along the seventeenth parallel in 1954 suggested that its impact as a political structure could be blunted by other political forces, notwithstanding its power. Furthermore, although the army was often described as pro-Moscow because of its dependence on the Soviet Union for weaponry and its modernization during the initial years, it also needed support from the population to compensate for its technological and material deficiencies. For this, the party was important for it helped to organize the people into labour gangs and military welfare groups. Party propaganda was also needed to stress the prestige of military work.

Ho's death on 3 September 1969 did not change the political structure to any significant extent. In accordance with the constitution, the aged vice-president, Ton Duc Thang, succeeded as president. However, Ho's powerful position as chairman of the Central Committee of the Lao Dong Party was left unfilled. Ton Duc Thang was old, and in poor health; his incumbency was largely ceremonial, and the presidency became a symbol, especially since he was a southerner—an important qualification in Hanoi's drive for reunification. If a change in the political structure was evident, it was the devolution of power to a quadrumvirate comprising of Le Duan (First Secretary of the Lao Dong Party), Prime Minister Pham Van Dong, Truong Chinh (the Chairman of the Standing Committee of the National Assembly) and Vo Nguyen Giap (the Defence Minister). In general, although power was divided among members in the quadrumvirate, the sharing was not even. At a time of war, it would not be surprising if Giap was in ascendance. From the early 1960s to late 1968, his influence was in fact very evident. The military strategy that was current then stressed the 'main-force' approach that would result in a 'final glorious victory'. When that failed, strategic planning was transferred to the National Defence Council where the non-military leaders also made decisions on military affairs. Truong Chinh, a vice president of that council in 1971, was able to push for a protracted 'people's war' strategy.

The post-Ho political arrangements were formalized in the new constitution adopted in mid-December 1980. This replaced the earlier constitution of 1969 in which the presidency—held by Ho—was the highest office. Now it was replaced by the Council of State whose members would form a collective presidency. The administrative arm of the Council of State remained the Council of Ministers headed, as before, by the prime minister.

Southern Vietnam

War and revolution in the south failed to galvanize the population as in the north. Nationalism served to widen the chasm between the ruling élites and the population at large. However, as in the north, the combination of war and revolutionary changes also contributed to the confusion of political structures in south Vietnam. On the one hand, there were the constitutional trappings of elections, referenda, new constitutions, and constituent assemblies. On the other hand, the extra-constitutional forces were the 'real' structures that deserve attention. These included the personal family rule of Ngo Dinh Diem and later the military oligarchies that emerged, with or without civilian participation. Also, the counter-élite of the National Liberation Front was a major structure.

Diem first came into power during the crisis following the partition of Vietnam in 1954. He deposed the emperor, Bao Dai; a referendum on 23 October 1955 resulted in his being chosen as chief of state; finally, his rise was completed with the proclamation, three days later, of Vietnam as a republic with himself as president. The hallmark of Diem's government was authoritarianism. Diem chose this option partly because of his personal disposition but also because he believed that the Vietnamese nationalist élite was hopelessly divided and only an authoritarian structure could overcome its weaknesses. Indeed, Vietnamese history demonstrated that the élite was split, manipulated, enticed and used by French, Japanese, communists and Americans.

However, there was still the need to secure the support of various sectors of the society for the national leadership. Following the Vietminh model, Diem and his supporters formed the National Revolutionary Movement, the Republican Youth, the Vietnamese Women's Solidarity Movement, and the Personalist Revolutionary Labour Party which was supposed to be the counterpart of the Indochinese Communist Party. These organizations were used in a top-down approach as propaganda and political control mechanisms. They had no life of their own.

The most significant characteristic of Ngo Dinh Diem and the rulers who followed was their position in the spectrum of Vietnamese leaders. They were the allies of the foreign powers. Diem was sponsored, installed and supported by the United States. At least eight out of fourteen cabinet ministers in the Diem government were civil servants (or collaborators) in the pre-1945 French colonial régime. All the military leaders who ruled from Saigon after Diem—Duong Van Minh, Nguyen Khanh, Nguyen Van Thieu, Nguyen Cao Ky—began their military careers fighting on the French side during the so-called First Indochina War, 1946–54. In contrast, all the top-level leaders of the north began their revolutionary careers fighting for Vietnamese independence.

A consideration of the role of the military oligarchy within the political structure in south Vietnam can start with the place of the military in society. As a general observation, it can be noted that the heavily Confucian-influenced environment in Vietnam did not accord the soldier much prestige. Bearing arms was not held in high regard. Rather, scholarship and intellectual pursuits offered better alternatives. Also, the military in Vietnam was not prominently associated with the nationalist movement. In fact, there were examples of Vietnamese military leaders within the living memory of people in the independent period who had fought with the French against the Vietnamese. Thus, there was no institutional base upon which the military could develop as a component of the political structure of which it was very much a part.

The governments that followed the fall of Ngo Dinh Diem on 1 November 1963 demonstrated the lack of roots in society by their short life span:

1. The Nguyen Ngoc Tho (civilian) government, in fact a facade for the military, lasted 86 days. Three generals were appointed to the cabinet in recognition of the military's role in deposing Diem.
2. The General Nguyen Khanh government lasted 260 days. Its aim was to forestall the neutralist tendencies of some army generals. Although its core group was the military, it tried to include lay leaders of the Buddhist movement.
3. The Tran Van Huong (civilian) government lasted 84 days. It represented an army-sponsored effort to restore south Vietnam to civilian rule.
4. The Nguyen Xuan Oanh (civilian caretaker) government lasted 19 days. This government marked the re-entry of the military into active political life. The cabinet members included Major General Nguyen Van Thieu and Vice Air Marshal Nguyen Cao Ky.
5. The Phan Huy Quat (civilian) government lasted 112 days. It was only a transitional government that emerged in the midst of political upheaval following a coup attempt, paving the way for the takeover by Thieu and Ky.
6. The Nguyen Cao Ky–Nguyen Van Thieu government lasted from 9 June 1965 till the fall of Saigon to the north Vietnamese forces. Although it showed more staying power, it had to be reshuffled many times.[4] Generally, the ultimate power holders under this military régime organized themselves into the Armed Forces Council (or Congress). A directorate served as the executive body of the council.

---

[4] I. Milton Sacks, 'Restructuring Government in South Vietnam', ibid., VII, 8 (1967).

By 1967, the Chairman of the directorate was Nguyen Van Thieu and, by virtue of this position, he was also head of state.

One aspect of the political structures created by these leaders was the lifeline provided by the United States. Their tenure and maintenance were made possible by the awesome power provided by this external body, which though not part of the domestic political structure, was certainly a great source of assistance. The American air-strikes, the search and destroy missions, the defoliation programmes, the Phoenix programme which applied 'selective terrorism' to ferret out the communists, the forced resettlement programme, all constituted an American presence which was a political structure in its own right.

The military governments after 1963 also permitted political parties to function. By the end of 1969, there was a total of twenty-seven active political parties and groups in south Vietnam. Most of them were based on personal ties and loyalties rather than specific programmes to mobilize mass support. Their divisiveness would have rendered them ineffective. But in any case mass participation was limited: President Thieu had made the conscious decision by the end of 1969 to limit his basis of support to the army, the Catholics and the parties rather than the population at large.[5]

The shallow roots of the Saigon authorities require the study of a counterpart political structure, but this is shrouded in obscurity. From what can be pieced together, it seems that Ho believed that the effort to recover territory in the south would be most decisive in the urban areas, either by elections or in the event of anarchy. This city strategy required a political structure that could realize Ho's objectives. Prior to 1951, the Central Committee of the Communist Party of Vietnam had been represented by the Nam Bo Regional Committee, then located in Ca Mau in the deep south. Difficulties of communication led to the reorganization of the Nam Bo Regional Committee into the Central Office for South Viet Nam (COSVN) in 1951. The COSVN headquarters was moved to Tay Ninh, just a short distance from Saigon. The establishment of the COSVN marked a considerable increase in its status and authority. While the Nam Bo Regional Committee was also an advance guard of the Central Committee, the COSVN included a number of Central Committee members assigned to permanent duty in the south.

The decision in 1954 to abandon the south was viewed with disappointment by the communist cadres there. It was not till 1959 that the relatively low profile recommended by Ho was jettisoned in favour of limited armed activity. Whether this change of strategy was responsible for the creation of the National Liberation Front (NLF) is not clear. The view that the NLF was a creature of Hanoi appears to be an oversimplification, while the idea of a southern organization acting independently or in spite of Hanoi is also difficult to stomach.

The NLF represented a counter-elite to Saigon's leadership. However, the fact that the former succeeded in ultimately defeating the latter tended to give the impression that it had roots in society that the Saigon government (both military and civilian) did not enjoy. That may not necessarily

[5] Allan E. Goodman, 'South Vietnam: Neither War Nor Peace', ibid., X, 2 (1970).

be the case. In Vietnam, the basic political structure was the village. Government had always been viewed as the predator, the tax collector, the police, the undisciplined soldier-bandit. At the time when the Saigon authorities tried to exercise control over the Vietnamese countryside, the NLF represented the protection of society against the government. It had the advantage of being local, though in the end, it too had to behave like a government, exercising its power of tax and control.

It is still necessary to explain the support the NLF enjoyed that made it a viable component of the political structure. Apart from the abuses of the Saigon government and other factors, the prospect of acquiring more land constituted another important motive for villagers to support the NLF. The NLF, after all, was a patronage organization, redistributing land from the well-to-do to poorer farmers. It should be noted, though, that the NLF did not issue deeds of ownership.

The issue of land distribution brings into focus the problem of the dynamics of the NLF and its antecedent, the communist movement in the south. Was the central engine of the political structure the appeal of issues and causes, or was it the organizational technique with its attendant administration and methods of coercion? There is no reason for accepting one and rejecting the other. The communists in the south had always combined both. During the period 1954 to 1960, organization and discipline were important. With the formation of the NLF and the beginnings of factionalism in the Saigon government, the communists could rely on economic and social programmes to generate support. However, as the pressure of war increased after 1966, more reliance had to be placed on the organizational infrastructure. Worse still, as the tide turned against the communists with heavier American military involvement, the communists were compelled to depend on the northern parent organization for survival.[6]

Dependence on its organizational superiority of course did not mean abandonment of political reform. In 1967, the NLF promulgated a new programme after the presidential election held by the Saigon authorities. This programme was modelled on the early Vietminh platform of a united front of all interest groups. The salient promises included land purchase for equitable distribution; property rights for religious institutions; protection of indigenous industries through restrictions on and prohibition of foreign manufacturing interests; ethnic and religious liberties; equal rights for women; and provisions for a social security system. A victory policy was envisaged rather than negotiations with the Saigon authorities. Reunification of north and south Vietnam was accepted as a long-range goal.

The prospects of reunification were enhanced when the death knell for the Saigon government under President Thieu was sounded at the signing of the Paris Peace Agreement in January 1973. The agreement was the culmination of efforts by the United States government to disentangle itself gracefully from military involvement in Vietnam. Little was said about the fate of the Vietnamese, whether north or south. The only

---

[6] Hammond Rolph, 'Vietnamese Communism and the Protracted War', ibid., XII, 9 (1972).

political structure provided in the agreement was the National Council for National Reconciliation and Concord which was to be formed for the purpose of enabling the contending Vietnamese sides to thrash out their differences. The council was never established.

Thieu also ignored the third force groups, a collection of non-communist opposition groups that had coalesced with the hope of forming some kind of coalition government with the communists within the framework of the Paris Peace Agreement. Rampant corruption within the Thieu government also resulted in the alienation of the Catholic Church which had been one of its strongest supporters. Nor did Thieu's narrow political structure embrace the Buddhist hierarchy or religious sects like the Cao Dai and the Hoa Hao. During the earlier years, especially under the presidency of Diem, these religious groups were principal players, operating within political structures in their own right.

With the Peace Agreement signed, the north Vietnamese increased their military activities in the Mekong delta and the border provinces of Tay Ninh and Phuoc Long. In January 1975, the entire province of Phuoc Long fell to northern control. The United States response was only the threat of possible retaliation. Encouraged, the north continued the offensive. The last great battle was the twelve-day long struggle for the control of Xuan Loc, a small town less than fifty kilometres from Saigon, in April 1975. When Xuan Loc fell, Thieu resigned and the northern troops with their southern allies finally captured control of Saigon on 30 April 1975.

The reunification of Vietnam opened the way for setting up new political structures. However, the rapidity with which Saigon fell took even Hanoi by surprise. Initially, the decision was taken to soft-pedal the reunification process. It was Truong Chinh who explained why Vietnam was still divided into two states. In November 1975, he reported:[7]

> On the State plane, although Vietnam is one country but [sic] nominally it is still divided into two states: in the North it is the state of the Democratic Republic of Vietnam while in the South it is the state of the Republic of South Vietnam. In the North, there is the Government of the Democratic Republic of Vietnam. In the South, there is the Provisional Revolutionary Government of the Republic of South Vietnam. The North has a national assembly, while the South has no National Assembly but an Advisory Council besides the Government. The North has a socialist constitution and legal system, while the South has no socialist constitution and legal system but only the programme of the National Front for Liberation and a number of regulations having the character of laws promulgated by the Provisional Revolutionary Government.

However, the decision to speed up reunification was taken soon after. When the war against the United States ended, there were only a few southern cadres left who could staff the political structure of a southern state. The northern leaders (including Truong Chinh) wanted to take advantage of the southern preparedness for change soon after the fall of

[7] Quoted in Huynh Kim Khanh, 'Year one of Postcolonial Vietnam', *Southeast Asian Affairs 1977*, Singapore, 1977, 300.

Saigon rather than allow the development of inclinations for independence. Also, the desire of the aged northern leaders quickly to realize their
dream of reunification could not be discounted.[8]

Towards this end, a Political Consultative Conference was held in
Saigon in November 1975 to discuss plans for reunification. It was decided
to conduct nationwide elections for a unicameral National Assembly which
would be the supreme organ of power, and which would write a new
constitution. The elections were duly held and the new National Assembly
met in June 1976, proclaiming the founding of the newly reunified Vietnamese state on 12 July 1976.

What can be said of the political structure in this new state by way of
conclusion? All through the postwar history of Vietnam until the invasion
of Kampuchea (Cambodia) in 1978, the party was perceived as the 'rock of
ages' that could not be eroded. A monolithic party, an omniscient leadership—these were the lodestars. Even when Ho was alive, the politburo
adhered closely to the principle of collective leadership. This continued
after his death, although in daily administration there were now two key
figures—Le Duan and Le Duc Tho. These two, together with three
others—Truong Chinh, Pham Hung and Pham Van Dong—formed the
inner circle of five. Whether it was one or two or five, the party remained
united. Yet this too could not last. The Kampuchean invasion, the economic
mess in the country, its isolation in the world, and an increasing dependence on the Soviet Union which undermined the much-vaunted Vietnamese sense of independence for which they had fought for decades to
win—all these began to coalesce in the 1980s to force upon the party
leadership acceptance of political changes.

Cambodia

Cambodia and Laos were drawn into the orbit of the revolution in
Vietnam. However, unlike the revolution in Vietnam, where nationalism
was the powerhouse, the revolution in Cambodia had to contend with
Prince Sihanouk whose monopoly over nationalism was almost unassail-
able. Before 1970, any mention of Cambodia must necessarily involve the
name of its ruler—Sihanouk. Given Sihanouk's charm and his capacity to
absorb opposition, the casual observer would be forgiven if the impression
was gained that there were no other political structures available to
Cambodia apart from that offered by the prince himself. Yet the lessons of
hindsight—especially obvious after his deposition—would demand studying the alternatives to Sihanouk: only thus can any attempt be made to
understand the chaos and diversity that emerged after 1970.

A Democratic Party (Krom Pracheathipodei) had been led by Prince
Sisowath Yuthevong (1912–47). Educated in France and married to a
French lady, Yuthevong wanted to establish democratic institutions *à la*
France in Cambodia itself. For this, of course, independence from France
was important. The party drew its support from Son Ngoc Thanh, an

[8] Ibid., 302.

erstwhile opponent of Sihanouk then living in exile, supporters of the Issarak movement (the nationalist group based in Bangkok that fought for independence from France), and other members of the Cambodian intellectual élite. The inclusion of Son Ngoc Thanh in the party naturally did not win the approval of Sihanouk. Nevertheless, in the September 1946 election for the Consultative Assembly to advise Sihanouk on a constitution, the Democratic Party won fifty of the sixty-seven seats. With this mandate, the party proposed a constitution in 1947 which gave power to the National Assembly, where the party was certain to hold the majority of seats. However, by that time the French had returned to Cambodia and were comfortably ensconced once more. In Phnom Penh, street names in honour of French heroes and events were restored. Holidays to commemorate Sihanoukist events were cancelled. Thus the power that the Democratic Party could amass, notwithstanding its electoral majority, was limited to what the French were prepared to grant. Not even the aura of Thanh's return in 1951 to join the Democratic Party helped. The intransigence of the French, the opposition from Sihanouk, and the death of the party's leaders (Yuthevong died in 1947 and his successor was assassinated in 1949) all conspired to ensure the lack of an alternative in the political structure in Cambodia.

Thanh himself left the Democratic Party and went underground in 1952, setting up his headquarters in Siemreap, somewhere near the Thai border. Within this zone, Thanh tried to establish political institutions that resembled those found in prewar Japan. His shadowy existence placed him outside the mainstream political structure throughout the 1950s and 1960s. In fact, his political strength was drained when Sihanouk pre-empted his nationalist appeal by a dramatic and successful 'crusade for independence'. Throughout 1953 and 1954, the population rallied to Sihanouk and essentially reduced Thanh's support to the minimum.

Sihanouk realized that with independence, new political structures would be necessary. In particular, the maintenance of the monarchy would require it to be revolutionized and linked to the people. At the same time, the prestige of the monarchy, a valuable input in the political structure, must not be left unexploited even though, by tradition, the throne was above politics. Therefore, in order to ensure that his political objectives were achieved, Sihanouk abdicated on 2 March 1955 in favour of his father, Prince Norodom Suramarit.

One of the most important contributions to the development of political structures in Cambodia made by Prince Sihanouk was the creation of the Sangkum Reastre Niyum (Popular Socialist Community), the mass movement that was born in March 1955. The Sangkum won every single seat in the elections of 1955, 1958 and 1962, each time with very high percentage votes. In the 1962 election, the Sangkum won all the seventy-seven seats in the National Assembly and garnered between 75 and 100 per cent of the votes depending on the constituencies.

Within Cambodia, there was no other political group that had the appeal of the Sangkum by 1955. The Sangkum was Sihanouk and his picture was its symbol. Independent candidates were frowned upon, and opposition to Sihanouk could mainly be found in the Sangkum. Indeed, Sihanouk used the Sangkum to absorb his opponents in the Democratic Party. However, even by 1962, the process of assimilation had not been entirely successful. Within the Sangkum, the young educated members complained of discrimination in favour of the old and corrupt. Hou Yuon was one of the younger members who criticized the cult of personality advanced by Sihanouk. There was also rivalry between the politically conservative and the radical élites within the Sangkum. Sihanouk's original intention in including both groups was to preserve national unity and to check the dominance of any one side. However, rebellions instigated by the radicals in April 1967 led Sihanouk to suspect that the left was getting the upper hand. When he warned that the rebel leaders would be severely dealt with, the two most prominent and vociferous of the radicals, Khieu Samphan and Hou Yuon, went underground.

The consolidation of the left-wing resistance to Sihanouk was a stage in the development of an alternative political structure. The left viewed the creation of an independent Cambodian state quite differently from Sihanouk or the earlier Democratic Party. For the latter two, independence was an end with hardly any effect on the political or social structures. For the left, independence was a pause in the Cambodian revolution after which complex issues of Cambodian nationalism and Cambodian socialism would have to be accommodated, domestically as well as at the regional level, in the history of Indochina (especially Vietnam) and at the international level, within the historically-determinist laws of Marx and Lenin.

The structure that harboured the Cambodian communists was the Khmer People's Revolutionary Party, founded in September 1951 after the dissolution of the Indochinese Communist Party earlier that year. At that time, the war against the French in neighbouring Vietnam was raging, and Vietminh combatants were using Cambodia as a staging area. With the support of these Vietminh, the Cambodian communists were able to control considerable portions of territory—estimates range up to one-half of Cambodia—including the power to levy taxes and contributions. The French military command estimated that the taxes they controlled equalled half the entire Cambodian budget and three times its expenditure on national defence.[9] By the time the Geneva Conference took place in 1954, the Cambodian communists and the Vietminh were significant forces.

The same Geneva Conference was to reduce the Cambodian left to insignificance. Sihanouk insisted that the indigenous communists should not be admitted to the Geneva Conference. At the same time, the Vietminh were prepared to abandon the cause of the Cambodian communists in order to earn the best concessions for Vietnam.

Right-wing political groups and the anti-communist military gained support from the United States which wanted an active anti-left government that would allow the open destruction of communist sanctuaries in Cambodia. The right-wing coup launched by Lon Nol who toppled Sihanouk in 1970 proved, however, only an interruption in the drive to establish a left-wing government that would provide protection for the communists. Lon Nol was toppled in 1975.

[9] J. L. S. Girling, 'The Resistance in Cambodia', *Asian Survey*, XII, 7 (1972).

The fall of Lon Nol and the emergence of the new communist leader, Pol Pot, marked an important phase in the development of political structures in Cambodia, now called Kampuchea. It was Pol Pot's aim to uproot society and reconstitute anew the existing political structures. His Communist Party of Kampuchea (CPK) was compelled to draw upon radical classist and anti-traditional themes because the mildly reformist and nationalist avenues were already monopolized by Sihanouk. The CPK was founded in 1960 and launched its armed struggle only in 1968. By then, a highly nationalistic home-grown autocracy had developed under Sihanouk. Sihanouk's credentials as the national liberator were almost impeccable. The CPK therefore had to out-do the nationalism of Sihanouk in order not to be tainted as anti-national. Thus radical classism and extreme forms of nationalism were embraced.

This position distinguished the CPK from the Vietnamese communists. In practical terms also, the experience of the Cambodian communists in co-operating with the Vietnamese was not encouraging. The fall of Sihanouk and his replacement by Lon Nol should have helped to cement relations between the CPK and the Vietnamese, but this was not the case. In 1973, when the Vietnamese signed the ceasefire agreement with the United States, the CPK found itself abandoned once again in its struggle against the pro-American Lon Nol régime. When internal opposition to the rigours of Pol Pot's rule became widespread, it was easy for other Cambodian leaders like Heng Samrin to seek Vietnamese support in order to depose Pol Pot. This happened in January 1979 when Vietnamese-led forces captured Phnom Penh and installed Heng Samrin at the head of a People's Revolutionary Committee to administer Kampuchea.

The invasion by the Vietnamese forces naturally had its own impact on the political structure in Kampuchea. However, its effects were not clearly seen because the invasion was not a clean surgical action. Rather, it degenerated into protracted guerrilla warfare. There was evidence, though, of the grand design of Vietnam. In 1980, there were meetings of foreign ministers in Phnom Penh (January) and Vientiane (July) to ensure more co-operation between Vietnam, Laos and Kampuchea.

Within Kampuchea itself, the Vietnamese-supported Heng Samrin régime appeared to be ensconced in power and capable of developing its own political structures to replace those of the old Pol Pot forces. In January 1979, a People's Revolutionary Council had been established, with Heng Samrin making it clear that there was no place in the new political structure for non-communist Cambodian groups. That ended any chance of an alliance with such groups as the Khmer People's National Liberation Front led by Son Sann, an opponent of Sihanouk, on the common basis of opposing Pol Pot—at least for the time being.

Meanwhile, a flurry of activities took place among the groups opposed to Heng Samrin to establish an alternative political structure. In a situation of war, this was extremely difficult. Son Sann's faction was militarily weak. The Khmer Rouge of Pol Pot and Khieu Samphan was a political embarrassment, but was better equipped and well trained. Sihanouk himself stood aloof. What emerged in the end was a coalition that allowed the

three main opposition factions to maintain their own identity, organization, structure and policies.

Laos

The theme of war and revolution is more difficult to pursue in respect of
Laos. There, the struggle against foreign influence—Vietnam, Thailand,
the United States—merged with an internal struggle among family-led
political structures. For the greater part of Laos' history as an independent
entity, war and revolution failed to produce the unity that would reverse
its earlier history of petty kingdoms and on-going diaspora of the Laotian
people. Seen from this perspective, the study of political structures should,
willy-nilly, start with the princely familes or Laotian élite that controlled
the kingdoms. The patterns that can be discerned should provide a picture
of the political institutions that emerged.

In the Lao political structure family-based centres were indeed prominent. Most of the Lao élite were descendants of the old royal families and
courtiers of Champassak, Vientiane, Xieng Khouang and Luang Prabang.
Only a limited number came from the provinces of Khammouane and
Savannakhet. None came from Nam Tha, Phong Saly, Sam Neua, Attopeu or
Sayabouri, areas not populated by the Lao. The élite was given access to
preferential education by the French colonialists and, after independence,
members of this privileged group occupied key government positions.
They included Prince Phetsarath; his brother, the neutralist Souvanna
Phuoma; and the communist sympathizer Prince Souphanouvong.

A second characteristic worthy of note was the kinship ties between the
various leaders. The three princes—Phetsarath, Souvanna Phouma and
Souphanouvong—were half-brothers, the first two having the same mother.
These kinship ties also extended into the bureaucracy and the armed
forces. The ties were not sacrificed even though Souphanouvong was
identified with the Pathet Lao which opposed the royal family.

These similarities did not result in the emergence of homogenous
political structures over all the territory that is currently called Laos. In
fact, two different types of structures could be identified, one symbolized
by the Royal Lao Government and the other by the Pathet Lao. The first
continued to rely on the traditional sources of power—the royalty, the
military and an obedient peasantry. All these were primarily Lao institutions and in fact, the royal leaders, Phetsarath and Souvanna Phouma,
were imbued with a traditional attitude of superiority toward the non-
Laotian tribal peoples. Their policy towards the latter was 'Laotianization',
though this policy was not pressed aggressively. As a result, a major
chasm existed between the Lao and non-Lao peoples under their leadership. Their preference for close relations with the United States also
tended to distinguish them from the rural Lao and even the Buddhist
monkhood. The Pathet Lao, on the other hand, was different. Souphanouvong operated in areas not heavily populated by the ethnic Lao, Xieng
Khoung, Phong Saly and Sam Neua. He was therefore compelled to carve
out new sources of support by appealing to the non-Lao as well as the

unorganized groups of disaffected intellectuals, youths and workers. Such different constituencies of support could not but affect the political structures of both sides.

At the same time as these different structures began to pull Laos into two main divisions, the French were led into a convention with Laos in 1949 which granted the territory autonomy within the French Union. Negotiations were therefore started to bring about a reconciliation between the Pathet Lao and the Royal Lao Government. For the latter, the problem was the method of accommodating Souphanouvong, whose dominant personality would overshadow any arrangements for co-operation. For Souphanouvong, the aim was to preserve his power base in the non-Lao ethnic areas as well as the continued control of his military units and influence over the cabinet.

The negotiations at Geneva in 1954 to settle the war in Vietnam after the French debacle at Dien Bien Phu provided the first opportunity for compromise. Laos was cast for a neutral role. The Pathet Lao was regrouped in the northern provinces of Sam Neua and Phong Saly. Plans were drawn up to integrate the armies of Souphanouvong and Souvanna Phouma. These were viewed as provisional arrangements pending an internal all-Laotian political settlement which was concluded only in 1957; but very quickly any semblance of political compromise ended in 1958 when seats for the National Assembly were contested in an election provided for under the 1957 settlement.

The pro-Pathet Lao parties won narrowly but this victory was pyrrhic because, instead of settling political differences, the prospect of communist control of Laos attracted the attention of the United States which began to interfere in the Laos political structure. The manoeuvring of the United States resulted in the establishment of the Phoui Sananikone government in Vientiane which was less accommodating than the earlier one led by Souvanna Phouma. The Sananikone government was succeeded by the pro-American Phoumi government. Prince Souphanouvong then terminated his connections with the government in Vientiane and returned to his territorial base. In 1960, in a bid to end the civil war, Captain Kong Le from the army paratrooper battalion staged a coup to bring Laos to a neutralist position. Far from achieving reconciliation, the coup segmented Laos into three parts: the neutralists joined by Souvanna Phouma in Vientiane, the pro-Americans led by Phoumi who retreated to Savannakhet in the south, and the Pathet Lao in the north.

From then on, the intrusion of foreign forces in Laos became a semi-permanent feature of the political structure. The Americans continued to supply arms to Phoumi, thereby enabling him to maintain his position in Savannakhet. At the same time, US economic aid to Vientiane continued, but Souvanna Phouma also decided to open another 'lifeline' to the Soviet Union, which soon came forward with assistance in the form of food and fuel. Such aid became even more important after Thailand imposed an economic blockade on Vientiane in protest against the neutralist coup which had ousted the pro-American Phoumi. In December 1960, the latter's military forces marched on Vientiane, forcing Souvanna Phouma to form a government-in-exile in Cambodia and pushing Captain Kong Le's forces to the Plain of Jars, at which place he was joined by the Pathet Lao forces and provided with Soviet military aid. The Pathet Lao, now also actively supported by the Soviet Union, then embarked on a vigorous campaign to capture territory controlled by Phoumi's forces.

The support given to the respective Laotian allies by the contending external powers led to a dangerous situation that required resolution. The result was the convening of the second Geneva Conference in 1962, where attempts were made to form a coalition government based on the warring factions. In June 1962, this was achieved. Foreign assistance was terminated and military personnel were ordered home. Superficially, the situation in 1962 suggested that there was a return to the arrangements of 1957, but in fact foreign intervention had completely altered the political structures. The coalition government that was formed boosted the power of the pro-American Phoumi: he was given the post of Minister of Finance in control of foreign aid funds for the payment of salaries of civil servants and military personnel. Souphanouvong's Pathet Lao had by 1962 become very much a pawn in the hands of the powerful Vietnamese in the north who needed control of the part of Laos through which their soldiers traversed to the south. The weakest chink in the armour of the coalition government was Souvanna Phouma, who had to balance the ambitious Phoumi and the powerfully-backed Souphanouvong. It should be noted that Souvanna himself did not enjoy any regional or genuine mass base of support. However, he was able to remain as part of the political structure because he cemented alliances with powerful families like the Sananikones of Vientiane and Sisouk na Champassak in the south. Also, he was the symbol of neutralism which was the anchor of the 1962 Geneva agreement. Thus foreign derivatives were also important in strengthening that segment of the political structure in Laos.

The coalition government did not last long. In 1963, Souphanouvong and his ally, Phoumi Vongvichit, left Vientiane abruptly. However, Souvanna Phouma was still committed to retain the tripartite system that had become frozen as a result of the 1962 Geneva agreement. He was also desirous of keeping the door open for the return of Souphanouvong and Vongvichit. This meant that the posts previously held by the two were left vacant and these were the important portfolios of deputy prime minister, minister of economy and planning, and minister of information and tourism. Government was largely hamstrung.

Meanwhile, plans to hold elections for fifty-nine deputies to the National Assembly proceeded apace and they took place on 18 July 1965. These elections were important because they marked a phase of new developments that cast considerable strain on the existing political structure. While the entire structure had previously been dominated by feudal or leading families, the elections introduced a new middle class which had benefited considerably from the economic aid furnished by the United States after the 1962 Geneva agreement. A commodity import programme was started by the United States, in which goods were made available for local merchants to import at a low rate and sell in Laos at a high rate. The difference represented a profitable source of new wealth which contributed to the emergence of the middle class. Their representatives were elected to the National Assembly as deputies in 1965 and they thus had a stake in government policy. When government became paralysed because of the differences explained above, irritation among the deputies increased. In 1966, Souvanna Phouma was forced to dissolve the National Assembly when it rejected the budget, and new general elections were called for 1967.[10]

By that time, political labels had become less important on the non-communist side. In 1967, Kong Le was compelled by his own men to go into exile in France. The right-wing leader, Phoumi Nosavan, was also forced to take refuge in exile in Thailand as his hopes for a political return faded. Laos became divided *de facto* into two roughly equal parts contested by the Pathet Lao and the Royal Lao Government. The military struggle that ensued till 1975 followed a predictable pattern: during the dry season from October to May, the Pathet Lao (backed by the Vietnamese, who probably totalled 40,000 in Laos by 1968) tended to take the initiative in order to seize tactically important positions and replenish their food supplies; during the wet season, the royalist forces appeared to have the advantage because of their greater mobility, thanks to American-supplied equipment and the use of aeroplanes.

The effect of this internal conflict on the political structure could only be guessed. Evidently, the longer the fighting, the more difficult it was to create a structure that would suit both the contenders. In fact, the Third Congress (1968) of the NLHS—the political arm of the military Pathet Lao—indicated that it planned to lay the groundwork for a broad political front having as a common programme the elimination of American influence from Laos, but it also made clear that cooperators with the United States, like Souvanna Phouma, would have no place in it. Thus the price for rejoining the coalition government that Souvanna was still trying to preserve was stated clearly.[11]

The signing of the Paris Peace Agreement on 23 January 1973 presented a new opportunity for the Laotian leaders. Article 20 of the agreement called on the signatories to abide by the 1962 Geneva agreement. This led to the signing in Vientiane on 21 February 1973 of the Agreement on the Restoration of Peace and Reconciliation in Laos. The agreement was encouraged by the Americans, the Soviets and the north Vietnamese. It provided for the establishment of a provisional government of National Union and a National Coalition Political Council. Specifically, both sides agreed that Souvanna would be prime minister of the provisional government. Each side also agreed to provide a vice-premier and five ministers. Each minister would be assisted by a vice-minister chosen from the other side. However, a minister's absence would be filled only by his own party and not by the other party's vice-minister. It was agreed that the Pathet Lao would chair the council which would operate on the principle of unanimity. Troops and the police from both sides would be used to ensure the neutralization of Vientiane and Luang Prabang. All other foreign forces would be withdrawn. However, pending an election, the date for which was not fixed, each side would retain control over its own territory. The

[10] Arthur J. Dommen, 'Laos: the troubled "neutral"', ibid., VII, 1 (1967).
[11] Paul F. Langer, 'Laos: preparing for a settlement in Vietnam', ibid., IX, 1 (1969).

careful balance that was struck ensured that only matters of consensus would be implemented.[12]

In hindsight, it is obvious that this was only a temporary arrangement. In 1975, after the fall of Saigon, the Pathet Lao seized power. Prince Souvanna Phouma, the prime minister, was appointed adviser to the government. The Lao king was deposed in December that year and the Lao People's Democratic Republic was proclaimed and ruled by leaders of the Pathet Lao.

Indonesia: The Revolution

Revolution did not occur only in the Indochina region. It also took place in Indonesia and there it shared some major similarities with that in Vietnam. Both aspired to overthrow colonial rule. Both were self-reliant and eschewed dependence on foreign aid. Both sought to unite their respective nations. Both revolutions reached a terminal point when the colonial or foreign powers made their official exit. This last feature had special meaning for the Indonesian case. The revolution in Indonesia ended in 1949 after a relatively short struggle of four years, compared to that of the Vietnamese which lasted from 1945 to 1975; the brief period of struggle meant that there was no need for long-drawn contention, agitation or dispute of the kind that would produce revolutionary dogmas. Unlike the Vietnamese revolution, the Indonesian revolution was not one phase in a series with each episode terminating on an expectant note because the continuation would unfold later. In Vietnam there was a pause in 1954 with the signing of the Geneva agreement and the division of Vietnam at the seventeenth parallel. Another pause—albeit a very short one—took place in 1973 after the signing of the Paris Peace Accords between the United States and north Vietnam. Each pause was succeeded by a renewed effort to complete the revolution. In contrast, the Indonesian revolution was completed at one go. There was no need for challenges to constituted authority to be repeated. A sovereign Republic of Indonesia— the antithesis of the Netherlands East Indies—was firmly established. Put another way, the Indonesian revolution did not require a sequel with its attendant ideological baggage beckoning towards a revolution yet to come and suggesting what form it might take.

Throughout its duration, revolution in Indonesia was almost a seamless web of political and armed struggle. Revolution imposed upon and demanded from the independent state of Indonesia a unity that was not previously possible. This unity was realized by the co-operation of two well-known leaders of the prewar nationalist movement—Sukarno and Mohammad Hatta. Together, they constituted a political structure that lasted for as long as that co-operation was required.

Sukarno was the president of the Republic of Indonesia proclaimed in 1945 and Hatta was vice-president. The 1945 constitution provided for a powerful executive president. However, during the early years of the

---

[12] MacAlister Brown and Joseph J. Zasloff, 'Laos 1973: wary steps toward peace', ibid., XIV, 2 (1974).

revolution, Sukarno could not exercise his constitutional powers. He was compelled to let Prime Minister Sjahrir take precedence because, in the immediate postwar world, it was not practical for Sukarno—tainted by collaboration with the Japanese—to deal with foreign powers. Sjahrir was noted for his non-collaborationism. Symbolically, however, the co-operation between Sukarno and Hatta was a significant political structure that fashioned consensus during the revolution. Indonesian society was sorely lacking in unity because it was a matrix of communal, ethnic, religious and cultural segmentation. Broadly speaking, Sukarno repre-sented the Javanese syncretistic religious strain; Hatta was Sumatran and more emphatically a Muslim. Sukarno was skilled at oratory, agitation and mass politics, whereas Hatta, an economist by training, was interested in restoring economic and administrative order to the chaos created by revolution.

Their co-operation provided the mechanism for driving a revolution towards its goal. On the one hand, Sjahrir and Hatta took up the task of hobnobbing with the Dutch and the post-1945 British occupation forces to negotiate international agreements, the Linggajati and Renville Agree-ments of 1947 and 1948 respectively. In particular, Sjahrir was publicly identified with the decision to concede many areas in the outlying territories to the Dutch as the latter's military strength increased in the islands outside Java. What Sjahrir and Hatta achieved turned out to be unpopular though necessary. On the other hand, Sukarno concentrated on propaganda, mobilization and agitation. Such a programme of activities encouraged guerrilla warfare against the Dutch, sabotage, revolutionary fervour and bravado. Sukarno was identified with the popular and attention-grabbing actions.

To be sure, the Sukarno–Hatta combination met considerable opposi-tion. The Dutch launched two military strikes (Police Actions, 1947 and 1948) against the Republic of Indonesia. The second one resulted in the arrest of Sukarno and Hatta. Internally, the national communists carried out an unsuccessful coup in 1946. The revived Communist Party of Indonesia (PKI) launched an abortive revolt at Madiun in east Java in 1948. Carried out during the Second Police Action, it was viewed by all as a stab in the back of the republic at its hour of need. Fundamentalist Muslims (Darul Islam) led a rebellion to establish an Islamic state in west Java, an uprising that was not crushed till 1962. Again, its timing—launched as it was in 1948—was unfortunate. Moreover, it inflicted casualties on the Indonesian army and impressed upon it an extremely unfavourable image of militant Islam. The revolution also meant different things to different groups. While Hatta and Sjahrir conceived the revolution in terms of a colonial uprising, there were independent and separate attempts at social revolution, e.g. overthrowing traditional aristocrats who had previously enjoyed the support of the Dutch. These took place in northern Sumatra and parts of Java.[13]

By and large, notwithstanding the opposition, consensus prevailed.

[13] See Benedict R. O'G. Anderson, *Java in a Time of Revolution: Occupation and Resistance, 1944–1946*, Ithaca and London, 1972 ch. 15.

Apart from the Darul Islam, the Muslims made concessions in the constitutional discussions just before the Japanese surrendered, and agreed not to include the specific mention of Islam in the state ideology of Pancasila. Instead, they settled for the Jakarta Charter, a draft prologue to be tagged on to but not part of the constitution, enjoining those who professed Islam to abide by Islamic laws. The Indonesian army was another political structure that acted as an instrument of consensus uniting the diverse population. In the dark days of 1948, during the Second Police Action, the army was the only source of hope and national authority in the republic.

PLURAL POLITICAL STRUCTURES

In the polyglot world that was Southeast Asia, revolution as a vehicle for consensus was not the remedy adopted by all the independent states. For many others, revolution conjured images of agrarian radicalism, a topsy-turvy world of political intrigue and conspiracy. A way to avoid revolution was to forge political structures that would win the support of large sections of a given population.

Burma: Aung San

The Burmese attempted to create political structures based on consensus of a kind. Post-colonial Burma (called the Union of Myanmar from 1989 onwards) can be studied in terms of its leaders' attempting to forge a civil ideology or a national culture that would provide the legitimacy needed for a consensual political order. Consensus was a vital ingredient if Burma was to exist as a state. In fact, Burma's independence was granted by the British only when an amicable settlement had been reached between Burma proper and the surrounding upland territories populated by ethnic minorities. Negotiations between Aung San on the one hand and the Shan *saw-bwas* and leaders of the Chins and Kachins on the other hand led to the formation of a Union federal government. In 1947, the frontier areas and the Shan states pledged their loyalty to the Union in the Panglong Agreement. Four states were envisaged in the non-Burmese territories, Shan, Karenni, Kachin, Karen, and also a Chin Special Division.

The first Burmese leader, General Aung San, visualized Burma as a plural society in which diverse political structures coexisted within a framework of overarching consensus. He was a prewar student leader later given military training by the Japanese. He had returned to Burma as the leader of the Thirty Comrades, who arrived in Burma at the head of the Burma Independence army, and whose achievements became legendary. Aung San was careful to avoid the development of political structures that would prove divisive in Burma. In his view, an authoritarian structure based on a resurrected and absolutist Burmese monarchy could not attract support. In a country where Buddhism played a central role in the lives of individuals and in the struggle for independence, Aung San was also noted for having argued for the separation of religion and state: 'In politics there is no room for religion inasmuch as there should be no insistence that the president of the Republic should be a Buddhist or that a Minister for Religion should be appointed in the cabinet.'[14] On the ethnic minorities, an important subject that plagued the later years of independent Burma, Aung San's position would have won much support. Never was there a more liberal political structure for the minorities than that proposed by Aung San in May 1947. He proposed that the status of 'Union State', 'Autonomous State' or 'National Area' should be conferred on those territories that possessed the following characteristics: (1) a defined geographical area with a character of its own; (2) unity of language different from the Burmese; (3) unity of culture; (4) community of historical traditions; (5) community of economic interests and a measure of economic self-sufficiency; (6) a fairly large population; and (7) the desire to maintain its distinct identity as a separate unit. It does not require much imagination to realize that Aung San's relatively relaxed views, if accepted, would lead to considerable autonomy for the important minority communities. Fortunately or unfortunately, for reasons that are not clear, Aung San omitted such detailed provisions from a later pronouncement in June 1947 on the same subject. He died soon after, the victim of an assassin's bullet, and his vice-president, U Nu, succeeded him.

Malaysia before 1969

Like Burma, Malaysia (and before 1963, Malaya) was also a multiethnic plural society. In both cases, the British delayed granting independence until suitable arrangements were made to provide for the accommodation of the ethnic minorities in the independent state structure. In Burma, the solution was embodied in the Panglong Agreement. In Malaya, arrangements were less formal but the Alliance 'formula' proved to be a more durable structure.

The evolution of the Alliance formula was an exercise in arriving at some sort of consensus among the principal races in Malaya. Malaya was not an entirely logical grouping of territories and peoples. It inherited from its colonial order several loosely linked administrative units: the Straits Settlements, the Federated Malay States and the unfederated Malay States. In 1963, Sabah, Sarawak and Singapore were added to the political state structure to constitute the new Federation of Malaysia. There were, of course, some common denominators. All of the above-mentioned states had experienced a history of British colonial rule. There was also a core of Malay nationalism in the peninsular part of Malaysia. However, the disintegrative forces were sufficiently potent. In 1948 and 1953, secessionist movements emerged in Penang, and the same happened in Johor and Kelantan in 1955. Singapore was forced to leave Malaysia in 1965. In Sabah, the Chief Minister—Tun Mustapha—acted like an autonomous head of state till he was toppled from power. As for the population, communal conflict was always lurking near the surface. From 1948 till

[14] Cited in *The Political Legacy of Aung San*, compiled by and with an introductory essay by Josef Silverstein, Ithaca: Cornell University Southeast Asia Program, 1972, 3–4.

1960, there was also a revolt launched by the Malayan Communist Party aimed at establishing a government led by communists, principally Chinese.

This environment of discord and conflict was temporarily tamed by the development of an alliance between the Malays and the Chinese. In effect, a consensual environment evolved whereby communal issues were not debated in public but settled through compromises in private. Essentially, this consensus operated on an avoidance principle—avoidance of open, public debate. It was called the Alliance because in 1952, the principal party organs of the Malays and the Chinese—the United Malays National Organization (UMNO) and the then Malayan Chinese Association (MCA) —entered into a co-operative alliance to contest the first municipal election held in Kuala Lumpur. The contested seats were allocated on the basis of an informal agreement. In this celebrated event, the Alliance won nine out of the twelve seats contested, showing that Sino-Malay co-operation was possible under this political structure. Similar arrangements in subsequent elections brought more electoral gains. The parties were so confident of its potency that the Alliance formula of private compromise was employed to produce the informal 'bargain' that lay at the basis of the independent state structure of 1957. An independent Malaya in which Malays and non-Malays were roughly equal in numbers was not viable unless the major ethnic groups agreed on the manner of sharing political and economic power. This bargain ensured the political primacy of the Malays by entrenching the position of the Malay Rulers in the political structure; by weighting rural electoral constituencies; by favourable admission ratios in the key sectors of the civil service and educational institutions; by special allocation of licences and other privileges. All these provisions were embodied in Section 153 of the constitution in the phrase 'special position of the Malays'. In return, the Chinese were allowed to retain their economic power. Also, they could attain limited political power through generous citizenship provisions.

For the Alliance to succeed in an independent state, several conditions had to be met. Leaders had to enjoy substantial support in their respective communities. For UMNO, this condition was fulfilled during the early years of its history. As a political structure, UMNO was *the* Malay party. Its branches reached the Malay village where it was not surprising to find village elders, teachers, or religious leaders holding membership in UMNO as an example to their followers. These party branches in turn followed the dictates of the *mentri besar* (chief minister) of each state in peninsular Malaya; since most of the states had *mentri besar* who were pro-UMNO, virtual bloc votes were ensured. Until the mid-1970s, votes at the crucial UMNO General Assembly were usually cast as a bloc in accordance with the wishes of the *mentri besar*. The considerable influence of the *mentri besar* meant that the votes of each state could be delivered to support the UMNO leaders at the national level. (From 1975 onwards, the formal bloc vote was replaced by the secret ballot, but the *mentri besar* were still able to influence the way votes were cast.) The relationship between the national leaders like Tunku Abdul Rahman and the state leaders remains an important area for further research but generally the latter tended to act in accordance with the dictates of the former, at least in the case of peninsular

Malaya. This pyramid-like political structure in UMNO, with the national leaders commanding rural votes, was a veritable phalanx. The MCA leaders also enjoyed undisputed control of Chinese votes during the early years of independence. The MCA began as a welfare organization in 1949 dedicated to help the Chinese squatters who were zoned to live in New Villages as part of a programme to isolate them from the influence of the MCP. The latter was the only party then that could pose a challenge to the MCA. When it was declared illegal in 1948, the MCA enjoyed the monopoly of legitimate political recruitment among the Chinese.

This is not to suggest that support for the Alliance formula was undiluted. In fact, the partners in the Alliance network were not the only political structure of note. For example, there were Malay groups which opposed the UMNO, considering it as an organization representing largely the administrative élite, scions of the royal houses and others who were willing to accommodate multiracialism. The religious ingredient, Islam, seemed to be under-represented in their scheme of things. There was, in fact, a vibrant tradition of Malay Muslim education since the colonial period, centred on the private institutions of the Maahad II-Ehya Assyarif Gunung Semanggul (Miagus) in the northern part of the state of Perak, and similar *pondok* and *madrasah*. The products of these educational institutions constituted a political structure that embarked on more radical politics than those represented in the Alliance network. Their religious training and their belief in God's reward for life after death contributed to the development of an altruistic and sacrificial attitude that led to radical politics. The Miagus was the educational institution which provided the seedbed for the birth of the Partai Islam se Tanah Malaya or PAS (Pan-Malayan Islamic Party or PMIP) and Partai Rakyat (People's Party). These parties formed an alternative political structure because, unlike those in the Alliance, their major characteristics were *bangsa* (race), *agama* (religion) and *tanah Melayu* (land of the Malays). The PAS, in particular, sought the establishment of a theocratic state, the recognition of Malay as the only official language and nationality, and the restriction of non-Malay privileges. The Partai Rakyat espoused an ideological amalgam of Malay nationalism, agrarian socialism and egalitarianism.

A remaining condition for the Alliance formula to work was the need for the leaders to enjoy close personal relations with one another. The Tunku was comfortable in non-Malay circles. He had a wide circle of non-Malay friends. His own mother was half Thai. It was also well known that he had adopted Chinese children. However, in the course of time and especially with the formation of the Federation of Malaysia in 1963, a more business-like and formal relationship replaced the hitherto informal and personal pattern of interaction among leaders. A whole new generation of Malays and non-Malays had grown up with no inkling of the 'bargain' struck by their elders. The formation of Malaysia in 1963 introduced new political forces into the structure that did not meet some of the conditions mentioned above. The proposal to bring Malaya, Singapore, Sabah, Sarawak and Brunei into a federation was a major change of and challenge to the political structure.

The entire sequence of events began with an almost innocuous

announcement by the then Malayan prime minister, Tunku Abdul
Rahman, on 27 May 1961, at a Singapore press luncheon:

> Malaya today as a nation realizes that she cannot stand alone and in isolation
> ... Sooner or later she should have an understanding with Britain and the
> peoples of the territories of Singapore, North Borneo, Brunei and Sarawak ...
> We should look ahead to this objective and think of a plan whereby these
> territories can be brought closer together in political and economic
> cooperation.[15]

Expanding the Federation of Malaya would seriously affect the communal nature of the political structure. The Bornean territories were populated by ethnic communities like the Iban who, apart from being 'sons of the
soil', had little in common with the Malays. Singapore was predominantly
Chinese with ideological tendencies towards the left. The nature of party
politics was also different. In Borneo, parties had an ethnic emphasis and
they were ephemeral. In Singapore, the dominant party was the People's
Action Party (PAP) which was urban, socialist, non-communal, and used
to governing a fairly homogenous island. It practised open debate on most
important issues. The Alliance, as already suggested, was communal, non-
ideological and used to private discussion of sensitive issues.[16] A political
structure founded on Malay primacy could not but feel the strains.

All the leaders were in fact aware of the changes that the political
structure would sustain, and they sought to find ways to limit the stresses.
Again, the search for a consensus among the major communities became
the main task. On the issue of representation in the House of Representatives, the inclusion of two million Chinese from Singapore would mean an
allocation of some 22 seats compared to the 104 for peninsular Malaya, 12
for Sarawak and 7 for Sabah. This would boost the influence of the Chinese
in federal policy-making. In the negotiations that followed, Singapore
agreed to a reduced representation of 15 seats in return for autonomy
in matters pertaining to labour and education, the latter a core issue in
communalism. At the same time, the representation of Sarawak and Sabah
was increased to 24 and 16 seats respectively. This assuaged the fears of
the Borneans that they would be submerged or eclipsed by the Malays,
who were considered more experienced in politics.

Closely related to representation was, of course, the matter of citizenship, which was a contentious issue on which consensus was difficult. The
extent to which the people in Singapore and the Bornean territories would
be accepted as Malaysian citizens would impact on the political structure,
since the communal balance under the Alliance would need readjustment.
For the Malay peninsula alone, before the formation of Malaysia, the
citizenship issue was not complicated. All persons who were citizens of
any state in the federation (mainly Malays), automatically became citizens
on independence day, 31 August 1957. In addition, all persons born in
Malaya after that date also became citizens (*jus soli*). Citizenship by

---

[15] Peter Boyce, *Malaya and Singapore in International Diplomacy: Documents and Commentaries*,
Syndey, 1968, 8.

[16] John S. T Quah, Chan Heng Chee and Seah Chee Meow, *Government and Politics of
Singapore*, Singapore, 1985, 155–6.

naturalization was also available. In 1962, the provisions regarding citizenship were redefined, effectively making it more difficult for non-Malays to qualify. In addition to *jus soli, jus sanguinis* (the condition that one of the two parents had to be a citizen or a permanent resident at the time of the child's birth) was also required.

The negotiations leading to the formation of Malaysia complicated the citizenship issue further. Two aims had to be satisfied, namely, Singapore politics had to be restricted to the island so that the communal balance in peninsular Malaya would not be upset, and Borneo had to be protected from the flood of Malay or Chinese entrepreneurs who might want to exploit the opportunities there. The latter aim was achieved quite simply. Travellers to Sabah and Sarawak, as it turned out, were required to obtain prior approval from the government of the state concerned. To achieve the former aim, provisions were enacted to ensure that Singapore citizens (who were mainly Chinese) could vote only in Singapore. Furthermore, Singapore citizens could stand for federal office only in a Singapore constituency. These features were necessary in order to make the inclusion of a predominantly Chinese Singapore acceptable to the predominantly Malay government of Malaya.

Money is the life blood that sustains any political structure. In peninsular Malaya before the formation of the Federation of Malaysia, the federal government in Kuala Lumpur controlled all the finances and did not hesitate to disburse funds in accordance with political criteria. With the formation of Malaysia, it was expected that Singapore and Brunei would contribute their revenue surplus while Sabah and Sarawak would be deficit states. (It was the management of finances that constituted one of the hurdles resulting in Brunei's refusal to join Malaysia. Sultan Omar of Brunei would not concede that the central government had the right to impose duties on Brunei's oil, while Kuala Lumpur insisted on that prerogative.)

In the end, almost on the eve of Malaysia Day, Singapore was given the right to collect and retain its own taxes, but 40 per cent of these had to be remitted periodically to Kuala Lumpur. The net effect of this arrangement was to grant considerable autonomy to Singapore within the new political structure, while Sabah and Sarawak also enjoyed some autonomy because they were granted the right to collect and retain export revenues on minerals and forest products.

The financial arrangements continued, however, to bedevil relations between Singapore and the federal government in Kuala Lumpur and formed one of the reasons leading to the former's eventual exit from the federation. While allocation of funds constituted a distinct area of disagreement and discord, it was not totally divorced from the communal issues because, indeed, Singapore's contribution gave the new member state a voice in how the money would be spent. In Singapore's view, the concept of the equality of races meant the practice of racial *laissez faire* which would allow equal treatment for all in order for the best to emerge unaided. That understanding of racial equality ran counter to the traditional practice of the Alliance in general and UMNO in particular. In the communal scheme of things, the government harboured no intention to change the heavy investment of public funds to support the Malays, believing that such preferential treatment would help them to become the equals of the non-Malays. Singapore's views therefore posed a direct challenge to the conventional approach to communalism. That, in itself, could have been accommodated if the views were confined to Singapore. However, Singapore's PAP also considered itself the representative of the Chinese in peninsular Malaya in addition to its multiracial constituents within Singapore.

In 1964, elections were called for the peninsular states; the PAP decided to contest several selected seats, hoping that success in six or seven would convince UMNO leaders that it would be more popular with the Chinese and therefore a more appropriate alliance partner than the MCA. This attempt to poach on Alliance territory failed, and the PAP won only one seat.

Meanwhile, even before the 1964 polls, the UMNO—in an act that foreshadowed the PAP's election participation—had also decided to enter the 1963 Singapore elections in an effort to present itself as the representative of the Malays there. Although it did not win any seats, UMNO continued its campaign for Malay support in Singapore. The vehicle used by UMNO was the Jawi-script, Malay-language daily—the *Utusan Melayu*—in which the PAP was vilified as a Chinese chauvinist party led by Lee Kuan Yew. The Malays in Singapore were encouraged to rely on Kuala Lumpur as the big brother who would protect them. Such constant harping on communal issues during 1963 and 1964 resulted in racial riots in Singapore on the occasion of the Prophet's birthday celebration on 21 July 1964. The bloodshed was stopped, but this event signalled the beginning of the end. Communal tension continued to be high.

In particular, the PAP's participation in politics in Malaya in 1964 and 1965, especially its programme of 'Malaysian Malaysia' (as distinct from the implied but unstated 'Malay Malaysia'), struck at the roots of the bargain. The only sensible way to avoid racial conflict was the separation of Singapore from Malaysia on 9 August 1965. This epochal event defused the communal threat somewhat, but the opposition towards the special position of the Malays was continued by the Democratic Action Party (DAP, successor to the PAP) and in a somewhat muted form by the Gerakan Ra'ayat Malaysia.

What was the effect of the separation on Malaysia's political structure? It showed the important role of leadership because the separation was decided by the Tunku while in London without consulting UMNO. Indeed, the Tunku had not held prior discussions with UMNO when he first broached the idea of Singapore joining the Federation of Malaysia.

If anything, the separation also strengthened the central control of the federal structure. No longer were attacks on the practice of communalism launched in the halls of parliament. The leadership provided by Singapore in criticizing Malay primacy also disappeared almost as it were overnight. However, communal problems did not then disappear.

In fact, one of the greatest legacies of the early experience of Malaysia was the increase in communal discord. Many Malays felt that their interests were pushed aside in order to accommodate the Chinese. For example, they felt that policies like the sole use of Malay as the official language by 1967 were not supported strongly enough. In fact, their demands for economic uplift could not be satisfied without affecting the non-Malays. The latter also felt discriminated against by what they discerned as pro-Malay policies. Slogans like 'Malaysian Malaysia' ignited heady visions of a new racial order. Dissatisfaction with the Tunku and the MCA leadership naturally emerged. The former was disliked for his relaxed attitude of multiracial tolerance. The MCA leaders were considered as unsuitable champions of Chinese rights. For the Malays within UMNO, opposition began to coalesce around the person of the Tunku's deputy, Tun Abdul Razak. The PAS also emerged as an alternative promoter of Malay rights. When general elections were held in 1969, opposition parties like the DAP and the PAS made significant inroads into the Chinese and Malay support of the MCA and UMNO respectively. Extremists from both races, the Chinese encouraged by the gains of the DAP and the Malays incensed by perceived Chinese betrayal of and defection from the Alliance, took to the streets on 13 May 1969 in an orgy of killing. The political structure of the Alliance was in sore need of repair.

The prospects for developing political structures designed to enhance consensus among the ethnic groups in Malaysia and Burma were not good. In both states, leaders who favoured plural structures under an overarching unity did not survive. Aung San was assassinated, while the Tunku was discredited by the 13 May riots. Future attempts at consensus-building proved to be less liberal and generous.

Burma: U Nu

In Burma Prime Minister U Nu tried to develop a political structure based on a synthesis of Buddhism and socialism, with an especially heavy dose of the former. The programme appealed to many Burmese who were Buddhists, but it also aroused the fear of the ethnic minorities who suspected that they would be marginalized since they were not Buddhists. Buddhism also opened the way to Burmanization and the demise of the non-Burman ethnic traditions. The programme also failed to receive support from the socialists.

U Nu's intended political structure of the state was therefore not akin to Aung San's. In fact, U Nu's tenure of office was marked by pressures from ethnic groups seeking greater autonomy. The ostensibly federal political structure that was granted to Burma at independence conferred statehood on the Kachin, Kayah and Shan frontier regions. In addition, Shans and Kayahs were given the right to secede after 1958. The Chins were administered in a special division, while the Karens were allowed to create a state in 1951. However, these liberal provisions for separate political structures were more form than substance. All the states or divisions were dependent on the central government for funds. Their governments were responsible not to state legislatures but to councils made up of members of the central parliament, albeit drawn from their states.

The ethnic minorities tolerated U Nu, if only because his government was so ineffective that proper exercise of authority was not consistently applied. In part, U Nu's erosion of power was due to the challenges posed to his leadership after 1948. For example, in March 1948, the communist party (later known as White Flags) revolted. A paramilitary force, the People's Volunteer Organization, joined the communists. The communists enjoyed considerable support because they championed popular causes in order to redress peasant grievances, such as cancellation of agricultural debt (owed mainly to Indians), returning ownership of land to the cultivators, reserving exploitation of natural resources to the Burmese. The ensuing civil war between the communists and Rangoon resulted in the collapse of the central administration. In the districts, local bosses (*bo* in local parlance) emerged, exercising control with their own paramilitary bands to defend their fiefs. By the time the civil war ended, the *bo* were managing local affairs and in fact operating a government structure parallel to the centre.

A challenge to U Nu's control of the government also emerged from his own party, the Anti-Fascist People's Freedom League (AFPFL). The AFPFL was the ruling party but U Nu's control over it was weak at best. Founded by Aung San, it was, in any case, not a monolith but merely an alliance of mass organizations (e.g. the All-Burma Peasants Organization, Federation of Trade Organizations), ethnic groups (e.g. Karen Youth League), independent individual members (e.g. U Nu, the prime minister) and at least one political party, called the Socialist Party. Many of the organizations were in fact the personal followings of certain leaders who jealously held tight control over them. The followers were often territorially based, and this feature and the fact that the leaders had to divide the spoils among the followers, only encouraged rivalries within the AFPFL. Cohesion as a party was lacking.

The large majority won in two national elections (1951–2 and 1956) tended to hide the fissures within the party, but these emerged at the third All-Burma AFPFL Congress in January 1958. At that meeting, U Nu declared that the AFPFL would be transformed from a coalition to an unitary party. All affiliates, henceforth, had to adhere to the party ideology and accept a status subordinate to the party hierarchy. At that time, U Nu rejected Marxism as the party ideology but opted for a form of socialism.

These developments resulted in the split of the AFPFL into two factions—the U Nu group and the Kyaw Nyein–Ba Swe group. The split led to a severe drop in the parliamentary majority for U Nu. The latter feared a vote of no-confidence in a forthcoming budget session. In an unconstitutional move, U Nu promulgated the budget without debate. An atmosphere of political tension followed. U Nu asked General Ne Win to form a caretaker government to restore order so that a climate of confidence could be created for elections to be held. Ne Win's caretaker government was in full control of the country for eighteen months. During this time, it stabilized the cost of living and increased exports and foreign-exchange reserves. It also attempted to exert central control over the various regions of Burma by eliminating the power of the *bo* and replacing them with the authority of appointed district officers and security and administrative committees.

When U Nu's faction won a resounding victory in the February–March 1960 elections and returned to power in the first peaceful transition from military to civilian rule, U Nu named his faction the Pyidaungsu or Union Party. His rivals retained the name AFPFL. The Union Party did not live up to its name. It soon succumbed to squabbling among the leaders. Two groups emerged. One called itself the Thakins, consisting of the leftist party members who had supported U Nu in the earlier 1958 split. The other group was the U Bo's who were relative newcomers and more conservative in their ideology. The internal divisions resulted in the party losing its credibility and this was in part responsible for the military takeover by Ne Win in 1962.

The parties in opposition to U Nu's earlier AFPFL (before 1958) and the later Union Party (after 1960) were not far different. Before 1958, the chief opponent of the AFPFL was the National Unity Front (NUF). It was also a coalition, but the members were almost equally strong constituent parties—ranging from the non-communist Justice Party to the Marxist Burma Workers and Peasants Party. Its only reason for cohesion rested on its opposition to the AFPFL. After its electoral failures in 1960, the coalition disintegrated leaving behind as its anchor group the Burma Workers and Peasants Party which was renamed the Burma Workers Party. By the time of the military takeover, it was clearly a Marxist-controlled coalition.

The other main political party in opposition to U Nu was the Kyaw Nyein–Ba Swe group which had retained the name of AFPFL. It never really posed a challenge to U Nu, being largely a party of personal followers of the principal leaders.

Two specific policies adopted by U Nu after 1960 were responsible for his downfall. The first was the call to establish Buddhism as the state religion. The Buddhist hierarchy was a substantial political structure because it provided a refuge from state laws but at the same time could pose as the conscience of the people. Relations between church and state could therefore be viewed in terms of contest or co-optation. Religion was a field in which U Nu appeared to have interfered most conspicuously from the 1950s. He believed that Buddhism was the means of making socialism possible because the economic system could not be changed unless human hearts were first transformed. In 1950, when the Buddha Sasana Council Act was enacted, U Nu created a state-financed agency for the promotion and propagation of Buddhism. Nu's support for Buddhism at that time was in part a programme to provide an ideological challenge to the left-wing forces. In 1954, in response to pressure from abbots, instruction in Buddhism was begun in state schools. Later, in 1961, he vowed to declare Buddhism as the state religion because of his own strong desire to perform this deed of merit, among other reasons. This move was of course opposed by the non-Buddhist minorities, and by the army which wanted the state religion to be limited to Burma proper. In essence, U Nu's proposal would have made little real difference since Buddhism was already so widely practised. However, the non-Buddhist ethnic minorities were incensed that an attempt to strengthen Buddhism was even made.

The second reason for Nu's downfall was the impact of his policies on the maintenance of the federal structure. In 1960, as an election promise,

U Nu proposed the establishment of separate states for the Arakanese and Mons. After the elections, he reneged and delayed the statehood bills, thus alienating the Arakanese, Mons and others. Insurgency increased and by the end of 1961, U Nu even admitted that the minority rebels controlled one-tenth of the country.[17]

It was the danger of the disintegration of the state structure that led to U Nu's being deposed by Ne Win in 1962. With Ne Win's accession to power, the focus shifted definitively from tolerance of plural political structures towards the creation of maximum government.

The Philippines before Marcos

Plural political structures were found in the Philippines at the inception of independence. However, the study of these structures presents a difficulty that historians must surmount, namely, the need to purge the mind of contemporary preoccupations in the analysis of the past. In the case of the Philippines, this advice is difficult to follow. In February 1986, President Marcos was overthrown in a peaceful, democratic revolution, called the 'second Philippine Revolution', in recognition of the first one that occurred in 1896 against Spanish colonial rule. On both occasions, the continuous trend of patriotism and the desire for democratic government with room for diverse political structures were the distinguishing features. The historian cannot but reflect on the similarities.

The key to understanding political structures in the Philippines is the family. Its importance had historical roots. The pre-Hispanic local settlements were kinship groups. The Spanish colonialists did not destroy the family ties but in fact strengthened them considerably. The Spanish government alienated the Filipinos because it was predatory, negative and burdensome. Without an ally in government, they had no alternative but to provide for their own welfare. The American colonial period and independence thereafter did not change this situation. The American régime gave the traditional élite opportunities for extending the family structure into politics. Aided by its economic strength, this élite was able to control the government upon independence. The result of this marriage of political leadership and economic power was the entrenchment of conservatism and family influence in government. The extended Filipino family system in which both paternal and maternal relations are considered as belonging to the family provided a made-to-order political structure.

What values did the family impart to the political structure? They included the priority given to the satisfaction of particularistic needs and the importance of personal and daily relationships. These ethics and norms were largely internalized in the individual. The head of the family therefore assumed importance as a leader with social and political clout. Members of the family and other retainers were able to share the good fortunes of the leader. A structure of dependency soon developed.

This aspect of a family-based political structure was further augmented by colonial legacies. Both Spanish and American rule bequeathed a highly

---

[17] Quoted in Richard Butwell, *U Nu of Burma*, Stanford, 1963, 227.

unequal system of land tenure. In the agricultural sector, this meant that there was a large exploitable class of tenants susceptible to influence by a politically powerful landowning class. Such a situation promoted a client framework. Leaders were supported because they were able to satisfy the demands of their followers: the former were patrons and the latter clients. Leaders themselves had patrons and in this way the entire political structure was vertically linked from the *barrio* to the national capital.

Two features of this patron–client relationship particularly marked the political structure. First, national leaders were not generally required to maintain direct ties with the population. For election to the presidency, the most important condition was the ability to dispense rewards to command the support of the voting blocs. Second, party loyalty was not important and therefore there was no need for parties to present identifiable pro- grammes. Parties were never distinct ideological entities. They resembled fiefdoms allied together. Party leaders could not therefore campaign on the basis of programmes because these would endanger the alliances within the party. After elections, the party leaders were sustained by local voting blocs controlled by local leaders who had to be rewarded. Such a situation encouraged the formation of two grand parties, the 'ins' and the 'outs'. This two-party feature distinguished the party political structure in the Philippines and extended even into the Muslim south.

This two-party political structure was interrupted only briefly by the Japanese occupation. When the ageing Sergio Osmena returned with General MacArthur to restore the Partido Nacionalista, his claim to leader- ship was challenged by Manuel Roxas—once the lieutenant of Osmena and a much younger, prominent prewar Nacionalista leader—who remained in the Philippines through the occupation. The result was a split in the party in the run-up to the presidential election in 1946, with Osmena's faction reconstituting itself as the Nationalist Party and Roxas' supporters calling themselves the Liberal Party. The sources of party alignment, however, remained the same and what Osmena and Roxas achieved was the splitting of support in each province.

As was to be expected, the two parties did not greatly differ. Both were conservative in the defence of private property and the existing social system. Both parties tried to win the middle ground, with neither going to the extremes so as to alienate the mainstream voters. Within this broad framework, there were certain regional differences. The Nationalist Party appeared to be strong in the Tagalog-speaking coconut-growing southern Luzon and in Cebu. The Liberal Party enjoyed strong support in the rice- growing Pampanga region of central Luzon and in the Ilocos provinces of the north where the people were members of the Philippine Independent (Aglipayan) Church and employees of the extensive tobacco industry. However, these regional links were very tenuous. For the purpose of the 1965 presidential election, Ferdinand Marcos, a Liberal Party member who was also Ilocano and Aglipayan, joined the Nationalist Party. As a result, the Nationalist Party, which was previously strong in southern Luzon, overnight became a heavyweight in the north. Thus regional identification was no sure indicator of the strength or weakness of the political party structure. On the whole, regional distinctions were not important because regional differences were slight, except for the stark but general contrasts between the Muslim south and the Christian north. Regional rivalry invariably meant rivalry for favours.

This line of analysis suggests that individual leaders could swing votes in very material ways. It should also be noted that these individuals were often heads of influential families which served as major components of the political structure. The Filipino tradition of authoritarianism probably had its origins in these hierarchically structured families. It was not uncommon to find political leaders and office-holders at the national and local levels of government wielding authority as if they were dominant patriarchs. Examples include scions of the Lopez, Aquino–Cojuangco, Osmena and Romualdez clans.

The independent state of the Philippines was therefore characterized by continuous political struggle between élite families represented in political parties which controlled votes from the *barrio* (village) through the patron–client system. The regular change of leaders in government through elections gave the impression that democracy was at work in the Philippines. In fact there was an almost monotonous political struggle between the élites. Two exceptions merit mention. The election of Ramon Magsaysay was significant because he was the first Filipino presidential candidate to employ the grassroots approach. The election in 1961 of Diosdado Macapagal was also noteworthy as the first real contest between the party machine and the grassroots. Macapagal's victory was viewed by some observers, prematurely as it turned out, as ending the domination of the upper class, not least because Macapagal was born of lower-class origin in Pampanga.

However, if democracy implies space for other political structures to exercise influence and control national policies, this was not the case in the Philippines. The political élite was small, and thus personal relations were important. Intimacy also served as a bulwark that prevented other structures from challenging the political élite families.

Of these, one that emerged as most important in the 1980s was the Catholic Church. With the population 85 per cent Catholic, it is not difficult to imagine how the Church can exercise considerable influence within the political structure of the Philippines and, indeed, be a part of it. The bishops exercised authority over the educated, the wealthy, and the masses alike. The clergy managed schools, welfare and other institutions. The Church also launched action programmes aimed at mass relief, thus providing a viable alternative to government. Above all, the Catholic Church was rich. The Archdiocese of Manila, first founded in 1579, was indeed reputed to be one of the wealthiest dioceses in the world.

During Spanish colonial rule, the church had been a partner of the state. The two co-operated to extend the empire and spread the faith. American colonial rule stressed the separation of church and state. After independence, this separation continued.

Organizationally, the Catholic leadership was centred principally in a body known as the Catholic Bishops' Conference of the Philippines, an alliance of eighty-one prelates with the power to decide official policy for 5000 priests in the country. Its long-term leader was Cardinal Jaime Sin, Archbishop of Manila from 1974 and a cardinal from 1976. He held a central moderating role between the conservatives on the one hand and the radical clergy on the other, the latter being supporters of socio-political activism. Traditionally, the bishops' conference had given its support to the government in power as long as its interests were not affected. Generally, the wealth of the Church implied that it was one of the social pillars of support of the status quo. But when martial law was proclaimed in 1972, and Marcos had suppressed all other opposition, the Church was to act as the conscience of the political structure.

Another political structure enjoying mass support was typified by the Hukbalahap. By any definition, the Huk movement was the best illustration of the widespread rural discontent in the independent period of Philippine statehood. From 1946 to 1953, the Huks were able to launch a full-scale rebellion in central Luzon, in part because the movement derived considerable support from the peasants who had been severely disadvantaged by the breakdown of the mutual support system between the upper and lower classes. According to traditional practice, the élite was expected to act as patrons, for example by contributing to community activities and providing help to their tenants in times of distress. In return, a member of the lower class was expected to show deference. In central Luzon, this two-class system was breaking down because of the increase of absentee landlords. The widespread use of the leasehold system instead of share tenancy also meant that the lower class was exposed to a less protected life. The backbone of the Huk movement was broken by President Magsaysay who offered land in the south to those Huk who surrendered. He also enacted agrarian reform legislation in 1954 and 1955.

Apart from the Huks, there seemed to be no political structure representing labour or the working class. This could be due to the reform measures of Magsaysay. The presence of strong family ties was also another explanation. In urban areas, splinter parties to woo the labour vote were not successful because the discontented among the working class tended to return to the *barrio* where relatives could provide subsistence.

Arguably, the propensity for conflict between political structures was greater in the Philippines than other Southeast Asian states. Society tended to be more adversarial than consensual. The most potent source of conflict was agrarian unrest which pitched peasants against landowners in a classic structural conflict of masses versus élite. The links between the structures in the Philippines are therefore characterized by discord. One of the principal explanations for this state of affairs lies in the failure of the élite in Philippine history to transcend its class affiliation.[18] For example, in 1896, this élite separated itself from the Katipunan, a populist movement. In 1899, many élite leaders abandoned the revolutionary government of Emilio Aguinaldo and opted for political freedom from Spain but not social or economic democracy. Later, in 1900–1, élite leaders collaborated with the United States to establish a colonial counter-revolutionary régime. The subsequent American policy of free trade meant an added economic advantage to them as producers of cash crops with open access to the

---

[18] Leslie E. Bauzon, *Philippine Agrarian Reform, 1880–1965*, Singapore: ISEAS Occasional Paper no. 31, 1975, 17.

United States market. At the same time, rural grievances were left unresolved. This situation continued little changed in the 1950s and 1960s.
Agrarian unrest continued to loom as a major theme in government
policies. Reform measures failed because of intense opposition by the
landlords, and the lack of supporting infrastructure that should have
accompanied declarations of sincere intent, for instance provision of credit
facilities, marketing outlets, co-operatives, attacks on bureaucratic obstruction and so on. When reform measures failed, governments adopted
coercion. In the early 1950s, during the height of the Huk rebellion,
President Elpidio Quirino even suspended the writ of *habeas corpus*—a
drastic measure for a state often described as the showcase of democracy.

Indonesia: The Political Parties

There was a time after the end of the Indonesian revolution when pluralistic
political structures abounded in Indonesia. One of the conditions for the
relinquishment of Dutch sovereignty in 1949 was in fact the establishment
of a federal state structure in the republic so as to accommodate the diverse
interests of a far-flung archipelago. The federal state did not last more than
a year: each of the constituent states elected to join the unitary Republic of
Indonesia by the end of 1950. Meanwhile, a provisional constitution of
1950 was enacted to accommodate the transition from federal to unitary
structures. It was a measure of the intense dislike for colonial-inspired
schemes that led to the rapid demise of the federal state. Anti-Dutch
feelings, however, soon lost potency as a cementing force contributing to
consensus. Attention had to be given to sorting out the chaos left by the
revolution. Economic stabilization was urgent. Then, too, decisions were
needed regarding the future of the Dutch investments, the return of West
Irian (which remained in Dutch hands), the conduct of foreign relations,
the demobilization of the revolutionary fighters. These problems challenged the consensus that was achieved during the revolution.

The task of solving them was entrusted to the political structure of party-
based cabinet governments. The early cabinets were headed by Hatta and
leaders of similar outlook. Their approach to the problems facing the
independent state was technocratic. Economic rationalization was emphasized. Foreign investments were encouraged. Forms of extreme nationalism
were eschewed. Their actions flowed from the assumption that the revolution had ended and the task of organizing the new-born nation beckoned.
Sukarno opposed this approach because it relegated him to a back seat,
requiring skills with which he was less familiar. After 1953, he supported
cabinets that adopted a more militant approach to nationalism. This meant
renewed emphasis on foreign policy issues or the recovery of West Irian or
programmes on which consensus could be easily obtained. At the same
time, economic rationalization or courses of action that would invite
disagreement were avoided. The political élite was divided on these lines.

This division, however, was linked to more fundamental cleavages in
political structures. Many of the Hatta-type leaders were members of the
Masjumi (Federation of Muslim Organizations) representing the reform

wing of Indonesian Islam. The Sukarno-type supporters identified with the Indonesian National Party (PNI) and the Muslim Scholars' Association (Nahdatul Ulama, NU) representing the more traditional Muslims. Each of these parties was the centre of a matrix of culturally discrete groups (called *aliran*) that extended from the level of national politics to schools or organizations at the village level. The dichotomy between the two groups of leaders also tended to parallel the division between the outer islands and Java. In short, party, cultural, ideological and geographical divisions reinforced each other. The independent state that emerged from the revolution appeared to be more fragmented than ever, and consensus was nowhere to be found.

The first nationwide election held in 1955 confirmed this fragmentation. The PNI obtained 22 per cent of the vote, the NU 18 per cent; both derived their votes from Java. The Masjumi obtained 21 per cent, most of its votes coming from the outer islands. A fourth party, the Indonesian Communist Party (PKI), netted 16 per cent. The strong showing of the PKI and the concentration of its votes in Java showed that it was a strong contender for the same religio-cultural community as the PNI and NU. The election therefore failed to fashion the political structures that would provide consensus.

The next measure taken to achieve consensus was the convening of a Constituent Assembly to draft a new constitution on which common agreement on the nature of the state could be achieved. Almost immediately, the structural cleavages represented by the political parties expressed themselves in argument over the kind of state structure Indonesia should adopt. Should it continue to be based on Pancasila formulated by Sukarno in 1945, in which religion was recognized by reference to belief in one's own God? Or should it be revamped to become a state explicitly expressed in terms of Islam, ostensibly the faith of the majority? The debates lasted from 1957 to 1959. They demonstrated how difficult it would be for an ostensibly Muslim-majority state to coalesce around a single, unified political structure under the banner of Islam.

Sukarno, despairing at the cleavages represented by diverse political structures, proposed a solution, namely, the establishment of a new structure called Guided Democracy under his leadership. A non-party leader, believing that his Javanese syncretism could be usefully employed to reconcile opposing viewpoints, Sukarno felt that Guided Democracy would eliminate the fundamentally divisive character of party-based cabinet governments. The PKI and a dominant faction in the army led by the Chief-of-Staff, Colonel Nasution, supported him, each with their own motives. The Masjumi strenuously opposed any attempt to establish Guided Democracy, considering the scheme inimical to the protection of Islam and other party-sponsored interests.

The proposal to establish a new political structure under the aegis of Guided Democracy also aroused the opposition of the inhabitants of the outer islands who saw it as another ploy by Javanese leaders to impose colonialism under a new name. Fear of growing communist influence in Java was also worrying to the outer islanders who were mainly Masjumi Muslim supporters. The result was the outbreak of regional revolts in

Sumatra and south Sulawesi, led by anti-communist and anti-Javanese army officers. By 1958, the rebellion had spread to the extent that a counter-government with its own prime minister was proclaimed in west Sumatra. The Masjumi and the Socialist Party (PSI) supported the rebellion. However, with the help of Nasution, Sukarno was able to crush the rebellion quickly.

Thus by the following year, 1959, the political structure had changed considerably. Political parties either were discredited by identification with the rebellion, or had agreed to accept Sukarno's superior role in Guided Democracy. Hatta had resigned from the vice-presidency in December 1956 and was no longer available to check Sukarno. The regional revolt had been crushed and unity had been restored, albeit one that was Java-oriented. The military had once again become a major political structure when martial law was proclaimed in 1957 on the outbreak of the regional revolts. Sukarno was now in a position to apply pressure on the Constituent Assembly to produce a constitution to his liking. When this body refused, he dissolved it and proclaimed the reinstatement of the 1945 constitution in 1959, thus heralding the era of Guided Democracy. In brief, a new political structure emerged in 1959 based on the narrow foundation of power-sharing between Sukarno and the military. The hoped-for consensus of diverse political structures contending in an overarching liberal system had proved beyond Indonesia's grasp.

MAXIMUM GOVERNMENT

While revolution continued in Vietnam, the other parts of Southeast Asia experienced a period of history that coincided with an economic boom. This boom meant a broad-based economic take-off for most of the independent states. Leaders emerged to take advantage of these conditions, many of them creating new political structures or refashioning existing ones. This they believed was essential in order to benefit from the boom. By and large, the political structures that emerged tended to concentrate power in the hands of a few. The ruling élite shrank in size, but at the same time government acquired the maximum influence possible.

Maximum government, of course, had its defenders. The most articulate was S. Rajaratnam, the former Foreign Minister of the independent state of Singapore, who argued that power was essential for many purposes, including legitimizing and modernizing the régime. Suitable political structures allowing for maximum government were therefore necessary. Certain political attributes, like separation and balance of power, multiplicity of political parties, and proliferation of opposition groups, were seen as inappropriate.[19]

---

[19] S. Rajaratnam, 'Asian Values and Modernization' in Seah Chee Meow, ed., *Asian Values and Modernization*, Singapore, 1977, 99–100.

The Philippines under Marcos

Another important defender of maximum government was President Ferdinand E. Marcos of the Philippines. Some credence should be given to the view that Philippine political structures experienced a major transformation when Marcos was re-elected president in 1969. During his second term, in 1972, Marcos declared martial law, suspended the writ of *habeas corpus* and closed the era of pluralistic politics that had existed since 1935. The political structures that emerged allowed for maximum government. This was a major change compared to the period before 1972 when government could not help but be minimal, faced as it was with serious differences within the élite as well as divisions between the élite and the masses.

Marcos' own explanation for dismantling democratic structures so entirely was simple. When declaring martial law, he cited the constitutional provisions that supported him. Such action was sanctioned 'in case of invasion, insurrection, or rebellion or imminent danger thereof'. He went on to note that lawlessness was perpetrated by Marxist–Leninist–Maoist elements. At the same time, he accused the Muslim minority of fomenting rebellion in the south and Christian vigilantes, like the Ilagas, of contributing to insecurity in that region.

Contemporary accounts attest to increased insurgency in Mindanao from 1969. This phenomenon, however, was not new. For the past four hundred years, there had been a simmering struggle to defend the Muslim heartland of Mindanao from the control of the Christian north. The Muslims themselves numbered only 8 per cent of the total Philippine population, and were concentrated largely in Mindanao, Sulu and Palawan. Such a small minority could have been accommodated in a Philippine polity but for government policies since the 1950s that exacerbated Muslim (or Moro) and Christian relations. The Muslim grievances were an expression of opposition to the continuing Christian migration to the south. This migration threatened to christianize the south as well as posing a danger to the Muslim control of land. The local economic infrastructure also came to be heavily dominated by the local Christian sector. Thus the Muslims formed the Moro National Liberation Front (MNLF) with its goal of secession from the Philippines.

The MNLF was to go to war against the Marcos martial-law government in late 1972 with the support of Libya, members of the Islamic Conference and the Malaysian state of Sabah. By the end of the 1970s, this war had resulted in the deaths of thousands of Filipinos, and many had become refugees. Excesses committed by the Philippine military units sent to fight the Muslim rebels did not endear Manila to the population in the south. In 1976, the MNLF was able to force the Manila government to sign an agreement in Tripoli in which the government agreed to grant the Muslim Filipinos an autonomous region. A ceasefire was proclaimed, but it was short-lived because both sides accused each other of bad faith. In particular, the Manila government appeared to have undermined the agreement regarding autonomy by holding plebiscites in the areas of the proposed autonomous region. War resumed in 1977.

The MNLF was not, however, able to meet the challenge. In addition to its military weaknesses, its political structure was also divided. The organization was a marriage of convenience between traditional Moro élites and Marxist-inspired radicals led by Nur Misuari who was the MNLF chairman. Ethnic antagonisms compounded the complications. When the Marcos government offered concessions as part of its autonomy programme, the MNLF split. Misuari and the radicals vowed to continue the struggle, while the traditional élite abandoned the secessionist goals in favour of working with Manila. In the end, the MNLF could not overcome the semi-feudal and communal structure of the Muslim community.

At the same time as the outbreak of the Muslim rebellion there had been increased insurgency in the central plains of Luzon under the leadership of the Marxist New People's Army (NPA). Drawing on the same roots of agrarian discontent as the Huks, the NPA provided an alternative political structure that had grave implications for the future of the Philippines.[20] The insecurity motivated many Philippine families to organize their own vigilantes. Since firearms were readily available, armed clashes occurred frequently. Investors were frightened off. The economy took a dive, made worse by the unfortunate coincidence of natural disasters and the lavish use of funds in the election year of 1969. The fear of a general insurrection in Luzon was also fuelled by two huge explosions on 21 August 1971 at the Plaza Miranda (Manila), killing and injuring many at a political rally. This incident provided the occasion for Marcos to proclaim martial law.

Under martial law, Marcos wanted to create a political structure called the 'New Society'. What this meant could be understood if juxtaposed against the pre-1972 situation. In a classic statement on the need for maximum government, he said: the 'old society was individualistic, populist. It tended to gravitate around rights. Naturally it was self-centred. Society broke down on the Jeffersonian principle of concentrating on rights instead of duties. It became a popular saying that that government was best which governed the least. Well, that is no longer valid.' In the New Society, people were expected to think 'more and more of the community ... This communality of feeling and spirit does away with the individualist, the selfish, and even class interest.'[21]

The common good demanded urgent attention to land reform. Within one month of the declaration of martial law, Presidential Decree No. 27 for the emancipation of the tiller of the soil from bondage was formulated in

---

[20] What would have been the nature of NPA control? Only glimpses are available from areas already under NPA authority. Peasants were allowed a share of their produce determined by the NPA. Exactions of local industries were fed into a network that transhipped food and supplies to party cadres. See the statement cited by Jose P. Magno and A. James Gregor, 'Insurgency and the Counterinsurgency in the Philippines', *Asian Survey*, XXVI, 5 (1986) 516: A lawyer whose region was subject to NPA control reported that its rule was 'terrible'. He recounted that 'when the NPA takes over an area, its control is absolute. They control thinking, behaviour, and the way of living ... At least under the military one may survive—under the NPA there is no question, they just liquidate you if you oppose them. There is no rule of law, just "people's courts" and executions.'

[21] *Asiaweek*, 1 Oct. 1976, no. 40, 17–18.

consultation between the president and a few close advisers. The decree conferred ownership of family-sized farms on all tenants on rice and corn land. However, promulgation was again not matched by implementation. The Department of Agrarian Reform charged with the task failed to clarify many points in its administrative policy. This itself raised questions on the extent to which the president, a major landowner, himself wanted to push land reform. Vagueness was also a weapon of the strong: the landlords could adopt evasive measures. The entire process of land reform—involving agricultural credit, legal manoeuvres, crop conversion to avoid land acquisition, vagaries in the compensation scheme—was also massively complicated for the tenants who simply wanted to own a piece of land for their livelihood.

In pursuit of the 'communality of feeling', Marcos also used martial-law powers to destroy the power of rival families. The fiercest opponent of martial law was Benigno Aquino. He was soon arrested and exiled. In the case of the Lopez clan, family business assets were seized. Marcos also tried to curb the powers of families which derived wealth from sugar. In this endeavour, he was assisted by a decline in world sugar prices and falling demand. He set up the Philippine Sugar Exchange to control all the marketing of sugar abroad: all sugar produced had to be sold to that authority. Land holdings exceeding 100 hectares were also purchased at low prices, resulting in huge losses to families with wealth based on land.[22]

As for the civil political structures, such as the constitution and the Philippine Congress, restructuring was the answer. Even before martial law was proclaimed, a Constitutional Convention had met in June 1971 to write a new constitution which would not contain unpopular American-inspired features found in the existing 1935 constitution. One of the most important topics discussed was executive power. The new constitution in its final approved version provided for a prime minister who shared power with a president. The precise division of powers is unimportant in this context, except to note that Marcos would continue to enjoy the powers of the presidency under the existing 1935 constitution as well as the powers of the prime minister under the new constitution during an interim period. Since the length of this interim period was indeterminate, Marcos could continue to exercise undiminished power. Given the regular change of leaders during the pre-1969 era to which people were accustomed, this marked a significant change in the nature of the political structure.

To replace Congress, Marcos organized a new political structure called People's Assembly, established in each *barangay* in the Philippines. Its membership included all citizens over the age of fifteen. It was intended to be consultative and was designed to provide a home-grown political structure that would draw its sustenance from indigenous sources. This structure would be free from the weaknesses and corruption of the liberal democratic system of the period before martial law that was modelled on the United States system. Marcos also organized his own political party, the Kilusang Bagung Lipunan.

---

[22] For details, see David Wurfel, 'Elites of Wealth and Elites of Power, the Changing Dynamic: a Philippine Case Study', *Southeast Asian Affairs 1979*, Singapore, 1979, 233–45.

The establishment of new structures would not have been possible without the support of the military. Under martial law, the military extended its influence in society. It was given control of the media, public utilities, and industries like steel.[23] The field campaigns against the NPA and the MNLF inevitably meant that the army had a greater decision-making role in the political structure. However, the emergence of the military as a structure with political significance was not an overnight affair: it had historical roots. In the 1950s, the Philippine military assumed an internal peacekeeping role, in addition to its customary duty of external defence, when it became clear that the Huks would challenge the Manila government. Magsaysay allocated non-military socio-economic activities to the defence establishment. Under the name of civic action, the military embarked on projects like land resettlement. It was also used to police the electoral processes in the 1950s and counter the influence of the Huks.

However, the intervention of the military in government was not an unmixed blessing for Marcos. Its growing influence later made it a decisive factor in the overthrow of the régime.

The maximum government of Marcos' political structure seemed to be impregnable and beyond challenge. Even when martial law was lifted in 1981, that facade of power remained. All proclamations and orders issued under martial law continued in force. It was therefore a significant event when, in February 1986, a hitherto unknown homemaker, albeit the wife of the slain Senator Benigno Aquino, was able to topple Marcos in a peaceful 'revolution'. The first sign of a crack in the facade of the New Society was the assassination of Aquino in 1983 as he was returning from self-imposed exile. The inability of Marcos to contain the NPA revolt also pointed to the danger of the extension of communist influence. This was unsettling for the United States, which maintained two military bases in the Philippines. American reluctance to support Marcos wholeheartedly, coupled with dissension within the military over Marcos' policies regarding the communists, provided the encouragement for opponents of the New Society to coalesce in a common endeavour. The Catholic Church was also outspoken. It supported Marcos' contention that the NPA posed a threat to security. It also endorsed attempts to combat corruption and to restrict the illegal use of firearms. However, it felt that the implementation of martial law was immoral. The heavy-handed treatment of Marcos' political opponents and the failure to satisfy the needs of the poor were considered as violations of human rights. It soon began to condemn the abuses of the New Society and in fact publicly proclaimed its withdrawal of support from Marcos.

An analysis of the downfall of Marcos might be started by asking why he, unlike Suharto and Lee Kuan Yew, was unable to create political structures that provided lasting maximum government. The answer probably lies in the fact that Suharto and Lee were developers of structures but Marcos was a destroyer.[24] The political structure that emerged to topple

---

[23] See Soedjati Djiwandono and Yong Mun Cheong, eds, *Soldiers and Stability in Southeast Asia*, Singapore: ISEAS, 1988, chs 8-9; Carolina G. Hernandez, 'The Philippines', in Zakaria Haji Ahmad and Harold Crouch, eds, *Military–Civilian Relations in South-East Asia*, Singapore, 1985, 157–96.

[24] William H. Overholt, 'The Rise and Fall of Ferdinand Marcos', *Asian Survey*, XXVI, 11, (1986).

Marcos was almost spontaneous—a Parliament of the Streets: a mass uprising that immobilized the functions of government. It disappeared as soon as its objective was attained and although Corazon Aquino rode to power on the back of this Parliament of the Streets, she no longer relied on it when she faced political challenges from the military during her presidency. While President Aquino actively tried to dismantle the objectionable political structures of the New Society, what emerged still remained fluid. Power was dispersed. Maximum government was clearly on the retreat and the emergence of private vigilante groups was indicative of a return to the old days of pluralistic political structures.

Malaysia after 1969

If 1972 was a watershed for political structures in the Philippines, the racial riots of 1969 in Malaysia also provided the occasion for a drastic overhaul of the structures in that country. The riots immediately resulted in the suspension of parliament, and in its place a National Operations Council, chaired by the deputy prime minister, was formed. The council had branches at the state level, and its membership included the armed forces. Its relationship with the cabinet was not clear but none of its decisions was ever over-ruled. With regard to the political structure, its principal contribution was the establishment of a National Consultative Council in January 1970 to examine the ethnic, political, economic and cultural problems affecting national unity. Its sixty-seven members included representatives from the trade unions, professions, religious bodies and most political parties, but it was boycotted by the Democratic Action Party and the left-wing Partai Sosialis Rakyat. It was intended as a forum for the government and other groups to discuss communal problems while parliament was suspended. Its deliberations resulted in the far-reaching decision to ban public (and parliamentary) discussion on first, the special position of the Malays and other indigenous groups; second, the use of Malay as the national language; third, the citizenship rights of any ethnic group; and fourth, the position of the Malay rulers. With this groundwork completed, parliament—now somewhat reduced in legislative authority—reconvened in 1971 as the nation's supreme law-making body. The National Operations Council was renamed the National Security Council, dealing mainly with security (principally communist) affairs. The armed forces returned to their strictly military role. The National Consultative Council was retained to discuss communal issues which parliament could not consider. A Department of National Unity was also set up to formulate a national ideology, called Rukunegara, to serve as a focus for the multiethnic population.

It was not, however, a simple return to the *status quo ante*, before 1969. It was the view of the National Operations Council that the riot originated from economic causes related to the communal distribution of wealth. One of the results of the riot was the launching of the New Economic Policy to eradicate poverty among all races and to eliminate the identification of race with occupation. Although the policy was socio-economic in orientation, it had serious implications for the political structure. Before 1969, the focus of Malaysia's economic policy was on rural development programmes that aimed at reducing disparities of income between the Malays and the urban Chinese. After the inauguration of the New Economic Policy, the objective was transformed so as to concentrate on the large-scale uplift of the *bumiputra* (son-of-the-soil) through urbanization and the creation of a *bumiputra* middle class.

Such a policy had major effects upon the political structures. It immediately aroused the suspicion of the non-Malay middle class which was established through the colonial economic system. The strengthening of the *bumiputra* middle class could not but undermine the support previously given to the Alliance by the non-Malays. Although this did not *ipso facto* mean a switching of allegiance to non-Malay parties in the opposition, like the DAP, it tended to weaken the personal links, trust and camaraderie shared by the Alliance leaders. Moreover, the emergent middle class was wholly dependent on the government for its continued growth. The process of urbanization itself would not have been possible without government support. Furthermore, the complex technologies, the expansion and accumulation of capital, and the sophisticated marketing operations—characteristic tasks facing the middle class in the late twentieth century—all tended to point towards the need for strong government, a strong bureaucracy, and a defined hierarchy within the political structure.

In later years various other political structures began to assume greater importance. One of these was the institution of the monarchy and the sultans in each state. The Malaysian king and his colleagues in the states occupied largely ceremonial positions. Under the constitution, they were required to act in accordance with the advice of the elected prime minister. There appeared to be no occasion for this role to change from 1957 till about 1981. During that period, the prime ministers were either scions of the royal houses or closely related to them. In 1981, with Mahathir bin Mohamad as prime minister, this changed. Mahathir was the son of a commoner. He believed that there should be less emphasis on a feudal style of government which stressed loyalty, and that more attention should be paid to ability, skill and achievement.

Friction soon appeared between the state rulers and the elected government. Sultan Haji Ahmad Shah of Pahang, who later became the Yang di-pertuan Agong (king), was one example. In 1978, he opposed the appointment by the prime minister of a *mentri besar* who was not supportive of the palace. After Sultan Haji Ahmad Shah became king, his son—the regent and heir apparent—withheld royal approbation from several state bills. In Johor, relations between the sultan, Mahmood Iskandar, and the *mentri besar* were also sour. In 1980, the latter had questioned the former's right to succeed to the Johor throne. Following the state and federal elections of 1982, another *mentri besar* was appointed in deference to the sentiments of the sultan.

Such interference in the political structure invited concern. What would happen when the strong-willed sultans of Perak and Johor had their turn to become king? Reaction to that possibility came in 1983 when constitutional amendments were submitted to reduce the powers of the king. A Conference of Rulers rejected the amendments. Go-betweens were sent to find a solution to the impasse. A compromise was finally reached without a face-to-face confrontation between the rulers and the elected government. This was entirely in keeping with Malay cultural norms because even Mahathir, a commoner, had to observe form and ritual when dealing with the rulers. After all, it was Mahathir himself who wrote in 1970, years before he became prime minister: 'Formality and ritual rate very high in the Malay concept of values. What is formal is proper. To depart from formality is considered unbecoming, rude and deserving of misfortune or punishment by God and man. This is essentially a conservative attitude.'[25]

Another political structure was the state. Constitutionally, a strong federal authority reduced the importance of the state as a political structure, but there was also sufficient diversity among the states in the whole of Malaysia to enable them to pull in different directions. Since money was often the lubricant that made a federal system workable, the viability of a state as a political structure independent of the central government depended on the revenue available. For peninsular Malaysia, subventions were critical for all the states, and offers of money for development were often used to attract votes in elections. A state like Kelantan which elected PAS-led governments might be denied federal assistance.

Unlike the other states in peninsular Malaysia, both Sabah and Sarawak joined the federation of Malaysia with safeguards which included a delay in switching to the use of Bahasa Malaysia and the control of immigration. In Sabah, the chief minister, Tun Mustapha, almost succeeded in creating a state within a state, asserting his independence to the extent of providing sanctuary as well as armed assistance to the Muslim secessionists in Mindanao, and, if the accusations of his opponents were to be believed, entertaining thoughts of secession. The central government dealt very patiently with Mustapha. It was not till September 1975 that he was forced to resign. In Sarawak, a three-tier political structure of councils ensured that a degree of state autonomy was retained. Essentially, a system of twenty-four district councils, directly elected by the population, formed the first tier. The second tier consisted of five divisional advisory councils made up of representatives elected from the district councils. The third tier was the Council Negri (State Legislative Council) in Kuching, consisting of representatives elected from the divisional advisory council. The Council Negri then proceeded to elect twenty-four representatives to sit in the federal parliament in Kuala Lumpur. This system was unlike that found in the other constituent states of Malaysia. It was established to provide training for representatives inexperienced in political practices. It ensured that the representative who finally secured a seat in the federal parliament would have served in all tiers. The structure therefore allowed local interests to be represented all the way up to Kuala Lumpur. Although that did not prevent the central authorities from interfering in the state political structure, the Sarawak case was unique. But it should be noted that, on 14 September 1966, a state of emergency was declared in Sarawak on the grounds that the political situation was being exploited by the communists. All state powers were immediately transferred to the federal

---

[25] Mahathir bin Mohamad, *The Malay Dilemma*, Singapore, 1970, 157.

authority and overnight the political structure in Sarawak was refashioned. The Sarawak constitution was amended to give substantially more powers to the governor (a federal appointee) over the chief minister, the Council Negri and its speaker.

Lastly, mention must be made of more populist political structures. Communism, though significant in its own right before 1960, failed to strike roots in Malaysia because it failed to overcome obstacles like Malay nationalism and communalism. In 1975 and early 1976, after a period of inactivity, there were reports of selective assassinations by communist hit squads in urban areas. But these ended in 1976, and guerrilla warfare also appeared to be on the decline. The MCP itself had split in 1970 and 1974, and by 1976 the three factions that were left were contending among themselves as much as against the government. The late 1970s and the early 1980s were also years of active *Dakwah* movements by Muslims to intensify the spread and practice of Islam. Various pressure groups also provided alternative centres of focus, e.g. the Aliran Kesedaran Negara (National Consciousness Movement), ABIM (Malaysian Islamic Youth Movement), and the Consumers' Association of Penang. They became well known because of their outspoken comments on government policies, but whether they had the potential to emerge as political structures in their right had yet to be seen.

Indonesia from Sukarno to Suharto

The development of maximum government was also most evident in Indonesia under the rule of presidents Sukarno and Suharto. The existence of maximum government was implied by the type of political structures that allowed Sukarno to dismiss the Constituent Assembly in 1959; to dissolve the legally-elected parliament in 1960; and to ban political parties like the Masjumi and the Socialist Party (PSI). Similarly, how else did Suharto derive the power to declare the mass communist party (PKI) illegal; to declare certain influential Muslim leaders disqualified from assuming leadership of the reconstituted Muslim political party (PMI); to manipulate the leadership of other political parties; and to dismiss fellow army generals from powerful positions? While charisma could have helped Sukarno to get his way, the same could not be said of Suharto. The more likely answer lies in the power of maximum government in the political structures available to the two leaders.

Sukarno had made his first move at establishing maximum government in 1956, when he proposed a new form of democracy, which he called Guided Democracy, to replace the liberal '50 per cent plus one' democracy then existing in Indonesia. Guided Democracy was finally proclaimed in 1959. Founded on the constitution of 1945 which provided for a strong executive presidency, Guided Democracy was seen by Sukarno as a political structure which would save the nation from the drift and purposelessness that had characterized Indonesia from 1949 to 1959. As president, he would 'guide' the nation to its proper path. In a speech in 1959, he said:

It was felt by the whole of the People that the spirit, the principles and the objective of the Revolution which we launched in 1945 had now been infected by dangerous diseases and dualisms.

Where is that spirit of the Revolution today? The spirit of the Revolution has been almost extinguished, has already become cold and without fire. Where are the Principles of the Revolution today? Today nobody knows where those Principles of the Revolution are, because each and every party lays down its own principles, so that there are those who have departed from even the principles of the Pantja Sila. Where is the objective of the Revolution today? The objective of the Revolution—a just and prosperous society—is now, for persons who are not sons of the Revolution, replaced by liberal politics and liberal economics. Replaced by liberal politics, in which the votes of the majority of the people are exploited, blackmarketed, corrupted by various groups. Replaced by liberal economics, in which various groups want only to grab wealth at the expense of the People.

All these diseases and dualisms were conspicuous in this period of investment, particularly the four kinds of disease and dualism of which I have several times warned: Dualism between the government and the leadership of the Revolution; dualism in men's perspective on society—a just and prosperous society or a capitalist society; dualism between 'the Revolution is over' and 'the Revolution is not yet completed'; and dualism as regarding democracy: Shall democracy serve the People, or the People democracy? . . .[26]

Although the opposition to Guided Democracy was weak, presidential power within the political structure was not unlimited. Sukarno depended on the military's tools of coercion. In return for its support, the military was given key positions in civil administration and economic management under the aegis of martial law. To balance the dependence on the military, Sukarno was forced to cement ties with the PKI. The latter supported Guided Democracy because it needed Sukarno's protection from persecution by the military. In return for this favour, the PKI provided the mass audience as well as the encouragement for Sukarno's increasingly strident and militant campaigns. Whether it was a question of the formulation of ideology (e.g. Political Manifesto or Manipol, Usdek, Nasakom), the anti-Dutch campaign to recover West Irian, or the confrontation against the newly-formed state of Malaysia, the PKI mobilized the crowds and supplied the adulation that Sukarno needed. In return, the party's programme of activities was allowed to proceed almost uninhibited. For example, the PKI pressed ahead with its *aksi sepihak*, a unilateral course of action to seize land for the landless. This alienated the landowners, many of whom were supporters of Muslim parties. By late 1964, the rural scene in Java was polarized between a radical left that purported to join Sukarno in continuing the revolution and a military–Muslim alliance that was fearful of a communist takeover. The consensus that Sukarno thought Guided Democracy could bring was only an illusion. Guided Democracy marked one further step towards maximum government.

---

[26] Speech reproduced in Roger M. Smith, ed., *Southeast Asia: Documents of Political Development and Change*, Ithaca, 1974, 197–8.

The military's opposition towards the communists was not only ideological and historical, harking back to the days of the Madiun revolt in 1948. The PKI represented a departure from the structure of the other political parties. These latter parties were élite organizations with little mass participation: the PKI was different. Once in power, non-élite masses were expected to succeed in redistributing political and economic privileges previously available only to a relatively small cohort. The PKI's support for Sukarno in fact doomed the latter because it alienated him from the rest of the élite: he was hobnobbing with a mass party. When an abortive coup took place on 1 October 1965 resulting in the murder of six generals, enough was enough. The PKI was accused of orchestrating the coup. Despite pressure from the military, Sukarno still refused to ban the PKI. A relatively unknown soldier, General Suharto, was given the task of restoring security since he was in charge of Kostrad, the military's strategic reserve; he emerged as the leader opposed to Sukarno. In an extended power struggle in which student and other groups participated, Sukarno was effectively deposed on 11 March 1966. The PKI was then banned. Suharto was named acting president in 1967, and in the following year became president. Meanwhile, the military allowed PKI supporters in central and east Java and Bali to be massacred by Muslims in a *jihad*. There were estimates of half a million to a million killed.

When Suharto became acting president in 1967, the political structure that he inaugurated came to be called the New Order. However, it shared certain similarities with the Old Order of Sukarno's Guided Democracy. Like Sukarno, Suharto kept political parties at arm's length. While Sukarno used the PKI to counter-balance the military and other political parties, Suharto employed the same tactic to play off the Muslims against the nationalist parties. In both cases, Suharto and Sukarno betrayed their Javanese religio-cultural bias against Islam, especially its militant version. Suharto refused to sanction the reconstitution of the banned Masjumi, even though its leaders quite logically expected that they would be permitted to resume their political activities, because they were the only ones who had dared to challenge Sukarno's Guided Democracy. In the end, Suharto agreed to allow the formation of the PMI, but insisted that its leaders should not be drawn from the ranks of the old Masjumi executive.

However, the differences between Suharto and Sukarno were equally significant. When Sukarno was president, attempts were made to mobilize the population for campaigns like the recovery of West Irian, confrontation against Malaysia and agitation for land reform, though such mobilization was not long-term but restricted to specific transient goals. When Suharto was president, the watchword was political passivity. Suharto's political structures were designed to reduce mobilization. Political parties were not permitted to organize in the villages and sub-districts, the home of 80 per cent of Indonesia's population. Instead, the population was conceived as a 'floating mass', free from the disintegrative pulls of party politics. To fill the political space that political parties were required to vacate, Suharto sponsored the organization of a functional group, popularly known as Golkar. Organizing the population into political structures that pivoted on parties embracing different ideologies tended to emphasize cleavages in society. It was believed that it would be less divisive if the population was organized in accordance with the function each sector served in society. Golkar was therefore an agglomeration of civil servants, the armed forces, intellectuals, women, youths, workers, farmers, veterans and even pedicab drivers. It was the instrument to mobilize votes in general elections. In July 1971, the country's second national election was held. With the help of some heavy-handed tactics, the Golkar won 236 seats out of the total of 360. The NU won 58 seats, making it the most important of the non-government parties. The revamped PMI followed with 24 seats while the PNI only garnered 20. In its election activities, the Golkar was no different from a political party.

The emphasis on political passivity also guided Suharto's handling of the student political structure. During the struggle to topple Sukarno, the students emerged as the moral conscience of the nation. They led demonstrations. The student organizations (KAMI, KAPPI) helped to bring down the old order. However, by 1969, the students were no longer a credible political structure. Suharto did not tolerate an independent moral authority and although students emerged again in later years to question the wisdom of some of Suharto's policies, for example in the 1974 anti-Japanese riots, they did not constitute a structure of long-term stamina and significance.

Political passivity was taken a step further in 1987 when all societies, including political parties, were required to declare as their sole guiding principle the state ideology of the Pancasila. This move was rationalized as the de-ideologization of the Indonesian political structure. Political parties were thus forcibly divorced from their primordial and traditional sources of power. Even Muslim groups, for example, had to acknowledge the Pancasila as their lodestar. The result of this move was to force all groups to subscribe to one ideology—the one approved by Suharto.

This measure was preceded by an earlier attempt to restructure the remaining nine political parties into two groups. All Muslim parties were forced to coalesce under the banner of the Development Unity Party (PPP). Similarly, the PNI was forced to co-operate with the Christian parties under the banner of the Indonesian Democratic Party (PDI). The result was more internal bickering and growing ineffectiveness. In the end the NU withdrew from the PPP and ceased to continue as a political party in 1985.

With the emasculation of the political parties, parliament—already weakened—ceased to be of major importance. During Suharto's presidency, the more important structure was the People's Consultative Assembly (MPR) which comprised the parliamentarians and appointed delegates. The assembly was empowered to elect and fire a president. It deliberated on the broad guidelines of state policy. The president was responsible to the assembly, but the latter's effectiveness was limited by the fact that it met only once in five years.

Another distinction between Sukarno and Suharto was the source of legitimacy. Sukarno's activist policies led to economic ruin. Suharto's distaste for political activism accorded with his view of the function of an independent state. He was deeply convinced that the New Order could be justified only by promoting orderly government, the rule of law, economic rationalization and internal consensus.

Given the concentration of power under Suharto, an ex-soldier, it is

relevant to examine the extent to which the military constituted a significant political structure. The Indonesian military embraced a cohesive
ideology for the greater part of its history. During the revolution, the army
commander, General Sudirman, described the military as belonging to the
people of Indonesia. This meant that it would not participate in the power
struggle of the political parties of the day. This position was widely
accepted and was instrumental in the military's contribution to the consensus achieved during the revolution.

With the end of the revolution, Sudirman's dictum was ignored. The
military became entangled in party politics. Pro-Sukarno officers intrigued
to sabotage the civilian government's attempts to demobilize soldiers. In
1952, Nasution led a group which tried to dissolve parliament for obstruct-
ing measures to professionalize the military. The divisions in the military
were not bridged till 1955. Shortly thereafter, regional revolts broke out,
with some army officers providing leadership to the rebels.

However, the dominant group of officers was opposed to the rebellion.
Led by Nasution, they realized that the military's role as a political
structure had to be accommodated in some manner. In 1958, Nasution
reinterpreted Sudirman's dictum to mean that the military would embark
on the 'Middle Way'. In his view, the Indonesian military would not follow
the path of coups widely practised by the Latin American military forces
in the 1950s. On the other hand, it would not be a lifeless tool of
the government.

In practical terms, the Middle Way could not be defined exactly. When
martial law was proclaimed, the military became a political structure in its
own right. This was also the time when the military assumed an economic
role in the country by seizing the management of Dutch investments.

The post-1965 situation provided a larger field for the expansion of the
military's political role. The term used to describe this new role was
'dwifungsi' or dual function. Army seminars constantly reiterated that the
military now had two roles to fulfil: a strictly defence role and a socio-
political role.

Perhaps the best example of an exponent of *dwifungsi* was Suharto
himself. By 1967, he occupied the top position in both military and civil
hierarchies. Until 1973, he was also the Minister of Defence and Security
in control of combat troops; he was commander of the armed forces too.
In themselves, the postings were not sufficient to ensure Suharto's control.
The Indonesian military had been plagued by warlordism since its inception, and top brass did not automatically exercise authority. The chain of
command had to be developed. Organizational changes were implemented in 1969 and 1973–4. The overall result was the transfer of operational
control of combat troops to Suharto. Other military organizations designed
to enhance security by removing opponents to the New Order were
strengthened. These included the Operations Command for the Restoration of Security and Order (Kopkamtib),[27] Special Operations Service
(OPSUS) and State Intelligence Agency (BAKIN).

In turn, military officers were given appointments in the judiciary, the

---

[27] In 1988, Kopkamtib was replaced by the Bakorstanas which had weaker authority.

executive branch of the civil administration, the top ranks of the diplomatic and consular corps, and business enterprises like Pertamina, the oil conglomerate. The provincial and local governments were also opened to military officers, including the post of village headman which usually went to army sergeants or policemen.

Thus benefits were allocated in exchange for control. The political structure of the military demonstrated the operations of a patron–client relationship. Its history demonstrated that as long as consensus was maintained, benefits would flow from the centre outwards.

Thailand

Not all states were rent by the same extent of communal or ethnic divisions as Indonesia or Malaysia. In Thailand, for example, there is a single tradition accepted by a unified nation, usually expressed in terms of Buddhism and the monarchy. This does not deny the existence of 'counter-structures'. The Muslims in southern Thailand represent a distinctly different tradition. Thailand is also not without its share of upland minority tribespeople. On the whole, however, these 'counter-structures' did not alter the major configurations of the Thai state.

Thailand has been called a 'consensus polity'.[28] For the greater part of Thai history, the monarchy was the focus of this consensus; it continues to be the source of political legitimacy and the reference point for national unity. The military-led revolution of 1932 displaced the political influence of the monarchy as a structure, although there was little change in the relationship between the monarch and the subject. Its incumbent since the end of World War II, Phumiphon Adulyadej, was able to mould the monarchy as an effective political tool. He ascended the throne in June 1946, after the death of his brother, the king, under mysterious circumstances. In 1950, he was crowned King Rama IX. By that time, the army was in control of the nation's political process and it was led by Field Marshal Phibun who had participated in the events of 1932 which led to the overthrow of the absolute monarchy. For the first seven years, the king distanced himself from the government.

In terms of executive power, the monarch was displaced by the bureaucracy—another political structure of note. The bureaucracy consisted mainly of ambitious civil servants and military officers. Its expansion took place under the early modernizing rulers of Thailand. A number of reasons account for its importance and continued prominence after 1945. Since Thailand was not colonized, and in fact embarked on a large-scale modernization programme under its kings, the bureaucratic élite remained in power and its influence was enhanced by its expansion. Its economic strength remained intact because its traditional role of extracting tribute on agricultural production and trade remained unaffected. Despite the commercialization of rice production, no new socio-political groups emerged to challenge the bureaucratic élite. For example, a landlord class did not

---

[28] David Morell and Chai-anan Samudavanija, *Political Conflict in Thailand: Reform, Reaction, Revolution*, Cambridge, Mass., 1981, Part 1.

emerge since tenancy was not a serious problem. Peasants without land did not have to seek patronage from a landlord class since there was land aplenty to exploit. The Thai political structure therefore remained in essence the same for a considerable length of time after 1945—a bureaucratic élite lording it over a large peasant mass.

This pattern of political structures—the monarchy and the bureaucracy—operated on the organizing principle of hierarchy. It has been said that 'Thais accept the fact that there are two categories of people: the powerful and the powerless, the important and the unimportant, the older and the younger . . .'.[29] Any analysis of political structures cannot evade the problem of authority. The sense of superordination and subordination constituted an intrinsic part of interpersonal relations. This notion of authority could even be detected in linguistic patterns of address in the Thai language.[30] It is therefore not strange that in Thailand, consensus was expressed by its leaders acting through the bureaucracy or the monarchy. Personalism remained the preferred expression of political action. What was important was not the institutionalization of new organizations or structures but the existence of leaders who could command confidence. The leader became the focal point. Such were the cases of King Chulalongkorn, Field Marshal Phibun, Field Marshal Sarit Thanarat. These leaders all fulfilled the function of a reference point in their lifetimes.[31]

Political activities were limited to a small ruling élite. The greater part of the Thai population had no share in the court intrigues or political manoeuvres. The dominance of this élite can also explain the weakness of radical alternatives to it. Because the commercialization of agriculture was confined to rice, which was the staple crop grown since time immemorial, there was little disruption to traditional patterns of political structure. This, coupled with the fact that land was relatively easily available, meant that radical intellectuals could not hope to attract the peasantry. Indeed, the Communist Party of Thailand was already formed in the early 1940s; it did not gain much support from the central plains area till the 1960s when tenancy began to pose a problem and the ratio of people to land began to worsen. Its base was confined to the northeast, which was poor and populated by people different from those in the central plains.

From 1947, it was the military group within the bureaucracy that was dominant. In that year, a coup on 8 November paved the way for the return of Phibun. The coup was a reaction against the former civilian government's concessions to the Allied war powers. These were viewed as damaging to the economy and humiliating to the monarchy. Moreover, that civilian government's recognition of the Soviet Union, the repeal of the anti-communist act, and the increased agitation in the Chinese community smacked of communism with its radical agrarian tendencies.

The 1947 coup was also important because it marked the emergence of Sarit Thanarat in national politics. Sarit was then a colonel and military commander of the 1st Regiment in the army's strategic First Division,

[29] Cited in Morell and Chai-anan, 22–3.
[30] Herbert P. Phillips, *Thai Peasant Personality: the Patterning of Interpersonal Behavior in the Village of Bang Chan*, Berkeley and Los Angeles, 1966, 143.
[31] Chai-Anan Samudavanija, *The Thai Young Turks*, Singapore: ISEAS, 1982, 2.

based in the Bangkok region. Knowing that many of his fellow officers wanted to take part in the coup, he realized that he had to lend his support if he wanted to retain his popularity among them.

Sarit himself launched a coup in 1957 which put him in power. Sarit's coup of 1957 marked the start of a 'revolution' in the sense that he tried to re-examine the political concepts that Phibun had borrowed from the West and give them a Thai flavour. This was not at all surprising because the promoters of the coup were the products of indigenous training. Sarit and his colleagues had started their careers during the Great Depression of the 1930s when there were no funds for study abroad. It was only in the 1950s that military officers were sent to the United States for training.

Sarit's own view of democracy centred on the need for it to be indigenous. He made a colourful analogy: 'Let us hope that our democracy is like a plant having deep roots in Thai soil. It should grow amidst the beating sun and whipping rain. It should produce bananas, mangoes, rambutans, mangosteens, and durians; and not apples, grapes, dates, plums, or horse chestnuts.'[32] The fundamental values he wanted to protect were the three ideals of king, religion and nation.

Sarit deliberately set out to cultivate the throne. None of the coup leaders could afford to offend the monarchy but it was clear that tension existed between the king and the country's leaders at various times after 1945 until Sarit became the sole leader in 1957. Phibun had been able to sideline the king because his own credentials dated back to the 1932 revolution, and because the king was still young and inexperienced. Sarit, however, treated the monarchy differently. He had no other credentials except that there were popular demands to remove the corrupt Phibun régime. He was therefore compelled to turn to the monarch for support and, indeed, one of his stated aims in the coup of 1957 was the need to protect the throne. Under Sarit's leadership, the king was given a greater role domestically and internationally. Through this exposure, the king was made to identify with the policies of the régime and thus enhance its prestige.

Domestically, for example, Sarit tried to identify the monarch with the army. The swearing of allegiance by the troops to the throne and flag became major military occasions under Sarit. The army's 21st Regiment was transferred to palace duties, and the queen became its honorary commanding colonel. The king also accepted various honorary command positions. Traditional ceremonies associated with the monarchy and also with Buddhism, discontinued since the 1932 revolution, were revived. The royal *kathin* procession, a Buddhist monarchist ceremony, was one such example. The exposure of the king to foreign countries began in late 1959 and early 1960. Three neighbouring countries were toured, south Vietnam, Indonesia and Burma. The visits were a major public-relations success for Sarit, who was not considered as 'sophisticated' in the Western sense because, totally trained and educated in Thailand, he did not have a good command of English. On the other hand, Rama IX had grown up in many foreign countries and was used to foreign ways. His beautiful consort was

[32] Thak Chaloemtiarana, *Thailand: the Politics of Despotic Paternalism*, Bangkok, 1979, 158.

another advantage. From 1960 till 1963 when Sarit died, the king made many trips, especially to those countries with monarchies.

Religion was another pillar in the Sarit political structure. The state religion in Thailand was Theravāda Buddhism which was different from the Mahāyāna Buddhism of Vietnam, Japan and China. An estimated 93.4 per cent of the Thai were Buddhists. This meant that the network of masses, monkhood and monarchy was very strong. The layman enters the monkhood and the monarchy has been a principal supporter of the monkhood for centuries. However, while the relationship between the masses and the monkhood was based to a large extent on personal ties, that between the monkhood and the monarchy (or the constitutional government after 1932) could not be taken for granted.

The religious order could be abused and used as a place for political refuge by anyone who merely shaved his head or donned the saffron robe. For the purpose of studying the hierarchy of the Buddhist Church in the postwar period, reference must be made to the Buddhist Order Act passed earlier in 1941. Under this scheme, a Supreme Patriarch was appointed by the king. The former would preside over an Ecclesiastical Assembly, an Ecclesiastical Cabinet and the Ecclesiastical Courts, each with separate powers to balance the influence of one another. This worked well, until two sects started squabbling over the appointment of a successor to the Supreme Patriarch who died in 1958.

The quarrels started shortly after Sarit came to power. As he was trying to enhance traditional Thai values of which Buddhism was one, the discord within the Buddhist hierarchy took place at an inappropriate moment. In 1962, he initiated measures to bring the monkhood under control. He pushed through the establishment of a centralized system under a Supreme Patriarch with strong authority. He abolished the checks and balances within the structure. As the Supreme Patriarch was a royal appointee, control over the Buddhist hierarchy was ensured.

Sarit believed that the ideal was a hierarchical political structure of three segments: government, bureaucracy and people. His preference was definitely not for a system of political parties with vertical links to the constituents. The three segments that constituted his political structure were intended to be static, and Sarit's policies and programmes were designed to maintain the boundaries between the hierarchical sectors.

Government, Sarit's first-order segment, must be paternalistic, despotic and benevolent. This was his expressed view at the 1959 Conference of Vice-Governors and District Chiefs:

> The principle to which I refer is the principle of *pho ban pho muang* [father of the family, father of the nation]. The nation is like a large family. Provincial Governors, Vice-Governors, District Chiefs are like the heads of various families. So it should be engraved on the minds of all administrative officials that the people under their jurisdiction are not just other people but their own relatives.[33]

---

[33] Quoted in Toru Yano, 'Political Structure of a "Rice-Growing State"' in Yoneo Ishii, ed., *Thailand: Rice-Growing Society*, Honolulu, 1978, 143.

Bureaucracy, Sarit's second-order segment, was the loyal servant of his benevolent paternalism. An oft-quoted statement attributed to him illustrates this view:

> I feel all of you [the bureaucrats] are my eyes and ears and heart toward the people. I am deeply concerned for the happiness and well-being of my people and I would like you to represent my concern. I want you to offer the people love and enthusiasm. I want you to help me hear, see, and above all think ... You occupy the same position as the old *khaluang tangcai* [local governors representing the king]; in short, I want you always to remember that you are representatives of my feelings. I love the people and I intend to devote myself to them and in the same way I want you to love the people and devote yourselves to them.[34]

Concerning the people, Sarit's idea of their position in the nation was clear and simple. They should have a livelihood and a place to live.[35]

Finally, if this static political structure could not continue in existence, there was always the army as another political structure to depend upon in the last resort. By Sarit's time, the Thai army had assumed the character of an internal force to be deployed for internal security. Even in the nineteenth century, there was no need for an army to defend Thailand from external invasions.

However, the army's importance was not solely as an internal political structure. It also served as a conduit by which foreign inputs were injected into the domestic political structure. This characteristic could first be observed soon after World War II. At that time, the British recommended that sanctions be applied to the Thai armed forces for fighting with the Japanese. However, the United States viewed this as continued interference in Thailand's domestic affairs. Thus the structure of Thailand's armed force remained intact after World War II and the unreconstructed army, used to power, could be expected to demand a major share of the government. Prime Minister Phibun immediately exploited the favour shown by the United States, then the world's superpower, by aligning Thailand with the fight against international communism. The United States accepted this support because the period after 1948 was characterized by the Cold War, and by communist successes in Czechoslovakia, China, Malaya, Vietnam and elsewhere. It was important for the United States to support strong, stable régimes, and military-led governments seemed to fit the bill.

The Thai–American relationship became mutually reinforcing. In July 1950, Phibun offered to send troops and rice to support the American war effort in Korea. The Americans responded by instituting the Fulbright educational exchange agreement and the Economic and Technical Co-operation Agreement of 19 September 1950. World Bank loans were secured for Thailand and military assistance was initiated in October 1950. In 1954, Thailand joined SEATO. When Sarit became prime minister, the United States viewed him as the perfect strongman with the power to act

---

[34] Quoted in ibid., 143.
[35] ibid.

decisively, often in their interests. Sarit's tough no-nonsense approach to government confirmed the American opinion of him. Strikes were banned; unions were dissolved; branches of foreign corporations were permitted to purchase land, gain exemption from taxation and freely import technicians, often bypassing the existing immigration laws. In turn, the United States decided to make Bangkok its regional headquarters for various activities. This support continued after the death of Sarit. In fact, under the latter's heirs—Thanom and Praphat—Thailand became a huge American base. By 1968, there were 50,000 American servicemen on Thai soil and this visible presence generated a boom in the construction, service and other sectors.[36]

The extended discussion on Sarit[37] is necessary because the consequences of his policies had a serious impact on the political structures in Thailand in subsequent years. They helped to create a new economic bourgeoisie. One of the most important of the policies was the lifting of the existing limit of 50 *rai* (about 8 hectares) on landholding. This policy laid the basis for large-scale speculation, especially in those areas where Americans intended to build major strategic highways. Land speculators with inside information bought huge tracts of strategically located land and sold them at high profits. Subsistence farmers were turned into tenants. By the 1960s, an increasingly large number of farms in the Bangkok area were no longer owner-operated. Thailand began to experience the dislocating effects of rural indebtedness and absentee landlordism that it had escaped because it was never colonized. The dispossessed led the exodus to Bangkok where they were unemployed, underemployed, or worked in the service sectors. Simultaneously, the new prosperity originating from American and Japanese investments created a great demand for education. In 1961, there were 15,000 students enrolled in a total of five universities. By 1972, the total was to reach 100,000 in seventeen universities.[38]

By the year of Sarit's death in 1963, an increasingly volatile situation both in the rural and urban areas was bequeathed to three strongmen: Field Marshal Thanom Kittikachorn, Field Marshal Praphat Charusathien and General Kris Sivara. This triumvirate, with Thanom as the prime minister, continued Sarit's policies. However, their weakness became evident as the forces of change impinged upon Thailand. Thanom, for example, did not exercise the same degree of control over the army as Sarit had. Praphat's commercial activities led to his being tainted with corruption and shady business deals.

With Sarit's passing, opposition began to coalesce around various alternative political structures. One of these was the revolutionary insurgents in the rural areas, mainly those identified with the Communist Party of Thailand. Communism, it should be noted, had always been regarded as contrary to traditional Thai values and Buddhist principles. Sarit and his

---

[36] Ben Anderson, 'Withdrawal Symptoms: Social and Cultural Aspects of the October 6 Coup', *Bulletin of Concerned Asian Scholars*, 9, 3 (1977) 15.

[37] The discussion on Sarit is based largely on Thak, *Thailand: the Politics of Despotic Paternalism*, Bangkok, 1979, *passim*.

[38] Anderson, 'Withdrawal Symptoms', 16.

successors were strong anti-communists. However, their neglect of the territories in the northeast broadened the basis for party recruitment. By 1973 the party constituted an alternative political structure that expressed an ideology different from king, religion and nation.

Farmers in the north and central plains of Thailand also experienced greater rural indebtedness, high rates of tenancy and rocketing land rents. Low productivity, low incomes, and land fragmentation became bugbears that somehow would not disappear. To be sure, these problems did not suddenly erupt in the 1970s. However, they simmered near the surface— neglected by a Bangkok government that never considered farmers in terms of meaningful political structures.

In the urban areas, students provided the framework for another political structure. Although students were not always politically passive, they were more concerned with problems on their own campuses prior to 1972 than with national issues. In that year, the National Student Centre of Thailand, an organization that had been revived in late 1969, spearheaded a public campaign to boycott Japanese goods. This move earned the centre its nationalist credentials, because Thailand was then suffering from a trade deficit with Japan. In October 1973, against a background of rice shortages in Bangkok, rising cost of living, and graft, the students led demonstrations in Bangkok. Violence erupted, and on 14 October, the nation was stunned when the king ordered Thanom, Praphat and Narong (Thanom's son and Praphat's son-in-law) into exile.

It is not the intention here to give the impression that the military-led government could be easily demolished by student groups feeding on general dissatisfaction in the country. The pressure from the students would not have produced results if the king had not intervened on their behalf. By 1973, King Phumiphon had ruled for twenty-seven years. Meanwhile, elections had been held, constitutions had been written and discarded, and cabinets had been formed and dissolved. The king continued in office through all these political vicissitudes. When he recognized that the military-led government was unpopular because it was unresponsive, he withdrew his support and it fell.

The downfall of Thanom and Praphat and the passing of the old Sarit order marked the onset of a three-year interregnum of open politics. This period was characterized by violence and conflict, against a background of aggressive communist threats. It was also marked by a bold experiment in democracy, the like of which Thailand had never experienced before. A new draft constitution was written in 1974, and it was decidedly ultra-liberal. It provided for the removal of many institutional devices by which the bureaucracy—civil as well as military—had dominated the mainstream political structure since 1932. To approve the draft constitution, a new National Assembly was elected pending national elections for a new legislature. Members of the new National Assembly, however, turned out to be no different from the representatives of the old élite, although the number of military and police representatives that were chosen was remarkably small. The liberal provisions of the draft constitution did not survive the review of the National Assembly.

The return to conservatism showed that the downfall of the military-led government in October 1973 was at least as much a result of internal military intrigues as of student pressure. From November 1971 onwards, the Thanom government had become faction-ridden mainly because of the likelihood that the unpopular Narong would succeed Thanom. General Kris Sivara led the faction that opposed Thanom and Praphat on this matter. The students served his faction well. In late 1973 and early 1974, they continued to attack those politicians and military leaders who supported Thanom and Praphat. This again was welcomed by Kris as a measure to enhance the power of his own faction.

The king's support for the students was also not a sign of disapproval of the military. In fact, by 1976, the monarchy was firmly in support of the military again. To a large extent, this was due to the king's perception that open politics as pursued since 1973 were tearing the fabric of the nation and undermining the monarchy. The post-1973 period was a golden opportunity for political parties—hitherto subservient to military dictates—to emerge as power brokers. Political parties of the right, left and centre proliferated. A coalition government, formed after the 1975 election, consisted of three parties—Social Action, Thai Nation, and Social Justice. However, there was no co-ordination and, in fact, three 'minigovernments'[39] existed. As a result of pressure from the military an election was called in April 1976. This turned out to be a bloody affair, augmenting the popular conviction that politics was disreputable ('len kan muang', a pejorative phrase suggesting that politics was an unprofessional, dirty and treacherous game). It should be noted that Thai political parties were not mass parties but parliamentary clubs that gave prominence to personal interests and individual links. Ideology or platform did not constitute the basis of party organization. When interests changed, party affiliation also changed. Permanent attachment to a party could be ensured only if there were incentives (monetary or otherwise) to stay. One Thai cabinet minister said: 'politicians are like birds sitting on a tree. The tree is analogous to the political party. When the tree bears lots of fruits, i.e, plentiful money and privileges, MP's will leave their parties and join it.'[40] To make things worse, the period from October 1973 was characterized by widespread strike action in Bangkok. All these events occurred against a backdrop of the reunification of north and south Vietnam, the frenzied retreat from Saigon by United States forces, and the fall of Laos and Cambodia to communist control. The profound sense of insecurity and uncertainty could not but influence the nation in general and the king in particular. The message was clear: insecurity threatened, and even the Chakri dynasty might be swept aside.

The reaction to open politics encouraged rightist groups like the Nawaphon, the Red Gaurs and the Village Scouts to be active. They were supported by the military and business groups, the latter fearful that the confusion in Thailand would harm their finances. The Village Scouts even received royal patronage. In October 1976, bloody clashes took place between students and rightist groups. On 6 October 1976, military units

---

[39] Morell and Chai-anan Samudavanija, 261.
[40] Thak, 63.

seized power from the civilian Seni government. Thus Thailand returned to military dominance and royal legitimacy after only three years.

However, the period after October 1976 was not merely a return to the consensual polity of the monarchy and the bureaucracy. The military had become faction-ridden in the absence of strong men. Its leaders no longer served their early years in the strategic command of the Bangkok troops, as had been the case with Sarit, Thanom, Praphat and Kris. In fact, the leader of the October 1976 coup was an admiral, Sangad Chaloryu. The new prime minister who was eventually appointed, General Kriangsak Cho-manand, did not have experience in army troop commands. His power base within the military was extremely narrow. The same was true of the next prime minister, General Prem Tinsulanond. He had to rely on the politicians, especially the members of the Social Action Party, for support. That made it necessary for him and for other military leaders to get entangled in the strange world of political bargaining and compromises. The machinations that abounded gave the impression that the military was weak and losing direction. Factions within the military began to manoeu-vre in an attempt to save the situation. A faction known as the Young Military Officers Group (or more popularly the Young Turks) was formed to find a solution. The group argued that the executive should be given strong political power to solve the problems of social and economic injustice. Only after that could a more open and participatory political system be gradually established. In 1981, the Young Turks led a coup against the Prem government, hoping to get their viewpoint accepted. However, they failed to prevent Prem from establishing a counter-coup headquarters in Korat, 260 kilometres northeast of Bangkok, with the royal family accompanying him. From Korat, General Prem made repeated broadcasts that the royal family was safe with him. That sealed the fate of the coup leaders, and ensured Prem's continuance in power. The abortive coup demonstrated that the monarchy was confirmed as the most signifi-cant political structure in Thailand. The leader who received royal endorse-ment was the one accepted by the state as the ruler.

This returns the discussion to the point made earlier that Thailand was a consensual polity with the monarchy as a principal focus. The pluralistic political structures of 1973–6 were an interregnum in Thailand's history of maximum government.

Burma: Ne Win

If Sarit was in full control of a monolithic structure, the neighbouring state in Burma was in disarray when General Ne Win assumed power after the coup of 1962. Ethnic consensus was lacking. Political feuds had racked the previous government of U Nu. Ne Win considered it his task to overcome the disintegrative tendencies. In the course of establishing political structures to achieve that goal, maximum government was also developed.

While U Nu's government was partisan, sectarian and communal, Ne Win planned to recast the political structures as non-partisan, non-sectarian and non-ethnic.[41] To a large extent, Ne Win's political models were drawn from his civil-war experience in the late 1940s.

The political structure that was created immediately after the coup of 1962 was the Revolutionary Council. The council combined all the powers of the state. It ruled by decree till 1974 when a new constitution was promulgated. The chairman was Ne Win.

Soon after the coup, the Revolutionary Council issued an ideological statement, The Burmese Way to Socialism (BWS), which served as a guide to government policies. The statement of belief read as follows:

> The revolutionary council of the union of Burma does not believe that man will be set free from social evils as long as pernicious economic systems exist in which man exploits man and lives on the fat of such appropriation. The Council believes it to be possible only when exploitation of man by man is brought to an end and a socialist economy based on justice is established; only then can all people, irrespective of race or religion, be emancipated from all social evils and set free from anxieties over food, clothing and shelter, and from inability to resist evil, for an empty stomach is not conducive to whole-some morality, as the Burmese saying goes; only then can an affluent state of social development be reached and all people be happy and healthy in mind and body.
>
> Thus affirmed in this belief the Revolutionary Council is resolved to march unswervingly and arm-in-arm with the people of the Union of Burma towards the goal of socialism.[42]

The purpose of the statement was to focus loyalty on as well as to mobilize popular support for the political structures of the state. Generally, the BWS specified that the state rested upon the people and not on a narrow capitalist or landlord class. The anti-capitalist and anti-imperialist rhetoric was derived from the civil-war experiences of the military. The BWS was also against parliamentary democracy, noting that it had failed to achieve unity under the previous government led by U Nu. A week after the proclamation of the new ideology, Ne Win commented that 'parliamentary democracy contains too many loopholes for abuse to be of value to a country like Burma'.[43] Inherent in the plan of action was the establishment of a single party that would lead the state to socialism.

The BWS was non-partisan because its socialist roots were indigenously Burmese. Drawing on experience of the civil war from 1948 to 1949, Ne Win tried to reconcile warring factions divided on ideology. When the Burmese Communist Party revolted against U Nu's government in March 1948, army officers had been compelled to support one against the other. This tore the army apart. Although Ne Win identified himself with U Nu, he appreciated the necessity of seeking accommodation with the communists too. The BWS can therefore be viewed as an attempt to establish consensus among opposing factions. He tried to unite the three major political parties in an effort to form a single national party, somewhat

[41] Robert H. Taylor, 'Burma' in Ahmad and Crouch, eds, 36.
[42] Roger M. Smith, ed, *Southeast Asia*, 134.
[43] Fred R. von der Mehden, 'The Burmese Way to Socialism' *Asian Survey*, III, 3 (1963) 132.

in the image of Aung San's AFPFL of 1945. The poor response led Ne Win to create a new party in 1962 called the Burma Socialist Programme Party (BSPP), also called the Burmese Way to Socialism Party or Lanzin in Burmese. Its aim was to steer the country towards the ideological goals of the BWS. At the beginning, it was not conceived as a mass party. Its members were individual cadres drawn mainly from the police and the military. Because of its urban bias, the Lanzin did not succeed in recruiting peasants. Minorities did not join, because they favoured a multi-party system which would ensure the articulation of their own interests by ethnic-based groups. In 1971, Lanzin was reconstituted as a mass party in an attempt to project a national image in a one-party political structure, but apparently this move only brought in members less committed to the party's ideology and more interested in securing favours or positions of power.

In his search for non-sectarian political structures, Ne Win showed that even during the caretaker period of 1958–60, he was against the religious practices of U Nu by lifting the ban on cattle slaughter and *nat* (spirit) worship. In 1959, Ne Win launched the 'Buddhism in Danger' campaign to prevent communist subversion of the Buddhist Church. However, this was seen as a cynical attempt to rally the Buddhists against U Nu, since only the monks who supported U Nu's political opponents participated in the campaign. Ne Win's non-sectarian stand led to the overwhelming electoral gains of U Nu in 1960. From 1962, however, Ne Win remained undaunted in pursuing his non-sectarian goals. He was firmly convinced that U Nu's promise to make Buddhism the state religion was divisive. Thus he was most intent on restricting the political activities of the Buddhist monks. In 1962, for example, he required all monks to register. This was aimed at the individual who wished to pass himself off as a monk by merely shaving his head and donning the yellow robe. In April 1964, the Revolutionary Council decreed that all Buddhist organizations must vow not to engage in political activities, though this had to be rescinded in May after protests. In March 1965, the Revolutionary Council sponsored a Buddhist conference which, among other things, outlined a programme of religious education reform. Several monasteries and individual monks objected to the results of the conference and Ne Win had to move forcefully against them. Subsequently Buddhist clergy were excluded from voting or holding office in many kinds of organizations.

Ne Win was also intent on destroying the autonomous ethnic political structures that U Nu had allowed to develop. Again, his civil-war experience reinforced his distaste for organizations based on ethnic grouping. In 1948, the army was still organized on a communal basis, and ethnic loyalty rather than loyalty to the state was the operating principle. In December of that year, Karen and then Kachin units revolted. They even succeeded in controlling the northen town of Mandalay briefly in 1949. Ne Win was left with the task of fighting the ethnic army rebels at the same time as fighting those army units that had joined the communists in revolt.

Therefore, it was understandable that shortly after the coup in 1962, Ne Win ordered the arrest or removal of hereditary leaders, especially among the Shans. Then the state councils with their chief ministers were abolished. In their place, state supreme councils consisting of local civilian leaders and military commanders were established, and these were linked in a hierarchy all the way up to the Revolutionary Council. The success of this administrative measure depended, of course, on whether the new leaders could displace loyalty to those who were jailed or leading the armed struggle. As well as the new administrative structure, the mailed fist was also employed as Ne Win deployed the Burmese army against the insurgents. However, military campaigns were never really successful, in part because of the difficult terrain. The continued challenge posed by the ethnic minorities can therefore be viewed as providing an alternative political structure to that of Ne Win. But the minorities were ultimately a peripheral, not mainstream, structure. They did not try to exploit the situation when the military government broke down for two to three months in 1988. The power structure ultimately lay in central Burma.

The potency of the ethnic political structures should not therefore be overstated. For example, secession especially among the Shan states was a much publicized threat to consensus in Burma. But what secession really meant is not easy to explain. True, the Shan were close linguistic relations of the Thai. In the nineteenth century, some Shan princes were sent to Bangkok to be raised and trained. However, the Shan ethnic and political identity also depended historically on the claim that the Shan system of principalities was connected with the Burman kingdom of Pagan. Shan Theravāda Buddhism was more akin to the Burmese style rather than the Thai. Much of the Shan language was influenced by Burmese, which made it less understood in Thailand.[44]

Despite the facade of non-partisanship, non-sectarianism and non-ethnicity, the enigma of Ne Win remained. Until the coup of 1962, Ne Win portrayed himself as a reluctant leader. Yet it was clear that Ne Win was the Revolutionary Council. Although there was a small military oligarchy in the council, it was Ne Win who called the shots. At the beginning, Ne Win's closest advisers were Brigadiers Aung Gyi and Tin Pe. However, when Aung Gyi disagreed with Ne Win over the pace and direction of socialism in Burma, he resigned in 1963 and was retired from the army. When the economic policies of Tin Pe failed, he too resigned in 1968. The next confidant until 1974 was Brigadier San Yu. Some civilians like U Ba Nyein and Dr Maung Maung were also appointed to the Revolutionary Council. The ease with which Ne Win dropped an individual from the council and supported another suggested the power he exercised. Even though he retired from the military in 1971 and entrusted the civil administration to a prime minister in 1974, he was still acknowledged as the leader in control. Ne Win himself did not promote a personality cult. Though his portrait was hung in government offices, it was always next to Aung San's. Indeed, it could be conjectured that a principal political structure in Burma was the Aung San–Ne Win complex. Ne Win was one of the Thirty Comrades and, indeed, a syndrome akin to that of China's Long March had been created in Burma, drawing upon the reputation of Aung San. This reservoir of legendary exploits was a major source of legitimacy for Ne

---

[44] F. K. Lehman, ed., *Military Rule in Burma since 1962*, Singapore, 1981, 2.

Win's political structures. When Ne Win established the Revolutionary Council in 1962, the inspiration was attributed to Aung San:

> The correctness and sagacity of the action of the Revolutionary Council will be fully appreciated if we consider only for a moment what the Founder of our Independence *Bogyoke Gyi* Aung San himself would have done in the situation that has just obtained if he were alive today. *No sane person would have doubted that the same steps would have been taken by that indomitable leader.*[45]

In the same vein, the BWS, the 'Revolution' (Ne Win's name for his period of rule) and the Lanzin were all attributed to the inspiration of Aung San. In fact, the Socialist Republic of Burma was the greatest tribute to Aung San. Since 1962, Aung San had also been cast as the fourth Great Unifier of Burma (after Anawrahta, Bayinnaung and Alaungpaya), and since Ne Win's portrait was often posted in government buildings in the company of Aung San, it could be argued that, by extension, Ne Win was identified with Aung San as a unifier.[46]

The power that Ne Win exercised in the political structure was, of course, backed by the Burmese army. The latter was a very confident group. It had overcome factionalism within itself. At the same time, it saved the civilian government of the day from the threats of the communist and ethnic rebels. With no or little foreign help, Ne Win's army was forced to rely on its own resilience to discharge its duties. The civilian politicians had little to offer by way of assistance. This accounted for the substantial claims throughout the 1950s on the national budget for internal security, one-third or even half of the total amount. The army budget was not challenged[47] and the army remained well-treated and well-provided compared to the rest of the population.

The Burmese army, however, was not impervious to change, even though the political leadership remained unchanged. Since 1962, the population in Burma had doubled. Large sectors of the official economy had disintegrated—a testimony to Ne Win's preference for self-reliance. In its stead a black market flourished. Opposition groups within Burma proper—principally students[48]—proliferated in an inchoate mass. Amidst all these changes, one thing became clear: Burma under Ne Win had hardly begun to address the economic issues that neighbouring Southeast Asian countries had tackled years before. Questions about Ne Win's leadership emerged.

In 1988, students launched massive demonstrations in Rangoon in a bid to topple Ne Win. For a period, Burma's government was paralysed or disintegrated. Ne Win resigned but in September 1988, the military made

---

[45] Jon A. Wiant and David I. Steinberg, 'Burma: The Military and National Development' in Soedjati Djiwandono and Yong Mun Cheong, eds, 301.

[46] ibid.

[47] Taylor, 'Burma', in Ahmad and Crouch, eds, 27.

[48] Students posed the strongest urban challenge to Ne Win. In 1974, students combined with workers to protest against inflation and food shortages. In the course of ending the protests, schools and universities were closed. Protests occurred again in December 1974 at the funeral of the former United Nations Secretary-General, U Thant, and again in 1975 when students camped at the Shwedagon Pagoda in protest.

a come-back and formed a Council for the Restoration of Law and Order. The events of September 1988 were likened to the military's taking over from the U Nu government in 1958. In both cases, the military intervened to re-establish political and economic order so that elections could be held.[49] However, the military in 1988 was no longer the same as that of 1958 or even 1962. The events in 1988 revealed that the military as a political structure was not the monolith of the earlier years.

In 1962, the Revolutionary Council comprised military officers who had forged bonds during the days of the Thirty Comrades. There was also a common desire to consolidate political power. These factors bound the Revolutionary Council together as a solid political structure.

However, as the years progressed, old comrades died, and the shared experience in the independence struggle disappeared as a bonding agent. Current issues also overshadowed history. After 1962, the Burmese military was required to second officers to new party organizations and government postings. Commanders who were then concentrated on fighting the insurgents took the opportunity to transfer their unwanted officers to administrative and party positions. This practice turned out to be a mistake. When the BSPP was transformed from a cadre to a mass party in 1971 and the First Party Congress was convened, combat officers found that their seconded party officers were now in charge. Much of the political manoeuvring in the subsequent party congresses was a reflection of this contest between combat and party officers, culminating in the victory of the combat officers after 1973. The latter, after all, commanded the field units and they would be pivotal in determining policy.[50]

In 1988, effective power lay with the combat officers. They had earned their spurs fighting against ethnic insurgents, not against British or Japanese soldiers as in Ne Win's generation. Many of these officers had observed that the old BWS had contributed to the economic mess that led to the student riots from the mid-1970s. Observers did not, however, rule out Ne Win's continued influence.

Singapore

Singapore shares with some other Southern Asian states political structures which allow for maximum government. However, while states like Indonesia, Burma, and the Philippines under Marcos fashioned their political structures in accordance with domestic needs, Singapore's political structures were shaped to a large extent by the external environment. Because the population was overwhelmingly ethnic Chinese, the communal pressure to identify Singapore with nearby China—a legitimate regional power—was very strong. Yet Singapore had always been located in a Malay world. Close affinity with China could interfere with the search for a consensus and arouse the suspicion of minorities. More cogently, it would definitely colour the perception of neighbouring states of what nationhood in Singapore meant.

[49] See Robert H. Taylor's article reprinted in the *Straits Times* (Singapore), 13 Feb. 1989, 20.
[50] Jon Wiant, 'Tradition in the Service of Revolution: the Political Symbolism of Taw-hlan-ye-khit', in Lehman, ed., 70–1.

The choice of a merged political structure within Malaysia was compelled, in part, by this external environment. There were, of course, domestic economic reasons why Singapore chose to join Malaysia. However, equally if not more important was the need to correct the leftward drift of communal politics among the Chinese-educated in Singapore. The most vibrant pre-Malaysia political structure of Singapore consisted primarily of the masses—students and workers—mobilized by the communist united front acting within the People's Action Party. Overt communist activities were declared illegal in 1948 and remained outlawed. It was hoped that with membership in a Malay-led Federation of Malaysia, the radical agitation of the Chinese-educated left wing would be circumscribed and even reduced to manageable proportions by a government in Kuala Lumpur which had fought communism since 1948. The Malaysia strategy was pushed by the English-educated Chinese leader, Lee Kuan Yew, together with non-Chinese colleagues in the moderate wing of the PAP. Even before Malaysia was formed, there were detentions without trial under the draconian Internal Security Act in 1961 with the connivance of the Kuala Lumpur government; these were harbingers of what could happen once Singapore entered the federation and internal security became a federal concern.

The Malaysian experience had a considerable impact upon the political structures of Singapore. First, for the PAP—the dominant political party—the emasculation of the left-wing resulted in the consolidation of a more cohesive political structure controlled by the English-educated moderates alone. Second, the confrontation between the communal structures of peninsular Malaya and the non-communal 'Malaysian Malaysia' group convinced Singapore leaders that multiracialism was the key to consensus. Third, it confirmed that Singapore's political structures could not be isolated from the external environment. Singapore joined Malaysia with restrictions on the rights of its Chinese citizens to vote other than in the island only. Despite this, Malay extremists in UMNO attempted to discredit Lee and participated in the Singapore general elections of 1964 to win the support of the Malay minority, thereby gaining a foothold in the political structure. Also, the structure of Singapore as a member state in a federal entity was challenged by Sukarno's *konfrontasi* (confrontation). The confrontation was a mixture of issues like neo-colonialism, ethnicity, hegemony and leadership in Southeast Asia, and Chinese dominance over trade. Thus it seemed that even changes in the political structure of Singapore could not be implemented without the endorsement of regional neighbours. Finally, with Singapore's exit from Malaysia, the issue of survival became imperative. In a crisis of that magnitude, political structures that stressed consensus and agreement on broad common goals found a fertile field for development. The economic security that statehood in Malaysia had conferred evaporated overnight. Yet Singapore had to make a living. Its only recourse was to plug into the global network of trade and investments. This meant further entanglement in an external environment that its political structures would not be able to control. The most it could do was to put its own house in order. Thus the management of its domestic political structures was crucial.

Lee began a programme of action to ensure that the dissent that characterized the 1950s would not be repeated. In the end, the measures adopted were so thorough that Singapore as a whole resembled a monolithic political structure in support of the leadership of Lee. Lee's no-nonsense style of government gave the structure an effectiveness that would not be possible under another kind of leadership. He stressed that there must be a core group within the cabinet to take tough and immediate decisions. In an interview with the *International Herald Tribune*, Lee had this to say about decisiveness: 'If you like good, you've got to oppose bad. If you want honesty, you fight and kill corruption. If you want men with principles, you must destroy men without principles. There are no half-way houses.'[51] Lee's use of the Internal Security Act to nip in the bud dangerous sources of opposition that would undermine the existing political structures was likened to a karate chop—clean, specific, direct and, of course, effective.

Parallel with this management style was the extension of Lee's control over parapolitical and parastatal structures.[52] One group of parapolitical bodies was the trade unions. In the 1950s, it was the control of the trade unions by the left-wingers within the PAP that gave them such great influence within the party. By 1965, the PAP-supported National Trades Union Congress (NTUC) had gained control over the trade unions from the left-wing Singapore Association of Trade Unions. The NTUC's main platform was to call upon the trade unions to discard their narrow self-interest and to 'modernize' by working towards accommodating rather than confronting government and the employers. Thereafter, with the support of the PAP, the NTUC leadership—which itself was drawn from the PAP ranks—reduced emphasis on its collective bargaining role and expanded upon its social role to provide members with educational, recreational and business opportunities. In 1972, the government set up the National Wages Council which was a tripartite wage-negotiation body consisting of labour, employers and the government. This further eroded the collective bargaining role of the trade unions. Thus, by 1972, the trade unions assumed a role within the political structure in which industrial relations were not the only concern.

Lee was emphatic that new forms of mass organizations be formed. He insisted that all members of parliament be faithful in conducting their weekly meet-the-people sessions which provided constituents with the opportunity to voice their problems. This also allowed the MPs to get a 'feel' of people's concerns. The exercise constituted a major component of the political structure. Cabinet ministers were also instructed to conduct 'walkabouts' in all constituencies on Sundays to provide a further channel between people and the government. MPs were required to chair residents' committees and management committees in community centres. All these links ultimately became more important than the formal structures that could be identified.

---

[51] Quoted in *Straits Times*, 14 Sept. 1988, 1.
[52] The terms 'parapolitical' and 'parastatal' were used in Seah Chee Meow, 'Parapolitical Institutions', in Jon S. T. Quah, Chan Heng Chee and Seah Chee Meow, eds, *Government and Politics of Singapore*,, Singapore, 1985, ch. 8.

What of the political structures within the government itself (the legislature and the bureaucracy)? The civil service was a parastatal institution that Lee thought should be integrated into the political structure in order to facilitate the achievement of government objectives. In 1959, the groundwork had been established by setting up the Political Study Centre to impart political education to civil servants and to raise their understanding of the problems of the people. After 1965, the importance of the civil sevice was further increased by a system of recruitment which emphasized talent and qualifications. Coupled with salaries and benefits that approximated those in the private sector, this served to promote the civil service as an important component of the political structure. The civil service also became a vital training ground for future members of parliament on the PAP ticket. The link thus established could not but enhance the role of the civil service within the political structure.

Extending maximum government controls through political structures, however, was not the same as building the structure of a nation. Nation-building was a particularly urgent task because of the abrupt circumstances in 1965 that surrounded the birth of an independent state. Singapore's exit from Malaysia left a residue of Malays who now found themselves a minority community in the Malay archipelago. Although the Malays constituted less than 10 per cent of the population, their existence made it probable that any fissures in a multiracial society would occur along ethnic fault lines. Notwithstanding the image of monolithism that Singapore's political structures portrayed, the Malay community contained the seeds of dissent and separation. An important issue relevant for the study of political structures had always been the representation of Malay interests in parliament.

As the dominant party in parliament, the PAP was always careful to field a sufficient number of Malay candidates. The experience of Lee and his senior colleagues in the communal politics of Malaysia and the importance they placed on the external environment demonstrated to them the crucial need to preserve multiracialism. However, various conditions emerged to threaten the continuance of this parliamentary tradition. The housing policy of the national Housing and Development Board tended to promote non-Malay residence in hitherto Malay-majority areas. In other words, there were no more electoral constituencies that could deliver block votes for a Malay candidate. At the same time, an increase in the number of younger non-Malay voters with no memories of the 'Malaysia' experience tended to place a premium on parliamentary candidates with professional skill, education and technocratic abilities, qualifications with which Malays were less equipped.

Such a situation could lead to a decline in the number of Malay representatives in parliament. In a political structure with elections based on one-person-one-vote and the first-past-the-post principle, there were very real dangers for the representation of the Malay community. If not resolved, these could render Singapore's position in a Malay archipelago untenable.

Indeed, results from several consecutive elections showed that the number of votes that Malay candidates could command was dropping compared to Chinese candidates in the same constituency. Chinese voters tended to vote for Chinese candidates. As a result, there was a trend towards a non-Malay parliament or a parliament with disproportionately low Malay representation. In short, Singapore's political structure was moving towards one in which the Malay minority would be marginalized and, of course, alienated. Given the geopolitical factors, this would send the wrong signals to Singapore's neighbours.

There were, of course, safeguards within the existing political structure to rectify the situation. In December 1965, soon after separation from Malaysia, a Constitutional Commission was appointed to provide for multi-racialism within the constitution. Generally, Article 89 recognized the 'special position' of the Malays. The commission also recommended the creation of a non-elected advisory body called the Presidential Council on Minorities. With members appointed at the discretion of the president, it was expected that this body would be able to check on any adverse impact of legislation in respect of racial issues.

Another solution was the Team-Member-of-Parliament concept and the creation of the Group Representation Constituency (GRC) in 1988. Under this scheme, certain constituencies were designated as GRCs. This meant that contestants for those electoral wards must include a member of the minority race (Malay or Indian as the case may be) as one of the candidates. This ensured that there would be a minimum number of representatives in parliament from each minority group. The GRC scheme was duly adopted in the amended constitution. In this way, multiracialism was legislated into the political structure. At the same time, all political parties, including the small or weak ones, were required to field at least three candidates on a single slate in order to contest the designated constituencies. This could be construed as a step towards the further development of maximum government, because only the stronger parties could fulfil the conditions.

Earlier, to ensure that all the measures taken to develop suitable political structures were not in vain, Lee had ordered the formation of the Singapore Armed Forces to defend the achievements that had been registered. The first decisive moves in this direction came soon after Singapore separated from Malaysia. When the July 1969 racial riots took Kuala Lumpur by storm and threatened to spill over into Singapore, Lee ordered the armed forces to display their tanks at the August national day parade in a show of force designed to instil confidence that the political structures in Singapore were sufficiently resilient to withstand any external pressure. Subsequently, in November 1972, in a move to pre-empt any attempt at merger with Malaysia which would change the political structures in Singapore, Lee persuaded the Parliament to amend the constitution so that thereafter any merger or any surrender of sovereign power over the police and the armed forces would require a referendum with two-thirds majority of the people voting. After that, the armed forces became an important component of the political structure, with 'bridges' linking them to the civilian segments. The stress on a citizen army, total defence, and the creation of a conduit by which high-ranking officers could cross over to participate in national politics or be seconded to the bureaucracy, all ensured that the armed forces would have a major role in the political structure but not a dominant one.

Brunei

Discussion on independent Brunei can best begin with the official view that the tiny state had never been colonized by the British. It had always been a protectorate. Hence, Britain's grant of independence to Brunei on 1 January 1984 was not similar to the independence experienced by its other colonies. It was in order to fulfil diplomatic requirements that Brunei needed a formal proclamation of independence.

This perspective provides for a 'longer view' of Brunei's political structures, in respect of which the year 1984 was not a watershed. Of these, the most important was of course the Malay Islamic sultanate.

An indication of the sultanate's importance was already revealed before Brunei became independent when it was negotiating with the Federation of Malaya on the terms of admission into the new state of Malaysia. The question of precedence of the Sultan of Brunei in the Conference of Rulers was evidently a major cause of the disagreement that brought about the breakdown in the Malaya–Brunei negotiations. Precedence, however, was not only an issue of protocol and ceremony. The sultanate of Brunei was one of the oldest in the Malay world and naturally the sultan thought it would be justified to claim a degree of pre-eminence in the line-up for the post of Yang di-Pertuan Agong, the titular head of state in the proposed Malaysia. The existing provisions stipulated that the incumbent should, generally, be selected on the basis of precedence. This in turn was determined by the date of accession to the throne. The Sultan of Brunei would have to wait his turn. The proceedings of the negotiations were not made public, but it was likely that the sultan asked for a position higher than his due in the hierarchy. When objections were raised, the discussions faltered.

The negotiations suggested that the sultan recognized the crucial importance of protecting the sultanate at all costs. Indeed, the history of modern political structures in Brunei was almost a history of the work of two sultans, the late Sir Omar, who was the twenty-eighth ruler of Brunei, and his son Sultan Hassanal Bolkiah.

In 1959, when a constitution was drafted to confer internal autonomy on Brunei, the decision was made to strengthen the sultanate by ensuring that power was transferred not to the people but to the ruling dynasty. For Sir Omar who negotiated the constitution, that was the principal way to replace the influence of the British resident with his personal rule. In his view the Islamic sultanate was the only political structure that could protect the non-Islamic ethnic groups. In an independent Brunei, the 1961 Citizenship Regulations would continue in force, allowing non-citizens (principally the Chinese who formed 23 per cent of the population) to enjoy residence rights and to travel on papers of identity after 1 January 1984. Moreover, applications for citizenship would continue to be entertained.[53]

[53] Roger Kershaw, 'Illuminating the path to independence: Political themes in *Pelita Brunei* in 1983', *Southeast Asian Affairs 1984*, Singapore, 1984, 69.

Maximum government in a political structure centred on the person of the ruler was the principal feature in Brunei. However, to counter criticisms against the accumulation of absolutism, measures were taken after 1984 to develop political structures apart from the sultanate and thus a ministerial cabinet was formed. But the substance remained the same. Sultan Bolkiah held a tight grip on the entire structure by assuming the offices of Prime Minister, Home Affairs and Finance. He appointed his father Minister of Defence, and two brothers also held important ministerial positions. When his father died on 7 September 1986, Sultan Bolkiah assumed the post of Minister of Defence. A new revised constitution was also promulgated. Based on the earlier 1959 document, it consolidated royal power further because it abolished the Legislative Council. Under the 1959 constitution, there were four other councils: the Council of Ministers, the Privy Council, the Religious Council, and the Council of Succession. There were also village and district councils linked with these councils. Such formal structures aside, it is also important to note that after 1980, the sultan made personal visits to the villages to hear grievances and this was an important political structure, albeit an informal one.

Since the granting of independence was not conditional on either elections or representative government, there was a limited role for the Legislative Council to play in the political structure. Up to 1962, this council had been controlled by the Party Ra'ayat, the party that formed the majority in fifty-four of the fifty-five district councils. In 1962 the party leader, A. M. Azahari, led a revolt against the sultan in order to launch his programme of re-establishing the former glory of Brunei. Azahari's action contributed a great deal to the monarchical distaste for such representative institutions as the Legislative Council. In theory, this council could exercise some powers. According to the 1959 constitution, all revenues were paid into the Consolidated Fund and the council must give its approval before monies could be spent. With the abolition of the council, state finances and reserves could in fact be treated as the personal wealth of the sultan.

There was some limited toleration of parties within the political structure, even after the Azahari revolt. In May 1985, the Brunei National Democratic Party was registered. The chairman was related to the sultan. In late 1985, a second party—a splinter group from the first—was registered as the Brunei National United Party. Despite these signs of change, Brunei's political structure remained essentially a modernizing autocracy.

An alternative political structure was therefore difficult to identify. If one existed at all, it was the Brunei Armed Forces, but even this institution was so closely associated with the sultan that it formed an extension of his authority.

CONCLUSION

The reference to the Sultan of Brunei returns the discussion to the importance of the leaders within the political structures in the independent states of Southeast Asia. It is submitted that in many instances, the exercise of power by several individuals, separately and independently of each other, gave meaning to the political structures.

In practically all the Southeast Asian states, leaders emerged to assume control of the political structures. Many of them were institution-builders. As creators rather than destroyers, they developed structures which endowed the societies they led with form, continuity and predictability. The study of Southeast Asian political structures cannot but mention the relatively long tenure of many leaders of governments whose extended role in office gave life and vigour to the structures. Indeed, leaders and the governments they led constituted a political structure of primary importance, sometimes to the exclusion of other structures, but endeavouring to absorb the diverse peoples in each of their states to achieve the elusive goal of nation-building.

Ne Win was credited with having said: 'There is no miracle worker. But a willing man with a stout and true heart can accomplish a lot. Placed in bad conditions, he can make them good. Placed in good conditions, he can make them better. With a few hundred of such men we can push the revolution through.'[54] Lee Kuan Yew, reminiscing about the past, spoke of the need for at least three persons who would not be moved under pressure.[55]

The study of political structures in Southeast Asia can therefore justifiably deal with the leaders who shaped the political structures almost in an *ad hoc* manner in response to problems and situations that emerged. A cursory survey of these leaders, by way of conclusion, reveals various interesting features that validate the need to study them in order to understand the political structures.

Of that breed of 'founding fathers' of the independent states in Southeast Asia, attention here focuses on four who were still alive at the end of the 1980s. The doyen of these must be Lee Kuan Yew of Singapore, who argued: 'I belong to that exclusive club of founder members of a new independent country ... Those who believe that when I have left the Government as Prime Minister, that I've gone into permanent retirement, really should have their heads examined.'[56]

Then there was Ne Win, who ruled Burma for twenty-six years (from 1962 to 1988, not including the short caretaker government that lasted from 1958 to 1960). Although he had resigned from the presidency of Burma in the wake of student-led unrest and riots, he was allegedly the *eminence grise* who appointed Sein Lwin as his successor and then, after eighteen days of further violence and killing, removed him from office. It was still believed that he was calling the shots even after the military coup of September 1988 although erstwhile close associates like Maung Maung thought that he had really retired.[57]

The third 'founding father' who still hankered after some degree of influence was Tunku Abdul Rahman, the first prime minister of Malaya and later Malaysia. Although wheelchair-bound and advanced in age, he

---

[54] Maung Maung, *Burma and General Ne Win*, Rangoon, 1969, 300.
[55] *Straits Times*, 16 Aug. 1988, 10.
[56] ibid., 15 Aug. 1988, 1.
[57] Seminar given by Maung Maung, 28 Feb. 1990, National University of Singapore.

flew from Penang to Johor (the southernmost state of peninsular Malaya) to campaign on behalf of a candidate who opposed the UMNO Baru (or New UMNO) party in a 1988 by-election. The Tunku, of course, was a strenuous opponent of the decision by Dr Mahathir, the incumbent prime minister, to replace the old UMNO (the Tunku's party which he led from 1955 till 1969) with the new UMNO. The outcome of the by-election is irrelevant to this discussion: the action of the Tunku suggested the strong determination of founder-leaders to exercise influence over the shape of political structures.

The last 'founding father' of note is, of course, the mercurial Prince Sihanouk. At the time of writing, this leader was still working towards a resolution of the Cambodia conflict despite many threats of retirement.

This survey of recent activities of the early leaders of independent Southeast Asia demonstrates their attachment to those political structures they had so painstakingly created. As Lee Kuan Yew said at a Singapore National Day rally on Sunday, 14 August 1988, 'And even from my sick bed, even if you are going to lower me into the grave and I feel that something is going wrong, I'll get up.'[58]

Not all the Southeast Asian leaders, of course, thought on the same wavelength as these men. Aung San, the Burmese leader who led the nationalist struggle against the British, was one of these. Shortly after the end of the Japanese occupation, he spoke on leadership:

> No man, however great, can alone set the wheels of history in motion, unless he has the active support and cooperation of a whole people. No doubt individuals have played brilliant roles in history, but then it is evident that history is not made by a few individuals only. I have already mentioned to you ... how history develops as the cumulative creation of generations of men responding to the demands of ever growing logical events. I am well aware that there is such a great craving in mind for heroism and the heroic and that hero-worship forms not a small motif in his complex. I am also aware that unless man believes in his own heroism and the heroism of others, he cannot achieve much or great things. We must, however, take proper care that we do not make a fetish of this cult of hero-worship, for then we will turn ourselves into votaries of false gods and prophets.[59]

It is not necessary to evaluate this view held by Aung San, save to say that its importance compared to the ones expressed by the other leaders was diminished because Aung San was assassinated while the others lived to establish structures of consensus.

What then were the circumstances that permitted the dominance of leaders and governments as a political structure? The low levels of political institutionalization in Southeast Asia allowed leaders, defined as those responsible for the orientation of their respective polities, to concentrate unto themselves influence and patronage by means that bore relatively little relationship to the formal political structures provided by the consti-

---

[58] *Straits Times*, 15 Aug. 1988, 1.
[59] Quoted in Roger M. Smith, ed., *Documents of Political Development and Change*, Ithaca, 1974, 93–4.

tution of each state.[60] The environment also increasingly made it easier for leaders to concentrate power in their hands. In the decades after the Southeast Asian states became independent, the pace of change was intense. One of the transformations that took place was the emergence of an international economy that was closely interdependent and becoming more and more integrated. The genesis of this transformation could be sensed even before the Southeast Asian states became independent. The colonial economies were meshed with the metropolitan economy. Various parts of Southeast Asia had already been drawn into the world system. However, this interdependence became more pronounced as the independent states grappled with the immense problems of heavy capital flows, demographic changes, commodity imbalances and unemployment problems. National markets increased in size. Transnational business corporations became prominent. In short, there was a change in scale, and only those political structures that could match the scale or forge links with other structures were big enough to adjust. Government power in Southeast Asia increased in every area because governments were placed in an advantageous position to adjust to the changes taking place in the world.[61] Leaders were thus provided with opportunities for amassing power.

However, this is not to suggest that the process was inexorable, sweeping everything to the side as leaders became more prominent. As Southeast Asia moved into an era in which states and their economies became more integrated, the role of the leaders could well be dwarfed by a change in scale. The narrow nationalism of the early leaders and the political structures they helped to shape may well have to adjust to the fit the globalization of the new era.

BIBLIOGRAPHIC ESSAY

The knowledge explosion has unleashed a torrent of publications on contemporary Southeast Asia history. Not all of them deal directly with political structures—the focus of the preceding pages—but collectively, they succeed in delivering a picture of the composition and dynamics of those structures. What is the basis of selection for mention in this bibliographic note? Standard works in English are cited and the new materials that have emerged in recent years are mentioned, especially those that can contribute to the quantum of primary sources.

Few authors have attempted on their own an encyclopaedic coverage of Southeast Asia. In the few instances where the whole of Southeast Asia is the subject, e.g. John F. Cady, *The History of Post-War Southeast Asia*, Athens, Ohio, 1974, the approach tends to settle along the fault line of a country-by-country analysis. Primary documents sourced from each country can be found in Roger M. Smith, ed., *Southeast Asia: Documents of*

---

[60] See Mohammed Ayoob and Chai-Anan Samudavanija, *Leadership Perceptions and National Security: The Southeast Asian Experience*, Singapore: ISEAS 1989, ch. 11.

[61] Daniel Bell, 'The World in 2013', *Dialogue*, 81, 3 (1988) 2–9.

Political Development and Change, Ithaca, 1974. Those who attempt compara-
tive regional studies usually seize upon a theme that could be pulled
thread-like across Southeast Asia. Examples include Fred R. von der
Mehden, *Politics of the Developing Nations*, Englewood Cliffs,. 1964; Lucian
W. Pye, *Southeast Asia's Political Systems*, 2nd edn, Englewood Cliffs, 1967;
Milton Osborne, *Region of Revolt: Focus on Southeast Asia*, Rushcutters Bay,
NSW, 1970; Michael Leifer, *Dilemmas of Statehood in Southeast Asia*, Sin-
gapore, 1972; Lucian W. Pye with Mary W. Pye, *Asian Power and Politics: the
Cultural Dimensions of Authority*, Cambridge, Mass., 1985.

Collective efforts have more often been the norm. Useful contributions
include John T. McAlister, Jr, ed., *Southeast Asia: the Politics of National
Integration*, New York, 1973, which has a section on national political
leadership.

Unavoidably, the student of contemporary Southeast Asia, whether of
political structures or other topics, is invariably referred to country studies
of which there is an abundant and exciting growth.

Vietnam

The continuing conflict in Indochina has spawned numerous publications.
Scholarship on Vietnam has developed far beyond the circle of writings
delimited by Paul Mus, Bernard B. Fall, P. J. Honey or Dennis J. Duncan-
son. On the impact of international dimensions of war on domestic
structures, see R. B. Smith, *An International History of the Vietnam War*,
London, 1983. An useful analysis of how a revolutionary movement was
able to gain ascendancy, albeit in one province only, is Jeffrey Race, *War
comes to Long An: Revolutionary Conflict in a Vietnamese Province*, Berkeley,
1972. Since the village is such an important unit in the political structure,
one useful reference is Gerald Cannon Hickey, *Village in Vietnam*, New
Haven, 1964. An extremely arresting account of events in Indochina after
1975 can be found in Nayan Chanda, *Brother Enemy: the War after the War*,
San Diego, New York, London, 1986.

Vietnamese writers have also published in English. Reading them will
give an impression, however superficial, of the workings of the political
structures in Vietnam. The writings of Vo Nguyen Giap are well known.
There are also *Ho Chi Minh: On Revolution. Selected Writings, 1920–1966*,
edited and with an introduction by Bernard B. Fall, New York, 1967;
Nguyen Cao Ky, *Twenty Years and Twenty Days*, New York, 1976; *No other
road to take. Memoir of Mrs Nguyen Thi Dinh*, Ithaca: Cornell University
Southeast Asia Program, 1976; Vo Nguyen Giap, *Unforgettable Days*,
Hanoi, 2nd edn, 1978; Nguyen van Canh with Earle Cooper, *Vietnam under
Communism, 1975–1982*, Stanford, 1983; Truong Nhu Tang, *Journal of a
Vietcong*, London, 1986; Tran Van Don, *Our Endless War: Inside Vietnam*,
San Rafael, 1978; Bui Diem with David Chanoff, *In the Jaws of History*,
Boston, 1987. There are interesting articles of tangential interest to political
structures written by Vietnamese in *Vietnamese Studies* (Hanoi), a review
founded in 1964.

Laos and Cambodia

For Laos and Cambodia, the offerings are as few as their respective territories are small. For Laos, the field is no longer confined to the writings of Fall, Langer and Zasloff. Significant contributions include the following: Martin Stuart-Fox, ed., *Contemporary Laos: Studies in the Politics and Society of the Lao People's Democratic Republic*, St Lucia, 1982; Martin Stuart-Fox, *Laos: Politics, Economics and Society*, London, 1986; MacAlister Brown and Joseph J. Zasloff, *Apprentice Revolutionaries: the Communist Movement in Laos, 1930–1985*, Stanford, 1986. Because much information readily available in respect of most countries is difficult to come by in the case of Laos, any contribution is welcome.

On Cambodia, a reliable account is Milton Osborne, *Politics and Power in Cambodia: the Sihanouk Years*, Camberwell, 1973. See also Ben Kiernan and Chanthou Boua, eds, *Peasants and Politics in Kampuchea, 1942–1981*, London, 1982: David P. Chandler and Ben Kiernan, eds, *Revolution and its aftermath in Kampuchea: Eight Essays*, New Haven, 1983; Michael Vickery, *Cambodia: 1975–1982*, Boston, 1984; Ben Kiernan, *How Pol Pot came to Power: a History of Communism in Kampuchea, 1930–1975*, London, 1985; finally, an account by a journalist, William Shawcross, *The Quality of Mercy: Cambodia, Holocaust and Modern Conscience*, London, 1984.

Few native Laotians or Cambodians have written about their respective countries, but Prince Norodom Sihanouk has published a defence of his role as leader in *My War with the CIA: the Memoirs of Prince Norodom Sihanouk*, New York, 1972, and *War and Hope: the Case for Cambodia*, New York, 1980.

Burma

In order to understand Burma's leadership as a core political structure, there are a number of useful publications by Burmese themselves, some of which must be read with care: Maung Maung, *Burma and General Ne Win*, London, 1969; U Nu, *Saturday's Son*, New Haven, 1975; Maung Maung Gyi, *Burmese Political Values: the Socio-Political Roots of Authoritarianism*, New York, 1983; Chao Tzang Yawnghwe, *The Shan of Burma: Memoirs of a Shan Exile*, Singapore, 1987.

However, the seminal contributions are still made by Western scholars, and their writings include those of Josef Silverstein who has published widely e.g., ed., *The Political Legacy of Aung San*, Ithaca: Cornell University Southeast Asia Program, 1972; ed., *The Future of Burma in Perspective: a Symposium*, Athens, Ohio, 1974; *Burma: Military Rule and the Politics of Stagnation*, Ithaca, 1977; *Burmese Politics: the Dilemma of National Unity*, New Brunswick, 1980. Others have also made substantial contributions, e.g. Frank N. Trager, *Burma: From Kingdom to Republic: a Historical and Political Analysis*, London, 1966; and Robert H. Taylor, *The State in Burma*, London, 1987.

Malaysia

One outstanding feature about publications on Malaysia is the recent prolific output of reminiscences and other accounts by former leaders and participants in the political process. These are led by Tunku Abdul Rahman Putra, the first prime minister: *Looking Back: Monday Musings and Memories*, Kuala Lumpur, 1977; *Viewpoints*, Kuala Lumpur, 1978; *As a Matter of Interest*, Kuala Lumpur, 1981; *Lest we Forget: Further Candid Reminiscences*, Singapore, 1983; *Something to Remember*, Singapore, 1983; *Contemporary Issues in Malaysian Politics*, Petaling Jaya, 1984; *Political Awakening*, Petaling Jaya, 1986; *Challenging Times*, Petaling Jaya, no date; *May 13 Before and After*, Kuala Lumpur, 1969. Except for the last three, most of the aforementioned were reproductions of articles previously published in the *Star* newspaper in Penang. The following are also worthy of note: *Strategy for Action: the Selected Speeches of Tun Haji Abdul Razak bin Dato Hussein Al-Haj*, Kuala Lumpur (?), 1969; Mahathir bin Mohamad, *The Malay Dilemma*, Singapore, 1970; Abdul Aziz Ishak, *Special Guest: the Detention in Malaysia of an ex-Cabinet Minister*, Singapore, 1977; Lim Kit Siang, *Time Bombs in Malaysia*, Petaling Jaya: Democratic Action Party, 1978; Tan Chee Khoon, *Malaysia Today: Without Fear or Favour*, Petaling Jaya, 1985; *Rukunegara: a Testament of Hope, Selected Speeches by Ghazali Shafie*, Kuala Lumpur, 1985; Lim Kit Siang, *Malaysia in the Dangerous 80s*, Petaling Jaya, 1982 and the later *Malaysia: Crisis of Identity*, Petaling Jaya: Democratic Action Party, 1986; A. Samad Ismail, *Journalism and Politics*, Kuala Lumpur, 1987. The writings of Chandra Muzaffar, winner of the 1989 Henry J. Benda Prize in Southeast Asian Studies, can also be included in this genre of participant-observer, e.g. *Protector? An analysis of the concept and practice of loyalty in leader-led relationships within Malay society*, Penang, 1979; *Freedom in Fetters: an analysis of the state of democracy in Malaysia*, Penang, 1986; *Islamic Resurgence in Malaysia*, Petaling Jaya, 1987.

Several doctoral dissertations have recently been revised and published. These include one on non-Alliance radical parties, one on centre–state relations, and one on the MCA, respectively: Firdaus Haji Abdullah, *Radical Malay Politics: its origins and early development*, Petaling Jaya, 1985; B. H. Shafruddin, *The Federal Factor in the Government and Politics of Peninsular Malaysia*, Singapore, 1987; Heng Pek Koon, *Chinese Politics in Malaysia: a History of the Malaysian Chinese Association*, Singapore, 1988.

Useful insights on political structures from a more narrow focus include Harold Crouch, Lee Kam Hing and Michael Ong, *Malaysian Politics and the 1978 Election*, Kuala Lumpur, 1980. Apart from Muzaffar's contributions, two of the few publications on Islam are Judith Nagata, *The Reflowering of Malaysian Islam: Modern Religious Radicals and their Roots*, Vancouver, 1984; and Mahathir Mohamad, *The Challenge*, Kuala Lumpur, 1986.

The standard reference works include K. J. Ratnam, *Communalism and the Political Process in Malaya*, Kuala Lumpur, 1965; James C. Scott, *Political Ideology in Malaysia: Reality and the Beliefs of an Elite*, New Haven, 1968; R. K. Vasil, *Politics in a Plural Society: a study of non-communal political parties in West Malaysia*, London, 1971; Mohamad Noordin Sopiee, *From Malayan Union to Singapore Separation: Political Unification in the Malaysia Region,*

1945–65, Kuala Lumpur, 1974; James P. Ongkili, *Nation-building in Malaysia, 1946–1974*, Singapore, 1985, with important contributions on Sabah and Sarawak.

Indonesia

Western scholarship has contributed immensely to an understanding of the political structures of Indonesia after 1945. The standard references must be repeated here: Herbert Feith, *The Decline of Constitutional Democracy in Indonesia*, Ithaca, 1962; Ruth T. McVey, ed., *Indonesia*, rev. edn, New Haven, 1967; Herbert Feith and Lance Castles, *Indonesian Political Thinking, 1945–1965*, Ithaca, 1970; J. D. Legge, *Sukarno: a Political Biography*, New York, 1972; Rex Mortimer, ed., *Showcase State: the Illusion of Indonesia's 'Accelerated Modernisation'*, Sydney, 1973; and Oey Hong Lee, *Indonesia facing the 1980s: a Political Analysis*, Hull, no date, for alternative views; C. L. M. Penders, *The Life and Times of Sukarno*, London, 1974; J. A. C. Mackie, *Konfrontasi: the Indonesia-Malaysia Dispute, 1963–1966*, London, 1974; Karl D. Jackson and Lucian W. Pye, eds, *Political Power and Communications in Indonesia*, Berkeley, 1978; Clifford Geertz, *Negara: the Theatre State in Nineteenth-Century Bali*, Princeton, 1980, which provides fascinating insights into political structures.

In particular, the cultural dimensions of political structures are studied in Claire Holt, ed., *Culture and Politics in Indonesia*, Ithaca, 1972.

More recent publications on very contemporary events include: Tengku Hasan M. di Tiro, *The Price of Freedom (The Unfinished Diary)*, Norsburg, Sweden, 1981; Heri Akhmadi, *Breaking the Chains of Oppression of the Indonesian People: Defense Statement at his Trial on Charges of Insulting the Head of State*, Ithaca, 1981; David Bourchier, *Dynamics of Dissent in Indonesia: Sawito and the Phantom Coup*, Ithaca, 1984; David Jenkins, *Suharto and his Generals: Indonesian Military Politics, 1975–1983*, Ithaca, 1984.

There continue to be major gaps in the literature on political structures. Standard references on Islamic and non-Islamic political structures are few. Studies of political parties include that of J. Eliseo Rocamora, *Nationalism in Search of Ideology: the Indonesian Nationalist Party, 1946–1965*, Quezon City, 1975. There is one recent publication on Golkar, David Reeve, *Golkar of Indonesia: An Alternative to the Party System*, Singapore, 1985. The political structure of communism has been studied by various scholars, but the one published with the hindsight of the PKI debacle was Rex Mortimer, *Indonesian Communism under Sukarno: Ideology and Politics, 1959–1965*, Ithaca, 1974. A major contribution on the military as a political structure is Harold Crouch, *The Army and Politics in Indonesia*, Ithaca, 1978.

Philippines

The events of martial law and the subsequent overthrow of President Marcos in 1986 have tended to affect the selection of materials to read on the Philippines and overshadowed political biographies of those leaders (e.g. Jose V. Abueva, *Ramon Magsaysay: a Political Biography*, Manila, 1971) who were dwarfed by the cataclysmic events from 1969 onwards. Pre-1972 books (e.g. Jose Veloso Abeuva and Raul P. de Guzman, eds, *Foundations and Dynamics of Filipino Government and Politics*, Manila, 1969) and materials published between 1972 and 1986 (e.g. David A. Rosenberg, ed., *Marcos and Martial Law in the Philippines*, Ithaca, 1979) therefore must be read in conjunction with those publications that used hindsight to advantage when discussing political structures. These include those collected in Carl H. Lande, ed., *Rebuilding a Nation: Philippine Challenges and American Policy*, Washington, 1987, and P. N. Abinales, *Militarization in the Philippines*, Quezon City: Third World Studies, 1982.

However, some of the standard studies remain reliable despite the political shifts: Carl H. Lande, *Leaders, Factions, and Parties: the Structure of Philippine Politics*, New Haven: Yale University Southeast Asia Studies, 1964; Onofre D. Corpuz, *The Philippines*, Englewood Cliffs, NJ, 1965; Jean Grossholtz, *Politics in the Philippines*, Boston, 1964. Various journals remain a valuable source of materials on political structures, e.g. *Philippine Studies* (Quezon City) and *Solidarity: Current Affairs, Ideas and the Arts* (Manila).

It should also be noted that the excitement of the 1986 overthrow of President Marcos resulted in the appearance of a number of publications providing personal accounts of martial law experiences. A most significant contribution was Benigno S. Aquino, *Testament from a Prison Cell*, Manila: Benigno, S. Aquino Jr Foundation, 1984. Not to be omitted from mention is Marcos' own defence of martial law: *Notes on the New Society of the Philippines*, 2 parts, Manila(?), 1973.

Thailand

Any attempt to study political structures in Thailand cannot ignore the following publications: John L. S. Girling, *Thailand: Society and Politics*, Ithaca, 1981; David L. Morell and Chai-Anan Samudavanija, *Political Conflict in Thailand; reforms, reaction, revolution*, Cambridge, Mass., 1981; Chai-Anan Samudavanija, *The Thai Young Turks*, Singapore, 1982; David K. Wyatt, *Thailand: A Short History*, New Haven, 1984.

Singapore and Brunei

Both Singapore and Brunei suffer from a lack of materials that can be recommended in a bibliographic essay of this nature.

In recent years, with the passage of time, the first-generation leaders of Singapore have become the source of publications, e.g. *Not by Wages Alone: Selected Speeches and Writings of C. V. Devan Nair, 1959–1981*, Singapore: National Trades Union Congress, 1982; and Chan Heng Chee and Obaid ul Haq, eds, *S. Rajaratnam: The Prophetic and the Political*, Singapore, 1987. Only one biography has been attempted: Chan Heng Chee, *A Sensation of Independence: a Political Biography of David Marshall*, Singapore, 1984.

Since 1970, when Thomas J. Bellows completed his study on the PAP, others have been published, e.g. Chan Heng Chee, *The Dynamics of One Party Dominance: the PAP at the Grass Roots*, Singapore, 1976. More survey-like accounts of the dominant structures in Singapore are Raj K. Vasil,

Governing Singapore, Singapore, 1984 (based, in part, on interviews with Lee Kuan Yew and S. Rajaratnam); and Jon S. T. Quah, Chan Heng Chee and Seah Chee Meow, eds, *Government and Politics of Singapore*, Singapore, 1985.

For Brunei as well as the rest of Southeast Asia, the reader is referred to the annual essays of *Southeast Asian Affairs* (Singapore) and *Asian Survey*. These publications rank with those which publish materials on Southeast Asian political structures occasionally: *Journal of Southeast Asian Studies* (Singapore), *Contemporary Southeast Asia* (Singapore), *Journal of Asian Studies* (Ann Arbor), *Modern Asian Studies* (Cambridge, Mass.).

One promising source of materials on political structures in Southeast Asia is the various publication series produced in the newer centres of regional studies in Australia and Southeast Asia. Examples include the Southeast Asian Studies Program of the Institute of Southeast Asian Studies in Singapore which produced three relevant books on Singapore (mentioned above), Malaysia and Thailand; the institute's Field Report Series (e.g. Lee Ting Hui, *The Communist Organization in Singapore: its Techniques of Manpower Mobilization and Management, 1948–66*, Singapore, 1976); and the Research Notes and Discussion Papers Series (e.g. R. William Liddle, *Cultural and Class Politics in New Order Indonesia*, Singapore, 1977; Ismail Kassim, *The Politics of Accommodation: an Analysis of the 1978 Malaysian General Election*, Singapore, 1978; Leo Suryadinata, *Political Parties and the 1982 General Election in Indonesia*, Singapore, 1982; Harold Crouch, *Malaysia's 1982 General Election*, Singapore, 1982; Albert D. Moscotti, *Burma's Constitution and Elections of 1974: A Source Book*, Singapore, 1977).

In Australia, the Centre of Southeast Asian Studies at Monash University has a series called Working Papers, e.g. Robert S. Newman, *Brahmin and Mandarin: a Comparison of the Cambodian and Vietnamese Revolutions* (1978) and Ivan Molloy, *The Conflicts in Mindanao. 'Whilst the Revolution Rolls on, the Jihad falters'* (1983). Another series is entitled the Monash Papers on Southeast Asia, e.g. Ken Ward, *The 1971 Election in Indonesia: an East Java Case Study* (1974). James Cook University of North Queensland also has an active Occasional Paper Series which has provided, for example, W. F. Wertheim, *Fissures in the Girdle of Emeralds* (1980); W. F. Wertheim, *Moslems in Indonesia: Majority with Minority Mentality* (1980); Ernst Utrecht, *The Military and the 1977 Election* (1980); R. Kreutzer, *The Madiun Affair: Hatta's Betrayal of Indonesia's First Social Revolution* (1981); Peter Burns, *The Decline of Freedom of Religion in Indonesia* (1985).

The Centre of South-East Asian Studies at the University of Kent at Canterbury also has an Occasional Paper series and a relevant publication is C. W. Watson, *State and Society in Indonesia: three papers* (1987).

Although many of the occasional papers appear to be preliminary expositions published in formats that are far from slick, they are useful accounts for those who wish to augment their knowledge on particular aspects.

CHAPTER

3

ECONOMIC AND SOCIAL CHANGE

World War II reduced the Southeast Asian economies, already weakened by the Great Depression, to their lowest levels in modern times. Warfare itself accounted for much of the destruction, particularly in Burma and the Philippines, where the Allied forces resisted longest and returned soonest. When the British retreated from Burma they blew up railways and refineries as they withdrew, and the American liberation of the Philippines employed massive concentrations of naval and aerial firepower; these operations probably accounted for most of the physical destruction in those two countries. By the end of the war Burma had lost all its oil refineries, 90 per cent of its boats, and 85 per cent of its locomotives (along with most of its rolling stock and bridges), while 70 per cent of its roads and most of its docks and factories were severely damaged. As one scholar put it, 'both in internal transport and external trade, Burma was thrown back a century, without warning or previous preparation'. The Philippines was scarcely better off; much of the damage occurred during the 1945 liberation of Manila, in which the country's industrial and modern services sectors—factories, warehouses, power plants, radio stations, telephone exchanges, newspapers, hospitals and universities—had been concentrated. By the end of the battle, the city was 80 per cent destroyed.[1]

Even where there was little or no combat, however, the war took its toll. Throughout the region, the Japanese demand for cotton and other war matériel, along with the extraction of labour and the destruction of draught animals, reduced food production dramatically. At the same time, however, the occupation forces requisitioned rice, leaving the people hungry and driving the death toll up. Many Southeast Asians fled the urban areas, where the food distribution system had virtually collapsed, to live in the villages, or even the forests, as best they could. Those without local connections, such as the Chinese and Indians, were peculiarly vulnerable. In terms of human lives, however, probably the greatest cost was paid in northern and central Vietnam, where 1–2 million perished in the great famine of 1944–5, while surplus rice from the south was shipped to Japan or used for fuel.

I am grateful for comments on earlier drafts of this chapter by George L. Hicks, Ronald D. Hill, Benedict J. Kerkvliet, Elfed V. Roberts, Ronald Skeldon, and all my colleagues on the *Cambridge History* project, particularly Robert Elson. Note that all monetary expressions in this chapter have been converted to current US dollars, and 'billion' is used to mean 'thousand million'.
[1] J. Russel Andrus, *Burmese Economic Life*, Stanford, 1948, 335; David Joel Steinberg, *Philippine Collaboration in World War II*, Ann Arbor, 1967, 114.

Everywhere there were local horror stories of assault, rape, and murder by the occupying Japanese forces, but there was also more systematic exploitation. In Indonesia, Malaya, and Burma, there were hundreds of thousands of *rōmusha* (literally 'labourer in the war effort', but glossed in Java as 'involuntary worker or convict');[2] they were recruited by force or deception for labour far from home on such projects as the 'Death Railway' between Thailand and Burma. Ill-fed, working in appalling conditions under brutal masters, denied any but the most rudimentary medical attention, a majority of them never returned.

Although mortality levels generally rose during World War II they do not seem to have exceeded fertility levels, except in certain subgroups (e.g., the predominantly male Indians of Malaya, whose numbers declined by around 100,000—15 per cent of their pre-war population—during the war). Even in Vietnam, Burma, and the Philippines the total population continued to grow, albeit slowly. Southeast Asians were survivors. When the monetary system was devastated by the issue of vast amounts of occupation currency (called 'Mickey Mouse money' in the Philippines) to pay for requisitioned goods, they turned increasingly to barter and the black market. Imported consumer goods—textiles, matches, needles, cooking oil—were often unavailable, so they did without or reverted to earlier arrangements, such as using coconut oil instead of kerosene in their lamps. The absence or inaccessibility of external markets virtually shut down several major export industries—tin, sugar, tea, coffee, pepper, coal, abaca—so workers turned to subsistence cultivation instead.

Not many Southeast Asians directly benefited from World War II, though a few black-market profiteers came out ahead. In a structural sense, however, the war created some of the preconditions for postwar change. Some Southeast Asians rose to positions of higher responsibility, both in government and production, than they had previously enjoyed. Others formed military and political alliances that led to later peasant and labour unions; where such groups were strongest, as in central Luzon and parts of Vietnam, there were even the beginnings of land reform during the war. The lack of trade helped to break the imperial nexus and push local economies toward greater self-reliance; Chinese tin-miners in Malaya, for example, were forced to diversify into farming. On balance, however, it is clear that the war did the Southeast Asian economy much more harm than good.

Not all of the hardships of Southeast Asians and the long-run damage to the regional economy can be blamed on Japanese iniquity, however. Many of the occupying troops were brutal and there was often a chilling lack of concern for the welfare of the local population, epitomized in the decision of one army command in 1944 to 'maintain the natives' standard of living at the lowest possible level'.[3] Some Japanese also looted gold and gems, with a total value estimated in billions of dollars.[4] At the same time, it must

---

[2] Theodore Friend, *The Blue-Eyed Enemy*, Princeton, 1988, 162–6.
[3] Quoted in ibid., 162.
[4] Sterling Seagrave, *The Marcos Dynasty*, New York, 1988, 99–119, 296–359, introduces the shadowy subject of 'Yamashita's gold' and suggests that much of it eventually wound up in the hands of Ferdinand Marcos.

be remembered that in wartime the Greater East Asia Co-Prosperity Sphere could not operate as it was designed to. The Sphere was to be based on the exchange of Southeast Asian raw materials for Japanese manufactured goods, a system no less workable in principle than Western colonialism, as the example of prewar Taiwan suggested. From 1942 to 1945, however, Japan's industrial capacity was devoted to the war effort and its shipping was devastated by American submarines. Thus it was unable to supply Southeast Asia with consumer goods in return for the primary produce it demanded, and what had been envisaged as a relationship of exchange (albeit unequal) turned out to be sheer exploitation.

After the surrender of Japan, economic reconstruction and political independence were frequently linked by Southeast Asians. Independence seemed to offer the opportunity to undertake economic policies designed to benefit themselves, not the colonial metropole. To many Westerners, however, rehabilitation of the economy was a priority that ought to precede any consideration of decolonization. Among the colonies of Southeast Asia only the Philippines, despite the lobbying efforts of advocates of 'reconsideration', was so far advanced along the road to independence as to make it inevitable. Even there, the perceived need for rehabilitation made post-colonial economic ties much closer than originally planned. The United States offered $620 million in aid, back pay for tens of thousands of guerrillas, and privileged access to the American market for Philippine goods. In return, it demanded the right of Americans to invest on the same basis as Philippine citizens, insisted that the peso be pegged to the dollar, and retained its military bases.

In Burma, British plans for reconstruction of the pre-war economy soon foundered on the intransigence of Aung San and his Anti-Fascist People's Freedom League (AFPFL). Postwar Britain was unable to provide substantial economic assistance, and hardships were created by its clumsy efforts to collect taxes, impose wage and price controls, and import and distribute essential commodities (through a Civil Supplies Organization that favoured British commercial interests); in view of this, most Burmese preferred independence to a continued colonial connection, and London soon acceded to their wishes. Even before independence the Burmese had established a national Economic Planning Board, and thus started to take policy into their own hands, though they were careful at first to avoid any talk of expropriation or restrictions on foreign investments.

France and the Netherlands, on the other hand, used the need for postwar reconstruction as part of their rationale for attempting the forcible reimposition of imperial control over Indochina and Indonesia, and thus precipitated renewed warfare, postponing effective independence for several years. The Indonesian Revolution (1945–9) was shorter, but probably more disruptive of the local economy, with trade paralysed and production virtually stagnant throughout the period. The First Indochina War (1946–54) lasted longer, but permitted some restoration of the export economy in rice and rubber, particularly in Cambodia and southern Vietnam. In both cases there are few precise data, but it is clear that there were high mortality (though relatively few died in actual combat), much destruction of physical infrastructure, interruption of trade, and rampant inflation; these were often accompanied by social conflict among indigenous forces, sometimes more violent than the war against the colonialists.

Britain's colonies in maritime Southeast Asia, on the other hand, were generally willing to accept rehabilitation rather than insist on independence on the immediate postwar period. Such conflict as did occur had more to do with disputes over the structure of the economy than the question of sovereignty. The British aimed to restore a cheap-labour export-oriented plantation economy, co-opting or suppressing incipient trade unionism; in this they succeeded, thanks to communal divide-and-rule tactics and the postwar rubber boom. They restricted the economic damage caused by the Emergency (1948–60) and eventually reached an understanding with a conservative coalition of Malay aristocrats and Chinese and Indian businessmen, leading to a peaceful transition to independence for Malaya in 1957. Radical nationalists protested that the profits from the rubber boom went primarily to finance the postwar reconstruction of Britain, desperate for dollars—it was later estimated that $720 million was remitted abroad, between 1947 and 1950[5]—but they were not successful in convincing a majority of their compatriots that they would be better off insisting on immediate independence. The comparative weakness of local nationalism ensured a late and smooth transition to independence in Singapore and the Borneo colonies.

Within a decade after the end of World War II, therefore, most of Southeast Asia was in a position to take control of its own economic destiny. Although most indigenous leaders were astute enough to admit, as Aung San did, that desired changes could not be achieved 'by the stroke of a magic wand, as he . . . [did] not possess one',[6] they had of necessity to imply that the solution was on the way. No-one could afford to admit that independence, so long sought, might not provide the answer to the continuing problems of poverty and developmental backwardness.

ECONOMIC POLICY IN INDEPENDENT SOUTHEAST ASIA

Although they differed in many other respects, the governments of independent Southeast Asia generally shared broad aims of economic growth, equity and nationalism, along with a belief that central planning and state intervention in the economy were necessary to achieve those aims. Growth—an increase in national wealth—was almost universally desired. Despite talk of other social and spiritual values, there were few Southeast Asian sympathizers for a Gandhian resistance to change or the deliberate abandonment of growth in favour of higher principles. There was no such clear consensus on the means to achieve growth, but it was generally acknowledged that they would have to include restructuring the

[5] Michael Stenson, *Class, Race and Colonialism in West Malaysia: The Indian Case*, St Lucia, Qld, 1980, 165–6, citing calculations by V. V. Bhanoji Rao.
[6] Quoted in Andrus, 85–6.

economy, particularly by expanding industry, which was believed to be the key to the wealth of the West. All postwar governments, even that in Democratic Kampuchea (1975–8), believed in economic growth and were at least rhetorically committed to industrialization.

Beyond contributing to a general sense of civic pride, economic nationalism tried to indigenize wealth and production, reduce foreign influence, and establish national self-sufficiency. In practice, this involved a number of different policies: discrimination against local aliens, usually Chinese or Indian, coupled with restrictions on further immigration; restrictions or restraints on foreign investors and transnational corporations; efforts to foster certain crucial sectors of the economy (particularly heavy industry) perceived as necessary to national strength and identity; and attempts to formulate an overall strategy that would somehow be distinctively indigenous.

Equity, at a bare minimum, implied lip-service to some kind of 'moral economy', particularly the belief that every person had a right to survive. What survival entailed, beyond mere physical existence, was not always clear, but some talked of 'basic human needs', including the right to employment, education, health care, and a 'decent' standard of living. Free compulsory elementary education was recognized in the Universal Declaration of Human Rights (1948) and ratified as a regional goal at the 1959–60 UNESCO conference in Karachi; the principle of medical care for all enjoyed similar widespread official backing in Southeast Asia. Only Democratic Kampuchea, in 'an excess of romantic peasantism', systematically downgraded education and Western (though not local) medicine.[7] For some Southeast Asians equity meant more: the right of all to share in the profits of development. Taken to the extreme, this implied an absolute equality of benefits for all, a time when there would be no rich and no poor. Many, however, accepted the differential distribution of rewards as just, or at least inevitable, though they hoped that the gap between rich and poor could somehow be narrowed. At most they envisaged an equality of opportunity, not one of wealth.

To achieve their stated aims of growth, nationalism, and equity, most of the new régimes became directly involved in the economy, both in planning and in direct participation. Despite a few flirtations with laissez-faire ideas, no Southeast Asian government ever seriously attempted to emulate the non-interventionist models praised by free-market ideologues. Instead they took over and expanded the managerial state of the late colonial period, enthusiastically if not always efficiently. Even Singapore, often cited as an exemplar of free-trade liberalism, consistently obtained nearly one-third of all its investment from the public sector and established the most comprehensive public housing programme in the world, accommodating three-quarters of the entire population by the early 1980s.

The process of state control began with the establishment of central banks in Thailand (1942) and most of the other states. In 1955 the World Bank acknowledged that 'a central bank has become a symbol of monetary independence, without which political independence is thought to be

7 Michael Vickery, *Cambodia: 1975–1982*, Boston, 1984, 170–3.

incomplete'.[8] Centralized economic planning, always a feature of socialism, was also urged on capitalist states by the World Bank in the 1950s and early 1960s. Soon almost every government in the region was issuing national plans, specifying growth targets (by sector) for the next few years. At times these merely represented wishful thinking, 'an expression of intent rather than a rigorous exercise in economic forecasting',[9] but increasingly they came to be important instruments of social engineering. Planning in Southeast Asia can be said to have come of age at the beginning of the 1970s. Indonesia's *Repelita I* (First Five-Year Development Plan) in 1969 was followed by the First Malaysia Plan, implementing the New Economic policy, in 1970. In 1972 came Burma's Twenty-Year Plan, subdivided into four-year plans; Thailand's Third Five-Year Plan, which signalled the shift to export-oriented industrialization; and the Four-Year National Economic Plan of Republic of Vietnam (RVN). The next year, the RVN announced a new Eight-Year Plan and the Philippines created its National Economic Development Authority; in 1976 the Socialist Republic of Vietnam (SRV), free at last from war, was finally able to introduce its Second Five-Year Plan.

Even before the rise of central planning, some Southeast Asian governments were acquiring or developing state corporations in utilities, energy, and industrial development. State corporations were not confined to nominally socialist governments, but were also undertaken by such stoutly capitalist states as Thailand under Prime Minister Phibun Songkhram. Generally they were motivated more by concerns for growth and nationalism than by whatever equity was implied by public ownership. By and large these ventures did not involve acquisition of, or even competition with, existing enterprises—Indonesia's expropriation of Dutch capital in 1957 was a notable exception to this general rule—but filled perceived national gaps, particularly the weaknesses of inherited infrastructure and industrial base. Few of the pioneering enterprises were well managed or lasted long, but they set a precedent for greater state participation in the economy. In Burma after 1962 and in communist Indochina the state virtually monopolized formal economic activity, but even in the nominally capitalist countries of the region great state enterprises developed: Singapore's Jurong Town Corporation and Singapore Technology Corporation; Malaysia's FELDA (Federal Land Development Authority), PERNAS (State Trading Company), and Majlis Amanah Raayat (Council of Trust for the Indigenous People); Indonesia's Pertamina (the state oil corporation) and Bulog (National Logistics Board); the Philippine Sugar Commission (Philsuco) and the Philippine Coconut Administration (Philcoa); and Thailand's Eastern Seaboard Development Committee.

Such enterprises, combined with the expansion of welfare services, made the state far more important economically in independent Southeast Asia than it had ever been in colonial times. Public consumption and

---

[8] *Report on the Economic Development of Malaya*, Singapore, 1955, 168, as quoted in Siew Nim Chee, 'Central Banking in Malaya', in S. Gethyn Davies, ed., *Central Banking in South and East Asia*, Hong Kong, 1960, 111–27.

[9] Hal Hill and Sisira Jayasuriya, *An Inward-Looking Economy in Transition: Economic Development in Burma since the 1960s*, Singapore: ISEAS, 1986, 11.

expenditures in the Philippines, Thailand, and Indonesia rose to almost 10 per cent of the gross national product (GNP) within a decade after World War II, and continued climbing until they averaged nearly 20 per cent by the late 1980s. In Brunei, Burma, Malaysia and Singapore, as well as the communist states of Indochina, they reached at times 40 per cent or more. Thus the modern Southeast Asian states were not mere arbiters in the economic arena, but potent players in their own right. Despite their growth, however, many remained what Gunnar Myrdal called 'soft states', unable or unwilling to implement the decisions they made, though over the course of the postwar period most of them noticeably hardened.

Although the governments of Southeast Asia shared the same broad goals, they varied sharply in their ranking of the priorities of these goals and their choices of strategies designed to achieve them. It was on the axis of attitudes toward equity that the clearest distinctions could be seen, though they were sometimes clouded by rhetoric. Pol Pot, Ho Chi Minh, Ne Win, Norodom Sihanouk, and Lee Kuan Yew each claimed to be a 'socialist', which suggests how empty of meaning that term could be. Nevertheless, we can distinguish on the one hand governments that viewed the great disparities of wealth that existed throughout the region as intrinsically unjust and set about dispossessing the rich, and on the other, those that accepted the basic principle of property rights and believed that the incentives offered by private ownership were necessary for development. Differences in commitment to specific growth strategies, to 'nationalist' policies, and to state enterprise were generally secondary to this fundamental distinction. Redistributionist policies, for example, inevitably involved increasing the size of the state apparatus and were in practice difficult to combine with openness to foreign trade and investment.

It is useful, therefore, in attempting to discern policy trends within Southeast Asia over the past four decades, to distinguish broad clusters of states by their basic orientation to property: capitalist, socialist, and 'third way'. At one end of the spectrum were those governments fundamentally committed to the preservation of private property: the Philippines, Malaysia, Singapore, Brunei and Thailand throughout almost the entire postwar period; southern Vietnam under the republic (1954–75), the Khmer Republic under Lon Nol (1970–5), and Indonesia under the New Order (after 1965). At the other extreme were Democratic Kampuchea (1975–8), which actually attempted the elimination of private property, northern Vietnam after 1954, Burma after 1962, southern Vietnam and Laos after 1975, and the People's Republic of Kampuchea after 1978. Somewhere in the middle were those governments that professed vaguely socialist principles, often explicitly interpreted in terms of local culture, but did little to redistribute wealth: Burma under U Nu (1948–62), Indonesia before 1965 (particularly under Guided Democracy, 1957–65), Cambodia under Norodom Sihanouk (1953–70), and perhaps Thailand under Nai Pridi Phanomyong (1945–7) and later civilian régimes (1973–6) or Laos under various of the coalition governments of the 1950s and 1960s.

Of these three clusters, the capitalist was the largest and achieved the most conspicuous economic success, to the point where it often came to represent the region as a whole. Many recent studies of the regional economy in fact tend to exclude the communist states of Indochina, and often Burma as well, thus effectively defining 'Southeast Asia' as equivalent to the Association of Southeast Asian Nations (ASEAN). Among the capitalist régimes, we can discern three major phases in postwar economic planning: first, rehabilitation and the reconstruction of a primary-producing export economy on the colonial model; second, beginning in the 1950s, the attempt to develop import-substitution industrialization, often accompanied by overt economic nationalism; third, starting with Singapore in the mid-1960s, the effort to convert to export-oriented industrialization. Differences between countries in the details and timing of these policy shifts have been the object of considerable study by economists. Over the whole postwar period, however, it is not the differences of policy within this bloc that are striking, but the broad similarities.

It is much harder to discern a general policy pattern among the socialist governments of Southeast Asia, beyond the immediate reconstruction required in the Democratic Republic of Vietnam after 1954 and the rest of Indochina after 1975 (and Cambodia again in 1979). Over the long run both Burma and Vietnam tended to follow periods of doctrinaire socialism with periods of relative pragmatism and greater scope for private enterprise. Over-enthusiastic land reforms in the DRV in 1953–6, for example, gave way to the public admission of errors and excesses, as did efforts in the late 1970s to impose a strong command economy on the southern half of the SRV. Similarly, the trend toward state ownership and international isolation of the Revolutionary Government in Burma after 1962 was reversed in part by the Twenty-Year Plan of 1972, which emphasized increasing production and re-establishing broader international economic relations. Only Democratic Kampuchea did not survive long enough to repent of its excesses.

The 'third way' economies of Southeast Asia are no more. Burma before 1962, Indonesia before 1965, and Cambodia before 1970 tottered the tightrope between capitalism and socialism as far as they could. The fact that all eventually succumbed to military coups prompted in part by their disappointing economic performances should not blind us to the fact that each managed to survive for more than a decade with ideologies that defied simple categorization and Cold War pressures. Their theories were syncretic and their policies were *ad hoc*, without any discernible tendency except a proud assertion that they were distinctively nationalist: the *Pyidawtha* (literally 'sacred-pleasant-country') welfare state of Nu's Burma, the 'Khmer Socialism' of Sihanouk, and Sukarno's Pancasila and 'Marhaenism'. As emblems of the intellectual history of modern Southeast Asia these formulations are fascinating, representing the rejection of Western economic thought, both classical and Marxist. They did not, however, represent a coherent guide to economic policy or embody a recognizable set of local or Asian principles leading to specific tendencies in decision-making.[10]

---

[10] Such rhetorical rejection of Western models was by no means limited to 'third way' states, as shown by Democratic Kampuchea's 'Angkar' (echoing classical Angkor), Ne Win's 'Burmese Way to Socialism', Mahathir's advice to Malaysians to 'Look East' and Lee Kuan Yew's evocation of Confucian values in Singaporean development.

Another aspect of the nationalism of these economies was a growing touchiness about 'foreigners', both internal and external. At times this xenophobia manifested itself in discrimination against local aliens (particularly the Chinese in Indonesia and the Indians in Burma), at times in rejection of foreign aid that diminished local dignity and autonomy. Such attitudes were certainly not absent from other Southeast Asian countries, but they seemed particularly significant in 'third way' economies, perhaps because of the absence of clear competing economic principles. 'To hell with your aid', Sukarno finally told the United States. 'We prefer to live in poverty, because at least we will be free', Sihanouk proclaimed, in repudiating American military aid in October 1963, asserting a month later that 'the most elementary dignity forbids Cambodia to accept any form of American aid, no matter how small'.[11]

Some scholars of postwar Southeast Asia distinguished 'inward-looking' from 'outward-looking' approaches to development; in terms of economic logic, the former emphasized self-sufficiency and sequestration, while the latter favoured expanded trade as the path to long-term growth. But the rhetoric of Sukarno and Sihanouk, along with the persistent pattern of Southeast Asian discrimination against local aliens, suggests that nationalism was the root, autarky just a rationale. New régimes sometimes attempted to legitimate themselves by carrying such chauvinistic practices even farther: revolutionary Burma by drastically reducing all contact with the outside world, New Order Indonesia by cutting off relations with China and sponsoring the 1965–6 pogrom of local Chinese, Democratic Kampuchea by expelling all Vietnamese and provoking a war with Vietnam, as well as by persecuting Chams and other ethnic minorities. Isolation was in practice more a manifestation of nationalism than a coherent development strategy.

Southeast Asian choices of development strategies were based on both ideology and self-interest. The appeal of capitalism included its resonance with traditional mercantile behaviour in the region and its association with the visible wealth and strength of the West and Japan. Socialism, on the other hand, connected with local ideas of mutual assistance (*gotong royong*, *bayanihan*), charitable redistribution of wealth, and usufruct, rather than absolute ownership, of land. Southeast Asians were also regularly exposed to the conventional wisdom of international economists, a wisdom which itself was evolving throughout this period, from restoration of primary production through to import substitution and then to export-oriented industrialization, accompanied by a growing recognition of the need for increasing agricultural productivity. Occasionally Southeast Asians anticipated these intellectual shifts; Burma's Hla Myint was perhaps the most distinguished regional contributor to the international world of development economics. More often they followed the trends as they evolved, through their exposure to Western advice and education. So heavily, in fact, did graduates of a certain American university dominate the shaping

---

[11] J. D. Legge, *Sukarno: A Political Biography*, rev. edn, Sydney, 1984, 292; Sihanouk, *My War with the CIA: The Memoirs of Prince Norodom Sihanouk as Related to Wilfred Burchett*, rev. edn, Harmondsworth, Mdx, 130, 134.

of economic policy under the New Order in Indonesia that they came to be known as the 'Berkeley Mafia'. Southeast Asian technocrats also shared ideas with each other under the auspices of such agencies as the United Nations Economic Commission on Asia and the Far East (ECAFE; later Economic and Social Commission on Asia and the Pacific, or ESCAP), ASEAN, and the International Rice Research Institute (IRRI), based in the Philippines.

Those who opted out of capitalism also had foreign models from which to choose. The evolving conventional wisdom of Marxism-Leninism clearly influenced Vietnam and its client states. Their emphases on heavy industry in the late 1950s and 'reform' in the 1980s (including the renewed exchange of tropical produce for manufactured goods from the Soviet bloc) were at least in part responses to Moscow's changing orthodoxy, while the original model for the DRV land reform was Chinese. They also, like their capitalist counterparts, had these orthodoxies reinforced by technocrats returning from education in more advanced communist states. Democratic Kampuchea and Revolutionary Burma, on the other hand, staked out more idiosyncratic economic strategies, based partly on indigenous concepts, partly on differing foreign influences—French academic Marxism and Maoism in the former case, Fabian socialism in the latter. The advocates of a 'third way' had no conventional wisdom of either the right or the left to refer to for guidance, and so drew on an eclectic range of sources.

Everyone favoured growth in the abstract, but not everyone was in a position to capitalize on it. Industrialization aimed at import substitution in particular lent itself to the support of vested interests, as it depended on tariff protection or the allocation of special licences or foreign-exchange quotas for its profitability. (Ironically, the Philippines, which pioneered import substitution in the 1950s, became the slowest-growing capitalist state in the region two decades later in part because entrenched interests resisted the full implementation of an export-oriented strategy.) In other contexts, other sectors or industries—oil, export agriculture, transport and communications—were favoured not because of what they were but because of who owned them. There is ample documentation of the link between policy-makers and favoured industrialists throughout the region. Richard Robison's study of ownership patterns in Indonesia—including the extensive holdings of the Suharto (Cendana) group and various military commands—is the most comprehensive, but there are also studies of the 'crony capitalists' of the Philippines and the 'Sino-Thai rapprochement' between businessmen and bureaucrats in Thailand.[12] Ne

[12] Robison, *Indonesia: The Rise of Capital*, Sydney: Asian Studies Association of Australia, Southeast Asia Publication Series no. 13, 1986; John F. Doherty, 'Who Controls the Philippine Economy?', in Belinda A. Aquino, ed., *Cronies and Enemies: The Current Philippine Scene*, Honolulu: University of Hawaii, Center for Asian and Pacific Studies, Philippine Studies Program, Occasional Paper no. 5, 1982, 7–35; G. William Skinner, *Leadership and Power in the Chinese Community of Thailand*, Ithaca: Cornell University, Association for Asian Studies Monograph no. 3, 1958; cf. Kevin Hewison, 'National Interests and Economic Downturn: Thailand', in Richard Robison, Kevin Hewison, and Richard Higgott, eds., *Southeast Asia in the 1980s: The Politics of Economic Crisis*, Sydney, 1987, 52–5.

Win of Burma became far more wealthy than his official salary could possibly justify, and three presidents of the Republic of Vietnam, or their close relatives, promoted the flourishing opium traffic there in return for a share of the profits. Decision-makers in communist Vietnam were less likely to enrich themselves substantially (though petty graft was rampant), but often fought for entrenched bureaucratic interests. Whether all this is regarded as simple corruption or seen as accepted 'patrimonial' practice, it cannot be ignored in the analysis of policy formation.

Nationalist policies, too, were reinforced by vested interests. Anti-Chinese and anti-Indian campaigns almost always received backing from indigenous traders and financiers, who genuinely wished to eliminate competitors, as well as from many officials and frontmen, who welcomed the opportunity to squeeze the outsiders more. Campaigns against transnational corporations similarly were favoured by many local entrepreneurs and officials, such as the outspoken Filipino businessman Alejandro Lichauco,[13] though they were resisted by others who profited from their connections with these corporations.

Equity, insofar as it implied redistribution of wealth, was not usually in the interests of the country's rulers, except perhaps in Indochina. They might expropriate foreign plantations or discriminate against Chinese merchants, but they could not readily advocate serious land reform without jeopardizing their own class base. Of the non-socialist states, only the RVN introduced any effective land reform, and there it was imposed and financed by the USA. Public campaigns for social justice elsewhere defused potential violence and thus benefited the whole proprietorial class, as well as the politicians who proposed them, though in this respect a well-run public relations exercise, such as accompanied most Philippine 'land reforms', could achieve almost as much as genuine redistribution, at much lower cost. To the extent that equity implied public spending on schools, roads, clinics, government credit agencies, etc., it of course created vested interests among those who obtained the contracts to build or manage them.

The state also came to be an interest group in its own right, growing in response to its own imperatives as well as the perceived needs of the country. The absence or weakness of competing interests had made it possible to erect state enterprises in the first place. As there was no strong indigenous bourgeoisie, Southeast Asian governments did not have to placate the private commercial sector by promises of non-interference, and there was no popular insistence on the sanctity of market forces. Once established in business, the bureaucracy tended to expand; this was particularly true of military enterprises in Thailand, Indonesia, Burma, and Vietnam, both capitalist and communist. Despite the arguments of economists who claimed that state-run ventures were always inefficient, Southeast Asian governments showed little interest in privatization until the 1980s, when Singapore started to undertake it (on a limited scale) and other governments started to talk about it. In general, however, the public proportion of national wealth always tended to grow.

---

[13] *The Lichauco Paper: Imperialism in the Philippines*, New York, 1973.

The danger in focusing on policy trends is the implicit assumption that they were wholly responsible for all that happened. Certainly much of the political debate within and about the region was framed in terms of legitimation by economic performance; it was implied that 'winners' won simply because they made the right choices, while 'losers' blundered. In practice, however, policy choices were often severely constrained, and performance depended to a considerable degree upon factors beyond the control of Southeast Asian governments. The decentralization of urban development in the DRV was primarily a response to the American bombing campaign; the forced evacuation of Phnom Penh in 1975 could be explained partially in terms of the inability of that swollen city to feed itself after five years of war; and the prosperity of Indonesia, Malaysia, and Brunei after 1973 was largely based on the global oil boom that began in that year. Policy-making in Southeast Asia was not simply the product of ideology and self-interest; it emerged from experience, from trial-and-error responses to a changing international environment.

ECONOMIC IMPLICATIONS OF INTERNATIONAL POLITICS

The world into which the independent states of Southeast Asia emerged was one that would not leave them alone. Governments outside the region persistently tried to influence local affairs. Such 'neo-colonialism' was not the principal determinant of modern Southeast Asian history, as its critics often implied, but its effects cannot be ignored. In the political sphere it ranged from attempts to manipulate local elections to full-scale military interventions. Economic assistance was often the handmaiden of political intent, though the gradual diminution of bilateral aid in favour of multilateral lending nominally depoliticized it. A host of cultural and educational institutions, from the Peace Corps to training programmes for Southeast Asian bureaucrats, officers, and academics, tended to reinforce these links at personal and intellectual levels.

In the immediate postwar period, the most significant attempts to influence Southeast Asia came from the former colonial powers. Once they had recognized Indonesian independence, however, the Dutch soon faded from the scene. The process of decolonization had left them with a bitter taste: many of their remaining investments were withdrawn or nationalized, and they were not in a strong position to supply much aid or advice. The French in Indochina and the British in Burma were little better off; economically shaken themselves, their continuing influence tended to depend on the goodwill of the new nationalist governments, which was never great. Britain did somewhat better in its former maritime possessions, at least until the 1970s, when it closed its naval base in Singapore and the Malaysian government began to indigenize foreign investments. The French and the British also retained some influence (in non-communist Indochina and Malaysia, respectively) in the field of education, capitalizing on what remained of the prestige of their language and culture through advisers for local ministries of education and study grants for some of their better students.

The USA, on the other hand, emerged from World War II with enhanced wealth and strength, becoming the dominant external influence on the region's economic affairs, the major agent of 'neo-colonialism' in the 1950s and 1960s. It acted not just on behalf of American trade and investment, but as the defender of capitalist interests in general against the perceived threat of global communism. It fought directly against overtly communist movements, particularly in the Second Indochina War, when it deployed over half a million troops; it engaged in the subversion of nominally neutralist but potentially left-leaning governments in Indonesia, Laos, and Cambodia; and it subsidized right-wing movements throughout the region, thus laying the groundwork for military coups in Indonesia (1965) and Thailand (1976) as well as for martial law in the Philippines (1972).

Economic assistance from the United States was generally correlated with political aims rather than need or prospective profitability. The countries of Indochina, where the Cold War became hot, were the most heavily subsidized. Over the course of twenty years (1955–75) the RVN received $16.8 billion in military aid and $8.5 billion in economic aid.[14] In proportional terms, the other non-communist states received even more: the Khmer Republic got aid in 1974 amounting to more than half its GNP, while in 1972 Laos was able to import twenty times as much as it exported, thanks to $250 million military aid (which actually exceeded the entire GNP by 16 per cent) plus another $50 million in economic aid. Thailand, as a site of major American military bases, was also rewarded handsomely for its co-operation. Between 1950 and 1975 Thailand received $650 million in economic aid, $1 billion in regular military assistance (nearly 60 per cent of the total Thai defence budget for the period), and another $1 billion in military operating costs, equipment transfers, subsidies for Thai troops in Vietnam, and base construction costs. In neutralist Burma and Indonesia, however, early efforts to use aid to sway them to the American cause were not particularly successful, although the 1965 coup in Indonesia was, like the imposition of martial law in the Philippines, rewarded by greatly increased aid over the next few years.

The Philippines was unique in the length and depth of its economic dependence upon a single external patron. In the immediate postwar period its government had little choice but to accept American imposi-tions, but over time the United States became less overtly imperious. Direct economic and military aid peaked in real terms between 1949 and 1952, when it totalled over $600 million, and though it continued at substantial levels thereafter it never represented a determinant component of the national budget; by the 1970s, it began to give way to multilateral and private lending. Individual Filipinos also benefited from military and

---

[14] Douglas C. Dacy, *Foreign Aid, War, and Economic Development: South Vietnam, 1955–1975*, Cambridge, UK, 1986, 200. Nguyen Anh Tuan, *South Vietnam: Trial and Experience: A Challenge for Development*, Athens, Ohio: Ohio University, Monographs in International Studies, Southeast Asia Series, no. 80, 1987, provides a slightly different breakdown, but the same total of just over $25 billion assistance.

civilian pension disbursements from the United States, which averaged over $120 million a year in the late 1970s. The Philippine demand for 'rent' for the military bases (though Americans refused to call it that) escalated from the 1970s onward and resulted in aid promises that rose from $50 million a year in 1979 to nearly ten times that a decade later; at the same time, bases-related spending slid from 2.3 per cent of GNP in the mid-1960s to 1.25 or 1.5 per cent in the mid-1980s.[15] The American share of Philippine trade and foreign investment also declined significantly over time, and by 1974 mutual special tariff concessions were finally terminated.

In spite of the diminution of direct leverage over the Philippine economy, the United States retained a disproportionate influence there, derived in part from the dominant American role in purveying advice to decision-makers and educating technocrats. Filipinos studied American textbooks, undertook postgraduate study at American universities, and engaged in joint research and planning projects with American counterparts; to a considerable extent, the hold that the USA had over the Philippine economy did not reside in ownership, but in the minds of the Filipinos themselves. The USA also attempted to exercise the same kind of personal influence elsewhere in the region, especially in the 1960s. One-fifth of the top level officials in the Thai bureaucracy in the 1970s had earned degrees from American universities, and roughly the same proportion of general officers in the Indonesian army had received training in US service schools.[16]

By the 1970s, however, the position of the USA in the region was changing. Imminent withdrawal from Indochina reduced its influence both there and in neighbouring Thailand, while the oil shocks of 1973 and 1979 reduced its economic strength relative to some of its capitalist rivals. Japan, in particular, emerged as a countervailing economic force in the region. Globally, its official development assistance rose from $244 million (6 per cent of the USA's) in 1965 to $3353 million (47 per cent) by 1980. Like its trade and investment, moreover, Japan's aid tended to be heavily concentrated in Asia, and before long Japan had become the major donor to most Southeast Asian countries. Japan outdid the USA in tying its aid to the utilization of its own goods and services; unlike American aid of the 1950s and 1960s, however, this was not usually accompanied by demands for ideological conformity. Members of the European Community, particularly the Federal Republic of Germany, also converted some of their rising prosperity into aid to Southeast Asia, as did Australia, newly aware of its near northern neighbours, and oil-rich Middle Eastern states, increasingly

[15] David Wurfel, *Filipino Politics: Development and Decay*, Ithaca, 1988, 193–5; Robert Pringle, *Indonesia and the Philippines: American Interests in Island Southeast Asia*, New York, 1980, 58–9; Charles W. Lindsey, 'The Economics of U.S. Military Bases in the Philippines', paper presented at Third International Philippine Studies Conference, Quezon City, 1989. Using a simple Keynesian-multiplier model of the Philippine economy, Lindsey estimated that the impact of this spending on the GNP declined from 3.5 to 2.0–2.3 per cent.

[16] Likhit Dhiravegin, *The Bureaucratic Elite of Thailand: A Study of Their Sociological Attributes, Educational Backgrounds, and Career Advancement Patterns*, Bangkok, 1978, 106–27; Bryan Evans III, 'The Influence of the United States Army on the Development of the Indonesian Army (1954–1964)', *Indonesia*, 47 (1989) 37.

conscious of their Islamic brothers around the world. Meanwhile, petro-dollars flooded international banking circles, and cheap loans, rather than direct grants, became the dominant form of foreign aid in the region.

As time went by, more and more economic assistance to Southeast Asia was channelled through multilateral organizations, such as the World Bank (International Bank for Reconstruction and Development), the Asian Development Bank (ADB), and the International Monetary Fund (IMF). In part this represented an acknowledgment that bilateral aid was perceived as manipulative. To many critics, however, the all-but-compulsory advice of the World Bank and IMF was no less an infringement of national sovereignty and a constraint on independent decision-making than the more overt 'neo-colonialism' of earlier years. To receive or renegotiate major loans, it was necessary to accept a package that almost invariably included devaluation, labour discipline, reduced government spending on social services, and greater opening to imports and foreign investment. Such measures were welcome to investors and often conducive to increased trade, but frequently they were also the cause of short-term hardship, particularly for the poorer classes.

Although the USSR and China inspired and supported revolutionary movements within the region, they had little economic impact outside Indochina. They made occasional efforts to influence Indonesia (before 1965) and Burma through offers of foreign aid, but to little avail; only in Vietnam, Laos, and Kampuchea did their contributions make a real difference. By the best estimates they contributed nearly $90 million a year to the Democratic Republic of Vietnam during 1955–65, rising to over $400 million a year in 1965–75.[17] In the earlier period, much of the aid was in the form of capital goods, but after 1965 it shifted to war matériel, food, and basic consumer goods. The breakdown of relations between Vietnam and China in the late 1970s drove the SRV into deeper economic dependence on the USSR and its Council for Mutual Economic Assistance (COMECON) bloc, to the tune of over a billion dollars a year by the mid-1980s. China, meanwhile, increased its support for Democratic Kampuchea and, after 1978, for the Khmer Rouge in exile. Communist aid, like that from the West, carried with it constraints; mostly it could be used only for goods from the donor countries and implied the acceptance of donor advice.

INTERNATIONAL MARKETS AND TECHNOLOGY

Beyond these governmental initiatives, Southeast Asia was also exposed to independent trends in markets and technology. The quarter-century after World War II was one of unprecedented global prosperity, with international trade growing at an average rate of well above 10 per cent a year and economic production increasing at the highest rate in modern history. This was due in part to improved productivity and lower transport costs,

---

[17] Melanie Beresford, *Vietnam: Politics, Economics and Society*, London, 1988, 143–4.

but there were political factors as well. Along with the absence of war between the major powers there was also a general worldwide reduction of trade barriers, mediated through such institutions as the General Agreement on Tariffs and Trade (GATT) and the United Nations Conference on Trade and Development (UNCTAD). Despite some efforts within UNCTAD to legislate in favour of the developing world, a disproportionate share of the expanded trade and wealth was claimed by the industrialized countries, as the terms of trade tended to move in their favour from the early 1950s onward. Globally, however, there was enough for everyone; even non-oil-producing Third World countries enjoyed an average increase in exports of more than 7 per cent a year.

Tropical products, on which Southeast Asia had depended so heavily during the colonial era, performed well in the first postwar decade. After a dip in the late 1940s, the Korean War created an enormous boom— 'a period such as commodity markets in general had never previously known'[18]—in the early 1950s, which helped regional recovery, particularly in Malaya and the Philippines, where productive capacity had largely been restored. Thereafter, however, prices tended to slip, although individual commodities rallied occasionally, particularly in the 1970s. Minerals generally held up better than agricultural products, despite enormous price fluctuations; ventures in copper, tin, bauxite, nickel, zinc, tungsten and chromium all proved profitable from time to time.

The major exception to the general downward trend, however, was oil, which shot to unprecedented heights when the Organization of Petroleum Exporting Countries (OPEC) discovered in 1973 how to flex its economic muscles, quadrupling world prices. Despite later fluctuations, including a second price hike in 1979 and a significant drop in 1982–3, oil prices thereafter were always far higher than they had ever been before. In many respects the first oil crisis marked a watershed in modern economic history, the end of a postwar golden age for world trade. Economic growth did not stop in 1973, however. Though OPEC had caused a short-term global recession and presented new challenges to importers of oil and petroleum-based commodities (such as fertilizer), it also brought substantial new wealth to countries with a surplus of oil or natural gas and supplied the international banking system with more money to lend to worthy—and unworthy—borrowers.

Another major development in the global economy was the growth of transnational corporations and banks. Between 1960 and 1980 the sales of the world's 200 largest industrial corporations increased from $200 billion to $2 trillion, or from 18 per cent to 29 per cent of the entire gross domestic product of the non-socialist world. Much of their investment was underwritten by huge transnational banks, the hundred largest of which had assets of $4.4 trillion by 1981. Their sheer size tended to give these firms substantial influence on multilateral agencies and governments, so that despite their non-official status they had to be taken into account in any analysis of 'neo-colonialism'. Although American corporations and

---

[18] J. W. F. Rowe, *Primary Commodities in International Trade*, Cambridge, UK, 1965, 103.

banks, such as Unilever, General Motors, and National City Bank of New York (later Citibank), were dominant in the early postwar period, from the 1960s onward Japanese and European firms began to gain ground. The share of USA-based firms in the total sales of the world's 200 largest corporations declined from 73 per cent in 1960 to barely 50 per cent in 1980, by which time Japanese banks actually owned greater total assets than their American counterparts.[19] Mitsubishi, Matsushita, Sumitomo, Toyota, Nippon Steel, and the Bank of Tokyo emerged among the major investors in Southeast Asia, where they often outstripped their Western rivals; at the same time, Japan became the leading trade partner of several countries in the region.

As they broadened their horizons, the transnational corporations took advantage of improved communications and tariff reductions to internationalize their operations. To them, Third World countries had once been simply sources of raw materials or markets for manufactures; later they were fields for import substitution investment; finally they became critical elements in a truly global economy, under a 'New International Division of Labour'. The corporations provided basic technology, sourced their production wherever labour was cheapest and taxes were lowest, and marketed the output globally, often taking advantage of special tariff concessions for goods from developing countries. Oil-rich banks, backed by their governments, were happy to supply the necessary capital for such investments. Third World countries bid against each other for the right to participate in manufacturing for the global market. The simple division between primary producers and industrial countries eroded; taking advantage of cheap labour, American department stores ordered children's garments from the Philippines, and Japanese computer firms subcontracted silicon chips from Malaysia.

Those Third World countries, including Singapore, that were first to establish export-oriented light industries, especially in the 1960s, became known as the newly industrializing countries. The manufacture of textiles, garments, toys, electrical goods and electronic components and the processing of primary products (e.g., canning tuna and pineapples, petroleum refining) became for these countries and those which wished to emulate them an opportunity to compensate for declining terms of trade. Another area of compensation was services, sold abroad or to visiting foreigners: banking, ship repair, personal services, and tourism. The Second Indochina War, particularly between 1965 and 1973, boosted such sales in Southeast Asia by the overspill from American military expenditures (e.g., from refitting of naval vessels and 'rest-and-recreation' spending by American troops) to Vietnam and nearby nations, particularly Thailand and the Philippines. By the 1980s Southeast Asia, which had been a net importer of labour and services in the colonial period, was exporting construction workers to the Middle East, maids to Hongkong, doctors and nurses to North America, and entertainers to Japan. Diversification had

---

[19] Robin Broad, *Unequal Alliance, 1979–1986: The World Bank, the International Monetary Fund, and the Philippines*, Berkeley, 1988, 38–43.

become a key to economic success in the postwar world. Except for the oil-producers, no Southeast Asian country in the 1980s was as dependent on a single commodity as Malaya once had been on rubber or Burma on rice; this helped cushion the effects of global market fluctuations, generally greater for primary commodities than for manufactures and services.

Technological developments also had significant consequences for the economies of postwar Southeast Asia. Perhaps the most significant of these were in the area of health. Beginning with the development of penicillin, sulfa drugs, and DDT in World War II, they led to a spectacular drop in mortality throughout the region. National crude death rates fell by an average of close to 20 per thousand in the four decades following the war, as annual population growth rates climbed to rates unprecedented in human history. New technologies of birth control also became available in this period, but as their utilization depended not just on accessibility but on motivation, which varied widely, the decline of fertility was not as rapid or universal as that of mortality.

The 'green revolution'—actually a complex package of new high-yielding variety seeds, irrigation, fertilizers, and pesticides—was the best-known example of technological innovation in postwar Southeast Asian agriculture. It was developed in the mid-1960s at IRRI and soon communicated to the rest of the region; within a decade traditional rice-deficit countries such as Indonesia and the Philippines became self-sufficient. Southeast Asian agriculture also profited from the development of high-yielding varieties of other crops, particularly rubber—Malaysian yields improved over 120 per cent between 1954 and 1970—and of farm machines such as tractors, combine harvesters, and water-pumps. Along with the extension and intensification of cropping, such technological developments enabled agricultural production in the region to remain ahead of population growth. At the same time, however, other improvements in technology—from the increased mechanization of Western agriculture to the development of synthetic rubber and nylon rope—drove down international market prices for many Southeast Asian crops.

Global developments in industrial technology also had both positive and negative effects on the postwar Southeast Asian economy. Although the computer industry was highly sophisticated at its core, it required components made by a large semi-skilled workforce, often located where labour was relatively cheap, such as in Singapore and the export-processing zones of the Philippines, Malaysia, and Thailand. Other innovations, however, were capital-intensive and extremely complex, reducing the likelihood that a labour-surplus economy could ever be independently competitive. Even when Third World countries obtained modern factories through foreign aid or investment, they often had difficulty keeping them up to date; the heavy industry introduced into Burma, Vietnam, and Indonesia in the 1950s was virtually obsolete two decades later. Southeast Asia was also affected by advances in transportation (cheaper trucks, buses, jeepneys, scooters, and motorboats) and communications (radios, televisions and telephones) which greatly increased the flow of people, goods, and information. Jumbo jets carried tourists, silicon chips, luxury imports and perishable export commodities across the oceans. All these different technologies had different local effects, but in general they tended to facilitate the creation of larger economic networks—provincial, national, and global—in which the wealthier centre tended to dominate the poorer periphery. Within Southeast Asia, national governments enormously increased their capacity to speak to and control distant rural populations; internationally, foreign governments and corporations enhanced their ability to plan globally and so override local initiatives.

The most spectacular new military technologies were those deployed by the USA in the Second Indochina War, which certainly caused more physical damage than any human agency in the history of Southeast Asia, including dropping five times the tonnage of bombs that fell globally in all of World War II. Advanced military technology was also used by Southeast Asians against local rebels and rivals. The campaigns of Jakarta against East Timor and of Manila against Sulu in the 1970s featured jets and helicopter gunships; rumours of chemical warfare also circulated about both of these campaigns, as well as those of the SRV in Cambodia and Laos. The state did not always prevail, as the forty-year Karen resistance in Burma indicated, but each advance in military technology tended to increase the extension of central control.

As independent states, of course, the countries of Southeast Asia could in theory control their exposure to international markets and their access to technology as well as their relations with foreign governments. What they encountered in practice was a package: trade, aid, investment, technology and compulsory advice on how to use them all. The developed capitalist countries accounted for 60–70 per cent of the world's trade and an even larger proportion of international aid and foreign investment, as well as most of the major technological innovations of the postwar period. To reject any element of their package was to risk losing the rest of it, as the 'third way' states came to realize.

The access of the socialist countries of Southeast Asia to new technologies was quite uneven, restricted sometimes by self-imposed quarantine, sometimes by foreign blockade, and always by the effects of war and poverty. After 1954 the DRV opted for the alternative package offered by the communist bloc, which controlled only about 10 per cent of the world's trade and a comparably reduced share of total aid, investment, and advanced technology. Revolutionary Burma and Democratic Kampuchea chose isolation instead, proclaiming self-reliance as a supreme virtue. This had certain benefits for Burma, which was buffered from the full effects of global market fluctuations and possible foreign intervention in its internal politics and cultural life, but it was not an optimal strategy in the postwar economic environment. The enormous expansion of world trade and the extraordinary advance of technology represented a unique opportunity for development, which Southeast Asian states missed out on at their own cost. The efforts of Indochina and Burma in the late 1980s to attract more non-communist trade, aid, investment and technology suggested both how attractive these were and how difficult they were to obtain without compromising national sovereignty.

ECONOMIC GROWTH AND STRUCTURAL CHANGE

There were many technical problems in defining and measuring growth in postwar Southeast Asia. Real GNP or gross domestic product (GDP) had to be calculated, making appropriate adjustments for inflation, the value of non-market production (always a sizeable proportion of local economic activity) and illegal trade (smuggling being a major industry in many of the region's borderlands). These figures were then converted into real income (or GDP per capita), allowing for rapid population increase. National economists and international agencies devoted a great deal of effort to all these calculations, yet admitted that the results were far from perfect.

The available data suggest, nevertheless, that the real income of most Southeast Asians grew in the postwar period, a pattern corroborated by other indicators, such as declining infant mortality and expanded literacy. Only for the countries of Indochina is this conclusion in doubt, in part because warfare and maladministration disrupted economic record-keeping as well as growth. In broad terms the capitalist economies clearly grew faster than the socialist economies, but that is at least partially explained by the fact that they suffered less from warfare and enjoyed greater access to foreign aid and trade. At the same time, it must be acknowledged that growth was usually neither as rapid nor as regular as Southeast Asians had hoped, and that most countries experienced extended periods of stagnation or decline, especially Democratic Kampuchea, 1975–8; but also Malaya, 1951–8; Indonesia, 1959–65; Burma, 1964–74; the DRV, 1965–72; the RVN and the Khmer Republic, 1970–5; the SRV and Laos, 1976–80; and the Philippines, 1981–6. Moreover, the increased prosperity implied by the gross data was not experienced by a substantial number of Southeast Asians, who would have been amazed to hear that they were better off than they had ever been before.

Singapore was the great Southeast Asian success story; over the whole postwar period it was second only to Japan in per capita growth and ranked with Hong Kong, Taiwan, and the Republic of Korea as one of Asia's four 'little dragons'. The British had developed it as an entrepôt, not an industrial centre, and its average annual growth rate through the troubled 1950s was under 2 per cent, though this figure may not fully reflect local earnings from the smuggling trade with Indonesia. With no agrarian sector to speak of, and an inconsequential domestic market after its departure from Malaysia in 1965, independent Singapore had no delusions of economic self-sufficiency. Its leaders realized that it would have to depend on export-oriented industrialization and services, financed by foreign investment if necessary, and set about planning to achieve those ends. A strategic location, an efficient and apparently incorruptible bureaucracy, a well-disciplined labour force (once the independent trade unions were broken), and a tough population planning programme contributed to Singapore's success. By the efficient development of modern banking and the stock market it not only mobilized its own domestic capital but tapped into regional resources as well, standing at the centre of a great Chinese financial network. It served (along with Hong Kong) as a clearing house for all manner of international financial transactions, legal and otherwise. Real per capita income grew at an average annual rate of over 7 per cent in the quarter-century after independence and reached $7500 a year by the late 1980s. Only Brunei did better, emerging from obscurity in the oil boom of the 1970s; its huge oil revenues, divided among a tiny population, gave it a per capita income of over $15,000 by the late 1980s.

Malaya based its postwar recovery on the restoration of primary production, and remained heavily dependent for two decades on the export of rubber and tin and the importation of rice. Its wealth per capita had long been among the highest in the region, and in the immediate postwar period high commodity prices and rapid recovery of production brought it to the top again. In the 1950s the Emergency disrupted production and real per capita growth was negligible, averaging barely 1 per cent a year over the decade. In the 1960s, however, import-substitution manufacturing grew rapidly (averaging 17 per cent a year, 1959–68) and earlier state investment in rubber replanting and the extension of oil palm cultivation began to pay off; GNP growth per capita climbed to average annual rates of 3–4 per cent. In the long run the new Federation of Malaysia was also to benefit from the natural resources of Sabah and Sarawak, especially oil and timber, though some of the proceeds had to be spent in raising the living standards of the poor farmers, fishermen, and hunter-gatherers of these states.

The New Economic Policy of the 1970s was designed to increase indigenous (*bumiputra*) ownership and participation in the economy; the only way this could be done without directly dispossessing the Chinese and Indians was by accelerated growth. One component of this was promotion of non-plantation agriculture through the green revolution, extension of cultivated area, and the introduction of new cash crops. Another was export-oriented industrialization; in the absence of indigenous entrepreneurs, this was operated by the state in trust for the *bumiputra* community. Foreign capital, particularly Japanese, was invited to participate in joint ventures (with 30 per cent of the stock reserved for *bumiputras*) and operate in special free-trade zones. Along with the oil boom, which made its offshore reserves and natural gas worth exploiting, these measures lifted Malaysia's per capita growth rates above 5 per cent in the 1970s, and growing diversification kept the average around 4 per cent in the 1980s, despite a mid-decade recession. With income per capita over $2000 and life expectancy approaching seventy years, Malaysia was clearly the most prosperous of the sizeable Southeast Asian nations.

After some early experimentation with state enterprises, the Thai government under Sarit Thanarat switched in the 1960s to infrastructural investment on behalf of private import-substitution industry and agriculture. Industry, primarily Sino-Thai in ownership, did in fact grow rapidly (averaging over 10 per cent annually); but the sustained growth of the economy as a whole—averaging over 3 per cent per capita in the 1950s, 5 per cent in the 1960s—was possible only because agriculture, from which most of the population still earned their living, also grew steadily. This was due in part to the expansion of irrigation (from 600,000 hectares in 1947 to 2.2 million by 1969) and the increased use of tractors and fertilizers, particularly in the central plain. Most of the growth, however, was attributable to the extension of cultivation, abetted by improved roads, rather than to increased yield. Some of this expansion was in traditional crops such as rice and rubber, but much of it was in new crops, particularly for the Japanese market: maize, kenaf, and cassava. By 1968 the export value of other crops passed that of rice for the first time in modern Thai history, having quadrupled in value over the previous fifteen years. Thailand also benefited from substantial American aid throughout the 1950s and 1960s.

The early 1970s, however, brought political instability, the oil crisis, and the end of most American aid, as well as signs that import substitution was reaching its ceiling. To the surprise of most experts the Thai economy kept growing, with GNP per capita increasing at an average annual rate of 4 per cent through the 1970s and 1980s. The civilian governments of the 1970s did not survive long enough to alter the broad development strategy pursued by the military and the technocrats. This was to promote agricultural development (the green revolution eventually arrived) and export industries, inviting foreign corporations, particularly Japanese, to participate along with local capitalists and a friendly government. Such new exports as textiles, computer components, prawns, and precious stones joined greatly increased tourism to diversify the economy and cushion it against commodity downturns. Thailand also benefited from a population planning programme that slowed demographic increase substantially in the 1970s and 1980s. By the end of the latter decade per capita income had reached $1000, passing the faltering Philippines. During the entire postwar period, in fact, Thailand was second in the region only to Singapore in average rate of growth.

Over the first decade and a half of the postwar period the Philippines was a regional leader in economic growth, thanks to American aid, a well-educated population, and relatively sophisticated institutional infrastructure. It was the Southeast Asian pioneer of import-substitution industrialization; between 1949 and 1957 this sector grew at over 12 per cent a year. The Korean War boom helped to pull GNP growth per capita to an average annual rate of nearly 4 per cent; per capita income remained higher than Taiwan and South Korea as late as 1960. During the 1960s, however, manufacturing growth slowed, due to limited demand and the chronic inefficiencies of over-protection. With commodity prices also sliding, and population increase climbing above 3 per cent a year, GNP per capita growth fell to just 2 per cent. Vested interests in import substitution (American as well as Filipino) prevented the serious implementation of an export-manufacturing strategy urged by both indigenous and foreign experts.

After the declaration of martial law in 1972, partially justified by the poor performance of the economy, growth did in fact pick up somewhat. Over the next eight years it averaged 3 per cent per capita—still the lowest rate in ASEAN—thanks to the green revolution, a construction boom, surging commodity prices, and above all to increased foreign borrowing. The total Philippine foreign debt, public and private, rose from $2.2 billion in 1972 to $9 billion in 1979; along the way, government borrowing passed private indebtedness for the first time. Much of this capital went directly into the pockets of Marcos and his 'cronies' rather than into productive investment, however. With the second oil shock of 1979 and the subsequent collapse in commodity prices, the 'debt trap' started to close. The Philippines had to borrow more than ever, and at worse terms; in just three years (1980–3) foreign indebtedness rose from 6.6 per cent to 49.4 per cent of the GNP, while growth per capita slipped from 2 per cent to zero. In the aftermath of the assassination of Benigno ('Ninoy') Aquino, Jr, public confidence collapsed, and the economy with it. The GNP actually fell over the next three years; by the February Revolution of 1986, it was back at the level of 1980, down 20 per cent on a per capita basis. Under Corazon Aquino there was an immediate improvement in both private investment and foreign aid, but even her most optimistic advisers acknowledged that it would be many years before the economy made up the ground it had lost. Before ameliorative 'restructuring' the foreign debt approached $30 billion and the ratio of debt-service to exports was estimated at close to 40 per cent, double what was usually considered the danger level for developing countries. Population growth also remained high, as planning efforts were left in disarray by the pro-natalist bias of the new régime.

The Indonesian economy, by contrast, began the postwar period poorly and achieved sustained growth only after 1965. The Revolution forced postponement of reconstruction to the 1950s, when the young republic had to struggle with problems of high mortality, food shortages, inflation, and the destruction of physical capital. A GNP growth rate of nearly 2 per cent per capita for much of the decade, though respectable under the circumstances, was disappointing to many Indonesians, particularly Sukarno, who took over effective control of the state apparatus between 1957 and 1959. His answer was nationalism: expropriation of Dutch property; discrimination against the Chinese; major state investment in heavy industry (to make Indonesia self-sufficient); and a rhetorical barrage levelled against 'neo-colonialism' in all its forms, culminating in 'confrontations' over Irian Jaya and Malaysia that increased military spending and reduced foreign aid and trade. The results, in economic terms, were disastrous: trade collapsed, industrial production plummeted, and hyper-inflation (over 2000 per cent a year by the mid-1960s) set in. GNP per capita actually declined between 1957 and 1965, as did food consumption in this already hungry country.

Between 1965 and 1967 the military wrested control from Sukarno and turned the economy over to the technocrats, who immediately sought and received the foreign aid and investment that had been frightened away in the period of Guided Democracy. The emphasis was on curbing inflation, promoting rice production (through the Bimas ['mass guidance'] agricultural extension programme, which provided physical inputs and credit), and fostering import-replacing industries (often with military participation). By the end of the 1960s the economy was well on the road to recovery, and even before the oil boom, annual growth per capita had climbed to 5 per cent. It maintained this rate for the remainder of the 1970s, despite the Pertamina scandal of 1975—possibly the largest defalcation in Southeast Asian history—but fell back to around 1 per cent after the decline of oil prices in 1982–3. To a considerable extent, moreover, this growth continued to depend on the exploitation of primary resources (including timber and minerals as well as oil) rather than on the manufacture of exports, which was always hampered by vested interests in import-substitution industries and an affinity for the ideal of national self-sufficiency. On the positive side, population planning slowed demographic growth somewhat, though Indonesia continued to have over two million new mouths to feed each year. By the end of the 1980s per capita income approached $600 and life expectancy approached sixty years, both the highest in Indonesian history but still the lowest in ASEAN.

Devastated by World War II and the civil war that followed independence (1948–52), Burma entered the 1950s as perhaps the poorest sizeable country in Asia, with a per capita income of less than $50 a year. From this low base it grew rapidly—over 4 per cent a year—throughout the decade, yet by 1960 the production of rice and teak, its two main exports, still had not reached prewar levels, while oil production was barely half what it had been in 1939 and other minerals fared even worse. Meanwhile, the prices of rice and other commodities kept slipping, and endemic insurgency inhibited the development of many outlying districts. Though its tiny manufacturing sector grew rapidly Burma, after more than a decade of independence, had not regained prewar income levels, much less started to catch up with the developed world.

As in Indonesia, disappointment at the performance of the economy led toward radical nationalism. Ne Win went even farther than Sukarno in cutting ties (aid, trade, and investment) with the outside world, discriminating against resident aliens, and plunging down the path of autonomous development, with an emphasis on heavy industry. Within two years of the 1962 coup the government had nationalized almost all mineral development, commerce in timber, import–export transactions, wholesale and brokerage trade, and banking. By the end of 1965 it controlled 60 per cent of manufacturing and 90 per cent of legal trade. Many Chinese and Indians, squeezed by 'inexorably comprehensive restrictive laws ... strictly applied',[20] emigrated. GNP per capita scarcely grew over the next decade, as external trade collapsed (dropping more than 10 per cent a year), agricultural production stagnated, and industry and mining suffered from the lack of expatriate expertise, capital goods, spare parts, and co-ordinated planning. Only a vast illegal trade, both internal and external, kept the economy afloat at all.

Adoption of more pragmatic policies in the early 1970s got the Burmese economy moving again, with GNP per capita growing at nearly 4 per cent a year for a decade (1973–83). External assistance, particularly from Japan and multilateral agencies, helped finance major projects in the extractive industries, though at a cost of increasing the ratio of debt-service to exports to 55 per cent by 1986. Agriculture, meanwhile, was boosted both by improved fertilizer supply and a revised marketing system that restored producer incentives; manufacturing also expanded, though it remained

[20] Yuan-li Wu and Chun-hsi Wu, *Economic Development in Southeast Asia: The Chinese Dimension*, Stanford, 1980, 88–9.

unbalanced and underdeveloped by regional standards. In the mid-1980s, however, growth was slowed by rising debt, reduced aid, and recession, even before political turmoil in 1988–9 led to the suspension of most foreign aid and declining GNP per capita once more. Burma remained in monetary terms among the poorest countries in the world, with per capita income under $200, though indicators of health and education suggested that the actual standard of living was not quite as low as this ranking implied.

The economic history of postwar Indochina was dominated and clouded by warfare: against the French, the Americans, the Chinese, and among its peoples. No reliable data are available for the period of the First Indochina War; descriptive evidence suggests a distinct improvement over the desperate conditions of 1945, but not much advance on the prewar economy. In the decade following the departure of the French, however, GNP per capita generally rose. The DRV rebuilt its economy almost from scratch, first with remarkable agricultural recovery (to 1959), then, as collectivization disrupted agriculture, with sustained increases in industrial output; the result was per capita rates averaging around 5 per cent. Growth rates in the RVN were comparable, and massive American aid enabled consumption (which regularly exceeded total GNP) to rise even faster. Even in Cambodia, GNP per capita grew at over 2 per cent a year between 1959 and 1964.[21]

The American military intervention ended this epoch of growth. Total RVN production continued to rise, thanks in part to the green revolution and a booming import trade, but it was only the aid-financed doubling of real expenditures on public administration and defence between 1965 and 1972 that enabled it to keep pace with population growth. DRV production declined under the impact of American bombing, 1965–8, and never fully recovered. Cambodia's GNP, already slowed by recession in the late 1960s, plummeted after Lon Nol took over in 1970, and fell more than 10 per cent a year over the next five years. The economy of Laos was brought almost to a standstill by American bombing, which made refugees of one-quarter of the population.

After 1975 the SRV fully expected a rapid recovery and dramatic transformation of its economy. 'Because we won the war, we thought we could do anything successfully', one official later admitted.[22] The government was aware of, and believed it could handle, the physical and demographic devastation of the south: fields and forests sprayed with herbicides, shattered infrastructure, food shortages, millions of refugees, an estimated three million unemployed, 500,000 prostitutes, 100,000 drug addicts,

---

[21] Calculated from data in G. Nguyen Tien Hung, *Economic Development of Socialist Vietnam, 1955–1980*, New York: Praeger Special Studies in International Economics and Development, 1977; Andrew Vickerman, *The Fate of the Peasantry: Premature 'Transition to Socialism' in the Democratic Republic of Vietnam*, New Haven: Yale University Southeast Asia Studies, 1986; Dacy, *Foreign Aid, War, and Economic Development*; Nguyen Anh Tuan, *South Vietnam*; and Remy Prud'homme, *L'economie du Cambodge*, Paris: Collection 'Tiers Monde', 1969. No comparable data are available for Laos.

[22] Quoted in Sue Downie, 'Shattered Vietnam on Road to Recovery', *South China Morning Post*, 25 June 1989.

800,000 orphans. What they failed to take into account was how much the economy and society had changed since 1954, and how difficult the 'socialist transformation' would therefore be. Farmers resisted collectivization, urban settlers sent to New Economic Zones returned to the cities, industrial and agricultural production fell, and efforts to crack down on private trade resulted only in the exodus of hundreds of thousands of boat people (mostly Chinese), taking with them both skills and capital. War with Kampuchea (Cambodia) and China in 1979 strained the economy further. On a per capita basis, national income declined at nearly 2 per cent a year during 1976–80. By late 1979 the government had embarked on an erratic series of 'reforms' intended to increase economic efficiency by restoring incentives in agriculture and accountability in industry. These were never whole-heartedly adopted, however, and recovery in the 1980s was uneven: steady growth (around 4 per cent per capita) in the first half of the decade was reversed by triple-digit inflation, agricultural stagnation, and general economic decline between 1985 and 1988.

Like Vietnam, Laos suffered in the late 1970s from the loss of aid, the departure of refugees and an abortive attempt at agricultural collectivization. It also recovered (at an annual rate of around 2 per cent per capita) in the 1980s, benefiting from rising agricultural production and expanded trade with Thailand, particularly the export of electricity from the Nam Ngum project. Both Laos and Vietnam remained heavily dependent on foreign aid, primarily from the Soviet bloc. Even with many loans on concessionary terms, their ratios of debt-service to exports were the highest in the region; Vietnam was 'in a position of de facto default' by the late 1980s.[23] Since much of their national wealth was still produced by agriculture, they were also extraordinarily vulnerable to unfavourable weather conditions. Estimates of per capita income by the late 1980s ranged around $150–200, although, as in Burma, indices of health and literacy were comparatively high.

The devastation of the Cambodian economy in the 1970s is well known, though the notorious atrocities committed by Democratic Kampuchea after 1975 tend to overshadow the deaths (at least half a million) and economic decline under the Khmer Republic before that date. By the most reliable calculations, excess mortality between 1975 and 1979 was in the order of 740,000 to one million—perhaps half of them executed, the rest dying of starvation or illness. Another half million Khmers and some 200,000 Vietnamese fled the country.[24] The harassment, execution, or exile of most engineers, teachers, and medical personnel ruined what there was of industry, education, and modern health care. The country, a surplus rice-producer as late as the 1960s, fell into enormous deficit in the early 1970s; efforts to reverse this by sheer force of political will failed, and famine ensued in some districts. Income estimates were meaningless, but there was little doubt that Cambodia was worse off in 1979 than it had ever been

---

[23] Economist Intelligence Unit, *Country Profile: Indochina: Vietnam, Laos, Cambodia: 1988–89*, London, 1988, 24.
[24] Vickery, *Cambodia*, 184–8, Vickery, letter to editors, *Bulletin of Concerned Asian Scholars*, 20, 1 (1988) 70–3.

in modern times. Recovery through the 1980s was slow, hampered by continuing insurgency and an embargo by most potential aid-donors and trade partners outside the Soviet bloc. In agriculture, industry, and infrastructure, the 1980s never even caught up to the 1960s. By most indicators— food supply, estimated GDP per capita (under $100), infant mortality (over 150 per 1000 births) and life expectancy (under fifty years)—Cambodia remained the poorest country in the region and one of the poorest in the world.

Growth in postwar Southeast Asia was generally connected with the shift from agriculture to industry, one of the defining characteristics of the era. In 1950 manufacturing accounted for 12 per cent of Philippine GDP; elsewhere in the region, 5–10 per cent or even less. Forty years later only in Brunei, Laos, and Cambodia did the proportion remain below 10 per cent; in Burma and Indonesia it had climbed into the 10–15 per cent range; in the Philippines, Malaysia, Vietnam, Thailand, and Singapore it averaged 25 per cent or more. The inclusion of mining, construction and utilities raised the total for all industry to 30 per cent or more in the ASEAN countries. 'Services'—a catch-all category that lumped together public administrators, petty traders, professionals and prostitutes—also tended to grow, except where a strong shift toward socialist autarky shrank the contribution of commerce, as in Burma after 1962 and Indochina after 1975. Agriculture (including fishing and forestry), which had once produced well over half the wealth of the region, slipped steadily in the non-socialist states to one-quarter or less of GDP, though it remained around 40 per cent in troubled Burma and Vietnam, much higher in Laos and Cambodia.

The shifting composition of the GDP was due in part to the movement of labour out of agriculture, which had employed an average of 70–80 per cent of the workforce before the war and in the immediate postwar period. As late as 1960 it still accounted for over 80 per cent in Thailand and Indochina and over 70 per cent in Indonesia. By the late 1980s, however, it had fallen to 60 per cent in Thailand, 55 per cent in Indonesia, 45 per cent in the Philippines, and below 35 per cent in Malaysia; only in Burma (65 per cent) and the states of Indochina (65–80 per cent) did it remain high. The transition from import substitution to export industry helped in this process, as the latter, more dependent on international market forces, was impelled to capitalize on the comparative advantage of cheap local labour, and therefore tended to generate more employment.

Industry's share of GDP also grew because of rising productivity, as output per industrial worker regularly grew faster than output per farm worker. In services, on the other hand, productivity tended to lag, as the numbers of featherbedding civil servants and underemployed street people increased almost as fast as total production; even so, output per worker remained substantially higher than in agriculture. Although some attributed differences in productivity to cultural values ('indolence' or the 'work ethic'), they were clearly due less to differential effort than to differential access to capital, including the technology that capital could buy. This was most obvious in heavy industry, transportation, communications, and utilities, but was true in other sectors as well. Agriculture soon regained prewar production levels using traditional technology, and continued to expand as long as land was available, but yields could not rise indefinitely without capital investment. Beyond a certain point (around two tons of paddy per hectare) further increases depended on costly new technologies, particularly the introduction of high-yielding varieties, chemical fertilizers, pesticides and improved water control. The inability to supply these inputs was, along with pricing and procurement policies that discouraged expansion, a major cause of the retardation of agricultural development in Burma and Indochina.

The formation and deployment of capital was thus a critical variable in postwar Southeast Asia. Some development capital was obtained from abroad, though this brought with it not only foreign influence but also, except in the case of outright grants, an eventual outflow of resources in the form of loan repayments or corporate profits. Only in Indochina did foreign aid represent more than half of capital formation; by the early 1970s, in fact, it accounted for 100 per cent of it in the RVN and the Khmer Republic. Elsewhere in the region domestic savings, including those provided by local Chinese, accounted for from 60 per cent to more than 90 per cent (in Thailand) of gross capital formation.

Throughout the region the state was responsible for a substantial portion (often one-third or more) of domestic capital formation, through taxation and such forced-savings institutions as Singapore's Central Provident Fund. Governments also tried to influence private savings by guaranteeing the security of savings institutions, facilitating the creation of profitable investment opportunities, and using taxes and foreign exchange controls to discourage unnecessary consumption. The traditional emphasis of Southeast Asians on the redistribution of wealth, creating or displaying merit through largesse, tended to reduce somewhat their propensity to save, whereas the traditional Chinese ethic placed greater value on accumulation for the good of the clan. This helped explain the disproportionate weight of Chinese capital in the region; it has been calculated—admittedly on rather tenuous grounds—that by 1975 some $16 billion in Chinese capital was invested in Southeast Asia, roughly twice the amount of foreign direct investment.[25]

Class was also a factor, as the poor understandably spent a much higher proportion of their income on necessities than did the rich, leaving less surplus for possible investment. Redistributionist policies therefore tended in the short run to reduce capital formation. One way or another, however, gross capital formation seems to have increased in the postwar period. In the ASEAN countries it rose steadily from an average of 8–15 per cent of GDP in the 1950s to around 25 per cent (40 per cent in Singapore) two decades later, before falling slightly in the 1980s. In Burma it fluctuated wildly, but averaged under 15 per cent for the postwar period. Vietnam, north and south, achieved levels of around 15–20 per cent in the decade of peace after 1954 and 10–15 per cent in the decade of reunification after 1976, though it suffered net losses during the wartime years.

Not all of this capital was invested to optimal developmental advantage. Much of it, particularly in the capitalist states, was simply 'rent-seeking';

[25] Wu and Wu, *Economic Development*, 31–4, 161–72.

the profitability of money-lending and landlordism, particularly in an era of rapid population growth, often outweighed the risks of investing in more productive ventures. Among productive investments, some turned out in practice to be more conducive to development than others. In postwar Southeast Asia growth was correlated most clearly with investments in basic infrastructure, agriculture, and light industry. Heavy industry rarely paid for itself. Energy was a high-risk venture; when a major power project or oil field was fully developed, it could boost the economy substantially, but before that there were usually years of uncertainty and delay. Import substitution, though important in early industrialization, soon ran up against market limits and developed inefficiencies which tended to cascade down to other industries. Export-oriented industrialization then provided a profitable alternative, though it became increasingly competitive over time; the early NICs found it easier than those who later hoped to emulate them.

Substantial investments in 'human capital'—health, education, and social services—were also common throughout the region, but cannot be clearly linked to economic growth. Most independent Southeast Asian states allocated 10–20 per cent of their budgets to education, with another 5 per cent or so for health and related services: inadequate to the task, but far more than had been spent in these areas before. The fastest-growing states in Southeast Asia generally provided the best and most extensive health and educational services, but this was as much a result of their greater wealth as a cause of it. On a proportional basis, relatively poor and slow-growing states such as Revolutionary Burma and the SRV often spent more of their available resources on human services than did such high achievers as Singapore and Malaysia, suggesting that the commitment to equity was even more powerful than the hope of growth.

Though differences in health and literacy remained, they were scarcely comparable in scale to differences in income and capital formation. By the late 1980s, average life expectancy in the region (Laos and Cambodia aside) ranged from around fifty-five years (Burma) to over seventy (Singapore and Brunei), with Indonesia, Vietnam, Thailand, the Philippines and Malaysia all within ten years of each other. Enrolments in primary school, which had ranged from under 10 per cent to over 70 per cent of the appropriate age group in 1950, were approaching 100 per cent throughout the region. Adult literacy rates climbed from well under 50 per cent to 80 per cent or more in most countries. Only in secondary and tertiary education were international discrepancies still wide, yet the cases of the Philippines and the SRV, with relatively strong educational (and health) systems but weak economies, challenged any simplistic 'human capital' interpretation of growth.

NATIONALISM AND EQUITY

Except in Singapore, a distinction was usually made between indigenous peoples and those identified as 'alien', even though some of the latter had been locally resident for several generations and were citizens of the newly independent states. The aliens were widely perceived as profiting at the expense of the indigenous population, a problem which governments took different approaches to solving. Where immigration had not already been severely restricted or prohibited before World War II, this was usually undertaken soon after, thus bringing to a close a century in which Southeast Asia had been open to a massive influx of foreign labour. The more drastic action of expelling resident aliens was rare, however; only Democratic Kampuchea undertook it on any significant scale. More common was a pattern of systematic discrimination that encouraged voluntary emigration, particularly of South Asians from Burma in the 1950s and 1960s, and of Chinese from Vietnam and Laos in the 1970s and 1980s. In Southeast Asia as a whole, however, the number of ethnic Chinese and Indians continued to increase, though it declined as a proportion of the total population (to around 5 per cent), since their fertility tended to be lower than the regional average.

Discrimination against aliens took a wide variety of forms: outright exclusion from certain occupations and industries; requirements that specified proportions of capital, management, or labour in private firms should be indigenous; restrictive quotas on business licences, foreign exchange allocations, and university places; insistence on the exclusive use of the national language in schools and official transactions, etc. Nominally nondiscriminatory policies affecting specific industries or sectors of the economy were also employed. The nationalization of retail trade, for example, was particularly hard on the aliens in Burma and Vietnam, where they had previously held a near monopoly in such commerce, while the promotion of rice-growing in Malaysia favoured Malay peasants at the expense of non-Malay urban and plantation sectors.

Despite such policies, the Chinese continued to play a dominant role in the modern sectors of Southeast Asian economies. Recognizing the capabilities of Chinese capital and entrepreneurship, national need and individual greed combined to circumvent anti-alien regulations through legal technicalities or 'Ali-Baba' arrangements, in which an indigenous businessman or official ('Ali') served as frontman for a Chinese capitalist ('Baba'), who continued to manage the enterprise. In response to governmental pressure some Chinese investment did shift from commerce toward manufacturing, but it remained strong in trade as well. Estimates from the 1980s that ethnic Chinese owned 70–75 per cent of private domestic capital in Indonesia and 85 per cent in Malaysia suggested their staying power.[26]

An alternative strategy was to deny the existence of a problem by expanding the definition of 'indigenous' to include naturalized immigrants and their descendants, allowing them full citizenship rights. This was Singapore's position from the start; official nationalism was carefully separated from ethnicity. Thailand started to adopt a similar policy in the late 1950s, with ethnic Chinese encouraged to take Thai names and participate as Thais in economy and society; the achievements of Sino-Thai

[26] Robison, *Indonesia*, 276; Yoshihara Kunio, *The Rise of Ersatz Capitalism in South-East Asia*, Quezon City, 1988, 51.

entrepreneurs in industry came to be regarded more as a source of national pride than as a target for discrimination. During the 1970s and 1980s, with the liberalization of citizenship laws under the Marcos régime, the Philippines seemed to be moving in the same direction. Throughout the region the process of assimilation was facilitated by the end of easy immigration, reducing 'resinification' and the flow of remittances out of Southeast Asia, which had always antagonized local nationalists.

The problem presented by foreign investment was comparable to that posed by resident aliens: popular nationalism insisted that it should be diminished, or even abolished, but the need for capital and technology, as well as the greed of individual decision-makers, argued for retention. In every independent state domestic enterprises were nominally favoured over foreign competitors, though until the 1970s the Philippines was virtually bound to treat American investments as domestic. In some cases there were actual attempts to dispossess foreign investors: communist Vietnam, followed in due course by Laos and Kampuchea, expropriated almost all foreign firms, though it found itself in the 1980s negotiating for investment again. Under Guided Democracy Indonesia abruptly nationalized Dutch holdings and threatened other investors, though after 1965 it reversed policy and welcomed foreign capital once more. Burma also effectively rid itself of most foreign capital by the mid-1960s, and later begged to get some back. In the 1960s and 1970s Malaysia and the Philippines both introduced legislation mandating a higher indigenous stake in the corporate sector, and were generally successful in achieving this within a few years, as foreign firms sold out, wholly or in part, to local investors or the government; at the same time these countries continued to solicit new investment. Only Thailand, Singapore, and Brunei did not at one time or another embark on a systematic attempt to diminish foreign investment; only Democratic Kampuchea did not sometime welcome it back.

The policy debates often became heated, with all sides claiming the mantle of nationalism. Even those who, like Marcos in the Philippines and Mahathir in Malaysia, advocated greater foreign investment in the short run justified it as necessary for increasing national strength and pride in the long run. In practice, the critical question had to do not with whether or not foreign investment existed, but on what terms. Unless they actually intended to expropriate or ban foreign firms, Southeast Asian governments could not simply dictate conditions. To tame transnational corporations they had to negotiate tariffs, taxes, wage rates and labour rights, infrastructural provision and costs, and a hundred other variables; often they wooed potential investors with promises of tax holidays and other special incentives. Foreign corporations in turn tried to prove that they were worth wooing, offering to train more local managers here, pay higher fees or royalties there. Joint ventures were negotiated with all the wariness that surrounded traditional marriage arrangements, and improbable unofficial alliances between transnational corporations, local Chinese entrepreneurs, and indigenous government officials often succeeded where more straightforward endeavours failed. Where their direct ownership was curtailed, foreign corporations often continued to control local production through subsidiaries or subcontractors.

Behind the bargaining lay the possibility of coercion, although it was rarely invoked. Britain did not fight to preserve its direct investments in Burma or Malaysia, nor the USA its in the Philippines, and though the Second Indochina War may have had economic roots, they did not involve direct foreign investment in Vietnam. More common were efforts to subvert governments, such as that of Sukarno, seen as hostile to foreign investment in general; Southeast Asian leaders came to realize that although advocating a tough line on foreign investment might evoke popular support, it also risked arming the opposition. Much of the postwar investment, however, came from Japan, Taiwan, Hong Kong, and Germany, which had no military presence in the region. What influence they exercised came from money, whether on the table or under it.

Over time direct military intervention became less likely, advice was rejected as often as accepted, and efforts at bribery and subversion became more expensive and less effective. In their dealings with foreign governments and corporations, local politicians (including military officers) and businessmen (including aliens) came to be manipulators, not just victims of manipulation. If they co-operated with foreigners, it was not because they were coerced, but because it was in their own interest—though not always that of their countries—to do so. It is impossible to assess who got the best of a myriad bargaining sessions in which all parties tested their ingenuity to the fullest. It would appear, however, that over the course of the postwar period the relative strength of the Southeast Asians improved, if only because as time went by their governments were more stable and their negotiators more experienced. Although they rarely bargained from a position of real strength, they were often able to play off one investor against another or borrow from multilateral institutions, and so escape from the direct dependency that characterized colonialism and the immediate post-colonial years. Certainly many foreign corporations in the 1980s made concessions that they would not have dreamed of making thirty years earlier.

The problem of foreign influence was inevitably tied up with the quest for economic autonomy. Many Southeast Asians hoped to restructure their economies so that they became more diversified and self-sufficient, capable of relying on their own resources rather than depending upon access to stronger economies, but this proved far more difficult than imagined. It was not sufficient simply to decree that the country should produce everything it needed. Heavy industry was inefficient; light industry could sustain prosperity only when it was aimed at international, rather than domestic, markets; and agricultural self-sufficiency generally depended on access to foreign inputs, particularly fertilizer. No Southeast Asian state became self-sufficient in machinery or advanced technology; only the oil producers were self-sufficient in energy; and there was little regional complementarity on which a common market might be constructed. The urge for autarky remained strong, yet almost every effort to achieve it resulted in retarding economic growth. This need for foreign capital, technology, and trade set effective limits on the progress of economic nationalism in postwar Southeast Asia. Though the independent states made some advances in dealing with individual corporations and foreign governments, they were unable to free themselves from the international economy as a totality—a 'world-system'—without sacrificing some of their hopes for rising national prosperity.

Equity was a prime goal of the socialist régimes of postwar Southeast Asia but only a secondary consideration for most of the capitalist bloc, with the 'third way' countries dithering in the middle. To judge by the descriptive evidence, the socialist régimes generally succeeded in reducing, though not eradicating, the gap between rich and poor. In practice this often meant levelling down rather than up; Democratic Kampuchea was the extreme in this regard, as in so many others, with most of the population reduced to an equality of grinding poverty. In Vietnam, land reform and the nationalization of most industry and trade removed the major source of disparities of income, though there remained differentials based on accumulated wealth (sometimes converted into gold, as the accounts of the boat people testify), occupation, and location. In Burma, the softest of the socialist régimes, there was significant accumulation in the hands of the powerful, but the general distribution of wealth within the country was more equal than it had been in colonial times or than it was in the capitalist countries of the region. The departure of many Indian landlords and moneylenders eliminated one of the major existing sources of inequality. Despite a rather half-hearted land reform that left 42 per cent of cultivators in tenantry in 1970–1, data from 1972 showed the top quintile of income earners earning just five times as much as the lowest quintile, as compared with ratios of 8:1 in Indonesia and 10:1 in the Philippines.[27]

The record of the non-socialist countries of Southeast Asia was much less clear. In part the problem was ideological: decision-makers tended to believe that directly redistributionist measures were inimical to growth. In the short run, they thought, a persistent or even increasing imbalance of wealth was one of the necessary and acceptable costs of growth. As Thai technocrat Puey Ungphakorn put it: 'If we pay too much attention to social justice, overall growth would be slowed down, therefore we should put economic development first. Even though the rich will get richer, and the poor get poorer, soon growth will filter down to the poor automatically.'[28] In part the problem was structural: many technological innovations, particularly those arising from foreign advice or investment, were capital-intensive, which resulted in rising unemployment, with a growing gap between possessors of the technology and those displaced by it. In part the problem was social: the régimes were controlled by men who had a vested interest in existing structures and no intention of dispossessing their own class. Even land reform, widely touted as a politically expedient prophylactic against insurgency, was not implemented with any enthusiasm outside the socialist bloc.

The linkage between capitalist policies and income inequality was reflected in the fact that the rural poor tended to be better off, relatively speaking,

[27] Robert H. Taylor, *The State in Burma*, Honolulu, 1987, 341–53; Hill and Jayasuriya, 64.

[28] *Glancing Back, Looking Forward* (1977), as quoted in John L. S. Girling, *Thailand: Society and Politics*, Ithaca, 1981, 84. Note that Puey also admitted that 20–30 years of practice of this method had been 'without success', however.

when central governments were weak. During World War II and postwar insurgencies in Vietnam, Malaya, the Philippines and Indonesia, tax collections fell, squatters occupied abandoned estates, many landlords were unable to collect rent, and popular pressure set limits on unfavourable tenure arrangements. Similar conditions prevailed under Guided Democracy in Indonesia, in parts of rural Cambodia under the beleaguered Khmer Republic, and generally in upland areas remote from central control. In such situations the restoration of stability and 'law and order' often meant the payment of back rent and back taxes, expulsion of squatter settlements, and the enforcement of contracts on terms unfavourable to the weaker parties.

Throughout capitalist Southeast Asia, those already wealthy held on to what they had. They benefited from the new opportunities offered by the postwar world, investing in land, producer goods such as fertilizer and machinery, modern services such as banking and tourism, and access to state power through vote-buying, bribery, and education, which opened up the legal system and the technocracy. Statistical measures of income-distribution tendencies, where they exist, show the inequality was already high by international standards in the 1960s and generally tended to rise thereafter, particularly in Thailand, though the Philippines remained the worst. Singapore was the major exception to this trend, having by 1970 reached that level of development at which (as Simon Kuznets predicted) inequality started to drop, though it was still very high. Data for Indonesia were ambiguous, with inequality tending to rise in some sectors and decline in others, but it was clear that overall income distribution, though somewhat better than in other ASEAN states, was badly skewed and little improving.

These gross measures of national income distribution incorporated imbalances of wealth along geographic, ethnic and gender lines, which persisted throughout the postwar period, even in the socialist bloc. The usual geographical bias was in favour of the 'core area' (inhabited by the dominant political group) over outlying hills, islands, and minority areas, urban over rural, and the capital city over everything else. In part this was deliberate, the rulers rewarding themselves for ruling. In part it was the consequence of the creation of centralized infrastructure and government pricing policies tilted against agriculture, such as the notorious 'rice premium' in Thailand, an export tax (of 25–35 per cent) imposed in 1955 that had the effect of reducing prices paid to farmers over the next two decades. In part it was simply the failure to envisage or implement policies that might have led to the decentralization of wealth.

Urban bias was particularly striking in the ASEAN states, where the political centrality of the capital cities combined with nascent industrialization there. (The cities of non-communist Indochina, where foreign aid dominated national income, may have been even more favoured over the countryside.) The average income in Bangkok around 1970 was nearly three times the average rural income, four times that in the impoverished northeast; differentials in the Philippines and Malaysia were not much better. The ratio between urban and rural income in Indonesia was lower at the time, but caught up substantially by 1980, while inequality within

Jakarta reached new heights. Comparable data are not available for the socialist states, but the slow growth of their industry and their occasional attempts to favour the peasantry suggest that urban dominance was probably less pronounced there.

Seen from the periphery, all central governments appeared to be exploiting local resources, such as plantations, mines, forests, and hydroelectric potential, while ignoring local needs and trampling on local rights. Perceived economic discrimination against fringe areas underlay the Indonesian regional rebellions of 1957–8, Muslim insurgencies in the Philippines and Thailand, persistent civil warfare in Burma, and outbursts of upland protest throughout the region.

Ethnic differentials in wealth received most public attention when certain minorities enjoyed a higher standard of living than the politically dominant group. Such minorities became, as we have seen, the object of deliberate nationalist discrimination, most systematically in Malaysia, where the income gap between Chinese and Malays widened throughout the 1950s and 1960s.[29] In the aftermath of the 1969 riots the government embarked on a long-term programme favouring the *bumiputra* (literally 'princes of the land') at the expense of citizens of Chinese and Indian descent; the second 'prong' of the New Economic Policy openly aimed at 'restructuring Malaysian society to correct economic imbalance, so as to reduce and eventually eliminate the identification of race with economic function'.[30] Though falling short of its targets, the policy succeeded to some extent in closing the ethnic income gap in Malaysia over the next two decades. Elsewhere in the region the outcome of racially discriminatory policies was visible only when they resulted in emigration.

Where minorities were poorer than the dominant ethnic group, very little was done to bridge the gap. They were not, in most cases, deliberately discriminated against, just overlooked in the process of development. Temporary exceptions occurred when the districts they inhabited became politically strategic; during the Second Indochina War the peoples of the Annamese Cordillera received economic as well as political attention both from the Americans and from the Pathet Lao and Vietnamese communists. By and large, however, fringe minorities tended to fall further behind, except as they could profit by their own efforts, such as growing opium in the Golden Triangle or smuggling in the Sulu Sea. Their access to national and international markets was enhanced through improved transport; but the same roads and boats brought in lowland settlers and entrepreneurs, who tended to seize new economic opportunities at the expense of local residents, often reducing the latter to wage labourers.

The economic gender gap also apparently widened in the postwar period, though the evidence is sometimes ambiguous. Among the rural majority men generally had better access to new technologies and the new

---

[29] It should be noted, however, that ethnicity alone accounted for only a small proportion—calculated at around 10 per cent—of economic inequality within Malaysia: Sudhir Anand, *Inequality and Poverty in Malaysia: Measurement and Decomposition*, New York, 1983.
[30] *Second Malaysia Plan, 1971–1975*, 1, quoted in V. V. Bhanoji Rao, *Malaysia: Development Pattern and Policy*, Singapore, 1980, 160.

political institutions that determined economic success, while women were more likely to be left in the subsistence sector. The spread of combine harvesters and labour gangs hired by middlemen cut into the income of rural women, who had traditionally seized opportunities for communal harvesting, and when rice hullers displaced hand-pounding it hurt the poorer women who had previously pounded rice for hire. As with other kinds of inequality, the gender gap tended to narrow in times of political stress and widen when 'normality' was restored. In the DRV, women gained administrative experience in agricultural co-operatives and village councils while men were away fighting, but demobilization brought a reversion to traditional roles. A Javanese landlord in the conservative 1970s justified ending the 'open' harvest: 'We can't allow women to get such high wages and even to sneak off with part of the rice: that's not just [adil]. Previously, [between 1955 and 1965] . . . the women received far too much. Then we couldn't do anything about it. But now everything is back to normal.'[31]

Not all changes in the postwar period were disadvantageous for women. The expansion of education was accompanied by a much better balanced sex ratio within schools and universities, and in some countries females actually came to outnumber males among both students and teachers. Government service provided employment for some women, though they tended to be shunted away from the key ministries of defence, justice, foreign affairs, and the treasury toward health, education, and tourism. Light industry, particularly exports, often employed young women because their wages were low and they were thought to be docile. Women also participated in the expanding services sector as clerks, shop assistants, waitresses, and entertainers; in the RVN, Thailand, and the Philippines women had superior access to the profitable market for 'services' to American military personnel. In Singapore, high employment and the rise of modern service industries during the 1970s and 1980s greatly increased female participation in the labour force, and helped bring the average wages of women slightly closer to—though still significantly below—those of men. By and large, women with education or urban connections stood a good chance of improving their lot in the postwar period.

For the region as a whole, however, the differential between average male and female incomes remained high throughout the postwar period, and probably tended to increase slightly. Official efforts to establish greater equality between the sexes were generally feeble; communist Vietnam seems to have done marginally better than the rest, with women obtaining child care, health care, and broader employment opportunities as well as rhetorical support from the government. Unlike imbalances of class, geography, and ethnicity, however, that of gender produced no rebellions in postwar Southeast Asia, perhaps because the majority of women operated within family environments in which basic resources

---

[31] Ann Stoler, 'Class Structure and Female Autonomy in Rural Java', *Signs*, 3, 1 (1977) 74–89; Beresford, *Vietnam*, 131; Frans Hüsken, 'Landlords, Sharecroppers and Agricultural Labourers: Changing Labour Relations in Rural Java', *Journal of Contemporary Asia*, 9, 2 (1970) 140–51.

were shared reasonably equitably (if not equally), as reflected in the fact that women still tended to live longer than men.

Though there is no doubt that the rich got richer in capitalist Southeast Asia, the question of whether the poor got poorer remains in dispute. There is some evidence that the living standards of the very poor—the rural landless and urban jobless—actually declined during much of the postwar period, sometimes even when GDP per capita was growing. The real incomes of a majority or a very substantial minority of the population fell during the 1960s in Malaysia and the 1970s in Indonesia and the Philippines; in the last of these food consumption per capita dropped to levels comparable to those in Bangladesh. Even by official definitions (which varied from country to country), the proportion of the population of ASEAN countries said to be living in 'poverty' in the mid-1970s varied from 30 per cent (Singapore) to near 60 per cent (Indonesia), which suggested the magnitude of the problem. If the data existed they would probably indicate that the proportion—perhaps even the number—of Southeast Asians in absolute poverty fell between the 1930s and the 1980s, but this would be of little consolation to the tens of millions of Southeast Asians who were still destitute, suffering real malnutrition as well as relative deprivation. However defined, equity remained more an aspiration than an achievement in most of postwar Southeast Asia.

POPULATION AND THE ENVIRONMENT

Unlike economic growth, nationalism and equity, population and the environment were not objects of serious consideration for planners in early postwar Southeast Asia, though the former began to become a policy issue in the 1960s and the latter in the 1970s. Population growth stemmed from reductions in mortality of 50–80 per cent, brought about largely by improved medical and health technology. Prewar crude death rates averaged around 25–30 (per thousand population); in the immediate postwar period they remained high, particularly in Vietnam and Indonesia. By the late 1980s, however, they had dropped to between 5 and 10 except in Burma, Laos and Cambodia, where they averaged about 15. Wars and spates of fratricidal violence, such as the massacres in Indonesia in 1965–6, reversed the downward trend at times, but rarely produced net population decline. World War II did not prevent demographic increase; the population of Vietnam, north and south, continued to grow throughout the entire postwar period; only in Democratic Kampuchea and East Timor in the late 1970s did deaths actually exceed births.

Detailed analysis shows that mortality varied by country, region, and class in a predictable manner, always favouring the wealthier. This was most evident in infant mortality, where by the 1980s the number of deaths of children in their first year (per thousand births) in Cambodia and Laos was more than ten times as high as it was in Singapore. Nevertheless, the pattern of overall mortality decline suggests a break with the past that can only be explained by technological advances. Even inhabitants of poor countries enjoyed better health in general than most Southeast Asians had ever enjoyed before.

When rates of natural increase reached 2.5–3.5 per cent a year—implying a doubling of population in 20–28 years—a 'population problem' began to be perceived. Planners soon realized that substantial economic growth would be required just to keep people fed and maintain incomes at the same level, to say nothing of improving welfare. The rapid rate of increase also altered the age structure of the population, with far more young people than ever before, often 40–45 per cent of the total population being under the age of fifteen. Besides increasing the dependency ratio (proportion of non-workers to workers), this meant an accelerating demand for schools and, a decade or so later, for jobs, adding to the headaches of planners.

The attitudes of Southeast Asian governments toward the population explosion varied widely. Some welcomed it as a contribution toward national strength—Sukarno once boasted that Indonesia could support 250 million inhabitants.[32] In other countries there was draconian state intervention in family planning—in Singapore fertility actually fell below replacement levels in the 1980s. Over time, there was a growing conviction that population ought to be controlled, a viewpoint consistently pushed by international agencies, which also funded many population planning efforts. Sometimes, however, other economic and political considerations outweighed this commitment. The hope of expanding the internal market (and of increasing the demographic edge of the faster-reproducing Malays over other ethnic groups) inspired Mahathir in the early 1980s to announce an ultimate target of 70 million people for Malaysia, which had just 15 million at the time; the opposition of the Catholic Church to most forms of birth control weakened the commitment of the Philippine government to population planning, especially under the Aquino administration. In Burma and communist Vietnam, population programmes, like many other state initiatives, tended to founder in a morass of contradictions and confusions. In Thailand and Indonesia after 1970, on the other hand, the state was unambiguously committed to population control, which helped reduce birth rates to 25 and 30 (per thousand population), respectively, by the late 1980s.

Throughout the region, in fact, fertility fell substantially after 1960, clearly reflecting not just official sponsorship of family planning but a phase of the global 'demographic transition'. It was a consequence of development, not simply a precondition for it. In broad terms the 'transition' was correlated with such economic and social indicators as rising per capita income and expanded education, particularly of women. In postwar Southeast Asia many women were postponing marriage for a few years while they took advantage of new opportunities for education and employment. They were also more inclined to control their fertility deliberately

---

[32] Terence H. Hull and Ida Bagus Mantra, 'Indonesia's Changing Population', in Anne Booth and Peter McCawley, eds, *The Indonesian Economy During the Soeharto Era*, Kuala Lumpur: East Asian Social Science Monographs, 1981, 264.

and, in some cases, to leave unsatisfactory marriages, though both contraceptive use and divorce rates generally remained much lower than in the West.

Differentials in the timing of the demographic transition between countries were paralleled by differences within countries: fertility fell faster in cities than in rural areas, in wealthier than in poorer districts, and among Chinese than among indigenous populations. Since mortality also continued to fall, annual rates of natural increase slowed only slightly, from a 1960s peak of over 2.5 per cent for Southeast Asia as a whole to around 2.0 per cent in the 1980s—somewhat more manageable, but still higher than in any earlier era. Thus the regional population kept climbing, from just over 150 million at the end of World War II to well over 400 million by 1990.

Among the rural majority, the population boom meant increased competition for land and for opportunities to labour; at these rates even sparsely peopled agricultural landscapes soon became crowded. Some of the increased number remained in the villages, farming smaller and smaller plots of land or trying to underbid other hungry claimants for tenancy rights and the chance to harvest wealthier peasants' rice. Others moved on to open new fields, but wherever they moved, they were likely to impose upon terrain previously used for shifting cultivation or hunting and gathering by earlier inhabitants, forcing them in turn to abandon or modify their traditional way of life, often at considerable human cost.

Urbanization was also associated with population growth. Before World War II the largest cities in the region—Manila, Bangkok, Singapore, Rangoon, and Batavia (Jakarta)—had between half a million and a million inhabitants; by 1980 Jakarta had nearly 7 million, Metro Manila nearly 6 million, Bangkok-Thonburi nearly 5 million, Ho Chi Minh City (Saigon) and Singapore over 2 million, and Rangoon, Hanoi, Surabaya, Bandung, Medan, Semarang and Metro Cebu between 1 and 2 million inhabitants. Kuala Lumpur would also pass 1 million early in the 1980s, and Phnom Penh had swollen to more than 2 million by 1975, though it fell dramatically later that year. Regional centres such as Davao, Chiengmai, and Danang also grew far faster than their rural hinterlands, and the proportion of the total population officially classified as 'urban' doubled between 1950 and 1980, when one out of every four Southeast Asians lived in a city. There were positive aspects to this urban growth, including the expansion of consumer demand and the accumulation of that critical mass of human and financial resources needed for development. Against this could be set the constant need to provide more jobs in industry and services, as well as crowding, pollution, and a recurrent drain on rural resources.

With the closing of borders to most migrant workers, immigration declined in demographic significance in postwar Southeast Asia. The RVN received nearly a million refugees from the north, many of them Catholic, after the division of the country in 1954, integrating them reasonably well into local society, though not without some political strains. Thereafter only Thailand, which accepted hundreds of thousands of refugees from Laos and Kampuchea during the 1970s and 1980s, recorded significant immigration. Even there it was of little demographic consequence in a population increasing naturally by over one million per year; in any event the refugees were generally kept in camps (financed by international agencies) rather than allowed to mingle with the Thai.

In the quarter-century after World War II there was almost no significant emigration from Southeast Asian countries except the exodus of Catholics from the DRV and the repatriation of Indians from Burma. In the 1970s, however, all of the states of Indochina suffered extensive emigration, with Vietnam probably losing the most in absolute terms (over one million), Laos and Kampuchea more proportionally (roughly 10 per cent and 20 per cent of their total populations, respectively). Continued natural increase and some return of emigrants in the 1980s compensated for these losses in demographic terms, though it hardly replaced the talent and capital the refugees took with them. There was also much emigration of skilled and semi-skilled workers from other Southeast Asian states, particularly the Philippines and Thailand, though it, too, was of more economic than demographic consequence. Remittances from Filipinos overseas became by the early 1980s the Philippines' largest single source of foreign exchange, yet cumulative migration amounted to just 1–2 per cent of the total population, less than the number added by natural increase every year.

Internal migration, meanwhile, became more widespread and extended than ever, as structural changes altered the job market and improved transport facilitated mobility. Millions upon millions of Southeast Asians left their farms for the city or the frontier or wherever opportunity shone brighter. Much of this migration was circular, often on a seasonal basis, which had important social implications both for the villages that sent out the migrants and welcomed them back and for the cities and 'industrial' areas that received them temporarily and gave them new ideas. Traditional migration in Southeast Asia had been predominantly male, but as services and light industry developed, female migration, especially to the cities, became more important; women actually outnumbered men among migrants in several countries. Young people of both sexes often relocated to provincial or national capitals for secondary and tertiary education. Sometimes they returned, often they did not; one survey of 150 Thai intellectuals showed 145 of them living in Bangkok, though fewer than half had been born and raised there.[33]

Throughout the region cities swelled and previously forested areas were opened for settlement and agricultural development, while older farming districts lost young workers. People also moved because of war (particularly in Indochina, where almost one-fourth of the population were refugees of one kind or another by 1975), because a new dam, airport, or other development project was planned for their village, or because they worked for an ever-growing government that assigned them to service far from home. Whenever possible, Southeast Asian migrants retained ties to their places of origin, visited them at festival time, summoned families or recruited friends from them when new needs or opportunities arose, and even remitted funds to them, but in practice they became part of new social and economic communities.

[33] Girling, *Thailand*, 89–90.

Although the state often inadvertently impelled migration, most South-east Asian governments did not have a clear policy toward it. Officials were well aware of the imbalance between overcrowded cities and rural districts in some areas and apparently underpopulated districts elsewhere, but only Democratic Kampuchea, Indonesia, and communist Vietnam attempted seriously to alter population distribution. The Khmer Rouge simply evacuated the inhabitants of Phnom Penh into the countryside; this was arguably a rational policy, but it was made quite irrational by the speed and brutality with which it was undertaken. The demographic effects were drastic, enormously costly in human terms, and relatively short-lived; after 1978 the new régime encouraged re-urbanization.

Elsewhere efforts were more restrained and sustained. The attempt to relieve population pressure in Java by transplanting its inhabitants to the outer islands actually dated back to the colonial period, but was always difficult to implement on a significant scale. Through the 1950s and 1960s Indonesia's 'transmigration' programme moved only about 400,000 people, but it accelerated in the 1970s and 1980s, transferring over 4 million Javanese to South Sumatra, Kalimantan, Sulawesi, and Irian Jaya. At the same time, however, immigration from the outer islands continued, and Java's total population grew by over 45 million between 1950 and 1990. From 1961 onward the DRV promoted New Economic Zones in the uplands as target areas for migrants from the cities and crowded Red River delta; around one million were resettled over the next fifteen years. After reunification, the SRV extended this system, aiming to develop new zones in the southern highlands with settlers from the north and the bloated cities of the south. Though falling far short of their target figures, they succeeded in moving more than 2.5 million people within the next decade —but the national population grew by nearly 14 million. As with smaller resettlement schemes in Thailand, Malaysia, and the Philippines, the impact on those who moved and the sites to which they moved was profound, but the alleviation of general population pressure was minimal.

Population growth and urbanization, along with the expansion of manu-facturing and extractive industries, accelerated what became a major regional problem during this era: environmental degradation. Visitors were often most struck by the noxious air and precariously potable water of such cities as Bangkok and Manila, which contributed to the incidence of disease and undermined the quality of life of all urbanites. Even greater damage, however, was done by massive deforestation, over-fishing, irresponsible mining, and the pollution of previously productive lands and waters.

Supporters of the state tended to put most of the blame for deforestation on shifting cultivators, while its critics cited loggers as the prime culprits. In practice the relationship was often symbiotic. Large local or trans-national corporations, well-connected with the national élite, obtained legal concessions from the central government for the extraction of limited amounts of timber. This was a major area of investment throughout the region, financing development programmes and political campaigns from upper Burma to Mindanao, by way of northern Thailand, Sabah and East Kalimantan. These legal concessionaires opened roads which were used in turn by illegal loggers, often backed by venal provincial and local officials, to finish stripping the primary growth. Shifting cultivators, including many former peasants who had lost their lands to economic and demographic pressure, then followed the same roads, slashing and burning whatever was left in order to create fields where they could scratch out a living. The collection of firewood also nibbled away at the forests; dam construction drowned them; and in southern Vietnam 12 per cent of the total forest area was bulldozed or sprayed with powerful herbicides during the Second Indochina War.

Definitions and estimates of deforestation varied widely, but all suggested losses on an unprecedented scale: half of the total forest area of Thailand, the Philippines, and Java was lost within twenty or thirty years; much of the rest was degraded from primary stands of hardwood to secondary softwood; and some experts projected the complete disappearance of the Southeast Asian tropical rainforest within a generation or two. Besides losses that could be dismissed as the price of development—disfigurement of the landscape, displacement of long-time forest-dwelling peoples, and depletion of the planetary atmosphere and gene pool—forest degradation also had immediate economic consequences. It meant greatly increased erosion, which exhausted the soil within previously forested areas and led to silting and flooding in the catchment area below. By the 1970s a few planners began talking about reforestation, but it was clear that this was at best a makeshift and stopgap measure. Even in the rare cases where it was implemented, the new forests were not in any biological sense a substitute for the rich diversity of the original growth which they replaced, though they did reduce the effects of erosion and provide some pulp and firewood.

The destruction of the marine environment was less visible than that of the forests, but no less costly. High-technology oceanic fishing fleets, including huge Japanese trawlers, destroyed the piscine population indiscriminately. Local shore-based fishermen in return resorted to such techniques as blast fishing (using dynamite or percussion grenades) and chemical poisoning, which helped maintain their livelihood temporarily at the cost of destroying coral reefs and further thinning marine life. By the 1980s 95 per cent of all Philippine coral reefs had been damaged, and 75 per cent were at least half destroyed; other maritime countries lagged behind in this destruction derby, but were catching up fast. The coastal environment, including mangrove swamps, was also damaged by mine tailings, great piles of mineral debris that were swept by rains down on to agricultural lands as well, turning previously productive valleys into desolate moonscapes. Pollution from pulp mills and other processing and industrial plants flowed down rivers, into lakes and across fields, poisoning freshwater fish, who were also adversely affected by the run-off of chemical fertilizers from the rice paddies.

In their search for economic growth (and, in many cases, personal profits) the policy-makers of Southeast Asia were generally unwilling to limit the profitable extraction of resources, in spite of the fact that most were non-renewable, at least at the rate at which they were being exploited. At times they actually 'imported' pollution; the Kawasaki sintering plant in northern Mindanao, for example, existed only to process iron ore bound from Australia to Japan without offending Japanese environmentalists, who had objected to its unhealthy presence in their own country. In the short run, Southeast Asian choices may have been economically defensible, though the costs of increased health care and of agricultural production lost by pollution, siltation, and flooding have never been adequately reckoned.[34] In the long run, however, the half-century after World War II may chiefly be remembered as the beginning of the end for the natural environment of Southeast Asia.

SOCIAL STRUCTURES AND STRATEGIES

World War II and postwar developments constantly challenged traditional Southeast Asian belief in natural hierarchy and community, already eroded by colonialism and capitalism. Natural hierarchy—the assumption that all living things existed in an innate relationship of ranked inequality—was challenged first by the rhetoric of democracy, which emphasized participation in decision-making rather than obedience and spoke of the equality of all men (and, in its extreme versions, women as well). Distinctions based on birth were increasingly difficult to uphold, at least in public; the deference due to kings, nobles, and hereditary headmen did not disappear, but it was no longer unquestioned.

The vision of a harmonious community of reciprocal obligations, beginning with, but not limited to, kin and the village, also came under ideological attack in postwar Southeast Asia. In the traditional ideal, any accession of wealth ought to be shared within the community; any unexpected need might be met from the resources of the community. (Outsiders were different; one economic advantage that aliens, such as the Chinese, were believed to have, in fact, was that they were not bound by local constraints.) Now this community was challenged by attempts to invoke higher values to which local obligations would be subordinate. Individual liberty—the right of a person to earn, to speak, to worship, and to do whatever else he or she saw fit, regardless of other claims—was preached by foreign advisers and enshrined in modern education. American-trained social scientists told Filipinos that they could achieve their potential only if they left their home villages, where personal obligations wore them down: 'If you want to get up, get out!' Larger entities such as the nation itself, the international proletariat, and the global brotherhood of Islam, also laid claim to Southeast Asian loyalties.

Southeast Asians encountered these ideological challenges amid political, demographic and economic changes that in themselves tended to undermine traditional institutions. Once, according to Vietnamese proverb, the emperor's laws had stopped at the village wall, but in the postwar era nothing could impede the penetration of the state apparatus into the

---

[34] Even in terms of maximizing the economic exploitation of forest resources, it has been shown that state policies in Malaysia, Indonesia, and the Philippines were extremely ill-advised. Robert Repetto and Malcolm Gillis, eds, *Public Policies and the Misuse of Forest Resources: A World Resources Institute Book*, Cambridge, UK, 1988.

village, undercutting local self-sufficiency and making access to higher political power more important than ever. On the national level, men who commanded mass support or the loyalty of troops or party cadres vied for power with traditional aristocrats, generally winning except when charismatic royal or princely rulers like Sihanouk and Tunku Abdul Rahman were able to exploit their own populist appeal. Locally, traditional élites had to forge links with the national apparatus or lose out to more adaptive rivals. As the state also engrossed an increasing share of production through taxation, it could reward its favourites through redistribution of central revenues, thus making them less dependent upon the communities in which they resided.

Demographic developments attenuated traditional community ties in various ways. Migration, facilitated by improved transportation, removed many Southeast Asians to cities or frontiers where they lived among strangers who did not recognize the same hierarchies or share the same values. The villages from which the emigrants departed were also affected by the loss of community members (particularly young adults), and if some of their places were filled it was by newcomers with strange customs and unpredictable loyalties. Meanwhile, rapid population growth not only increased the sheer size of almost all communities, weakening face-to-face contact, but also made labour abundant, and so caused it to depreciate relative to land and capital. Landlords and factory owners felt less necessity to maintain relations of reciprocity and respect with individual tenants or workers when they could easily replace them.

In the economic sphere, there was not only increasing inequality but an attrition of the personal relationships that had traditionally reinforced community ties. More and more Southeast Asians, previously accustomed to flexible working conditions arranged on an individual basis, were drawn into wage labour, which demanded the disciplined acceptance of impersonal rules. This was particularly true in extractive industries and the booming cities, where wage labour dominated the lives of miners, factory workers, construction labourers, and government clerks, and came to shape the outlook even of many who were employed in the 'informal sector'.[35] Though it often involved health risks and exploitative practices (particularly for women and children), it generally represented a profitable alternative to unemployment or precarious self-employment. Wage labour also made considerable inroads in rural areas, as a rising proportion of Southeast Asians lost regular access to land, even as tenants, and had to earn their living by selling their labour to the highest bidder. Since double-cropping tended to increase the demand for hired help, those who exchanged marginal subsistence farming for wage labour were not necessarily worse off in monetary terms. Socially, however, the gap widened between those with access to land and those without.

The decline of local markets similarly counterpoised economic gain with loss of social cohesion. In these markets, traditional gathering points for

---

[35] Michael Pinches, '"All that we have is our muscle and sweat": The Rise of Wage Labour in a Manila Squatter Community', in Pinches and Salim Lakha, eds, *Wage Labour and Social Change: The Proletariat in Asia and the Pacific*, Clayton: Monash University Centre of Southeast Asian Studies, Monash Papers on Southeast Asia no. 16, 1987, 103–40.

local produce and distribution points for consumer goods, raw economic forces were socially mediated. Prices were arrived at in discrete bargaining sessions that reflected not just supply and demand but personal relationships between buyers and sellers. In the postwar period these markets became less and less relevant: wholesalers or government agencies contracted for farmgate delivery of produce, and consumers sought a better selection of goods in nearby towns or even city supermarkets. Prices tended either to be fixed, or to be negotiated between virtual strangers, so the role of markets in structuring human interdependence was reduced.

Great disparities of power and wealth were not new to Southeast Asia, but traditionally they had been softened by respect, reciprocity, and redistribution, at least in theory. In the postwar capitalist states, however, economic inequality was growing even as traditional status markers were weakening, with the result that people were increasingly defined by their economic position. This new stratification was most visible at the top, where a class of Southeast Asians (including local Chinese) with spectacularly conspicuous wealth emerged, more reminiscent of pre-colonial kings than the prosperous but subordinated élites operating under colonialism. Some of these super rich, like the Sultan of Brunei, were traditional rulers, but others found their way to great wealth through politics (Marcos), the military (Ibnu Sutowo), export production (Lee Kong Chian), retail trade (the Chirathivat family), banking (Chin Sophonpanich), utilities (the Lopez family) or even entertainment (the Shaw brothers). The visible discrepancy between such concentrations of wealth and the misery in which so many other Southeast Asians lived was an obvious source of social tension.

More significant in terms of overall social structure was the increasing number of Southeast Asians who lived comfortably from property, salaries, or business, and did not have to worry about where their food or rent was coming from. (There was some upward mobility, but in most cases those who rose farthest not only exhibited commercial and political acumen, but chose their parents well. Very few exemplars of 'rags to riches' actually started out in anything resembling rags.) Even when their income was rurally derived, they tended to congregate in the growing cities. The urban élite, though small and weak by comparison with the middle classes of the West, was still larger, richer, and politically more consequential than any such group the region had known before. Much intellectual effort, especially on the left, was devoted to defining the precise relationship of this class to the means of production, but they were actually easier to identify in terms of consumption: Western-style clothes, access to tertiary education and private vehicles, occupation of solidly-built houses with modern conveniences, and employment of domestic servants. Many of them also enlivened their discourse with a smattering of English, the new lingua franca of the region. Often they worked in the high-rise international-style office buildings that characterized the great cities of Southeast Asia, which little by little became more like each other and less like the countrysides from which they had originally sprung.

Without the need to struggle for mere survival, the urban élite developed concerns that increasingly overlapped with those of the bourgeoisie elsewhere: education, culture, democracy, development, fashion, law and order, and the quality of life. Some of them evinced liberal values, which took political form in the non-violent revolutions in Thailand in 1973 and the Philippines in 1986, as well as movements for greater democratic freedoms elsewhere. Their concerns were reflected in Intje Hassan's lament over Jakarta:

> Jakarta . . .
> This is no slum
> Only a village
> Four hundred years old
> Dipped in modernity
> Granted a . . .
> Quantum of kilowatts
> For streetlamps
> To chase shadows . . .
>
> Prostitutes . . .
> in darkness, waiting
> Nightclubs and casinos opening
> To pass the leisure time
> School, as partial gift
> To develop ambitions later
> Still empty and unanswered
> And tomorrow . . .
> The frustrated generation, waiting—
> Of enormous problems to overcome—
> in the developed city.[36]

Another example is Catherine Lim's gentle satire on official values in Singapore:

Mr Sai Koh Phan . . . looks at the many campaign posters around, and the pride and gratitude once more surges into his heart, in recollection of years of total fidelity to their admonitions:

> Don't litter
> Don't spit
> Don't stop at two
> Don't dirty public toilets
> Don't sniff glue
> Don't waste water
> Be courteous
> Eat more wheat
> Eat frozen meat
> Don't breed mosquitoes
> Don't change lanes while driving

---

[36] 'The Developed City' (1972), quoted in Gerald H. Krausse, 'From Sunda Kelapa to Jabotabek: A Socio-Cultural Profile of Indonesia's Capital City', in Krausse, ed., *Urban Society in Southeast Asia, II: Political and Cultural Issues*, Hong Kong: Asian Research Service, Asian Studies Monograph Series, 1988, 159–60.

Say 'Good morning' and 'Thank you' in Mandarin
Don't fill your plates to overflowing at buffet lunches
Don't be 'kia su'
Plant a tree
Don't grow long hair
Don't grow
Don't[37]

Below this comfortable class were the numerous urban poor, who, like the élite, to some extent emulated the fashions of the West by wearing T-shirts, drinking Coca-Cola, and listening to pop music. There was no real economic convergence, however; the gap between rich and poor actually widened, with the juxtaposition of luxury and squalor particularly glaring in Manila and Bangkok. The poor were divisible in terms of both level and security of income; in many cities the proletariat who received regular wages or salaries in the formal sector were a minority of the labour force, with the majority being casuals or self-employed, fitting into the interstices of the urban economy as best they could: day labourers, street hawkers, taxi and pedicab drivers, piece-work producers, beggars, guides and would-be gigolos. Some lived in huge government-built blocks of flats, others in squatter settlements; some were brand-new immigrants from the provinces, others were city-born and bred. Along with differences in employment and ethnicity, this made for a wide diversity of interests and a corresponding lack of social and political unity most of the time.

Social stratification was generally less visible in rural areas, where even the well-to-do were often poor by external standards and the consumption of modern goods and services was less conspicuous. Out in the provinces it was sometimes still possible to believe in the pure 'traditional' village, unchanged from time immemorial, sharing poverty as it shared everything else. Local studies throughout the region, however, suggest that in the course of economic development the gap between the relatively well-off and the truly poor was widening, exacerbated by state policies that deliberately courted the rural élite at the expense of their tenants and neighbours. This was accompanied by a general deterioration of relationships of reciprocal obligation within the village, which struck at the heart of the traditional sense of community.

The local community—that face-to-face group in which all knew each other and accepted their mutual responsibilities to each other—had already been attenuated by migration to the frontier and the city. Within the village, however, there persisted conventions of a 'moral economy' in which custom and propriety set limits on avarice. This ideal had long been honoured in the breach, but seems to have been eroded even further in the postwar period, particularly in the 1970s, when new agricultural technologies and enhanced state power allowed landowners, no longer dependent on local labour or goodwill, to ignore the claims of the poor. In Java, harvests that had once been open to all were reserved for a selected few; in

---

[37] From 'The Malady and the Cure' in *O Singapore*, Singapore, 1989. *Kia su*, literally 'afraid to lose', may also be translated as 'afraid of getting involved' or 'afraid of losing face'.

Malaysia, machinery replaced casual local labour; in the Philippines, tenants were evicted to make room for export plantations; everywhere there were complaints that alms and low-interest loans were less frequently bestowed. The logic of capitalism tended to reduce previous patron–client reciprocity to account-book calculations of profit or loss.

The concepts of 'dual economy' and 'plural society' were hard to sustain in postwar Southeast Asia, as both economic and cultural links between various segments of national populations became stronger and more visible. Subsistence farmers were forced into the market economy by higher taxes and rents, or lured in by education and consumer goods; soft drinks and rubber-soled sneakers reached where development experts could not penetrate. The diffusion of national cultures through schools, movies, and the radio tended to homogenize previously diverse societies, and led to the decline of many local arts, customs and dialects.

Even in the remotest hills and islands, traditional structures and values were under attack. Upland communities generally lacked the military capacity to cope with the private armies of logging companies, the legal resources to cope with intrusive government agencies, and the commercial acumen to cope with lowland merchants. The result was often economic dislocation and demographic decline. The only way some of the smaller groups could physically survive was by accepting deculturation and the eventual extinction, not just of individual communities, but of their entire tribal identity.

In socialist Southeast Asia, the challenges to hierarchy were even stronger. Ideological attacks on aristocracy and customary rights were pressed more vigorously than under capitalist régimes, as the militant egalitarian state claimed uncontested supremacy over all rivals. Temporary tactical accommodations were sometimes made with 'patriotic' mandarins, monks, or minorities, but the logic of socialism implied the eventual reduction or homogenization of these groups. The prerogatives of traditional élites were systematically whittled away, along with most of their economic base. In their place emerged an 'official class' of bureaucrats, military officers, and party members, whose prestige and economic base derived from their position in the state apparatus. Our information on this new class remains extremely sketchy, but it seems to have enjoyed, like ruling élites elsewhere, privileged access to travel, education, and certain consumer goods. Unlike them, however, it could not overtly accumulate great wealth or reinvest in profit-making enterprises. Whether, as is likely, its members found ways of transmitting their privileges to their descendants is something that at present we simply do not know; the party represented a hierarchy that was supposed to be self-renewing but not actually hereditary.

As for the traditional community, in principle it too had to be sacrificed for the greater good of the nation and the socialist future, as the imposition of agricultural collectivization on the various states of Indochina made clear. The Khmer Rouge in particular were ruthless opponents of the claims of the village and the extended family. Upland societies in socialist Southeast Asia were also profoundly challenged by war, economic strains, and intrusive officials preaching the priority of development and the superiority of lowland civilization. If some of these societies remained slightly less transformed and deculturated than their counterparts in the capitalist states, it reflected differences in communications and effective political and economic penetration more than in actual policy.

Although challenges to hierarchy and community in Southeast Asia were often triggered by Western contact and associated with Western values, they were primarily mounted by Southeast Asians who had internalized the ideas and institutions that they were propagating. Some scholars overlooked this fact, their own judgements distorted by romantic prejudices. In moving from rural to urban poverty, for example, many Southeast Asians gave up picturesque bamboo houses in a lush green landscape for rude hovels made out of packing crates and corrugated iron in apparently unmitigated squalor. Observers tended to interpret this as a clear worsening of circumstances, yet such moves were often viewed by the migrants as steps toward a better life for both themselves and their children; there were 'slums of hope' as well as 'slums of despair'. Similarly, *kerajaan* (royal government) in northern Sumatra was swept away in the 'social revolution' of the 1940s not by Westerners or conscious Westernizers, but by local Acehnese, Bataks and Malays who had no use for their traditional rulers.[38]

To some Southeast Asians the weakening of hierarchy and community implied a number of desirable ends: equality, personal freedom, dignity, mobility, and, above all, economic opportunity. This was most visible among national leaders and the prosperous urban élites, who were almost unanimous in favour of 'modernization', despite occasional lamentation for their vanishing cultural heritage. Capitalists and socialists argued bitterly with each other on many other points but agreed that the future was different from, and more important than, the past. Farther down the social scale, a similar outlook was implied when the poor voluntarily left their villages to seek a better life elsewhere or forsook traditional rituals in favour of modern (often Western) icons. The rising demand of women for education and greater participation in the public sphere represented another aspect of the indigenous challenge to traditional authority.

Social scientists of the 1950s and 1960s devoted much attention to this topic, seeing in 'modern' values the key to automatic improvement both in economics and politics. Secularism and rationality were contrasted with 'traditional' beliefs in supernatural powers and mystical processes; their eventual triumph was assured, though it might be hastened or retarded. The hindsight of twenty years has suggested that this triumph was neither inevitable nor necessarily beneficial, and the debate over exactly how the spread of 'modern' values might be monitored and promoted was in certain respects one of the least productive Western intellectual efforts ever devoted to Southeast Asia. (Recent studies have focused instead on the economic advantages putatively associated with 'Confucian' culture, an

[38] Aprodicio A. Laquian, 'The Asian City and the Political Process', in D. J. Dwyer, ed., *The City as a Centre of Change in Asia*, Hong Kong 1972, 41–55 (employing a distinction first articulated by C. Stokes); Anthony Reid, *The Blood of the People: Revolution and the End of Traditional Rule in Northern Sumatra*, Kuala Lumpur, 1979.

equally dubious endeavour.) But the phenomenon that they attempted to analyse was no less real for being difficult to define; in the postwar period significant numbers of Southeast Asians did in fact perceive the world, and their role in it, in new ways.

Although there were some efforts to retain symbolic hierarchy in the political sphere—particularly in the systematic glorification of the Thai monarchy—there was little evident desire to revert to a world of ascriptive authority. In its place, where there was not actual equality, stood an implied hierarchy of achievement, based on military prowess, political dedication, education or entrepreneurship. When skilled politicians like Suharto and Ne Win could invoke a regal style of rule, radiating 'natural' authority capable of either great benevolence or irresistible anger, they got the best of both worlds. Socialists and feminists also attempted to use history to justify their own visions of the future, arguing that in the good old days before colonialism and 'feudalism' there had been no private property and women were the equal of men. For many Southeast Asians traditions of hierarchy and community had been reduced to symbols to be manipulated toward more modern ends.

When traditional communities faltered, Southeast Asians invented new institutions to serve in their place. Migrants often created new locational groups based in urban villages (*kampung*) and squatter settlements or frontier towns. Such groups were weaker than traditional villages, as they lacked the full weight of custom and authority and possessed no village shrine or common burial ground. In time, however, some of them developed a vitality of their own, sponsoring ritual feasts, providing local services, building community projects, organizing youth activities, and creating networks of credit, alliance, and kinship almost as complex as those in the villages left behind. Normally these groups operated with state tolerance or backing, but upon occasion they could help the neighbourhood defend itself against government-backed intruders or developers, as Manila's Zone One Tondo Organization (ZOTO) demonstrated in the early 1970s.[39]

Other Southeast Asians devoted their energies to vocational groups, including professional organizations, labour unions, and student movements. Some found that religious organizations, whether based in relatively new sects (such as Hoa Hao or the Iglesia Ni Kristo) or in revitalized older faiths, gave them a home beyond their home. These provided, in addition to whatever deeper religious significance they embodied, an opportunity for regular contact with other like-minded people, a chance to share worldly goods and stand shoulder-to-shoulder in a worthy struggle. For some adherents they were a kind of enclave within an anonymous urban environment; for others they represented a counter-culture within villages dominated by those who professed a majority faith.

Politics served the same social functions for other Southeast Asians.

---

[39] Patrick Guinness, *Harmony and Hierarchy in a Javanese Kampung*, Singapore: Asian Studies Association of Australia, Southeast Asia Publications Series no. 11, 1986; *Reason to Hope: A Study of Five Urban Poor Communities in Metro Manila*, Manila: Share and Care Apostolate for Poor Settlers, 1983.

Belief in the 'imagined community' of the nation found institutional expression in political parties ranging from the Vietminh to UMNO (the United Malays National Organization), each with auxiliary women's groups and youth groups as a framework for social gathering. For those to whom the nation—despite state sponsorship and the dissemination of official culture—was an unwieldy or uncongenial focus for the community they sought, the politics of opposition sometimes offered affiliation with a set of associates sharing an ideal. Indigenous minorities found and reasserted their identity as 'Moros', 'Igorots', 'Isan', 'Karen', or *ana chu* (sons of the mountain) through supra-village organizations in the postwar period. The potential of local branches of political parties to offer social cohesion and cultural meaning independent of state orthodoxy was suggested by the ban on them in New Order Indonesia.

To the extent that all of these groupings were voluntary, they allowed greater freedom of self-definition. Those who had once been simply 'Chinese' or *orang Kelantan* (people of Kelantan) now had the option of trying instead to define themselves primarily as residents of a certain urban neighbourhood or as 'Malaysians' or 'socialists' or 'Muslims' or 'professionals'. A few of the new organizations attempted to replace the traditional community entirely, creating spiritual and economic brotherhoods complete unto themselves; but most simply supplemented or combined with it, adding a dimension that had been erased or eroded by other pressures. Many of the groups tended to be unstable; Filipinos described the speed with which they appeared and disappeared as like grass fire (*ningas kugon*).

In socialist Southeast Asia, the range of permissible alternatives was more limited. Religious and political organizations outside the state orthodoxy were discouraged or prohibited entirely, and all other groupings were brought under state or party control as much as possible. Anecdotal evidence suggests that the results of this attempted state monopoly of 'community' varied widely. Sometimes an agricultural collective, a neighbourhood committee, a military unit or a women's group would be infused with a genuine sense of harmony and give meaning to people's lives. More often such organizations were subject to manipulation by party officials or petty bureaucrats, and so became, in social terms, hollow shells. Descriptions of life in communist Vietnam suggest that in times of war (1946–54, 1965–75) patriotism tended to fill state-sponsored organizations with a sense of fellowship and purpose that emptied rapidly once the fighting was over.

Along with welcoming the new, many Southeast Asians clung to the old, retaining what they could of traditional hierarchy and community. At a national level, though royalty and aristocracy lost their power to command, they retained considerable influence. In rural areas millions of people lived in ancestral villages and reaffirmed ancestral ways, exhibiting not blind traditionalism but prudent conservatism. Most Southeast Asians were well aware that new opportunities and arrangements did not in fact benefit everyone equally. Opposition to the introduction of farm machinery was based on the sound calculation that it would displace labour;

scepticism as to the wisdom and benevolence of public officials was all too frequently justified; and the perception of modern education as a potential threat to customary values was largely correct.

The most vocal reassertion of traditional community values came from certain religious groups. Islam, they claimed, meant giving alms and not profiteering; Buddhism implied charity and the rejection of material accumulation; Christianity included the gospel of social justice, in which all believers were brothers. This kind of appeal lent force to such organizations as the Partai Islam (PAS) in Malaysia, the Federation of Buddhists in Thailand, and the Basic Christian Communities in the Philippines. They had only limited success, however, and to some extent their position as defenders of tradition was paradoxical. They were themselves modern organizations, designed to fight modern political and economic battles, and when they did win, it was a victory for a new community, not the old one.

With virtually all other political leaders favouring modernization, overt resistance to it was difficult, and most Southeast Asians could deploy only what James C. Scott described as the 'weapons of the weak': avoidance, non-compliance, sabotage, and veiled insolence.[40] To a considerable extent they succeeded in slowing down the march of what passed for progress, as shown by comparisons between the visions of planners (indigenous and foreign) and what actually happened to their plans. The village proved far more resilient than anyone had imagined. Southern Vietnamese peasants resisted both the 1960s 'strategic hamlet' programme of the RVN and the collectivization efforts of the SRV a decade later, and throughout the region efforts of landlords to alter traditional leasing and harvesting arrangements had to be postponed or reversed, at least temporarily. Over the long run, however, this was a rearguard action fought against a force advancing on many different fronts: official policy, educational expansion, population pressure, the extension of transport and communication networks, and the imperatives of economic growth, from the green revolution to hydroelectric and mining development. Eventually most of the landlords and planners and developers had their way.

When they were unable to ward off the challenges to traditional hierarchy and community, Southeast Asians had to adapt to the new. At worst, violent crime, prostitution, drug addiction, and psychological disorders suggested anomie. Certainly no description of the region that did not include the armed gangs of Mindanao, the bar girls of Bangkok, and the heroin addicts of Saigon could be regarded as complete. It is not easy, however, to confirm that such activities were actually on the increase in the postwar ear (compare banditry and opium use in the colonial period); nor can it be assumed that they were all dysfunctional. If a waitress or an armed guard was an aspirant to upward mobility, why not a prostitute or a professional 'goon'? Deculturation, drug abuse, and severe mental disturbances, on the other hand, were clearly unhealthy concomitants of change.

---

40 Scott, *Weapons of the Weak: Everyday Forms of Peasant Resistance*, New Haven, 1985; cf. Scott and Benedict J. Tria Kerkvliet, eds, *Everyday Forms of Peasant Resistance in South-East Asia*, London, 1986.

Most Southeast Asians, however, achieved some kind of compromise between retaining old communities and accepting the new. They still lived in the village, but sometimes travelled beyond it, or even worked elsewhere for a while. They kept going to the *wayang* (puppet theatre) and temple festivals, but also listened to transistor radios and read *komiks*. They formed patron–client alliances with local officials, not as an anachronistic holdover from the past, but as a creative response to the fact that the state was a growing source of benefits. They increased the flexibility of their discourse, using deferential styles to those who still appreciated it and more democratic forms of address where appropriate. They ploughed behind water buffaloes and rode Hondas; they participated in *slametan* (ritual feasts) and mass political rallies; they attended both the herbalist and the government clinic. Even under communism they adapted traditional institutions to their needs, regardless of official policy:

> If you come to Thai Nguyen City
> You will see an awful sight,
> For the market, morn till night,
> Bustles with venality.
> Anything you want to buy
> On the sidewalk is displayed—
> Even what the state forbade.
> God may know how, but not I![41]

One element of continuity in their lives was kinship. The Southeast Asian family had been subjected by migration to the strain of distance. It had been denigrated by modernizers and attacked by the Khmer Rouge. But it survived the decline of the village community and permeated many of the newer organizations that replaced it. Politically, postwar Southeast Asia was characterized by nepotism, even incipient dynasticism; Ferdinand and Imelda Romualdez Marcos merely carried to excess what other regional leaders more quietly aspired to. In business, family loyalties accounted for much of what unsympathetic Westerners saw as 'corruption', but locals regarded as simple fulfilment of familial obligations. Micro-studies of geographic and social mobility show the importance of kinship there; most Southeast Asians who moved to cities or frontiers did so along 'chains' of kinship, while those who found new work often did so through the good offices of relatives. Where family connections were not widespread enough to achieve social ends, they were extended artificially; 'kinship', noted Jeremy H. Kemp, '[was] far too valuable to be limited to the facts of biology!'[42] The persistence of traditional kinship does not refute the significance of social change, any more than the persistence of scholastic philosophy and witch-burning in seventeenth-century Europe refutes the significance of the Renaissance. If anything, it acts as confirmation;

---

[41] Nhu Van Lo, 'Flea Market in Thai Nguyen' (1977), quoted in Nguyen Van Canh (with Earle Cooper), *Vietnam Under Communism, 1975–1982*, Stanford, 1983, 43–4.
[42] 'The Manipulation of Personal Relations: From Kinship to Patron–Clientage', in Hans ten Brummelhuis and Kemp, eds, *Strategies and Structures in Thai Society*, Amsterdam: Universiteit van Amsterdam, Antropologish-Sociologisch Centrum, Publikatieserie Vakgroep Zuid- en Zuidoost-Azie, no. 31, 1984, 55–69.

kinship may have persisted simply because it was the only constant in an otherwise kaleidoscopic world. Its reliability, at a time when old values were being questioned and old institutions were crumbling, gave kinship its ongoing importance.

PROTEST AND REBELLION

A final strategy was open to Southeast Asians who could neither sustain the old ways nor tolerate the new: protest and—when protest was unavailing—rebellion. Perhaps at no time in its history had the region heard so many expressions of discontent as in the postwar era, though some of these undoubtedly reflected rising expectations and improved communications rather than declining socio-economic circumstances. Protests took a variety of forms, including petitions, rallies, strikes, marches, boycotts, and a host of symbolic actions. Buddhist monks in Saigon burned themselves to death to protest against the policies of Ngo Dinh Diem; white-collar workers in Makati shredded telephone directories for yellow confetti to honour the martyrdom of 'Ninoy' Aquino. Riots, which rocked most of the great cities at one time or another, may also be considered as a form of protest, though once under way they often seemed to transcend the specific grievances that sparked them.

Protest movements were more common in cities than in rural areas, in part because of such safety from reprisal as the relative anonymity of urban activism might provide. Mostly they were reactive responses to developments seen as harmful to the immediate interests of urbanites, rather than part of a coherent strategy for long-term change. Southeast Asians protested against rising rice prices, bus fares, and school fees; the presence of exploitative aliens (Chinese traders, Japanese investors, American troops); and threats to political or religious freedom (stolen elections, invasions of monasteries). Such unrest rarely escalated into full-scale rebellion, though when it was supported or instigated by elements of the elite it was capable of toppling already shaky governments, as happened in the RVN in 1963, Thailand in 1973, and the Philippines in 1986. Usually, however, the police and armed forces were able to contain or roll these protests back while higher authorities conceded little or nothing.

In rural areas the success rate of peaceful protests was even lower, as it was generally more difficult for the protestors to co-ordinate their actions and easier for the state to suppress them without fear of offending national or international opinion. For many Southeast Asian peasants, therefore, there appeared to be little middle ground between employing the 'weapons of the weak' (including migration) and actual armed rebellion; those without military capacity had little choice but to be polite and avoid direct confrontation.

Although many protest movements in Southeast Asia began as spontaneous responses to local grievances, those that were sustained over the course of years generally had a core identity based on religion, ethnic minority status, or economic class. Armed challenges to the state by religious movements ranged in scale from Darul Islam, which mobilized millions of Sundanese against the Republic of Indonesia for fourteen years (1948–62) to cults like Lapiang Malaya, which engaged the Republic of the Philippines in a single day of conflict (in 1967), at a cost of fewer than one hundred casualties.[43] Other religious leaders—Buddhist monks, Muslim *ulamā*, Catholic priests—also engaged in non-violent protests against the state from time to time. The spiritual meaning of these movements is not the concern here: all that is noted is the possible, though generally unacknowledged, link between religious protest and diffuse socio-economic discontent.

The causes of most separatist movements were relatively easy to discern, as were the limits to their strength. Ethnic minorities far from the national capital felt—often correctly—that they were politically slighted and economically exploited by the dominant ethnic group, and believed that only through independence or communal autonomy could justice be achieved. By virtue of the fact that they were minorities, outnumbered and outgunned, they could hardly hope to win, yet the strength of their commitment (often reinforced by the excesses of government forces) and their familiarity with local terrain allowed some of the movements to persist over decades. Parts of Burma were in a state of active rebellion during the entire postwar period. Separatist activities elsewhere were intermittent but virtually inextinguishable, now flaring up, now in remission, but never wholly healed. Rebellion seemed particularly recurrent where physical remoteness from the centre was coupled with religious differentiation, as among Muslims in southern Thailand and the Philippines, Christians in Maluku, and animists in Irian Jaya and the highlands of Indochina.

Rebellion based on class, rather than ethnicity, potentially had a wider demographic base, as well as access to a systematic ideology and structure of resistance, which most separatist movements lacked. By any calculation most Southeast Asians were poor, and the presence of wealthy landlords and capitalists in their midst must have suggested that their poverty was due in part to exploitation. Marxist logic indicated as early as the late 1940s that Southeast Asians should be ready to throw off their chains, yet of the many rebellions that occurred throughout the region at that time only those in Indochina ultimately succeeded. Elsewhere the early uprisings were defeated; though some of these movements made later comebacks— particularly in Indonesia in the early 1960s and the Philippines in the 1970s and 1980s—the history of postwar Southeast Asia in general confounded those whose analysis was predicated on the centrality of class and the class struggle.

Class, as a category of analysis, can be useful to scholars of Southeast Asia, provided that it does not capsize on the attempt to specify the precise relationship between 'feudalism' and capitalism and makes due allowance for the occasionally opposing interests of class fractions: 'national' and

[43] Karl D. Jackson, *Traditional Authority, Islam, and Rebellion: A Study of Indonesian Political Behavior*, Berkeley, 1980; David R. Sturtevant, 'Rizalistas—Contemporary Revitalization Movements in the Philippines', in *Agrarian Unrest in the Philippines*, Athens: Ohio University Monographs in International Studies, Southeast Asia Series no. 8, 1969, 18–30.

'comprador' bourgeoisies, poor tenants and landless labourers, etc. Where it falters is as a phenomenological category, a representation of indigenous consciousness. Southeast Asians were certainly aware of gradations of prestige and social ranking, and at the most basic level consistently distinguished between 'big people' and 'little people'. What they did not do, by and large, was identify their own interests with those of a broader class and then act in accordance with those collective interests.

Although they avoided the term itself, there was probably greater 'class' solidarity within the upper strata than among the masses. Despite rhetorical flourishes in favour of democracy, and the occasional defection of individual members, the ruling élites were essentially unified on basic principles of governance. Land, they agreed, should not be redistributed without compensation; no need to look further for an explanation for the failure of land reform in most of Southeast Asia. Labour should be disciplined and denied effective participation in either economic or political decision-making—and so it was, even in nominally progressive states such as Singapore. Temporary deviations from these principles in Thailand after 1973 and the Philippines after 1986 were corrected when it was fully recognized just what was at stake. Perhaps the most successful demonstration of upper-class solidarity was the Alliance (and its successors) in Malaya, which overrode ethnic differences to maintain a political system based firmly on the protection of property and order.

Among the masses it was more problematical. Widespread horizontal solidarity was extraordinarily difficult to achieve, even in peaceful protest movements, and in the search for new forms of social organization most Southeast Asians seemed to prefer either vertical links based on patron–client relationships, or limited egalitarian groupings based on personal acquaintance. Even when a vanguard party spelled it out for them, most Southeast Asian workers and peasants were reluctant to accept the abstraction of a 'working class', or at any event to commit themselves to its defence. The Malayan Communist Party was unable to transcend its ethnic base in the Chinese community, and the PKP (Partido Komunista ng Pilipinas) and PKI (Partai Komunis Indonesia) had great difficulty transcending their geographical bases in central Luzon and Java, respectively. Similarly, whereas local strikes were occasionally successful, general strikes and boycotts were not, and those legal political parties that professed a class basis rarely accomplished much in the electoral arena.

Why did such movements fail? To some extent it was the weight of traditional cultural values. Class consciousness was profoundly strange; to understand human relations as based primarily on the opposition of economic roles required overcoming centuries of Southeast Asian thinking about the nature of the world. To some extent it was due to the complexity of new economic and social structures. In the cities there were many different kinds of workers with different interests, while even in rural areas landless labourers, seasonal workers and part-time proletarians were mixed in with the familiar class of tenants. At the same time the expanded involvement of the state and large corporations in the local economy increased the physical and social distance between ordinary workers or peasants and those who controlled their means of livelihood. It was harder to comprehend and confront a governmental development agency, a transnational corporation, or the World Bank than an exploitative landlord or factory owner, and it was harder to develop solidarity with workers five hundred miles away than with fellow tenants.

Class consciousness was also undermined by rising prosperity, in that many of the poor, though more exploited than ever (in the sense of retaining less of the value they helped to create), were actually better off in material terms than they had been before. A different kind of prosperity helped to explain why most military personnel failed to identify with the labouring classes into which they were born. (Officers were usually recruited from the propertied classes.) The state was usually a reliable paymaster, sometimes even a generous one, and in much of the region soldiering also offered occasional opportunities for the receipt of bribes or even armed robbery. It was thus in the economic interest of the troops either to support the government or to try to remove it in favour of one that might treat them even more kindly.

It was official mystification and repression, above all, that inhibited the development of class consciousness in Southeast Asia. At an intellectual level the capitalist states followed colonial precedent in denying that 'class' existed as a significant social factor. In its place they offered either myths of national unity or divisions based on ethnicity which left the rulers among the majority (e.g., Malays) rather than the minority (e.g., landlords). In a sense, every discussion of race or 'the Chinese problem' was a distraction from more dangerous questioning of the socio-economic structure. Many governments censored publications that openly challenged the official orthodoxy, and often persecuted the authors as well. The term 'class' itself became suspect, associated with Marxism and therefore, by implication, with subversion.

Even where the press was relatively free, however, as in the Philippines (before and after martial law), those who tried to translate class consciousness into action were subject to harassment or worse. Almost the surest way to invite trouble in Southeast Asia was to be a union or community organizer, even one committed to peaceful change. Effective unions, both industrial and agrarian, were systematically broken up by legal restriction, bribery or violence; some were replaced by tame unions that could be trusted not to ask more than the government or the company was willing to concede; others simply vanished. Organizers were fired, beaten up, blacklisted, imprisoned, or even killed; if they enjoyed some kind of religious immunity, they were put under great pressure to stay out of politics. The human rights record of the independent states of Southeast Asia, never bright, was particularly dim when it came to activities designed to empower ordinary workers or peasants.

In the face of implacable hostility to peaceful change, actual rebellion was an act of desperation. The most convincing analyses of leftist insurgencies—e.g., Jeffrey Race's study of the National Liberation Front in southern Vietnam and Benedict J. Kerkvliet's study of the Huk rebellion in the Philippines—suggest that they were rooted in local economic and social injustice. Those who joined the movement and risked their lives for it (not necessarily the party leaders, who were often from the disaffected élite) did so because they saw the modicum of economic security and dignity that they had traditionally enjoyed being eroded, while their pleas for justice and attempts to ameliorate their lot within the system proved fruitless. 'We wanted the landlords or the government to guarantee us enough to eat and a roof over our heads', one former Huk told Kerkvliet, while another claimed: 'I didn't want to fight for my life and my share of the harvest. These bastards—landlords, civilian guards, soldiers—they all made me take up a gun.'[44] Most of the rebels were not wild-eyed fanatics deluded into grandiose utopian dreams; they fought to retain basic human rights.

That they lost more often than they won in postwar Southeast Asia is largely attributable to the sheer state power they confronted, a power frequently reinforced by external assistance. The state not only had superior firepower and communications, but the resources to wage effective public relations campaigns and to grant judicious concessions. It could build roads, fly in medical teams, monopolize the media, and sometimes buy off rebel leaders or factions. It could also stir up popular violence against its enemies, particularly in Indonesia, where village lanes ran red with the blood of suspected PKI sympathizers in 1965–6.

In this context the victory of the Vietnamese Communist Party was all the more remarkable, and many books have been devoted to explaining it. (The success of the communists in Cambodia and Laos is easier to comprehend, as those societies were radicalized by the overspill of the Second Indochina War.) Some of the explanations emphasized the strengths of the party itself—continuity of leadership and a sophisticated organization combining central direction with strong local initiative—but the more interesting focused on the sources of its appeal to ordinary Vietnamese. First, the party successfully identified itself with Vietnamese nationalism, offering a new framework for the sense of cultural community that many believed had been lost and portraying its opponents (first the French, then the USA-backed RVN) as the enemies of that community. Second, it appeared to be working on a local level in the concrete interests of ordinary people by reducing rents and allowing the people a greater voice in decision-making.

Unrest did not disappear once socialist or communist régimes were established, however. Continuing insurgencies in Burma, the clumsy and brutal land reform campaign in the DRV in the 1950s (even if it was not the full-scale 'bloodbath' its detractors claimed), the flight of the boat people from the SRV in the 1970s and 1980s, and the horrors of Democratic Kampuchea all suggested that the new régimes had altered, rather than removed, the bases of social conflict. The one-party state replaced the landlord and capitalist as the main source of oppression and the primary target of protest. Official mystification and repression were even stronger than in capitalist Southeast Asia. In communist Indochina the significance

---

[44] Kerkvliet, *The Huk Rebellion: A Study of Peasant Revolt in the Philippines*, Berkeley, 1977, 164–5; cf. Race, *War Comes to Long An: Revolutionary Conflict in a Vietnamese Province*, Berkeley, 1972.

of 'class' was officially acknowledged, but only as something exterior or rooted in the past; the suggestion that the state and party apparatus itself represented a new kind of exploitative class structure was taboo. Alternative parties and non-official unions were proscribed; suspected resistance led to severe chastisement, extended 're-education', or even death. Burma was less systematic in extirpating resistance than the Indochinese states, but no less savage toward opponents who fell within its grasp.

The half-century after the outbreak of World War II saw more rapid and drastic social and economic change in Southeast Asia than any comparable period in its history. Starting almost from scratch after the war, the states of the region became politically independent just as the global economy was becoming increasingly interdependent, and this paradox framed much of the debate over specific economic policies throughout the region. Eventually, some states chose to defend property and open themselves to international aid, trade, and investment; they achieved unprecedented but extremely uneven growth, with rising GNP per capita frequently concealing persistent poverty. Others opted for enforced equality and attempted to distance themselves from the capitalist world-system; the price they paid was much slower economic growth and endemic warfare. Throughout the region population grew; agricultural production (thanks to the green revolution) grew even faster; industrial production grew faster yet; and the state apparatus grew fastest of all, while the physical environment began to deteriorate visibly.

The social consequences of these economic changes were complex. Traditions of hierarchy and local community were challenged not just by new ideologies of equality, individualism (or socialism) and nationalism, but by major changes in demographic patterns and economic structures. In the postwar era very few Southeast Asians spent their lives where basic human values and relationships were constant and shared by the entire community. If they themselves did not move, or undertake some different kind of work, or accept the new ideas, they were surrounded by others who did. Although some rejoiced in the liberty and opportunity offered by the new order, most evinced a certain unease as they attemped to uphold traditional institutions or invent new ones.

The limited participation of Southeast Asians in movements of protest and rebellion reflected contentment by some, but simple prudence by many others. Faced by the strongest states—capitalist or socialist—that had existed in Southeast Asian history, they chose to acquiesce and adapt, rather than confront state power. (The recent work of Scott and others on 'everyday' resistance is a useful corrective to the assumption that silence automatically signifies assent.) Yet the minority who chose open defiance left important clues as to how the kinds of changes that occurred in postwar Southeast Asia were perceived by those at the bottom, as well as by planners at the top. They show that, despite nominal prosperity, for many Southeast Asians independence led not to social harmony but to injustice so great that it had to be challenged, sometimes even at the risk of death.

BIBLIOGRAPHIC ESSAY

Information on economic and social change in postwar Southeast Asia has been compiled from a myriad of monographs, articles, and official publications; those listed here did not provide all the data, but suggested ways of viewing them. Gunnar Myrdal, *Asian Drama: An Inquiry into the Poverty of Nations*, A Twentieth Century Fund Study, 3 vols, New York, 1968; Hla Myint, *Economic Theory and the Underdeveloped Countries*, London, 1971; Lloyd G. Reynolds, *Economic Growth in the Third World, 1850–1980*, New Haven, 1985; and Harry T. Oshima, *Economic Growth in Monsoon Asia: A Comparative Survey*, Tokyo, 1987, offer useful comparative perspectives on economic growth. Frank H. Golay et al., *Underdevelopment and Economic Nationalism in Southeast Asia*, Ithaca, 1969, is the best introduction to economic nationalism in the region. Yoshihara Kunio, *The Rise of Ersatz Capitalism in South-East Asia*, Quezon City, 1988, is helpful on sources of investment; cf. Yuan-li Wu and Chun-hsi Wu, *Economic Development in Southeast Asia: The Chinese Dimension*, Stanford, 1980. Robin Broad, *Unequal Alliance, 1979–1986: The World Bank, the International Monetary Fund, and the Philippines*, Berkeley, 1988, analyses the political implications of multilateral aid.

Data on the socialist states are particularly likely to be faulty or biased. A reasonably balanced view can be found in Melanie Beresford, *Vietnam: Politics, Economics and Society*, in the series Marxist Regimes, London, 1988; see also Michael Vickery, *Kampuchea*, and Martin Stuart-Fox, *Laos*, in the same series (both 1986). For Burma, Hal Hill and Sisira Jayasuriya, *An Inward-Looking Economy in Transition: Economic Development in Burma since the 1960s*, Singapore: ISEAS, Occasional Paper no. 80, 1986, is most useful. Douglas C. Dacy, *Foreign Aid, War, and Economic Development: South Vietnam, 1955–1975*, Cambridge, UK, 1986, is the best analysis of official data for that controversial country, but see Alfred W. McCoy et al., *The Politics of Heroin in Southeast Asia*, New York, 1972, for a dimension otherwise overlooked.

For the rest of Southeast Asia the actual economic data are somewhat less problematic. Insightful interpretations are provided in Richard Robison, *Indonesia: The Rise of Capital*, Sydney: Asian Studies Association of Australia Southeast Asian Publications Series no. 13, 1986; Michael Stenson, *Class, Race and Colonialism in West Malaysia: The Indian Case*, St Lucia, 1980; Jomo K. Sundaram, *A Question of Class: Capital, the State, and Uneven Development in Malaya*, East Asian Social Science Monographs, Singapore, 1986; Richard Higgott and Richard Robison, eds, *Southeast Asia: Essays in the Political Economy of Structural Change*, London, 1985; and Robison, Kevin Hewison, and Higgott, eds, *Southeast Asia in the 1980s: the Politics of Economic Crisis*, Sydney, 1987.

Among the hundreds of local studies of social and economic change in postwar Southeast Asia, a few may be singled out: James F. Eder, *On the Road to Tribal Extinction: Depopulation, Deculturation and Adaptive Well-Being among the Batak of the Philippines*, Berkeley, 1987; Clifford Geertz, *Peddlers and Princes: Social Change and Economic Modernization in Two Indonesian*

Towns, Chicago, 1963; Patrick Guinness, *Harmony and Hierarchy in a Javanese Kampung*, Singapore: Asian Studies Association of Australia Southeast Asia Publications Series no. 11, 1986; Gillian Hart, *Power, Labor, and Livelihood: Processes of Change in Rural Java*, Berkeley, 1986; Gerald Cannon Hickey, *Village in Vietnam*, New Haven, 1964; Hickey, *Free in the Forest: Ethnohistory of the Vietnamese Central Highlands, 1954–1976*, New Haven, 1982; Benedict J. Kerkvliet, *The Huk Rebellion: A Study of Peasant Revolt in the Philippines*, Berkeley, 1977; Manning Nash, *The Golden Road to Modernity: Village Life in Contemporary Burma*, New York, 1965; Jeffrey Race, *War Comes to Long An: Revolutionary Conflict in a Vietnamese Province*, Berkeley, 1972; James C. Scott, *Weapons of the Weak: Everyday Forms of Peasant Resistance*, New Haven, 1985; Lauriston Sharp and Lucien Hanks, *Bang Chan: Social History of a Rural Community in Thailand*, Ithaca, 1978; G. William Skinner, *Leadership and Power in the Chinese Community of Thailand*, Ithaca: Cornell University Association for Asian Studies Monograph no. 3, 1958; Ann Laura Stoler, *Capitalism and Confrontation in Sumatra's Plantation Belt, 1870–1979*, New Haven, 1985; and Maria Cristina Blanc Szanton, *A Right to Survive: Subsistence Marketing in a Lowland Philippine Town*, University Park, PA, 1972.

CHAPTER

4

RELIGIOUS CHANGE IN CONTEMPORARY SOUTHEAST ASIA

Seagoing trade made Southeast Asia a fertile meeting ground from early history, and at the close of World War II Landon aptly characterized the region as a 'crossroad of religion'. He emphasized that up to then imported religions had been subordinated to ancestral spirit cults which were grounded in relatively autonomous villages, and noted that even the Westernized élites had adapted modern ideas within a world-view shaped by local traditions. In the same breath he suggested that the middle of this century marked a turning point because the closing years of colonial rule and the disruptions of the war had definitively shaken the foundations of local life.[1] Despite the range of changes since then, the region remains a site of encounter between deeply held and widely divergent world-views. A rich tapestry of ancient local traditions is still sustained with remarkable force, and significant communities derive their practices from all of the major world faiths in many of their forms. The diversity, vitality and depth of religious commitments within the region combine so that it remains an especially rich laboratory for the exploration of religion.

The region is filled with vibrant ritual enactments, such as those in Hindu Bali, and many people routinely enter altered states through ritualized trance, as in Malaysia's annual Thaipusam festival, touching realms of consciousness which are remote for most people in industrialized societies. Meditation practices of Javanese syncretic mystics and the Theravāda forest monastries counterpoint orthodox Islam and ritual Buddhism. Vigorous communities of new Christians exist alongside animists and some, mainly in urban contexts, who live without knowing religious meanings. These diverse experiences of reality, shaped by magical animism, esoteric mysticism, traditional piety, scriptural literalism and modern scepticism, intersect routinely in villages, markets and offices. At the same time, because most people feel their religion is both substantive and significant, contention over spiritual convictions in relation to other spheres of life is regularly in the foreground of the cultural politics of the region.

Every major historical transformation in Southeast Asia has been attended by changes in religion, and some have been especially facilitated by the emissaries of new faiths. In the late twentieth century pragmatic utilitarianism

---

[1] K. P. Landon, *Southeast Asia: Crossroad of Religions*, Chicago, 1949, 202–3.

may be the most powerful missionary force and the communities of that faith are expanding. But focus on the urban surfaces of local life can obscure the persistence of patterns which are rooted in the animistic and rice-growing village substratum of the region. Beneath surface transitions the structures of popular perception and belief remain remarkably cohesive. Changes have generally had their greatest impact on the élites linked to trading ports and temple cities. Even in those contexts whenever local peoples domesticated imported tools of thought and organization, including religious systems, they gave local flavour to patterns which were used otherwise elsewhere. The idioms of imported religions accommodated local meanings. Indian deities came as universal terms for spirit forces known already by different names; Confucianism shaped Vietnamese courts while villagers self-consciously retained ancestral culture.

On the other hand the past fifty years have brought previously unimaginable challenge to the spiritual beliefs and practices rooted in regional prehistory. The depth of social transformation has immense implications in every sphere, and the population explosion has compounded the pace of change. Most people may still live in villages but recently urban populations have mushroomed dramatically. The demographic revolution means that an increasing majority has grown up in a postwar world dominated by modern states rather than ethnicity, by education in schools rather than village ritual religion, and by monetarized economies rather than communal co-operation. Changes occur not only through the ways in which geographically distinct communities are being tied together, but also through transformations in generational, class and gender relations. At the same time the radical transitions of mid-century ensured that the generation which came of age during and after World War II has dominated socio-political institutions through most of the region since then, establishing the predominant tones of cultural evolution into the 1980s.

Change is channelled through metropoles which exemplify the trends they mediate. Pre-modern capitals, such as Mandalay, Chiengmai, Surakarta or Klungkung provide contexts for limited maintenance of traditional arts, but insofar as they do they are like the eye of a cyclone. It is the capital cities which provide a paradigm for the nature of wider changes. Their early colonial centres were already superseded by prewar expansion in the late colonial period. The initial bursts of construction in the 1950s, dramatic as they seemed then, now appear hesitant. Singapore, Bangkok, Manila, Kuala Lumpur and Jakarta have seen such profound expansion in the 1970s and 1980s that their origins have been overwhelmed. Where there were canals and tree-lined avenues in 1950, we see cement in Bangkok. Skyscrapers and multilane highways reshape the spaces of Jakarta so that suburbs like Kebayoran, created only in the 1950s, are now almost unrecognizable. Though restructuring is especially concentrated in these metropoles, they also reach out to reshape the ambience of their hinterlands; changes in cities properly indicate the depth and pace of wider transformation in the past half-century.

In this context, recent reformulations of religion are evident through representations in politics as well as through participation in institutions which are conventionally recognized as religious. Spiritual impulses are implicit within national political culture, cultural policies, and popular practices. We will start by considering religious change at the macro level and in its external dimensions, by dealing with patterns of cultural change and the institutional levels of religious life. In the most general terms recent political cultures have often aimed to reconstruct essentially religious meanings through neo-traditionalism. Resonance with earlier meanings can be surprising and religious nuances are quite clear, but whenever contemporary élites invoke indigenous spiritual cultures it is within new frameworks which make the process one of reinvention rather than strictly of preservation. It is viewed in that light, as a process of creative reinvention, that neo-traditionalism must be considered a theme of cultural politics in the independent states of the region.

Policies of integration, related to education and the formation of national ideologies, threaten tribal and ethnic minorities such as the Karen and Chin of Myanmar (Burma), the Meo of Thailand, the Jarai in the hills of Vietnam and the Mentawai, Punan or Asmat in remote parts of the archipelago, jeopardizing what were until now relatively autonomous identities. Implicitly these policies lead to homogenization, to inadvertent or intended cultural genocide. This mirrors the green revolution in rice agriculture. In that field the spread of new hybrid species increases uniformity of genetic stock, making crops at once more productive and more vulnerable to pests. Through the self-confident modernism of national governments, monocultures extend in the social domain with vigour and the same double edge. Even within the dominant ethnic communities, the restructuring of recognized religion is influenced by instruments of control which facilitate previously impossible regulation, extending to licensing of folk healers, and new forms of opposition, including militant fundamentalisms.

The micro level involves identification of the major types of religious expression in Southeast Asia and exploration of changes within explicitly religious communities. After considering the varieties of recent local religious expression, we will move toward reflection on the ways in which 'experience of what is real' has been evolving. In the innermost dimension this leads toward probing the nature of shifts in the experiential sphere of individual consciousness. Religious changes are not simply a matter of shifting objects of belief or ideology, of altered allegiance to clearly designated organizations, or even of changes in the degree to which people are spiritual in orientation. Religion, as we now understand increasingly, is a matter of what we experience as real, of how we know truth—indeed of whether we can believe there is such a thing—and equally of how our ways of knowing influence our interactions. This account will outline the diversity of explicitly religious movements and then move beyond that. Symbolic structures, on the surfaces of cultural life, have been either evolving, as old symbols accommodate new contexts, or shifting, as new systems replace old ones. At the same time and at a deeper level we can also note that the very nature of the relationship between individual experience, cultural structures and social life is also changing. New contexts and mediations have brought new modes of access to what Southeast Asians of this era are able to know or believe as real.

APPROPRIATIONS OF INDUSTRIAL CULTURE

It is most instructive to view the second half of the twentieth century as the period in which Southeast Asian peoples have been gaining control over and creatively adapting their cultures to industrially derived structures. Though usually considered as the era of independence, this historical phase ironically involves the consolidation of interdependence. Local peoples may directly control their domestic politics once again, but their context is clearly one of increasing interdependence and emergent internationalism. Whether through extended warfare, as in Vietnam, or commitment to trade, as in Singapore, new networks of communication and tools of organization connect people ever more profoundly into world patterns. Where there have been counter-currents, such as those ostensibly aiming to establish locally self-sustaining systems in post-1962 Burma or the Kampuchea of the Khmer Rouge in the late 1970s, they have had the flavour of rearguard actions. Focus on movements of local élites to replace colonial masters directs attention away from critical continuities between colonial and independent systems.

Increasing authoritarianism, economic interdependence, and monocultural modernism are all aspects of the Southeast Asian situation. Early anti-colonial resistance movements, such as the Aceh or Java wars in the archipelago in the nineteenth century or the Saya San rebellion in Burma during the 1930s, centred on revival of social harmony through traditional institutions. In those instances opposition was filtered through and identified with ethnicity, language, or kinship, and we thus see peasant, court and religious movements as the dying gasps of traditional entities. Though they were connected with nationalism through common underlying aspiration and in the mythologies of subsequent activists, they contained no vision of a modern state. In contrast nationalists have competed to create and control modern integrating institutions and Westernized local élites appear as their cutting edge. As the first to experience themselves as members of multi-ethnic states, their target has consistently been control of the apparatus which produced them.

In social historical terms the consolidation of modern state systems and increasing interpenetration are powerful themes which cross the boundary between the eras of colonialism and independence. Governments are now connected with populations through extensions of the very legal systems, bureaucratic networks, educational and military channels that were established in the first half of the century under colonialism. The second half of this century has seen forces of transformation which were only hinted at in the colonial era assume increasing pace. The fruits of the Industrial Revolution at once tie local states to global patterns and bond peoples to each other with new force. Systems of government and taxation; warfare, trade and tourism; state-run education and electronic media; all these intrude increasingly in the lives of even remote peoples. Modern states entail instruments of intervention, through the mechanics of printing and the reach of electronic communications, far more pervasive than those available to earlier systems of power.

Southeast Asian appropriations of new communications media and the apparatus of statehood have been taking place within a context of severe limitation. Everywhere the legacies of colonialism, extremes of political contention, international imbalance, dislocations attending warfare, poverty and rapid urbanization have imposed heavy costs. To grasp recent changes in religious culture, we must understand how economic shifts and population movements threaten the capacity of village communities to sustain old rituals. Warfare, internal migration, new agricultural régimes and deforestation have restructured the physical as well as social environments of tribal minorities and shifting cultivators. Javanese transmigrants to Kalimantan, factory women in Malaysia, Visayan street people in Manila or prostitutes from the northeast in Bangkok cannot imagine cosmological realities or relate to ultimate meanings in the way their relatively settled rice-farming grandparents did as they bowed to Indic-style royalty. In extreme cases, minorities like the Muslim Chams under Pol Pot's Kampuchea (Cambodia) from 1975 to 1979, and others elsewhere, have been faced with apparently genocidal policies.[2] These factors deeply condition cultural process and establish a vital gestalt for understanding changes in popular culture and religion.

Putting cultural and religious history in the foreground facilitates recognition of local volition in a way even social history may not. The appropriation of new media is not simply a matter of the obvious, of acquiring indigenous control over print, radio, film and television. It is also a way of talking about the wider correlates of new industries, forms of entertainment, militaries, bureaucracy and government. As in earlier phases of evolution, adjustments in world-view occur as local peoples enter wider circles of contact beyond the region. Earlier cultural and religious changes have been comprehensible only as shifts in vision accompanied by social changes as intensified commerce brought Sinic, Indic and Islamic vocabularies into the region. In those instances, as their environment changed local peoples found their own purposes fulfilled more clearly through new modes of cultural discourse. Recent trajectories of local development do not match expectations dictated by political economic logic alone, and events are still shaped by or refracted through persistently religious cultures. Southeast Asians are once again claiming to speak with a new voice, though now through their adaptation of industrialized media.

An overview is naturally more easily attained for early and thus distant appropriations of systems of government, writing, trade or agriculture. Insofar as we can achieve such a perspective on the present, it marks a distinctive phase of cultural evolution; there is a change at least as profound as the emergence of states, made more dramatic by the compression of time. Recent changes do not seem incremental, as changes may through earlier history: time itself stops appearing as a constant as interpretation nears the present, appearing to accelerate along with technological innovation and population growth. Just as early societies adapted new patterns in unique ways, contemporary peoples now adapt technological

[2] B. Kiernan, 'Orphans of Genocide: The Cham Muslims of Kampuchea under Pol Pot', *Bulletin of Concerned Asian Scholars*, 20, 4 (1988).

structures and rework their world-views through a modernity which is not static in any of its manifestations. The undercurrents of indigenous cultural voices are not always obvious, especially as political and economic realities tend to dominate our perception of recent social life. Nevertheless localization continues even when the warping pressures of circumstance, including extremes of social dislocation and international intervention, are pervasive.

The extension of modern media into village societies has been remarkable. Newspaper and radio communications began to be widely disseminated before World War II, and now television and films have been reaching villages as well as towns. Increasing consumerism in Thailand, Malaysia and Indonesia has fed the communications revolution from the 1970s onward. Burma has been less affected by modern media, as it has been relatively isolated under Ne Win. Radio programmes, extension education and new farming methods have all changed cultural attitudes and social relations as well as agricultural practices. In Java some villagers report that only the older strains of rice are connected to spirits; the realms of the *devas* become distant and the connections loose as new miracle strains and chemical fertilizers move in. Spirits are also less central to social life as customary law is replaced with rationalized and centrally administered justice. Formerly village heads and councils interpreted customs with a view to resolve disputes in an atmosphere theoretically guided by sensitivity to local spiritual atmospheres. Now decisions are coded by parliaments and, at least in principle, interpreted through bureaucratic representatives.

Every structural reorganization crystallizes new classes, and the germinal intelligentsias of the late colonial era, mainly drawn from earlier élites, became the seed for rapidly expanding and increasingly cosmopolitan supercultures. The revolutionary transitions of the postwar era brought other groups into the new élite. The economic strength of migrant Chinese and Indians has given them a central position, however ambiguous and uncomfortable, in major cities. In most parts of the region the military has became a prime channel for upward mobility, allowing some villagers into the newly forming national élites. Secular education, though still underpinned by patronage systems and thus tied to older class divisions, has offered a channel for others who had less scope through traditional monastic or religious schooling. The extent of their socio-economic and political power gives the new élites a magnetic influence in their cultural environment. As the prime mediators of advanced industrial culture, the new élites are mediators of foreign influence and produce modes of modernity which are distinctive and local.

National boundaries have been sharply defined on maps only in this century, and nationalism is only the political face of response to modernity as mediated by imperialism. Similarly sharpened lines characterize other spheres, as every facet of organization and consciousness is modernized. As literatures and religions have been articulated increasingly through print, they also become defined as text. This has militated against the performance modes and syncretic styles which were predominant in earlier local practices. Scripturalist emphasis on vernaculars brought a shift from an intuitive and participatory ritual style to intellectual sermonizing and a contingent preoccupation with ideologically defined purity. Boundaries between worlds of symbolic meaning have sharpened as much as have those between spheres of power. Other domains also become distinct. To question how religion relates to nationalism, as we may wish to do, reflects a mentality once entirely foreign to the region. Traditional validations of power construed politics as one aspect of a process that was also spiritual; their apparent separability, increasingly institutionalized, is one consequence of recent changes.

SPIRITUAL VISIONS OF REVOLUTION AND INDEPENDENCE

From a spiritual perspective, colonialism was a magical spell as well as a mechanical mastery of institutions, guns and economies. In magical idiom the suppression of will, as in any hegemony, rests on tacit convictions about the way things are, and can thus shift suddenly. So in Southeast Asia at the end of the war, as in Europe more recently, change was a matter of how human will was mobilized and perceptual gestalt configured as well as of who held what instruments of social control. Thus an opening through glasnost led to a dramatic shift in perspective on Soviet dominance and this rapidly reconfigured social realities in Eastern Europe at the end of the 1980s. Similarly the enforced quiet of colonial twilight in the years of the Great Depression was broken dramatically when the Japanese punctured the myth of white supremacy. As the occupation drew to a close in mid-1945 for most Indonesians, Burmese, Vietnamese and Filipinos the prewar order was definitely past, and they prepared for an independence which seemed both imminent and cosmologically destined. European blindness to the spiritual depth and nature of this popular sentiment contributed to the protracted and painful transitions which ensued. It is not surprising that the millenarianism of many Southeast Asians has been difficult to grasp for many Westerners. Such systems appear simply irrational unless it is recognized that the reference is to shifts in atmosphere which everyone registers through different idioms.

Only remote minority groups were untouched by the disruptions of the depression and war years. For the urban-based intelligentsias, independence meant opportunity to replace Europeans in controlling modern communication infrastructure. The political narratives which constitute most histories focus on contention between those élites, but social historians have been consistently drawing attention to the plurality of motives and crosscurrents in the transition years. However sweeping the changes of the postwar years, most people nevertheless retained continuing social practices, wanting mainly to be left alone. For them the grand narratives of political drama appeared as tangents which only occasionally intruded. Insofar as most subsistence-oriented rice-cultivating villagers considered independence, it usually meant aspiration for what was imagined as return to an idealized normality and balance in a context of minimized demands from the state. For many other people, whether embracing Christianity as an appropriation of modernity or celebrating established faiths, the momentous shifts at the end of the war opened new spiritual, as well as social and economic, territories.

From most established religious perspectives in the region the transitions and revolutions have been the outer layers of a reshaping which was also taking place spiritually. In the Theravāda, Confucian, Muslim and Catholic regions there has been widespread assent to notions that the state is responsible for regulating or providing a positive context for spiritual life. Reformation-style separation of political and religious spheres touched prominent élites, but at the roots of social life traditional visions predominated. Thus, among the plurality of interests and ideologies shaping transitions to independence, we register powerful groups who pursued visions dominated by spiritual senses of purpose. These resonances are most apparent in the movements toward an Islamic state, termed 'Darul Islam' in Indonesia. But similar convergence was also evident in Buddhist senses of the Burmese revolution, in Confucian spirituality implicit within Vietnamese communism, and in widespread peasant-based millenarianism. These perspectives influenced the transitions to independence, and moulded social trends of the postwar era.

The strongest root of religious tension in Indonesia lay in Dutch efforts designed precisely to prevent Islam from becoming a focus for nationalist sentiment, to emasculate it by forging strong bonds between the colonial and *adat* élites. This alliance had deepened an existing polarity between religious and political élites, for instance in Java continuing the subordination of mosque officials (*penghulu*) to the bureaucratic élite (*priyayi*). Under the Japanese, however, Islam gained momentum through efforts to orchestrate anti-Western sentiments. Recognizing the influence of religious teachers, the Japanese aimed to mobilize Islamic support throughout the archipelago. By giving separate authority to the Office of Religious Affairs and creating the forerunner of Masjumi (Masyumi), with authority over local Islam, they established a basis for postwar Muslim power, as Masjumi was to became the leading Muslim party during the Indonesian struggle for independence.[3] Thus, in the lead-up to independence, Islam was able to assert a claim toward establishment of an Islamic rather than secular state. Throughout the occupation, Japanese reliance on Sukarno gave him access to radio other nationalists did not have and, as that tool was well suited to his oratorical strengths, his domination of it elevated him to primacy in the public eye. Though secular nationalists thus regained relative strength as the occupation came to an end, the new institutional basis of Islam irrevocably altered the balance of local power.

Anderson suggested that Japanese training of a local militia served, like earlier religious training in hermitages or Islamic schools (*pesantren*), spiritually to prepare youth for the revolution. The deprivations of the occupation focused senses and concentrated energies; it was like an enforced asceticism tempered by conviction that freedom (*merdeka*) would follow.[4] This imagery suggests the special qualities of the energies which were unleashed during the period of suspension and excitement in which the republic was

---

[3] H. Benda, *The Crescent and the Rising Sun*, The Hague, 1958.
[4] B. R. O'G. Anderson, *Java in a Time of Revolution: Occupation and Resistance, 1944–1946*, Ithaca and London, 1972.

born. Though different participants hold variant views, certainly the early days of the revolution were a turning point many have looked back on with nostalgia. Most leaders of the republic since then have recalled what seemed a spiritual unity of purpose which, however momentarily, drew diverse classes and ethnic groups into united effort and aspiration. Whatever the degree of actual unity, most were touched by the intensity of the time and those of formative age remained indelibly marked as they moved on to assume leading roles in the republic. Stringent wartime circumstances and policies combined with chauvinism eventually to alienate most locals, but many Javanese initially saw the Japanese as liberators, those predicted by the prophecies of Joyoboyo, a twelfth-century king of Kediri.[5]

Their imagery presented the revolution as a momentary vacuum, a phase of upheaval resulting from the departure of divine sanction (*wahyu*) from those in power, a time of craziness which sets the stage for a new golden era. Defeudalization was a prominent theme alongside decolonization, millenarian senses of the revolution underpinned populist idiom, and many new mystical sects crystallized during the revolution.[6] The collapse of the outer walls of the Yogya palace (*kraton*) was read by some as a physical parallel to a symbolic opening which was connected to deep spiritual changes. Power (*kasekten*), which had been concentrated in kings and courts, flowed outward so that the communion between human and cosmic planes, previously mediated through royalty, became accessible for all who could receive it. Traditional imagery, as throughout Indianized Southeast Asia, consistently presented events within the human microcosm as interwoven with and parallel to changes in the social and natural orders of the macrocosm. Thus, in the idiom of some of these movements, the spiritual struggle within the revolution was directed at unseating the imperialism of the mind within the body, an internal reorganization which was seen as simultaneous with the displacement of Dutch power over national culture.

At the same time more orthodox Muslims' aspirations had been long suppressed and were already tuned, through longstanding contacts with Mecca and Cairo, to awareness of European colonialism as a dampening force throughout the Islamic world. Throughout the archipelago Japanese appeals to Islam enhanced conviction that the occupation foreshadowed the creation of the *dar-al islam* (the house of Islam). Movement towards an Islamic state had already been a leading current in prewar nationalism and played an especially consistent and powerful role in Aceh, which was never regained by the Dutch. Elsewhere, in Sumatra, Sulawesi, west Java and even along Java's north coast and within its heartlands, Islamic teachers (*kyai*) and the ideal of Islamic statehood sparked movements which competed with secularism at local and national levels right through the 1940s and 1950s. At their roots these movements were not simple expressions of purism: they also drew from millenarian and magical

---

[5] B. Dahm, *Sukarno and the Struggle for Indonesian Independence*, Ithaca, 1969, ch. 1.

[6] C. Geertz, based on fieldwork in an East Javanese town in the early 1950s, in *The Religion of Java*, Chicago, 1976, notes both the emergence of sects (pp. 112–18, 339–52) and the fact that activists connected changes in spiritual practices to the revolution.

strands of Islam. In the Darul Islam there was common emphasis on the internal spiritual facet of the holy war, the jihad. It was not only highly educated leaders such as Kartosuwirjo, but also many followers who understood that the establishment and expansion of the house of Islam involved an inner purification rather than only an external war.[7]

Though framed as banditry by the victors, from an internal perspective both the Darul Islam movements and the Moro nationalism of Mindanao and Sulu have expressed widespread conviction that national revolutions remained unfinished so long as the resulting states built on European rather than Islamic models. Like Marxists, for whom the revolution was incomplete without radical social transformation, some Muslims fought for a revolution they never won. In Aceh and along the north coast of Java changes were deep rooted, often spontaneously reflecting populist or religious impulses qute contrary to the thrust of what European cultures could register as national political development. In the southern Philippines the Muslim struggle began later, but it parallels the Darul Islam in representing revolutionary nationalism in an Islamic mould. The Indonesian nationalist leadership contained these aspects of revolution by standing against changes which could have jeopardized negotiations. The relatively secularized *priyayi* were heirs to Indic court traditions but Dutch educated; since they controlled the bureaucracy, they ensured limits to social and religious versions of the revolution, especially those of the Darul Islam.

Implicitly religious conflict contributed to the elimination of communism as a component of Indonesian nationalism. In 1948 Sudirman's guerrilla armies threatened to break with Sukarno, and in the same year enforced demobilization of communist regiments precipitated killings, particularly in the Madiun area of east Java. The Indonesian Communist Party (PKI) was eliminated, as it had been by the Dutch in 1926, and many thousands died in local conflicts, this time overseen by the firmly Muslim West Javanese Siliwangi division. By surmounting these populist guerrilla and communist 'threats to nationalism', the leadership gained ground for negotiation, but at the expense of elevating the cleavage between Islam and Javanism to a new order of intensity which persisted into the 1960s. The post-independence period witnessed a divergence between Muslim parties—the traditionalist Nahdatul Ulama and modernist Masjumi—and the syncretic or secular parties—the nationalists (PNI) and communists—which certainly coincided with difference in cultural orientation and related to differing underlying spiritual senses of what the national revolution aimed to accomplish.

In Vietnam traditional images presented the end of the war as implying an irrevocable end to the French order, one which had still held a place for imperial rituals. According to local spiritual culture the name for 'village' (*xa*) itself meant at root 'the place where people come together to worship the spirits'. In the Vietnamese variant of the Chinese model it had still been held, even within the French order, that imperial rituals such as

---

[7] C. van Dijk, *Rebellion Under the Banner of Islam*, The Hague, 1981, 34, 391–6.

the Nam Giao drew on the power and goodwill of ancestors, especially those of the royal clan, to guarantee both crops and the social welfare of the population. Rulers had to be tuned to nature and changed according to rhythms which, even when not apparent on the surface, were felt in the tight village communities. When Emperor Bao Dai abdicated on 22 August 1945 he sanctioned the Democratic Republic led by the Vietminh and entrusted it with the maintenance of his ancestral temples. To villagers, still bound to the land through cults of tutelary spirits focused on ancestral founders, this act represented more than a change of dynasty. It did not stop all ancestral practices, as festivals like Tet, the lunar New Year celebration of ancestors, continued to have symbolic force as a way of reforging bonds between the ancestors, nature and society. Nevertheless it foreshadowed the end of a profound constellation of relationships between heaven and earth.[8]

Their deeply imbued vision of social order implied for Vietnamese contestants that the tensions at the end of the war would lead to the emergence of one victor from among the many who initially appeared as candidates, not to pluralistic accord. In the end it appeared that the communists had made the most successful effort to assimilate modern Western notions to the universe of Vietnamese discourses. This implied that their victory was not only tactical, but also cultural. In local idiom it was cosmologically determined, a shift in the mandate of heaven which could not be reversed by ploy or strategy. According to Mus's argument the revolution was decided in popular eyes in the critical period from August 1945 to March 1946 and this marked a whole generation of leadership, as the same period also did in Indonesia.[9] This culturally rooted sense of the revolution remained largely invisible to French or American analysts and strategists. By focusing on ideologies, institutional structures and urban centres, they consistently failed to register that the mobilization of popular will, conceived locally as spiritual even when communist, influenced events more than formalized ideologies.

Imperial powers did note that in the Mekong delta the Hoa Hao variant of Buddhism attracted a following, as did analogous Javanese movements, around the founder's visionary projection of the colonialists' defeat in 1940. Within it practices of individual spiritual enlightenment clearly intermeshed with the impending revolution. As Woodside noted, 'classical culture had been more discredited at the upper levels of society than at the lower and ... the eighth-century Chinese poet Li Po (whose spirit regularly entered Cao Dai mediums in the 1920s and 1930s) still touched the hearts of more Vietnamese peasants than did the Paris commune'.[10] Within the movement much was made of ethnic myths of origin which saw the primordial spiritual strength of the people as lying in a magical prowess which would defeat the technical advantages of modern powers. The strength of the Hoa Hao movement, which had an independent military-administrative structure in the villages of the Mekong delta, provoked violent elimination of its leader in 1947. Hoa Hao prophecy held

[8] Landon, 194–7.
[9] D. McAlister and P. Mus, *The Vietnamese and Their Revolution*, New York, 1970, 118, 126.
[10] A. B. Woodside, *Community and Revolution in Modern Vietnam*, Boston, 1976, 188.

true in the end, but as a statement about communist rather than syncretic Buddhist power.

In urban centres a vigorous but limited modern revival of Buddhism (with in 1935 some 2000 adherents) competed with Marxism in attracting intellectuals to a vision of independence in Vietnam. These new movements, though rooted in older Mahāyāna Buddhism, emphasized the explication of original scriptures in the vernacular. They especially competed with Catholic missionaries, who had begun to succeed in communicating to villagers through local language, at a time when local Buddhists seemed esoteric and technical, making Mahāyāna appear as a preserve of monks. At the same time and on another front, examination of how communist intellectuals were drawn together led Marr to note significant resonances between communism and ingrained millenarianism. Terms in prison functioned to politicize many who had not previously been radical, forging spiritual bonds which underpinned revolutionary cells.[11] While for many millenarian religious impulses converged with revolutionary commitment, at the same time intellectuals also opted for Marxism as a liberation from what appeared as a stasis-oriented Confucian traditionalism.

In Burmese theorizing the interchange between Marxism and Buddhism was more direct and profound. Sarkisyanz established that underpinning the ideology of U Ottama in the 1920s there were notions that political struggle for independence paralleled the stages of Buddhist progression toward enlightenment. Pursuit of 'nirvana within this world', what appeared as a Buddhist 'social gospel', evoked ideals of how the state houses spiritual endeavour which can be traced as far as the Indian Emperor Asoka. Communal values of selflessness and an ethos of levelling were related at once to Buddhism and communism within the Thakin movement of the 1930s.[12] Even popular readings of terms such as 'revolution' and 'liberation' were shaped at critical junctures by Buddhist imagination and constraints. While diverging radically in other respects, this convergence fed into the thinking of most nationalists. Aung San's leadership of the revolution brought emphasis on separation of religion and politics and on socialist militancy in modern secular terms. But the culturalist anti-Western traditions of U Ottama and Saya San became especially relevant again under U Nu's leadership, after Aung San's death and up to 1962.

Shifts to national sovereignty in both Burma and Indonesia saw movement from the relatively Westernized ethos of Aung San, Sjahrir and Hatta to the culturalist orientations of U Nu and Sukarno. In Burma this shift happened quickly. Overt dedication to fostering the Buddhist basis of the state was foreshadowed in 1950 and firmly in place by 1951. U Nu reasserted the traditional role of the state as the protector of religion, seeing it as embodying the cultural values which, following the era of colonial suppression, needed to be enhanced to facilitate spiritual liberation. Socialism continued to be invoked in Burma and Indonesia, but communism was disavowed by the political philosophies which became

[11] D. Marr, *Vietnamese Tradition on Trial*, Berkeley, 1981, 305–6, 316.
[12] E. Sarkisyanz, *Buddhist Backgrounds of the Burmese Revolution*, The Hague, 1965.

dominant in both contexts. From 1949 onwards the presence of communist insurgents in the hills led governments, first under U Nu then Ne Win, to emphasize the incompatibility of Buddhism and Marxism, even while they have consistently advocated a Burmese Buddhist socialism.

Revolutionary transitions to independence, as in Indonesia, Vietnam and Burma, sharpen collective focus on spiritual issues in the same way that the prospect of death does for individuals. But even where the political order was relatively stable or transitions less violent, we can see a parallel configuration in that religious aspirations have been interwoven with revolutionary movements. In the Philippines the hierarchical organization of the Catholic Church tied its leadership closely to the state. This paralleled the social link between the Thai *sangha* and royalty, those cases being more aligned in this respect than either was to the pattern of Muslim organization in the archipelago. But at the grass roots of society, Catholic idiom was often also appropriated to converge with calls by the poor for social justice. Within the Church liberation theology, influenced by currents from Latin America from the 1960s onward, appealed to sectors of the priesthood who identified their mission simultaneously with social and spiritual welfare. The people-power revolution, which contributed to the end of the Marcos era in 1986, involved even the hierarchy of the Church and made candlelight prayer vigils a weapon of protest.

In the Thai context it is especially clear that religious purposes inspire modern state construction. Ironically the strength of continuities there have allowed a less ambiguous pursuit of modernity. Some correllates of modernity, repudiated aggressively as too Western elsewhere, have been embraced. Nevertheless, as Tambiah has argued, religious purposes continue to inspire government visions of progress:

> From early times Buddhism has been positively related to a conception of an ideal politico-social order, whose cornerstone was a righteous monarch who would promote a prosperous society and religion. ... Given this interlaced totality of religion and politics, of national consciousness and religious identity, of righteous morality and politics, it is difficult to see in Thailand a secular nationalism dispensing with Buddhist referents in the near future.[13]

Variations of this image of the relationship between religious and sociopolitical domains have continued to apply throughout the region.

The fundamentalist revivalism of the 1970s and 1980s make nonsense of assumption that either Muslims or Buddhist populations would distinguish, any more than Confucianists ever did, between spiritual and social spheres. Religious impulses intersect with political-economic purposes in postwar state construction throughout the Islamic and Theravāda regions. Political process has been consistently construed by most local peoples as a sphere of cultural and spiritual contention. This has often remained the case even when revolutionary actions and political ideologies have appeared to be secular on the surface. At the rice roots of village societies, even ostensibly secular ideologies such as Marxism have intersected with

---

13 S. J. Tambiah, *World Conqueror and World Renouncer*, Cambridge, UK, 1976, 431.

millenarian spirituality. Nevertheless, it is apparent that economic concerns and secular politics have appeared to be increasingly separable from spiritual concerns during the past decades.

THE GENERATION OF NATIONAL CULTURES AS RELIGIOUS CONTENTION

Religious and ethnic identities within each state have been multiple, and competing claims to national identity have thus produced prominent fracture lines within all postwar societies. The relationships which were consolidated implicitly in the territories mapped by colonialism have carried into national structures. States like Aceh and ethnic groups such as the Karen and Meo were drawn, more through colonialism than by any earlier states, into social units dominated by Burmese, Thai, Vietnamese, Javanese, Malay and Tagalog speakers. These majorities are for the most part the occupants of core areas, the centres from early times of intensive rice cultivation, dense population and state formation, and those areas now house the dominant populations of most of the new states. At the same time the social boundaries between local peoples and migrant Indian, Arab and Chinese groups hardened from the turn of the century onward. The fragility of unity and fragmentation of identities have been self-evident. Throughout the region postwar constructions of national culture have self-consciously aimed to produce a dominant mould which would override these profound differences.

Most of the dominant political philosophies of the postwar period can be characterized as 'neo-traditional', and insofar as they are they infuse religious meanings within modern politics. Confucianism resonated in Diem's South Vietnam; U Nu's socialism was also Buddhist; and Sukarno's Nasakom suggested how Javanist impulses could guide the formation of national ideologies. This is to speak of a positive rather than strictly negative process—when these modern actors appeal to Buddhism or the *wayang*, they are actively constructing, rather than cynically manipulating older popular symbols. Even Vietnamese communists have prioritized communal values, usually in a manner consonant with Confucian-tinged spirituality which some Western Marxists have found hard either to grasp or to correlate with their politics. Suharto built his striking family grave next to the grave complex of the Mangkunegaraan court, to which his wife is distantly related, and modelled it on the temples of Indic Majapahit. By doing so he clearly aimed to memorialize his role as the man who has guided the nation into modernity, but his manner of doing so emulates the way Indic kings commemorated their accomplishments. New national rituals, including ostensibly Western elections, build on senses of ceremony embedded within local society; religious holidays are designated state holidays, and new memorial rites commemorate revolutionary heroes as founding ancestors. These patterns reflect choices guided by deeply worn tracks, even if what was once a dirt path may now have become concrete.

Though the power of kings is circumscribed, royalty is a continuing centrepoint of ceremonial life in significant parts of Southeast Asia, and wherever it remains it carries religious significance. Kingship remains a central institution in Thailand and Brunei; it continued in Laos through the 1950s; and it existed in modified form in Cambodia until 1975. When Sultan Hamengku Buwono IX, of Yogyakarta in Java, died in 1988, the commemoration of his passing drew extraordinary crowds and was widely noted. Ironically he had maintained the magical power of royalty precisely by the strength of his support for the revolution and his role as vice-president of the republic in the 1970s. In Cambodia Sihanouk evoked similar sentiments, and for similar reasons, throughout the 1950s and 1960s. By adjusting to constitutional monarchy, he preserved the sacral power of royal tradition, accepting homage as had been the due of earlier kings. Considered more widely, as complexes of belief relating to courts and in terms of their residual roles within society at large, traditional courts retain significance in Yogyakarta, Surakarta and in the Malay sultanates, where they still retain religious influence, as well as in Thailand and Brunei, where they are obviously vigorous.

Modernization was spearheaded by royalty in the Thai case and the nexus bonding the court to the *sangha*, to village and to distant regions has been gaining strength consistently. The 1932 constitutional revolution turned what was Siam into today's Thailand and repositioned, but did not eliminate, the kingship. Kings have thus retained a powerful ritual and ceremonial place within Thai society. In the postwar period Buddhism has been even more firmly enshrined, theoretically at least, than ever. Along with the monarchy it is a key ideological basis of the nation. Field Marshal Sarit Thanarat, whose views dominated the 1950s and early 1960s, reinstated some of the lapsed ceremonial functions of kingship and looked to Buddhism as a bulwark against what he perceived as the threat of communism. On the other hand the modern forms of Buddhism which have been promoted by the state have also reflected twentieth-century adaptations. The most prominent modernist forms, within all of the religions in the region, bring a shift of emphasis toward social action. In any event in Thailand traditional institutions have been reformed and enhanced, now underpinned as they are by modern media, as a basis for the cultural integration of the state.

In Burma virtually all residues of the monarchy were eliminated by British colonialism. Nevertheless the independent state resurrected traditions rooted in local religious notions of kingship. U Nu, who was premier for most of the period from 1948 to 1962, adhered to a version of socialism which departed from that of his more secular Thakin colleagues of the 1930s. Observers uniformly note the genuine qualities of a personal spiritual commitment which he underpinned with a simple lifestyle. U Nu's Buddhism was inseparable from the cult of the *nats*. He justified propitiation ceremonies through references to the scriptures; his Pyidaungsu Party gave annual offerings to the spirits and he spent lengthy periods at sites sacred to them, even when deciding economic matters. In 1961 he initiated the construction of 60,000 sand pagodas with iron spires and, as opposition to the declaration of Buddhism as the state religion grew, he spent forty-five days in spiritual retreat on the sacred Mount Popo.[14] Elements of the *saṅgha* accused him of prioritizing the cults at the expense of Buddhism, but there is no doubt that he sincerely believed the spiritual health of the population would be enhanced by proclamation of a Buddhist state.

National regeneration and the enhancement of Buddhism were seen as coterminous within a vision of the socialist state framed by Buddhist values. The revival which U Nu led emphasized the Buddhist nature of Burma and the importance of its world role as 'the strongest home' of its contemporary practice. The Ministry of Religion was established in 1950, and from 1952 onwards the government employed monks to facilitate the incorporation of hill tribes into the nation. It sponsored Mahasi Sayadaw's insight (*vipassana*) meditation centre in Rangoon, a showpiece of modern Buddhist practice to which foreign visitors of the time were regularly introduced. The Sangayana, the Sixth Great Buddhist Council of 1954–6, was the centrepiece of revivalism, and associated activities coloured the whole decade. It marked the 2500th anniversary of the Buddha, and to some extent became the world event it was intended, as representatives from thirty countries met. Building of the Kaba Aye Peace Pagoda began in 1950, on a site selected on the basis of a visionary experience, and the council took place in the Great Sacred Cave, constructed next to the Peace Pagoda to house 10,000 representatives. At the same time the rebuilding of old derelict pagodas became an object of government policies.

When U Nu campaigned for re-election in 1959, he announced preference for establishment of Buddhism as the state religion, but the ensuing controversies divided even Buddhists. Recurrent disciplinary and factional problems, a residue of the fragmentation resulting from the colonial removal of royal patronage, plagued the *saṅgha*, the monastic order, throughout the 1950s. In 1951 a fight followed a refusal to allow *pongyis*, Burmese monks, free admission to a theatre; in 1954 two *pongyis* died in a clash over control of a temple school (*kyaung*); in 1956 factionalism led to rioting of monks in Mandalay; and in 1959 the police resorted to tear gas, arresting eighty-nine monks after student rioting in Rangoon. When legislation was pending to amend the constitution, monks objected to the protection it offered to minority religions. It appeared to allow them increased scope for growth by promising minority religions a share of state religious funds. In November 1961 monks went so far as to burn down mosques on the outskirts of Rangoon.[15] When the constitutional change went through in 1961, the minorities seethed because the bill did not bring the unexpected counterbalance of federalism. On the other hand, because the final version of U Nu's legislation proclaiming Burma as a Buddhist state was a mild statement, the Buddhist *saṅgha* remained divided over endorsing it.

State-sponsored revival of Buddhism lost momentum with Ne Win's coup of 1962. The philosophy of the military has been relatively secular, though even it has theoretically prioritized material development only 'in balance with spiritual life'. The Revolutionary Council announced its guiding philosophy through the Burma Socialist Programme Party

---

[14] M. Mendelson, *Sangha and State in Burma* (ed. J. P. Ferguson), Ithaca, 1975, 273–4, 350.
[15] D. Smith, *Religion and Politics in Burma*, Princeton, 1965, 206–7, and Mendelson, 353.

in January 1963. Elements of both Marxism and Buddhism found a place in that philosophy, but key traditional notions relating to the *nats* (guardian spirits), Buddhist philosophy of *samsara* (the 'wheel of rebirth') and *kamma* (karma) were omitted. Its thrust was humanistic, appealing to spiritual values and affirming that the state had responsibility for the improvement of the spiritual life of its citizens. Ne Win has not tolerated respect for *nats*. His government launched a concerted attack on spirit beliefs, even banning film productions centring on them. Following Ne Win's coup, the proclamation of a Buddhist Burma was rescinded to pacify minorities and the government made new and concerted efforts to exclude *pongyis* from politics. After 1962 the Union Buddha Sasana Council was abolished; in 1965 the Vinasaya Act of 1949, the Dhammacariya Acta of 1950 and the Pali Education Board Act of 1952 were all repealed, and thus the major elements of U Nu's legislation to strengthen the *saṅgha* were all eventually eliminated.

Among Vietnamese activists, articulate spokespeople like Thien Minh held that Buddhism represented a choice of values not present in either Western or communist countries. He commented that 'we are convinced that Buddhism can build up a nation because it represents a unified force and because it teaches the doctrine of tolerance and understanding.'[16] Represented by a relatively small *saṅgha*, Buddhists were strongest in central Vietnam. The postwar revival of Buddhism there began in 1951, when a national conference was attended by fifty monks and lay people in Hué. They joined the World Fellowship of Buddhists, which had been formed in Sri Lanka in 1950. Buddhists took issue with the Diem government because it so often appeared unwilling to recognize a role for them. Diem's policies appeared to be based on patronage models of government, common throughout the region, more than on Catholicism as such, and the Vatican was at pains to dissociate Catholicism from them.

Tensions mounted around the ceremony of Waisak, the celebration of the Buddha's birth, enlightenment and passing, in early May 1963; crowds in Hué were met with tanks and nine died, precipitating lengthy petitioning and a series of demonstrations in Saigon as well. The self-immolation of Thich Quang Duc on 11 June followed a lengthy period of unsuccessful petitioning to Diem on behalf of the Buddhists that year. In August 1964 Buddhist antagonism to the Saigon government led as far as rioting in Danang, where Buddhist-led mobs burned down the huts of Catholic refugees. Buddhist neutralists pressured the Saigon government continually. As General Ky assumed power in mid-1965 and the war situation worsened, lay Buddhists reduced their activism in order to concentrate on education and social welfare activities. They published magazines and periodicals, ran 135 primary and 35 secondary schools and a Buddhist university, and also recruited youth to show their strength.[17]

Throughout 1966 tense negotiations continued between Catholic, Hoa Hao, Cao Dai and Buddhist groups and the Ky government over the holding of elections and prospective representation in the constitutional

16 J. Schecter, *The New Face of the Buddha*, New York, 1967, 160.
17 ibid., 210.

assembly. Periodic violence between the military and Buddhist student groups in Danang and Hué failed to bring responses from the government. In May Thanh Quang, a 55-year-old nun, immolated herself before the Dieu De pagoda in Hué. Her action unquestionably indicated the spiritual depth of distress at United States support for Ky's government, making her death an appeal to the hearts of Americans and symbolizing commitment to the spirit of non-violence. But the power of Buddhist activism, strongest in 1963, dissipated gradually in 1966. The appeal to Buddhism as a basis for nationalism was undermined by Cao Dai dominance of Tay Ninh Province, Hoa Hao power in the western Mekong delta and the semi-autonomy of the Montagnard animists, Khmer border people, and Muslim Cham remnants.

In Indonesia the Western notion of division between secular and religious spheres has had only narrow purchase. The few genuinely secular nationalists have always had to address religious—especially Muslim—people, movements and interpretations. At the same time, though 90 per cent of the population profess to be Muslim, the nation is not characteristically Islamic in the way its cousins of that religion's heartlands are. Variants of animism and mysticism remain significant counterweights to the strength of Islam. Within Sukarno's PNI, Javanese spiritual philosophy underpinned political thought; even the communist PKI converged with millenarianism insofar as it extended into Javanese rural life. The place of Islam was a major issue in the lead-up to the proclamation of independence, resulting in an ambiguous compromise called the Jakarta Charter. Some Muslims thought this draft preamble to the constitution, stating that Muslims would be legally required to adhere to Islamic law, would be official. Secularists prevented acceptance of the compromise, arguing that it would have endangered the revolution, but until the 1970s recognition of the charter remained an active objective for Islamic politicians.[18]

Subsequent social tensions have often corresponded with cultural and religious cleavages. Divergence between Muslim orthodoxy and Javanism underlay the rhetoric of the 1950s and remained an explicit focus of tension into the 1970s, as the New Order effectively required membership in a recognized religion. Most Indonesians do believe in God and experience a spiritual dimension as real; one corollary is that they see the national identity as palpable, as a spirit rather than just an abstraction. Insofar as identities are seen as spiritual, the reflexive implication has also been that national reconstruction involves a spiritual struggle. For some this has meant movement toward collective realization of submission to the will of Allah; for others it means repetition of the endless tension between desires, linking us to the material plane, and impulses toward spiritual release. These views, the one Islamic, the other Indic, are suggestive of the major contenders which have been asserting the right to define the spiritual identity of the national entity in independent Indonesia.

Both the Ministry of Religion and the Islamic parties have had a clearly

---

[18] Important discussions of the Islamic perspective are presented in van Dijk, 45–58, and in B. J. Boland, *The Struggle of Islam in Modern Indonesia*, The Hague, 1982, 17–39.

Muslim interpretation of the national commitment to freedom of religion. As Van Nieuwenhuijze observed, at the time of independence many Muslims viewed religion as synonymous with Islam and interpreted religious freedom as meaning 'freedom for Islam', since 90 per cent of the population was supposed to be Muslim. Even purist Muslims now realize that this assumption was superficial, but the notion of Islamic domination remains strong. Muslims have gradually and reluctantly accepted that they remain a fractional element within a plural religious scene. Many Muslims continued to feel, as they had under the Dutch, that only political repression prevented them from setting the mould for a nation they ought to have dominated. Until the 1955 elections the leading Islamic parties assumed that all Muslims would vote for them. They were shocked to find that in the event only 42 per cent of the population voted for them, and this contributed to Islamic and outer island separatism in the late 1950s.

The elections of 1955 and 1957 remain markers of religious commitments in the country. Masjumi, representing modernist Islam, was strongest in the outer islands, in west Java and in urban areas. The traditionalist Muslim Nahdatul Ulama, the nationalists (PNI) and communists (PKI), all had their roots in the heartlands of Java. After the elections, both Muslims and Christians feared growing PKI strength, and resented Java-oriented economic policies. The Darul Islam movements had been continuing in Aceh, west Java, and south Sulawesi intermittently through the 1950s. The association of Masjumi with the PRRI rebellion in Sumatra and the Permesta revolt in north Sulawesi in 1958 was used to push modernist Islam to the political margins. The suppression of Darul Islam, the PRRI and Permesta revolts and nationalization of businesses, all in the late 1950s, drew the military into civilian administration, transforming it also into the primary new vehicle of national integration and reducing Islam's political relevance.

The concept of Guided Democracy elaborated by Sukarno framed politics from 1959 to 1965 and tacitly revived the ethos and style of *kraton* culture[20] Both purist senses of Islam and Western pluralistic notions of democracy were excluded in favour of syncretic thought and the politics of consensus. Magical senses of power underlay the effort to concentrate energy on glorification of the capital and on unifying struggles to liberate Dutch New Guinea and confront 'neo-colonialist' Malaysia. Sukarno recalled the traditional glories of Majapahit as a peak of the past and model for the present. His populist images of the primal peasant (*marhaen*) and of principles of cooperation (*gotong-royong*) and consensus (*musyawarah-mufakat*) were elevated as national ideology. Nasakom (the acronym for 'nationalism-religion-communism') was proclaimed as a synthetic and transcendent ideology, and Sukarno presented himself as the mouthpiece of the people, meaning that he conceived of his personal consciousness as being linked to the collective as its prime mechanism of representation. His charismatic invocations of the spirit of 1945 came with opposition, inflation

[19] C. A. O. van Nieuwenhuijze, *Aspects of Islam in Post-Colonial Indonesia*, The Hague-Bandung, 1958.
[20] B. R. O'G. Anderson, 'The Idea of Power in Javanese Culture' in Claire Holt et al., eds, *Culture and Politics in Indonesia*, Ithaca, 1972, and C. Geertz, *Islam Observed*, Chicago, 1972.

and unresolved ills, so that in retrospect even usually sympathetic Javanists felt that it fell short in practice.

Social tensions led toward the coup and counter-coup of 1965. The land-reform laws of 1959 were never implemented, leading communist cadres to stimulate unilateral seizures which provoked a powerful Muslim counter-offensive. The Aidit PKI implicitly remained a vehicle for *abangan* expression, finding numerical strength mainly as a counter to rural Islam. Suharto consolidated control when he manoeuvred Sukarno into providing an authorization to re-establish order on 11 March 1966, through a letter known by the acronym 'SuperSemar'. If Sukarno aimed to transcend ideology through synthesis, Suharto has aimed to purge politics of ideology; if the 'theatre state' resurrected Indic courts, the New Order can be represented as a surfacing of village temperament. Suharto is a committed Muslim, but in Javanist terms—a foster father; and several of his early advisers participated in a prominent cult of the guardian spirits. The group emphasizes pilgrimage to the power points of Dieng and Srandil, both linked to Semar as the guardian (*danhyang*) of Java, as a route to power. Ironically this Javanist ethos is obscured by cultural defensiveness: it is less articulate than either Indic-style syncretism or traditional religions, and the official status of mysticism remains insecure.

Thus the underlying spiritual ethos of the governments led by both Sukarno and Suharto have been inspired by a Javanism within which Islamic sensibility is framed by syncretism. There has been self-conscious emphasis on a corporatist 'family principle' which rationalizes a consensual basis for the politics of the state. That philosophy was clearly articulated in the nationalist educational philosophy of Dewantoro in the 1920s, and it remains relevant. Dewantoro's prewar Taman Siswa movement fed into the national educational system, but has much more significance at present through its relation to national political philosophies. In it a holistic emphasis on collective corporate identity and consensual politics was tied to commitment to develop the whole person in balance by engaging the mind, feeling and will through awareness of all of the senses. Taman Siswa philosophy was connected to mystical theories through Suryomataram, one of the most famous prewar mystics of Yogyakarta, and resonated with the teachings of the Theosophical Society and Maria Montessori.[21]

This philosophy converged with what was to become the dominant philosophy of the nation as expressed in the 1945 constitution, the Pancasila (the five principles articulated by Sukarno which underlie the state philosophy), Guided Democracy in the late 1950s and, not least, the Golkar organization under Suharto. It is pointedly stressed in the exclusive emphasis on the Pancasila demanded by New Order in the 1980s. In 1981 Suharto conflated criticism of himself with that of the Pancasila and in 1983 the MPR (parliament) formalized the separation of religion and politics, undermining Islamic parties implicitly in the process, by legislating the requirement that all political organizations had to adopt the Pancasila as their basis. This was extended to all social organizations and is tied to consistent and self-conscious argument that democracy had to be tuned to

---

[21] D. Reeve, *Golkar of Indonesia*, Singapore, 1985, 355–6.

the 'Indonesian soul'. Islamic parties commanded about 30 per cent of the vote, despite adverse circumstances in elections in the 1970s, making Islam the clearest oppositional force to the New Order. But recent assessments of Islam in Indonesian politics point out that Muslims have become a majority with a 'minority mentality' and that the faith is 'an outsider'.[22]

STATE REGULATION AND INSTITUTIONAL RELIGION

The consolidation of new states has led to increasing centralized control over institutional religious life; the same powers which limit smuggling or collect revenue have been exercised in regularizing religious hierarchies which are increasingly articulated at national level. This trend is a corollary of the general process of reorganizing social life and it is also due to special interest in mobilizing religious institutions for political, cultural and economic purposes. At the same time it is linked to the view, which governments share even when they are ostensibly secular, that the ambit of state authority includes the spiritual welfare of its population. As many prominent neo-traditionalist political philosophies carry religious senses of purpose, intervention by governments in the religious sphere has usually been sanctioned by postwar states.

Within the Theravāda states the spread of modern education, as a reorganization of *saṅgha*-based education or as a vehicle of new national values, contributes to the reshaping of even popular perceptions of Buddhism. There has been notable progress in this area, with massive rises in adult literacy being achieved during the 1950s. Despite the fact that governments have emphasized secular education, religious schooling continues to be strong. At the same time the lines between traditional religious and modern secular education have also blurred in the postwar period. Religious schools give increasing attention to secular subjects, government sponsorship has extended to religious education, and religious education has even expanded within secular systems.

Burma's first constitution, of 1947, recognized only a 'special place' for Buddhism; this was in deference to the Karen, Kachin and Chin minorities and with a view to induce them to join the union. Naturally neither Christian Karens nor animists elsewhere were attracted to the prospect of Buddhism as a state religion. Once U Nu was in office in 1948, he concentrated on promoting the Buddhist revival as part of his vision of the national revolution, notwithstanding that Burma was not declared as a Buddhist state. The Vinicchaya–Htana Act of 1949, for example, aimed to remove religious disputes from the jurisdiction of civil courts by establishing ecclesiastical courts at the town level throughout the country. It was modified in 1954 to take account of the strength of divergent sects within Burmese Buddhism, as sectarian fissures are prominent and abbots have

[22] W. F. Wertheim, 'Moslems in Indonesia: Majority with a Minority Mentality', Townsville: James Cook University, Southeast Asian Studies Committee, 1980, and R. McVey, 'Faith as the Outsider: Islam in Indonesian Politics', in J. Piscatori, ed., *Islam in the Political Process*, Cambridge, UK, 1983.

had more power within their temples (*kyaungs*) than their colleagues elsewhere.

The Ministry of Religious Affairs was established in 1950, partly to restore cohesion to what had become a fragmented religious structure. Meanwhile the Ministry of Education engaged actively in regulating and supporting monastic examinations and standards within the larger monastic universities. From 1947 onwards there was discussion of establishing a Pāli university. On the one hand these moves were designed to counterbalance the long period of absence of royal sponsorship, on the other they served to strengthen government intervention in the affairs of the *sangha*. This combined with periodic debates through the 1950s over registration of monks and the holding of monastic parliaments. These interventions provoked some Buddhists, such as the Anti-Hlutdaw Association, to demand the abolition of the Ministry of Religious Affairs in 1959. Registration was a touchy issue partly because revolutionaries in many instances worked through the *sangha*, gaining a mobility through that they would not otherwise have had.[23]

One notable intervention in Buddhist developments, the Institute for the Advanced Study of Buddhism, was founded through collaboration with the American Ford Foundation in 1954. It implied a mixture of secular and religious objects which sat uncomfortably within Burmese traditions, which did not separate those spheres. Emphasis on English-language learning and both the domestic and international missionary expansion of Buddhism went hand in hand with what became a Burmanization of the curriculum and personnel.[24] This new style of government- and foreign-sponsored training was tied to social service. Promotion of Buddhism was directly linked at once to consolidating the state internally and to projecting its image in the international environment. In Burma by 1962 there were eighty-four temple schools which had enough highly trained monks to register as colleges. The Ne Win government has given no encouragement to *kyaung* schools. They nevertheless remain a vital component of Burmese education, even if the 70 per cent who attended religious schools in 1952 must have declined signficantly since.[25]

In Thailand in 1967 half the primary schools were still *wat* schools where teaching was done by monks. Monastic examination regulations which came into effect in 1910 remain in force and there were 6634 Nak Dhamma schools and 615 Pāli schools. The two *wat* institutes in Bangkok, Mahamakuta Rajavidyalaya and Mahachulalongkorn Rajavidyalaya, became the basis of modern universities in 1945 and 1947, from that point offering a wide range of modern studies along with Buddhist Pāli studies.[26] All of these schools served not only to link the modern state to religious institutions, but also to introduce religious specialists to secular modes of learning. According to figures from 1968 there were about 25,000 *wat* and 185,000 monks, perhaps one-third of them 'temporary', in a Thai population of around 34 million. The hierarchy of monastic institutions, leading

[23] Mendelson, 240–62, 341–5.
[24] ibid., 299–306.
[25] F. von der Mehden, *Religion and Modernization in Southeast Asia*, Syracuse, 1986, 136.
[26] R. Lester, *Theravada Buddhism in Southeast Asia*, Ann Arbor, 1973, 97.

up toward the élite 'university *wat*' of the capital, matched the socio-political hierarchy of cities. In this context, as often in earlier times, the *saṅgha* offered a prime channel for upward mobility and high status, especially for the relatively poorer villagers of the northeast.[27]

The Thai government has been in the strongest position to patronize Buddhism and it has not held back from fostering and attempting to manipulate the very strong local *saṅgha*. The government attitude was reflected in a 1963 pamphlet which indicated that 'the complexities of living in the modern world . . . necessitate a close cooperation and mutual understanding between the State and the Sangha working harmoniously together for the economic and spiritual well-being of the people'.[28] The 1963 Sangha Act, initiated under Sarit, constituted a powerful intervention in the life of the *saṅgha*. The previous Acts, of 1902 and 1941, had ironically contained significant democratic features. The 1963 Act centralized power in the name of defusing sectarian rivalry between the cohesive, and hence relatively better represented, modernist Dhammayut and more diffuse Mahanikai sects within the *saṅgha*. This restructuring reflected Sarit's recognition that Buddhism and the monarchy remained critical to the achievement of modernizing objectives. Each adjustment in state policy with regard to the *saṅgha* has matched modernizing reforms, relating first to the reforms of the nineteenth century, then to the 1932 revolution, and finally to Sarit's coup of 1957.[29] Continuous strengthening of the bonds between religion and the state, as hierarchical ties have tightened through the Ministry of Religion, has decreased the prestige and autonomy of local *wat*.

It is recognized in all village studies of the Theravāda countries that throughout the period since the war monks continued to play a key role as counsellors and advisers, as well as officiating at religious ceremonies. Now their traditional centrality in this respect has been counterbalanced by community development training. In Cambodia Sihanouk held that 'our 70,000 monks are the "officers" conducting our people to work, just as the officers conduct the troops into combat'.[30] In the late 1960s Maha-chulalongkorn University in Bangkok sponsored community development training for monks in centres dispersed through the country. Monks who attended were expected to return to their villages and apply the skills and perspectives gained in whatever way they could, and there is little doubt that many, as in the purely secular cadre training programmes in Vietnam, absorbed and applied the lessons learned.

In Laos roughly 25 per cent of schools were religious and in 1962 there were ninety-five Pāli schools. There were only a few vernacular high schools up to the time of Pathet Lao victory in 1975. The French did not cut the tie between royalty and the *saṅgha* in Laos or Cambodia, and it remained relatively tight until the socialist revolutions of the mid-1970s. In Cambodia, as in Laos and Thailand, the state and *saṅgha* were also much

[27] S. J. Tambiah, 'Sangha and Polity in Modern Thailand', in Bardwell Smith, ed., *Religion and the Legitimation of Power in Thailand, Laos, and Burma*, Chambersburg, 1978, 123–4.
[28] Quoted in Lester, 104.
[29] Tambiah, *World Conqueror*, 252–5.
[30] Lester, 126.

closer than in Burma. There Buddhist schools included 600 primary, two secondary and one tertiary, the Preah Sihanouk Raj Buddhist University of Phnom Penh.[31] Traditionally schooling reached young males in most villages through the *wat*, but by 1967 all but 10 per cent of schools were in the government system and enrolments were increasing rapidly.[32]

The French and Americans looked to the *saṅgha* as a potential counter-weight to communism in Laos throughout the 1950s and 1960s, and its strength was undermined as a result. The *saṅgha* was particularly deeply divided between Mahanikai and Dhammayut sects, a tension lending itself to factionalism, and at the same time strongly committed to a vision of itself as the prime vehicle of Lao culture, a mission easily construed as counter to American secularism. By the early 1970s, especially as the Pathet Lao gained strength through growing anti-Americanism, the politicization of the *saṅgha*, ironically facilitated by its own initiatives to broaden its base through encouraging lay missionizing and meditation, had undermined its role within Lao society. With its victory in 1975, the Pathet Lao made every effort to use monks in order to extend its message to the population. It announced policies of religious freedom; there was already a strong basis for collaboration, as notions of Buddhist socialism were well established. At the same time the new government set out to re-educate monks, restrict their privileges and bypass their central social and symbolic role. By 1979 the number of monks was said to have dropped from 20,000 to 1700, and the subordination of the *saṅgha* to politics appeared to be complete.[33]

A subordinate position in political terms has limited Muslim influence over national institutions in Indonesia, but in the cultural and religious arenas the balance of power differs. In that domain other parties respond increasingly to Islam in the sense that discourses about religious issues are framed increasingly in Islamic idiom. The state endorses an Islamic sense of God and requires citizens to identify with a religion Muslims can acknowledge as such; it sees itself as having an active responsibility in the religious sphere in terms no secular Western state does. In each of these spheres Islamic discourses define the context of Indonesian spiritual life, influencing other strands of religion implicitly and pervasively. Even Suharto was always guarded in reference to his early Javanist preferences, and Muslims still associate related practices with the residue of pre-Islamic traditions. International *tarekats* have remained active but at the national level their significance declined until the 1980s, when a revival became noticeable. Mysticism is often seen now as irrational, a projection or fantasy contrary to the realities of development and modernity, and related practices have been consistently on the defensive, certainly vis-à-vis government agencies.

Though it failed to claim the Indonesian nation fully for Islam, the strength of Masjumi as an umbrella Muslim party was sufficient to ensure rapid establishment of a Ministry of Religion. This was dominated by the

[31] ibid., 96–7.
[32] C. Keyes, *The Golden Peninsula*, London, 1977, 293.
[33] M. Stuart-Fox and R. Bucknell, 'Politicization of the Buddhist Sangha in Laos', JSEAS, 13, 1 (1982) 78.

Nahdatul Ulama until 1971, at which point the New Order effectively displaced that party as the dominating force behind the ministry. Though it is responsible for all religious communities, funds within it are allocated according to census statistics and Islam has thus dominated it heavily. The ministry administered government subsidies to more than 13,000 primary, 776 secondary and 16 higher *madrasas* in 1954 and to a total of 22,000 *madrasas* and *pesantren* by 1965, and these figures kept increasing in the 1970s.[34] The separate Islamic educational network has come increasingly into its own, especially since the 1970s through the tertiary level IAIN (State Islamic Institutes), when substantial oil money went toward it, and this network established the basis for a new wave of nationwide Islamization. The ministry became the main stronghold of Muslim influence within the bureaucracy and a counter to Javanist domination of the Ministries of Information and of Education and Culture.

Given the importance of law within Islam, the establishment of the Ministry of Religion had immense practical implications for local religious life. Islamic courts came under its jurisdiction rather than that of the Justice Department. In issues of family law, notably divorce and inheritance, a legal basis for religious authority was established. From the mid-1950s to 1974 there was intermittent and severe controversy over marriage legislation, especially concerning polygamy and non-Muslim marriages. Muslim reaction to the government's proposed civil legislation of 1974 provoked such extreme reaction that the bill was withdrawn. For Muslims frustration has often focused on the codification of customary (*adat*) law undertaken by the Dutch. The ministry channelled funds and created institutions in a way that strengthened Islamic organizations. At the same time it also implicitly limited the potential for Muslim activists to challenge the basis of the state, as its very establishment implied Muslim endorsement of the state. NU control of the ministry, which was firm by 1954, led it to endorse the state which underpinned it. Other Muslims protested because they wanted to challenge the basis of the state more fundamentally.[35]

Dominance of Islam within the Ministry of Religion is reflected in its definitions of religion and in its role in promoting Islamic senses of what can be religious. When the ministry was established in 1946, it was acknowledged that Protestants and Catholics deserved places, as even in the strictest Islamic terms Christianity is legitimate, a religion of the Book. Other religions were initially lumped under the rubric of 'ethnic'; those of Asian origin had to struggle for recognition, their status remaining problematic in some respects to the present. Each had to reorganize to match essentially Semitic senses of what constitutes religion—they are legitimate now to the degree that they emphasize belief in one God, a clear system of law, a holy scripture, and a prophet. To date, the official list of acceptable religions is largely that promulgated in Sukarno's presidential decree of 1965: Islam, Protestantism, Catholicism, Hinduism, Buddhism and Confucianism. The only exception is Confucianism, which has been relegated to the status of Judaism, being viewed essentially as an ethnic faith rather than an international religion.

[34] Boland, 117.
[35] D. Lev, *Islamic Courts in Indonesia*, Berkeley, 1972, 50.

This restricted sense of the term does not allow animism, folk spirit cults, new religions or independent mystical practices as 'religion'. Even the Balinese had to struggle actively before gaining official recognition in the 1950s. Hindu, Buddhist, and Confucian communities were forced to conform to monotheistic conceptions of divinity. The recasting of Buddhist idiom gave an advantage to Mahāyāna groups, as Theravāda Buddhists faced particular difficulty before they agreed finally that the Adi Buddha, roughly referring to the innate Buddha nature in everything, could be identified as 'God'. In the process of gaining recognition, scriptural factions within each community gained strength at the expense of traditional syncretists. Whether in scholarly debate, public discussion or government legislation, the accepted Indonesian definition of religion now accords with the Islamic model of what can constitute one.

Perhaps more critically, Islam conditions government views of its responsibility in the religious arena. The Indonesian government sees itself as having the responsibility to ensure that its citizens follow an acceptable religious faith as an obligation of citizenship. In the Five-Year Plan for 1969–74 (in Chapter IX on 'Religion') it is stated that 'the Government of the Republic of Indonesia has the responsibility of giving guidance and assistance to facilitate the development of each religion according to its own teachings, and to maintain supervision such that each citizen maintains their religious practice according to their beliefs'. This sense of responsibility distinguishes Indonesian views of religious freedom from those held by Western liberal régimes. In secular Western states professions of belief in God play a passive role, mainly meriting rhetorical invocation. Indonesia may not be an Islamic state, but it nevertheless takes from Islam its sense that authorities should intervene to guide the spiritual lives of citizens. Under the New Order the first principle of the Pancasila, that the nation is founded on belief in the one God, is read as a programme for action, and all citizens have generally been required to list an accepted religious affiliation on their identity cards. This view of religious freedom, obviously in marked contrast to that which pertains in the West, is essentially consistent with the Muslim view of the responsibility of the state vis-á-vis religion.

Government regulation of mystical movements extends colonial policies. Traditional courts were transformed through colonialism into an element within the new state, but policies aimed mainly to contain Islam. This alliance, with what were coincidentally the syncretic, mystical and Indic segments of the population, continued an opposition between Islamic and court powers of the pre-colonial era. That opposition is consistent again with the tension between Islam and the New Order. However, the Dutch were also sensitive to the dangers of millenarian and mystical movements, and surveillance has been continued since independence through Pakem, an agency of the Department of Justice since 1954. Offices in major cities supervise meetings and keep records. Even routine sessions of a spiritual nature in individuals' homes and the practices of traditional healers (*dukun*) require licence and registration. The Ministry of Religion also researched folk practices, indicating until 1978 that mysticism lay within its authority. It aimed to guide adherents toward orthodoxy by clarifying that mysticism originated from Islam.

In the New Order lobbying centred on winning legitimacy independent of religion. In opting for designation as *kepercayaan* in 1970, the movements staked a claim to legitimacy within the provisions of the 1945 constitution. That had been readopted by Sukarno in 1959 and remains sacred, together with the Pancasila as the essence of national political philosophy, under Suharto. During the hasty sessions in which the provisional 1945 constitution was drafted discussion of paragraph 29 of part XI (religion) was extended. The paragraph reads: 'The nation is based on faith in God [*Ketuhanan Yang Maha Esa*]; The nation guarantees each citizen the freedom to choose their own religion and to pray according to his own religion or faith (*kepercayaan*).' For independent-minded mystics the key was inclusion of the term 'faith' (*kepercayaan*); they read it as legitimizing practices outside religion so long as those were also directed toward the one God. Golkar, the government functional grouping, indirectly sponsored a congress in Yogyakarta in late 1970 in which mystics argued that they had been wrongly deprived of their rights, that their status was in principle already supposed to be equal to that of the religions. In 1973 the independent movements were recognized as legitimate options within the terms of the 1945 constitution, making it legal for citizens to list a mystical movement instead of a religion on their identity cards. In practice local authorities viewed it as subversive to broadcast this legislation, and when the census took place in 1980 no record of mystical affiliation was registered.

Then the marriage law of 1974 resulted in broader guidelines, easing the requirement for Javanese to adhere to Islamic ritual. Though the government attempt to establish civil marriage was withdrawn, some mystical groups conducted their own marriage ceremonies after 1974. In early 1978, responsibility for supervising the independent mystical sects, until recently usually called *kebatinan* (literally 'the science of the inner') was shifted from the Ministry of Religion to that of Education and Culture, weakening the legal claim of Islam to jurisdiction over them. Legislative changes had limited effects, and in many areas it has been considered provocative to publicize the new laws. The laws have provoked Islamic polemics and confusion in practice. Subud, the Javanese movement which is best known internationally, withdrew from the umbrella organization in early 1978 after its east Javanese SKK officers appeared to pressure adherents to identify themselves only as such, rather than by religious affiliation.

The establishment of a Directorate in the Ministry of Education and Culture theoretically ended subordination of *kebatinan* to religion. It began an inventory of movements, published significant documentation and initiated contact with non-Javanese movements. Recently changes within the Directorate coincide with what appears to have been a shift in government thinking about the relationship between *kebatinan* and religion. During the 1970s activists argued that identification with *kebatinan* was sufficient to fulfil requirement that citizens pursue belief in God. Recently interpretation has become more narrow, and affiliation with mystical movements is separated from the question of religious membership, which is still essential. The pendulum has swung back toward the position of the late 1960s. Most Javanists continue to hold that their mystical practice is interior and separate from religious identification. Pressure for members of movements also to maintain religious identification is again increasing.

Elsewhere in the Islamic zone, as in Sulu and Mindanao, changes have been coloured by social dislocation. In the largely Catholic Philippines, the Church has been basically conservative and closely tied to élite-dominated governments. Notwithstanding currents of liberation theology from Latin America and the critical stance of some Church leaders, such as Cardinal Sin in respect of President Marcos, the general tenor of the church has been conservative. This stance is rooted both in the social origins of its leadership and its staunch anti-communism since the Huk movement of the 1950s. From the vantage point of the Manila government, its policies in the south were strategies for development and national integration, associated with the migration of northern Christian settlers and businesses into what seemed a relatively underdeveloped south; for Muslim locals these programmes represented imposition of intense colonialism in the guise of nationalism.

It is impossible to separate changing religious practices, in this context of intermittent bloodletting, from the socio-economic and political strains of relations between poor Muslim southerners and relatively rich northern patronage powers. Marcos' policies provoked the founding of the Philippine Muslim Nationalist League in 1967. That became the Moro National Liberation Front (MNLF), with a military arm which grew rapidly through the 1970s. Misuari, the most public and astute leader of the movement, eventually sought support from Libya and blended Islamic nationalism with Marxist populism. Religious connections also became a bridge, along with ethnicity, complicating relationships between Manila and Kuala Lumpur. The Tausug, living in both Sulu and Sabah, established a working relationship across the border. Between 1973 and 1978 important steps were taken to regularize trade between Sulu and Sabah and to adjust the national legal system to account for local Muslim law. These steps took some of the fire from separatism, but it remained a running sore, among the many inheritances of the Marcos era which also plagued the Aquino government.[36]

In the Malaysian context, Islamization has been intensified through its role as a vehicle of Malay cohesion. Governments have contributed by proclaiming Muslim holidays, by upholding Islamic values in education and economics, and by encouraging internal conversion (dakwah) movements. The relationship between Islamic and national law in Malaysia remains complex, partly due to variations between states. In the sultanates colonial policies allowed distinct religious rights to remain with sultans, and in the modern states local authorities still retain significant powers in this area. Tun Mustapha made especially notable appeals to Islam when he was chief minister in Sabah, working against Christian influences and promoting conversion to Islam.

[36] T. J. S. George, *Revolt in Mindanao*, Kuala Lumpur, 1980, 195–207, 234–5, 266-7.

Since 1960 the government had administered collection of the *zakat*, the religious tithe. States administer the collection of 10 per cent of the paddy and at the same time villages levy their own *zakat*. In urban areas people pay an extra tax instead. In 1968 roughly $US3.5 million was collected: funds have gone to religious buildings and education, in direct subsidies to the poor, even to some business-oriented programmes.[37] Elsewhere national governments have no direct involvement in collecting religious taxes. In Indonesia it is only through private organizations, such as the Muhammadiyah, that *zakat* is collected and disbursed at a local level.

Throughout postwar Southeast Asia, the *haj* has been facilitated by increased air travel and, in Indonesia and Malaysia, it has been encouraged by centralized government co-ordination of arrangements. By the 1980s over 70,000 Indonesian pilgrims went to Mecca annually; Malaysian pilgrims increased from about 5000 to 15,000 between 1965 and 1980 and in the same year over 7500 pilgrims went from elsewhere in Southeast Asia.[38]

Christian missions and churches have remained active through most of Southeast Asia, representing an avenue of continuity for Western influence through education and health work. In areas like Timor, Irian Jaya or among the Karen, as noted already, Christian institutions have constituted independent networks which may threaten, or at least appear to undermine, state control. In this respect churches may parallel the function of Muslim networks in Mindanao and Sulu. In Indonesia and Malaysia, governments have been pressed to respond to Muslim sensitivity by actively restricting Christian missions, especially in areas like Aceh, where there have been popular protests against even locally initiated Christian church construction. In the late 1970s the Indonesian government pressed overseas missions to replace foreign missionaries with local people.

Even in the secular and materialistic city state of Singapore, the government has actively concerned itself with both promoting and regulating religious life. By the late 1970s Confucianism was promoted as an ethos convergent with government interest in social stability; in the 1980s this encouragement was underlined as a way of promoting extended family support for the elderly—to reduce welfare demands on the state. By the end of the 1980s the government was concerned with the rise of fundamentalisms and contingent discord. A white paper on the 'Maintenance of Religious Harmony' was tabled in parliament in December 1989 and noted incidents of social conflict in the late 1980s involving aggressive Protestant and Muslim fundamentalists. Muslims reacted indignantly when Protestants used the term 'Allah' for 'God', a translation which had already been banned by the Malaysian government. Dravidian and Aryan Hindus complained of each other and they also complained that the Christians were too aggressive. At the same time Sikhs and Hindus brought the tensions of South Asia into Singapore.

Resonances of religious difference continue to underlie or interlink with politics, and tensions have been most explicitly religious within the nations of the archipelago. The Muslim south and Catholic north have been at odds throughout the history of the modern Philippines. Religion

---

[37] von der Mehden, 58.
[38] ibid., 62.

converges with race in Malaysia—the requirement that Malays practise Islam implicitly reflects tension between Chinese and Malay groups. Indonesian politics have certainly been shaped significantly by the underlying division between syncretic traditional and modern orthodox Islam. In the 1950s the communists drew support mainly from syncretic Javanese, and opposition was strongest among the Muslim youth who helped the army eliminate it in the 1960s. Though less prominent, similar tensions have been clear through the mainland states as well. Religious issues wove into the politics of the thirty-year-long Vietnamese revolution. Catholics from the north sometimes worked together with syncretic southern cults during the 1950s and 1960s in opposition to the socialist revolution. In Burma, Buddhist Burmese speakers from the lowlands have been resisted by Christian Karens even since independence. In Thailand the Malay-speaking Muslim minority of the south has not easily endorsed or been integrated into a state which makes so much of the conjunction of Thai ethnicity, Indic-style royalty and Theravāda Buddhism.

REFORMULATIONS IN POPULAR PRACTICE

On the whole, colonial rule did not integrate tribal minorities into states any more than earlier indigenous lowland states had. On the peripheries or margins of centralizing colonial states, modern forces took effect mainly through channels such as missionizing. From the late nineteenth century Protestant missionaries brought communities like the Karen in Burma and the Batak and Sumatra into contact with both Christianity and, not incidentally, modern education. In the postwar era the independent states, dominated by speakers of Burmese, Thai, Vietnamese, Tagalog and Javanese, have spearheaded vigorous new policies of cultural integration. These threaten, ironically often more than earlier Western systems did, to lead to the disappearance of the hundreds of tribal or ethnic minority groups which have inhabited the less-trafficked zones of the region. The residual autonomy of tribal communities in remote parts of the Shan plateau and Mindanao, the Mentawi islands, and interior Borneo or New Guinea have all been brought into direct and increasingly routine contact with new institutions of government, foreign capitalized businesses, national education, and modern health care.

Thus we may observe that if colonialism defined our current maps of the region, the independent states have been left to effect the policies which aim culturally to integrate the peoples living within those boundaries. Similarly in rice-growing village society, still the foundation for the dominant populations of the region, there has been a penetration of state control in the postwar era far surpassing colonial interventions. Through most of the region, village heads and councils had functioned to represent local communities; by their mediation they muted the intervention of outside forces in the village sphere. Now village heads are increasingly the bottom rung of bureaucracies; their responsiveness to local demands has weakened, along with the claims of residents to land and the related strength of contacts with local spirit realms.

Notwithstanding these interventions, traditional and explicitly religious activities remain rich and varied. Many tribal and village cultures remain vigorous, and their commitment to rituals still goes with respect for the spirits of sacred sites. Spiritually linked healing practices remain widespread, as are possession cults and magical undercurrents. Ordinary people everywhere still use amulets and folk medicines; rituals at sacred springs help people find lovers; and students still visit the graves of grandparents to contact spirits, if now to aid success in modern examinations. In village societies the maintenance of traditional beliefs is associated with continuing agricultural and life-cycle rituals.

Continuities within ritual life can be remarkable: even in Bali, long inundated by tourism, ritual practices still mirror those of the prewar era.[39] In the Philippines fiestas celebrate not only holy days and national holidays but also harvests and life-cycle events. Patron saints occupy a position similar to that of guardian spirits in other parts of Southeast Asia. Even among Southeast Asia's widespread Chinese migrant population, the cohesion of spirit-medium cults remains.[40] In Java village life continues to centre on communal rituals, despite the fact that they have become expensive. Financial stresses have not stopped villagers in Kalimantan (Borneo), Bali or Burma from competing to outdo each other in funeral or initiation ceremonies, and often these lead hosts into severe debt. While orthodox Muslims in Indonesia or Malaysia are less likely to overextend in this fashion, the same impulse is displaced among them into excesses of giving in conjunction with Hari Raya, at the end of the fast month of Ramadan.

The syncretic traditional religions, notably local versions of Buddhism, Islam and Christianity, blended with these undercurrents of local culture, and still remain the largest formal communities of believers. But, according to Gourou for example, the central social focus in every village of the Red River delta in northern Vietnam was never the Buddhist temple, but the *dinh*. As the site for major agricultural rituals and other communal celebrations, it is the building in which ritual meetings aim to establish or maintain harmony with deities, the patron spirits of the village. For the populace in general, ancestral spirits have appeared unquestionably real; though Buddhist monks were usually also present, they were not often central to village life. The resilience of such village beliefs was evident in the 1970s when, even after several decades of communist rule, 'village elders were found to be restoring the old ritual processions to the *dinh*, the village communal house, whose mystique—and the politics associated with it—had supposedly been transformed and transposed with the downfall of colonialism'.[41]

In the archipelago periodic conflict in Mindanao relates to government efforts to subordinate the Moros within the Catholic- and Manila-dominated state. In Malaysia the so-called 'Emergency', a war between Chinese,

39 This remarkable continuity is evident in the three-part documentary film by John Darling, 'Bali Triptych' (Bozado Pty Ltd, 1988). Part two, 'The Path of the Soul', especially compares footage of rituals performed in the 1930s, taken by Mead and Bateson, with his own from the 1980s.
40 Cheu Hock Tong, *The Nine Emperor Gods*, Singapore, 1988.
41 A. B. Woodside, *Community and Revolution in Modern Vietnam*, Boston, 1976, 259.

British and Malays, extended through the 1950s and drove guerrilla fighters into the forest areas of the Semang, forcing some to cross the border into Thailand and others into resettled villages.[42] Indonesian confrontation with Malaysia in the early 1960s similarly drew armies to the boundary of Sarawak and Kalimantan. Indonesian military action against the Dutch, in what became Irian Jaya, had already established a military channel for integrating Irian into the state. Christian missions and churches became intensely active there only in the 1950s, in the last decade of Dutch control, and since its *de facto* incorporation into Indonesia in 1962 they have remained the major alternative network to the government in Irian Jaya. Subsequently the protracted war against Fretilin in East Timor, beginning in 1975, has had a similar complexion, aiming to subsume ethnic identities into the nation and facing resistance which has sometimes drawn on Catholic networks. The resettlement of Visayans in Mindanao or of Javanese in Sumatra, Irian Jaya, Sulawesi and Kalimantan, like the rapid expansion of forestry, has also worked to destroy the shifting lifestyles which underpinned the earlier rich diversity of local cultures.

Traditional ceremonial, political or economic exchange between hill and valley peoples had built-in mechanisms to moderate inequities and maintain distance; modernizing governments work to incorporate local chiefships or village councils into national administrations. As in the colonial era, conversion to Christianity sometimes appeared an attractive option. Even in Thailand, where extension of Theravāda into the hills is under way, some hill groups have become Christian instead. Missionary work directed at Biblical translation has facilitated conversion of predominantly oral traditions into writing, providing a route to literacy which is especially relevant for minorities interested in maintaining their language while accessing modern education. This competed with nationalist policies which have usually emphasized literacy through schooling in the language of the dominant ethnic group. Among the Karens, many of whom were converted by Baptists or Buddhists during the past century, natural (*Y'wa*), ethnic cultural (*Mu Kaw Li*) and ancestral (*bgha*) spirit forces continue to interact even among the large number who became Christian. Since 1962 the Ne Win government has actively pursued a policy of assimilation, but militant Karen nationalism remains in residual form along the Burmese–Thai border. In the Democratic Republic of Vietnam, which adopted Chinese policies with regard to ethnic minorities, promotion of literacy was channelled through indigenous tribal languages.[43]

Warfare and its attendant disruptive modes of central intervention have shaped the experience of most tribal areas of the mainland through much of the past four decades. The Vietminh defeated the French in the hills at Dien Bien Phu only through alliance with hill peoples whom they had depended on throughout their struggle. This alliance laid the basis for an unusual degree of autonomous tribal power in the Democratic Republic of Vietnam. The Annamite chain, bordering Vietnam, Kampuchea and Laos, has for decades been a key channel supplying guerrilla armies: first for

---

[42] C. Keyes, *The Golden Peninsula*, London, 1977, 38.
[43] ibid., 28–9.

Vietnamese against the French and then Americans, then for the Khmer resistance to the Vietnamese. In the Shan plateau the mainly Christian Karens, separate communist groups and opium warlords have been fighting intermittently since 1948. Similarly until the early 1970s at least, Sihanouk self-consciously considered Theravāda Buddhism as the prime instrument of national integration for Cambodia. In Thailand's northeast, north and south there have been periodic communist or ethnic guerrilla movements, and since the war the Thai government has felt that the security of its borders depended on assimilating the minorities into lowland Theravāda culture.

Thus in 1963 the Dhammajarig (travelling *Dhamma*) programme began self-consciously to promote the extension of Buddhism to the hill tribes with an assimilationist objective. By 1967 one hundred monks had been sent and instructed to explain their practices whenever local people inquired.[44] Observers of lowland villages uniformly note that the village *wat* remains the prime socially integrating institution of rural Thai society. Some have argued that the bounds of the village in central Thailand are defined by participation in specific *wat* communities. Everywhere participation involves both explicitly religious rites, associated with agricultural cycles, and normative Buddhist celebrations. Village monks are commonly youth who involve themselves increasingly in labour projects as well as with spiritual or secular teaching. While they may now help build roads or advise local military officers, the respect which villagers and officials alike demonstrate is still both strong and rooted in religious sensibilities. Villagers view monks as a separate class, despite the fact that most men have, if briefly, been ordained themselves.

Throughout the village societies of the lowland, Theravāda Buddhist Lao, Burmese, Khmer and Thai regions villagers maintain animistic as well as Buddhist beliefs. Students like Spiro have seen animism and Buddhism as though they are separate systems interacting, but most now concur with Tambiah, who presented them as sub-complexes within one system.[45] Rites oriented toward summoning and ensuring the presence of the 'vital essence' of life (*leipya* in Burmese, *khwan* in Tai, *pralu'n* in Khmer) represent ongoing animistic conceptions. Respect for village guardian spirits and interest in the sacred power of places and amulets or ritual objects combine with indigenous systems of astrology, tattoos and sexual magic and those with systems of merit making, monastic schooling and the doctrine of karma. These are most elaborated in the *nat* cults of Burma, but everywhere through the region practices of spirit possession and healing, linked to beliefs in life essence, remain powerful at the village level.

In Kampuchea and Laos the *saṅgha* lost ground under communist governments, but did not disappear. The proportion of monks relative to the overall male population halved in Thailand between the 1920s and 1970s, but remained high, at about 1:34. In Burma and Thailand the number of village youth ordaining for the annual rain retreat is still high, though expanding secular education has competed with the *saṅgha* as a

---

[44] Lester, 123–5.

[45] M. Spiro, *Buddhism and Society*, New York, 1970, and S. J. Tambiah, *Buddhism and the Spirit Cults in North-east Thailand*, Cambridge, UK, 1970.

vehicle of social mobility and thus fewer choose the monkhood as a long-term vocation. In Burma it was claimed that the *sangha* had declined from some 100,000 in royal times to 70,000 in 1941 and then, even more rapidly, to 45,000 in 1958.[46] In the Philippines, where the Catholic priesthood has a very different relationship to the general population, there were fewer than 4000 priests in the 1960s. Nevertheless there too the role of religious specialists at the local level has been changing: they have functioned more directly as agents of change, whether on behalf of the government or through their own perception of themselves as agents of change in the social, as well as specifically religious, spheres.[47]

This sort of shift in the role of religious specialists was noted in the Indonesian context by Geertz, who observed that in the 1950s the politicization of rural life through parties led the rural *kyai*, Javanese Islamic teachers, to become brokers for modern politics and ideas as well as continuing to function as teachers within the religious schools, the *pesantren*, which housed them.[48] At the same time the *penghulu*, in charge of mosques, and *hakim*, religious judges, have become even more directly part of national structures through their integration, via the Ministry of Religion, into the national bureaucratic network. In Indonesia at the local level the prewar Muhammadiyah has remained a powerful organization through its school system. It has been joined since the 1970s by a series of newer *dakwah* movements. Religious impulses of all sorts were strengthened in Indonesia through the coup of 1965, as they had been earlier through the revolution. A combination of political pressure and personal trauma led many Javanese to fill the mosques for Friday noon prayers. Many people since the 1970s have undoubtedly found renewed commitment to a more purely Islamic faith in the process.

Islamic efforts to purify Javanese Islam of syncretic beliefs and the insistence that all Muslims must rigorously obey the injunctions of their faith had the unintended effect of pushing committed Javanists to define themselves in non-Islamic terms. In the late 1960s several hundred thousand converts joined Christian churches. Hindu, Buddhist, and mystical movements were also injected with a new vitality. Hinduism, Hindu Dharma in Indonesia, was exclusively Balinese until 1965, when scattered villages, especially in the mountainous regions of east and central Java, chose to identify themselves as Hindu. Whether opting for Hinduism or Buddhism, villagers in Java have often done so out of conviction that, among the alternatives presented, the Indic religions are closest to the reality of their continuing traditional practices. At the same time new requirements have challenged most local religious communities to redefine themselves in scriptural terms in order to gain recognition from the new national bureaucracy.

This challenge forced Balinese Hindus to redefine their practices during the 1950s. A new generation of postwar Balinese began to establish direct

---

[46] Mendelson, 336.
[47] von der Mehden, 86.
[48] C. Geertz, 'The Javanese Kijaji: the Changing Role of a Cultural Broker', *Comparative Studies in Society and History*, II (1959–60).

contact with Indian Hindus in order to gain recognition from the Ministry of Religion. Geertz observed, on the basis of his studies in the late 1950s, that this reformation of Balinese religion resulted in the formalization of teachings on a more literal basis, the invention of new rituals, and the construction of sometimes bizarre new temples.[49] At the same time the continuing strength of earlier ceremonial religion is exemplified in Bali, where temple ritual cycles have been maintained. Associated dramatic performances and artistic activities have as often been strengthened as weakened by tourism, since foreign audiences supplement income for hamlets which channel new money into old rituals. The most spectacular demonstration, exceeding even the drama of royal cremation, was the Ekadasa Rudra ceremony at the mother temple of Bali at Besaki. This two-month-long ceremony was initiated in 1963, as 8 March of that year was the end of the Saka year 1884, and marked a 100-year cycle from the previous ceremony. Because that ritual cycle was interrupted by the eruption of Mount Agung, it was only 'completed' through cleansing rituals in 1979. The successful second attempt showed the markings of New Order Society as well as a powerful depth of local commitment to enact a traditional magical ceremony.[50]

Changes have been necessary within all the other Asian-based religions in Indonesia. Several of the small, previously exclusively urban, modern Buddhist movements have become mass movements.[51] Modern Indonesian Buddhism has roots within both the local Chinese communities and in *priyayi* circles, as some of them came to identify with it through the Theosophical Society in the prewar period. Even within the reformed Hindu and Buddhist spheres there have been rebels. Some Javanists hark back to syncretic Majapahit, looking to mysticism rather than scriptural modernism. In the 1970s the Surakarta-based Sadhar Mapan advanced Javanist Hindu yogic rather than Balinese ritual practice, as contained in the mainstream Parisada Hindu Dharma; Kasogatan, a small Tantric-style group, also looked to the Majapahit text *Sanghyang Kamahayanikan* rather than to the purism of many modern Buddhists.

'Religion' had meant the nexus of ritual magic and mystical theory which everywhere wedded private and communal practices with performance and textual traditions. In opting for the new versions of Hinduism or Buddhism, villagers were often expressing their sense that even modernist versions of those conformed to their actual tradition of practice more than modernist versions of Islam did. From village perspectives or for traditionally minded Javanese or Balinese, religious identification was never an exclusive matter. In any event, all of the dominant national organizations of the world religions in Indonesia are now modernist in tone and exclusive in structure, emphasizing ritual, text, and doctrine to the exclusion of mysticism and traditional magical praxis.

[49] C. Geertz,' 'Internal Conversion' in Contemporary Bali' in his *The Interpretation of Cultures*, New York, 1973.
[50] A. Forge, 'Balinese Religion and Indonesian Identity' in J. Fox, ed., *Indonesia: the Making of a Culture*, Canberra, 1980, 227–32.
[51] J. D. Howell, 'Modernizing Religious Reform and the Far Eastern Religions in Twentieth Century Indonesia' in S. Udin, ed., *Spectrum*, Jakarta, 1978.

MAGICAL, MILLENARIAN AND MYSTICAL PRACTICES

Just as modernizing governments have established powerful channels to integrate, dominate and reform the cultures of geographically remote peoples, so they have intruded with increasing directness on the magical practices of villagers even within the centrally positioned lowland societies. The postwar communications revolution has reconfigured cultural relations both horizontally, through space as it were, and vertically, cutting downward across social classes. Most new national governments have actively suppressed the most obviously magical and millenarian elements of local religion, in effect favouring formalized orthodoxies—not surprisingly, as those usually have hierarchies which can be manipulated by centralizing powers. Whether they have been socialist or capitalist in orientation, recent governments have all endorsed older imperial views of folk practices as reflections of 'pre-scientific superstition' which impede 'modern progress'.

In socialist Vietnam there has been willingness to compromise with Buddhism, allowing it a central committee. Support has even extended to the establishment of a High Level School of Vietnamese Buddhist studies. The government is nonetheless actively hostile to anything representing popular millenarianism, which it sees as representing a throwback to definitely outdated superstitions.[52] Folk rituals combined spiritualist séances with Buddhism. An element of animism, through the contacts with spirits implied, made local traditions similar to many others throughout the village cultures of the region. About 10 per cent of the population in southern Vietnam were Catholic in the early 1960s; an estimated 35–40 per cent were considered strong believers in Mahāyāna Buddhism; the remainder were regarded as nominal, meaning that they adhered to a mixture of animism, Taoism and Confucianism.[53]

Alongside traditional religious practices there have been substantial new sectarian movements everywhere in Southeast Asia. In Vietnam the Hoa Hao sect, founded in 1939, claimed a membership of 450,000 in 1964 in Ang Giang Province alone, and two million overall. It has been essentially a local form of Buddhism, but with emphasis on traditional folk practices rather than the more scriptural style of the Thien (Zen) revivalist monks, who began to gain strength from the 1930s onward. Teachings included not only a strong element of millenarianism, but also emphasis on moral reform. In 1966 the Cao Dai, founded in 1925, was estimated to have between one and two million members. It recognized the revelations received by the prophets of all the major world religions, somewhat in the fashion of Ba'hai, presenting them all as vehicles of God's purpose in the world in the past. In it, presence of belief in the one God stands above notions of karma and reincarnation, as is also the case in many Javanese movements. Sect activities were most notable during the 1950s through their political implications, but the indications are that the syncretic sects remained healthy under socialism. Recent visitors have reported not only that attendance at Sunday mass in the cathedrals of Hanoi and Ho Chi

---

[52] D. J. Steinberg, ed., *In Search of Southeast Asia*, Sydney, 1987, 465.
[53] Schecter, 180.

Minh City has been spectacular, but also that sect temples in the delta are in excellent repair.

In Burma large numbers of the Chin followed a syncretic movement which, like other millenarian movements since the late nineteenth century, adopted aspects of Christianity. The Pau Chin Hau can be interpreted as a movement which adopted elements of Christianity as an indigenous democratization movement which countered both traditional chiefly authority and the intensification of Burmese control.[54] While sectarian cults have been important in Burmese villages, new forms of vipassana meditation have been notable in cities and of more international significance. This movement had roots early in the century, but after 1950 was formally encouraged, particularly by state sponsorship of meditation centres. These were recognized in varying grades and then registered and granted subsidies. From an early stage these centres catered to foreign students of Buddhism. Since the 1950s small groups of foreign students have always been present, and in this sector Burma has never been completely closed. Within that sphere Mahasi Sayadaw occupies a special place, due especially to the patronage provided to him during the 1950s by the U Nu government.

In Thailand the most internationally known exponent of modern Buddhist meditation has been Bhikkhu Buddhadasa, who has presided over the forest hermitage of Suan Mokh in the South. While doctrinally orthodox and borrowing from Zen, he presents a view of Buddhism grounded in 'this-worldly' action. His view is that Buddhism is relevant not only cosmologically, as though only in some future life, but also in terms of its relation to continually evolving living situations. He emphasized, as core doctrines of Buddhism in fact always have, that the states of *samsara*, the worldly condition of attachment, and *nirvana*, the bliss of release, are interiorized conditions in the here and now. Setting himself early on against the notion that Buddhism was fatalistic, he stressed in relation to the teachings of all world religions that they focused ultimately on the practical realization of principles. In a political context his teachings can be styled a form of Buddhist socialism, one which rejected both communist and capitalist materialisms. He has been able to speak to many young educated Buddhists who aim to reconcile traditional faith with modern civic action.

Popular stereotypes of Buddhist monks as intensive meditators have long been dismissed. Though the forest tradition of intensive insight meditation practice has an ancient history with lineages into the present, the vast majority of Theravāda monks in Thailand neither teach nor even practise meditation. Nevertheless several significant schools of *vipassana* practice have emerged from the *sangha*, extending to lay followers who may undertake ten-day retreats on a regular basis. Several teachers have gained overseas followings. In the early twentieth century the meditation master Achaan Mun, who spent most of his career in the northeast of Thailand, revived the longstanding tradition of forest monastic disciplines. His disciples are scattered throughout the country, having founded their

54 Keyes, 49.

own schools of meditation and catering to both monks and laity. His most noted follower, Achaan Chaa of Wat Pah Pong in Ubon Province, attracted continuous patronage from Bangkok and has sent disciples to establish forest meditation centres in England and Australia.

Whether through modern forms of meditation or in other ways, through education and community action, increasing numbers of monks are actively concerned with trying to reconcile their practices with modern life. Many who aspire to move upward socially also show serious commitment to meditation. The overall effect of modernizing meditative practices is a new strength of emphasis on the possibility of contributing positively through social action by being more tuned and egoless. Whatever the traditional conjunction, it appears increasingly that in contemporary Buddhism there is a positive evaluation of ameliorative social action. The gap between monk and laity, at least with respect to spiritual practices, is also being reformed and in certain respects closed. The meditation movements, both within and beyond the *sangha*, represent an active repositioning and continuation of commitment to spiritual realization.

In Malaysia the formal status of Islam as *the* religion of 'Malays' militates powerfully against syncretic cults of the type allowable in Theravāda or Javanese environments; local healers and urbanites nevertheless participate in magical practices or in marginal 'new' religious movements. Just as the *dakwah* movements represent a reinvigoration of Malay identity through strengthening of a pure Islamic commitment, among local Chinese and Indians there have been many followers not only of charismatic Christianity but also of the Indian saint Satya Sai Baba and of the Baitiangong. The latter, founded by Zhao Chongming after a vision in 1976, attempted to unite spirit-medium cults in middle-class Kuala Lumpur.[55] These movements indicate, just as do the urban followers of *vipassana* meditation in Rangoon and Bangkok or the adherents of faith healers in Manila, that magic, millenarianism and mysticism remain popular among Western-educated middle-class Southeast Asians as well as in villages, where it is easier to see such beliefs as a residue of earlier tradition.

Within Indonesia the relationship between politics, religion, and mysticism has been transformed since independence, in the process altering both the context and internal structures of local variants of mysticism. Sukarno's voice had joined others in warnings against black magic, which was a recurrent focus of public debate throughout the 1960s. Since the mid-1960s recognized movements have had firmly to abjure interest in political power, giving official legitimacy only to movements which were at least ostensibly apolitical. In the classical context such a separation was inconceivable; mysticism, culture, and politics were inextricably interwoven in theory and practice. The modern context of religious plurality, Islamic strength, and outwardly secular government all worked to pressure Javanists, those who tended to be the most mystical in their spirituality, into formal organizations. Within this context such organizations

[55] S. E. Ackerman and R. L. Lee, *Heaven in Transition: Non-Muslim Religious Innovation and Ethnic Identity in Malaysia*, Honolulu, 1988, 127–36.

have to be defined as purely mystical, in the classical sense that the core of all mysticism is union with the divine, and this separates mysticism from the magical and millennial elements to which it was bound by tradition. The term *kejawen* now most often refers specifically to the traditional styles within which spirit relations, magic powers, and millennial expectations were fundamental. This style remains powerful, even though it is restricted in organizational expression, as a substratum of popular outlook and cultic movement. At the same time new forms of mysticism have risen out of Javanist orientations.

Repression of millennial movements has been continual, constituting a continuing theme of religious politics in the postwar period. In 1967 the Mbah Suro movement was suppressed after it spread rumours of radical change from its centre near Ngawi; in 1968 the Java-wide Manunggal movement was outlawed after a public trial. Tens of thousands of members, some of them highly placed military and civilian officials, paid homage to their guru, Romo Semana, in a style that the government felt evoked Indic courts. Defenders argued that their behaviour merely reflected ordinary expression of respect for an elder. This incident demonstrated the extent to which power-oriented and magical spirituality, tied closely to normal social patterns, had become problematic in a context of commitment to modernizing and centralizing state power.

When the Suharto government announced that it had uncovered an attempted coup in September 1976, it became clear quickly that it centred on a mystic, until then unknown, named Sawito. He had visited power points and, at Gunung Tidar at the centre of Java, claimed to have been given the authority previously held by Semar, the guardian of Java. Subsequently he gathered a remarkable collection of signatures to attach to a document criticizing the moral fibre of Suharto. Former Vice-President Hatta and all the prominent religious leaders whose signatures appeared on the document quickly denied having known what was in it, but it was nonetheless taken seriously. From the Western standpoint Sawito's threat seemed trivial, but the magnitude of Suharto's response demonstrated his sense of vulnerability in those Javanist terms. This special fear, in the face of mystical claims that he lacked the *wahyu*, the divine sanction on which power is supposed to rest, itself indicated the continuing wider relevance of the underlying complex of beliefs to which the challenge related.

Kebatinan movements have been noted since independence in Indonesia. Generally emphasizing experiential realization of the Absolute, they are mainly Javanese in origin and composition, and see their practices as rooted in an ageless indigenous wisdom which predates Indian influences. In this context mysticism refers, as everywhere in its classical meaning, to the inner, spiritual and esoteric dimension within all religion, and also more especially to beliefs, practices and movements which are defined by their focus on individual realization. There are hundreds of identifiable movements in the country. Subagya listed 288 in 1973; an inventory in 1980 registered 160; but there can be no definitive listing.[56] Many groups are so small, local, ephemeral and informal that they never merit note, though some of them may be quite significant. The *tarekats*, the Sufi movements,

---

[56] R. Subagya, *Kepercayaan dan Agama*, Yogyakarta, 1973, 129–38.

are also mystical, but their affiliation with Islam is intrinsic and they are thus not generally bracketed with the independent movements. Several dozen movements have Java-wide or genuinely Indonesian membership. These include Pangestu, Subud, Sapta Darma, Ilmu Sejati, Sumarah and Hardopusoro. A few of those claim more than one hundred thousand members, but most have at best several thousand who are centrally motivated by their practice.

Kebatinan groups existed within the Dutch colonial framework, but were necessarily secretive in that context. They came into public view during the revolutionary fighting of the late 1940s. Then, paralleling the organizing process of the 1950s through all sectors of society, major movements adopted formal patterns with elected officers, minutes and conferences. This process was in part spontaneous, in part a response to the new demand for records of membership and meetings on the part of government agencies. In the early 1950s a number of movements argued that they deserved recognition as separate religions, suggesting that in the context of national independence it would be an anomaly if only 'imported' religions received government approval. Sapta Darma maintained that argument into the 1970s, but most accepted early on that they were unlikely to be recognized as religions because of the violent response which that would have brought from Muslims.

In the traditional setting, mystical consciousness and social power were cosmologically bound together. Both the Indic notion of the *devaraja* and the Islamic ideals of the state as guardian of religion implied that the ruler had a special relation to the sacred. Insofar as mystics claimed direct contact with divinity, they walked a delicate line to avoid appearance of separate claim to secular authority. Under the Dutch such movements attracted surveillance as potential focal points of rural unrest; in the period since independence the political sensitivity of, and pressures on, religious life have increased. Increasingly autonomous and exclusive definition of each element in the religious scene naturally extended into intensified competition, both to participate in the newly established power structures of the state and to determine how the national identity would relate to religious convictions.

Popular association of *kebatinan* with occultism, no less than analytical association of mystical gnosis with instrumental effects, represents confusion of forms with essence. All of the major national movements dissociate themselves from *kejawen* occultism, emphasizing direct consciousness of God rather than culturally rooted symbols and spirits. This shift of emphasis from powers to consciousness is not simply a response to the politicized context of Javanese mysticism. The same polarity is rooted within early Indic culture; it also represents a penetration of Semitic forms of monotheism, which stress distinction between magic and divine revelation, into the Javanist world. Although Javanist tradition still prioritizes a Tantric-style identification of consciousness and powers, it also already contained a Buddhist-style emphasis on the void as a powerful counter to that; the extension of monotheism resonated with that existing strand of local spirituality. Tantric patterns continue implicitly to have strength in village practices, the *danhyang* cults, and in movements such as Sadhar Mapan and Manunggal. But the Buddhist tradition and mystical separation of consciousness from any visible effects are profoundly rooted in a tradition extending back over a millennium, one which has dovetailed with modern pressures to produce more exclusive emphasis on consciousness.

The movements are not equivalent to Sufism, which is integrally tied to a 'world religion', but rather to culturally based traditions such as Taoism or Shinto. Sufism and Zen place emphasis on lineages connecting living masters to Muhammad and the Buddha. In Javanism such lineage is denied not just as a counter to Islamic claims that it is derivative, but also as an assertion that religious knowledge comes direct from God: in short, an assertion that *kebatinan* is mystical in the fundamental sense of the term. Throughout the 1970s public tension frequently focused on the manoeuvring, partly inspired by the Suharto government, to confer greater legitimacy to the mystical movements. Islamic reaction has been intense and each step toward independent legitimacy has been geared, as much as possible, to avoid stirring reaction. Related debates, such as those surrounding the effort to bring in secular marriage laws in 1973 and 1974, have touched the same sensitive area of religious conflict. In 1973 it became legal to belong to mystical movements without also claiming membership in a 'world religion'; in 1978 these movements were given a new basis of legitimacy when they were released from the jurisdiction of the Ministry of Religion and given their own Directorate within the Ministry of Education and Culture.

Members use Javanese in daily life and group meetings, but Indonesian is used for organizational matters. Traditional cults focused on a charismatic guru; modern movements have semi-rationalized structures. Leaders are distinguished from spiritual teachers; if the patronage model remains strong in practice, theory no longer places it at the heart of organization. Organizations adopt the administrative hierarchy common to all national organizations, but growing care in the keeping of membership lists is often mainly to facilitate relations with supervising bodies. Major sects are relatively open in structure and streamlined in practice, and esoteric tendencies decline together with the decreasing emphasis on instrumental magic, ancestral spirits, and occult powers. Healing plays a major role in sects such as Subud and Sapto Darmo, but is balanced by emphasis on 'God's responsibility' for effecting cures. Monotheistic emphasis is reflected in often puritanical distaste for the possession cults characteristic of most local traditions. Similarly, people in most movements speak of meditation as *sujud* (surrender) or *panembah* (prayer) rather than *semadi*. The Indic resonance of the latter renders it suspect to Islam; which sees *semadi* as implying entry into a 'Godless void', because it usually comes without a notion of personalized divinity.

The strongest evidence of an essentially Islamic framing of discourse about religion lies in the very extent of public debate about and between 'Islam and *kebatinan*'. The relationship has been problematic from the earliest days of the republic in formal contexts of legal clarification; in the press; and down to the village level in relations between branches of mystical movements and local authorities. Umbrella organizations emerged in the 1950s when the leading national spokesperson for them was Wongsonegoro. He headed the Congress of Indonesian Mystics (BKKI), which petitioned Sukarno to request status equal to religions in 1957. In Malang in 1960 a subsequent congress stressed that *kebatinan* and religion differed only in emphasis—mysticism focused on perfecting the individual spirit while the latter emphasized prayer to God. In 1961 a seminar considered the relationship between *kebatinan* and Sukarno's political philosophy; in 1962 another stressed the relationship between spiritual practice, national struggle and world peace. The BKKI aimed to clarify that *kebatinan* represented an indigenous spiritual tradition of high standing, not a jumble of superstition and magic. Participants felt a special relationship to the national identity, arguing that the foundation of the nation's belief in God lay in the strength of *kebatinan* within it. In 1958 the BKKI affirmed that the 'essential characteristic of the Indonesian national identity lies in emphasis on life of the spirit'.

There is strong pressure behind the growth of a literalist monotheism. The first principle of the Pancasila is an underscoring of the profession of faith in one God, though omitting reference to Muhammad, in Islamic terms. Islam may not have established itself as the religion of Indonesia, but there is no doubt that its sense of religion defines, shapes and constrains discourse about religion and spiritual life. This pressure is conveyed through the government bureaucracy, and has influenced private practices as well as public expression of religious life. A disposition to rearguard action, rationalization and justification of practices, pressures even mystics toward literal Islamic terms of discourse. At the same time, as a separate vector of change, there is growing emphasis on a restricted range of dimensions. Indonesian Muslims define religion increasingly in terms of its socio-cultural dimensions. From the perspective of the mystics it appears that orthodoxy itself loses sight of the fact that religion and spirituality are not only mediated and expressed through human symbols and actions but also exist as a sphere in themselves.

In reflecting generally on the range of magical, mystical and millenarian movements through the Southeast Asian region, we can note strong common patterns. Differences relate partly to varying dominant 'world religions' and national governmental policies, as those appear as moderating forces shaping local expression. Everywhere an explicit ideology of scientific modernism colours dominant formal perspectives on folk magic. Conversely, whether in Filipino faith-healing practices in Luzon or in the thinking of the Cao Dai in the Mekong delta of Vietnam, local sects attempt to 'domesticate' science both by incorporating reference to it in magic and by attempting to validate practices by pseudo-scientific criteria. In any event folk magical healing, related to shamanism, remains present, however substantially reformed and defensive.[57]

Like magical healing, millenarianism also remains powerful as a framework for folk perception and practice. An underlying conviction in the

[57] The strengths of these currents are evident in studies such as R. W. Leiban, *Cebuano Sorcery*, Berkeley, 1967; M. E. Spiro, *Burmese Supernaturalism*, Englewood Cliffs, 1967; and L. Golomb, *An Anthropology of Curing in Multiethnic Thailand*, Urbana and Chicago, 1985.

cosmological meaning of earthly events, implicitly always including politics, continues to lead people throughout the region to frame social process within their spiritual senses of what constitutes humanity, implying ultimately that life leads toward resolution and balance within nature and that that may be expressed socially through radical shifts in power. These impulses are expressed through national political philosophies as 'neo-traditionalism', as we noted in observing the convergences which relate Marxist and millenarian formations in both Vietnam and Java. The same forces have also operated separately, as a distinct pattern evident through the region, in the form of purely local expressions centring on charismatic teachers who have eschatological visions of social process.

While the magical and millenarian strands of postwar religious practice are most rooted in and pervasive through the villages of the region, newly formed mystical sects and meditation practices cross the urban–rural divide and have often been urban-based. Within them the reformed contemporary élites have essentially rescued aspects of their traditional esoteric spirituality; but they have done it by disentangling consciousness-raising practices (as we may reframe meditation) from the magic and hierarchies of older orthodox Buddhism or Islam, within which such practices had earlier been embedded. *Vipassana* practitioners following the Burmese master Mahasi Sayadaw or the Thai Achaan Chaa, Javanese members of Pangestu, Subud or Sumarah, Tagalog disciples of faith healers, and Vietnamese followers of Cao Dai, have all practised meditation or entered trances; these are new ways of exploring essentially the same spiritual domains which older local traditions have accessed through the mediation of religious specialists such as village shamans, Catholic priests, Islamic *ulamā* or Buddhist monks.

PURIST REVIVAL AND SECULAR MODERNISM

The breakdown of communal structures by rapid socio-economic change has brought a variety of responses. Nevertheless the majority of Southeast Asians still pursue folk customs or syncretic traditional religions. Those derive from practices which were fully formed in earlier periods of history, including the variations of orthodoxy and mysticism already alluded to. Distinctive new currents, such as secularism and fundamentalism, may appear as stark counterpoints to each other, but they equally embody the specifically modern situation. Earlier scriptural modernism was a feature of prewar religious reform and paralleled nationalism in the political arena: it arose essentially as a correlate of the print media.

Now new fundamentalisms, like contemporary areligious secularism, are more especially a reflection of electronic mass media. Fundamentalist revivalism, popular purist movements of regeneration and internal conversion, may be especially apparent in the Islamic sphere, but similar movements appear in all other local communities. The groundswell of revivalist religion calls into question the assumption that industrialization and the pressures of urban life would decrease the social role of religion.

Just as the intensity of fundamentalism in the United States and Iran has confounded expectations, so in Southeast Asia one of the clearest responses to the pressures of modern life has been intensified literal faith. These belief patterns are not, as some secularists imagine, explicable mainly as a residue of earlier traditional faith. They are facilitated by the effectiveness of electronic media and are a specifically modern phenomenon. Earlier forms of reformism were 'modernist' rather than areligiously secular or fundamentalist.

Extending outward from urban areas, and reflecting the outlook of those educated in Western styles, many variants of the scriptural modernism which have prewar origins can still be identified. Rationalizing reformists have emerged separately from within each local Southeast Asian community: they have certainly not been only reflections of the activity of missions from beyond the region, as indigenous modernism arose beyond the sphere of direct colonial impact as a process of independent innovation. Generally they have argued at once for adjustment to modernity and for a return in more critical and rational terms to the original canons of their religion. In the process they attempt to disentangle scripture from myth and faith from magic, claiming a rationalism almost in the terms of modern science.

In Thailand the continuing link between the *sangha* and royalty has meant that modernist forms of religious consciousness were pioneered through dominant religious and political institutions rather than as a counter to them. Mongkut, king of Siam in the mid-nineteenth century, had been a monk for two decades before he assumed the throne. Through contacts he pursued with missionaries he undertook studies of Latin, English, mathematics and astronomy, and he became critical of monks, including those who had trained him: he felt they engaged in chanting without understanding the scriptures. The emphasis on comprehension of texts he initiated through the Dhammayutikaya movement, first founded in 1833, aimed to reduce the related 'confusion' of orthodoxy with popular magic, and the related reformist sects which resulted have become especially important in all of the mainland *sanghas*.

In Thailand, Laos and Cambodia the traditionalist group is known as the Mahanikaya, or 'Great Order', and the reformists belong to the Dhammayuttikaya. In Burma the traditionalists generally belong to the Sudhamma, the 'Good Dhamma' order, while the reformists belong to the Shwegyin, also founded in the nineteenth century. The modernist groups are more committed to emphasis on the study of Pāli texts and the practice of meditation, and are more strict with regard to prohibitions on the handling of money. Only a small minority of monks belong to the reformist orders, but they have strong royal patronage and greater influence than numbers alone would suggest.

Where Western imperialism had divided religious and secular power from each other, politics and religious reformism nevertheless went hand in hand. Because the link between politics and established religion had been cut by imperialism in Burma, with the elimination of the traditional state, the *sangha* was weakened due to the absence of royal patronage. As a result, lay movements, such as the Young Men's Buddhist Association, became the most visible foci of anti-colonial resistance. Religious issues nevertheless remained prominent within political nationalism, as suggested by the fact that its first notable victory early in the century came when agitation gave abbots the right to insist that even the British had to take their shoes off upon entering temple compounds. The prominence of lay practices of *vipassana*, insight meditation, through teachings such as those of U Ba Kin and Mahasi Sayadaw, reminds us of the internal and non-political aspects of modernizing religion. Religious styles self-consciously adapt to changing urban lifestyles and modern education, without always being a response to political issues and objectives.

Malay Islamic modernism has had roots in Cairo, where Al-Azhar University housed Mohammad Abduh's influential effort to reconcile religious doctrine with scientific thought, making it a focus of Islamic intellectual life worldwide. Nationalism went hand in hand with renewal of religion; since independence Malay ethnicity has been identified increasingly with Islam, adding force to purism, and influencing the complexion of religious practices on the ground. In one sense this recent trend is simply a continuation of the longstanding process of *'masuk Melayu'*, that is of 'becoming Malay'. Whether in Indonesia, especially in Kalimantan, or in Malaysia, as minority groups come increasingly into contact with urban currents they often adopt Malay-Indonesian language and Islam simultaneously. The modern context extends a longstanding process, but now usually with more direct movement to purist forms of Islam.[58] In Indonesia the Muhammadiyah movement, founded in Yogyakarta in 1911, established a network of schools with a curriculum including mathematics, science, and social studies. Most Javanese, even in cities, have experienced Islam as part of a synthesis including deeply rooted Indian thought and animistic spirit beliefs. Muhammadiyah, like other modernisms, stressed revamping of Islam to expunge what it saw as outdated elements, setting itself against the syncretism present within the *pesantren* pattern of tradition.

Contemporary purism is not simply a continuation of prewar scriptural modernism; it takes a sharper form. In Malaysia the *dakwah* movements do some external missionizing but can be generally characterized as movements of internal conversion. Notable groups within this ambit include Darul Arqam, a small group centring on a commune near Kuala Lumpur; Jemaat Tabligh, an international movement originating in India; and, most importantly, ABIM, a nation-wide and locally rooted movement. Like Muhammadiyah in Indonesia or the Dhammayut sect in Thailand, the Darul Arqam has power beyond its numbers due to tight organization and the high profile of its school and clinic. In both it draws strongly from traditional practices. The Jemaat Tabligh came to the peninsula in the 1950s and exists throughout the country, but with little formal organization. ABIM, the Muslim Youth League of Malaysia, was founded in 1971 and now has a membership of over 35,000. It sponsors rallies and is well

[58] D. Miles, *Cutlass and Crescent Moon*, Sydney: University of Sydney, Centre for Asian Studies, 1976, and R. Hefner, *Hindu Javanese*, Princeton, 1985.

organized throughout the school and university system. It has been strongly connected with international revivalism in Iran and the Arab Middle East, raising consciousness of those areas locally. It attracted a young and well-educated membership under the leadership of Anwar Ibrahim and continues to emphasize internal purification of practices.

Generally in Malaysia during the 1970s and 1980s, explicit and publicly indicated adherence to Islamic practices has been strongly on the upswing within the Malay community. The conflation of Malay ethnic and Muslim religious identity has been longstanding, but it is only recently that it has become a focus of constant invocation. Muslim holidays have become more definitively national in scope. Civil servants dress more conservatively, moving away from the British conventions which many had adopted in the colonial era. Religious issues have converged with ethnic conflict to a remarkable and uncomfortable degree. As Malays have moved increasingly into urban environments, largely facilitated by patronage through the bureaucracy but also by movement toward factory labour and away from the farms, they have confronted Chinese domination of the economy and conflict with Western values more directly. These contexts have sharpened, rather than decreased, movement toward local values in a more purist form. Local movements have also been powerfully influenced by the increase in self-confidence throughout the Islamic world since the oil boom. In part this is related to a worldwide Islamic movement to reject the philosophical baggage which appears to accompany Westernization. The new strength of economies throughout the Islamic world provided an underpinning for this revival.

Indonesian *dakwah* movements have been increasing in strength since the early 1970s. The government has promoted renewal and re-emphasis on Islam, almost in spite of itself. Though significant elements of the national leadership might be privately otherwise inclined, contributions from Suharto's discretionary funds to the *pesantren* have been consistently high from the late 1970s onward. The Ministry of Religion, still preponderantly Muslim in composition and orientation, carries out missionary activities, produces publications, and co-ordinates legal and educational offices which encourage purism. Government ironically goes farther in this respect than even many of those it is presumably catering to would want. Now that the policy in all government buildings is to have a prayer room to cater to Muslims, there is social pressure for those present to appear to be using these new facilities. Muhammadiyah continues to be active through its many schools and hospitals and, while relatively moderate by the standards of many groups, it contributes to continuing Islamization. The Dewan Da'wah Islamiyah Indonesia has been under the leadership of Muhammed Natsir, former Masjumi leader and one-time Prime Minister.

The previously apparently conservative Nahdatul Ulama has been reinvigorated since the 1970s. A dynamic new generation of activists, including Abdurrahman Wahid and Nurcholish Madjid, both thoroughly cosmopolitan products of highly charged modern *pesantren* education, present it with a radically new image. The *pesantren* networks have been revitalized; the *tarekats*, which were linked strongly to them earlier on, have recently regained a new legitimacy, which has perhaps strengthened as the lingering predispositions of Protestant Christian imperialists fade. It appears as though the modernist disdain for mysticism of the prewar era, one which drove those so inclined to distance themselves from Islam by associating with independent and explicitly syncretic movements, has shifted. Since the late 1970s radical movements have increased the political sensitivity of Islam. One indication of the government's attitude is that Libya and Iran are listed, along with Israel and China, among the countries which citizens may not enter with an Indonesian passport.

While from many points of view the government has, in the past two decades, made powerful gestures to neutralize Islamic fundamentalism, within the Islamic community dissatisfactions have remained strong. Many have certainly felt that the New Order's willingness to accommodate mysticism (*kepercayaan*) by legitimizing it in 1973, threatened the position of Islam within the country. There have been only a few public demonstrations, but the incidents which have come to the surface have attracted a great deal of publicity. The 'Kommando Jihad' movement was banned in the late 1970s through association with movements to overthrow the government. In 1978 the Gerakan Pemuda Islam (Islamic Youth Movement) was banned. Libyans were associated with movements in Aceh; in 1981 another group was accused of having support from the Ayatollah Khomeini; a Bandung group commandeered a plane in 1980; and in 1985 the bombing of Borobudur was blamed on Muslim extremists.[59]

Reformism and fundamentalism have appeared in every religious community. Vietnamese Buddhism has been a syncretic blend of spirit beliefs and Confucianism, but was reshaped during the 1920s and 1930s. In the most dynamic phase of the postwar period for Buddhists there, a Vietnamese Buddhist Reunification Congress took place in the week of the New Year of 1964 at Xa Loi Pagoda in Saigon. The congress aimed to unite the South's Mahāyāna and Theravāda followers through a new modern structure, but only perhaps a million joined the resulting United Buddhist Association.[60] Six regional groups of monks and two million estimated Theravāda followers (mainly from provinces along the Cambodian border) remained unconnected to the federation.

Migrant Chinese Buddhism was so emphatically syncretic in Indonesia that it was officially called 'Tridharma', meaning 'the three teachings' and referring to a blending of the philosophies of Lao-tzu, Confucius and the Buddha. Local temples, *klenteng*, have generally invoked all three while emphasizing one, and at the same time housed spirit-medium practices related to folk ancestral cults. While increasing numbers of Indonesian Chinese have converted to Christianity, many have remained within the ambit of their own traditions. A few opted for modernized versions of Confucianism, which had a brief and tentative flowering but which is now discouraged in Indonesia, as it is viewed as an 'ethnic' rather than 'world' religion. More often local Chinese communities have effectively converted to new forms of Buddhism, some even to Japanese offshoots of Nichiren or to an Indonesian version of the Taiwanese-based Unity Sect.

[59] von der Mehden, 110.
[60] Schecter, 204.

Southeast Asian 'Hindus' have also experienced significant reformation. Just as folk practice of Balinese Hinduism is now complemented by a nationally administered orthodoxy, reflecting postwar contacts with India, elsewhere Hinduism has taken new forms which reflect the Hindu renaissance of the Indian homeland. Spillovers from the religious tensions of the South Asian subcontinent, such as those between Tamils, Sikhs and Hindus, have already been noted, as even in Singapore local communities extend the religious politics of new fundamental versions of their faiths. Movements such as the Arya Samaj, which allow non-Indians to convert to Hinduism, have been active in Malaysia. Just as South African experience shaped Gandhi, Malaya was the home of one particularly noted modern Indian teacher. Swami Sivananda, many of whose disciples have a worldwide following, worked initially as a medical doctor in the peninsula early in this century. Revivals of Vedantic philosophy such as his now complement Tamil trance rituals such as Thaipusam.

To indicate the full extent of scripturalism and fundamentalism, we can note that as a style of religious commitment it is identifiable even within some ostensibly mystical religious communities. In Indonesia modernism is usually associated with Muslim organizations, but some Javanese movements are equally defined by revealed texts. Even their practices, as in the large and well-established Pangestu movement for instance, can be more intellectual than meditative; in this they resemble Protestant, Muhammadiyah or Dhammayut groups more than they do stereotypes of mysticism. If our purpose is to identify major strands of religious sensibility at the local level within Southeast Asia, it is certainly important to note that traditionalism, magic, millenarianism, mysticism, scripturalism and fundamentalism crosscut and exist as types of religiosity within all of the varied world religions and ethnic communities of the region.

Even in contexts of radical modernization, traditional practices are often reformulated rather than dropped, as is evident in the vicinity of Kuala Lumpur through the way spirit possession works among factory women from village origins.[61] Though modernity does appear to lead to a streamlining of beliefs, it clearly does not always lead to secularization. However, if we are considering religious and cultural change in the broadest sense, we must be consistent with the suggestion at the outset that 'religion' refers fundamentally to any mediating system which connects people to what they can imagine as 'really real'. In those terms it is important to touch, however briefly, on aspects of world-view and conviction which fall beyond the spheres conventionally designated as 'religious'.

Implicitly this survey has already done so, through suggesting some of the ways in which the national revolutions and the construction of new cultures resonate with traditional spiritual and religious senses of social life. In dealing with variants of local practice, with new Southeast Asian ways of knowing what is real, it is equally important to note the power and extent of secularism, even if ironically framing that here as a variant 'faith community'.

[61] A. Ong, *Spirits of Resistance and Capitalist Discipline*, Albany, 1987.

The extension of basic literacy to the general population through modern schools must be considered one of the great achievements of the postwar states. The temple schooling of Thailand and Burma had effected levels of literacy well above those of premodern Europe; it has already been noted that religious schools remain influential throughout the region and that religious subjects remain prominent in the curriculum of state schools, excepting in the socialist states of Indochina. Conversely it can even be argued that religious senses of knowledge suffuse the theoretically secular schools. Secular schools present knowledge virtually as a 'substance' which is communicated through mantric-style rote repetition. Sometimes it is seen virtually as passed by osmosis from teacher to pupil, and the pattern of learning thus echoes the patronage model of discipleship which characterized earlier transmissions of craft skills or sacred lore.

At the same time it can be argued that, just as capitalism may be the most revolutionary force in transforming local societies, in the cultural sphere secularism is the most aggressive of the new faiths. Middle-class urbanites are increasingly cosmopolitan through the nature of their lifestyles, with white-collar jobs, extensive travel and education in increasingly secular systems both at home and abroad. These new middle classes are composed of people who are situated to control new economic activities, the apparatus of states and local adaptations of modern communications; naturally they have power and prominence well beyond their statistical strength. As they are also often in the cultural vanguard, farthest removed from the mystical and magical inheritance of their traditional religions, the forces of genuine secularism are undoubtedly increasing in significance.

However, even modern art forms which appear quite secular on first glance can be read as the new social rituals of everyday life in urban contexts. *Ludruk* theatre, a proletarian drama still popular in Java, teaches the urban public in the postwar era in the same way that the older *wayang* still carries a spiritual message to villagers. Traces of the earlier arts remain present within even such radical steps into new urbanism. So Peacock's study of *ludruk* theatre presented it as a 'rite of modernisation'. In both thematic content and dramatic form the theatre invoked formulaic visions of material progress, now for urbanites. But the modes of presentation nevertheless replicated traditional dramatic codes, even in the nature of the concentration displayed by actors as they virtually unconsciously drew on bodily modes of learning and dance forms which resonated unselfconsciously with the traditional court-derived arts.[62]

Radical though the changes of the postwar period have been, spiritual values and issues remain pervasively important. It is instructive, for example, that in the secular state of Vietnam a self-conscious appeal to spirituality remains. Vietnamese communist literary critics commented in 1970 on the American Susan Sontag's critique of the *Tale of Kieu*, the classic of the early 1800s. They observed without reservation that she was deeply socialized into the individualistic consciousness of the modern West and thus unable to grasp the 'limitless richness' of the Vietnamese soul and with that the value and emphasis within its culture on cummunal

62 J. Peacock, *Rites of Modernization*, Chicago, 1968, 242–3.

sharing.[63] Spiritual values can thus appear to remain prominent even within cultures which adhere to what most Westerners identify as a materialistic ideology.

TRAJECTORIES OF CHANGING ACCESS TO THE REAL

Through the cycles of history Sinic, Indic, Islamic, and European forces have been superimposed on Southeast Asia. Each worked in some sense to claim it, to recast society within borrowed models. Local cultural memories nevertheless preserve senses of primal identity, and at the moment struggle to assert that through modern forms. Nationalist culture began to take root at the turn of the century, just as the colonial framework defined the boundaries of the contemporary state. Now metropolitan super-cultures radiate from the new national centres, promoting new languages and the growth of a supra-ethnic identity spread through the bureaucracy, schools, literature, electronic media, and, not least, the military. National revolutions have not been just a matter of achieving political and economic independence: they also involve the assertion of identity in autonomous rather than derivative terms. Following the revolutions, the forces of modernity appeared to define national governments through models borrowed from the West; the dominant élites, whether secular or religious, comprised the most Westernized Southeast Asians. Tension between trajectories of growing global integration and resurgent primal identity combine to generate the extraordinary pressures under which contemporary Southeast Asians still labour.

Everywhere clearer demarcation of religious communities has paralleled the modern establishment of national boundaries which was mediated initially by colonialism. Syncretic styles of religion had not focused on boundaries, but on courts, schools or monasteries. Those had existed in a hierarchical world conceived as requiring progress through layers of knowledge, guided by apprenticeships analogous to those in other domains of traditional learning, to a mystically conceived centre. Scripturalism redefined individual experience as literal, and social identification as exclusive; thus tensions increased, intersecting also in new ways with political process. Buddhists felt their faith as an element of revolution in Burma, and many Muslims held that their revolutions should lead to an Islamic state. Paradoxically the strength of adherence to exclusivism undermined its realization in a context crosscut by social and religious pluralism.

There has been a clear trajectory within the religious sphere in postwar Southeast Asia, and it has been a major area of domestic concern. The dominant trend has been that of increasing scripturalism, the strengthening of outlooks associated with the West but reflected locally in a wide range of unique adaptations. Colonial students of Theravāda or of Islam often suggested that the Thai or Javanese were not 'really' Buddhist or Muslim. Their view derived from a textual sense of religion, and in the face

[63] Woodside, 307.

of animistic practices they could see claims to membership in world religions only as a facade. The traditional syncretism of Southeast Asians did not mean that they did not belong within the sphere of the world religions they associated with: it meant that the religions themselves were syncretic. The nature of tensions between communities was transformed through the growth of the scripturalist community. Scripturalism has meant that religion has been defined in increasingly concrete terms. Scriptures, rituals, and doctrines are definable; the mystical is not. Modern structures have meant that definition and distinction have been of increasing importance. This has highlighted differences and increased tensions by sharpening the lines of contrast.

In the traditional context it seemed possible to be what modern syncretist leaders like U Nu or Sukarno said they were—in the latter's case at once mystic, Muslim, and Marxist. Now some can accept those possibilities, but many cannot. Within the traditional religious world there was a very clear sense of a layered cosmos, a hierarchical structure in nature and within human consciousness. Traditionally Indianized states were defined cosmologically and by their centres; now states are defined geographically by their borders. The same shift has taken place within religions as modernity has flattened even local senses of religious space. Religious communities tend now to be closed and with clear boundaries, not open-ended and fluid; the boundaries have arisen in precisely the same way that political boundaries have, and as a result of the same forces.

New meditation movements and styles of mystical, millenarian and syncretic spiritual practice have appeared throughout the region, counterpointing the equally vigorous emergence of secular modernism. At the same time the spirit realms, once central to local maintenance of balanced relations with ancestral culture and the physical environment, now appear to be receding along with the forests as a modern developmental worldview advances. Finally we must note the emergence of secular practices within the urban middle classes and among industrial workers and itinerant traders. For the first time there is a vigorously growing sphere of agnosticism but modernity does not necessarily lead to secularization. Changes are not confined to shifts of membership from one religion to another, or from being religious to becoming agnostic or atheistic. Those shifts are significant and allegiances have been fluid in the region. But at the same time notable internal transformations have occurred within every community of belief. Though the nexus between cultural and spiritual life has been weakened, this has led more often to restructured belief than to secular disbelief.

In the development of tourist industries there is also an ironic rebound affecting local cultures. Even the urban and internationally oriented Southeast Asians are themselves increasingly positioned as tourists in relation to village communities who retain what is now packaged, for tourist purposes, as 'indigenous' and authentic culture. In areas particularly geared to tourism, such as Bali or Toraja in Indonesia, production of art is usually separated in new ways from its previous ritual context. This has an effect also, inadvertent but nevertheless profound, on those who create the works of art. They begin to imagine themselves as, even to become, museum specimens; this is what the commodification of culture, through packaging of tourism as a national industry, aims to turn them into.

Within some sectors of the modernizing élites of the region there is strong and often repeated support for the view that continuing adherence to beliefs in the supernatural is a prime inhibitor of development. This belief is common throughout the Third World as a borrowing from the scientism of the developed world. It applies particularly with respect to modernizing medical systems, which are one of the strongest forces contesting traditional beliefs and practices relating to healing. There is, apart from the self-confidence evident in specific radical and especially religious and mystical circles, little confidence that Western systems of knowledge can be challenged on their own grounds. But much of this is strictly rhetoric. This is to say that, in public life within modern institutions, educated people often play the roles they believe they are expected to according to the logic 'modernity' appears to represent. Tambiah argues that the commitment to Buddhism, for example, has not declined, though its expression in social organizations, such as numbers in the monkhood, may have dropped as a proportion of the male population.[64] It is most likely that it is not the extent and depth of religiosity which has changed, but the way it is socially articulated and publicly expressed.

Modernist styles of commitment have implications for personal experience. Traditional practices emphasize the intuitive aspects of religion; modern styles give priority to the intellectual. The Dhammayutikaya and the Muhammadiyah movements demythologize Buddhism and Islam respectively, echoing themes in contemporary Christian theology. Each modernism presents the essence of religion, disentangled from the ritual, mythic participatory, and intuitively apprehended aspects which used to be fundamental. Traditional education in Theravāda *wat* or Islamic *madrasah* was defined by attunement through sacred language. The significance of chanting in those contexts lay not in whether words were understood but in the act itself: emphasis was on experience as such, not on understanding of or abstraction about it. Within modernism emphasis falls on written words which everybody has equal access to, and the defining features of belief are outside and apart from inner experience— emphasis on rational apprehension is a natural corollary. As community is defined increasingly through literally seen and logically understood forms, there has also been a shift in emphasis from the heart to the head, from the intuition to the intellect within individual experience. Using Geertz's terminology, we can note that people are now more likely to have faith in religion rather than accepting it implicitly as a system everyone belongs to.[65]

The intensity of Southeast Asian experiences of the spiritual remains, despite the challenges of materially directed ideologies from above and social stresses from below. The most significant changes have been occurring not in outward allegiances, but more subtly in the ways in which cultural symbols now mediate access to what Southeast Asians in this era are able to know or believe as real. The most obvious axis of change in this

[64] Tambiah, *World Conqueror*, 267–8.
[65] C. Geertz, *Islam Observed*, Chicago, 1972, 61.

respect has been in the nature of adherence to beliefs, in the growing tendency to hold religious convictions as though they are ideological systems. In earlier periods most peoples of the region breathed their religion, experiencing it as an integral and multidimensional part of an inevitable social atmosphere. Within the now more obviously pluralistic world, religious experiences in the region assume increasingly distinct conceptual and institutional forms. In this era of internationalization and cultural encounter no specific culture or religion, indeed no system of symbols, appears able comfortably to claim the exclusive grip it used to.

BIBLIOGRAPHIC ESSAY

The information explosion of the postwar era is reflected in scholarship on Southeast Asian religions. This is thus strictly a preliminary guide to monographs in English which focus on religious changes in postwar Southeast Asia, and the concentration is on works which connect religion to general processes of cultural change. Only especially critical ethnographies have been included, though almost every ethnography contains important sources of insight into practices of and changes in religion. Many important contributions to the subject are contained in collections which appear here only as such.

For the Southeast Asian region as a whole the study by Kenneth Landon, *Southeast Asia: Crossroad of Religions*, Chicago, 1949, remains important both as an introduction and for the insight it provides into the state of religion at the close of the war. The most helpful recent general work of synthesis is Fred von der Mehden's book on *Religion and Modernization in Southeast Asia*, Syracuse, 1986. Two important collections, one edited by Alton Becker and Aram Yengoyan, *The Imagination of Reality*, New Jersey, 1979, and another by Mark Hobart and Robert Taylor, *Context, Meaning and Power in Southeast Asia*, Ithaca: Cornell University Southeast Asia Program, 1986, contain excellent insights. Relevant related shifts in communications systems, especially in media and drama, are covered in the survey by James Brandon, *Theatre in Southeast Asia*, Cambridge, Mass., 1967.

Charles Keyes' study, *The Golden Peninsula*, New York, 1977, is a superb survey treating social and religious changes on the mainland, including Vietnam, and Robert Lester's introductory survey, *Theravada Buddhism in Southeast Asia*, Ann Arbor, 1973, is a reliable starting point for exploration of the Buddhist countries. A more technical collection, edited by Manning Nash, *Anthropological Studies in Theravada Buddhism*, New Haven: Yale University Southeast Asian Studies, 1966, contains essays which map the field as it has been explored by postwar students of Theravada, and the journalist Jerrold Schecter's work, *The New Face of the Buddha*, New York, 1967, is grounded enough to trust and useful for the scope of its coverage of postwar changes in Asian Buddhism.

There are excellent studies of the interplay between religion and politics in the Theravāda countries. Emanuel Sarkisyanz, *Buddhist Backgrounds of the Burmese Revolution*, The Hague, 1965; Michael Mendelson, *Sangha and*

State in Burma, ed. J. P. Ferguson, Ithaca, 1975; Donald Smith, *Religion and Politics in Burma*, Princeton, 1965; and Stanley Tambiah, *World Conqueror, World Renouncer*, Cambridge, UK, 1977, are each landmark works with very wide relevance. Similar themes are touched on in the essays in Bardwell Smith's edited collection, *Religion and Legitimation of Power in Thailand, Laos, and Burma*, Chambersburg, 1978, and in a symposium on religion and society in Thailand in the *Journal of Asian Studies* 36, 2 (1977), including essays by Kirsch, Reynolds, Keyes and Tobias. A more recent study by Peter Jackson, *Buddhism, Legitimation, and Conflict*, Singapore: ISEAS, 1989, includes particularly instructive material on urban sects in Thailand.

Notable ethnographies deal with the interface between normative Buddhism and folk magic in the postwar era. These include Manning Nash, *The Golden Road to Modernity*, Chicago, 1965; Melford Spiro, *Buddhism and Society*, London, 1971, and *Burmese Supernaturalism*, Englewood Cliffs, 1967; Stanley Tambiah, *Buddhism and the Spirit Cults in Northeast Thailand*, Cambridge, UK, 1971; and Bas Terweil, *Monks and Magic*, London, 1975. Louis Golomb's fine and ranging study, *An Anthropology of Curing in Multiethnic Thailand*, Urbana and Chicago, 1985, and Ruth-Inge Heinze's more narrow one, *Tham Khwan*, Singapore, 1982, deal more exclusively with folk religion on its own terms. Apart from studies of village practice, there are a number of sources for insight into forest meditation practices. The most prominent is by Stanley Tambiah, *The Buddhist Saints of the Forest and the Cult of Amulets*, Cambridge, UK, 1984. Excerpts from the teachings of these teachers are well presented by Jack Kornfield in *Living Buddhist Masters*, Santa Cruz, 1977, and pertinent commentary on the same movements can be found in Donald Swearer, 'Thai Buddhism: Two Responses to Modernity', *Contributions to Asian Studies*, V.4 (1973).

Studies of Islam in Southeast Asia have only recently begun to achieve the depth the subject deserves. Ahmad Ibrahim, Sharon Siddique, and Yasmin Hussain have collected many of the most important postwar essays or excerpts on the subject in their *Readings on Islam in Southeast Asia*, Singapore, 1985. Michael Hooker's edited collection, *Islam in South-East Asia*, Leiden, 1983, is solid and the essays in it by Roy Ellen, on the ethnography of Islam, and Deliar Noer, on politics, are especially pertinent to exploration of postwar religious change. Taufik Abdullah and Sharon Siddique present a more patchy but still useful selection of essays in *Islam and Society in Southeast Asia*, Singapore, 1986. Like the latter, the collection edited by Raphael Israeli and Anthony Johns, *Islam in Asia: Southeast and East Asia*, II, Boulder, 1984, is uneven, but includes useful works.

Because Indonesia has been relatively open to Western scholars, a huge range of studies deals with social and religious change there. Rita Kipp and Susan Rogers have edited a collection of excellent recent studies, *Indonesian Religions in Transition*, Tucson, 1987, and an earlier book edited by Claire Holt, *Culture and Politics in Indonesia*, Ithaca, 1972, remains critical reading for any student of religion, society and politics in Indonesia. Three less uniform collections, each also containing much that is useful, are Gloria Davis, ed., *What is Modern Indonesian Culture?*, Athens: Ohio University

Center for International Studies, Southeast Asia Program, 1979; James Fox, ed., *Indonesia: The Making of a Culture*, Canberra: Faculty of Asian Studies, Australian National University, 1980; and Paul Alexander, ed., *Creating Indonesian Cultures*, Sydney, 1989. There are a number of highly useful survey articles on cultural change and religion in Indonesia. The most notable include Hildred Geertz, 'Indonesian Cultures and Communities', in Ruth McVey, ed., *Indonesia*, New Haven, 1963; Gavin Jones, 'Religion and Education in Indonesia', *Indonesia*, 22 (1976); and Julia Howell, 'Indonesia: Searching for Consensus', in Carlos Caldarola, ed., *Religion and Societies: Asia and the Middle East*, The Hague, 1982.

The political face of Islam up to the 1970s is treated at length by B. J. Boland in *The Struggle of Islam in Modern Indonesia*, The Hague, 1982, and recent currents are covered by Ruth McVey's essay, 'Faith as the Outsider: Islam in Indonesian Politics', in J. P. Piscatori, ed., *Islam in the Political Process*, Cambridge, UK, 1983. Deliar Noer's monograph on the *Administration of Islam in Indonesia*, Ithaca: Cornell University Modern Indonesia Project, 1978, and Daniel Lev's exploration of *Islamic Courts in Indonesia*, Berkeley, 1972, deal with the most important institutional changes in Islamic life. The most valuable study of militant Islam in Indonesia in the immediate postwar period is C. van Dijk, *Rebellion Under the Banner of Islam*, The Hague, 1981. Clifford Geertz provides the most probing suggestions about internal changes within the Muslim community in *Islam Observed*, Chicago, 1971. James Peacock, *Muslim Puritans*, Berkeley, 1978; Douglas Miles, *Cutlass and Crescent Moon*, Sydney, 1976; Mitsuo Nakamura, *The Crescent Arises over the Banyan Tree*, Yogyakarta, 1983, and Mark Woodward, *Islam in Java*, Tuscon, 1989, each bring grounded local perspectives which open insights into important aspects of change.

The most outstanding treatments of Javanese religion are Clifford Geertz's classic, *The Religion of Java*, Chicago, 1976, and Koentjaraningrat's *Javanese Culture*, Kuala Lumpur, 1985. Robert Jay's monograph, *Religion and Politics in Rural Central Java*, New Haven: Yale University Southeast Asian Studies, 1963, broke ground in connecting village religion to national politics. Studies by Niels Mulder, *Mysticism and Everyday Life in Contemporary Java*, Singapore, 1978, and Harun Hadiwijono, *Man in the Present Javanese Mysticism*, Baarn, 1967, concentrate on syncretic mysticism in Java. Robert Hefner's book, *Hindu Javanese*, Princeton, 1985, provides a historically and ethnographically grounded exploration of Tengger society and its interaction with Islam. Frank Cooley's *Indonesia: Church and Society*, New York, 1968, outlines the postwar position of Christian churches and Paul Webb, *Palms and the Cross*, Townsville: Southeast Asian Studies Centre, James Cook University, 1986, has explored the changing position of Christians in the lesser Sunda islands.

John McAlister and Paul Mus, in *The Vietnamese and Their Revolution*, New York, 1970, treated the intersection between spirituality and politics in Vietnam; Gerald Hickey's *Village in Vietnam*, New Haven, 1964, includes a solid account of village ritual and the local chapter of the Cao Dai sect; and Jayne Werner's monograph on *Peasant Politics and Religious Sectarianism: Peasant and Priest in the Cao Dai in Viet Nam*, New Haven: Yale

University Southeast Asian Studies, 1981, concentrates on the organizational face of the same sect. Martin Stuart-Fox and Rod Bucknell, in the 'Politicization of the Buddhist Sangha in Laos', JSEAS, 13, 1 (1982), and George Condominias, in 'Phiban Cults in Rural Laos', in G. W. Skinner and A. T. Kirsch, eds, *Change and Persistence in Thai Society*, Ithaca, 1975, provide insight into Lao practices. Ben Kiernan's essay, 'Orphans of Genocide: The Cham Muslims of Kampuchea under Pol Pot', *Bulletin of Concerned Asian Scholars*, 20, 4 (1988), chronicles the particularly disastrous experience of one of Southeast Asia's many pressed minorities.

Important aspects of religious change elsewhere are treated by Clive Kessler, *Islam and Politics in a Malay State*, Ithaca, 1978; Aihwa Ong, *Spirits of Resistance and Capitalist Discipline: Factory Women in Malaysia*, Albany, 1987; Susan Ackerman and Raymond Lee, *Heaven in Transition: Non-Muslim Religious Innovation and Ethnic Identity in Malaysia*, Honolulu, 1988; Alfred McCoy, 'Baylan: Animist Religion and Philippine Peasant Ideology', in D. Wyatt and A. Woodside, eds, *Moral Order and the Question of Change: Essays on Southeast Asian Thought*, New Haven: Yale University Southeast Asian Studies Program, 1982; Peter Gowing, *Muslim Filipinos*, Quezon City, 1979; Richard Lieban, *Cebuano Sorcery*, Berkeley, 1967; Michelle Rosaldo, *Knowledge and Passion*, Cambridge, 1980; John Blofeld, *Mahayana Buddhism in Southeast Asia*, Singapore, 1971; Tham Seong Chee, 'Religion and Modernization: a Study of Changing Rituals among Singapore's Chinese, Malays, and Indians', *East Asian Cultural Studies*, 23, 1–4 (1984); and Cheu Hock Tong, *The Nine Emperor Gods*, Singapore, 1988.

5

REGIONALISM AND NATIONALISM

For Southeast Asia the immediate postwar years (1945–8) were a time of change and turmoil. Dominating this era were problems of rehabilitation and aspirations for independence in the face of returning colonial régimes. The Philippines and Burma, along with India, Pakistan and Ceylon (Sri Lanka), parted from their paramount powers in a comparatively amicable way, and guidelines were laid down for an orderly advance to independence by Malaya and British Borneo; but there was little prospect for a peaceful transfer of power in Indonesia and Vietnam, and decolonization was to come to those countries through violence.

Between 1949 and 1959, Indonesia, Cambodia, Laos, Vietnam and Malaya attained independence, while Singapore acquired internal self-government, but these years coincided with the Cold War's spillover into Asia. While this was cold war between the superpowers, there were active war and revolution in many parts of Southeast Asia, where countries were often aligned with Western or communist blocs and faced internal struggles which moulded them according to rival ideological models. Intense power-bloc rivalry in Southeast Asia added to the strains of newly won independence. This contest led to the formation of the South-East Asia Treaty Organization (SEATO), backed by the United States, on the one hand and to Russo-Chinese support for left-wing movements on the other. Superpower competition accentuated internal divisions between radicals and traditionalists, subversives and constitutionalists. It also deepened rifts between states: communist and anti-communist, 'non-aligned' and 'neo-colonialist'. While the 1955 Afro-Asian Bandung conference was a significant step in the emergence of the non-aligned movement, in which Third World nations attempted to develop an independent stance in international affairs, this failed to spread harmony in Southeast Asia.

The following period, up to 1975, covered the Second Indochina War, which brought foreign involvement on a massive scale and dominated developments throughout Southeast Asia. It also coincided with the Cultural Revolution in China. But during this time the first steps were taken to develop regional co-operation. An Association of South-East Asia and aspirations to Malay brotherhood (the Maphilindo concept) foundered on the creation of Malaysia, which led to disputes about Sabah and to armed confrontation between Malaysia and Indonesia (1963–6). The first major breakthrough came with the formation of the Association of

South-East Asian Nations (ASEAN) in 1967. In the early 1970s the sharp divide of the East–West Cold War began to blur. The beginnings of détente between the United States and the Soviet Union were overtaken by the more dramatic rapprochement between the United States and China, the American withdrawal from active participation in the Vietnam war, and subtle changes in Japan's policies towards the region.

The communist victories in the three Indochinese countries in 1975 were seen as a major turning point at the time, and indeed had immediate repercussions for the rest of Asia. But in some ways the events of 1975 only confirmed certain trends already under way. China's Cultural Revolution came to an end soon afterwards, with the death of Chairman Mao Zedong (Mao Tse-tung) in 1976, followed by the beginnings of China's open-door policy, which would have significant effects on Southeast Asia. The new situation, intensified by Vietnam's invasion of Kampuchea (Cambodia) in 1978, put pressure on ASEAN to improve regional co-operation and achieve stability. By the late 1980s the communist countries of Indochina, the non-communist countries of ASEAN, and non-aligned Burma showed promise of peaceful co-existence.

THE CONCEPT OF SOUTHEAST ASIA

The concept of Southeast Asia as a political entity emerged almost by accident from World War II when, at the Quebec Conference in August 1943, the Western Allies decided to establish a separate South East Asia Command (SEAC), embracing Burma, Malaya, Sumatra and Thailand. The Potsdam Conference in July 1945 extended SEAC's responsibility to cover the rest of the Netherlands East Indies and Indochina south of the sixteenth parallel, excluding only northern Vietnam, the Philippines and Laos.

This military expedient provided a cohesive framework for a region which had never previously been seen as a distinct geopolitical area. No single empire had dominated the whole region in pre-colonial times. At the outbreak of the Pacific war, apart from Thailand, Southeast Asia comprised a collection of colonies and protectorates under the tutelage of Western imperial powers. And even Thailand's sovereignty and freedom of international action were limited. The external relations of the region were determined as part of each metropolitan country's foreign policy, without heed to pre-colonial feuds or friendships.

Although the period of consolidated colonial rule in Southeast Asia was comparatively brief, it produced fundamental effects not only on the various subject states but on their relationships with each other and the outside world after independence. Occasionally colonial rule strength-ened existing political structures and tried to take over their regional relationships, but more often Western rule had the opposite effect. The divisiveness was most notable in the separation of Sumatra and the Malay peninsula by the Anglo-Dutch treaties of 1824 and 1871. Elsewhere it smothered bitter feuds such as the traditional enmity between Burma and Thailand, or stemmed age-old developments like the southern expansion of the Vietnamese people and the waning of Cambodia. Often it encouraged the immigration of people from outside the region, notably Chinese and Indians who found opportunities in the colonial economies.

While there were stirrings of nationalism before World War II, the similarities of the imperial experience did not provide a stimulus for co-operation, and nationalism developed at a varied pace and in different forms in the individual countries.

The closest to a regional association before World War II was the Nanyang Chinese National Salvation Movement. The Chinese term 'Nanyang' or Southern Ocean had long been in use but acquired a new significance as Nationalist China tried to bind its overseas compatriots together in the service of the motherland. The Nanyang Chinese National Salvation Movement, which reached its zenith in 1938 in opposing the Japanese invasion of China, had its headquarters in Singapore and branches throughout Southeast Asia. For a short time Japanese aggression against China drew the Nanyang Chinese together in unprecedented unity. This was not proof against the political and cultural divisions within the Chinese community, but the concept—or spectre—of the Nanyang Chinese was a potent force in shaping postwar regional policies and attitudes of newly independent states.

Other external ideological and religious influences exerted some sway at certain periods but were generally divisive. Communism in Southeast Asia was fragmented and weak after the disastrous communist revolt in Java in 1926, followed by the split between the Kuomintang and the Chinese Communist Party in 1927 and the failure of the Comintern to establish an effective Nanyang Communist Party. The pan-Islamic movement, which played a dominant role in early Indonesian nationalism, lost credibility with the downfall of Sarekat Islam in the 1920s, while international Buddhism could not transcend ethnic and sectarian differences.

Yet despite the divisions, Western imperialism stamped a pattern across Southeast Asia. After wars of resistance by subject people and friction among the colonial powers themselves during the early days of their takeover, by the twentieth century territorial boundaries were clearly delineated and civil wars were over. Western imperialism brought peace and stability to the region, which was broken only by occasional upheavals, such as the Saya San rebellion in Burma. The various colonial régimes had many similar features: secular administration, a modernized bureaucracy and judiciary, Western-educated élites, an urban middle class, and economies partially geared to the international world system.

The colonial pattern was shattered by the Japanese invasion and interregnum. The Japanese Greater East Asia Co-prosperity Sphere, in which Southeast Asia was to play a vital role, proved to be more a political firebreak than a catalyst for regional cohesion. It disrupted colonial economies and political administrations without substituting an enduring new system. Nations emerging in the postwar world had to establish their own identity and create a new regional order. The variety of ethnic, cultural and religious differences added complexity to the situation, as did the revival of some traditional issues. Once more the region came under the influence of its powerful neighbours, India and China, which were themselves undergoing great changes. Southeast Asia was drawn into the superpower struggle between the United States and the Soviet Union. And later still it was to fall under the economic influence of Japan.

THE POSTWAR SCENE

A number of factors complicated the immediate postwar scene: the unexpectedly sudden end of the Pacific War, the problems of reconstruction and reorganization in war-torn Southeast Asia, the varied circumstances in which independence was attained, and the desire to create unity. All these were bound to complicate the regional and international relationships of inexperienced new states. There were additional problems: the presence of minorities with external links, the inertia of colonialism which continued after formal political independence had been achieved, the beginning of the Cold War, the communist victory in China in 1949, and the growing involvement of the United States in the area.

In the last stage of their occupation, the Japanese encouraged dialogue between Indonesian and Malay nationalists. Tokyo gave nominal independence to Burma and the Philippines in 1943, to Indochina in March 1945 and to Indonesia on the eve of the surrender in August 1945. But no metropolitan power was prepared to accept this, nor did the nationalists feel themselves strong enough to resist outright the return of colonial rule. While insisting on real independence within a short space of time, initially they preferred negotiations. This was true even in Indonesia among moderate nationalists, such as Mohammad Hatta, and in Vietnam, where in 1946 Ho Chi Minh was prepared to accept membership in the French Union for his Democratic Republic of Vietnam as a 'bourgeois democratic republic' in the first stage towards communism.

The 'firebreak' effect of the Japanese occupation made it nigh impossible to revive the ancien régime, even in places such as Malaya and the Borneo territories where the British were at first welcomed back. The Japanese victories revealed the vulnerability of the colonial powers, which were further weakened by the wartime drain on their economic resources. Japanese rule alienated the Nanyang Chinese vis-à-vis host ethnic groups, some of which collaborated with the Japanese. The occupation had given a taste of pseudo-freedom, while the Atlantic Charter and the founding of the United Nations provided international legitimacy for nationalism. This was further encouraged by disillusionment among the liberated peoples over economic difficulties, shortages and hardships in the aftermath of war.

Although all the Western powers attempted to reimpose their rule after the war, within twelve years most of the area had gained independence. Singapore, Sarawak and Sabah were to follow in 1963 as part of Malaysia, and two years later Singapore became a separate republic. Portuguese East Timor was annexed by Indonesia in 1975 and Brunei became independent in 1984. By that time the region comprised ten independent nation-states:

Brunei, Burma, Cambodia (Kampuchea),[1] Indonesia, Laos, Malaysia, the Philippines, Singapore, Thailand and Vietnam.[2]

The new nations were almost invariably the successor states of former colonies and dependencies and, with the exception of Timor, modern frontiers largely followed the lines laid down by the colonial powers at the high noon of empire. Despite Thailand's initiative during World War II in reclaiming sovereignty over parts of the Shan states, the northern Malay states and territory on the eastern border with Cambodia, the winning of independence did not lead in general to a reversion to the pre-colonial scenario. Indeed working out external policy was determined by many new factors: domestic needs; economic priorities; the continuing relationship with the former colonial powers; the reactions to the great powers; and the evolution of intra-regional relationships, which might involve both conflict and co-operation.

The two most important factors affecting regionalism and international relations in the immediate postwar years were the decolonization process itself, and the problems of creating national identity within the (often artificial) former colonial boundaries.

THE IMPACT OF DECOLONIZATION

The colonial powers returned with different approaches towards their dependencies in Southeast Asia. The United States and Britain had the advantage of returning as liberators against a repressive Japanese régime, but France and the Netherlands, themselves occupied during the war, appeared as imperial masters after the euphoria of liberation had dissipated. The United States honoured its prewar pledge to grant independence to the Philippines, but continued close economic and defence links, which were to be of new significance when the United States came to play a wider role in post-colonial Southeast Asia. France and the Netherlands planned to give their colonies equal status in a French or Netherlands Union. But the vagaries of domestic politics in Paris and The Hague, and the failure to meet Asian nationalist aspirations, led in both cases to wars of liberation. These ended with the breaking of political links—and, to a great extent, economic links—with the paramount power.

The British connection lasted longer, partly because colonial policy in Southeast Asia was not a matter for political rivalry in London, and also because legitimate movements to independence were allowed to

---

[1] The country adopted a variety of names in this period. Known as the Royal Kingdom of Cambodia when it attained independence in 1953, it became the Khmer Republic after Lon Nol took over in 1970. The Khmer Rouge adopted the term Democratic Kampuchea in 1975. The Heng Samrin régime established a People's Republic of Kampuchea in 1979 but reverted to the name Cambodia in 1989. For convenience, the name Cambodia is generally used here.

[2] Papua New Guinea, which became independent in 1975, is excluded from this study as being more traditionally linked with Australasia, although it has had observer status in ASEAN since 1976.

take a more peaceful constitutional path. Thus British economic links and defence responsibilities continued beyond political independence. Further, the Commonwealth concept was already well tried in the case of the old Dominions, and was sufficiently flexible to attract most newly independent countries, except for Burma.

Despite its legal independent status, prewar Thailand had suffered quasi-colonial infringements of its sovereignty, and its declaration of war on the United States and Britain and seizure of British and French colonial territory in World War II left the country in a vulnerable position in 1945. The resignation of premier Phibun Songkhram in 1944 helped to soften Allied hostility, since the successor civilian government was a front for Pridi Phanomyong's Free Thai resistance movement, which was closely in touch with the British and Americans. Nevertheless Britain and France wanted to penalize Thailand for its pro-Japanese wartime role, but were overruled by the United States, which in the early postwar years adopted an anti-imperial stance when it suited national interests. Britain insisted on compelling Thailand to supply rice at fixed low prices to the rest of Southeast Asia—a measure considered essential for the stability of the region—but otherwise the country's integrity was not infringed. In 1946 Thailand was admitted to the United Nations, where it aligned itself with the West. Bangkok welcomed American protection against Anglo-French retribution, and this broadened into a more general reliance on the United States in the difficult postwar world. After Phibun took over once more in 1948, the American alignment became even closer.

While Washington kept its promise of political independence for the Philippines, nothing had been done about the islands' economic reliance on the United States. In July 1946 the Americans transferred power to a conservative oligarchy, and for nearly thirty years the country remained their firm ally, economic dependant and military collaborator.

The British came back to Southeast Asia with new policies of advancing former dependencies to self-government. For Burma, which had achieved a fair measure of autonomy in the 1930s, the British War Cabinet proposed full independence as part of the Commonwealth as soon as the country was ready and the interests of non-Burman minorities assured. In the Malay states, the Straits Settlements and the Borneo protectorates, where there had been little overt nationalism before World War II, the British had approved schemes to streamline the political structure and prepare the way for eventual self-government.

In 1946 Britain separated Singapore as a Crown Colony and organized the peninsula into a Malayan Union, which in 1948 became the Federation of Malaya. Sarawak and British North Borneo were brought under direct colonial administration, but Britain deferred plans for changing the status of Brunei, which continued to be a protected sultanate. Subsequently the orderly transfer of power in Malaya and Singapore and the constitutional incorporation of Sarawak and British North Borneo into the Federation of Malaysia facilitated continuing military and economic links with Britain and membership of the Commonwealth.

But in Burma the apparent strength of the nationalists largely determined the pace of political events. Aung San's Anti-Fascist People's

Freedom League (AFPFL) emerged from the war with such ostensible popular support that the British, with too many other priorities on their hands, went along with Burmese demands without securing adequate safeguards for minorities or achieving the degree of preparedness London had considered necessary. A constitution was agreed in April 1947, but three months later Aung San and most other AFPFL cabinet leaders were assassinated, and the premature granting of independence in January 1948 immediately plunged the country into civil war. Vulnerable and weak, the Union of Burma Republic was preoccupied with its internal problems. It joined the United Nations but not the Commonwealth, and to a large extent reverted to its traditional pre-colonial policy of isolation from the outside world.

Dutch attempts to force its colonies into a Netherlands Union and to isolate and undermine the newly declared Republic of Indonesia soured the independence settlement negotiated at The Hague in 1949. Provision for continued Dutch investment and commercial links laid down in the agreement foundered during the ensuing troubled years.

In Indochina the returning French administration did not recognize the independent régimes created by the Japanese. Paris re-established its authority in Cambodia and Laos in 1946, signing agreements with both countries providing for constitutional monarchies. But in Vietnam the French were unable fully to reimpose their power or come to terms with Vietnamese nationalism. By the end of 1946 France was engaged in outright war against the Democratic Republic of Vietnam, which was dominated by the Vietminh.[3]

NATIONAL IDENTITY AND UNITY

While international frontiers were a consequence of imperialist interests and not necessarily designed to create nationhood, they proved to be the least contentious issue in the post-independence period. With the notable exception of the Philippines claim to Sabah and the multinational claim to the Spratly Islands, there were few serious territorial disputes. Nevertheless the variety of sometimes incompatible racial groupings, including immigrant communities, formed during the colonial period left problems and tensions which affected regional and international relationships.

Some political leaders stressed cultural nationalism. They tried breaking free from the colonial past to build up a sense of national cohesion by using the language, religion or ethnic affinity of the politically dominant group as a unifying factor. This happened with the Buddhist religion in Burma and the Malay language in the Federation of Malaya. But such emphasis highlighted minority differences and tended to look back to conservative tradition. Elsewhere, as in Indonesia, or later in Singapore, nationalist leaders stressed a unity in diversity, acknowledging ethnic, religious and linguistic distinctions but adopting a secular approach with such common

[3] Vietminh: Vietnamese Independence Brotherhood League, founded in 1941 as a front organization of the Indochina Communist Party.

goals as modernization. On occasions independence meant transferring power from foreigners into the hands of a traditional élite or Westernized privileged class, which tried, at least in the early years, to maintain the economic and social status quo with the minimum disruption, as in the Philippines and Malaya. But more radical nationalists aimed, in overthrowing alien rule, to restructure society, eliminate poverty, and redistribute wealth more equitably.

Even Thailand, which had never been colonized, needed to establish an identifiable nationalism, which it had failed to do despite the 1932 revolution. While the British and French had annexed many of the ethnically non-Thai border areas, postwar Thailand still had to come to terms with Malay Muslim separatism in its southern provinces and the influx of hill tribes in the north. Meanwhile, in Bangkok the pendulum continued to swing between military and civilian bureaucracy, usually in bloodless coups which caused little internal upset but made for unstable and shifting government policies.

Before World War II the Muslim Moro population of the southern Philippine islands had raised objections to the proposed granting of independence, which might subject them to the rule of the Christian majority, and indeed communal problems were to flare up later. But the immediate concern of the newly independent régime under President Manuel Roxas was to cope with agrarian unrest and communist Huk guerrilla warfare. For this the Roxas régime needed aid and recognized its economic reliance on the Americans, both for the immediate needs of postwar rehabilitation and for long-term development. In March 1947 the Philippines granted the United States military bases on 99-year leases and made a mutual defence assistance agreement. The interdependent questions of military bases and economic assistance would continue to dominate Philippines foreign and domestic policy.

Burma's chief need was to absorb non-Burman states and defeat communist guerrillas, while at the same time avoiding provoking its potentially dangerous neighbour, China. Prime minister U Nu, the AFPFL vice-president, who took over the leadership after Aung San's murder, was respected as an individual but did not command the allegiance of either the army or the left wing of his party. Within a year of independence Burma was torn apart by the insurgency of communists, former Burma Independence Army soldiers, Karens and hill tribes, so that the U Nu government exerted little control outside the urban areas. The consequent instability and preoccupation with establishing national cohesion, combined with its vulnerability, reinforced Burma's inclination to isolationism.

Some sense of Indonesian nationality evolved through the long struggle for independence, yet at the same time the bitterness of those years left many divisions, a fragile federal organization, a ravaged economy, and a dearth of administrators. The unleashing of guerrilla warfare during the anti-Dutch campaign bequeathed a legacy of violence, which was to characterize the new nation and perpetuate rifts between moderate secular nationalists, aggressive *pemuda* (youths), left-wing socialists, and Muslim fundamentalists. Indonesia's experiences during the fight for independence made it suspicious of the West—not only of the Netherlands but also of the United States and Britain. British troops had reoccupied the Indies on behalf of the Dutch at the end of World War II, and Britain had withdrawn from the scene after helping to produce the unsuccessful Linggajati agreement.

Since the majority of Indonesians were Muslims, there was a natural inclination to look to fellow Islamic countries for moral support. In 1947, during the struggle against the Dutch, Haji Agus Salim, Vice-Minister of Foreign Affairs for the Republic of Indonesia and a fluent Arabic speaker, toured the Middle East. He negotiated a treaty of friendship with Egypt and obtained recognition for the republic from Syria, Saudi Arabia, the Lebanon and Iran. But Indonesia's internal needs meant tolerating diversity in order to achieve national unity, which led it to play down an Islamic image.

In Indochina the French and Vietminh remained at war, while independence for Malaya and Singapore still seemed a distant prospect in the late 1940s. Progress in the Federation was complicated by the outbreak of a communist uprising in 1948, and by the need to provide for the various racial groups in a country where the indigenous Malays were now outnumbered by Chinese and Indian immigrant communities.

REGIONAL LINKS IN THE IMMEDIATE POSTWAR ERA

Widespread anti-colonial sentiment in the immediate postwar years did not prove a regional bond since Southeast Asian nationalism was fragmented. This was true even before the lines were under-scored in the Cold War and the area became involved in superpower rivalry. In these early days independent countries often found that pressing internal needs precluded the ability to devise sound foreign policy, so that what policy there was usually stayed in a state of flux, engendering a fluid and complex international situation. Regional ties among the newly independent countries were slow to develop.

There was no obvious regional leader. While the Philippines boasted a nationalist movement dating back to the 1870s and was the first Asian colonial territory to gain independence—predating even India in this respect—its ongoing links with the United States made it a spokesman and docile ally of that country rather than an acknowledged pace-setter of regional nationalism. This was accentuated by the strong social and cultural influence of the Spanish and American colonial period, which left a Christian majority and the largest Western-educated community in Southeast Asia. Filipino statements praising the United States at an Asian Relations Conference held in New Delhi in March 1947, only months after the Philippines became independent, shocked other delegates, as did a statement at the Manila Treaty conference in 1954 that Filipinos did not regard themselves as Asians.

Thailand's status as the only traditionally independent country in Southeast Asia and the first to become a member of the United Nations, might have qualified it for a leadership role in the rest of the region. During the decade prior to World War II Thailand had shaken itself free of extra-territorial jurisdiction and in the period from 1938 to 1944, under Phibun Songkhram, had pursued an aggressively nationalist policy. Pridi Phanomyong, who headed the immediate postwar civilian government in Thailand, was a forward-looking radical intellectual, sensitive to the forces of nationalism in the region. Critical of the way the French were reimposing their rule in Vietnam, he showed sympathy with Vietminh aspirations and gave countenance to a large Viet-Nam News Service, which was the Vietminh's spokesman in Bangkok. Thai ministers joined the executive of a Vietminh-sponsored South-East Asia League, formed in Bangkok in 1947, which collected together nationalists from Vietnam, Laos, Cambodia, Burma, Indonesia, Malaya and Thailand.

Sutan Sjahrir, then leader of the Republic of Indonesia, visited Bangkok in April 1947 and the Pridi government appeared ready to recognize the Republic of Indonesia. But Pridi was ousted in November 1947 and Phibun Songkhram returned to power, first as Supreme Commander of the Armed Forces and three months later as prime minister. A practical patriot, anxious to preserve his country's safety, as he had done so skilfully during World War II, Phibun took a more simplistic and less visionary view of foreign affairs than his predecessor. The South-East Asia League was banned as an alleged instrument of communist subversion, and the Phibun government refused to recognize or aid the Indonesian Republic in its struggle against the Netherlands, or to assume responsibility as a neighbour for the nationalist movement in Vietnam, insisting these were matters for the United Nations and the Great Powers to determine. In effect Thailand turned its back on left-wing movements and became increasingly aligned with the United States.

Despite the Union of Burma's genuine sympathy towards the Republic of Indonesia in its struggle for independence, the Rangoon government's general weakness and relative isolation prevented it from giving concrete assistance or playing any significant regional role.

Indonesia was the largest and most populous of the new states and gained prestige through its independence struggle. When the ill-fated Linggajati Agreement in late 1946 was seen as heralding the emergence of a United States of Indonesia, the Republic's Prime Minister Sjahrir was fêted in Malaya and Singapore. But the Indonesian leaders at that time eschewed any ambitions to link the Malay peninsula with Indonesia, and such a union would have been anathema to non-Malays and to many Malay nationalists in the peninsula. Indonesia hosted the Afro-Asian Bandung conference in 1955; it was to be acknowledged later as *primus inter pares* in the Association of South-East Asian Nations (ASEAN); and it had a special regard for Vietnam which it saw as the only other Southeast Asian country which was forced to fight the former colonial power to achieve independence. But Indonesia was too deficient both in men of stature and in resources to give any immediate regional or international leadership.

In the unstable and fragmented situation of Southeast Asia, the concept of regionalism in the immediate postwar years was a reaction to events rather than some preconceived plan. It was shaped in the main by a variety of sometimes conflicting external influences, ranging from personal initiatives to the activities of United Nations agencies and of foreign governments.

Individuals needed to be brought together before organizations could be formed, and often this was easier to do in Europe than in Southeast Asia itself. In the late 1940s the Malayan Forum, established by Asian students in London, provided a meeting place for the future leaders of Malaysia and Singapore and helped introduce them to prominent European left-wingers. In the same period the London-based Union of Democratic Control, run by Dorothy Woodman, attracted Indonesian, Vietnamese, Burmese and Thai nationalists and gave them a voice through radical members of parliament and the *New Statesman* journal. Indeed John Coast, a protégé of the Union of Democratic Control who worked for the Indonesian revolutionaries, claimed to have masterminded the Bangkok-based South-East Asia League, as a means of bringing together nationalists from the various countries.[4]

The United Nations provided an effective forum for Southeast Asia during this period, notably in Indonesia through the work of its Good Offices Committee in promoting the January 1948 agreement, and by channelling international pressures to secure the eventual transfer of power. The United Nations' Economic Commission for Asia and the Far East (ECAFE), which was set up in March 1947 with its headquarters in Bangkok, was important in providing a regional organization.

But the major force encouraging co-operation at this stage came from the overlapping and sometimes contradictory initiatives of Britain and India. In the closing stages of World War II the British government had envisaged a postwar regional commission in Southeast Asia, involving collaboration with France and the Netherlands, as part of a worldwide scheme for colonial development. But this concept was set aside in view of the strength of anti-imperialist sentiment, and concern that a regional organization might open the way to interference from the United States or the United Nations. Instead, in February 1946 Britain appointed a Singapore-based Special Commissioner, whose main function was to co-ordinate the distribution of essential supplies for the area. In May 1948 this post was upgraded to Commissioner-General for the United Kingdom in South-East Asia, whose parish embraced the whole region, apart from the Philippines which were seen as an American sphere of interest. His role would be to build up political influence so that—as the British Foreign Office saw it—Southeast Asia would look to Britain for 'spiritual leadership'.[5] At the same time Britain shifted the focus for co-operation from the other colonial powers to the Commonwealth, hoping that Australia, New Zealand, and newly independent India, Pakistan and Ceylon would become involved.

While the British considered that India in particular was essential to its plans for co-operation, Prime Minister Jawaharlal Nehru preferred to adopt the role of independent champion against imperialism. New Delhi

---

4 John Coast, *Recruit to a Revolution: Adventure and Politics in Indonesia*, London, 1952, 52.
5 Foreign Office minute, 9 Oct. 1948, FO 371/69683, Public Records Office, London.

tried to play a positive part, with varying success, in sponsoring nationalism in other parts of Asia through its embassies and by leading the anti-
colonial lobby in the United Nations. In March 1947, in the run-up to its
own country's independence, the Indian Council of World Affairs called
an Asian Relations Conference in New Delhi, assembling representatives
from more than thirty Asian countries, including Thais, Indonesians,
Malayans, Burmese and Vietnamese.[6] While disclaiming any ambitions on
the part of New Delhi, Nehru stressed that India was 'the natural centre
and focal point of the many forces at work in Asia' and that to create '"One
World" we must . . . think of the countries of Asia co-operating together for
that larger ideal'. But the small Southeast Asian countries were reluctant to
come under the thumb of India or the rival Asian giant, China. There was
no support for Nehru's proposal to create a permanent Asian organization,
and the communist defeat of the Nationalists in China killed the plan to
hold a second conference there in 1949.

In January 1949 Nehru called another inter-Asian conference to deal
with the situation in Indonesia at a time when the Dutch had seized
Yogyakarta and arrested Sukarno, Hatta, Sjahrir and Agus Salim. The
New Delhi conference demanded the release of the Republican government leaders, the withdrawal of Dutch troops from the whole of Indonesia
and the transfer of sovereignty to a United States of Indonesia by 1 January
1950. A few days later the United Nations Security Council ordered an end
to hostilities, the restoration of the Yogyakarta government and the
reopening of negotiations; they led to The Hague agreement and independence. While many Asian countries were sympathetic towards the
Indonesian struggle for independence, only India gave concrete support.
The two countries shared a cultural heritage, and Nehru knew and
respected both Hatta and Sjahrir. In turn the Indonesian leaders admired
the Indian National Congress and were also attracted by New Delhi's
independent policy in steering clear of power blocs. Nevertheless, neither
Indonesia nor other Southeast Asian countries wished to pass from Western imperial rule to domination by an Asian neighbour, and Thailand, for
instance, sent only an observer and not a representative to the January
1949 conference. Despite the bitterly anti-colonial tone of the proceedings,
the delegates did not respond to Nehru's call to form a South and
Southeast Asian body to oppose Western imperialism.

THE BEGINNING OF THE COLD WAR, 1948–1954

The effects of the Cold War soon spread to Asia, compounding the
confusion and turbulence of the period, when governments were buffeted
by conflicting ideologies and the backlash of Great Power rivalry. The

---

[6] Asian Relations Organization, *Asian Relations—being a Report of the Proceedings and Documen-
tation of the First Asian Relations Conference, New Delhi, March–April 1947*, New Delhi: Asian
Relations Organization, 1948. For a detailed account of the conference see Tilman Remme,
'Britain, the 1947 Asian Relations Conference, and regional co-operation in South-East
Asia', in T. Gorst, L. Johnman and W. S. Lucas, eds, *Postwar Britain, 1945–64: Themes and
Perspectives*, London, 1989, 109–34.

superpowers sought to manipulate newly emerging countries, which were faced with a choice between the conflicting role models of communism and capitalism as the means of achieving national cohesion and general development. Thus the dominating factor became ideology rather than the welding of different ethnic and religious groups into a national entity: it was the contest between left-wing and moderate nationalists that determined the character and international ties of these states.

Up to that point the Soviet Union and the United States were only peripherally involved in mainland Southeast Asia. Even after the formation of the anti-imperial Cominform in September 1947, Stalin dismissed Southeast Asia as a region of low priority. This view seemed to be confirmed by the speedy collapse of the Madiun revolt, staged by the Indonesian Communist Party in 1948. Nor, prior to 1954, did Russia see any advantage to be gained from the war in Vietnam.

While American activities were such that the thirty years from 1945 to 1975 have sometimes been described as 'the American era', in fact the United States was not significantly involved on the mainland until the advent of the Cold War, and even then it was a slow build-up. As the colonial systems crumbled, a relatively untried State Department was groping for a viable policy towards Asia. For a time, despite their anti-colonial bias, the Americans deferred to Britain's longer experience and greater immediate stake in Southeast Asia. In its global defence strategy the United States saw the British forces in Singapore and Malaya as a regional stabilizing factor.

Indeed in the early days it was Britain who tried to persuade the United States to become more involved. Despite lack of direct evidence, London suspected Moscow's prompting behind the communist risings which took place in Burma, Malaya and Indonesia in 1948. In November 1948 the Commissioner-General for the United Kingdom in South-East Asia warned London about the consequences of a communist victory in China, which would make Southeast Asia 'a major theatre in the Cold War'. In May 1949 he predicted that once China fell, Indochina would probably succumb in six months, followed by Siam (Thailand), then Burma and Malaya. By this time the British government was convinced of the roll-on effect of communist subversion, whereby the triumph of communism in one country would destabilize its neighbour, each falling in turn until the region was engulfed by communism. This was to crystallize as the 'domino theory' after President Eisenhower drew this analogy in April 1954. But in 1948–9 Washington rebuffed repeated British urgings to offer aid to South and Southeast Asia along the lines of the Marshall Plan in Europe.

Washington also discouraged the idea of an American-backed anti-communist Pacific Pact, which was mooted by President Elpidio Quirino of the Philippines as a parallel to the North Atlantic Treaty Organization (NATO), created in 1949 to contain communism in Europe.[7] President Syngman Rhee of South Korea and Generalissimo Chiang Kai-shek supported the idea, hoping to bolster their own flagging régimes. Chiang and Quirino met at Baguio in July 1949, when, with South Korea's support,

---

[7] Charles M. Dobbs, 'The Pact that Never Was. The Pacific Pact of 1949', *Journal of Northeast Asian Studies*, 3, 4 (1984) 29–42.

they agreed to invite India, Australia, New Zealand, Thailand and Indonesia to form an anti-communist Pacific front, as 'our answer to the threat of Red imperialism'. Australia, New Zealand and Thailand showed some initial interest, but from the start the Truman administration poured cold water on this scheme, and Quirino argued his case before the American Congress to no avail. Subsequently Quirino organized a conference in Baguio in May 1950, but felt compelled to exclude South Korea and Taiwan and to change from an anti-communist to a non-communist stance. Economic, social and cultural matters were discussed, but not security issues, and no organization was set up.

But behind the scenes the Americans were secretly reviewing their policies towards Southeast Asia, while keeping their options open on establishing relations with the new communist régime in China. In November 1949 Washington gave the first indication of its willingness to send aid to the region, and as Cold War battle lines became entrenched, United States policy became dominated by its commitment to contain communism.

China's intervention in the Korean War seemed to confirm American fears about a master plan for communist expansionism. At the end of World War II Korea had been divided into two states. When the communist north invaded the south in June 1950, the United States responded immediately and persuaded the United Nations Security Council to rally behind the south. China's entry into the war in support of North Korea, in November 1950, brought it into conflict with United States and other United Nations forces.

Deep-seated Sino-American hostility persisted for the next twenty years, throughout the Eisenhower, Kennedy and Johnson administrations. Washington backed Taiwan against the People's Republic of China, encouraged the British suppression of communist insurrection in Malaya, and gave considerable material support to the French in their fight against the Vietminh. In August–September 1951, the secretary of state, John Foster Dulles, main architect of American anti-communist foreign policy, negotiated three treaties: a mutual defence pact between the United States and the Philippines; a tripartite treaty with Australia and New Zealand (ANZUS); and a security pact with Japan. These were all part of the worldwide race between the two superpowers to secure the support of the Third World.

Meanwhile Britain pressed ahead with its plan to use the Commonwealth to build up regional co-operation against communism. Commonwealth Foreign Ministers, meeting in Ceylon in January 1950, resolved on a plan to provide economic and technical aid for South and Southeast Asia. Initially the Colombo Plan[8] was confined to a six-year programme for economic aid with a Commonwealth focus, but Britain hoped that it would extend its scope to include security matters and enable London to wield political influence in the region.

In every Southeast Asian country colonial or independent governments already faced communist-led subversive movements, which attracted a

[8] *The Colombo Plan* (Cmd 8080), HMSO 1950; Colombo Plan, *Report of the Consultative Committee on Economic Development* (Cmd 8529 of 1951–52).

strong following among some patriots, discontented minorities, and the poor. As an ideology, Marxism-Leninism had little relevance in Southeast Asia except in the minds of a small number of intellectuals. There was no large urban proletariat. Communism often conflicted with religious beliefs and the traditional order of society, including the attitude of both landlords and peasants towards property rights. Prewar communism generally made little headway whenever the Comintern insisted on hardline orthodoxy, which precluded a united front with religious groups, traditional élites or nationalists. But communism flourished during the 1937–45 Sino-Japanese War, when the Chinese Communist Party contrived to identify itself with Chinese patriotism. And during the Pacific War communist-led guerrilla armies attracted followings of patriots and used nationalist resistance as the foundation on which to build up a disciplined organization with a detailed political programme, as in the case of the Hukbalahap (the People's Anti-Japanese Army in the Philippines), the Vietminh, the Malayan People's Anti-Japanese Army, or the Burmese Anti-Fascist People's Freedom League.

In postwar nationalist movements the role of communism was ambivalent: in theory the international aims of communism negated nationalism, but nationalist movements in the region were often useful tools. During the long years of struggle against the French, for instance, the communist-led Vietminh and Pathet Lao attracted a large following of nationalists and anti-colonialists who were not necessarily communists themselves. Sometimes communists failed to keep their hold over nationalist movements. In Burma, for example, although the Anti-Fascist People's Freedom League grew out of the Burmese Communist Party, the decision of Hubert Rance, the British governor, to appoint non-communist AFPFL leaders to the executive council in 1946 split the nationalists, and when Burma became independent in 1948 the communists took up arms against their former comrades. The Malayan Communist Party, which had provided leadership for the Malayan People's Anti-Japanese Army, found itself divorced from the mainstream of Malayan nationalism by the outbreak of the 1948 Emergency. But communism had special appeal for some minority communities, as in Laos and Burma. To many people in Southeast Asia, communism was the hope of the underdog, promising a fairer society with freedom from foreign domination, land for the peasants, and a better standard of living for the poor. It was difficult to rouse similar popular enthusiasm for anti-communism, particularly if this was identified with foreign rule or a wealthy indigenous élite. Also newly independent countries became disillusioned when they discovered that political independence did not remove economic dependence on the industrialized nations.

In the late 1940s communism appeared to be in the ascendancy, and many in the Third World perceived it as the way to the future and modernization. The major international communist conference held in Calcutta in March 1948 focused attention on communist activity in Southeast Asia at a time when the communists were gaining the upper hand in China. The West feared the Chinese communists would support revolutions in neighbouring territories, either by direct military intervention or by logistical and moral support, particularly through their Nanyang Chinese compatriots. While rooting out communism, the colonial authorities and their non-communist successors needed at the same time to allay the political, economic and social discontent on which communism thrived.

In fact the period was one of confused ambitions for the communists. Their various revolts and wars in Indonesia, Malaya, Vietnam and Burma, were no part of a grand pre-planned Soviet strategy, such as Lenin's dream of communist revolution in Asia, or the Comintern's ambitious design to use China in the 1920s as the means of realizing this dream.

While the Soviet Union had shown little interest in Southeast Asia, apart from the 1920s Comintern interlude, the Chinese Communist Party posed a more immediate threat. From the late Ch'ing and Kuomintang régimes the People's Republic inherited the tradition of harnessing the Nanyang Chinese to China's cause. But as early as the mid-1950s Beijing (Peking) began to find the Overseas Chinese more an embarrassment than an advantage, and the People's Republic put its own foreign policy interests before concern for its overseas compatriots. Nothing approaching the prewar Nanyang Chinese National Salvation Movement re-emerged, and these expatriates remained divided by education, dialect, ideology and local loyalties. Nevertheless the perception of them as a potential danger and fifth column continued to play a significant part in shaping the attitudes and policies of Southeast Asian governments.

As the Cold War intensified, so did competition between Western and communist blocs for support in Southeast Asia. Direct interference further complicated the independence process and the task of nation-building. Ideology was not merely a question of the nationalists' chosen path in developing their states; it was also a reflection of Great Power influence. Southeast Asian countries faced often conflicting demands to counter militant insurgency while seeking constitutional advance, economic development and an improving quality of life.

Many nationalist leaders claimed to be socialists, although their interpretation of socialism could range from orthodox Marxism-Leninism to a liberal mixed economy. While the Democratic Republic of Vietnam looked to the communist world as its model, Malaya, Singapore, the Philippines and Thailand adopted a market economy as part of the international capitalist system. Others, such as Sukarno's Indonesia, while avoiding communism at home, wanted to break free from Western-style economies. Burma followed its own unique brand of Buddhist socialism.

Despite the obvious dangers of the Cold War, small nations could extract benefits in the form of economic and military aid as the price for their support for the superpowers. But often countries came to rely on foreign aid and put too much emphasis on suppressing dissidence and insurgency and not enough on fostering development.

The Philippines, for instance, relied on American military aid to suppress the Huk insurrection, which reached its height in 1950 and was only gradually brought under control over the next five years under the leadership of Ramon Magsaysay. As secretary of defence and from 1953 as president of the republic, Magsaysay succeeded in overcoming Huk resistance by a combination of military firmness, resettlement and amnesty. But transferring landless Christian peasants from Luzon to Muslim Mindanao promised trouble for the future. And while Magsaysay himself was a guerrilla leader and man of the people, United States support for suppressing communism had the effect of bolstering the ruling oligarchy even further. After Magsaysay was killed in an aeroplane crash in 1957, the Philippines returned to élitist dominance under his successors.

Manila became a natural anti-communist ally of Washington during the Cold War, and in January 1950 Dean Acheson, the American secretary of state, described the Philippines as a vital link in the world-spanning island chain that was the forward defence line of the United States. Filipino troops, financed by the United States, fought in the Korean War from August 1950, and in August 1951 the two countries signed the further Mutual Defence Treaty. For many years the United States tended to take the Philippines for granted. The republic gained considerable advantage from the relationship with the United States, but at the cost of economic and military dependence, which became increasingly unpopular at home and detracted from its standing abroad.

Meanwhile in Thailand Phibun's government moved steadily to the right and gained further American approval by sending Thai troops to fight in the Korean War, while keeping Thailand comparatively stable. The loyalty of the two million ethnic Chinese in Thailand was suspect, particularly in the wake of the 1949 communist takeover in China and because the Thai Communist Party at that stage was predominantly ethnically Chinese. Consequently Phibun revived some of the anti-Chinese measures which had characterized his earlier 1938–44 administration.

The bitter struggle for independence preoccupied Indonesia in the late 1940s to the exclusion of any concern about international Cold War politics. While the Indonesian Communist Party (PKI) was the largest in Asia outside China, it had recurrent problems because of its anti-religious bias. The 1948 Madiun revolt, which endangered the nationalists at a critical time in the anti-Dutch struggle, discredited the party for some years, branding communists as traitors to the national cause in league with foreign interests.

The PKI slowly rebuilt its strength in the early 1950s but was only one of several elements—albeit a major one—in Indonesia's precarious political balance. Within a year of independence the federal structure was abandoned in favour of a unitary state, and a provisional constitution was promulgated in August 1950. Agreement on a permanent constitution was delayed for years, since the provisional parliament was hampered by party discord and frequent changes of cabinet. With the end of the economic boom arising from the Korean War, political conflict became more intense.

The communist insurgency in the Federation of Malaya in 1948 resulted in the declaration of a state of Emergency which lasted for twelve years. Although guerrilla warfare did not extend to Singapore, the colony was subject to the same emergency regulations, which enabled the colonial government to counter communist guerrillas and left-wing organizations. At the same time the British and local establishment wished to undermine the Malayan Communist Party's claim that its Malayan Races' Liberation

Army was fighting for independence on behalf of all communities. For a time official policy discouraged legitimate radical dissent as well as driving extremists underground. But behind the scenes in 1949 the Commissioner-General convened a Communities Liaison Committee, which brought together the leaders of the different ethnic groups and, over a period of many months, hammered out agreements on the question of citizenship and economic development. The British also encouraged the formation of an anti-communist Malayan Chinese Association. From this developed a pact between the United Malays National Organization (UMNO), the Malayan Chinese Association and the Malayan Indian Congress, which formed a national Alliance to demand independence. A further part of the Commissioner-General's remit was to draw Singapore and the Federation of Malaya together and to create a Borneo federation comprising Sarawak, Brunei and North Borneo, as a prelude to forming a wider confederation embracing all five territories. But these plans proceeded slowly in the early 1950s.

While Burma's communists were strongly entrenched neither Russia nor China gave support to the insurgents at this stage, and with help from India by 1953 the Rangoon government was able to contain the communist rebels. Thus Burma seemed to be relatively immune from early Cold War tensions, immersed in its own internal problems but keeping a wary eye on its powerful Chinese neighbour. Burma was the first non-communist country to recognize the People's Republic of China, which it treated with particular circumspection, despite the fact that many of its border minority guerrillas were identified with communism. The end of civil war in China added to Burma's troubles when defeated Kuomintang troops fled across the frontier, taking to banditry which plagued the northern provinces for more than ten years. The authority of the AFPFL declined steadily as internal unrest persisted and the economy stagnated.

Indochina assumed increasing importance to the United States. In the last stages of World War II, the Americans were de facto allies of Ho Chi Minh's anti-Japanese guerrillas and were critical of French measures to reassert their rule in Vietnam. But after the People's Republic of China confronted the Americans in the Korean War, the United States saw the French régime in Vietnam as the best bulwark against the southern expansion of Chinese communism, and by 1954 Washington was paying two-thirds of the cost of the 'French' war.

But the French failed in their attempts to establish a non-communist nationalist government in Vietnam, which would attract the support of moderate nationalists favouring parliamentary democracy as an effective alternative to the Vietminh. The only leader with the ostensible standing for such an administration was the former emperor Bao Dai, whom the French persuaded to return to Vietnam in April 1949. Despite a series of weak coalition governments in Paris giving inadequate support to Bao Dai, he became widely regarded as a Westernized French puppet. The United States and Britain tried to persuade other independent Asian countries to recognize his régime. But neighbouring Thailand felt too vulnerable itself to take the risk. And India, whose approval would have carried the most weight with other Asians, refused to accept the legitimacy of a government which was backed by French troops.[9] Britain hoped the conference of seven Commonwealth countries, which was held in Ceylon in January 1950 to launch the Colombo Plan, would agree to support Bao Dai, but Pandit Nehru remained adamant in his stance.

Cambodia and Laos became Associated States within the French Union in 1949, but King Sihanouk sought more independence in defence and foreign affairs. He assumed the premiership in 1952 and the following year France transferred full control of military affairs to his government. A few Khmer Issarak (Free Khmer) guerrillas launched sporadic attacks in Cambodia, but in neighbouring Laos the situation was more tense. Refusing to recognize the country's status as a constitutional monarchy within the French Union, left-wing nationalists formed the Pathet Lao (Patriotic Front) under Prince Souphanouvong to fight for complete independence. By mid-1953 Pathet Lao troops, in conjunction with Vietminh forces, had overrun half of the country.

The People's Republic of China gave substantial help to North Vietnam, where the whole population was marshalled into conducting a people's war, under the brilliant leadership of General Vo Nguyen Giap, and in 1954 Hanoi inflicted a crushing defeat on the French at Dien Bien Phu.

While the fighting was still going on in Vietnam and Laos, negotiations were in train at Geneva to settle the future of Indochina. The Geneva Agreement of July 1954 ended French rule but did not bring a lasting peace, and Hanoi failed to get the immediate reunification of Vietnam. Instead the country was partitioned along the seventeenth parallel, with provision for nationwide elections to be held two years later. Assuming that the agreement would exclude American military interference in Indochina and that the elections would reunite the country, Russia and China persuaded the Vietminh to accept less than their spectacular military victory might justify. But these assumptions did not materialize. Failure to fulfil the Geneva Agreement perpetuated the division of Vietnam for more than twenty years and led eventually to massive direct American intervention.

THE SOUTH-EAST ASIA TREATY ORGANIZATION

The South-East Asia Treaty Organization (SEATO), brain-child of John Foster Dulles, the US secretary of state, was formed consequent to the 1954 Geneva Agreement on Indochina. Delegates from Australia, France, New Zealand, Pakistan, the Philippines, Thailand, Britain and the United States, meeting in Manila in September 1954, agreed on a South-East Asia Collective Defence Treaty.[10] At the same time, at the urging of President Magsaysay of the Philippines, they promulgated a Pacific Charter, which undertook to uphold the principle of equal rights and self-determination under the United Nations and to try by peaceful means to promote self-government and independence of 'all countries whose peoples desire it

[9] C. M. Turnbull, 'Britain and Vietnam, 1948–55', War and Society, 6, 2 (1988) 102–24.
[10] South-East Asia Collective Defence Treaty (Miscellaneous No. 27 of 1954), Cmd 9282 of 1954–55; ratified by the United Kingdom, 19 Feb. 1955, Cmnd 265 of 1956–57, Treaty series, 1957.

and are able to undertake its responsibilities'; to co-operate in promoting higher living standards, economic progress and social well-being in the region; and, under the South-East Asia Collective Defence Treaty, to prevent any attempts in the area to subvert freedom or destroy sovereignty or territorial integrity.[11]

The United States and Britain were the two main pillars of SEATO, but the negotiations for its formation underlined the growing division between the two allies. Britain's foreign secretary, Anthony Eden, hoped the Geneva conference would bring a lasting peace to Southeast Asia, based upon a compromise between all the parties involved, communist and non-communist. But Dulles had no confidence in the outcome of the conference, and in March 1954, even before it convened, he called for a joint Western stand to prevent the communists getting control in Indochina and for a formal collective security treaty, comprising the Western powers and Washington's Thai and Philippine allies. As Dulles declared publicly in March 1954:

> Under the conditions of today, the imposition on Southeast Asia of the political system of Communist Russia and its Chinese Communist ally, by whatever means, would be a grave threat to the whole free community. The United States feels that that possibility should not be passively accepted but should be met by united action.[12]

Eden refused to jeopardize the conference by opening negotiations for such a pact while the meeting was in session, and preferred a non-aggression Locarno-type arrangement which would include India and other Asian countries. Eventually, after the Geneva conference ended, a compromise was agreed in which Britain dropped the broad non-aggression concept and wider Asian membership, while the United States gave up the idea of a military alliance with a unified field command. It meant that from the beginning SEATO was flawed by dissension between the two main architects.

The Pacific Charter claimed to be 'inspired by the highest principles of justice and liberty', but SEATO roused intense suspicion among communist countries—particularly the People's Republic of China and Vietnam—which charged, with some justification, that the organization went much further than merely reinforcing the Geneva Agreement, as the United States and Britain claimed. In February 1955 Chinese premier Zhou Enlai alleged that the Manila Treaty was a charade and 'developments since signature of the Agreements have shown that the United States were using every method to wreck the Geneva settlements'.[13]

Even among the non-communist Southeast Asian countries, SEATO was seen as a foreign-dominated organization and 'regarded by some of its potential members as a more dangerous enemy than the enemy it is

---

[11] Pacific Charter, Manila, 8 Sept. 1954, Miscellaneous No. 32 (1954), Cmd 9299 of 1954.

[12] Department of State, *Bulletin*, XXX, no. 772 (12 Apr. 1954), 540, quoted in Charles O. Lerche, 'The United States, Great Britain and SEATO: a case study in the fait accompli', *Journal of Politics*, 18, 3 (1956) 459–78.

[13] Humphrey Trevelyan (British Chargé d'Affaires in Beijing) to Foreign Office, 26 Feb. 1955, FO 371/116921/1071/127.

supposed to guard against'.[14] But in view of recent Vietminh successes in Vietnam and the possibility of communist régimes in Cambodia and Laos, SEATO was welcomed by Phibun's Thailand when it established its headquarters in Bangkok, and the United States stepped up its economic and military aid to Thailand.

THE BANDUNG CONFERENCE AND THE NON-ALIGNED MOVEMENT

The polarization of international politics, with rival blocs and military alliances, in turn inspired the first Southeast Asian initiative for independent co-operation at Bandung in April 1955. The first Afro-Asian conference attracted representatives from twenty-nine countries, including all the independent states of Southeast Asia. It arose indirectly from the Colombo Plan, which by the end of 1954 had drawn in all the countries of Southeast Asia, apart from the Democratic Republic of Vietnam. While the Colombo Plan continued to concentrate on economic affairs, it strengthened contacts between the nations of South and Southeast Asia, and it was the 'Colombo powers' that sponsored the Bandung conference.

The conference did not result in the creation of a permanent organization for Asian co-operation, but it was the springboard for the non-aligned movement. As early as 1949 Pandit Nehru had said that India should adopt non-alignment as 'a positive and vital policy that flows from our struggle for freedom'. Non-alignment did not mean negative neutrality or pacifism but active independent participation in international relations. It was an expression of independence and separate identity, with peaceful co-existence as one of its central principles. This philosophy appealed to other nations newly emerging from the colonial experience and seeking a role for themselves in world politics divorced from any subservience to contending blocs.

Nehru and Zhou Enlai were the dominating characters at the Bandung conference, and Pancasila (Five Principles of Peaceful Co-Existence) became the stated instrument of Indian and Chinese foreign policy. But while China could claim to be a Third World country its commitment to communism excluded it from the non-aligned movement which formally emerged in the early 1960s.

Up to this point India enjoyed a special place and prestige in Southeast Asian affairs, and it chaired the International Control Commission, comprising also Poland and Canada, which was appointed to oversee the implementation of the 1954 Geneva Agreement. But in the late 1950s India's prestige and influence waned for a variety of reasons, including the continuing dispute with Pakistan over Kashmir, the rift with China, and the declining powers of the ageing Nehru. Even at his peak, Nehru's approach to foreign policy tended to be simplistic and naive. His rather negative attitude towards the attempts at building up an independent

[14] Rupert Emerson, 'South and South-East Asia as a Political Region' in Saul Rose, ed., *Politics in Southern Asia*, London, 1963, 4 (being papers of a 1961 Oxford symposium).

non-communist government in South Vietnam in the early 1950s contrasted with the positive support which his government gave to the Indonesian republic in its fight against the Dutch in the late 1940s. While Nehru wanted to discourage the spread of communism in India itself, he misjudged Ho Chi Minh as a simple nationalist at heart rather than a hardline 'Kremlin communist'. And he failed to keep on good terms with China. China's brutal suppression of a rebellion in Tibet in 1959 sent refugees flooding into India and brought the two countries face to face across disputed boundaries, escalating into open war in 1962.

While Nehru gave birth to the idea of non-alignment, which the Bandung conference promoted, the decline of Indian influence, the exclusion of China and the admission of European and increasing numbers of African states to the non-aligned movement, shifted its focus away from Asia, and its relevance to Southeast Asian countries became vague.

REGIONAL TENSIONS AND PROBLEMS

Many tensions within the region acted as a brake on regional co-operation in the late 1950s: the continuing division of Vietnam and the Vietminh government's ambitions for hegemony in Indochina, set against internal subversion and instability in most Southeast Asian countries. Fears about the spread of communism were countered by allegations of neo-colonialism and Western imperialism. By the late 1950s most of the region was free from direct Western colonial rule, but all countries, whether independent or aspiring to early independence, still faced internal strains and external pressures. Inevitably the transfer of power disrupted administrative efficiency, sometimes to a major degree. Far from healing internal divisions, independence often exacerbated them, and all states faced the same continuing communist-led insurgencies as their colonial predecessors had done. Not all revolutionary leaders possessed the qualities needed to rule effectively in the more mundane post-independence climate. Some countries experienced disappointment when political independence did not bring immediate economic benefits, while in some cases the continued economic or military dependence on former colonial powers led to charges of neo-colonialism.

The Sino–Soviet split in 1960 created new problems for communists and their sympathizers in Southeast Asia. While President Sukarno had accepted a great deal of Russian equipment, after 1960 he and the Indonesian Communist Party leaned towards Beijing rather than Moscow. In Malaysia and the Philippines bitter feuds between rival pro-Russian and Maoist sects and sub-sects weakened the communist cause. Ho Chi Minh hoped for reconciliation between the two communist giants right up to the time of his death in 1969, and in the short term North Vietnam profited by keeping on good terms with both countries, which vied in giving Hanoi their support. Ho continued to emulate the Maoist Chinese model of development, which he considered more relevant to Vietnam. But it was the Soviet Union which supplied substantial economic aid for the Democratic

Republic's first five-year economic development plan (1961–5), and Hanoi turned increasingly to Moscow for vital military equipment and aid.

Meanwhile in Saigon the United States gave support to Ngo Dinh Diem, an ambitious Catholic politician, who became prime minister in 1954 and president of South Vietnam after a rigged election the following year. On the grounds that South Vietnam was not a party to the Geneva Agreement, Diem, with American backing, refused to hold the nation-wide elections laid down for July 1956, which would undoubtedly have resulted in a communist-dominated reunification. This refusal, and the excesses of Diem's régime, led to the creation in 1959 of a communist-led Vietminh-backed National Front for the Liberation of South Vietnam, known as the Vietcong. It formed a Provisional Revolutionary Government to work in the countryside in South Vietnam, setting up its own schools, seizing and redistributing land to peasants and encouraging them not to pay taxes to the Diem government.

By 1961 the Geneva settlement had completely broken down and Vietnam had reverted to all-out civil war. In October 1961 Diem declared a state of emergency and obtained full powers from the National Assembly. He arrested thousands of political opponents, appointed his own family and friends to high office, and his attacks on the Buddhist church brought opposition from the General Association of Vietnamese Buddhists, sparking off protests and public self-immolation by monks. While opposition mounted against Diem, the Vietcong attracted support not only from radicals but from anti-Diem patriots and peasants, who were disillusioned with only token land reforms. By the end of 1962 the Vietcong claimed to control two-thirds of the villages in the south.

For many years Washington saw Diem as a bulwark against communism and poured in resources to back him. In 1961 President John Kennedy sent the first American military advisers, thus taking the first major step leading to a dramatic escalation of American involvement. But while Diem was regarded in Saigon as an American puppet, in fact he refused to bend to Washington's will and became increasingly an embarrassment, until in 1963 the Americans allegedly connived at a plot by Vietnamese army officers to oust and kill Diem.

A Revolutionary Military Council took over after Diem's death, and the war intensified, leading to the build-up of conventional American forces during the presidency of Lyndon Johnson (1963–8). In 1965 the Johnson régime began the systematic heavy bombing of the north, and by 1967 the United States had more than half a million men under arms in support of the Saigon régime. Diem's successors proved more amenable puppet material, notably Major General Nguyen Van Thieu, who became president of South Vietnam in 1967 under a new American-style constitution and remained in power until the republic fell in 1975.

Although Laos was on the periphery of the Cold War, its proximity to Vietnam gave it strategic importance. Under the Geneva Agreement the Pathet Lao were permitted to occupy the two northern provinces 'temporarily' but this developed into a permanent occupation, leaving the royal government weak and vulnerable. The United States poured in aid and sent advisers to Vientiane in an endeavour to shore up the administration.

But Laos lacked the means effectively to channel foreign aid, which was of little help to the remote and poverty-stricken rural population. Consequently, over the years the communist Pathet Lao was able to consolidate its support among the peasantry.

In 1961 a second international conference was called at Geneva to try to resolve the problems of Laos and provide international guarantees for its neutralization. After fifteen months' debate the conference achieved a degree of accord, setting up a coalition régime under neutralist Prince Souvanna Phouma, with Pathet Lao participation. But the treaty arrangements soon broke down, and Laos degenerated into civil war. This intensified as the war escalated in neighbouring Vietnam, and the United States bombed North Vietnamese-held territory in Laos.

Cambodia seemed more settled. Guerrilla fighting ended after the Geneva Agreement was signed, with French and Vietminh troops withdrawing and the communist-led Khmer Issarak giving up the struggle. In January 1955 the country cut remaining economic and financial ties with the French Union and the other Associated States of Indochina to become fully independent. The following month Sihanouk abdicated as king in favour of his parents, but formed a People's Socialist Community party (*Sangkum Reastr Niyum*), which won every seat in the September 1955 national election and swept the polls again in elections held in 1958 and 1962. On his father's death in 1960, Sihanouk retained political power as chief of state without reverting to being king. He seemed firmly in control, supported by the Buddhist hierarchy, which helped his government to promote 'Buddhist Socialism'. Cambodia tried to conduct a neutral foreign policy and at that stage received aid from the West, the Soviet Union and China. But, wary of the dangers of becoming enmeshed in the Vietnam war, Sihanouk tried to keep on good terms with his communist neighbours, turning a blind eye to the Vietminh's use of Cambodian territory as part of the 'Ho Chi Minh trail', by which North Vietnam supplied the Vietcong. At the same time Sihanouk complained loudly about American violations of Cambodian territory, repudiated American aid in 1963, and broke off diplomatic relations with Washington two years later.

In Thailand, under pressure both within the country and from the West to liberalize the régime, Phibun legalized political parties, lifted press censorship and held general elections early in 1957, in which he managed to scrape only a bare majority in spite of blatant corruption. Later that year General Sarit Thanarat overthrew Phibun in a bloodless coup and arranged for fresh elections. But parliamentary government lasted only a few months and in October 1958 Sarit reimposed military rule. Sarit dealt firmly with the radical opposition, particularly the Communist Party of Thailand, while promoting economic development, education and social reform in order to dispel discontent. He also encouraged King Bhumibol to play a strong public role. But Sarit died suddenly in 1963.

Neighbouring Burma's elections in 1956 showed further decline in the ruling AFPFL's popularity, and U Nu retired into the background in order to reform the party and its policies. He returned to office in 1958, with a programme of conciliation involving concessions to the left wing and to the Shans, and an offer to consider setting up separate Mon and Arakan states. But these proposals roused much opposition in the AFPFL and the army. The AFPFL split into two factions, and, faced with the threat of chaos, in October 1958 U Nu invited General Ne Win to form a caretaker administration, which in the next eighteen months succeeded in restoring law and order, and curbing corruption and inflation.

New elections were held in February 1960, when U Nu's supporters were returned to power with a strong majority, but his liberal policies provoked great discord. In particular the adoption of Buddhism as the state religion, together with the concession of toleration to all religions, pleased neither Buddhists nor non-Buddhists. U Nu's announcement of his intention to resign as party leader that year, and as premier in two years' time, generated further uncertainty, and in March 1962 General Ne Win staged a coup. He suspended the constitution, imprisoned many politicians, and set up an army-led Revolutionary Council, with himself as chairman with full executive, legislative and judicial powers.

The 1962 coup was at first welcomed as only a temporary measure promising more orderly and efficient administration. But the Revolutionary Council ruled the country for the next twelve years. In July 1962 the council established its own political party, the Burma Socialist Programme Party, which became the sole legal party two years later.

A Revolutionary Council declaration in April 1962, entitled 'The Burmese Way to Socialism', aimed to complete the independence process by giving Burma control over its economy as well as its political system. It was an attempt to combine Theravāda Buddhism with Marxism-Leninism in a typically Burmese formula, by a pseudo-socialist economic system which it hoped would free the country from social evils and income inequalities. All foreign and most large domestic businesses, banks and trading houses were nationalized early in 1963; private trade was marginalized; and many thousands of Indians and Pakistanis were forced out of work and returned to their countries. Land was nationalized, land rents abolished, and the government took control of the rice trade. The aim was to do away with capitalism and entrepreneurial profit, but the economy remained stagnant; rice production dropped, with no surplus for export; and foreign earnings declined.

Immediately on seizing power, the Revolutionary Council confirmed its commitment to the principle of non-alignment, and Burma maintained good relations with both India and China, even when those countries went to war with each other. After 1962 Burma had even fewer contacts with international economic, educational and cultural bodies, refused to send students abroad and discouraged tourism. But Rangoon retained membership of the United Nations, the International Bank for Reconstruction and Development (the World Bank), the International Monetary Fund and the Asian Development Bank.

After the first national election held in 1955, the Indonesian parliamentary system soon disintegrated under the strains of the country's internal dissension and economic chaos. By that time the Indonesian Communist Party was recovering from the consequences of the abortive 1948 revolt, and Soviet President Khrushchev saw potential in Indonesia as part of his general policy of building up Russian influence in the Third World. In spite of its disasters of 1925 and 1948, the Indonesian Communist Party was still second only to the Chinese Communist Party in Asia. President Sukarno remained a revolutionary leader, eager to supplant Western orientation of the Indonesian economy, and he had personal ambitions to become a Third World leader of the movement against Western imperialism.

Sukarno's leanings towards the communists led Hatta to resign and displeased the army. Further resentment in the outer islands against increasing centralization by the Javanese sparked off revolts in late 1956 by army commanders who set up independent governments in Sumatra and Sulawesi. Martial law was declared throughout the archipelago in March 1957.

In mid-1959 President Sukarno formally abandoned the parliamentary constitution in favour of Guided Democracy under his personal rule, and the following year he formed a mass National Front organization, which stressed mutual co-operation between all elements of society. Although a brilliant revolutionary and a spell-binding orator with great charisma, Sukarno lacked statesmanlike qualities, and the six years of Guided Democracy (1959–65) brought economic chaos to Indonesia, with hyper-inflation, the collapse of its export trade, and shortages of food and other essential commodities.

The continuing campaign to suppress the rebels gave more power to the Indonesian army, who assumed control of much of the administration, including management of expropriated Dutch enterprises. As the army gained the upper hand over the rebels in the early 1960s, the dangers of a break-up of Indonesia receded and the rebellion formally ended in August 1962. Sukarno still needed army support but looked to the communists to counter domination by the military. He tried to run both the army and the left wing in tandem, playing one off against the other, yet turning increasingly to the communists, both at home and abroad.

In such areas as the build-up of the armed forces, President Sukarno bargained with the rival power blocs to secure advantageous terms. While the Russians were the ostensible winners, it was always on strictly commercial terms, and essential supplies dried up as Indonesia could no longer meet the Soviet bills. After the Sino–Soviet split, Sukarno threw in his lot with Beijing.

To divert attention from domestic ills, Sukarno embarked on foreign adventures, first claiming West Irian (Dutch New Guinea), which had been excluded from the territories transferred from the Netherlands under The Hague Agreement. Jakarta had abrogated the last links with the Netherlands Union in February 1956 and repudiated its debt to Holland six months later. When the West Irian claim was rejected by the United Nations Assembly in December 1957, Sukarno's government confiscated all Dutch property and enterprises and drove out Dutch nationals, including thousands of local-born Eurasians who had maintained Dutch citizenship. In 1960 Indonesia severed diplomatic relations with the Netherlands, and launched a further tirade against continuing Dutch rule in West Irian. The Netherlands put West Irian under United Nations administration in 1962 and the following year the territory was transferred to Indonesia.

Sukarno's next move was to denounce the formation of the Federation of Malaysia as a neo-colonialist plot.

MALAYSIA, BRUNEI AND CONFRONTATION

Proposals for a confederation of all British dependent territories in Southeast Asia were complicated from the mid-1950s by differences in political momentum in the various territories. Malaya gained independence in 1957, and progress towards self-government was speeded up in Singapore, but the Borneo territories remained political backwaters.

After the Alliance gained a sweeping victory at the first Malayan federal elections in 1955, the country moved rapidly to full independence two years later. The Alliance was a grouping of anti-communist communal parties, dedicated to preserving and expanding the export-oriented free economy of Malaya, and maintaining links with Britain and the Commonwealth, with its defence guaranteed under the Anglo-Malayan Defence Agreement.

With independence agreed, the Alliance offered an amnesty to the communist guerrillas, but this failed to end the Emergency which continued, officially, up to 1960. And the problem of reconciling economic divisions between the different racial groups—and notably between the Chinese and Malays—was further complicated by racial affinities either to communist China or to the concept of a Greater Indonesia.

Meanwhile the neighbouring colony of Singapore had embarked on cautious constitutional reform in 1948 when, for the first time, a small number of legislative councillors were elected by a restricted franchise. The pace of change quickened after a more liberal constitution was granted in 1955, and in 1959 Singapore attained internal autonomy with a People's Action Party (PAP) government, under Lee Kuan Yew, which was pledged to attain full independence by merger with the Federation of Malaya. Singapore's turbulent politics in the late 1950s and early 1960s, combined with the constant wariness of the island's Chinese majority and its commercial dominance, at first deterred Kuala Lumpur from any closer association. But by 1961 political unrest in Singapore reached a pitch where Lee Kuan Yew's government was in danger of falling to left-wing extremists, and the Malayan prime minister, Tunku Abdul Rahman, decided that merger with Singapore would be less dangerous than the risk of an independent 'second Cuba' on Malaya's doorstep.

To minimize the problem of absorbing Singapore, Tunku Abdul Rahman decided on a wider federation, which would also incorporate the three Borneo territories. This was welcomed by Britain as a means of providing a secure independence for these small, seemingly unviable states, and after protracted and at times acrimonious negotiations, the Federation of Malaysia was formed in 1963. The 1957 Anglo-Malayan Defence Agreement was extended to cover the whole of Malaysia, which incorporated Malaya, Singapore, Sarawak and British North Borneo (renamed Sabah).

The sultanate of Brunei opted out. London considered Brunei too small to stand on its own, but Sultan Omar preferred to seek internal autonomy, while retaining British protection. In 1959 a new but cautious constitution had been agreed, whereby Britain remained responsible for foreign affairs, defence and internal security, but Brunei acquired internal self-government. The sultan was to rule with the aid of executive, legislative and district councils, but only the latter were directly elective, and the sultan retained dominant power as chief executive.

Sultan Omar's wish to direct nationalism from above by means of paternal enlightened despotism brought him into conflict with the protagonists of democracy, led by Ahmad Azahari, whose left-wing Parti Rakyat Brunei (PRB) had links with radical peninsular Malays and with the Indonesian Communist Party. The PRB demanded immediate independence for Brunei, with full parliamentary democracy, as part of a federation of the three northern Borneo states. The party staged mass rallies and demonstrations, attracting considerable popular support. As a counter-weight, Sultan Omar at first favoured joining the proposed Malaysia, as a means to acquire greater protection for Brunei from both external aggression and internal dissidence. But the PRB, fighting on an anti-Malaysia platform, swept the polls at the first district board elections held in August 1962. The following month Azahari formed an Anti-Malaysia Alliance with left-wing politicians in Sarawak and North Borneo, and rallied support in the Philippines.

Despite the strength of his constitutional position, in December 1962 Azahari needlessly resorted to armed force and declared himself prime minister of a unitary state of Kalimantan Utara (North Borneo). This alienated his more moderate supporters, and, with the intervention of British troops from Singapore, the sultan was able to crush the revolt within days. He proclaimed a state of emergency, proscribed the Parti Rakyat Brunei, imprisoned or drove its leaders into exile, and proceeded to rule by decree.

Initially the rebellion reinforced the sultan's enthusiasm to join Malaysia, but the final negotiations in June 1963 broke down, partly because of insensitivity on the part of peninsular Malays to the special nature of Brunei nationalism and the sultan's status in the proposed Council of Rulers, but mainly because of arguments about Brunei's oil revenues. In consequence, despite pressure from London and summit meetings between the sultan and prime minister Tunku Abdul Rahman, Brunei refused to join the federation.

The factors affecting Indonesia's opposition to Malaysia were complicated. There was an element of personal ambition in Sukarno's motives for promoting perpetual revolution and destabilizing the area. But there was also a measure of principle in his contention that colonial territories would achieve true independence only by cutting economic and defence ties—as well as political ties—with former colonial masters. Indonesia contrasted its own protracted fight for independence with the negotiated settlements achieved through constitutional means in Malaya and Singapore. Sukarno denounced as neo-colonialism the continuing links with Britain, and in particular the Anglo-Malaysian defence arrangement. Indonesia also felt some genuine fear that the far-flung Federation of Malaysia posed a physical threat. The proposed new grouping cut traditional links in the Malay world: the centuries-old contacts between Sumatra and the Malay peninsula; prewar Young Malay Union nationalism; the combination of Sumatra and the Malay peninsula into one administrative zone during the Japanese occupation; the aspirations of Ibrahim Yaacob's KRIS movement and the Malay Nationalist Party; the shadowy concept of an Indonesia Raya, which would embrace all Malay people. Malaysia was an artificial colonial creation, a consequence of British imperial rule. Sukarno's Indonesia itself was also an artificial relic of Dutch imperialism. But Indonesia gave support to Azahari's revolt in Brunei, and argued in the United Nations Assembly against the Malaysia proposal.

The Philippines also objected, and in 1962 officially laid claim to Sabah on the grounds that this came within the fief of the former sultanate of Sulu. In 1963 the Philippines convened meetings in Manila with representatives of the governments of Malaya and Indonesia to try to settle their differences, and the three countries tentatively agreed to a 'Maphilindo' (Malaya-Philippines-Indonesia) confederation. But this was unworkable. Sukarno launched a 'Crush Malaysia' campaign, leading to armed confrontation between the two states after the Malaysian federation was formed. This lasted for nearly three years and was marked by raids along the Sarawak–Kalimantan border and incursions into Singapore and the Malay peninsula. In January 1965 Indonesia left the United Nations in protest at the admission of Malaysia to the Security Council. While the Philippines did not join Indonesia in armed confrontation, it broke off diplomatic relations with Kuala Lumpur, and the Sabah claim was to be an irritant in Philippines–Malaysia relations for more than twenty years.

Confrontation was brought to an end only after a coup in Jakarta in September–October 1965 following an abortive attempt, which the army attributed to the Indonesian Communist Party, to eliminate the entire top military command. Hundreds of thousands of communist supporters were massacred over the ensuing months, and the party was outlawed in March 1966. In that same month General Suharto, the most senior surviving army officer, took over executive authority. Sukarno, who three years earlier had been made president for life, remained as nominal head of state for another eleven months, but finally surrendered all his powers to Suharto in February 1967. Suharto introduced a New Order to replace Guided Democracy. He called a halt to Sukarno's aggressive foreign policy, including confrontation with Malaysia, which formally came to an end in August 1966, and Indonesia rejoined the United Nations a month later.

THE REPUBLIC OF SINGAPORE

Meanwhile Singapore's incorporation into the Federation of Malaysia ended on a sour note in August 1965, when the island state became an independent republic. While merger with the federation and access to a Malayan Common Market had been central to PAP policy, the union was flawed by conflicting priorities, intolerance and distrust, aggravating communal tensions in peninsular Malaysia and sparking racial riots in Singapore. Secular urban Singapore did not lie easily with monarchist Muslim agrarian Malaysia. Arguments among leaders and resentment at interference in each other's affairs culminated in Singapore's attempt to mobilize the opposition parties in a cry for a 'Malaysian Malaysia', which by implication attacked the traditional role of the host Malays. Faced with the choice of separation or imposing direct rule on Singapore, the Kuala Lumpur government chose to let Singapore go.

This created new problems for the region. Singapore had long been regarded as an economic parasite, which produced nothing itself but battened on its neighbours' resources, conducting most of the area's rubber, tin and palm oil trade and prospering from smuggling into Indonesia. To complicate the issue, the republic was ill prepared for any form of separate existence, since no responsible Singapore politicians considered the island as viable if divorced from the rest of the Malay peninsula. To create a sense of nationhood and in an aggressive bid for survival, at first Singapore leaders adopted abrasive policies. As a cosmopolitan international trading city, Singapore needed to change its conception of itself from a largely immigrant Chinese colony to a multiracial society. To do this the republic stressed the rugged, energetic, competitive nature of its people as a whole, which often involved scathing comparison with its neighbours. This was particularly marked in regard to Malaysia, where initially prime minister Lee Kuan Yew promoted Singapore self-interest at the expense of future good relationships with Kuala Lumpur.

At the time of separation Singapore and Malaysia agreed to enter into a treaty for mutual assistance and external defence, but in the early years of independence Singapore continued to be dependent on the British military bases, both for a valuable (20 per cent) part of its economy and for military defence. At the same time the republic was keen to assert its independence and to avoid charges of neo-colonialism. To this end, in the immediate aftermath of independence, top ministers toured the world to explain Singapore's position vis-à-vis Commonwealth defence. The republic felt vulnerable, as a Chinese island in a predominantly Muslim sea. It therefore deflected resources it could ill afford into defence, both to deter aggression from unfriendly neighbours and to create a Singaporean identity by compulsory military service. But by using Israeli military advisers, it antagonized its Muslim neighbours.

In fact Singapore was no longer perceived as a threat to regional political stability. During the island's brief interlude as part of Malaysia, Kuala Lumpur had helped Lee Kuan Yew to neutralize local political extremists and in so doing had strengthened Lee's own position. The republic was a member of the United Nations and the Commonwealth, sheltered by the Anglo-Malaysian defence umbrella, firmly committed to developing its economy on free-market lines and to suppressing communism. And despite its precarious regional relationships, Singapore was eager to be a founder member of the Association of South-East Asian Nations.

THE FORMATION OF ASEAN

The Association of South-East Asian Nations was created by the governments of Indonesia, Malaysia, the Philippines, Singapore and Thailand through the Bangkok Declaration, which was signed by the deputy prime minister of Malaysia and the foreign ministers of the other four countries in August 1967.[15]

ASEAN replaced an earlier Association of Southeast Asia (ASA), comprising Thailand, the Philippines and Malaya, which had been created in 1961. Soon after Malaya became independent, Tunku Abdul Rahman mooted the idea of regional co-operation to combat communist subversion, and at talks with President Garcia of the Philippines in Manila in January 1959 agreed to a proposed Southeast Asian Friendship and Economic Treaty. Thailand's foreign minister, Thanat Khoman, was attracted to the idea of economic co-operation and tried to bring in all the other countries of the region, apart from North Vietnam. This failed, but in July 1961 the three governments agreed to set up an Association of Southeast Asia, as a loose association stressing economic co-operation.

From the start President Sukarno of Indonesia opposed ASA. While the association did not touch on security, its aims of economic development were designed to keep communism at bay, and the three signatories were aligned with the Western bloc for their defence: the Philippines and Thailand as allies of the United States and Malaya under the Anglo-Malayan Defence Treaty. Indonesian Foreign Minister Sumitro commented: 'The spirit behind the proposal is anyway anti-this and anti-that . . . and Indonesia does not want any part in a negative policy in international affairs'.[16]

The proposal to form a Malaysian federation not only intensified Indonesian opposition but drove a wedge between the ASA partners themselves, when, in June 1962, the Philippines formally laid claim to Sabah. President Macapagal of the Philippines favoured the Greater Malay Confederation, or Maphilindo, as an alternative to Malaysia. It was stillborn.

ASA remained dormant throughout the period of confrontation between Indonesia and Malaysia, although Thanat Khoman did much to restore diplomatic ties between Malaysia and the Philippines. The association continued to exist in name until 1966, by which time the new régime in Indonesia was eager to bury the enmity of confrontation and seek regional collaboration. But Jakarta wanted no part of ASA, preferring to see the creation of a new organization, which would embrace the whole of Southeast Asia. While ASA failed to develop into an effective organization through lack of common ground between the partners, it was significant since it arose from local initiatives and referred specifically to Southeast

---

[15] ASEAN Declaration, in Association of South-East Asian Nations, *ASEAN Documents Series, 1967–1985*, ASEAN Secretariat, Jakarta, 1985, 8.

[16] Sumitro interview in *Far Eastern Economic Review*, 13 July 1961, quoted in Arnfill Jorgensen-Dahl, *Regional Organization and Order in South-East Asia*, London, 1982, 18.

Asian needs. Neither the New Delhi nor Bandung conferences had resulted in setting up any permanent organizations, and the Colombo Plan and SEATO were externally inspired.

While Burma and Cambodia refused to join ASEAN, the circumstances surrounding its birth were more auspicious than those of the early 1960s, which led to the rapid disintegration of ASA and Maphilindo. Adam Malik, who became Indonesian foreign minister in March 1966, was a statesman of high calibre and, while seeing the vital role of Indonesia as the largest country in Southeast Asia, was prepared to exercise restraint. Confrontation between Malaysia and Indonesia was over, and under General Suharto's New Order Jakarta was eager to restore harmonious relations with its neighbours. Ferdinand Marcos, who became president of the Philippines in January 1966, restored diplomatic relations with Malaysia five months later. As a newly independent republic, Singapore was still nervous about its prospects for survival. Moreover, these changes were set against the threatening background of escalating war in Vietnam. For the first time in the postwar era, there were genuine grounds for the non-communist powers to bury their differences and seek regional co-operation.

The first priority was conciliation: to heal the wounds arising from recent conflicts. From the start ASEAN saw itself as 'an Association for Regional Co-operation' but avoided any suggestion of forming a defensive alliance, relying rather on 'collective political defence'. This was a term coined by Thanat Khoman, who was largely responsible for reconciling the varied priorities and attitudes of the founding members of ASEAN. In theory security and stability took second place to the association's primary objective: 'to accelerate the economic growth, social progress and cultural development in the region'. But achieving peaceful accord would enable resources to be concentrated on fostering strong economies and social harmony, which were seen as essential to counter internal communist subversion and deter external interference. Apart from Indonesia, all the signatories depended upon the United States or Britain for their defence, but the Bangkok Declaration stated that foreign bases were temporary, maintained only with the express agreement of the country concerned, and not prejudicial to national development.

The Bangkok Declaration provided for collaboration in matters of common interest and maintaining close co-operation with existing international and regional organizations with similar aims. It was not meant to be exclusive: it held the door open for other Southeast Asian states to join, provided they subscribed to ASEAN's policies.

The highest policy-making body was the Meeting of Foreign Ministers, which convened annually in each ASEAN country in turn, and there were also regular meetings of ASEAN Economic Ministers and other subordinate committees.

The ASEAN countries were all anti-communist, bound together by fear of an aggressive North Vietnam and the perceived threat from communist China. Their governments tended towards authoritarianism, but with open economies. They were reliant on the market system of world trade dominated by the industrialized nations, committed to develop using foreign capital. They hoped to promote ASEAN commerce within and outside the region, to collaborate in practical matters such as transport and communications, to encourage tourism, and to foster cultural, scientific, educational and administrative exchanges.

But for many years ASEAN developed slowly. Its member states were a motley collection of diverse cultures and competing economies, paying only lip service to the association's ideals, and there were many points of friction. Tensions remained between Thailand and Malaysia in policing their common frontier: Malaysia was dubious about Bangkok's commitment to flushing out Malayan Communist Party remnants who had sought sanctuary over the border, while Bangkok was suspicious of Malaysian encouragement of the Muslim separatist movement in Thailand's southern provinces. Singapore's expulsion by Malaysia in 1965 embittered their relationship for many years, and the Philippines claim to Sabah continued to rankle. Singapore's insistence on executing Indonesian saboteurs in 1968, long after confrontation had ended, despite personal pleas for clemency by President Suharto, provoked violent demonstrations in Jakarta, during which the Singapore ambassador had to flee for his life.

By the late 1960s the polarization of the Cold War era was giving way to a more fluid and complicated situation, involving not only the United States and the Soviet Union but the People's Republic of China, the economic power of Japan and the growing cohesion of Europe through NATO and the European Economic Community (EEC). The most dramatic change arose from the total breakdown of Sino–Soviet relations, opening the way to eventual rapprochement between the United States and China. Consequently the measure of détente achieved in the Nixon era (1969–74) resulted in an ambivalent relationship between America and the communist world. These were unsettled times in which Southeast Asian nations had to adapt rapidly.

Meanwhile economic stringency forced the British to give up most of their defence commitments in the region. The cost of the Indonesia confrontation led to the British government's decision in 1966 to pull out its forces east of Suez by the mid-1970s—and two years later to accelerate this withdrawal date to 1971—leaving the United States with the prime responsibility for Western defence support for the region.

The Anglo-Malaysian Defence Agreement was replaced by a watered-down Commonwealth Five-Power Defence Arrangement (ANZUK), under which Britain, Australia and New Zealand kept small military contingents in Malaysia and Singapore with obligations to consult but not necessarily to act in the event of any external threat. Its effectiveness was never put to the test, and British, Australian and New Zealand involvement was whittled down in the ensuing years as Malaysia and Singapore built up their own military capability.

THE SECOND INDOCHINA WAR

The escalation of the Vietnam War from the mid-1960s drew Cambodia and Laos deeper into the conflict. While Sihanouk veered to the left in his foreign policy, at home he was authoritarian and anti-communist, combining traditional royal mystique with repression.

But criticism of Sihanouk was mounting by the late 1960s. The growing educated élite was against his idiosyncratic style of government, his frequent overseas travels and his intolerance of opposition. Peasant resentment of the heavy demands by the state and the Buddhist church was fertile ground for communism. The Cambodian Communist Party, or Khmer Rouge, had been in disarray since independence, but it began to revive from 1962 with the appointment of a French-educated schoolteacher, Saloth Sar, as secretary of the party's central committee; later, in 1976, he was to adopt the name Pol Pot. The Khmer Rouge supported a large-scale peasant revolt in the Samlaut region of northwest Cambodia in 1967, but this was put down with great brutality by Sihanouk, who continued to suppress left-wing activity, driving the Khmer Rouge leaders into hiding. Nor did the Khmer communists receive comfort from abroad. The Indonesian Communist Party was destroyed in 1965–6, and the North Vietnamese continued to foster their symbiotic relationship with Sihanouk. Hanoi's concern to safeguard the Ho Chi Minh trail and sanctuary areas in Cambodia outweighed any ideological considerations. Consequently the Khmer Rouge remained weak and divided, with Saloth Sar urging armed resistance to overthrow Sihanouk, while others preferred to lie low until a communist victory was achieved in Vietnam.

The most formidable opposition towards Sihanouk at this stage came from the right, notably among army officers who favoured a more pro-American policy, which would restore the benefits of foreign aid. While Sihanouk was away on one of his many overseas trips in March 1970, the National Assembly deposed him. The new régime, under General Lon Nol, tried to keep out of the Vietnam war, although in May 1970 the United States launched a month-long incursion into eastern Cambodia to attack the Ho Chi Minh trail. In October that year the country became the Khmer Republic, with aspirations towards parliamentary democracy, but the Lon Nol government became more repressive in the face of continuing resistance from Sihanouk's supporters and the Khmer Rouge.

In Vietnam, meanwhile, a surprise all-out offensive by Hanoi in the spring of 1968 (the Tet offensive) failed in its immediate military objective, but it helped to foster the growing disillusionment in the United States about the war and sapped the morale of its mainly conscript army. It led directly to President Johnson's decision not to stand for re-election in 1968, while Hanoi and Washington agreed to meet for peace talks in Paris later that year. Richard Nixon came to the presidency early in 1969 committed to ending American participation in the war, and in July that year he enunciated the Guam Doctrine, heralding the United States' military withdrawal from Vietnam.

This presaged a fundamental change in the international situation. The Eisenhower, Kennedy and Johnson administrations had seen South Vietnam as essential in stemming the tide of communist expansion, which the Americans believed would undermine the rest of Southeast Asia if the Saigon administration fell. A bi-partisan anti-communist policy in Washington had meant consistent antagonism to the People's Republic of China from its founding. Beijing reciprocated this hostility, but its break with the Soviet Union left China virtually isolated throughout the 1960s. Premier

Zhou Enlai realized that China could not confront both superpowers simultaneously, and overtures were made to Washington. Increasing opposition to the war at home, combined with a belated comprehension of the widening Sino–Soviet rift, led to changed perceptions of American interests overseas. The result was a dramatic rapprochement between China and the United States. In October 1971 the People's Republic replaced Taiwan as the Chinese representative in the United Nations and as permanent member of the Security Council, and in February 1972 President Nixon visited China.

The Sino–US accommodation appalled North Vietnam, which had regarded China as a staunch supporter for more than twenty years, during which time Beijing had given generous military and economic aid. China now urged North Vietnam to accede to American terms which would have meant the withdrawal of all foreign troops from South Vietnam. But Hanoi refused, and continued to fight with undiminished zeal. Under the peace terms finally agreed at Paris in January 1973, North Vietnam was allowed to keep its troops in the south after the American forces had withdrawn, while the participation of the Vietcong's 'provisional revolutionary government' in the peace negotiations implied its legitimacy. Although Washington continued to supply arms and equipment, the Thieu régime lacked any semblance of popular support and survived only on American economic and military aid. It was corrupt, it ignored the constitution, and it aroused opposition from a wide variety of people.

Similarly in Cambodia Lon Nol was largely dependent on United States support, while Sihanouk and the Khmer Rouge joined forces in an unlikely but effective united front. For several months in 1973 the Americans carried out heavy bombing of guerrilla positions in order to prop up the Lon Nol régime. But in December 1973 Congress ordered the bombing stopped, and by early 1975 the guerrillas controlled the countryside and were closing in on Phnom Penh.

THE ASEAN STATES

ASEAN was not yet sufficiently effective to take a common stance in face of the confusing and complicated changes brought about by Sino–American rapprochement, the entry of Communist China into the United Nations, and American disengagement from the Vietnam war. While for most ASEAN member states the traumas of the independence struggle were receding, in the late 1960s and early 1970s they were still largely absorbed with the tasks of nation-building and were unprepared for the dramatic transformation of the international political scene.

Malaysia survived the expulsion of Singapore without a major crisis, and after some initial friction Sarawak and Sabah gained materially from this wider association. But bitter communal riots in Kuala Lumpur and some other parts of peninsular Malaysia following elections in May 1969 were interpreted to mean that the policy of relying on a free-market economy to reduce racial inequalities was not working. Preferential opportunities made a minority of upper-class Malays richer, but left the mass of the Malay peasantry poor.

For a time parliament was suspended, and prime minister Tunku Abdul Rahman put administration in the hands of a National Operations Council under Tun Abdul Razak. Parliamentary government was restored in September 1970 and Abdul Razak became prime minister, putting renewed emphasis on consensus and unity. The new prime minister set out with considerable success to create a bigger Alliance by bringing most parties, including many from the opposition, under one National Front. A national ideology, the *Rukunegara*, demanded loyalty to the king, country and constitution, belief in God, and moral behaviour. Debate was banned on sensitive issues, notably the status of the Malays and the Rulers. And the government introduced a New Economic Policy, which was designed, through a series of development plans over a twenty-year period, to redress the economic imbalance between the different races. The policy did not aim to redistribute by large-scale transfers from one sector to another, but rather to give *bumiputra* (literally 'sons of the soil') a more equitable share in relation to foreigners and other Malaysians in an expanded economy.

While Malaysia continued to depend to a large extent on foreign investment and on world markets for selling its primary produce, Abdul Razak steered the country away from its traditional pro-Western stance towards the non-aligned movement and contacts with communist countries. At the non-aligned summit held in Lusaka in 1970 he put forward a proposal to make Southeast Asia a Zone of Peace, Friendship and Neutrality (ZOPFAN), guaranteed by the Great Powers. In 1974 Malaysia was the first ASEAN country to establish diplomatic relations with the People's Republic of China.

Singapore continued its policies of achieving national cohesion and rapid economic expansion. The 1968 announcement of the accelerated British military pull-out threatened the republic's economy as well as its security. Yet in practice the withdrawal proved beneficial, since the British handed over valuable defence installations and a trained workforce, together with a £50 million soft loan, just as Southeast Asia's boom in the search for offshore oil was starting. The crisis also enabled the government to instil new social discipline. The ruling People's Action Party swept the polls in 1968 and, from this position of power, the government took vigorous steps not only to build up its own armed forces, but also to accelerate industrialization and pass tough labour legislation. Political stability and economic drive enabled Singapore to reap the maximum benefit from the international boom of the late 1960s and early 1970s.

Of all the countries of Southeast Asia, Singapore was most dependent on world markets and the friendship of the Great Powers, yet it was determined to assert its sovereignty, control its own economy, and pro- mote regional solidarity. As the immediate worries about survival faded, the infant republic's strident nationalism began to soften. From 1971 the government encouraged Singaporeans to invest in the Second Malaysian Plan, which was languishing for lack of public confidence following the May 1969 riots. Relations with Indonesia were repaired in an amicable exchange of visits between Lee Kuan Yew and President Suharto in 1973, with the Singapore prime minister putting flowers on the graves of the marine saboteurs his government had executed five years earlier. Some of these moves pre-dated the change in United States policy and were a positive regional initiative as distinct from a response to external activities.

Brunei's decision not to join Malaysia in 1963 soured its friendship with Kuala Lumpur, and allegations about Indonesia's involvement in the December 1962 revolt strained relations with Jakarta. The Brunei government officially revived a claim to the Limbang valley, which had become part of Sarawak under the Brookes in the late nineteenth century at the request of the local chiefs but without the then sultan's consent. Now Sultan Omar himself crossed into Limbang to drum up support. Brunei was isolated, more than ever dependent on Britain, while its autocratic government and semi-colonial dependent status laid it open to international censure. At a time when London was preparing to withdraw most of its forces from east of Suez, the Labour government in Britain was impatient at the slow progress of constitutional reform. To prepare for smooth constitutional change, Sultan Omar abdicated in 1967 in favour of his 21-year-old son, Hassanal Bolkiah, but for many years the ex-sultan remained the guiding power behind his son. A new treaty, signed with Britain in 1971, left the sultan in control of all internal matters and confined Britain to continuing responsibility for foreign affairs and defence. Brunei forged friendly ties with Singapore, after the island state was expelled from the Federation of Malaysia in 1965, but relations with Kuala Lumpur continued to be indifferent for many years.

In the late 1960s the internal stability of the Philippines was threatened by Muslim rebels in the south and by the communist New People's Army. The influx of Christian settlers from Luzon into predominantly Moro Mindanao compounded deep-seated Muslim hostility to Manila, leading in 1968 to the formation of the Moro National Liberation Front (MNLF). Pledged to fight for independence, the MNLF received material support from Sabah, whose ambitious chief minister, Tun Mustapha, was of Moro extraction. At the same time radical young communists revived the communist party, now renamed the Communist Party of the Philippines Marxist-Leninist, which created the New People's Army.

As President Ferdinand Marcos of the Philippines neared the end of his second term of office, which was the limit imposed by the constitution, he faced a challenge from the old traditional families, and notably from Benigno Aquino, who expected to be elected as the next president. In a bid to perpetuate his power, in September 1972 Marcos, warning of a communist takeover, suspended the constitution and proclaimed martial law.

The martial-law régime promised to build a New Society, based on stability, peace, substantial land reform and a more equitable distribution of wealth: 'constitutional authoritarianism' in place of the 'old order'. In the early years it seemed set to achieve its aims. A much-vaunted land-reform scheme was announced in 1973. The army was brought into mainstream Filipino politics for the first time since independence and strengthened to cope with the Muslim and communist insurgencies. Law and order were enforced in Manila by rigorous policing of crime combined with suppression of political dissidence. By 1976 resistance from both the New People's Army and the MNLF was broken. The top communist leaders were imprisoned, and a ceasefire was agreed with the MNLF, which lost its main outside support when Tun Mustapha was toppled in a 1976 Sabah election. Foreign investors regained confidence in the Philippines, and the economy boomed.

Marcos's New Society also aimed to win greater independence for the Philippines in foreign policy by drawing the country away from its close alignment with the United States. He put more stress on regionalism, strengthening ASEAN, and developing trade and diplomatic relations with communist countries, and identified the Philippines more closely with the Third World.

Whereas Malaysia, Singapore and the Philippines, while preserving links with the Western powers, simultaneously sought to gain control over their own economies and establish friendlier relations with non-Western countries in this period, Indonesia abandoned its left-wing orientation and looked more to the West.

The Suharto régime continued to consolidate its New Order under the slogan of 'national resilience'. Where Sukarno had championed anti-colonial revolution, Suharto stressed development and anti-communism. With an accent on stability, the army maintained its dominant position both in politics and the economy. Golkar, the government's party, comprising the military, bureaucrats and technocrats, won ever greater landslide victories at successive elections from 1971 onwards.

The aims of internal stability and economic growth also determined the New Order's foreign policy. Indonesia broke with the Soviet Union and China, holding the latter largely responsible for the activities of the Indonesian Communist Party and the attempted 1965 coup. While leading the way in encouraging the development of ASEAN, Indonesia refused to follow its allies in establishing diplomatic relations with China, and this suspicion of Beijing persisted into the late 1980s. Instead Suharto turned to the West and Japan for the aid, investment and technical expertise needed to revive the country's rundown economy. One of the New Order's early successes was to stabilize the rupiah and control inflation, and within a short time the economy was on the road to impressive growth. This underpinned the political stability of the early Suharto years.

The remaining ASEAN country, Thailand, under the rule of Sarit's chosen successor Marshal Thanom Kittikachorn, was increasingly affected by the escalation of the Vietnam war in the 1960s. Bangkok was anxious about Sihanouk's neutralism and displeased with the outcome of the 1961–2 conference, which set up a neutralist government in Laos. Thailand obtained guarantees of American support if it were seriously threatened and in exchange gave active help to the United States in the Vietnam war, providing troops and air bases.

Massive US financial aid helped to develop Thailand's communications and, in an attempt to deflect support from the communists, the Thanom government poured funds into social and economic development in the impoverished northeast. But by the late 1960s there was serious rural insurgency not only in the northeast but also in the extreme north and south, fomented largely by the Communist Party of Thailand, which by that time had lost its Chinese character and was predominantly ethnic Thai.

In 1969 elections were held to implement a new more liberal constitution, but Thanom reimposed military rule late in 1971 at a time when the first signs of American withdrawal from Vietnam caused Bangkok to fear the effects on Thailand. The clamp-down after this brief experience of more democratic government led to student unrest and violent mass demonstrations in Bangkok in October 1973. Thanom fled abroad and a civilian government took over.

Three years of uncertainty followed. This was a time of fluid volatile politics with coalition governments, first under Seni Pramoj, then under his brother, Kukrit, followed again by Seni. Groups of students, workers, professionals and intellectuals sought to take over from the military and bureaucrats who had dominated Thai politics since the 1932 revolution. The close alignment with the West also came under scrutiny. The turbulent period of civilian rule in Thailand from 1973 to 1976 occurred while there was radical change on the international scene: the 1973–4 world oil crisis, which halted economic growth; a slump in world commodity prices; and the communist victories in Indochina in 1975.

Meanwhile civil war continued in Burma, but over the years the government gained the upper hand. Beijing, during the early days of the Cultural Revolution in the late 1960s, denounced the Ne Win government as reactionary and gave help not only to the Burma Communist Party but also to the Kachin Independence Army. But Chinese aid to the insurgents dried up as relations with Rangoon improved from the early 1970s. By that time the Karen National Liberation Army was also in difficulties, and the government was able to exert its authority over much of the country. Twelve years of military rule came to an end in 1974 when a new constitution replaced the Revolutionary Council by a one-party state: the Socialist Republic of the Union of Burma. General Ne Win remained chairman of the Burma Socialist Programme Party, and elected People's Councils replaced the Security and Administration Committees in local government. But the government continued to endorse centralized economic development.

In Burma, Indonesia and the Philippines authoritarian régimes emerged partly in response to the need for security, and partly in the hope of achieving maximum efficiency in economic development and combating poverty.

As Cold War tensions eased and suspicions of ideological conspiracy faded, Southeast Asian nations responded in a variety of ways. Countries which had depended on an external defence umbrella had to rethink their defence strategy, building up their own defences, while working harder for regional security and co-operation. Partly because of the distancing by the Western powers, the non-communist countries of Southeast Asia came to review their own standing with their neighbours and the outside world. ASEAN countries responded less cautiously to overtures from the Soviet Union. They viewed Tun Abdul Razak's proposal for a Zone of Peace,

Friendship and Neutrality (ZOPFAN) with varying degrees of enthusiasm, and agreed to adopt it in November 1971 in modified form. Jakarta in particular was wary of Great Power policing for fear this might involve Beijing. The Indonesian foreign minister, Adam Malik, had long envisaged developing stability in Southeast Asia, so that its nations could preserve their own security without recourse to the support of outside powers. In consequence, the declaration by ASEAN establishing ZOPFAN was a vague document, aspiring to neutralization but providing no machinery or provision for Great Power involvement.

While the individual ASEAN countries gained in confidence and prosperity, ASEAN itself remained a relatively ineffective organization, and its members continued to confront each other on matters such as rights of navigation in the Straits of Melaka, establishing diplomatic relations with Beijing, and the nature of economic co-operation.

1975: THE COMMUNIST VICTORIES IN INDOCHINA

Paradoxically the consequences of the fall of Indochina to communist forces in 1975, long dreaded under the domino theory, were not realized. Instead the communists' triumph triggered off dissension and conflict within their own camp, which coincidentally set the stage for a move towards a measure of regional stability and cohesion in the rest of Southeast Asia. After thirty years in which nationalism and international alignments were strongly influenced by ideological reactions, from the 1970s the emphasis shifted to more conventional power politics. While external forces continued to be important in Southeast Asia, regional ties—notably ASEAN and the Vietnam-dominated bloc—assumed a more significant role in determining how those forces exerted their influence. Small nations found their bargaining position with great powers was often lost or reduced. Instead the Southeast Asian countries turned to closer co-operation with each other. Usually through self-interest, nations put behind them the disputes of earlier days and sank their differences to seek security through collaboration.

Nevertheless the speed and scale of the final communist victories in Indochina came as a shock. A triumphant Khmer Rouge proclaimed a revolutionary government in Phnom Penh in mid-April 1975. Saigon fell to North Vietnamese troops less than two weeks later, when Hanoi launched a final attack which ended in rout and the flight of Americans and their supporters by helicopter from the roof of the United States' Saigon embassy. In Laos the coalition government disintegrated over the next few months and the king abdicated, leaving the communist Pathet Lao as sole masters of a Lao People's Democratic Republic by November 1975. While these events had been foreseen, nevertheless they were recognized at the time as a dramatic turning-point for the region. The next few years were dominated by developments in Indochina and their effect on Southeast Asia.

While many of the dangers of the Cold War were receding, the communist domination of Indochina meant potential conflict within Southeast Asia itself, through a confrontation of two opposing blocs. Of the ASEAN states, Thailand and the Philippines had actively supported the United States' war in Vietnam and Cambodia, while the other three states had given moral backing and derived material benefits from supplying the American forces. Vietnam saw ASEAN as an anti-communist alliance, which could be used by the United States instead of SEATO to promote Western imperialism and neo-colonialism. ASEAN countries in turn feared the emergence of a militant communist Indochina Federation. With the largest battle-trained army outside the major powers, Hanoi had shown a taste for conquest. Residual worries about the domino theory still lingered, and ASEAN countries were alarmed lest Vietnam should sponsor communism throughout the region, either by direct military intervention or by encouraging or supplying local communist guerrilla movements from the stock of American military hardware left over from the war.

The situation remained confused for some months. While Vietnam, Cambodia and Laos declared 'militant solidarity', no Indochina Federation emerged.

In Vietnam the feared bloodbath of retribution did not take place, and a disciplined Hanoi leadership addressed itself to the task of reconstruction. In September 1975 the Vietnamese premier, Pham Van Dong, speaking on the thirtieth anniversary of the founding of the Democratic Republic of Vietnam, heralded a new period of peaceful reconstruction, in which Vietnam wished to strengthen existing friendships and build relations with the rest of Southeast Asia and all other countries on the principles of mutual respect, equality and non-interference in internal affairs. Vietnam at that time still hoped for normal relations with the United States and American aid on the basis of the 1973 Paris Agreement.

Vietnam proceeded with its prime object of reunification, and the two states were merged to form the Socialist Republic of Vietnam in July 1976. A five-year plan for 1976–80 concentrated on economic development and national unity. But, alongside repairing the ravages of war, the new republic aimed to promote socialist ideology and culture and to transform the economy from private ownership to socialism and state control within fifteen to twenty years. This demanded huge resources, and Vietnam was willing to accept aid from any quarter. It joined the World Bank, the International Monetary Fund and the Asian Development Bank, and forged trading links with Japan, India, Singapore, Australia, Sweden and western European countries. It was clear that a unified Vietnam must put greater priority on national rehabilitation than on continuing to spread international communism, at least in the short term.

In Laos initial hopes of peace and moderate reform turned sour in 1976 when the authorities began a programme of collectivization and the use of re-education camps. But over the years the régime stabilized, slowing the pace of collectivization, tolerating Buddhism, and accepting a fair amount of foreign aid from various sources. The leadership remained stable under prime minister Kaysone Phomvihane, secretary-general of the Lao People's Revolutionary Party, who continued to hold office into the 1990s. In foreign policy Laos stood firmly with Vietnam. Kaysone Phomvihane himself was half-Vietnamese, and senior members of his cabinet had close

Vietnamese connections. The republic made an agreement for co-operation with Hanoi in February 1976, but denied it was a Vietnamese satellite and insisted that the relationship was one of mutual friendship and respect.

The most dramatic change came in Cambodia, where the Khmer Rouge leaders, devoted to communist ideology but lacking practical experience of government, were determined to transform what they regarded as a stagnant and semi-feudal society as quickly as possible. On occupying Phnom Penh they ordered the immediate evacuation of all inhabitants from 'this wasteful consuming city' to labour in the countryside. A new constitution for a Democratic Kampuchea state of 'workers, peasants and other labourers' was proclaimed early in January 1976. Prince Sihanouk stepped down and, after some months under house arrest, went into exile in Beijing, while Pol Pot set out to eliminate the old régime, with mass killings of peasants as well as former leaders and intellectuals, and a ruthless purge of the communist party itself. Reportedly, more than one million Cambodians perished in the three years that followed, including five of Sihanouk's children and fifteen grandchildren. The entire population was drafted into restructuring society. Private property was nationalized, the Buddhist church was proscribed, the use of money was abolished, and people were forced into communal living.

Anxious to assert its independence, the Pol Pot régime preferred to rely on mobilizing Cambodia's own resources and regimenting the people rather than have recourse to general international aid. The Democratic Kampuchea constitution specified a policy of non-alignment, but, fearing a revival of traditional Vietnamese encroachment, which had been halted during the French colonial period, the Khmer Rouge leaders looked to China as a check against Hanoi's ambitions. In August 1975 Kampuchea signed an agreement for economic and cultural co-operation with Beijing.

ASEAN REACTIONS

Because of fears about Indochina, in May 1975 ASEAN foreign ministers met to try to work out a common policy, but member states were still divided in their attitudes towards Vietnam and the changed political climate. While Malaysia was willing to consider admitting the Indochina states into ASEAN, others were concerned that incompatible member states would undermine the character of the association.

Initially Malaysia, Indonesia and Singapore responded to the communist victories in Indochina by setting out to strengthen internal cohesion within their own frontiers: while stressing the need for enhanced economic development and social justice in order to maintain stability, the three governments also stepped up measures to counter communist subversion at home. Both Malaysia and Singapore took repressive measures against alleged communist subversives in the next eighteen months, while Indonesia increased its military capability with the help of American subsidies.

President Marcos of the Philippines and the Bangkok civilian government had already begun to draw away from their countries' military alignment with the United States. Marcos visited the Soviet Union and China, establishing diplomatic relations with both and with the new communist régimes in Vietnam and Cambodia. In 1976 the Philippines insisted on renegotiating its military agreements with the United States, agreeing to the continued presence of air and naval bases and US ground forces but at increased rents, for a limited period, and with a recognition of Filipino sovereignty over the bases.

As the only ASEAN country having common frontiers with Cambodia and Laos, Thailand was most directly affected by the communist victories: thousands of Indochinese refugees fled into Thai territory. Thailand was already engaged in combating serious insurgency on its borders with Indochina, and clashes with Lao communists on the Mekong River led Bangkok to close that frontier for a time in December 1975. But as early as January 1975 the North Vietnam government had put out feelers towards establishing friendly relations, and a Vietnamese delegation came to Bangkok immediately after Saigon fell. Hanoi's wish to see American bases and troops removed from Thailand and SEATO dismantled was in line with Thailand's current policy of distancing itself from the United States. This had started with the October 1973 civilian takeover in Bangkok in response to left-wing pressure, and the Kukrit government now ordered an American military pull-out, which was finally effected under the succeeding Seni government in July 1976. Thereafter full diplomatic relations were established with Hanoi, and Thailand then looked to the People's Republic of China as the best guarantee of containing any future Vietnamese ambitions. In 1976 Seni also compelled Malaysia to withdraw the police field force which it had maintained in southern Thailand under a 1964 Malaysia–Thai agreement facilitating hot pursuit of communist terrorists over their common border.

THE BALI SUMMIT

By the end of 1975 there was less Great Power involvement in Southeast Asia than at any point since the end of World War II. At the same time the non-communist states of the region had established some national cohesiveness and made big strides in establishing order and containing internal subversion. After the initial panic occasioned by the communist takeover of Indochina had died down, the other Southeast Asian states concluded that their best defence was to ensure internal stability and prosperity and seek a more effective regional consensus.

The ASEAN leaders assembled in Bali in February 1976 for the first summit meeting in the organization's nine-year history, which was preceded by a flurry of visits by leaders to each other's capitals. The occasion was clouded, a few weeks before it was due to meet, by the sudden death of Tun Abdul Razak, the chief advocate of the proposal for regional neutralization, but his hand-picked successor, Tun Hussein Onn, reaffirmed commitment to his predecessor's foreign policies. The Bali summit was a milestone, revealing a new atmosphere of confidence and a desire for effective co-operation. Two documents were issued: a Declaration of ASEAN Concord and a Treaty of Amity and Co-operation. A permanent ASEAN secretariat was also established in Jakarta, headed by a secretary-general to be chosen for a three-year term from each member state in turn.[17]

Invoking the United Nations Charter, the Ten Principles adopted by the Afro-Asian Bandung conference in April 1955 and the ASEAN Bangkok Declaration of August 1967, the Bali Declaration reaffirmed the goal of economic co-operation and the association's commitment to an early establishment of the Zone of Peace, Freedom and Neutrality agreed in 1971. It resolved to eliminate threats of subversion, but made no move to convert ASEAN into a military pact, its member states believing that such groupings tended to provoke hostile reaction without guaranteeing security.[18] The accompanying Treaty of Amity and Co-operation bound ASEAN leaders to rely exclusively on peaceful negotiations to settle intra-regional differences.

The Bali summit marked a progression from the aims of regional conciliation, which had been uppermost at the time of ASEAN's founding in 1967, to the goal of collective internal security, based upon promoting political stability and economic development within all member states. It followed the lead of President Suharto of Indonesia in seeing 'regional resilience' emerging from 'national resilience'.

When Vietnam was united in July 1976, Hanoi propounded a pragmatic policy of economic transformation, seeking trade and technical exchange with Southeast Asia, but Vietnamese statements about neutrality and co-operation were received suspiciously in ASEAN countries. At the non-aligned summit conference in Colombo in August 1976, Vietnam supported Laos in blocking the reaffirmation sought by Malaysia of its ZOPFAN declaration, which had been accepted at the last non-aligned conference in 1971. Instead Laos and Vietnam called for support for 'the struggle of the people of Southeast Asia against neo-colonialism', which brought shocked protest from Singapore and disappointment to the other ASEAN members, since it implied a challenge to their governments' legitimacy, and support for subversion.

Indochinese offers of friendship to individual ASEAN states did not extend to acceptance of ASEAN itself. While the Soviet Union and China spoke positively about the Bali summit, Vietnam vociferously criticized the organization as a substitute for SEATO, and Laotian prime minister Kaysone Phomvihane described ASEAN in 1976 as 'an organization set up by the US imperialists ... to defend the interests of US neo-colonialism'. This feeling had probably intensifed as a result of President Gerald Ford's visit to Indonesia and the Philippines at the time of his China tour in late 1975, when he reaffirmed Nixon's Guam Doctrine and issued his own Pacific Doctrine, which drew a new American offshore defence line from Korea through to Japan, Guam, the Philippines and Indonesia.

[17] See A. Broinowski, *Understanding ASEAN*, London, 1982.
[18] A view propounded by Adam Malik at this time during a meeting at the ISEAS in Singapore.

Hanoi continued to call for the removal of foreign military bases, and urged developing countries dependent on commodity exports to co-operate in breaking the alleged Western imperialist hold on the world economic order.

Communist subversion was of greater concern to the ASEAN states than any fear of external aggression at this time. Establishing diplomatic relations with China did not bring relief from domestic communist insurgency, as Tun Abdul Razak had discovered. Indeed guerrilla activity increased in both rural and urban areas in Malaysia in the mid-1970s, following the Indochina takeover by the communists and continued moral support by the Chinese Communist Party (CCP) for its ideological comrades in Malaysia. Until the early 1980s the Chinese government adhered to its theory that friendly government-to-government relations were not incompatible with friendly party-to-party ties between the CCP and its counterparts in Southeast Asia, even if those parties were engaged in open revolt.

Singapore and Malaysia co-operated in clamping down on internal subversion, and in 1976 unmasked an international network of agents. This mainly comprised intellectuals and professionals, among them two prominent Malay editors and two Malay deputy ministers, showing that communism had penetrated even the United Malays National Organization.

In Thailand criticism of the inept Seni Pramoj government came to a head in October 1976 when the army intervened to suppress student riots at Thammasat University. General Kriangsak Chomanand, secretary-general of the National Reform Advisory Council, installed a new régime under prime minister Thanin Krivichien, who toured ASEAN capitals and found a ready response to his call for closer regional co-operation against communism. The Thanin government revived the border policing agreement with Malaysia which had run into trouble under the Seni administration. One year later, in October 1977, General Kriangsak took over the government himself, reaffirming Thailand's commitment to regional solidarity.

While the local Indonesian Communist Party remained shattered after the 1965 crackdown, the Suharto régime was concerned at the possible emergence of a left-wing state in East Timor. Following a revolution in Portugal in April 1974, Lisbon decided to abandon its imperial role and grant independence to its colonies. In January 1975 it pulled out of East Timor, leaving a weak coalition government comprising a right-wing Timorese Democratic Union and a militant Revolutionary Front for an Independent East Timor (Fretilin). Portugal's rapid disengagement caught Jakarta by surprise. While some Timorese favoured integration with the republic, Indonesia had never laid formal claim to East Timor, and indeed Adam Malik had earlier written unequivocally that the former Portuguese colony had a legitimate right to self-determination. The coalition government quickly broke down, plunging the territory into civil war, and in November 1975 Fretilin declared unilateral independence for a Democratic Republic of East Timor. Despite protests by the United Nations, Indonesia sent 'volunteers' to support the Timorese Democratic Union. The Fretilin leaders fled, and in July 1976 President Suharto accepted a petition from

the pro-Jakarta government in East Timor to integrate the territory as
the twenty-seventh province of Indonesia. Despite continuing Fretilin
resistance and widespread international protest, the ASEAN countries
overcame some initial hesitation to defend Indonesia's actions in the
United Nations. International criticism died down, and Australia, New
Zealand and the United States saw it in their own interests to accept the
fait accompli, which averted the danger of East Timor's becoming a
communist state.

While all ASEAN countries took measures to check subversion and
strengthen security, they recognized that raising general living standards
was the best answer to communism. As an outcome of the Bali ASEAN
summit, a genuine attempt was made towards economic co-operation on
programmes where each member was allocated a product to manufacture
for tariff-free sale throughout ASEAN: diesel engines in Singapore; urea
in Indonesia and Malaysia; soda ash in Thailand; and superphosphate in
the Philippines. ASEAN ministers and officials met regularly to settle
everyday problems: to co-ordinate policies on extradition treaties, sea
pollution, anti-drug campaigns, and to work out a common stand on
various international issues. But ASEAN was slow in breaking down tariff
barriers, let alone establishing a free-trade zone. While developing friendly
co-operation and combining effectively in economic negotiations with
other countries, individual ASEAN countries were for the most part
economic competitors.

They were even less prepared to sacrifice political nationalism, although
they showed some solidarity in adopting a common voting pattern in the
United Nations Assembly vis-à-vis the Soviet Union and Hanoi. But they
did succeed in playing down traditional territorial and political disputes,
notably the Philippines' claim to Sabah. At a second ASEAN summit
meeting, held in Kuala Lumpur in August 1977 to celebrate the association's tenth anniversary, President Marcos indicated that the Philippines
would take steps to waive the claim, although no formal action was taken
to confirm this promise.

Despite a call by Singapore's prime minister for the Kuala Lumpur
summit to give regional co-operation 'substance rather than form', the
meeting did little in concrete terms to advance either economic or political
co-operation. It was marked, however, by increasing international respect
for the organization, notably by the participation of the prime ministers of
Australia, New Zealand and Japan in post-summit discussions.

Most significant was the statement made in Manila by Japanese prime
minister Takeo Fukuda at the end of a visit to Southeast Asian capitals. The
Fukuda Doctrine of August 1977 committed Japan to the role of a peaceful
economic power, working closely with ASEAN on terms of equal partnership, but acting as a 'bridge' to establish economic links between ASEAN
and the rest of Southeast Asia. After the ASEAN summit Fukuda also
visited Burma, where he offered similar grants, technical aid and trade
facilities.

Japan had made spectacular progress in the third quarter of the century.
The Korean War (1950–3) lifted the economy from its post-1945 trough,
and the country prospered even more from the Vietnam War boom of the

1960s and early 1970s. Private Japanese investment in Southeast Asia increased from the late 1960s. Prime Minister Kakuei Tanaka visited ASEAN capitals in 1974 and after the end of the Vietnam War the Japanese government took steps to increase its influence in the region. In 1978, after six years of negotiations, Japan signed a Treaty of Peace and Amity with China and normalized its relations with Beijing.

As American interest in Southeast Asia waned, Japanese influence became more important. Some anti-Japanese feeling persisted; grim memories of the Japanese wartime occupation, coupled with resentment at perceived Japanese arrogance, sparked some hostile demonstrations against the Tanaka and Fukuda visits. Despite its disclaimer of political or military ambitions, Japan's economic strength provoked jealousy and suspicions of economic nationalism. Tokyo's main interests in Southeast Asia were its raw materials and its markets for Japanese manufactures, and the effects were to create uneven trade balances. Nevertheless, there was growing admiration for Japan's economic success, and many Southeast Asians looked to Japan and Japanese values as a role model for themselves. With its stress on economic development as the key to political stability, Japanese policy was in tune with ASEAN's aspirations. It was in Tokyo's interests to have peace, harmony and equilibrium in the region, to promote prosperity, to raise living standards, and to keep the Straits of Melaka open as an international waterway.

VIETNAM, CAMBODIA AND CHINA

Vietnam's relationship with China soured in reaction to Chinese détente with the United States in 1972, when Hanoi suspected that Beijing had abandoned Vietnam's cause in a deal with Washington over Indochina. This ended a friendship between the Chinese and Vietnamese Communist Parties which dated from the early Comintern days in the 1920s. The Chinese Communist Party had helped Ho Chi Minh to set up the forerunner of the Indochinese Communist Party, and the Democratic Republic of Vietnam remained closely aligned with Mao's China up to the death of Ho Chi Minh in 1969. While Beijing had given large-scale support to North Vietnam during its struggles against the French and the Americans, the People's Republic had no greater wish than the imperial China of the past to see a powerful united Vietnam on its southern frontier. Once the United States withdrew its forces from Vietnam, China gave no further encouragement for the unification of the country.

Beijing and Hanoi also quarrelled about claims to islands in the South China Sea and discrimination against ethnic Chinese in Vietnam. China occupied the Paracels in January 1974 and the Spratly Islands in the following year. Hanoi's nationalization of private trade in March 1978, as part of its economic restructuring, bore heavily on the Chinese community. Their dual citizenship was withdrawn and many fled as refugees to escape resettlement, starting the mass exodus of 'boat people' which was to become a major problem for the region.

But the Sino–Vietnamese conflict had wider implications because China resented Vietnam's growing dependence on Moscow. As friendship with China cooled, Vietnam drew closer to Eastern Europe and the Soviet Union, which supplied most of Hanoi's needs in the decisive last months of the Vietnam war. Russia was recovering from its disillusionment following its rebuff in Indonesia, where the Indonesian Communist Party had first turned away from Moscow to Beijing and had then been shattered. By 1968, as its rift with China deepened, the Soviet Union was contemplating setting up a collective security system for Asia, and building up Russian influence in Southeast Asia, particularly to safeguard its naval interests in the Indian Ocean and the Straits of Melaka. Soviet contacts with ASEAN countries in the early 1970s were increasingly cordial, but ASEAN's adoption of the ZOPFAN neutralization principle offered less scope for Russian ambitions than Indochina.

Accordingly Moscow invited the Vietnamese leader, Le Duan, to visit the Soviet Union in December 1975 and the following year signed agreements to give Hanoi immediate economic aid and long-term help in its five-year plan. In June 1978, one month before Beijing withdrew the last of its aid and technicians, Hanoi joined the Council for Mutual Economic Assistance (COMECON),[19] the Moscow-dominated communist trading bloc. Five months later Vietnam signed a 25-year friendship treaty with the Russians, and Beijing, fearing encirclement on the southern frontier, accused the Soviet Union of hegemony.

Beijing's worst fears seemed to be realized when, within a month of signing the Russian treaty, Vietnam invaded Kampuchea in December 1978 and established a client government in Phnom Penh. This removed the traditional buffer between Thailand and Vietnam and brought renewed Great Power conflict to Southeast Asia, dragging the region further into the ambit of Sino–Soviet rivalry and threatening to make Indochina the focus of a global war.

From early 1977 the Pol Pot régime had harassed the Vietnamese border; this escalated into fierce fighting, with the Vietnamese Communist Party giving support to a Kampuchean National United Front for National Salvation, led by Heng Samrin and Hun Sen, who had broken away from the Khmer Rouge in reaction to Pol Pot's reign of terror. When their forces backed by the Vietnamese seized Phnom Penh in January 1979, they established a People's Republic of Kampuchea with Heng Samrin as president and Hun Sen as prime minister. This pro-Hanoi government was to rule Cambodia for more than ten years, but thousands of Cambodian refugees settled along the Thai side of the border, and guerrilla bands continued to fight.

Hanoi's intervention brought a speedy reaction from China, which launched an incursion into the northern border zone of Vietnam in March 1979. The stated object of Beijing's attack was 'to teach Hanoi a lesson'. Although the conflict was bitter and costly to both sides, the Chinese

---

[19] The Council for Mutual Economic Assistance, formed about 1949 by the Soviet Union and East European countries to promote co-operation and socialist economic integration. By 1988 it comprised 21 members, plus observers who included Laos, but the organization was wound up in 1991.

withdrew within a few weeks without forcing any concessions from Vietnam. Beijing's brief expedition achieved little, except to make Vietnam even more dependent on the Soviet bloc, and the continued Vietnamese occupation of Cambodia remained the most vexing problem in Sino–Soviet relations for a decade.

The Sino–Soviet quarrel, Vietnam's invasion of Kampuchea and Beijing's retaliatory strike against Hanoi destroyed any concept of ideological solidarity, and marked yet another return to conventional power politics.

The Heng Samrin régime continued to be strongly supported by Vietnamese troops and advisers and kept a close relationship with Hanoi. Although foreign-backed, it was welcomed with some relief, since it put an end to the Pol Pot terror, tolerated the revival of Buddhism within limits, and modified the extreme socialism of the previous régime.

Although the People's Republic of Kampuchea had established fairly firm control over most of the country, the United Nations supported an ASEAN-sponsored resolution in November 1979 refusing to recognize it as the legitimate government. It was seen as in ASEAN's interests to achieve a comprehensive political settlement of the Kampuchea problem, and the association tried to promote a coalition of all opposition groups in Kampuchea, which would be more acceptable than the notorious Khmer Rouge. But the resistance was divided into three: Prince Sihanouk's monarchists; the non-communist Khmer People's National Liberation Front, under the leadership of former prime minister Son Sann; and the Khmer Rouge led by Khieu Samphan. For years the opposition factions bickered among themselves, and a United Nations conference on Kampuchea held in New York in July 1981 came to nothing. Eventually, in June 1982, the opposition groups sank their differences to form a coalition, which the United Nations recognized as the government-in-exile, with Prince Sihanouk as president, Khieu Samphan as deputy president and Son Sann as prime minister. But this was very much a marriage of inconvenience, and the Khmer Rouge remained the most effective force and the biggest threat to the Phnom Penh régime.

THE DEVELOPMENT OF ASEAN

The Vietnamese invasion and occupation of Kampuchea—the first sign of any substance to the domino theory—impelled the ASEAN countries for the first time to adopt a common stance in rejecting Hanoi's intervention as an affront to national sovereignty. Over the next ten years ASEAN was to lead the way in barring the Hanoi-backed régime's admission to the United Nations and supporting a government-in-exile. In so doing ASEAN acquired enhanced international respect as a body with political and diplomatic influence, promoting a policy in Indochina which found favour both in the United States and China.

Behind this public accord remained substantial differences in attitudes and interests among the ASEAN partners, ranging from frontline Thailand, who turned to China as a bulwark against its traditional Vietnamese rival, to the more remote Indonesia, which retained considerable respect for Vietnam's militant nationalist record and saw Beijing as a more ominous long-term threat. Most countries were concerned about increased Chinese involvement in the region, but all resisted becoming enmeshed in the Sino–Soviet dispute.

By the late 1980s most of the ASEAN countries had achieved fairly strong and secure governments through various forms of autocratic or quasi-autocratic régimes. In general, populations seemed content to sacrifice a degree of personal freedom in the interests of stability and strong government. The ruling parties of Malaysia and Indonesia drew different elements into their coalitions: the National Front and Golkar respectively. In Indonesia General Suharto was president, prime minister and minister of defence, with Golkar, the army's political wing, consistently winning overwhelming electoral victories. In Singapore, through successive elections, the ruling People's Action Party monopolized parliament for thirteen years from 1968 to 1981 and continued into the 1990s with only a minuscule opposition. Military rule persisted in Thailand until 1988 but was less autocratic than it had been in the days of Phibun, Sarit and Thanom. In July 1988 Thailand returned to civilian rule—as it turned out, for only eighteen months—under an elected prime minister, Chatichai Choonhavan. The Thai army remained in a strong position but, like its Indonesian counterpart, was committed to a 'war against poverty' in a nation where economic development was the first priority.

In 1984 ASEAN expanded its membership for the first time by admitting the newly independent state of Brunei, which had enjoyed observer status since 1981. This helped Brunei to re-establish harmonious relations with Malaysia and Indonesia and to gain a stake in the development of the region.

After the 1962 rebellion, Kuala Lumpur had given shelter to former PRB members and remained critical of Brunei's undemocratic system of government and continued dependence on Britain. In 1977 the United Nations adopted a Malaysia-sponsored resolution calling for the Brunei people to choose their own government, for the removal of the ban on political parties, and for the return of all political exiles to Brunei. But the sultan saw the tie with Britain as giving the greatest freedom for himself and his state, viewing the link as a protection against neighbouring governments, secessionists and political opponents within Brunei itself.

The sultanate was reluctant to revise the terms of its 1971 treaty with Britain until it received assurances that Malaysia and Indonesia would respect Brunei's independence, but in 1979 the sultan was compelled to sign an agreement under which Brunei was to become a sovereign independent state at the end of 1983. On the eve of independence, Brunei obtained a new defence agreement with the United Kingdom, whereby, at its own expense, it would continue to employ a battalion of British Gurkhas to protect the oilfields.

Unprecedented prosperity helped to preserve internal political calm in Brunei throughout these years, since, beginning in 1963, large offshore oil and natural-gas fields were discovered, and after the international oil crisis of 1973–4 export earnings from oil and gas soared, although Brunei itself was not a member of OPEC. This enabled wide-ranging welfare benefits to be given, which contributed to political contentment. Brunei became independent in January 1984, and the following year the sultan relaxed the ban on political parties. But the sultan and his brothers continued to head the top ministries in the cabinet, the emergency laws remained in force, and there was little popular demand for constitutional reform.

After independence Brunei became a member of the United Nations, the Commonwealth and the Organization of the Islamic Conference as well as ASEAN. In 1988 it offered to help finance economic development in the Philippines.

Brunei remained heavily reliant on Britain and Singapore for defence, but its major problems were its anachronistic political system and its almost total dependence on oil and gas, which were wasting assets. Beginning in 1953 five major National Development Plans stressed the need to diversify the economy, and in 1985 the Brunei government proposed a 20-year master plan to this end, but despite ample funds for development, by the late 1980s comparatively little had been accomplished within the state itself.

The offshore oil boom also helped Malaysia, Thailand, Singapore and Indonesia to achieve considerable economic growth and enhanced standards of living. Singapore joined the ranks of the newly industrialized countries and Thailand was well on the way to doing so by the late 1980s.

The odd one out was the Philippines, which faced economic chaos in the last years of the Marcos régime, because of its inefficient agrarian economy and large-scale corruption beyond the state's capacity to absorb. While Marcos staged a series of plebiscites which confirmed the continuation of martial law and his own tenure of power, by the 1980s there was mounting criticism of the flamboyant lifestyle of him and his wife, Imelda, and the corruption of influence peddling or 'crony capitalism'. Muslim insurgency flared up again in 1977 when the Moros were disappointed at the degree of autonomy accorded to them. And Marcos's repressive measures encouraged the rise of radical young Maoists, who won new converts as the peasants became disillusioned with the failure of land reform. The church and the middle classes became increasingly critical of the Marcos family's corruption and self-aggrandizement, and this opposition found a mouthpiece in Senator Benigno Aquino. The assassination of Aquino in August 1983, which was widely attributed to the Marcos clique, roused popular anger, and Aquino's widow challenged Marcos at a presidential election in February 1986, where emotions reached fever pitch. Marcos was proclaimed the victor although the elections were glaringly fraudulent, and this sparked mass demonstrations. Army leaders turned against Marcos, who fled abroad, and Corazon Aquino became president.

The collapse of Marcos's régime in face of 'People Power' brought in a more democratic but inherently unstable government. Corazon Aquino promulgated a new more liberal constitution and held elections in 1987 to confirm her presidency. But against a background of burgeoning population growth combined with rising expectations, and faced with crippling debts, she was hamstrung by the unsolved problem of the élite privileged class that had always bedevilled Filipino politics. Consequently, the Aquino régime battled with limited success to end the communist and Moro insurrections, to introduce land reform, and to overhaul the economy.

Over the years the reformists and experienced politicians of the original Aquino cabinet gave way to more conservative lawyers and businessmen. President Aquino's popularity waned amid renewed criticism of inefficiency, corruption and 'crony capitalism', and a series of military coups attempted to topple her. While these were unsuccessful, only American intervention saved the Aquino government in December 1989, when rebels held the commercial area in Manila for several days.

But there was no credible rival, with the exiled Marcos dying in Hawaii in September 1989, and little public support for Aquino's erstwhile colleagues: Senator Juan Ponce Enrile and vice-president Salvador Laurel. The defence secretary, Fidel Ramos, who had led the revolt against Marcos in 1986 and quashed attempts to overthrow President Aquino, commanded more popular support but he remained loyal to her. Internal instability continued to make the Philippines ASEAN's weak link, and a question mark hung over the future of the American military bases, whose lease was due to expire in 1991. While the bases were still very important for the republic's political and economic survival, they remained a badge of subservience.

The third ASEAN summit, marking the end of the association's second decade, met in Manila in December 1987. It was the first time the heads of state had assembled since the Kuala Lumpur gathering ten years before, despite calls to stage another summit which had been voiced from the early 1980s. The Philippines was next in line to host the conference, but this was delayed because of growing disapproval of the Marcos régime and because Malaysia's prime minister refused to visit Manila until the Sabah claim was formally laid to rest. Even at that late stage President Aquino's attempts to legislate finally to end this last remaining source of territorial dispute in ASEAN were qualified by the Philippines Congress. But the meeting, held at considerable personal risk to the leaders, was an expression of support for the precarious Aquino régime.

BURMA

Despite some signs of opening up to foreign investment and aid in the early 1980s, Burma still remained largely aloof, at the cost of stagnation of a once prosperous export economy and growing political unrest. Poverty, coupled with the alienation of educated youth, erupted in violence in 1988. General Ne Win stepped down from office in that year but continued to manipulate the government. He repressed the incipient opposition under the spirited leadership of Aung San's daughter, Aung San Suu Kyi, head of the National League for Democracy and the most effective spokeswoman for the pro-democracy opposition to Burma's military government. Aung San Suu Kyi was put under house arrest in July 1989, while many of her party members were jailed. The party swept the polls in a general election held in May 1990 but were not permitted to take up office, and in

July 1990 the ruling State Law and Order Restoration Council issued a decree confirming its retention of executive, legislative and judicial powers.

INTERNATIONAL COMMUNISM IN THE 1980s

While anti-imperialism had failed to unite Southeast Asia, concern about communist subversion and the Vietnamese threat became effective catalysts. But over the years the communist danger receded, both internally and externally.

This was partly because the People's Republic of China, in giving priority to good relations with the ASEAN countries in its own modernization drive, withdrew its moral support from communist parties in other countries during the 1980s. Local dissident movements became increasingly isolated and their activities were more a reaction to the shortcomings of national governments than part of a coherent international movement. The communists also lost ground on account of internal divisions, such as the splintering of the Malaysian communists into three rival factions, while subversion was effectively monitored and countered by the vigilance and co-operation of ASEAN governments. The most dramatic rift in the communist camp was Vietnam's invasion of Cambodia followed by China's retaliatory campaign.

Increasingly the Marxist-Leninist model for development in the region became discredited in face of the excesses of the Cultural Revolution in China, the brutality and degradation of the Pol Pot régime in Democratic Kampuchea and the floundering of Vietnam's economy, despite the massive Chinese and Soviet aid which had flowed into the country for more than twenty years. By the late 1980s Vietnam itself was torn between clinging to orthodox ideology and moving to a more open, less centralized economy.

A variety of factors contributed to dilute fears of communism: Vietnam's continuing confrontation of China and concern for economic revival; China's preoccupation in the 1980s with modernization; the stagnation of USSR and East European economies, with Poland and even the Soviet Union itself looking for Western aid by 1989; President Mikhail Gorbachev's new *glasnost* and *perestroika* policies in the Soviet Union and their dramatic impact in Eastern Europe; Russian withdrawal from Afghanistan and Moscow's disillusionment with the economic drain involved in supporting Vietnam. After some initial concern at the Soviet military presence in Cam Rahn Bay, ASEAN saw Vietnam as its own political master.

In 1975 Thailand and the Philippines followed Malaysia in establishing diplomatic ties with the People's Republic of China, and Singapore forged strong economic links with Beijing (although at the same time maintaining its ties with Taiwan). But in view of its predominantly Chinese population, Singapore deferred establishing formal diplomatic relations with the People's Republic until Indonesia did so in 1990.

Despite the general slackening of tension, these developments were not without problems. The modernization of China revived nagging fears that the Overseas Chinese could be used as a means to secure both investment and export markets, thereby becoming an 'economic fifth column'. The Vietnamese refugees also became an increasing burden. In the early days most were ethnic Chinese, fleeing from political persecution or relocation to rural areas, but increasingly the refugees were Vietnamese trying to escape from poverty, over-population, and the failures of the nation's economy. While their ultimate goal was to reach the developed countries of the West, notably the United States, they fled in the first place to Southeast Asia and Hong Kong.

There was also the doubt whether communist countries were abandoning the traditional goal of world revolution or merely seeking temporary accommodation with the West in order to build up their strength for renewed aggressive policies.[20] The Vietnamese constitution of 1980 provided for a proletarian dictatorship and talked of mobilizing the masses for revolution in production and opposing counter-revolutionaries. Hanoi's leaders took an even tougher line after the the suppression of the pro-democracy student movement in Beijing and the breakdown of communist solidarity in Eastern Europe in 1989.

In a comprehensive statement issued on National Day in September 1989, Vietnamese Communist Party secretary-general Nguyen Van Linh resolutely rejected any multi-party system or speeding up of democratic reform in Vietnam. Linh was an economic reformer, who in the past had promoted a certain measure of political liberalization, but he feared change might lead to similar disturbances in Vietnam itself.

The Indochina situation remained the most immediate threat to the peace and stability of Southeast Asia. The United Nations continued to reject the Heng Samrin régime as the legitimate government of Cambodia and to demand the withdrawal of the Vietnamese army. But Hanoi stood firm on its insistence that the Khmer Rouge should be excluded from any future government. In an attempt to break the deadlock, Sihanouk withdrew temporarily from leadership of the Democratic Kampuchea government-in-exile and in December 1987 began a series of informal talks with prime minister Hun Sen.

As economic difficulties mounted at home, Hanoi announced it would withdraw its troops unilaterally by September 1989. France called a high-powered conference of nineteen nations, co-chaired by Indonesia, in Paris for July–August 1989 in an attempt to reach a peaceful settlement for Cambodia. But the conference ended in failure, and Prince Sihanouk resigned once again, leaving the resistance in disarray. No agreement could be reached between Hun Sen and Sihanouk on quadri-partite power-sharing in the interim government prior to elections.

On the wider international level, the end of the Cold War offered better prospects for a Cambodian settlement. Soviet President Gorbachev's visit to Beijing in May 1989 was disrupted by anti-government student demonstrations, culminating in the Tiananmen Square incident. But the warming of Sino–Soviet relations promised to set a new scenario for Southeast Asia

---

[20] Sinnathamby Rajaratnam (former Deputy Prime Minister of Singapore), 'Riding the Vietnamese Tiger', *Far Eastern Economic Review*, 4 May 1989.

and pave the way for restoring diplomatic ties between Beijing and Vietnam, which had been broken since 1978.

In September 1990 the four warring factions in Cambodia agreed to accept a United Nations role in an interim administration leading to free elections, and two months later the United Nations Security Council, including China and the Soviet Union, agreed on a draft peace plan to end the twelve-year war. This provided for a ceasefire and eventual elections, with an interim UN administration involving a Supreme National Council composed of representatives of the Hun Sen government and the three guerrilla groups. The agreement was finally signed in October 1991.

WESTERN INVOLVEMENT

Links with the West continued to weaken. SEATO, which was described at this time as 'a long moribund strategic basketcase',[21] was disbanded in June 1977. The weak presidency of Jimmy Carter (1976–80) combined with American negative reaction against involvement in the Vietnam War to compound Washington's neglect of mainland Southeast Asia.

The Colombo Plan was no longer a British nor even a Commonwealth-dominated organization, but had developed into a broader and more permanent international body. After being renewed for periods of five years, in 1980 the plan was extended indefinitely. By that time membership had expanded from the original seven Commonwealth nations to an international organization of twenty-six countries, including all the countries of Southeast Asia except Vietnam and Brunei. Its area was extended to cover Asia and the Pacific, with most aid coming from the six developed member countries, namely Australia, Canada, Japan, New Zealand, the United Kingdom and the United States. By 1988–9 Japan was the largest donor, supplying more than twice the amount of aid provided by the United States, which itself contributed more than the original four developed Commonwealth member countries combined.[22] In addition the Colombo Plan provided assistance, training and research, including technical co-operation among developing countries themselves. For example a Colombo Plan Staff College for Technician Education was established in Singapore in 1975 and transferred to the Philippines in 1987.[23]

In 1984 Britain and China issued a joint declaration arranging to hand Hong Kong back to China in 1997. Subsequently a similar document was signed between the Portuguese and Chinese to cover Macau, which would revert to the People's Republic in December 1999. These heralded the final disappearance of European political colonialism from the region by the end of the century.

As Anglo-American involvement declined, Japan became more important

---

[21] Justus M. Van der Kroef, *The Lives of SEATO*, Singapore: ISEAS, Occasional Paper no. 45, 1976, 1.

[22] *The Statesman's Year-Book, 1988–89.*

[23] *Colombo Plan Annual Reports* (HMSO, London, 1952–71); followed by *Colombo Plan Bureau* (Sri Lanka, 1971 onwards).

as mentor and model, achieving economic influence and material advantages beyond the dreams of the Greater East Asia Co-Prosperity Sphere of the militarist era. But Tokyo's impact was confined to the economic sphere.

NON-ALIGNMENT

Over the years ASEAN countries became disillusioned with the non-aligned movement, which was often out of step with their policies. At its first summit meeting at Belgrade in 1961, the so-called non-aligned movement had adopted an anti-colonial political stance. It grew more militant as membership expanded to incorporate newly independent nations, laying most ASEAN countries open to charges of neo-colonialism because of their continuing defence and economic ties with the West. The 1976 Colombo meeting, which was the first non-aligned summit to be held after the end of the Vietnam War, refused to re-endorse ASEAN's ZOPFAN proposal. It also issued a Declaration for a New Economic Order, calling for a restructuring of the world economy at the expense of the advanced nations. This attracted hostile comment from Singapore in particular, since it ran counter to co-operation with the West, an essential ingredient of ASEAN economies.

Burma withdrew from the movement at the Havana summit meeting in 1979 because other members, such as Cuba and the Philippines, were aligned to either communist or Western blocs. But by the late 1980s the non-aligned movement itself was changing: the Belgrade summit meeting in September 1989 agreed that it must adapt to the new situation of East–West détente by downplaying its traditional diatribes against colonialism and superpower domination in favour of concern over terrorism, human rights and protecting the environment. While some hardline African and Latin American states protested and insisted on including the customary references to the 'struggle against imperialism, colonialism, neo-colonialism, racism, apartheid and all forms of domination', Asian countries, and particularly Southeast Asia, were content to go along with the new realism.

By the end of the 1980s the countries of Southeast Asia seemed secure within their frontiers and were more concerned with economic prosperity than strident nationalism. Even Vietnam and Burma gave some priority to emerging from the economic stagnation to which their respective ideologies had brought them.

The search for security drew non-communist Southeast Asian countries into more urgent co-operation in ASEAN, yet it did not give ASEAN a military role. In principle member states still accepted the ideal of Southeast Asia as a zone of peace, freedom and neutrality, although they managed to attach a variety of meanings to this. But the prospects of Burma or the Indochina states joining ASEAN were still remote.

While only limited progress had been made in the economic, social and cultural fields, ASEAN was more successful in political and diplomatic co-operation, and by the late 1980s had achieved a major international standing. From the beginning ASEAN was important in providing a framework for co-operation and reconciliation in the post-colonial—and especially the post-confrontation—era, and from the early 1970s its members adopted some concrete measures of mutual help. But for many years the outside world had dismissed the association. Its value came to be recognized only after the Bali summit of 1976, when the ASEAN countries stood together in the face of the communist victories in Indochina and later when they maintained a common stance against the Vietnamese-backed Heng Samrin régime in Kampuchea throughout the 1980s. This showed what could be achieved by diplomatic and political pressure, without a parallel military pact. ASEAN's international prestige increased further over the years as it achieved dialogue with the advanced industrialized countries: the United States, the European Community, Australia, Canada, New Zealand and Japan.

While they remained committed to integration into the international economy, ASEAN countries tried to avoid dependence on, or the drain of profits to, their more powerful capitalist partners. Yet they relied to some extent on Great Powers—notably the United States and Japan—for the rapid economic development they saw as essential to political stability. Generous economic and military aid, technical help and development loans stimulated the economy of most Southeast Asian countries, but sometimes this benefited only a privileged few and fuelled further discontent. The new economic opportunities also encouraged corruption, particularly when most development funds were administered by the bureaucracy. The Pertamina scandal in Indonesia in 1976 highlighted bribery at the highest level of public life, while ten years later dishonesty in the Philippines reached such a scale that it jeopardized the economy and toppled the Marcos régime. The irregularities revealed in the running of Malaysia's Bank Bumiputra, linked to the Carrian group in Hong Kong, demonstrated how widespread the problem was and how the corruption network reached the highest level of government and permeated the region.

After a slow start ASEAN had succeeded in reducing political tension and eventually led to limited economic rationalization. While rural poverty, unequal development, and inequitable distribution of wealth were still serious problems in ASEAN countries, these were not so acute as in most other parts of the Third World. Its population was as large as the European Community, while its resources of primary produce made it one of the richest regions in the world. The Great Powers were beginning to see ASEAN as a political power bloc in its own right, and by the last decade of the century ASEAN was probably the most effective of Third World organizations.

The ASEAN countries had largely settled their traditional disputes and developed machinery for negotiating day-to-day problems. The initial objective of promoting regional security through reconciliation had largely been achieved, with an emphasis on consensus and not confrontation. Individual members generally remained unwilling to sacrifice political or economic nationalism to regionalism, but sought friendly co-operation.

The security of Singapore and Brunei within ASEAN showed that small states could not only survive but prosper in the late twentieth century, and the experience of both countries in relation to Malaysia indicated that it was not necessary or even desirable to seek a post-colonial future as part of a larger unit or federation. Tiny oil-rich Brunei enjoyed a high per capita income but one based almost entirely on two wasting assets. The feudalism of the sultanate, combined with its great wealth, posed the question whether this could ultimately create another Azahari-type problem that could split ASEAN.

Despite their common Marxist-Leninist ideology, the Indochina bloc was much less harmonious than ASEAN. While committed to rapid economic development through fundamental reconstruction, the socialist economic road they chose was a failure, despite massive aid from the Soviet Union and COMECON. Unlike ASEAN, the Indochina countries suffered from the revival of traditional rivalries such as those between Vietnam and Cambodia, and between Vietnam and China. At the same time the waning fear of communism opened the way for smoother relationships in the region, since communism was no longer seen as a monolithic movement which threatened internal stability or international peace. Outside the Philippines, communist insurgency ceased to be a danger, and in December 1989 the Communist Party of Malaya formally renounced its armed struggle. China continued to loom over the region, but as a large power rather than an ideological threat.

Thus as Southeast Asia reached the last decade of the most turbulent century in its history, it had come a fair way to determining the character of its nations and to establishing regional cohesion. As in the past, its strategic economic position at the cross-roads of international trade made it the continuing object of big-power interest, yet at the same time the small states of Southeast Asia were firmly established with sufficient regional co-operation to ensure at least some measure of control over their own destiny.

BIBLIOGRAPHICAL ESSAY

There is a wealth of literature on this topic, and most of the works mentioned in this brief note have detailed bibliographies.

Michael Leifer, *The Foreign Relations of the New States*, Melbourne, 1974, deals with Southeast Asia in the period from 1945 to the early 1970s. See also Evelyn Colbert, *Southeast Asia in International Politics, 1941–1956*, Ithaca, 1977; Russell H. Fifield, *The Diplomacy of Southeast Asia, 1945–1958*, New York, 1958; and Peter Lyon, *War and Peace in South-East Asia*, London, 1969.

Bernard K. Gordon, *The Dimensions of Conflict in Southeast Asia*, Englewood Cliffs, 1966, explores efforts at regional co-operation as well as conflict in the twenty years following World War II. Arnfinn Jorgensen-Dahl, *Regional Organisation and Order in South-East Asia*, London, 1982, deals with the development of regional organization from 1945 and particularly with ASEAN. Charles E. Morrison and Astri Suhrke, *Strategies of*

Survival: The Foreign Policy Dilemmas of Smaller Asian States, New York, 1978, includes Vietnam, all the founder ASEAN states and ASEAN itself.

On ASEAN see the *ASEAN Documents Series, 1967–1988*, 3rd edn, Jakarta: ASEAN Secretariat, 1988; Alison Broinowski, ed., *Understanding ASEAN*, London, 1982; and Michael Leifer, *ASEAN and the Security of South-East Asia*, London, 1989.

Leszek Buszynski, *SEATO: Failure of an Alliance Strategy*, Singapore, 1983, deals in detail with the origins, development and winding up of SEATO. See also the organization's journal *Spectrum* and its annual reports.

Indonesian foreign policy from independence to the early 1980s is covered by Michael Leifer, *Indonesia's Foreign Policy*, London, 1983. Franklin B. Weinstein, *Indonesian Foreign Policy and the Dilemma of Dependence: From Sukarno to Suharto*, Ithaca, 1976, concentrates mainly on the 1960s and early 1970s. Jon M. Reinhardt, *Foreign Policy and National Integration: the case of Indonesia*, New Haven: Yale University Southeast Asian Studies, 1971, relates nation building to foreign policy up to the end of the 1960s. Firsthand accounts are given by a variety of Indonesian diplomats and foreign ministers: Ide Anak Agung gde Agung, *Twenty Years Indonesian Foreign Policy 1945–1965*, The Hague and Paris, 1973, the detailed memoirs of a former Minister of Foreign Affairs, who was imprisoned by Sukarno; Ganis Harsono, *Recollections of an Indonesian Diplomat in the Sukarno Era*, edited by C. L. M. Penders and B. B. Hering, St Lucia, 1977, the memoirs of a pro-Sukarno minister who was imprisoned by Suharto; and Adam Malik, *In the Service of the Republic*, Singapore, 1980, covering the period from 1945 to 1980 including Malik's career as Foreign Minister.

For the Malaysia issue see Peter Boyce, *Malaysia and Singapore in International Diplomacy: Documents and Commentaries*, Sydney, 1968. J. A. C. Mackie, *Konfrontasi: the Indonesia-Malaysia Dispute 1963–1966*, Kuala Lumpur, 1974, is the most comprehensive study of confrontation. Chin Kin Wah, *The Defence of Malaysia and Singapore: The Transformation of a Security system, 1957–1971*, Cambridge, UK, 1983, covers the period of the Anglo-Malay(si)an Defence Agreement. For broader aspects of the relationship, see Stanley S. Bedlington, *Malaysia and Singapore: the Building of New States*, Ithaca, 1978.

Milton W. Meyer, *A Diplomatic History of the Philippine Republic*, Honolulu, 1965, covers the period from the formative years 1945–6 to the end of the Garcia administration in 1961. Michael Leifer, *The Philippine Claim to Sabah*, Zug, 1968, provides a concise historical background to this controversy, and Lela Garner Noble, *Philippine Policy towards Sabah: A Claim for Independence*, Tucson, 1977, deals in detail with the period from 1962 until Marcos abandoned pursuit of the claim in 1976.

On Indochina, the diplomatic background to the immediate postwar period is examined in R. E. M. Irving, *The First Indochina War: French and American Policy 1945–54*, London, 1975. The first two volumes of R. B. Smith's projected five-volume *An International History of the Vietnam War* cover the period 1955–65, I: *Revolution versus Containment, 1955–61*, London, 1983, and II: *The Struggle for South-East Asia, 1961–65*, London, 1985. William S. Turley, *The Second Indochina War*, Boulder, 1986, is a concise political and military account. Gene T. Hsiao, ed., *The Role of External Powers in the Indo-china Crisis*, Edwardsville, 1973, goes up to the 1973 Paris Peace Agreement.

The 1954 Geneva Conference and the events leading up to it are covered comprehensively. See Melvin Gurtov, *The First Vietnam Crisis: Chinese Communist Strategy and United States Involvement, 1953–54*, New York, 1967, and Robert F. Randle, *Geneva 1954: the Settlement of the Indochinese War*, Princeton, 1969. Kenneth T. Young, ed., *The 1954 Geneva Conference: Indo-China and Korea*, New York, 1968, is a collection of documents on the conference itself, and James Cable, *The Geneva Conference of 1954 on Indo-china*, London, 1986, is a lively eye-witness account.

Michael Leifer, *Cambodia: Search for Security*, London, 1967, deals with the post-1954 Geneva settlement years. Roger M. Smith, *Cambodia's Foreign Policy*, Ithaca, 1965, is a detailed study of the period from 1954 to the 1962 Laos settlement. On Laos, see MacAlister Brown and Joseph J. Zasloff, *Apprentice Revolutionaries: The Communist Movement in Laos, 1930–1985*, Stanford, 1986. Malcolm Caldwell and Lek Tan, *Cambodia in the Southeast Asian War*, New York, 1973, presents a radical left-wing analysis going back to French colonial days but concentrating mainly on the period from 1954 to the early 1970s. Donald Weatherbee, ed., *Southeast Asia Divided. The ASEAN-Indochina Crisis*, Boulder, 1985, includes 1979–84 documents.

William C. Johnstone, *Burma's Foreign Policy: A Study in Neutralism*, Cambridge, Mass., 1963, analyses Burma's policy in the 1948–62 period.

Much has been published about the role of the various external powers. Russell H. Fifield, *Americans in Southeast Asia: The Roots of Commitment*, New York, 1973, traces the US relationship from pre-war days to the aftermath of the 1954 Geneva Agreement. Andrew J. Rotter, *The Path to Vietnam: Origins of the American Commitment to Southeast Asia*, Ithaca, 1987, is a perceptive study of the late 1940s and early 1950s. See also R. Sean Randolph, *The United States and Thailand: Alliance Dynamics, 1950–1983*, Berkeley: Institute of East Asian Studies, University of California, 1986.

Charles B. McLane, *Soviet Strategies in Southeast Asia*, Princeton, 1966, explores Soviet policy from 1917 to the death of Stalin, with a useful final chapter on the 1948–54 period. Leszek Buszynski, *Soviet Foreign Policy and Southeast Asia*, London, 1986, is important for post-1969 policy and particularly developments following 1978. Douglas Pike, *Vietnam and the Soviet Union: Anatomy of an Alliance*, Boulder and London, 1987, traces the relationship from pre-Soviet contacts to the 1980s.

Phillip Darby, *British Defence Policy East of Suez*, London, 1973, deals with the postwar situation up to the changes of the late 1960s.

On China's involvement see David Mozingo, *Chinese Policy towards Indonesia 1949–1967*, Ithaca, 1976; Joyce K. Kallgren, Noordin Sopiee and Soedjati Djwandono, eds, *ASEAN and China: An Evolving Relationship*, Berkeley: Institute of East Asian Studies, University of California, 1988; and Leo Suryadinata, *China and the ASEAN States: The Ethnic Chinese Dimension*, Singapore, 1985.

On Australia, Alan Watt, *The Evolution of Australian Foreign Policy 1938–1965*, Cambridge, UK, 1967, has a chapter on relations in Asia 1945–65. A. W. Stargardt, *Australia's Asian Policies: The History of a Debate 1839–1972*,

Wiesbaden, 1977, deals extensively with the post-1945 period. J. A. C. Mackie, ed., *Australia in the New World Order: Foreign Policy in the 1970s*, Sydney, 1976, is largely concerned with the changed situation in Southeast Asia following Sino-American detente and the US withdrawal from Vietnam. Alan Watt, *Vietnam: An Australian Analysis*, Melbourne, 1968, gives a concise historical background, mainly of the post-1954 period.

From 1974 onwards *Southeast Asian Affairs*, an annual publication of the Institute of Southeast Asian Studies, Singapore, provides detailed reports and commentaries on domestic and international affairs throughout the region.

Dean Forbes, 'Towards the "Pacific Century": Integration and Disintegration in the Pacific Basin', in *The Far East and Australasia 1998*, pp. 25–32, has a comprehensive and up-to-date bibliography.

BIBLIOGRAPHIES

Besterman, Theodore (ed. J. D. Pearson). *A World Bibliography of Oriental Bibliographies*. Oxford: Basil Blackwell, 1975.
Bibliographic Index: A Cumulative Bibliography of Bibliographies. New York: H. W. Wilson, 1945– .
Brewer, Annie M., ed. *Indexes, Abstracts, and Digests: A Classified Bibliography Reproduced from Library of Congress Cards Arranged According to the Library of Congress Classification System*. Detroit: Gale Research Co., 1982.
Commonwealth National Bibliographies: An Annotated Directory. London: Commonwealth Secretariat, 1977.

ASIA

Asian Studies Indexed Journal Reference Guide. University of Pittsburgh, 1978.
[Association of Asian Studies]. *Cumulative Bibliography of Asian Studies 1941–1965*. Boston: G. K. Hall, 1969.
[Association of Asian Studies]. *Cumulative Bibliography of Asian Studies 1966–1970*. Boston: G. K. Hall, 1972.
Bibliography of Asian Studies. Ann Arbor: Association for Asian Studies, 1970– .
Birnbaum, Eleazar. *Books on Asia from the Near East to the Far East*. Toronto: University of Toronto Press, 1971.
Chen, Virginia. *The Economic Conditions of East and Southeast Asia: A Bibliography of English-Language Materials, 1965–1977*. Westport: Greenwood Press, 1978.
Embree, Ainslie T. *Asia: A Guide to Basic Books*. New York: Arno Press, 1976.
Goil, N. K. *Asian Social Science Bibliography with Annotations and Abstracts*. Delhi: Vikas Publications, 1970.
Hall, David E. *Union Catalogue of Asian Publications*. London: Mansell, 1971.
Kumar, Girja, et al. *Documentation on Asia*. New Delhi: Allied Publishers, 1963.
New York Public Library. Reference Department. *Dictionary Catalog of the Oriental Collection*. Boston: G. K. Hall, 1960.
Ng, Elizabeth W. *Directory of Current Hong Kong Research on Asian Topics*. Hong Kong: Centre of Asian Studies, University of Hong Kong, 1978.
Nunn, G. R. *Asia and Oceania: A Guide to Archival and Manuscript Sources in the United States*. London and New York: Mansell, 1985.
Nunn, G. R. *Asia: A Core Collection*. Ann Arbor: Xerox University Microfilms, 1973.

Nunn, G. R. *Asia: Reference Works—A Select Annotated Guide*. London: Mansell, 1980.
Orientalische Bibliographie. Berlin: H. Reuther's Verlagshuchhandlung, 1887– .
Pearson, J. D. *A Guide to Manuscripts and Documents in the British Isles relating to South and South-East Asia*. London and New York: Mansell, 1989.
Pearson, J. D. *Oriental and Asian Bibliography: An Introduction with Some Reference to Africa*. London: Crosby, Lockwood and Son, 1966.
Royal Commonwealth Society, Library. *The Manuscript Catalogue of the Library of the Royal Commonwealth Society*. London: Mansell, 1975.
Royal Empire Society. *Subject Catalogue of the Library of the Royal Empire Society*. London: Dawson of Pall Mall, 1967.
de Silva, Daya. *The Portuguese in Asia: An Annotated Bibliography of Studies on Portuguese Colonial History in Asia, 1498–c.1800*. Zug: Inter Documentation Co., 1987.
Toho Gakkai. *Books and Articles on Oriental Subjects Published in Japan*. Tokyo: Toho Gakkai [annual].
University of London. School of Oriental and African Studies. *Library Catalogue*. Boston: G. K. Hall, 1963.
Wainwright, M. D., and Matthews, Noel. *A Guide to Western Manuscripts and Documents in the British Isles Relating to South and South East Asia*. London: Oxford University Press, 1965.

SOUTHEAST ASIA

Senarai Bibliografi Mengenai Asia Tenggara Dalam Perpustakaan Universiti Kebangsaan Malaysia. Bangi: Perpustakaan Tun Seri Lanang, Universiti Kebangsaan Malaysia, 1981.

Arief, Sritua. *Southeast Asian Politics, 1967–1979: A Bibliography*. Kuala Lumpur: META, 1980.
Asian Studies Indexed Journal Reference Guide. University of Pittsburgh, 1978.
Attar Chand. *Southeast Asia and the Pacific 1947–1977*. New Delhi: Sterling Publishers, 1979.
Berton, Peter, and Rubinstein, Alvin Z. *Soviet Works on Southeast Asia: A Bibliography of Non-Periodical Literature, 1946–1965*. Los Angeles: University of Southern California Press, 1967.
Bibliografi Kaum Tani dan Pembangunan di Kawasan ASEAN. Bangi: Perpustakaan Universiti Kebangsaan Malaysia, 1980.
Bixler, Paul H. *Southeast Asia: Bibliographic Directions in a Complex Area*. Middletown, Conn.: Choice, 1974.
Carlson, Alvar W. *A Bibliography of the Geographical Literature on Southeast Asia, 1920–1972*. Monticello, Ill.: Council of Planning Librarians, 1974.
Chand, Attar. *Southeast Asia and the Pacific—A Select Bibliography: 1947–1977*. New Delhi: Sterling Publishers, 1979.
Chantornvong, Sombat, and Sonsri, Sida (Chety). *The ASEAN View: An Annotated Bibliography of ASEAN Theses and Dissertations on Southeast Asia from 1976 to 1984*. Bangkok: Foundation for the Studies of Democracy and Development, 1987.
Checklist of Southeast Asian Serials. Southeast Asia Collection, Yale University Library. Boston: G. K. Hall, 1968.
Chen, Virginia. *The Economic Conditions of East and Southeast Asia: A Bibliography of English-Language Materials, 1965–1977*. Westport: Greenwood Press, 1978.

Classified Catalogue of Books in Western Languages on South-East Asia in the Toyo Bunko (edited by the Seminar on South and South-East Asian History). Tokyo: Toyo Bunko (Oriental Library), 1978.

Clifton, Merritt et al., eds. *Those Who Were There: Eyewitness Accounts of the War in Southeast Asia, 1956–1975, and Aftermath*. Paradise, Calif.: Dustbooks, 1984.

Cordier, H. *Bibliotheca Indosinica*. New York: Burt Franklin, 1967 (1st edn, 1912). Vol. 1: *Burma, Assam, Siam, Laos*. Vol. 2: *Malay Peninsula*. Vol. 3: *French Indochina*. Vol. 4: *French Indochina*. Vol. 5: *Index*.

CORMOSEA (Committee on Research Materials on Southeast Asia). *Bulletin*. Ann Arbor: Association for Asian Studies.

Cornell University Libraries. Southeast Asia Program. *The John M. Echols Collection: Southeast Asia Catalog*. Boston: G. K. Hall, 1976 [Supplement Pertama, 1983].

Cornell University Libraries. *Accessions List: The John M. Echols Collection on Southeast Asia*.

Echols, John. 'Southeast Asia' in Howe, George F., *The American Historical Association's Guide to Historical Literature*. New York: Macmillan, 1961.

Embree, John F., and Lillian Ota Dotson. *Bibliography of the Peoples and Cultures of Mainland Southeast Asia*. New Haven: Yale University, Southeast Asian Studies, 1950.

Great Britain. Colonial Office. *An Annotated Bibliography on Land Tenure in the British and British Protected Territories in South East Asia and the Pacific*. London: HMSO, 1952.

Hay, Stephen N., and Case, Margaret H. *Southeast Asian History: Bibliographic Guide*. New York: Frederick A. Praeger, 1962.

Hobbs, Cecil. *Southeast Asia: A Bibliography of Writings, 1942–1978*. Carbondale: Center for Vietnamese Studies and Office of International Education, Southern Illinois University, 1980.

Hobbs, Cecil, *Southeast Asia: An Annotated Bibliography of Selected Reference Sources in Western Languages*. New York: Greenwood Press, 1968.

Hobbs, Cecil. *Southeast Asia Materials in the Australian National University Library: A Programme for Development and Use*. Canberra: Australian National University Library, 1975.

Huffman, Franklin E. *Bibliography and Index of Mainland Southeast Asian Languages and Linguistics*. New Haven and London: Yale University Press, 1986.

Ichikawa, Kenjiro, ed. *Southeast Asia Viewed from Japan: A Bibliography of Japanese Works on Southeast Asian Societies, 1940–1963*. Ithaca: Department of Asian Studies, Cornell University, 1965.

Insular Southeast Asia: A Bibliographic Survey, 1971. Washington, DC: Department of the Army, 1971.

Irikura, James K. *Southeast Asia: Selected Annotated Bibliography of Japanese Publications*. New Haven: Human Relations Area Files, 1956.

Iwasaki, Ikuro. *Japan and Southeast Asia: A Bibliography of Historical, Economic and Political Relations*. Tokyo: Library of the Institute of Developing Economies, 1983.

Johnson, Donald Clay. *A Guide to Reference Materials on Southeast Asia: Based on the Collections in the Yale and Cornell University Libraries*. New Haven: Yale University Press, 1970.

Johnson, Donald Clay. *Index to Southeast Asian Journals, 1975–1979: A Guide to Articles, Book Reviews, and Composite Works*. Boston: G. K. Hall, 1982.

Land Tenure Center, University of Wisconsin. *A Bibliography on Agrarian Economy in Southeast Asia* (1972).

Lim, Patricia, et al. *ASEAN: A Bibliography.* Singapore: ISEAS, 1984.

Lim Pui Huen, P. *Directory of Microfilm Facilities in Southeast Asia.* Singapore: ISEAS, 1973.

Lim Pui Huen, P. *News Resources on Southeast Asian Research.* Singapore: ISEAS, 1976.

List of Theses and Dissertations concerned with South East Asia 1965–1977. London: Centre of South East Asian Studies, School of Oriental and African Studies, University of London, 1977.

Loofs, H. H. E. *Elements of the Megalithic Complex in Southeast Asia: An Annotated Bibliography.* Canberra: Australian National University Press, 1967.

McVey, Ruth T. *Bibliography of Soviet Publications on Southeast Asia: As Listed in the Library of Congress Monthly Index of Russian Acquisitions.* Ithaca: Department of Far Eastern Studies, Cornell University, 1959.

Morrison, Gayle, and Hay, Stephen. *A Guide to Books on Southeast Asian History (1961–1966).* Santa Barbara: ABC-Clio, 1969.

National Library of Australia. *Southeast Asian Periodicals and Official Publications.* (In 5 Parts.) Canberra: National Library of Australia, 1970.

Northern Illinois University. Library. *List of Recent Southeast Asia Acquisitions in the Swen Franklin Parson Library.* DeKalb: Northern Illinois University. 1970–

Northern Illinois University. Library. *Revised List of Southeast Asia Holdings in the Swen Franklin Parson Library, Northern Illinois University.* DeKalb: Northern Illinois University, 1968.

Pendakur, V. Setty. *Urban Transport in South and Southeast Asia: An Annotated Bibliography.* Singapore: ISEAS, 1984.

Oey, Giok Po. *Survey of Chinese-Language Materials on Southeast Asia in the Hoover Institute and Library.* Ithaca: Southeast Asia Program, Department of Far Eastern Studies, Cornell University, 1953.

Oey, Hong Lee. *Power Struggle in South-East Asia.* Zug: Inter Documentation Co., 1976.

Partaningrat, Winarti. *Masterlist of Southeast Asian Microforms.* Singapore: Singapore University Press, 1978.

Peninsular Southeast Asia: a Bibliographic Survey of Literature (Burma, Cambodia, Laos, Thailand). Washington, DC: Headquarters, Department of the Army, 1972.

Pryon, Robin J. *A Bibliography on Internal Migration in South East Asia.* Canberra: Department of Demography, Research School of Social Sciences, Australian National University, 1977.

Quah Swee Lan. *Oil Discovery and Technical Change in Southeast Asia: A Bibliography.* Singapore: ISEAS, 1973.

Rhodes House Library. *Manuscript Collections in Rhodes House Library.* Oxford: Bodleian Library, 1970.

Rhodes House Library. *Manuscript Collections in Rhodes House Library, Oxford (Supplementary Accessions to the End of 1977 and Cumulative Index).*

Rony, A. Kohar. *Southeast Asia: Western-Language Periodicals in the Library of Congress.* Washington, DC: Library of Congress, 1979.

Scott, James C., et al. *A Bibliography on Land, Peasants and Politics for Malaysia, Indonesia and the Philippines.* Madison: Land Tenure Center Special Bibliography, 1972.

Senarai Bibliografi Mengenai Asia Tenggara dalam Perpustakaan Universiti Kebangsaan Malaysia. Bangi. Perpustakaan Tun Seri Lanang, 1981.

Smith, Myron J. Jr. *Air War Southeast Asia, 1961–1973.* Metuchen, NJ, and London: Scarecrow Press, 1979.

Sternstein, Larry, and Springer, Carl. *An Annotated Bibliography of Material Concerning Southeast Asia from Petermanns Geographische Mitteilungen, 1855–1966*. Bangkok: Siam Society, 1967.

Tregonning, K. G. *Southeast Asia: A Critical Bibliography*. Tucson: University of Arizona Press, 1969.

Union Catalogue of Documentary Materials on Southeast Asia (5 vols). Tokyo: Institute of Asian Economic Affairs, 1964.

United States of America. Library of Congress. Orientalia Division. *Southeast Asia Subject Catalog*. Boston: G. K. Hall, 1972.

University of Malaya, Library. *Literature, Drama and Dance in Southeast Asia*. Kuala Lumpur: Library, University of Malaya, 1976.

Van Niel, Robert, *A Survey of Historical Source Materials in Java and Manila*. Honolulu: University of Hawaii Press, 1970.

Willer, Thomas F., ed. *Southeast Asian References in the British Parliamentary Papers, 1801–1972/73: An Index*. Athens: Ohio University Center for International Studies, Southeast Asia Program, 1978.

MALAYSIA, SINGAPORE AND BRUNEI

Ding Choo Ming. *A Bibliography of Bibliographies on Malaysia*. Petaling Jaya, Selangor: Haxagon Elite Publications, 1981.

Arief, Melanie Sritua. *The Malaysian Economy and Politics, 1963–1983: A Bibliography*. East Balmain, NSW: Rosecons, 1984.

Aziz, Ungku A., and Yip Yat Hoon. *Projek-Projek Penyelidikan dan Penerbitan Universiti Malaya, 1959–1976*. Kuala Lumpur: University of Malaya, 1977.

Bibliografi Buku-Buku dalam Bahasa Malaysia, 1967–1970. Kuala Lumpur: Perpustakaan Negara Malaysia, 1981.

Bibliografi Buku-Buku Nadir dalam Perpustakaan Negara Malaysia. Kuala Lumpur: Perpustakaan Negara Malaysia, 1982.

Bibliografri Buku-Buku Nadir Malaysiana. Kuala Lumpur: Perpustakaan Negara Malaysia, 1982.

Bibliografi Negara Malaysia. Kuala Lumpur: Perpustakaan Negara Malaysia, Arkib Negara Malaysia, 1969–

Bibliografi Negeri Perak. Kuala Lumpur: Perpustakaan Negara Malaysia, 1983.

Bibliografi Negri Sabah. Kuala Lumpur: Perpustakaan Negara Malaysia, 1985.

Bibliografi Negri Trengganu. Kuala Lumpur: Perpustakaan Negara Malaysia, 1985.

Bibliografi Sejarah dan Politik. Kuala Lumpur: Perpustakaan Negara Malaysia, 1982.

Bibliografi UMNO dan Perjuangan Kebangsaan. Kuala Lumpur: Perpustakaan Negara Malaysia, 1985.

Bottoms, J. C. 'Some Malay Historical Sources: A Bibliographical Note', in Soedjatmoko et al., *An Introduction to Indonesian Historiography*. Ithaca: Cornell University Press, 1965.

Brown, Ian, and Ampalavanar, Rajeswary. *Malaysia*. Oxford, Santa Barbara, Denver: Clio Press, 1986.

Bryant, C. R. *Recent Bibliographical Activities in Malaysia and Singapore: A Brief Survey with a Selected, Annotated Bibliography*. New Haven: Yale University, 19– .

Challis, Joyce, ed. *Annotated Bibliography of Economic and Social Material in Sabah (North Borneo) and Sarawak*. Singapore: University of Singapore, 1969.

Challis, Joyce, ed. *Annotated Bibliography of Economic and Social Material in Singapore and West Malaysia: Governmental Publications*. Singapore: University of Singapore, 1969.

Challis, Joyce, ed. *Annotated Bibliography of Economic and Social Material in Singapore and West Malaya: Non-Governmental Publications*. Singapore: University of Singapore, 1969.

Cheang, Molly, Sng Yok Fong and Wee, Carolyn. *Index to Singapore/Malaysia Legal Periodicals, 1932–1984*. Singapore and Kuala Lumpur: Malayan Law Journal, 1986.

Cheesman, Harold. *Bibliography of Malaya: Being a Classified List of Books Wholly or Partly in English Relating to the Federation of Malaya and Singapore*. London: Longmans, 1959.

Chng, David K. Y. *A Select Bibliography of Chinese Sources for Nineteenth-Century Singapore*. Singapore: Singapore National Library, 1987.

Cotter, Conrad P. *Bibliography of English-Language Sources on Human Ecology, Eastern Malaysia and Brunei*. Honolulu: Department of Asian Studies, University of Hawaii, 1965.

Cotter, Conrad P. *Reading List of English-Language Materials in the Social Sciences on British Borneo*. Honolulu: Reference Bureau, University of Hawaii Library, 1960.

Drake, P. J. 'The Economic Development of British Malaya to 1914: An Essay in Historiography with some Questions for Historians', JSEAS, 10, 2 (Sept. 1979).

Habsah Hj. Ibrahim and Zainab Awang Ngah. *Bibliografi Aspek-Aspek Sosio-Budaya Penanaman dan Penggunaan Padi di Malaysia*. Kuala Lumpur: Perpustakaan Universiti Malaya, 1981.

Heussler, R. *British Malaya. A Bibliographical and Biographical Compendium*. New York: Garland Publishing, 1981.

Hill, Lewis. *A Checklist of English-Language Fiction Relating to Malaysia, Singapore and Brunei*. Hull: Centre for South-East Asian Studies, University of Hull, 1986.

Hill, R. D. 'Materials for Historical Geography and Economic History of Southeast Asia in Nineteenth-Century Malayan Newspapers', JMBRAS, 44, 2 (1971).

Index of Articles in the Journal of Southeast Asian History (1960–1969) and the Journal of Southeast Asian Studies (1970–1979).

Ismail Hussein. *Bibliografi Teks Cetakan Sastera Tradisi Melayu*. Kuala Lumpur: Jabatan Pengajian Melayu, Universiti Malaya, 1978.

Johore: A Bibliography. Kuala Lumpur: Perpustakaan Universiti Malaya, 1982.

Karni, R. S. *Bibliography of Malaysia and Singapore*. Kuala Lumpur: Penerbit Universiti Malaya, 1980.

Katalog Koleksi Melayu: Catalogue of the Malay Collection of the University of Malaya Library. Kuala Lumpur: Perpustakaan Universiti Malaya, 1980.

Khoo Kay Kim. 'Recent Malaysian Historiography', JSEAS, 10, 2 (Sept. 1979).

Krausse, Sylvia C. Engelen, and Krausse, Gerald H. *Brunei*. Oxford, Santa Barbara, Denver: Clio Press, 1988.

Kuah Sim Joo, Monica, and Che Puteh binti Ismail. *Prehistory and Archaeology of Malaysia and Brunei: A Bibliography*. Kuala Lumpur: Perpustakaan Universiti Malaya, 1982.

Leigh, Michael B. *Checklist of Holdings on Borneo in the Cornell University Libraries*. Ithaca: Southeast Asia Program, Department of Asian Studies, Cornell University, 1966.

Leong, Alice. *Select List of Singapore Parliamentary Papers, 1948–1976*. Singapore: Chopmen Enterprises, 1977.

Lent, John. *Malaysian Studies: Present Knowledge and Research Trends*. DeKalb: Center for Southeast Asian Studies, Northern Illinois University, 1979.

Lim, Beda. *Malaya: A Background Bibliography*. Kuala Lumpur: Malaysian Branch, Royal Asiatic Society, 1962.

Lim Huck Tee, Edward, and Wijasuriya, D. E. K. *Index Malaysiana: An Index to the Journal of the Straits Branch, Royal Asiatic Society, and the Journal of the Malayan Branch, Royal Asiatic Society, 1878–1963*. Kuala Lumpur: Malaysian Branch, Royal Asiatic Society, 1970. Supplement 1 (1964–1973), 1974; Supplement 2 (1974–1983), 1985.

Lim Pui Huen, Patricia, ed. *The Malay World of Southeast Asia, A Select Cultural Bibliography*. Singapore: ISEAS, 1984.

Lim Pui Huen, Patricia, ed. *Newspapers Published in the Malaysian Area, with a Union List of Local Holdings*. Singapore: ISEAS, 1970.

McIntyre, W. David. 'Malaya from the 1850's to the 1870's, and Its Historians, 1950–1970: From Strategy to Sociology' in C. D. Cowan and O. W. Wolters, eds, *Southeast Asian History and Historiography*. Ithaca: Cornell University Press, 1976.

Malaysian Historical Society. *An Index to 'Malaysia in History'*. Kuala Lumpur: Malaysian Historical Society, 1981.

Padma, Daniel. 'A Descriptive Catalogue of the Books Relating to Malaysia in the Raffles Museum and Library', JMBRAS, 19, 3, no. 141 (Dec. 1941).

Pelzer, Karl J. *Selected Bibliography on the Geography of Southeast Asia. Part 3. Malaya*. New Haven: Human Relations Area Files, 1956.

Pelzer, Karl. *West Malaysia and Singapore: A Selected Bibliography*. New Haven: Human Relations Area Files, 1971.

Quah, Stella R., and Quah, Jon S. T. *Singapore*. Oxford, Santa Barbara, Denver: Clio Press, 1988.

Roff, Margaret. *Official Publications of Malaysia, Singapore and Brunei in New York Public Libraries*. New York: Columbia University, 1971.

Roff, W. R. *Bibliography of Malay and Arabic Periodicals Published in the Straits Settlements and Peninsular Malay States 1876–1941*. London: Oxford University Press, 1972.

Roff, W. R. *Guide to Malay Periodicals, 1876–1941*. Singapore: Eastern Universities Press, 1961.

Roff, W. R. *Southeast Asian Research Tools: Malaysia, Singapore, Brunei*. Honolulu: Southeast Asian Studies, Asian Studies Program, University of Hawaii, 1979.

Saw Swee-Hock and Cheng Siok-Hwa. *A Bibliography of the Demography of Malaysia and Brunei*. Singapore: University Educational Press, 1975.

Saw Swee-Hock and Cheng Siok-Hwa. *A Bibliography of the Demography of Singapore*. Singapore: University Educational Press, 1975.

Shaika Zakaria, Datin, ed. *Poverty in Malaysia: A Bibliography*. Kuala Lumpur: Library, University of Malaya, 1986.

Singapore National Bibliography. Singapore: National Library, 1969– . Quarterly, with annual cumulations, 1977– .

Singapore National Library. *The Birth of a Nation—Singapore in the 1950s: A Select Bibliography*. Singapore: Singapore National Library, 1984.

Singapore, National Library. *Books About Singapore, 1970*. Singapore: National Library, 1970, 1975, 1979, 1982, 1984.

Soosai, J. S., and Kaw, H. W. *Fifty Years of Natural Rubber Research, 1926–1975: A Bibliography of Contributions from the Rubber Research Institute of Malaysia*.

Kuala Lumpur: Rubber Research Institute of Malaysia, 1975.
Stockwell, A. J. 'The Historiography of Malaysia: Recent Writings in English on the History of the Area since 1874', *Journal of Imperial and Commonwealth History*, 5, 1 (Oct. 1976).
Subbiah, Rama. *Tamil Malaysiana*. Kuala Lumpur: University of Malaya Library, 1969.
Tay Lian Soo. *Classified Bibliography of Chinese Historical Materials in Malaysia and Singapore*. Singapore: South Seas Society, 1984.
Tong Suit Chee. *Bibliography of Penang*. Pulau Pinang: Perpustakaan Universiti Sains Malaysia, 1974.
Tregonning, K. G. *Malaysian Historical Sources*. Singapore: History Department, University of Singapore, 1962.
Turnbull, C. M. 'Bibliography of Writings in English on British Malaya, 1786–1867'. Published as Appendix to Lennox A. Mills, *British Malaya, 1824–1867* (1966 edn). Kuala Lumpur: Oxford University Press, 1966.
Universiti Kebangsaan Malaysia. Perpustakaan. *Islam dalam Peradaban Melayu: Suata Bibliograpfi*. Kuala Lumpur: Universiti Kebangsaan Malaysia, 1976.
Universiti Malaya. Perpustakaan. *Koleksi Za'ba*. Kuala Lumpur: Perpustakaan University Malaya, 1976.
University of Singapore. Library. *Catalogue of the Singapore/Malaysia Collection*. Boston: G. K. Hall, 1968.
Wong Lin Ken. 'The Economic History of Malaysia: A Bibliographic Essay'. *Journal of Economic History*, 25, 2 (June 1965).
Wong Lin Ken, '20th Century Malayan Economic History: A Select Bibliographic Survey', JSEAS, 10, 1 (Mar. 1979).
Zainab Awang Ngah. *Kelantania di Perpustakaan Universiti Malaya*. Kuala Lumpur: Perpustakaan Universiti Malaya, 1979.

Manuscripts

Howard, Joseph H., ed. *Malay Manuscripts: A Bibliographical Guide*. Kuala Lumpur: University of Malaya Library, 1966.
Juynboll, H. H. *Catalogus van de Maleische en Sundaneesche Handschriften der Leidsche Universiteits Bibliotheek*. Leiden: E. J. Brill, 1899.
Manuskrip Melayu Warisan Budaya Negara. Kuala Lumpur: Perpustakaan Negara Malaysia, 1984.

THE PHILIPPINES

Bernardo, Gabriel., comp. [ed. by Natividad P. Verzosa]. *Bibliography of Philippine Bibliographies, 1593–1961*. Quezon City: Ateneo de Manila University Press, 1968.
Houston, Charles O. Jr. *Philippine Bibliography, I: An Annotated Preliminary Bibliography of Philippine Bibliographies (since 1900)*. Manila: University of Manila, 1960.
Hart, Donn V. *An Annotated Bibliography of Philippine Bibliographies: 1965–1974*. DeKalb: Center for Southeast Asian Studies, Northern Illinois University, 1974.
Saito, Shiro, *The Philippines. A Review of Bibliographies*. Honolulu: University of Hawaii, East-West Center Library, 1966.

Antonio, Celia M., and Tan, Allen L. *A Preliminary Bibliography of Philippine Cultural Minorities*. Quezon City: Commission on National Minorities, Republic of the Philippines, 1967.

Baradi, Edita R. *Southeast Asia Research Tools: The Philippines*. Honolulu: University of Hawaii, 1979.

Baylon, Concepcion S. *The National Library: guide to doctoral dissertations on microfilm (1937–68) in the Filipiniana Division*. Manila: National Library, 1971.

Bernardo, Gabriel A., and Vergosa, Natividad P., comps; Schumacher, John N., ed. *Philippine Retrospective National Bibliography: 1523–1699*. Manila: National Library of the Philippines and Ateneo de Manila University Press, 1974.

Bibliography of the Philippine Islands, Vol. 1: *A List of Books (with references to Periodicals) in the Library of Congress*. By A. P. C. Griffin. With Chronological List of Maps in the Library of Congress. By P. Lee Phillips. Vol. 2: *Biblioteca Filipina*. By T. H. Pardo de Tavera. Washington, DC: GPO, 1903.

Catalogue of Filipiniana Materials in the Lopez Memorial Museum (5 vols). Pasay City: Lopez Memorial Museum, 1962–71.

Conklin, Harold. *Ifugao Bibliography*. New Haven: Southeast Asian Studies Program, Yale University, 1968.

Doeppers, Daniel F. *Union Catalogue of Selected Bureau Reports and Other Official Serials of the Philippines, 1908–1941*. Madison: Center for Southeast Asian Studies, University of Wisconsin-Madison, 1980.

Eggan, Frederick Russell. *Selected Bibliography of the Philippines, topically arranged and annotated*. New Haven: Philippine Studies Program, University of Chicago, 1956.

Elaner, Emma Osterman. *Checklist of Publications of the Government of the Philippine Islands, September 1, 1900 to December 31, 1917*. Manila: Philippine Library and Museum, 1918.

Ferrer, Maxima Magsanoc. *Union Catalog of Philippine Materials* (2 vols). Quezon City: University of the Philippines Press, 1970.

Foronda, Marcelino A., and Cresencia R. *A Filipiniana Bibliography, 1743–1982 (A Classified Listing of Philippine Materials in the Marcelino A. and Crescencia R. Foronda Private Collection)*. Manila: Philippine National Historical Society, 1981.

Golay, Frank H., and Hauswedell, Marianne H. *An Annotated Guide to Philippine Serials*. Ithaca: Department of Asian Studies, Cornell University, 1976.

Griffin, Appleton Prentiss Clark. *List of Works Relating to the American Occupation of the Philippine Islands, 1898–1903*. Washington, DC: GPO, 1905.

Lietz, Paul S. *Calendar of Philippine Documents in the Ayer Collection of the Newberry Library*. Chicago: Newberry Library, 1956.

Medina, Jose Toribio. *La Imprenta en Manila desde sus origines hasta 1810*. Amsterdam: N. Israel, 1964.

Netzorg, Morton J. *The Philippines in World War II and to Independence (Dec. 8, 1941–July 4, 1946): An Annotated Bibliography*. Ithaca: Department of Asian Studies, Cornell University, 1977.

Palao, Trinidad E. *A Bibliography of Filipiniana Imprints: 1800–1850*. Manila: University of the Philippines, 1973.

Pardo de Tavera, Trinidad H. *Biblioteca filipina; o sea, Catalogo razonada de todos impresos tanto insulares como extranjeros, relativos a la historia, la etnografia, la linguistica, la botanica, la fauna, la flora, la geologia, la hidrografia, la geografia, la legislacion, etc. de las Islas Filipinas, de Jolo y Marianas*. Washington, DC: GPO, 1903.

Perez, Angel y Guemes, Ceciliio. *Adiciones y continuacion de 'La Imprenta en Manila' de D. J. T. Medina, O Rarezas y curiosidades bibliografico Filipinas de las bibliotecas de esta Capital.* Manila: Impr. de Santos y bernal, 1904.

Philippine Bibliography. Quezon City: Library, University of the Philippines, 1965–73.

Philippine National Bibliography. Manila: National Library of the Philippines, 1974.

Philippine Studies Program, University of Chicago. *Selected Bibliography of the Philippines.* Westport: Greenwood Press, 1973 (first published 1956).

Rebadavia, Consolacion B., comp.; Verzosa, Natividad P., and Austria, Pacifico M., eds. *Checklist of Philippine Government Documents, 1917–1949.* Quezon City: University of the Philippines Library, 1960.

Retana y Gamboa, Wenceslao Emilio. *Archivo del Bibliofilo Filipino. Recopilacion de Documentos Historicos, Cientificos, Literarios y Politicos y estudios Bibliograficos* (5 vols). Madrid, 1895.

Retana, W. E. *Aparato Bibliografico de la Historia General de Filipinas deducido de la Colleccion que Posee en Barcelona La Compania General de Tabacos de Dichas Islas* (3 vols). Madrid: Imprenta de la Sucesora de M. Minuesa de los Rios. Manila: Pedro B. Ayuda y Compania, 1964.

Richardson, Jim. *Philippines.* Oxford: Clio Press, 1989.

Robertson, James A., and Blair, Emma H. *The Philippine Islands, 1493–1898*, vol. 53: *Bibliography of the Philippines.* Mandaluyong, Rizal: Cachos Hermanos, 1973.

Robertson, James A. *Bibliography of the Philippine Islands.* New York: Kraus Reprint Co., 1970 (first published 1908).

Saito, Shiro. *Philippine Ethnography: A Critically Annotated and Selected Bibliography.* Honolulu: University Press of Hawaii, 1972.

Siega, Gorgonio D., et al. *A Classified Annotated Bibliography of Selected Filipiniana Materials at the Silliman University Library, Dumaguete City, Philippines.* Dumaguete City: Silliman University, 1977.

Tiamson, Alfredo T. *Mindanao–Sulu Bibliography.* Davao City: Ateneo de Davao, 1970.

Tubangui, Helen R. *A Catalog of Filipiniana at Valladolid.* Quezon City: Ateneo de Manila University Press, 1973.

University of the Philippines. Library. *Filipiniana 1968. A Classified Catalog of Filipiniana Books and Pamphlets in the University of the Philippines Library as of January 1, 1968.* Diliman, Quezon City: Library, University of the Philippines, 1969.

Welsh, Doris Varner. *A Catalogue of Printed Materials Relating to the Philippine Islands, 1519–1900 in the Newberry Library.* Chicago: Newberry Library, 1956.

INDONESIA

Tairas, J. N. B. *Indonesia: A Bibliography of Bibliographies.* New York: Oleander Press, 1975.

Anderson, Benedict R. *Bibliography of Indonesian Publications: Newspapers, Non-Government Periodicals and Bulletins, 1945–1958 at Cornell University.* Ithaca: Department of Far Eastern Studies, Cornell University, 1959.

Arief, Sritua, and Arief, Melanie Sritua. *The Indonesian Economy, 1967–1977: A Bibliography.* Jakarta: Sritua Arief Associates, 1978.

Australia. National Library. *Daftar Pengadaan Bahan Indonesia/Indonesian Acquisitions List*. Canberra: National Library of Australia.

Ave, Jan, King, Victor, and de Wit, Joke. *West Kalimantan: A Bibliography*. Dordrecht and Cinnaminson, NJ: Foris Publications, 1964.

Baal, Jan Van. *West Irian, a bibliography*. Dordrecht: Foris Publications, 1984.

Bhatta, J. N. *A Science Bibliography on Indonesia*. Djakarta: Departemen Angkatan Darat, 1965.

Bibliography of Indonesian Materials for the Humanities and Social Sciences (1960–1970). Djakarta: LIPI, 1972– .

Bibliografi Nasional Indonesia. Djakarta: Kantor Bibliografi Nasional, 1953– .

Boland, B. J. and Farjon, I. *Islam in Indonesia: A Bibliographic Survey, 1600–1942 with Post-1945 Addenda*. Dordrecht and Cinnaminson, NJ: Foris Publications, 1983.

Cense, A. A., and Uhlenbeck, E. M. *A Critical Survey of Studies on the Languages of Borneo*. s'-Gravenhage: Martinus Nijhoff, 1958.

Coolhaas, W. Ph. *A Critical Survey of Studies on Dutch Colonial History*. s'-Gravenhage: Martinus Nijhoff, 1960.

Damian, Eddy, et al. *Bibliografi Hukum Indonesia, 1945–1972*. Bandung: Lembaga Penelitian Hukum dan Kriminologi, Fakultas Hukum, Universitas Pengadjaran, 1974.

Dengel, Holk H. *Annotated Bibliography of New Indonesian Literature on the History of Indonesia*. Stuttgart: Franz Steiner Verlag Wiesbaden GMBH, 1987.

Excerpta Indonesica. Leiden: Centre for Documentation of Modern Indonesia, Royal Institute of Linguistics and Anthropology, 1971– .

Hicks, George L., and McNicoll, Geoffrey. *The Indonesian Economy, 1950–1965: A Bibliography*. New Haven: Yale University, Southeast Asian Studies Program, 1967.

Hicks, George L., and McNicoll, Geoffrey. *The Indonesian Economy, 1950–1965: A Bibliographic Supplement*. New Haven: Yale University, Southeast Asian Studies Program, 1967.

Hebig, Karl M. *Die Insel Borneo in Forschung und Schrifttum*. Sonderdruck aus den Mitteilungen der Geographischen Gesellschaft in Hamburg. Band 52. 1955.

Hooykaas, J. C. *Repertorium op de Koloniale Literatuur, of Systematische Inhoudsopgaaf van hetgeen voorkomt over de Koloniën, (beoosten de Kaap) in mengelwerken en tijdschriften, van 1595 tot 1865 uitgegeven in Nederland en zijne overzeesche besittingen*. Amsterdam: P. N. van Kampen & Zoon, 1877.

Indonesian Monographs: A Catalogue of Monograph Publications, 1945–1968. Zug: Inter Documentation Co., 1974.

Institute of Social Sciences, Waseda University. *The Nishijima Collection: Materials on the Japanese Military Occupation in Indonesia*. Tokyo: Waseda University, 1973.

Jang Aisjah Muttalib. *The History and Society of South Sumatra: Publications in New York Libraries*. New York: Columbia University Southern Asian Institute, 1971.

Joustra, M. *Overzicht van de Literatuur betreffende de Minangkabau*. Amsterdam: Minangkabau Instituut, 1924.

Karyeti, and Nurasin V. Suwahyono. *Daftar Koleksi Literatur tentang Nusa Tenggara Timur*. Jakarta: Pusat Dokumentasi Ilmiah Nasional, Lembaga Pengetahuan Indonesia, 1985.

Kennedy, R. *Bibliography of Indonesian Peoples and Cultures*. New Haven: Yale University Press, 1945.

Koentjaraningrat. *Anthropology in Indonesia: A Bibliographical Review*. 's-Gravenhage: Martinus Nijhoff, 1975.

Lan Hiang Char. *Southeast Asian Research Tools: Indonesia*. Honolulu: Southeast Asia Studies, Asian Studies Program, University of Hawaii, 1979.

Lev, Daniel S. *A Bibliography of Indonesian Government Documents and Selected Indonesian Writings on Government in the Cornell University Library*. Ithaca: Department of Far Eastern Studies, Cornell University, 1958.

Muljanto Sumardi. *Islamic Education in Indonesia: A Bibliography*. Singapore: ISEAS, 1983.

Nagelkerke, G. A. *Bibliografisch Overzicht uit Periodieken over Indonesië 1930–1945*. Leiden: Bibliotheek Koninklijk Instituut voor Taal-, Land- en Volkenkunde, 1974.

Nagelkerke, G. A. *A Selected Bibliography of the Chinese in Indonesia, 1740–1974*. London: Library of the Royal Institute of Linguistics and Anthropology, 1975.

Naim, Asma M., and Naim, Mochtar. *Bibliografi Minangkabau*. Singapore: Singapore University Press for ISEAS, 1975.

The Nishijima Collection: Materials on the Japanese Military Administration in Indonesia. Tokyo: Institute of Social Sciences, Waseda University, 1973.

Nolthenius, A. B. Tutein. *Overzicht van de literatuur betreffende de Molukken (exclusief Nieuw-Guinea)*, vol. 2 (1921–33). Amsterdam: Molukken-Instituut, 1935.

Ockeloen, G. *Catalogus van in Ned.-Indië verschenen Booken in de Jaren 1938–1941*. Batavia-Soerabaia: G. Kolff, 1942.

Ockeloen, G. *Catalogus van boeken en tijdschriften uitgegeven in Ned. Oost-Indië van 1870–1937*. Amsterdam: Swets and Zeitlinger, 1966.

Ockeloen, G. *Catalogus dari Boekoe-boekoe dan Madjallah-madjallah jang diterbitkan di Hindia Belanda dari tahoen 1870–1937*. Batavia-Amsterdam: G. Kolff, 1940.

Ockeloen, G. *Catalogus dari Buku-Buku jang diterbitkan di Indonesia*, Djilid 1: *1945–1949*. Djilid 2: *Buku dalam Bahasa Melaju, Djawa, D.L.L., 1937–1941*. Bandung: G. Kolff, 1950.

Ockeloen, G. *Catalogus dari Buku-Buku jang diterbitkan di Indonesia, 1950–51*. Bandung: G. Kolff, 1952.

Ockeloen, G. *Catalogus dari Buku-Buku jang diterbitkan di Indonesia, 1952–53*. Bandung: G. Kolff, 1954.

Ockeloen, G. *Catalogus dari Buku-Buku jang diterbitkan di Indonesia, 1954*. Bandung: G. Kolff, 1955.

Polman, Katrien. *The Central Moluccas: An Annotated Bibliography*. Dordrecht: Foris Publications, 1983.

Polman, Katrien. *The North Moluccas: An Annotated Bibliography*. The Hague: Martinus Nijhoff, 1981

Postma, Nel, Aeina Hadad, Sudarsono, B. *Bibliografi Wanita Indonesia*. Jakarta: Kantor Menteri Muda Urusan Peranan Wanita and Pusat Dokumentasi Ilmiah Nasional, Lembaga Limu Pengetahuan Indonesia, 1980 [with supplements in 1983 and 1985].

Rouffaer, G. P., and Muller, W. C. *Catalogus der Koloniale Bibliotheek van Het Koninklijk Instituut voor de Taal-, Land- en Volkenkunde van Ned.-Indië en het Indisch Genootschap*. 's-Gravenhage: Martinus Nijhoff, 1966.

Ruinen, W. *Overzicht van de Literatuur betreffende de Molukken*. Amsterdam: Molukken-Instituut, 1928.

Sherlock, Kevin. *A Bibliography of Timor, including East (formerly Portuguese) Timor, West (formerly Dutch) Timor and the Island of Roti*. Canberra: Research School of Pacific Studies, Australian National University, 1980.

Singarimbun, Masri. *The Population of Indonesia: A Bibliography*. Yogyakarta: Institute of Population Studies, Gadjah Mada University, 1974.

Soekanto, Soerjono. *Bibliografi Hukum Adat Indonesia: Akhir Abad XIX–1975*. Bandung: Alumni, 1976.

Stall, R. N. A. *A Bibliography of Indonesian Politics since 1966*. Bentley: Department of Library Studies and Department of Asian Studies, Western Australian Institute of Technology, 1979.

Stuart-Fox, David J. *Bibliography of Balinese Culture and Religion*. Jakarta: KITLV and LIPI, 1979.

Sukanda-Tessier, Viviane, with Sukanda Natasasmita, Haris. *Bibliographie d'une documentation Indonesienne Contemporaine, 1950–1970*. Paris: Ecole française d'extreme-orient, 1974.

Suzuki, P. *Critical Survey of Studies on the Anthropology of Nias, Matawi and Enggano*. 's-Gravenhage: Martinus Nijhoff, 1958.

Tan Sok Joo and Tan Hwee Kheng. *ASEAN: A Bibliography*. Singapore: ISEAS, 1976.

Teeuw, A., with Emanuels, H. W. *A Critical Survey of Studies on Malay and Bahasa Indonesia*. s'-Gravenhage: Martinus Nijhoff, 1961.

Telkamp, Gerard J. *Bouwstoffen voor de sociaal-economische geschiedenis van Indonesië van ca 1800 tot 1940; een beschrijvende bibliografie*. Amsterdam: Koninklijk Instituut voor de Tropen, 1977.

Thung, Yvonne, and Echols, John M., eds. *A Checklist of Indonesian Serials in the Cornell University Library, 1945–1970*. Ithaca: Southeast Asian Program, Cornell University, 1973.

Uhlenbeck, E. M. *A Critical Survey of Studies on the Languages of Java and Madura*. s'-Gravenhage: Martinus Nijhoff, 1964.

Van Baal, J., Galis, K. W., and Koentjaraningrat, R. M. *West Irian: A Bibliography*. Dordrecht and Cinnaminson, NJ: Foris Publications, 1984.

Van Delden, E. E. *Klein Repertorium. Index op tijdschriftartikelen met betrekking tot voormalig Nederlands-Indië*. Amsterdam: Koninklijk Instituut voor de Tropen, 1900.

Van Doorn, Marlene. *Bouwstoffen voor de sociaal-economische geschiedenis van Indonesië van ca 1800 tot 1940: een beschrijvende bibliografie*. Amsterdam: Koninklijk Instituut voor de Tropen, 1979.

Voorhoeve, P. *A Critical Survey of Studies on the Languages of Sumatra*. s'-Gravenhage: Martinus Nijhoff, 1955.

Wellen, J. W. J., and Helfrich, O. L. *Zuid-Sumatra. Overzicht van de Literatuur des Gewesten Bengkoelen, Djambi, de Lampongsche Districten en Palembang*. 's-Gravenhage: De Nederlandsche Boek- en Steendrukkerij, 1923.

Yayasan Idayu. *Bung Karno: Sebuah Bibliografi Memuat Daftar Karya oleh dan tentang Bung Karno*. Jakarta: Yayasan Idayu, 1981.

Manuscripts

Girardet, Nikolaus, et al. *Descriptive Catalogue of the Javanese Manuscripts and Printed Books in the Main Libraries of Surakarta and Yogyakarta*. Wiesbaden: Franz Steiner Verlag GMBH, 1983.

Juynboll, H. H. *Catalogus van de Maleische en Sundaneesche Handschriften der Leidsche Universiteits Bibliotheek*. Leiden: E. J. Brill, 1989.

Ricklefs, M. C., and Voorhoeve, P. *Indonesian Manuscripts in Great Britain*. Oxford University Press, 1977.

BURMA

Aung-Thwin, Michael. *Southeast Asia Research Tools: Burma*. Honolulu: University of Hawaii, 1979.

Barnett, L. D. *A Catalogue of the Burmese Books in the British Museum*. London: Longmans, 1913.

Bernot, D. *Bibliographie Birmanie (1950–1960)*. Paris: Editions du Centre National de la Recherche Scientifique, 1968.

Griffin, Andrew. *A Brief Guide to Sources for the Study of Burma in the India Office Records*. London: India Office Library and Records, 1979.

Morse, Ronald A., et al. *Burma: A Study Guide*. Washington, DC: Wilson Center Press, 1988.

Shulman, Frank Joseph. *Burma: An Annotated Guide to International Doctoral Dissertation Research, 1898–1985*. Lanhan, New York, London: University Press of America for the Wilson Center, 1986.

Tan Sok Joo. *Library Resources on Burma in Singapore*. Singapore: ISEAS, 1972.

Trager, Frank N. *Furnivall of Burma: An Annotated Bibliography of the Works of J. S. Furnivall*. New Haven: Southeast Asia Studies, Yale University, 1963.

Trager, Frank N. *Japanese and Chinese Language Sources on Burma: An Annotated Bibliography*. New Haven: Human Relations Area Files Press, 1957.

Whitbread, Kenneth. *Catalogue of Burmese Printed Books in the India Office Library*. London: HMSO, 1969.

THAILAND

Hart, D. V. *Thailand: An Annotated Bibliography of Bibliographies*. DeKalb: Northern Illinois University, Center for Southeast Asian Studies, 1977.

Amyot, Jacques, with Soontornpasuch, Suthep. *Changing Patterns of Social Structure in Thailand, 1851–1965: An Annotated Bibliography with Comments*. Delhi: UNESCO Research Centre, 1965.

Bernath, Frances A. *Catalogue of Thai Language Holdings in the Cornell University Libraries through 1964*. Ithaca: Department of Asian Studies, Cornell University, 1964.

Bibliography of Thammasat University Library. Bangkok: Thammasat University Library, 1979.

Bitz, Ira. *A Bibliography of English-Language Source Materials on Thailand in the Humanities, Social Sciences and Physical Sciences*. Washington, DC: Center for Research on Social Systems, The American University, 1968.

Chety, Sida. *Research on Thailand in the Philippines: An Annotated Bibliography of Theses, Dissertations, and Investigation Papers*. Ithaca: Southeast Asia Program, Cornell University, 1977.

Chulalongkorn University, Central Library. *Bibliography of Material about Thailand in Western Languages*. Bangkok: Chulalongkorn University, 1960.

Kawabe, Toshio. *Bibliography of Thai Studies*. Tokyo: Tokyo University of Foreign Studies, Institute of Foreign Affairs, 1957.

Keyes, C. F. *Southeast Asia Research Tools: Thailand*. Asian Studies Program, University of Hawaii, 1979.

Mabbett, Ian, ed. *Early Thai History: A Select Bibliography*. Clayton: Monash University, Centre of Southeast Asian Studies, [1978].

Mason, John Brown, and Parish, H. Carroll. *Thailand Bibliography*. Gainesville: Department of Reference and Bibliography, University of Florida Libraries, 1958.

National Library (Bangkok). *Periodicals and Newspapers Printed in Thailand between 1844–1934: A Bibliography*. Bangkok: National Library, 1970.

Raksasataya, Amara, with Veeravat Kanchanadul, Prachak Suthayakom, et al. *Thailand: Social Science Materials in Thai and Western Languages*. Bangkok: National Institute of Development Adminstration, 1966.

Saengthong, M. Ismail. *Library Resources on Thailand in Singapore*. Singapore: ISEAS, 1974.

Sangtada, Rattporn. *Isan (Northeast Thailand): A Select Bibliography*. Sydney: University of Sydney, 1986.

Sharp, Lauriston, et al. *Bibliography of Thailand*. Ithaca: Southeast Asia Program, Department of Far Eastern Studies, Cornell University, 1956.

Thrombley, W. G., et al. *Thai Government and Its Setting: A Selective, Annotated Bibliography in English and Thai*. Bangkok: National Institute of Development Administration, 1967.

Thrombley, W. G., and Siffin, W. J. *Thailand: Politics, Economy and Socio-Cultural Setting: A Selective Guide to the Literature*. Bloomington: Indiana University Press, 1972.

Watts, Michael. *Thailand*. Oxford, Santa Barbara, Denver: Clio Press, 1986.

Wyatt, David K. *Preliminary Thailand Bibliography*. Ithaca: Published privately by the author, 1971.

VIETNAM, CAMBODIA, LAOS

Auvade, Robert. *Bibliographie Critique des Oeuvres Parues sur l'Indochine Française*. Paris: G.-P. Maisonneuve & Larose, 1965.

Boudet, Paul, and Bourgeois, Remi. *Bibliographie de l'Indochine Française, 1913–1935*. Hanoi: Imprimerie d'Extreme-Orient, 1921–1943. 4 vols. Hanoi: IDEA, 1929–1932, 1943.

Burns, Richard D., and Leitenberg, Milton. *The Wars in Vietnam, Cambodia and Laos, 1945–1982: A Bibliographic Guide*. Santa Barbara: ABC-Clio Information Services, 1984.

Chen, John H. M. *Vietnam: A Comprehensive Bibliography*. Metuchen, NJ: Scarecrow Press, 1973.

Cotter, M. G. *Vietnam: A Guide to Reference Sources*. Boston: G. K. Hall, 1977.

Fisher, Mary L. *Cambodia: An Annotated Bibliography of Its History, Geography, Politics and Economy since 1954*. Cambridge, Mass: Center for International Studies, MIT, 1967.

Gaspardone, E. 'Bibliographie annamite', Hanoi: BEFEO, 1934.

Halpern, Joel, and Hafner, James A. *Bibliography of Miscellaneous Research Materials on Laos*. Bruxelles: Centre d'Etude du Sud-Est Asiatique et de l'Extreme Orient, 1971.

Halpern, Joel, and Hafner, James A. *A Bibliography of Miscellaneous Research Materials Pertaining to Laos, Cambodia, Vietnam and the Mekong River*. SEADAG (mimeo), n.d.

Hobbs, Cecil, et al. eds. *Indochina: A Bibliography of the Land and People.* New York: Greenwood Press, 1969 (first published in 1950).
'Indochine annamite', BEFEO, 21 (1921).
Jumper, Roy. *Bibliography on the Political and Administrative History of Vietnam, 1802–1962.* Saigon: Michigan State University Vietnam Advisory Group, 1962.
Keyes, C. F. *Southeast Asia Research Tools: Cambodia.* Honolulu: University of Hawaii, 1979.
Keyes, C. F. *Southeast Asia Research Tools: Laos.* Honolulu: University of Hawaii, 1979.
Keyes, Jane Godfrey. *A Bibliography of Vietnamese Publications in the Cornell University Library.* Ithaca: Department of Asian Studies, Cornell University, 1962.
Keyes, Jane Godfrey. *A Bibliography of Western-Language Publications Concerning North Vietnam in the Cornell University Library.* Ithaca: Southeast Asia Program, Department of Asian Studies, Cornell University, 1971.
Lafort, Pierre-Bernard. *Bibliographie du Laos* [Vol. 1: *1666–1961*; Vol. 2: *1962–1975*]. 2nd edn. Paris: EFEO, 1978.
List of Vietnam and Southeast Asia Holdings. Carbondale: Southern Illinois University, 1971.
Mekong Documentation Centre of the Committee for Coordination of Investigations of the Lower Mekong Basin. *Cambodia: A Select Bibliography.* Bangkok: Mekong Documentation Centre, 1967.
Mekong Documentation Centre of the Committee for Coordination of Investigations of the Lower Mekong Basin. *Viet-Nam: A Reading List.* Bangkok: Mekong Documentation Centre, 1967.
Ng Shui Meng. *Demographic Materials on the Khmer Republic, Laos and Vietnam.* Singapore: ISEAS, 1974.
Nguyen The-Anh. *Bibliographie Critique sur les Relations Entre Le Viet-Nam et L'Occident: Ouvrages et articles en langues occidentales.* Paris: G.-P. Maisonneuve & Larose, 1967.
Oey, Giok Po. *Checklist of the Vietnamese Holdings of the Wason Collection, Cornell University Libraries, as of June, 1971.* Ithaca: Southeast Asia Program, Department of Asian Studies, Cornell University, 1971.
Peake, Louis A. *The US in the Vietnam War, 1954: A Selected Annotated Bibliography.* New York and London: Garland Publishing, 1986.
Phan Thien Chau. *Vietnamese Communism: A Research Bibliography.* Westport: Greenwood Press, 1975.
Pretzell, Klause A., and Bode, Jutta. *Indochina: A Select Bibliography* [Vol. 1: *Indochina, Laos, Cambodia*; Vol. 2: *Vietnam*]. Hamburg: Institut fur Asienkunde, 1980.
Rony, A. Kohar. *Vietnamese Holdings in the Library of Congress: A Bibliography.* Washington, DC: Library of Congress, 1982.
Ross, Marion W. *Bibliography of Vietnamese Literature in the Wason Collection at Cornell University.* Ithaca: Southeast Asia Program, Department of Asian Studies, Cornell University, 1973.
Sage, William W., and Henchy, Judith A. N. *Laos: A Bibliography.* Singapore: ISEAS, 1986.
Sugnet, Christopher L., Hickey, John T., and Crispino, Robert. *Vietnam War Bibliography: Selected from Cornell University's Echols Collection.* Lexington, and Toronto: Lexington Books and D. C. Health, 1983.
Tanby, Zaleha. *Cambodia: A Bibliography.* Singapore: ISEAS, 1982.
Tran Thi Kim Sa. *Bibliography on Vietnam, 1954–1964.* Saigon: National Institute of Administration, 1966.

SPECIAL TOPICS

American Geographical Society. *Research Catalogue of the American Geographical Society*, Vol. 13: *Asia*. Boston: G. K. Hall, 1962.

American Geographical Society. Map Department. *Index to Maps in Books and Periodicals*. Boston: G. K. Hall, 1968.

Bartlett, H. H. *Fire in Relation to Primitive Agriculture and Grazing in the Tropics. Annotated Bibliography*. 1956.

Catalogue of the Colonial Office Library, London. Boston: G. K. Hall, 1964.

Catalogus der Koloniale Bibliotheek van het Koninklijk Instituut voor de Taal-, Land- en Volkenkunde van Ned. Indië en het Indisch Genootschap. The Hague: Martinus Nijhoff, 1980.

Conklin, Harold C. *The Study of Shifting Cultivation*. Washington, DC: Union Panamericana, 1963.

Coolhaas, Willem P. *A Critical Survey of Studies on Dutch Colonial History*. 's-Gravenhage: Martinus Nijhoff, 1960.

Cox, Edward Godfrey. *A Reference Guide to the Literature of Travel*. Seattle: University of Washington, 1935.

Ensor, A. G. S. *A Subject Bibliography of the Second World War: Books in English, 1939–1974*. London: André Deutsch, 1977.

Fan Kok Sim. *Women in Southeast Asia: A Bibliography*. Boston: G. K. Hall, 1982.

Farrington, Anthony. *The Records of the East India College, Haileybury, and Other Institutions*. London: HMSO, 1976.

Great Britain. Colonial Office. Library. *Catalogue of the Colonial Office Library*. London: G. K. Hall, 1964.

Great Britain. Colonial Office. *Reading List on Colonial Development and Welfare*. London, 1951.

Great Britain. Foreign and Commonwealth Office. *Accessions to the library, May 1971–June 1977*. Boston: G. K. Hall, 1979.

Halstead, John P., and Porcari, Serafino. *Modern European Imperialism: A Bibliography of Books and Articles, 1815–1972*, Vol. 1: *General and British Empire*; Vol. 2: *French and Other Empires; Regions*. Boston: G. K. Hall, 1974.

Hufner, Klaus, and Naumann, Jens. *The United Nations System—International Bibliography*. München: Verlag Dokumentation, 1976.

Nagelkerke, G. A. *A Selected Bibliography of the Chinese in Indonesia*. Leiden: Library of the Royal Institute of Linguistics and Anthropology, 1975.

National Maritime Museum. *Catalogue of the Library*. London: HMSO, 1968.

Nevadomsky, J.-j., and Li, A. *The Chinese in Southeast Asia: A Selected and Annotated Bibliography of Publications in Western Languages, 1960–1970*. Berkeley: University of California, Center for South and Southeast Asian Studies, 1973.

Postma, Nel, et al. *Bibliografi Wanita Indonesia*. Jakarta: Kantor Menmud UPW/LIPI, 1980.

Royal Empire Society. *Subject Catalogue of the Library of the Royal Empire Society*. London: Dawsons of Pall Mall for the Royal Commonwealth Society, 1967.

Tiele, P. A. *Mémoire bibliographique sur les Journaux des Navigateurs Neerlandais*. Amsterdam: N. Israel Publishing Dept, 1960.

UNESCO. *Bibliography of Publications Issued by UNESCO or under Its Auspices (The First Twenty-Five Years: 1946 to 1971)*. Paris: UNESCO, 1973.

United States of America. Library of Congress, Geography and Map Division. *The Bibliography of Cartography*. Boston: Micropublications, G. K. Hall, 1973. First supplement, 1980.

Winton, Harry N. M. *Publications of the United Nations System: A Reference Guide*. New York and London: R. R. Bowker and Unipub, 1972.

INDEX